THE HISTORY OF AL-ṬABARĪ

AN ANNOTATED TRANSLATION

VOLUME I

General Introduction

and

From the Creation to the Flood

The History of al-Ṭabarī

Editorial Board

Ihsan Abbas, University of Jordan, Amman

C. E. Bosworth, The University of Manchester

Jacob Lassner, Wayne State University, Detroit

Franz Rosenthal, Yale University

Ehsan Yar-Shater, Columbia University *(General Editor)*

SUNY

SERIES IN NEAR EASTERN STUDIES

Said Amir Arjomand, Editor

The general editor acknowledges with gratitude the support received for the execution of this project from the Division of Research Programs, Translations Division of the National Endowment for the Humanities, an independent federal agency.

Bibliotheca Persica
Edited by Ehsan Yar-Shater

The History of al-Ṭabarī
(Ta'rīkh al-rusul wa'l-mulūk)

VOLUME I

General Introduction
and
From the Creation to the Flood

translated and annotated
by

Franz Rosenthal

Yale University

State University of New York Press

The preparation of this volume was made possible by a grant from the Division of Research Programs of the National Endowment for the Humanities, an independent federal agency.

Published by
State University of New York Press, Albany

Printed in the United States of America

For information, address State University of New York Press, State University Plaza, Albany, N. Y. 12246

Library of Congress Cataloging in Publication Data

Ṭabarī, 838?– 923.

[Ta'rīkh al-rusul wa-al-mulūk. English. Selections]
General Introduction, and, From the Creation to the Flood / by Franz Rosenthal.
p. cm. – (SUNY series in Near Eastern studies) (The history of al-Ṭabarī=Ta'rīkh al-rusul wa'l-mulūk; v. 1) (Bibliotheca Persica)
Translation of extracts from: Ta'rīkh al-rusul wa-al-mulūk.
Bibliography: p.
Includes Index.
ISBN 0-88706-562-7. ISBN 0-88706-563-5 (pbk.)
1. History, Ancient. 2. World history–Early works to 1800. 3. Bible. O.T. Genesis I-IX–History of Biblical events–Early works to 1800. 4. Bible. O.T. Genesis I-IX–History of contemporary events–Early works to 1800. I. Rosenthal, Franz, 1914–. II. Title, III. Title: From the Creation to the Flood. IV. Series. V. Series: Ṭabarī, 838?– 923. Ta 'rīkh al-rusul wa-al -mulūk. English : v. 1. VI. Series: Bibliotheca Persica (Albany, N.Y.)
DS38.2.T313 1985 vol. 1
[D17]
909'. 1 s—dc19
[930'.2]
10 9 8 7 6 5 4 3 2 1

Contents

General Editor's Preface / ix

Guidelines for Translation, Annotation, and Indexing / *xii*

Acknowledgments / *xix*

General Introduction

Translator's Foreword / *3*

The Life and Works of al-Ṭabarī / 5

A Remark on the Sources / *5*
His Early Life / *10*
His Fifty Years of Scholarly Activity in Baghdad / *31*
His Death / *78*
His Works / *80*

The History *and Its English Translation / 135*

The *History* in Islam and the West / *135*
The Text / *141*
Previous Translations / *144*

Appendix A: A Partial Translation of Tafsīr *on Qur. 17:79 / 149*

Appendix B: A Classification and Chronology of Ṭabarī's Literary Production / 152

From the Creation to the Flood

Translator's Foreword / *157*
Invocation / *165*
Introduction / *166*
What Is Time? / *171*
How Long Is the Total Extent of Time . . .? / *172*
The Proofs for the Origination of Momentary and Extended Time . . . / *186*
Whether God, before He Created Time . . . Created Any Other of the Created Things / *187*
Explaining the Annihilation of Time . . . and That Nothing Remains Except God / *193*
The Proof for God Being Eternal . . . / *194*
The Beginning of Creation: What Was Created First? / *198*
Those Who Put the Creation of the Pen in Second Place / *203*
What God Created on Each of the Six Days . . . / *213*
Night and Day . . . the Creation of the Sun and the Moon . . . / *228*
The Story of Iblīs / *249*
The Story of Adam / *257*
Adam Is Taught All the Names / *266*
God's Testing of Adam / *274*
The Duration of Adam's Stay in Paradise . . . His Fall . . . / *282*
The Moment on Friday When God Created Adam and the One When Adam Was Cast Down to Earth / *286*
The Place on Earth to Which Adam and Eve Came When They Were Cast Down / *290*
Perfumes, Fruits, and Other Things Adam Brought from Paradise / *296*

The Events That Took Place in Adam's Time after He Was Cast Down to Earth / *307*
Eve Giving Birth to Seth / *324*
Adam's Death / *327*
From Seth to Mahalalel / *334*
The Events That Took Place . . . from the Rule of Adam's Son to the Days of Jared / *337*
Persian Kings after Ōshahanj: Ṭahmūrath / *344*
From Enoch to Noah / *345*
Persian Kings from Ṭahmūrath to Jamshēd and al-Ḍaḥḥāk / *348*

The Events that Took Place in Noah's Time / *354*

The Use of Eras / *370*

Bibliography of Cited Works / *373*

Index / *387*

General Editor's Preface

The History of Prophets and Kings (*Ta'rīkh al-rusul wa'l-mulūk*) by Abū Ja'far Muḥammad b. Jarīr al-Ṭabarī (839–923), rendered in the present work as the *History of al-Ṭabarī*, is by common consent the most important universal history produced in the world of Islam. It has been translated here in its entirety for the first time for the benefit of non-Arabists, with historical and philological notes for those interested in the particulars of the text.

Ṭabarī's monumental work explores the history of ancient nations, with special emphasis on biblical peoples and prophets, the legendary and factual history of ancient Iran, and, in great detail, the rise of Islam, the life of the Prophet Muḥammad, and the history of the Islamic world down to the year 915.

In 1971, I proposed that UNESCO include a complete translation of Ṭabarī's History in its Collection of Representative Works. At a meeting chaired by the late Roger Caillois, UNESCO agreed; but the Commission in charge of Arabic works favored other priorities, mostly of a literary kind. At the time I was in charge of UNESCO's Collection of Persian Representative Works, a program which was managed within the framework of the activities of the Iranian Institute of Translation and Publication (*Bungāh-i Tarjama wa Nashr-i Kitāb*). Failing to enlist the support of the Arab Commission, I persuaded the Institute to undertake the task.

My interest in the translation of Ṭabarī's history derived not only from the desire to see an outstanding historical work made available to non-Arabists, but also from the fact that Ṭabarī is the most important source for Iranian history from the rise of the Sasanian dynasty in the third century to the year 915. By rights, the task should have been undertaken by a scholar of Islamic history and classical Arabic, in neither of which fields can I claim any expertise; but I thought it a pity to let the rare opportunity presented by the sponsors of the project to be lost. Fully aware of my limitations and convinced of the importance of the participation of specialists in the project, I enlisted the assistance of a number of excellent scholars in the field.

Preliminary work on the project began in 1974 and I invited Professor Franz Rosenthal of Yale University to bring the benefit of his scholarship and experience to this venture. An Editorial Board originally consisting of Professors Rosenthal, Ihsan Abbas of the American University in Beirut, and myself was envisaged. I later invited Professors C.E. Bosworth of the University of Manchester and Jacob Lassner of Wayne State University to cooperate as members of the Board of Editors. We then began a steady search for able and willing scholars to take part in the project. Ideally we were looking for historians of medieval Islam with a command of classical Arabic.

The Leiden edition was the obvious text on which to base the translation of the History as it is thus far the only critical and scholarly edition. It was prepared by a number of competent scholars in the last quarter of the nineteenth century under the able direction of the Dutch scholar M.J. de Goeje, and published by E.J. Brill of Leiden, Holland, in fourteen volumes with an index volume and a supplementary volume, between 1879 and 1901.*

One of our first tasks was to divide the text into manageable sections to be assigned for translation and annotation. The text was divided arbitrarily into 38 sections of about 200 pages each, but in a manner that allowed each section, as far as possible, to be used independently. The general size of the sections was dictated by the desire to leave adequate space for annotation, and to make it possible for the best and busiest scholars in the field to participate. Each section was given a separate title as a short guide to its contents.

It was obvious that in a project of this size, given the differ-

*See pp. 141 ff. of Professor Rosenthal's introduction to the present volume for more details on this edition and the merits of the Cairo edition.

ent viewpoints on translation among scholars and their different styles of rendering Arabic into English, we needed clear guidelines to ensure an essential modicum of consistency. It was necessary to make the translation of some frequently used phrases and expressions uniform. For instance, Amīr al-mu'minīn, the title of the caliphs, can be, and has been, translated in different ways. It was important that we used a single rendering of the term ("Commander of the Faithful"). Furthermore, we had to insist on uniformity in the spelling of place-names. To accommodate these concerns, we established a series of guidelines which addressed the questions of format, rubrics, annotation, bibliography, and indexing. According to the guidelines, which were communicated to participating scholars, the project aimed at a translation both faithful and idiomatic—an ideal which we realized was nevertheless far from easy to accomplish. Concern for consistency required that the volumes be carefully edited by an Arabic scholar thoroughly familiar with the guidelines established by the Editorial Board.

This task was originally entrusted to Professor Lassner, but as the number of manuscripts claimed more of his time than he could devote to editing, Professor Bosworth's assistance, too, was enlisted; Professor Rosenthal has also been generously giving of his time for editorial purposes. Naturally this does not mean that all the volumes of Ṭabarī follow the same style or that all Arabic terms have been translated in exactly the same way. Variations do occur, but every effort has been made to ensure not only accuracy and readability, but also consistency.

The system of romanization commonly employed by present-day Arabists and Islamicists in the English-speaking world was chosen. Although the system is not universally accepted in all its details, it is hoped that it meets the requirements of accurate transliteration.

Ṭabarī very often quotes his sources verbatim and traces the chains of transmission (*isnād*) to an original source. The chains of transmitters are, for the sake of brevity, rendered by the individual links in the chain separated by a dash (—). Thus, "according to the Ibn Ḥumayd—Salamah—Ibn Isḥāq" means that Ṭabarī received the report from Ibn Ḥumayd who said that he was told by Salamah, who said that he was told by Ibn Isḥāq, and so on. The numerous subtle variations in the original Arabic have been disregarded.

The table of contents at the beginning of each volume gives a brief survey of the topics dealt with in that particular volume. It also includes the headings and subheadings as they appear in Ṭabarī's text, as well as those occasionally introduced by the translator.

Well-known place-names, such as Mecca, Baghdad, Jerusalem, Damascus, and the Yemen, are given in their English spellings. Less common place-names, which are the vast majority, are transliterated. Biblical figures appear in the accepted English spelling. Iranian names are usually transcribed according to their Arabic forms, and the presumed Iranian forms are often discussed in the footnotes.

Technical terms have been translated wherever possible, but some, such as imām and dirham, have been retained in Arabic forms. Others that cannot be translated with sufficient precision have been retained and italicized as well as footnoted.

The annotation aims chiefly at clarifying difficult passages, identifying individuals and place-names, and discussing textual difficulties. Much leeway has been left to the translators to include in the footnotes whatever they consider necessary and helpful. Initially, each volume was to have a brief, general introduction; however, after the first few volumes, it was deemed useful to expand the scope of the introductions so that they would include a discussion of the historical context of the volumes and Ṭabarī's method of relating the events. Again, it was left to the translators to decide what was pertinent and helpful to say in their introductions. Translators were also encouraged to provide maps and genealogical tables.

Rather than give further detail of the editorial policy and principles, I reproduce here, for those who may be interested, the Guidelines set forth by the Editorial Board.

Guidelines for Translation, Annotation, and Indexing

I. Translation

1. The purpose of the translation is to provide an accurate but literate text.

2. Mecca, Baghdad, Jerusalem, Damascus, Aleppo, Medina and the

like retain their accepted English forms. Less well-known place names are to be romanized accurately.

3. Amīr al-mu'minīn should be rendered "Commander of the Faithful". The English spelling "Caliph" is retained.

4. *Bāya'a, bay'ah* should be consistently translated as "to give/render the oath of allegiance".

5. Familiar technical terms, when reasonably accurate English equivalents are available, should be translated; thus, vizier *(wazīr)*, judge *(qāḍī)*, cubit *(dhirā')*. Other technical terms should be retained in transliteration without italics, e.g., muftī, imām, ṣūfī, dirham (drachma), dīnār (denarius), shaikh. In general, Arabic terms should be avoided as much as possible.

When a less familiar term like dihqān is left untranslated, an explanatory footnote with reference to the secondary literature (usually *EI*) may be called for. Unfamiliar and untranslatable technical terms, e.g., *raṭl* or *dāniq*, should be rendered in italics and footnoted.

6. Referents should be supplied for pronouns as required by English usage.

7. It is unnecessary to translate the common terms of blessing after God, the Prophet, etc., except when the formula has some special import.

8. It is not always obligatory to follow the exact sequence of Arabic syntax or literary style; this should be determined by the text and idiomatic English usage. Occasionally, it may be useful to turn direct Arabic speech into indirect speech in the translation to enable the English text to flow smoothly. However, direct speech adds to the liveliness of the translation and preserves the flavor of the original text; thus it should be retained unless other considerations prevail.

II. Annotation

1. Annotations are meant to provide a better understanding of the text. Proper names as well as technical terms unfamiliar to the non-specialist require annotation.

2. A search should be made for relevant parallel sources, and these should be cited when deemed necessary.

3. Philological and stylistic comments are for the benefit of the Arabist. They should be limited to explicating the text where it presents problems.

4. Major geographical areas, e.g., Ḥijāz, Khurāsān, Sind require no comment. Less well-known places should be identified by referring to the secondary literature, such as *EI*, *EIr*, Le Strange, Yāqūt's *Muʿjam al-Buldān*, or Schwartz's *Iran*. Fuller comments are necessary only when identification of a particular place is critical to understanding the sense of the text.

5. In rare cases when the explication of the text requires more extensive treatment, this should take the form of an excursus at the end of the translation.

6. Maximum space allowed for the annotation of each volume, including excursuses, should not exceed about one-third of the text.

7. Authors should be cited by name only, except in those cases where the same author has written other works likely to be cited. Thus, Ṭabarī III/I, 250 but Yaʿqūbī, *Taʾrīkh* (Leiden), I, 250 or Yaʿqūbī, *Buldān* (BGA, VIII), 250.

8. Titles should be abbreviated and follow the format of *EI*² and *EIr* (but with the romanization used in this series).

9. References should generally be to standard editions. Where several editions exist, the translators should indicate their choice.

10. Passages that pose textual problems should be romanized and reproduced in footnotes.

III. Editions of the Arabic Text

The Leiden edition should serve as the basis of the translation (see above, p. x). The Cairo edition should, however, be consulted and, if the Topkapı Sarayı manuscripts used in this edition differ significantly from the Leiden edition, the difference should be taken into account and footnoted.

IV. Format and Style

A. General

1. The pagination of the Leiden edition is to be indicated in the margin in square brackets.

2. Hijrah dates are always given with corresponding Western dates; the two are separated by a /, e.g., 145/762.

3. Chains of transmission *(isnād)* should be introduced by "according to" followed by the names of the transmitters in sequence, separated by a —, with a colon after the last name; e.g., "According to Abū Jaʿfar—Muḥammad b. ʿUmar—Muḥammad b. Ṣāliḥ."

4. *Kunyah* and *nisbah* are always romanized and not translated, e.g., Abū al-Ḥasan al-Khayyāṭ (not "Father of al-Ḥasan the Tailor").

5. Translations are followed by a bibliography giving full publication details for all works cited.

6. The translation of a *bayt* consisting of two hemistichs should be typed as two lines. The first line should begin with a capital letter and be indented; the second line should be further indented and begin with a lower case (small) letter, unless the first line ends with a period, in which case the second line should begin with a capital letter. If any of the hemistichs exceeds one line, the remainder is placed on the next line and is similarly indented. *Bayts* should be separated by an extra space.

B. Rubrics

1. Reigns of Caliphs should be capitalized, e.g.

THE CALIPHATE OF MARWĀN B. MUḤAMMAD

2. The year should be capitalized and beneath it the equivalent Western date should be given parentheses, e.g.,

THE YEAR 280
(March 23, 893—March 12, 894)

When indicated in the text add:

The Events of This Year

3. Other rubrics should be rendered as English titles and underlined, e.g.,

The Reason for...

4. Rubrics may often be cumbersome and difficult to translate, particularly when introduced by "mention of" or the like. In the interest of brevity, one may omit this element of the formula, e.g., instead of:

Mention of the Accounts Concerning the Death of...

translate:

The Death of...

5. The form for rubrics that merge with the text is:

The Reason for this was the killing of...

C. Pre-Islamic Names and Letters

Ancient Iranian names should be romanized according to their Arabic spelling. For biblical names, the standard English forms (see *The Westminster Bible Dictionary)* should be used. Classical names are to be rendered according to standard English practice.

In the case of titles, it will at times be desirable to put the original forms in brackets after the translation, e.g., "general" *(iṣbahbadh).*

D. Paragraphs

Translators may exercise considerable license in paragraphing; however, the introduction of an *isnād* as a rule calls for a new paragraph.

Occasionally, transmitters insert lengthy addresses, sermons, documents, etc. into the text. These should be set off in special paragraphs in quotation marks. Key short passages of this kind need not be set off.

V. The Index

A. Contents

1. There is to be only one index.

2. It should be as complete as possible (too much is better than too little).

3. It should contain:
 a. All personal proper names in Ṭabarī's text.
 b. All geographical names (cities, countries, rivers, etc.) in Ṭabarī's text.
 c. All personal and geographical names in the notes as far as they refer to the medieval context. For instance, if a note states that M.b.A. al-Baghdādī is not identical with the M.b.A. al-Kūfī mentioned by Ṭabarī, M.b.A. al-Baghdādī requires a separate entry in the index.

References to medieval sources are also to be included. Thus, if Miskawayh is cited in the note, "Miskawayh" will appear in the index.

However, proper names of modern scholars are not to be included. With respect to the notes, some selective judgment will be needed; however, if in doubt, add!

B. Form

1. Place a capital A, B, etc. at the head of each new letter of the alphabet.

2. The definite article is to be disregarded for purposes of alphabetization. al-Ṭabarī thus appears under Ṭ, but "al-" is retained.

3. If an entry under Ibn is needed, it should appear under I. Thus: Ibn M. (The same applies to Bint).

4. Abū M. appears under A. (Also Akhū; Umm under U).

5. The main entry of a name with page references is listed under the forms of the name considered to be most characteristic. Of course, the "most characteristic" form is not always obvious; one's choice may be arbitrary at times. If different forms of an individual's name appear in the text, all must be listed separately, with cross references to the main entry. For instance, assuming that Ṭabarī appears in the text or the notes under the various components of his name, the following entries are needed:

Abū Ja'far, see al-Ṭabarī
Ibn Jarīr, see al-Ṭabarī
Muḥammad b. Jarīr, see al-Ṭabarī
al-Ṭabarī (Abū Ja'far Muḥammad b. Jarīr), 35, 46, 109 (n.83), 72

In the main entry, the other forms of the name should be repeated; however, it is not necessary to supply them where they do not occur. Thus "Miskawayh" is sufficient; his given names need not be supplied.

VI. General

1. The translators are expected to provide a substantial introduction that places the volume in historical perspective. The introduction may contain not only a summary of the volume's contents, but also comments on the significance of the events, an evaluation of Ṭabarī's reporting, and a discussion of parallel sources.

2. Maps and genealogical tables are helpful, in fact, welcome, provided the translator is able to furnish them.

E.Y.

Acknowledgments

My foremost thanks to the National Endowment for the Humanities and its Division of Research Programs for their continued support and encouragement.

I also wish to thank sincerely the participating scholars, who have made the realization of this project possible; the Board of Editors for their valuable assistance; Professor Franz Rosenthal for his many helpful suggestions in the formulation and application of the editorial policy; Professors C.E. Bosworth and Jacob Lassner for their painstaking and meticulous editing; Professor Michael Morony of the University of California at Los Angeles for undertaking the task of dividing the text into volume portions; and Dr. Susan Mango, formerly of the National Endowment for the Humanities, and her successor, Dr. Martha Chomiak, for their genuine interest in the project and their advocacy of it.

I am grateful to the State University of New York Press for volunteering to undertake the publication of the series; to its Director, Mr. William D. Eastman, for showing himself earnestly committed to the project; and to Professor Said Arjomand, the editor of the Middle Eastern Series of SUNY Press, for bringing the project to the attention of the Board of the Press.

Special thanks are due to Dina Amin, who as Executive Secretary has managed with great care the administrative aspects of the project, and to Mrs. Patsy King of Columbia University's Office of Projects and Grants for her patient handling of the bureaucratic matters pertaining to the project. I trust that the completion of the project and the publication of the index volume will provide me with a second opportunity to express my gratitude to others who have assisted the project.

E.Y.

General Introduction

Translator's Foreword

This volume contains the first part of the Ṭabarī translation, a biographical sketch, and a discussion of what can be said at present about Ṭabarī's literary output, as well as some remarks on the English translation of the History. Much work remains to be done before all the data are clarified and Ṭabarī's works and his intellectual position in his environment have been fully studied. Although considerable effort has been expended to this end in recent years, it can truly be said that the task has just begun.

It has been deemed advisable that the General Introduction and the translation of Volume I be kept as separate as possible, even if they appear under the same cover. However, continuous pagination has been adopted, and entries for the Bibliography and for the Index have been combined. On the other hand, the numbering of footnotes starts afresh in the Translation. Therefore, in the General Introduction, cross-references to footnotes in the Translation are prefaced by "translation." Inversely, in the Translation, cross-references to footnotes in the General Introduction are marked accordingly. In view of the different character of this volume as compared to the other volumes of this series, the Index should, perhaps, have been considerably modified, but this has been done only to a very small degree, as stated in the note at the head of the Index.

Some of Ṭabarī's works still in manuscript have remained inaccessible to me. I am grateful to the Escorial Library for having provided me with a microfilm of the manuscript of *Tabṣīr* and to the Beinecke Library of Yale University for making me a copy of the Ṭabarī biography from the Landberg manuscript of Ibn ʿAsākir. I have discussed the "praiseworthy position" (below, 71 ff.) with a number of colleagues—foremost among them Josef van Ess to whom I am indebted for essential references. Gerhard Böwering helped me out with a xerox from his copy of the biography of Ṭabarī in Dhahabī's *Nubalāʾ*. My former student, Dr. Elise Crosby, was instrumental in obtaining for me a copy of the *Ḥadīth al-himyān*. Yale University Library and its former Near East librarian Dr. Jonathan Rodgers have been as helpful to me in connection with this work as the library staff has always been during the past thirty years.

Franz Rosenthal

The Life and Works of al-Ṭabarī

A Remark on the Sources

The information we have on Ṭabarī's life and works is unusually instructive in a number of ways, but it leaves many large gaps in our knowledge. Important questions have to be asked for which no definite answers are available. In writing his biography, it is also necessary, and has been attempted here, to distinguish as clearly as possible between securely known data and what appears to be valid information but in fact remains the result of unverifiable speculation.[1]

Ṭabarī shows himself very reluctant to talk about his personal life, at least in the preserved works, which constitute only part of his large literary production. Although it is by no means certain, he may have revealed more about his personal situation in some of his lost writings, for instance, the original *Dhayl al-mudhayyal* in which he discussed his teachers.[2] He does provide his biographer with the names of numerous scholars with whom he had personal contact. There can be no doubt that the "I was told" and "we were told" at the opening of the chains of transmitters [3] have as a rule to be taken literally as indicating direct personal contact or contact within the setting of public lectures and instruction. In most cases, however, it is unfortunately not clear how close such

1. Biographical notices such as the one by R. Paret in the first edition of *EI*, s. v. al-Ṭabarī (see also *Shorter Encyclopaedia of Islam*, 556 f.), contain the elementary data and may serve for quick information.

2. See below, 89 f. For the *Ḥadīth al-himyān*, see below, 98 ff.; whatever one may think about its genuineness, it does not qualify as a "work by" Ṭabarī.

3 See below, 147.

contact may have been. Knowledge of the circle of individuals among whom Ṭabarī moved is invaluable for understanding the events of his life. It has been imperative therefore to try to learn as much as possible about his authorities, colleagues, students, and acquaintances, and to establish their relations with him. Conversely, where it proved impossible to identify an individual, we are left in the dark with respect to potentially important, even crucial, nexuses.

As a scholar convinced of the preeminence of the material with which he dealt, Ṭabarī was not inclined to waste time and space on such mundane matters as when and where he had contact with his authorities. Occasionally, he might very well have indicated such data, for it was the custom to keep notes including the name of a teacher and the time of attendance at his classes. In fact, Ṭabarī did so as a young student; he may have continued the custom later in his life, but for his own information and not for publication.[4] It must also be assumed that he often referred to someone with whom he undoubtedly had some personal contact; but later, he used the source that was transmitted to him by that individual in its written (published) form and quoted from it while pretending all the time to rely upon oral transmission. This was no doubt the manner in which he handled quotations in *Tafsīr* from earlier Qur'ān commentaries. It also seems very likely that he relied on written (but presumably unpublished) "books" when transmitting information that had been preserved as the heirloom of a particular family such as that of Muhammad b. Sa'd.[5] In certain cases, the function of Ṭabarī's direct informant seems to have been hardly more than to legitimize the use of a recension of a work in its written form, as in those of Aḥmad b. Thābit al-Rāzī as the transmitter of Abū Ma'shar,[6] or of al-Sarī b. Yaḥyā as a transmitter of Sayf b. 'Umar.[7] Al-Sarī, it should be noted, transmitted Sayf's historical information to Ṭabarī by written communication; under the circumstances, it is rather doubtful whether there was indeed personal contact between him and Ṭabarī where

4. See *Irshād*, VI, 431, ed. Rifā'ī, XVIII, 51, and below, 21.
5. See below, translation, n. 337.
6. See Sezgin, *GAS*, I, 292; Ṭabarī, *History*, I, 1141 and frequently. It seems uncertain whether Aḥmad b. Thābit al-Rāzī is identical with the person listed in Ibn Abī Ḥātim, I,1, 44; Ibn Ḥajar, *Lisān*, I, 143, as suggested in Sezgin, *GAS*, I, 796.
7. See Sezgin, *GAS*, I, 311 f.

the formula "he told me/us" is used.[8]

In sum, we are faced with the fact that Ṭabarī's own works, as far as they are preserved, are a very limited source of hard biographical data. They do provide us with many important leads, and they are of the greatest value to us because they reveal his scholarly personality and attitude.

No biographies of any length appear to have been written during Ṭabarī's lifetime, but there were a number of men who had known him personally and who wrote on his life and works.

Abū Bakr Aḥmad b. Kāmil (260–350/873[4]–961),[9] who had a distinguished career as a judge and productive scholar, was on familiar terms with him. He was among those present when Ṭabarī died. An early follower of Ṭabarī's legal school, he seems to have veered away from it later in his life.[10] His monograph became a prime source for Ṭabarī biographers.

While Ibn Kāmil's prominence earned him obituary notices in a number of reference works, another individual who wrote a biography and seems to have been close to Ṭabarī, Abū Muḥammad ʿAbd al-ʿAzīz b. Muḥammad al-Ṭabarī, remains obscure. We can place neither him nor his supposed monograph.[11]

Abū Muḥammad ʿAbdallāh b. Aḥmad b. Jaʿfar al-Farghānī (282–362/895[6]–972[3]),[12] prepared an edition of Ṭabarī's *History* and wrote a continuation (*Ṣilah*) to it. He had personal contact with Ṭabarī as a student, but it is difficult for us to say how extensive this contact may have been. He devoted a long obituary notice to Ṭabarī in his *Ṣilah*, which served as an important source

8. As, for instance, Ṭabarī, *History*, I, 1845, 1848, 1851, etc., as against the use of the verb "to write" in I, 1749, 1921, etc. Written information from a certain ʿAlī b. Aḥmad b. al-Ḥasan al-ʿIjlī is mentioned in Ṭabarī, *History*, I, 1311. See also, in particular, the reference to Ziyād b. Ayyūb in I, 3159, below, n. 210. See also below, n. 455, on al-Masʿūdī's relationship with Ṭabarī.

9. See Sezgin, *GAS*, I, 523 f. We cannot pinpoint the exact location of Ibn Kāmil's East Baghdad residence on Shāriʿ ʿAbd al-Ṣamad in Suwayqat Abī ʿUbaydallah (see *TB*, IV, 357, l. 11; Miskawayh, in *Eclipse*, II, 184; Lassner, *Topography*, 78–80). It was probably closer to Ṭabarī's mosque in Sūq al-ʿAṭash than to his home. Miskawayh, who made very extensive use of *History*, studied the work with Ibn Kāmil. He read some of it to him and received his permission (*ijāzah*) to use the rest, see *Eclipse*, II, 184. Cf. J. Kraemer, *Humanism*, 223.

10. See below, nn. 251 and 301.

11. His work, as that of Ibn Kāmil, is specifically stated by Yāqūt to have been a monograph; see *Irshād*, VI, 462, ed. Rifāʿī, XVIII, 94.

12. See Sezgin, *GAS*, I, 337, and *History*, translation, Vol. XXXVIII, xv, n. 7.

of biographical information. Another valuable document from al-Farghānī's hand is an *ijāzah* giving permission to a certain ʿAlī b. ʿImrān and (?) a certain Ibrāhīm b. Muḥammad to teach a number of Ṭabarī's works which al-Farghānī himself had studied with Ṭabarī. It was originally affixed to a volume of *Tafsīr,* no doubt the one used by the mentioned student(s), and dated from Shaʿbān 336/February–March 948.[13]

Another follower of Ṭabarī's legal school inserted much information on Ṭabarī in his historical work that depended on (continued?) Ṭabarī's work. We know not much more about him than his name, Abū Isḥāq Ibrāhīm b. Ḥabīb al-Saqaṭī al-Ṭabarī. He can be assumed to have lived while Ṭabarī was still alive.[14]

Among those who were born during Ṭabarī's lifetime but had no personal contact with him, the Egyptian historian Abū Saʿīd b. Yūnus (281–347/894–958) may be mentioned. It was natural for him to include a notice on Ṭabarī in his work on "Strangers in Egypt," because Ṭabarī had visited Egypt for purposes of study.[15] Others in his generation who wrote biographical works would certainly not have overlooked a man of Ṭabarī's stature. However, as far as our information goes, another biography in monograph form was not written for about three hundred years, at which time the Egyptian scholar al-Qifṭī (568–646/1172–1248) compiled a Ṭabarī biography, entitled *al-Taḥrīr fī akhbār Muḥammad b. Jarīr.*[16] Al-Qifṭī was a great admirer of Ṭabarī, for he not only wrote this monograph but took the opportunity to list Ṭabarī in other works of his, such as his dictionaries of grammarians and of poets named Muḥammad; neither work, especially the latter, necessarily required mention of Ṭabarī.

None of the early biographies, including al-Qifṭī's monographs, has come down to us. We have to rely on excerpts preserved by later scholars. These excerpts give us some idea of the contents of those biographies, and they furnish the most reliable information at our disposal. Among the biographical sources that are

13. The text of the *ijāzah* is quoted in *Irshād,* VI, 426 f., ed. Rifāʿī, XVIII, 44 f. Two recipients of the *ijāzah* seem to be mentioned, but a singular pronoun is used to refer to them.

14. See Ibn al-Nadīm, *Fihrist,* 235, l. 24.

15. Ibn Yūnus is referred to in connection with Ṭabarī by Ibn ʿAsākir, LXXII, and Ibn Khallikān, *Wafayāt,* IV, 192. For Ibn Yūnus, see *EI*², III, 969b, s. v.

16. See Qifṭī, *Inbāh,* III, 90, and *Muḥammadūn,* 264.

preserved, the oldest is the *History of Baghdad* by al-Khaṭīb al-Baghdādī (392–463/1002–71), cited here as *TB*.[17] The Khaṭīb's biographical notice was quoted by practically all later biographers. Since Ṭabarī spent some time in Damascus on his western journey, Ibn 'Asākir (499–571/1105–76) devoted to him a long and informative entry in his *History of Damascus.* He went beyond *TB* and added much information from the old sources.[18] By far the most extensive coverage of Ṭabarī's life and works is the one we owe to the great geographer and biographer Yāqūt. He was a contemporary and long-term associate of al-Qifṭī, whose enthusiasm for Ṭabarī he apparently shared. Yāqūt's article on Ṭabarī in his *Dictionary of learned men and litterateurs,* cited here as *Irshād,* reproduces long excerpts from the old sources. It seems that he quotes them quite literally. The available text is not free from mistakes. In all likelihood, however, they do not affect anything essential.[19]

Ṭabarī's fame was such that no biographer in subsequent centuries who touched on Ṭabarī's age and fields of scholarly activity could afford not to mention him. Biographical notices are numerous, if often quite perfunctory. Some provide valuable bits of additional information not found elsewhere, but that is rare.[20] As a rule, they do not offer noteworthy biographical data beyond what is found in the works of al-Khaṭīb al-Baghdādī, Ibn 'Asākir, and Yāqūt. Among the longer notices, reference may be made here, without prejudice, to those in the *Muntaẓam* (VI,

---

17. See *TB*, II, 162–9.

18. Attention to Ibn 'Asākir's biography of Ṭabarī was first drawn by Goldziher, "Die literarische Thätigkeit." In a letter to T. Nöldeke, he mentions that this edition was a difficult task, see Róbert Simon, *Ignác Goldziher*, 197. Goldziher published only the part dealing with Ṭabarī's works. The manuscript he used is now in the Yale University Library, Ms. L-312 (Cat. Nemoy 1182), fols. 109a–117b. On the basis of the same manuscript, the complete text was published in Ṭabarī, *Introductio etc.*, LXIX–XCVI, with comparison with and additions from other biographies, in particular, those of Ibn al-Jawzī, *Muntaẓam*, and al-Maqrīzī, *Muqaffā*, also Subkī, *Ṭabaqāt*, as well as brief passages from al-Dhahabī and al-Nawawī. (Al-Dhahabī's source is now available, see Mu'āfā, *Jalīs*, I, 472, quoted in *TB*, X, 98 f., in the biography of Ibn al-Mu'tazz, see below, n. 464).

19. See *Irshād*, VI, 423–62, ed. Rifā'ī, XVIII, 40–94. Rifā'ī offers some suggestions and corrections. For Yāqūt's sources, see Bergsträsser, "Quellen," 201 f. For his biography, see Sellheim, "Neue Materialien," 87–118, and *Materialien zur arabischen Literaturgeschichte*, I, 226–31.

20. See, for instance, below, n. 123.

170–2) of Ibn al-Jawzī (507–97/1126–1200), the *Nubalā'* (XIV, 267–82) of al-Dhahabī (673–748/1274–1348),[21] and the large *Ṭabaqāt al-Shāfi'iyyah* (III, 120–8) of Tāj al-Dīn al-Subkī (727–71/1327–70). Other works have, of course, been mentioned here wherever indicated.[22]

Not surprisingly, the critical evaluation of the available material presents difficult problems. The reports we have are expectedly partial to Ṭabarī. In fact, they can be suspected of an attempt to idealize him. Since Ṭabarī expressed views on nearly every aspect of religion, law, and society, he inevitably made many enemies. They left no biographical notices known to us, and their views are rarely heard.[23] We may question whether the anecdotes told about him actually occurred and whether he did in fact do all the things and make all the remarks attributed to him. Furthermore, there was, and is, the temptation to suppose that a famous person had contact with any other famous person in his time and place. Thus, there is occasionally some doubt as to whether the individuals named in anecdotes, on which we must rely for reconstructing some of the data of Ṭabarī's life, were accurately reported.[24] In view of these and other difficulties, the only sound procedure is the one followed here: Unless there is irrefutable proof to the contrary, we must assume that the reports reflect reality, and that idealizing descriptions depict, if not reality, then something equally or more important, namely, the perception of contemporaries. In either case, they provide legitimate material for the biographer, to be used, it is true, with appropriate caution.

His Early Life

Abū Ja'far Muḥammad b. Jarīr al-Ṭabarī was born in Āmul, the principal capital city of Ṭabaristān, located in the lowlands of the

21. Al-Dhahabī had occasion to come back to Ṭabarī in other works. His *Ta'rīkh al-Islām* presumably contained a lengthy obituary notice. It was not available to me.

22. For instance, the biographies in Ibn Khallikān and al-Nawawī were already edited and translated by Hamaker, *Specimen*, 21–32. For Ḥājjī Khalīfah and d'Herbelot, see, in particular, below, 138.

23. Some hostile Ḥanbalite information seems to have entered the biographical mainstream; see below, 73 f.

24. The often crucial dates for individuals connected with Ṭabari are unfortunately not always as certain as we might wish; see below, translation, v f.

region at a distance of about twenty kilometers from the southern shore of the Caspian.[25] It was sometime during the winter of A.D. 839, when al-Muʿtaṣim ruled as caliph in Baghdad. Ṭabarī himself was not quite sure whether his birth fell near the end of the hijrah year 224 or in the beginning of 225. According to local memory, it coincided with some noteworthy happening, but those whom he asked at some later time in his life were uncertain what that happening had been. Ṭabaristān certainly went through an eventful time at this period of its history, though the political circumstances may not have been responsible for the particular happening by which Ṭabarī's birth was remembered. In the years 224 and 225, the governor of the region, Māziyār b. Qārin, a recent convert to Islam and a member of the Bāwandid dynasty who were still non-Muslims,[26] rebelled against control by the Ṭāhirid dynasty of governors and thus against the central authorities of the caliphate. In the course of the rebellion, heavy taxes were placed upon the landowners of Āmul, and the city itself was laid waste. We do not know in which way and to what degree these events affected Ṭabarī's family. It is possible that the attempt to levy new taxes on farms and real estate had a temporary unsettling effect on it. With the victory of the Ṭāhirids, Āmul seems to have entered upon a prosperous phase of its history.

Ṭabarī retained close ties to his hometown throughout his life. At some later date, he wrote an essay detailing his religious principles, and addressed it to the people of Ṭabaristān. He felt that erroneous doctrines, such as those propounded by Muʿtazilites and Khārijites, were spreading there.[27] Shīʿah influence also was strong. ʿAlids and their supporters achieved political hegemony when the Zaydī dynasty came into power in 250/864. Probably about 290/903, on his second (and, apparently, last) of his recorded visits home, his outspoken defense of the virtues of the first two caliphs against Shīʿah attacks caused him much trouble. Reportedly, he had to leave the region in a great hurry. An old man who had given him timely warning of the danger awaiting him was severely beaten by the authorities; cognizant of his indebtedness

25. See "Āmol" in *Encyclopaedia Iranica*, I, 980 f.

26. See "Bāwand" in *EI*[2], I, 1110. On the Ṭāhirids, see, for instance, C.E. Bosworth, in *The Cambridge History of Iran*, IV, 90 ff.

27. On *Tabṣīr*, below, 126 f.

to him, Ṭabarī had him brought to Baghdad where he treated him hospitably.[28] There may be no special significance to the fact that men from Ṭabaristān were rather numerous in the historian's circle of acquaintances and that *History* pays a good deal of attention to events in Ṭabaristān, but it could be another indication of Ṭabarī's attachment to the land of his birth.

Information on the more remote history of Ṭabarī's family is restricted to the names of his ancestors on his father's side. Yazīd is reasonably well-established as the name of his grandfather. It is mentioned regularly, and it also occurs in Ṭabarī's own works, though rarely and with somewhat doubtful authenticity.[29] Beyond Yazīd, the names of Ṭabarī's great-grandfather and great-great-grandfather appear as Kathīr b. Ghālib in one tradition, while another less common one knows only of a great-grandfather named Khālid.[30] These are all good Arabic Muslim names and as such contain no hint at ancient non-Muslim roots on his father's side. They would lead into the mid-second/eighth century before Ṭabaristān came, in a way, fully under Muslim control. It is thus not entirely excluded, if far from certain, that Ṭabarī's paternal forebears were Muslim colonists who migrated to Āmul and settled there at some date. Ṭabarī himself discouraged speculation about his ancestry. When he was asked by a certain Muḥammad b. Ja'far b. Jumhūr[31] about his ancestry, he replied by quoting a verse of Ru'bah b. al-'Ajjāj, in which the famous Umayyad poet deprecated pride in one's pedigree.

(My father) al-'Ajjāj has established my reputation,[32] so call me

28. See *Irshād*, VI, 456, ed. Rifā'ī, XVIII, 85 f.

29. We can never be sure whether "b. Yazīd" goes back to Ṭabarī's own text or was added in the course of the manuscript transmission. See *Tafsīr*, III, 107, l. 14 (beginning of sūrah 3). The subscription of the ancient manuscript of *Ikhtilāf*, ed. Schacht, x, refers to Yazīd, but the text later on (p. 242) does not have it. It is, however, frequent in Kern's edition of *Ikhtilāf*.

30. Thus Ibn al-Nadīm, *Fihrist*, 234, l. 9. His source was al-Mu'āfā, who might have had reliable information; still, the majority opinion seems to be correct. See also Ibn Khallikān, *Wafayāt*, IV, 191.

31. He cannot be further identified. He appears to have been a follower of Ṭabarī's school. His name is given only in Ibn 'Asākir, LXXIII f., who indicates that his information goes back to al-Mu'āfā.

32. Cf. Qur. 94:4. Ru'bah's *Dīwān* does not have "my." A reading *dhikrā*, and not *dhikrī*, has nothing to recommend itself.

by my name (alone)! When long pedigrees are given
(for others), it suffices me.[33]

Perhaps, Ṭabarī wished to express disdain for the view that merit was based upon ancestry rather than individual accomplishment (even if Ru'bah's verse is not a good example for it). This was a topic hotly debated in Islam at all times. On the other hand, it could merely mean that Ṭabarī did not have memorable ancestors whom he knew about or cared for.

A strange family relationship was claimed for Ṭabarī on the basis of a couple of verses ascribed to the well-known poet Abū Bakr (Muḥammad b. al-ʿAbbās) al-Khuwārizmī, whose death is placed about 383/993 or a decade later.[34] The verses speak about the poet's relationship to the "Jarīr family (*banū Jarīr*)." He states that he was born in Āmul and boasts that the Banū Jarīr were ʿAlid extremists *(rāfiḍī)* through the female lineage *(ʿan kalālah)*, while he himself was a *rāfiḍī* by paternal inheritance.[35] The relationship was supposed to be as close as that of nephew and uncle (?), which would be chronologically impossible. The little we know about Ṭabarī's family does not support such a relationship or the existence of an extended "Jarīr family." As suggested by Yāqūt, the connection of the verses with the historian may have been the work of hostile Ḥanbalites who wished to brand him as a Shīʿite. But we also hear from a Shīʿite source that the other Abū Jaʿfar Muḥammad b. Jarīr al-Ṭabarī, whose grandfather's name was Rustam and who was the likely author of *al-Mustarshid* (see below, 118 f.), applied the verses to himself, with the difference that he claimed maternal relationship while someone else claimed paternal lineage for their Shīʿah loyalties.[36] At any rate, the story can be safely disregarded as absurd and unhistorical, as far as Ṭabarī is concerned.

His father, Jarīr, was a man of property, although he was not

33. See Ru'bah, *Dīwān*, 160, no. 57, ll. 8 f., translation, 215; Ibn ʿAsākir (above, n. 31); *Irshād*, VI, 428, ed. Rifāʿī, XVIII, 47.

34. See Sezgin, *GAS*, II, 635 f. Abū Bakr al-Khuwārizmī was also called al-Ṭabarkhazī, because his father came from Khuwārizm and his mother from Ṭabaristān; see Samʿānī, *Ansāb*, IX, 37 f.; Ibn Khallikān, *Wafayāt*, IV, 400; and Ṣafadī, *Wāfī*, III, 191. See further *EI²*, IV, 1069, s.v. al-Khʷārazmī.

35. See Yāqūt, *Muʿjam*, I, 68. Yāqūt rejects the story as malicious Ḥanbalite slander picked up by the Shīʿah poet, but it appears to have been accepted by scholars such as Ibn Khallikān, *Wafayāt*, IV, 192, and Ṣafadī, *Wāfī*, II, 284, III, 192.

36. See Ibn Abī al-Ḥadīd, *Sharḥ*, I, 301.

rich. As long as he lived, he provided his son with an income, and Ṭabarī inherited (his share of) the estate after his father's death, the date of which is not known to us. According to an anecdote placed in the time of the wazirate of Muḥammad b. ʿUbaydallāh b. Khāqān, who became wazīr in 299/912, even at that late period of Ṭabarī's life, the pilgrim caravan brought the proceeds from his lands *(ḍayʿah)* in Ṭabaristān to Baghdad—as usual, it seems, in the form of merchandise rather than cash. It was Ṭabarī's custom to use the occasion to make gifts to friends and acquaintances to whom he was obligated. This time, he selected[37] a sable estimated to be worth fifty dīnārs, wrapped it up in a large parcel, and had it conveyed to the wazīr, who was surprised when the parcel was opened in his presence and he saw the valuable gift. He accepted it, but he indicated that he did not want Ṭabarī to give any more such presents to him in the future. On his part, Ṭabarī had intended the precious fur as a countergift for one the wazīr had offered him, and it was to serve as a hint that as a matter of principle, he felt he could not accept any large gifts from the wazīr or anybody else.[38]

The modest degree of financial independence which Ṭabarī enjoyed throughout his life enabled him as a student to travel, and it gave him some freedom to follow his scholarly and moral ideals when he was an established scholar and other potential sources of income were readily at his disposal. Living and traveling at rather large distances from his source of income, it could happen that his father's stipend did not reach him on time, and he experienced some temporary inconvenience. Once, he was forced to sell some of his garments, such as the long sleeves characteristic of the scholar's robe.[39] In Egypt, he and his friends even had to go

37. Yāqūt is not very clear as to whether Ṭabarī bought the fur from the proceeds or whether it was part of the merchandise he had received. There is good reason to assume the latter. It could conceivably suggest that the total value of the merchandise was substantial.

38. See *Irshād*, VI, 457 f., ed. Rifāʿī, XVIII, 88 f. The informants here, Abū al-Ṭayyib al-Qāsim b. Aḥmad b. al-Shāʿir and Sulaymān b. al-Khāqānī (if these are the correct forms of their names), cannot be identified. Ṭabarī's attitude toward gifts will come up repeatedly here, as it is a recurrent motif in his biography. The exchange of gifts played an important role in Muslim society and found much attention among jurists (see, for instance *EI*², III, 342-40, s. v. hiba). For Ṭabarī's views on the acceptance of gifts from non-Muslims—a subject that had major political implications—one may compare his discussion in *Tahdhīb, Musnad ʿAlī*, 207–21.

39. See below, n. 69. Ibn Abī Ḥātim, *Taqdimah*, 363 f., reports a similar experi-

hungry until a local dignitary miraculously came to their rescue and sent them a large amount of money.[40]

At a young age, Ṭabarī displayed his precociousness, which was remarkable even in a world where precociousness was not unusual and was carefully nurtured by parents and teachers. As an old man probably in his seventies, he recalled that he knew the Qur'ān by heart when he was seven, served as prayer leader when he was eight, and studied (lit., "wrote down") traditions of the Prophet when he was nine. This remark may sound a little boastful, but there is no reason to doubt it. The words appear to be those actually used when he wanted to convince the father of a nine-year-old boy, the young son of his future biographer Ibn Kāmil, that it was not too early for Ibn Kāmil to have the boy study with him and that he should not use the boy's tender years and lack of preparation *(qillat al-adab)* as an excuse for not doing so. In order to stress his point, he told Ibn Kāmil of a dream which his own father had once had about his young son. "My father," Ṭabarī reminisced, "had a dream concerning me. He saw me standing before the Prophet with a bag filled with stones, and I was spreading some of them in front of him. A dream interpreter told my father that the dream signified that I would be a good Muslim as an adult and a strong defender of the religious law of the Prophet. As a consequence, my father was ready to support my studies ('my quest of knowledge' *ṭalab al-ʿilm)* when I was still a small boy."[41]

Whether it was an actual dream or a literary fiction does not really matter. Dreams commonly served as a means to express basic convictions. In this case, the dream mirrored the desire of Ṭabarī's father to further his son's education, although he himself most likely had no specialized scholarly training. He encouraged him to leave home "in quest of knowledge," when he reached puberty *(taraʿraʿa)*. We are told reliably that young Ṭabarī left home

ence of his father.

40. See below, n. 109. It was, of course, nothing rare for students and many other young men to live on paternal bounty. Thus, Tanūkhī, *Faraj*, II, 179, tells about a Khurāsānian who every year received his annual allowance through the pilgrim caravan. Unable, or unwilling, to stretch it to last the entire year, he compiled debts to be paid off when next year's caravan arrived, only to get into a very tight situation when the caravan did not bring anything for him one year because his father had been seriously ill.

41. See *Irshād*, 429 f., ed. Rifāʿī, XVIII, 49. On Ṭabarī's good-humored banter with the boy's names on this occasion, see below, n. 163.

in 236/850–1, when he was only twelve.[42] It often was a wrenching decision, especially for a mother, to send a child off to college, for this is what "traveling in quest of knowledge" really meant in cases of young boys such as Ṭabarī. The situation was aggravated by the fact that there were no organized "colleges" in his day (as there were in later centuries) which could have provided institutional support. Providing for proper living arrangements for the youngsters was left to individuals, family connections, or, preferably, teachers. We know nothing about Ṭabarī's mother, not even if she was still alive when he left home. If she was, she might have felt like the mother of Ibn Bashshār, one of Ṭabarī's influential teachers, when her son was faced with the decision of going away to study. She did not want him to leave, and he heeded his mother's advice and stayed, at least for the time being. Later, he felt that it was on account of this act of filial piety that he was blessed with a successful career.[43]

Young Ṭabarī left to receive his further schooling in the nearest metropolis, al-Rayy, on the site of present-day Teheran. The teachers in Āmul whom his father had engaged for him naturally did not measure up in prestige to those in al-Rayy. It was there that, during a stay of apparently close to five years, Ṭabarī received the intellectual formation that made him the scholar he was to become. There is no record of his having visited other scholarly centers before leaving for Baghdad, where he arrived "shortly after the death of Ibn Ḥanbal" in the latter half of 241, that is, late in 855 or early in the following year.[44] "Traveling in quest of knowledge" could mean brief visits to famous authorities. Frequently, however, and no doubt in the case of very young students such as Ṭabarī, it entailed an extended stay and the systematic attendance at regular courses rather than occasional lectures. A teacher would quiz his students in the evening on the material they had taken down during the day. When the students happened to take a course with a teacher who lived outside the city limits, they had to run back "like mad *(ka-al-majānīn)*" in order to be on time for

42. The source for the precise date is Maslamah b. al-Qāsim, as quoted by Ibn Ḥajar. See below, n. 123.

43. See *TB*, II, 102, ll. 3 f.

44. See *Irshād*, 430, l. 18, ed. Rifāʿī, XVIII, 50.

another class.[45]

Most prominent among his teachers in al-Rayy was Ibn Ḥumayd. Abū ʿAbdallāh Muḥammad b. Ḥumayd al-Rāzi[46] was in his seventies at the time, and he died a decade later, in 248/862. He became one of Ṭabarī's most frequently cited authorities. Ibn Ḥumayd had lectured in Baghad and had been welcomed there by Ibn Ḥanbal, who is even said to have transmitted traditions on his authority. If it is correct that Ibn Ḥanbal's son ʿAbdallāh (213–90/828[9]–903)[47] had studied with him, his stay in Baghdad cannot have been very much in the past, unless, of course, ʿAbdallāh was a small child when he attended his lectures, which is quite possible. In Ṭabarī's time, Ibn Ḥumayd had apparently retired to his native city. We have no information that he returned to Baghdad during his remaining years, in which case Ṭabarī could have continued his studies with him there. Thus, the material he quoted on Ibn Ḥumayd's authority was acquired by him in al-Rayy. No doubt he filled his notebooks with it for future reference, but he can also be assumed to have checked it all against the books upon which Ibn Ḥumayd had based his teaching, and supplemented it from them.

Another teacher from Ṭabarī's days in al-Rayy was al-Muthannā b. Ibrāhīm, whose *nisbah* was al-Āmulī (rather than al-Ubullī as found in *Irshād*).[48] Practically nothing more is known about him, but he also served as an important source of information for Ṭabarī's writings. Another, even less-known teacher of Ṭabarī was a certain Aḥmad b. Ḥammād al-Dawlābī. His main claim to distinction was that he had been a student of the reputable Sufyān (b. ʿUyaynah).[49] It must be said that our lack of knowledge about these men does not mean that their standing in the world of contemporary scholarship was low in any respect.

It is significant that the instruction which Ṭabarī received from Ibn Ḥumayd in al-Rayy extended to the historical works of Ibn

45. See *Irshād*, 430, ed. Rifāʿī, XVIII, 49 f.

46. For Ibn Ḥumayd, see below, translation, n. 26. *Irshād*, VI, 424, l. 2. ed. Rifāʿī, XVIII, 41, l. 2, had Aḥmad for Muḥammad by mistake (misprint ?).

47. See below, 70. For Ibn Ḥumayd's connection with Ibn Ḥanbal and the latter's son ʿAbdallāh, see *TB*, II, 259, ll. 4 f., 12, and 260, ll. 4 f.

48. See below, translation, n. 179.

49. See *History*, below, I, 1806; *Tafsīr*, VI, 3, l. 21 (*ad* Qur. 4:148), XI, 94, l. 21 (*ad* Qur. 10:64), XVIII, 60, l. 8 (*ad* Qur. 24:5).

Isḥāq, famous above all as the author of the life of Muḥammad *(al-Sīrah)*. He thus learned about pre-Islamic and early Islamic history. Knowledge of it was needed by religious scholars in general. In Ṭabarī's case, more importantly, it would seem that in the process, the seeds were planted for his wider interest in history which later culminated in the writing of his great *History*. According to Yāqūt, Ibn Kāmil is supposed to have reported that it was under the guidance of the just-mentioned Aḥmad b. Ḥammād al-Dawlābī on the authority of Salamah[50] that Ṭabarī studied Ibn Isḥāq's *Mubtada'* and *Maghāzī* and thus laid the groundwork for *History*.[51] However, in *History* itself, the *isnād* is always Ibn Ḥumayd—Salamah—Ibn Isḥāq. The reference to Ibn Ḥammād in this connection is no doubt a mistake, which, however, could hardly have occurred in Ibn Kāmil's original text but must have crept in during the course of transmission.[52] Ṭabarī later on continued his study of Ibn Isḥāq. In al-Kūfah, both Hannād b. al-Sarī and Abū Kurayb transmitted to him information from Ibn Isḥāq according to another recension, that of Yūnus b Bukayr (d. 199/814[5]).[53] At that time, Ṭabarī probably did not receive instruction in special courses devoted entirely to Ibn Isḥāq. It was rather through incidental reference that he learned more about him there.

Ibn Ḥumayd's status as an authorized transmitter of Ibn Isḥāq's *Maghāzī* through Salamah was attacked by an otherwise unknown ʿAlī b. Mihrān. Ibn Mihrān claimed plagiarism on the part of Ibn Ḥumayd. According to him, Ibn Ḥumayd did not receive the material directly from Salamah but through him. Therefore, he contended, a certain Isḥāq b. Manṣūr (possibly the bearer of the name who died in 251/865?), who had studied with Ibn Ḥumayd just like Ṭabarī, was right when he classified Ibn Ḥumayd as

50. For Salamah b. al-Faḍl, judge of al-Rayy, see below, translation, n. 49.

51. See *Irshād*, VI, 430, ed. Rifāʿī, XVIII, 50.

52. It is possible that both Ibn Ḥammād and Ibn Ḥumayd (who also taught Qur'ān commentary) lectured on the same material from Salamah from Ibn Ishāq in al-Rayy at the same time, but it does not seem very likely.

53. For Hannād (below, translation, n. 71), see *History*, I, 970, and for Abū Kurayb (below, translation, n. 77), see *History*, II, 311, III, 52. For Ibn Bukayr's recension, see Sezgin, *GAS*, I, 289, and Ibn Ḥajar, *Tahdhīb*, XI, 434 f., where Hannād and Abū Kurayb are listed among Ibn Bukayr's transmitters.

a "liar."[54] Quarrels of this kind were not uncommon, but even if there was some truth to the accusation directed against Ibn Ḥumayd, it would in no way reflect upon Ibn Ḥumayd's decisive role in Ṭabarī's development as a scholar.

A continuation of his studies in the center of the Muslim world, the capital city of Baghdad, was a natural choice for Ṭabarī, who by then was not yet seventeen years old. Baghdad not only counted many of the greatest representatives of Muslim scholarship among its residents, but scholars as well as litterateurs also came to lecture there for longer or shorter periods. Many stopped over on their way to or, more commonly, from the pilgrimage to Mecca, offering students the opportunity to add to their store of knowledge. In fact, if we can believe the *Story of the Belt* (below, p. 99), Ṭabarī himself went on the pilgrimage in 240/855, possibly before his first arrival in Baghdad (and not in the time between his arrival in Baghdad and his study trip to southern Iraq). The date of Ṭabarī's arrival in Baghdad is fixed by the statement that what attracted him to Baghdad was the expectation to study with Aḥmad b. Ḥanbal (164–241/780–855), but Ibn Ḥanbal died shortly before his arrival.[55] It cannot be entirely ruled out that this report was invented to defuse later Ḥanbalite animosity against Ṭabarī. There is, however, nothing inherently impossible in it, even though Ibn Ḥanbal was no longer fully active at the time. Ibn Ḥumayd might very well have suggested to his bright young student that it was advisable for him to profit from contact with the great traditionist, no matter how slight such contact would be.

Rather soon,[56] Ṭabarī left Baghdad in order to continue his study and research in the great towns south of Baghdad, al-Baṣrah and al-Kūfah, including Wāsiṭ on the way. A number of famous authorities, mostly men already at least in their seventies, lived and taught there. It would have been possible for Ṭabarī to make repeated trips while spending some time in between in Baghdad, but a student was hardly likely to do this; thus, it can be confidently

54. See *TB*, II, 262 f.
55. See above, n. 44.
56. The assumption of Hūfī, 35, that Ṭabarī left Baghdad right away seems unlikely. *Irshād*, VI, 430, ll. 19 f., ed. Rifāʿī, XVIII, 50, states that he began to study in Baghdad and then left for al-Basrah. His tutorship, which has been assigned by me to a later date (see below, 21 f.), could conceivably fall into this time, but this would seem improbable.

assumed he undertook just one extended journey. The date when it started can be established with reasonable accuracy. Some of the authorities with whom he studied, such as the Baṣrans Ḥumayd b. Mas'adah, who is often quoted in *Tafsīr,* and Bishr b. Mu'ādh al-'Aqadī,[57] died at the latest in 245/859–60; but one of the Kūfan scholars, Hannād b. al-Sarī, who also provided him with much information for *Tafsīr,* is said to have died already in 243/857 as a man in his nineties.[58] Assuming that this date is correct, Ṭabarī's first stay in Baghdad lasted hardly more than a year, and he had gone south already in 242/856–7.

Scholars in al-Baṣrah whom Ṭabarī met during his visit there included men quoted again and again in his works. Among them were Muḥammad b. 'Abd al-A'lā al-Ṣan'ānī (d. 245/859[60]),[59] Muḥammad b. Mūsā al-Ḥarashī (d. 248/862),[60] and Abū al-Ash'ath Aḥmad b. al-Miqdām (d. 253/867).[61] Others, such as Abū al-Jawzā' Aḥmad b. 'Uthmān (d. 246/860), are cited less frequently.[62]

In al-Kūfah, he encountered, among others, Ismā'īl b. Mūsā al-Fazārī (d. 245/859), whom Ṭabarī considered to be a grandson of al-Suddī,[63] and Sulaymān b. 'Abd al-Raḥmān b. Ḥammād al-Ṭalḥī (d. 252/866), an expert in Qur'ān reading who showed himself willing to test Ṭabarī's knowledge and qualifications in the field.[64]

The two men from whom he profited most in those years were Muḥammad b. Bashshār, known as Bundār (167–252/783[4]–866),[65] in al-Baṣrah, and Abū Kurayb Muḥammad b. al-'Alā' (d. in his

57. For Ḥumayd b. Mas'adah, see Ibn Ḥajar, *Tahdhīb,* III, 49. He is often quoted in *Tafsīr* as well as *Tahdhīb, Musnad 'Alī,* index, 429. For Bishr, see below, translation, n. 196.

58. See above, n. 53.

59. See below, translation, n. 101.

60. See Ibn Ḥajar, *Tahdhīb,* IX, 482, no. 778.

61. See below, translation, n. 970.

62. See Ibn Ḥajar, *Tahdhīb,* IV 206 f. He is mentioned in *Tahdhīb, Musnad Ibn 'Abbās,* index, 1051, and *History,* I, 1147.

63. For al-Fazārī, see Ibn Ḥajar, *Tahdhīb,* I, 335 f. His relationship to al-Suddī (below, translation, n. 276) was disputed.

64. For Sulaymān al-Ṭalḥī, see Ibn Ḥajar, *Tahdhīb,* IV, 206 f.; Ibn al-Jazarī, *Ghāyah,* II, 107, and I, 314, ll. 13 f. (*'araḍa 'alayh al-imām Muḥammad b. Jarīr al-Ṭabarī*). Ibn al-Jazarī, like al-Maqrīzī, *Muqaffā* (Ṭabarī, *Introductio etc.,* XCVI), depends on al-Dānī. Ṣafadī, *Wāfī,* II, 285, l. 5, and Subkī, *Ṭabaqāt,* III, 121, also mention that Ṭabarī studied Qur'ān reading with him. It is not certain that he met him in al-Kūfah. Al-Ṭalḥī is mentioned in *Tafsīr,* XVI, 61, l. 3 (*ad* Qur. 19:31).

65. See below, translation, n. 44.

eighties in 247 or 248/861–2)[66] in al-Kūfah. As appears from the innumerable times that they are cited as transmitters, both Ibn Bashshār and Abū Kurayb exercised a great influence on him. Abū Kurayb was a difficult person, but Ṭabarī did not fail to mollify him from the start of their acquaintance by his extraordinary ability. When he came to his house together with other *ḥadīth* students clamoring for admission, he found the great scholar looking out of a window and asking for those who could recite from memory the traditions they had written down on his dictation. The assembled students looked at each other and then pointed to Ṭabarī as the one who would be able to do that. Abū Kurayb examined him and found him able to recite every tradition he was asked, with the exact day on which Abū Kurayb had taught it.[67]

Ṭabarī probably spent less than two years traveling in southern Iraq and may have returned to Baghdad about 244/858–9. It was not until eight years later that he undertook his next major research trip that took him to Syria and Egypt. During that interval between journeys, we should possibly date his first attested gainful employment. He accepted a position as tutor to a son of the wazīr ʿUbaydallāh b. Yaḥyā b. Khāqān.[68] The boy was called Abū Yaḥyā. As the story suggests, he probably was the wazīr's son by a slave girl. Since Ibn Khāqān was out of office and in exile between 248 and 253, Ṭabarī would have held his tutorial position sometime between 244/858–9 and 248/962. The report we have is introduced by the words "when Ṭabarī entered Baghdad" and could refer to his first arrival in the capital. However, a rather high salary is involved, which seems more than could have been commanded by a very young and unknown student such as Ṭabarī was when he first came to Baghdad. Moreover, the story shows Ṭabarī already firmly committed to legal ethics, which is hardly in keeping with someone seventeen years of age. Ṭabarī, we are told, had merchandise to provide for his living expenses (sent, no doubt, by his father). It was stolen, and he was in dire straights,

66. See below, translation, n. 77.

67. See *Irshād*, VI, 431, ed. Rifāʿī, XVIII, 51. "Difficult person" renders *sharis al-khuluq*. This characterization, which fitted other scholars as well, is also used for the grammarian Thaʿlab (*Irshād*, VI, 438, l. 7, ed. Rifāʿī, XVIII, 60).

68. See EI^2, III, 824a, s. v. Ibn Khāḳān (2). The future wazīr was a student of Ibn Ḥanbal; see Ibn Abī Yaʿlā, *Ṭabaqāt*, I, 204. On another son, the wazīr al-Khāqānī, see below, n. 129.

so much so that he had to sell part of his clothing.[69] A friend of his knew that the wazīr was looking for a tutor for his son, and the friend asked Ṭabarī whether he was willing to accept the position if it was offered to him. Ṭabarī agreed, no doubt eagerly. The friend was able to arrange matters. After first providing him with the proper clothes, he introduced him to the wazīr. Ibn Khāqān gained a good impression of him. He offered him the position and agreed to pay ten dīnārs per month. In addition, he had a contract drawn up specifying the time Ṭabarī[70] was allowed to devote to study, prayer, eating, and resting, and even gave him upon his request a one-month advance. A well-equipped classroom *(ḥujrat al-ta'dīb)* for the boy was assigned to Ṭabarī. He instructed him in writing, and his pupil appears to have quickly learned how to write. The writing tablet that demonstrated the boy's newly acquired skill was taken by servants to his mother and the other slave girls who had borne children to their master *(ummahāt al-walad)* as proof of the good news. The overjoyed ladies filled a tray with dirhams and dīnārs and sent it with the servants back to Ṭabarī. He, however, refused to accept the money. He had, he said, a contract with the wazīr to be paid a certain sum and was not entitled to any further compensation. The matter was submitted to the wazīr who summoned him and told him that he was wrong to reject the well-meant gift of the women and had offended them by not accepting it. Ṭabarī argued that the women were slaves and legally owned no property of their own. He obviously implied that it was really the wazīr who was the source of the money and who therefore was paying more than had been agreed upon in the contract. Ṭabarī learned a lesson from this occurrence. Later on, when friends would bring him a gift of food, it was his established custom *(sunnah)* to accept it as being, in contrast to money, merely a token gift; but, prompted by his socially proper attitude *(muruwwah)*, he would make an appropriate return gift. This taught

69. The manuscript of Ibn 'Asākir has *k-s-y qamīṣ-h*, which was emended to *kummay...* "the long sleeves of his shirt" in Ṭabarī, *Introductio etc.*, LXXV. The correction is confirmed by Dhahabī's quotation in *Nubalā'*, XIV, 271 f. In a brief statement reported by Subkī, *Ṭabaqāt*, III, 125, Ṭabarī is quoted by al-Farghānī as having said, "My father's allowance for my living expenses did not arrive on time, so that I was forced to cut off the sleeves of my shirt and sell them." Al-Subkī no doubt refers to the same event.

70. The Arabic pronoun clearly refers to Ṭabarī, and not to his young pupil.

his friends that it would be inadvisable to press gifts on him.[71]

Being in his late twenties, Ṭabarī was an acknowledged scholar—a "recent Ph.D." in our parlance—when he left Baghdad for further study in the West, that is, in the countries located to the west of Iraq. His goal was Egypt, but his journey included visits to Syria and Palestine both on the way to Egypt and on a sidetrip from Egypt before his eventual return to Baghdad. Beirut was an especially important stop because it gave him the opportunity to study with al-'Abbās b. al-Walīd b. Mazyad al-'Udhrī al-Bayrūtī (ca. 169–270/785[6]–883[4]).[72] Al-'Abbās instructed him in the variant readings *(ḥurūf)* of the Qur'ān according to the Syrian school. Moreover, he was instrumental in conveying to him through his father al-Walīd the legal views of al-Awzā'ī, Syria's most prominent jurist who had died in Beirut about a century earlier.[73]

Ṭabarī's precise itinerary in Syria and Palestine is not known to us. Some of the places he visited can be deduced from the names of the authorities cited in his works. The scholars named Ḥimṣī, Ramlī, or 'Asqalānī could, of course, have been in Iraq or in Egypt when Ṭabarī studied with them. However, even if it is not expressly attested that a given scholar resided in his native town at

---

71. See Ibn 'Asākir, LXXV f., and Dhahabī, *Nubalā'* (above, n. 69).

72. See Ibn 'Asākir, LXIX and LXXII; Ibn al-Jazarī, *Ghāyah*, I, 355, II, 107; al-Maqrīzī, *Muqaffā* (Ṭabarī, *Introductio etc.*, XCVI). For al-'Abbās and his father (who was also always the source of his traditions in *Tahdhīb, Musnad Ibn 'Abbās*, index, 1061), see below, translation, n. 98. Al-'Abbās b. al-Walīd's authority is said to be Khallād b. Khālid (d. 220/835; see Ibn al-Jazarī, *Ghāyah*, I, 274 f.). Ṭabarī, according to *Irshād*, VI, 427, ll. 9–12, ed. Rifā'ī, XVIII, 45, taught Qur'ān reading—which he supposedly did rarely, and only to selected individuals—according to the tradition of 'Abd al-Ḥamīd b. Bakkār al-Kalā'ī. 'Abd al-Hamīd was also a teacher of Qur'ān readings (*ḥurūf*) to al-'Abbās b. al-Walīd; see Ibn Ḥajar, *Tahdhīb*, VI, 109; Ibn al-Jazarī, *Ghāyah*, 355, 360. No contradiction is involved here, inasmuch as al-'Abbās b. al-Walīd transmitted material from both authorities to Ṭabarī.

In his second passage, Ibn 'Asākir quotes a work entitled *Talkhīṣ qirā'āt al-Sha'miyyīn* by a certain Abū 'Alī Aḥmad b. Muḥammad b. al-Ḥasan al-Iṣbahānī. Regrettably, the quotation is out of context: "Abū Ja'far, that is, Muḥammad b. Jarīr al-Ṭabarī, stayed in Beirut several days, spending seven nights in the main mosque until he finished the Qur'ān according to this (!) transmission, reciting it to al-'Abbās b. al-Walīd. Then, after the reading, he listened to the Book being read by al-'Abbās. He informed him that he had thus read the Qur'ān to 'Abd al-Ḥamīd b. Bakkār twice, and so on."

73. For al-Awzā'ī, see below, translation, n. 95. The *isnād* "al-'Abbās b al-Walīd—his father—al-Awzā'ī" occurs, for instance, in *Ikhtilāf*, ed. Kern, 20, l. 4, etc., ed. Schacht, 148.

about the time Ṭabarī visited there, there are additional indications for their places of residence, such as, for instance, their permanent close ties to a given town, their having been visited there by contemporary students such as Ibn Abī Ḥātim al-Rāzī (ca. 240–327/854[5]–939) and his father Abū Ḥātim (195–277/810[1]–90[1], their interconnections with other scholars of the region, their failure to be listed in *TB*, and the like.[74]

Ḥimṣ (Ḥomṣ, Emesa) was famous for its special tradition of *ḥadīth* transmission. Among the Ḥimṣīs who were Ṭabarī's authorities, mention may be made of ʿImrān b. Bakkār al-Kalāʿī,[75] Abū al-Jamāhir Muḥammad b. ʿAbd al-Raḥmān,[76] a certain Abū Shuraḥbīl,[77] Sulaymān b. Muḥammad b. Maʿdīkarib al-Ruʿaynī,[78] Muḥammad b. Ḥafṣ al-Waṣṣābī,[79] Saʿīd b. ʿUthmān al-Tanūkhī,[80] and the outstanding representative of the Syrian *ḥadīth* school at the time, Muḥammad b. ʿAwf al-Ṭāʾī.[81] Another Ḥimṣī, Saʿīd b.

74. Another father-and-son team traveling in quest of knowledge among Ṭabarī's contemporaries was Abū Bakr b. Abī Dāwūd (see below, n. 229) and his father Sulaymān b. al-Ashʿath; see *TB*, IX, 464.

In connection with these pages, it is particularly regrettable that most of Ibn ʿAsākir's *History of Damascus* was unavailable to me.

75. ʿImrān b. Bakkār died in 270/883–4; see Ibn Ḥajar, *Tahdhīb*, VIII, 124. His family had old roots in Ḥimṣ. Ṭabarī refers to him frequently, for instance, *History*, I, 210; *Dhayl*, III, 2425, ed. Cairo, XI, 591; *Tahdhīb, Musnad Ibn ʿAbbās*, index, 1066, *Musnad ʿAlī*, index, 435 f.; *Tafsīr*, II, 353, l. 8 (*ad* Qur. 2:238), V, 163 f. (*ad* Qur. 4:11), on *ṣalāt al-khawf*, etc. In *Aghānī*, VIII, 161 (= *Agh.*3 „ IX, 273), Ṭabarī is quoted as reporting an Umayyad family tradition through him.

76. See Ibn Abī Ḥātim, III,2, 327, where Ibn Abī Ḥātim says that he studied with him in Ḥimṣ; *Tahdhīb, Musnad Ibn ʿAbbās*, index, 1054; *Tafsīr*, XIV, 15, l. 28 (*ad* Qur. 15:22). His authority in the *Tafsīr* passage, Abū Rawḥ ʿAbd al-ʿAzīz b. Mūsā, was also a Ḥimṣī. Abū Ḥātim al-Rāzī studied with Abū Rawḥ in Salamyah, see Ibn Abī Ḥātim, II,2, 397.

77. See *History*, I, 1140; *Tafsīr*, XIV, 32, l. 11 (*ad* Qur. 15:75), XXI, 56, l. 27 (*ad* Qur. 31:34); *Tahdhīb, Musnad ʿAlī*, index, 432.

78. See Ibn Ḥajar, *Tahdhīb*, IV, 217; Ibn Abī Ḥātim, II,1, 140 f.: "he died before I came to Ḥimṣ." In *Tafsīr*, XX, 53, l. 8 (*ad* Qur. 28:48), his authority is another Ḥimṣī, al-Baqiyyah b. al-Walīd.

79. See Ibn Abī Ḥātim, III,2, 237. He is cited in *Tahdhīb, Musnad Ibn ʿAbbās*, index, 1071; *Tafsīr*, XXVII, 108, ll. 29 f. (*ad* Qur. 56:37).

80. See Ibn Abī Ḥātim, II,1, 47. He is cited in *Tahdhīb, Musnad Ibn ʿAbbās*, index 1058, *Musnad ʿAlī*, index, 431; *Tafsīr*, XVI, 80, l. 7 (*ad* Qur. 19:65); *Dhayl*, III, 2501, 2512, ed. Cairo, XI, 646, 655.

81. Abū Jaʿfar Muḥammad b. ʿAwf al-Ḥimṣī died in 272–3/885–6; see below, translation, n. 56; Ibn Abī Ḥātim, IV,1, 52 f.; Laoust, in *Mélanges Massignon*, III, 13. He appears also, for instance, in *Tahdhīb, Musnad Ibn ʿAbbās*, index, 1074, *Musnad ʿAlī*, index, 440 f.; *Tafsīr*, VI, 184, l. 4 (*ad* Qur. 5:54), XXIII, 17,l.17 (*ad*

ʿAmr al-Sakūnī,[82] is almost always cited by Ṭabarī together with the Ḥimṣī Baqiyyah b. al-Walīd[83] as his authority; it is most likely that Ṭabarī's contact with him took place somewhere in Syria or Palestine, if not directly in Ḥimṣ. The same applies to Abū ʿUtbah Aḥmad b. al-Faraj, although he is known to have been a frequent visitor to Baghdad.[84]

Ramlīs, from al-Ramlah in Palestine and presumably visited there by Ṭabarī, included Mūsā b. Sahl,[85] ʿAlī b. Sahl,[86] ʿĪsā b. ʿUthmān b. ʿĪsā,[87] Ismāʿīl b. Isrāʾīl al-Sallāl,[88] al-Ḥasan b. Bilāl (who had moved from al-Baṣrah to take up residence in al-Ramlah),[89] and ʿAbd al-Jabbār b. Yaḥyā.[90] Ayyūb b. Isḥāq b. Ibrāhīm lived and

---

Qur. 36:65), XXVII, 130, ll. 7 f. (*ad* Qur. 57:14); *Dhayl* III, 2397, 2414, 2422 f., ed. Cairo, XI, 569, 582, 588 f.

82. See Ibn Ḥajar, *Tahdhīb*, IV, 67 f. Cited in *Tahdhīb, Musnad ʿAlī*, index, 431; *Tafsīr*, III, 104, l. 31 (*ad* Qur. 2:286), etc.; *Dhayl*, III, 2391. ed. Cairo, XI, 565.

83. For Baqiyyah (115–97[8]/733–813), see Ibn Ḥajar, *Tahdhīb*, I, 473–8.

84. Aḥmad b. al-Faraj died in Ḥimṣ in 271/884–5; see *TB*, IV, 339–41; Ibn Ḥajar, *Tahdhīb*, I, 67–9. See, for instance, *Tahdhīb, Musnad Ibn ʿAbbās*, index, 1051, *Musnad ʿAlī*, index, 424; *Tafsīr*, IX, 80, l. 29 (*ad* Qur. 7:172), X, 15, l. 1 (*ad* Qur. 8:50), XV, 98, l. 26 (*ad* Qur. 17:79, on *maqāman maḥmūdan*), XXII, 23, l. 14 (*ad* Qur. 35:36 f.), XXVII, 4, l. 16 (*ad* Qur. 51:41).

85. See below, translation, n. 232; Ibn Abī Ḥātim, IV,1, 146. Cited in *Tahdhīb, Musnad Ibn ʿAbbās*, index, 1076; *Tafsīr*, V, 120, l. 9 (*ad* Qur. 4:86), XIII, 114, l. 30 (*ad* Qur. 13:39), XVI, 142, l. 22 (*ad* Qur. 20:73); *Ṣarīḥ*, 195 f.

86. See below, translation, n. 45. Cited in *Tahdhīb, Musnad Ibn ʿAbbās*, index, 1064, *Musnad ʿAlī*, index, 434; *Tafsīr*, XVI, 29, ll. 22 f. (*ad* Qur. 18:107), XVIII, 54, l. 13 (*ad* Qur. 24:2), XXVII, 142, l. 2 (*ad* Qur. 57:28); *Ikhtilāf*, ed. Schacht, 146; *Ṣarīḥ*, 198; *Dhayl*, III, 2369, 2490, 2492, ed. Cairo, XI, 549, 638 f. Although he was a Ramlī and transmitted from Ramlīs, it is not certain that Ṭabarī met him in his hometown.

87. According to Ibn Ḥajar, *Tahdhīb*, VIII, 220, ʿĪsā b. ʿUthmān died in 251/865. The date, if correct (which may not be the case), would mean that Ṭabarī could not have met him in al-Ramlah but presumably met him earlier in Baghdad. ʿĪsā b. ʿUthmān's chief authority, his uncle Yaḥyā b. ʿĪsā (d. 201/816[7], was a well-known Ramlī. See, for instance, *Tahdhīb, Musnad Ibn ʿAbbās*, index, 1066, *Musnad ʿAlī*, index, 436; *Tafsīr*, II, 84, l. 31 (*ad* Qur. 2:184), VI, 87, l. 15 (*ad* Qur. 5:6), VII, 168, l. 11 (*ad* Qur. 6:82), VIII, 71, l. 17 (*ad* Qur. 6:158), X, 51, l. 4 (*ad* Qur. 9:3), XIV, 42, l. 25 (*ad* Qur. 15:90 f.), XVII, 80, l. 33, 82, l. 7 (*ad* Qur. 21:105), XIX, 26, l. 28 (*ad* Qur. 25:68), XX, 51, l. 21 (*ad* Qur. 28:46), XXI, 43, l. 23 (*ad* Qur. 31:12), XXVII, 50, l. 28 (*ad* Qur. 54:1).

88. See Ibn Abī Ḥātim, I,1, 158. Ibn Abī Ḥātim has al-Sallāl, whereas *Tafsīr* has al-Laʾʾāl (?); see VII, 63, l. 6 (*ad* Qur. 5:105), XXVII, 78, l. 33 (*ad* Qur. 55:29). A Muḥammad b. Ismāʿīl b. Isrāʾīl al-Dallāl occurs *Tafsīr*, V, 144, ll. 25 f. (*ad* Qur. 4:97). Read Abū Muḥammad Ismāʿīl... (?).

89. See below, translation, n. 601.

90. See *Tafsīr*, IV, 8, l. 16 (*ad* Qur. 3:96), XIII, 65, l. 7, 68, l. 14 (*ad* Qur. 13:4), XVIII, 3, l. 18 (*ad* Qur. 23:1 f.), XX, 24, l. 5 (*ad* Qur. 28:10). His authority was Ḍamrah b.

taught in Baghdad and Egypt in addition to al-Ramlah, and he died in Baghdad in the 250s or 260s (ca. 865–82); thus, we cannot be quite sure where Ṭabarī studied with him.[91]

ʿAsqalānīs are represented by Muḥammad b. Khalaf,[92] ʿUbayd b. Ādam b. Abī Iyās,[93] and ʿIṣām b. Rawwād b. al-Jarrāḥ.[94] It may have been in Jerusalem that Ṭabarī met ʿUbaydallāh b. Muḥammad al-Firyābī.[95] Ibrāhīm b. Yaʿqūb al-Jūzajānī died between 256/870 and 259/872–3 in Syria, probably in Damascus, and Ṭabarī may have studied with him there a few years earlier. He is described as the leader of the anti-ʿAlid faction in Syria. In the course of time, he was mistakenly identified as a follower of Ṭabarī's legal school, as his *nisbah* Ḥarīzī was misread Jarīrī; this error caused later Muslim historians to exercise their critical acumen.[96]

The individuals mentioned, numerous as they are, do not exhaust the list of those who were Ṭabarī's informants during his stay in Syria and Palestine. In many cases, we know quite little about them, but they all enjoyed great esteem as scholars in their time. Their number is a good illustration of the intensity with which scholars such as Ṭabarī (but, of course, not only he)

Rabīʿah al-Filasṭīnī al-Ramlī (see Ibn Ḥajar, *Tahdhīb*, IV, 460).

91. See *TB*, VII, 9 f. Cited in *Tahdhīb*, *Musnad Ibn ʿAbbās*, index, 1052, *Musnad ʿAlī*, index, 426; *Tafsīr*, X, 128, l. 11 (*ad* Qur. 9:74).

92. See below, translation, n. 621; Ibn Abī Ḥātim, III,2, 245. Cited in *Tahdhīb*, *Musnad Ibn ʿAbbās*, index, 1071, *Musnad ʿAlī*, index, 439; *Tafsīr*, V, 80, l. 23 (*ad* Qur. 4:48) and elsewhere; *Dhayl*, III, 2379, 2414, 2515, ed. Cairo, XI, 557, 582, 657.

93. ʿUbayd b. Ādam died in 258/872; see below, translation, n. 221. His father, a prominent scholar of Marwan origin, was born in Baghdad and died in ʿAsqalān; see Ibn Abī Ḥātim, I,1, 268. Cited in *Tafsīr*, XXI, 39, l. 14 (*ad* Qur. 31:6); *Dhayl*, III, 2424, ed. Cairo, XI, 590.

94. See Ibn Abī Ḥātim, III,2, 26; and, for his father Rawwād, I,2, 524. Cited in *Tafsīr*, III, 54, l 29, 55, l. 26, 56, ll. 24 ff. (*ad* Qur. 2:267), XVII, 69, l. 17 (*ad* Qur. 21:96), XVIII, 20, l. 13 (*ad* Qur. 23:50), XX, II, l. 5 (*ad* Qur. 27.82), XXII, 72, l. 23 (*ad* Qur. 34:51).

95. Ibn Abī Ḥātim, II,2, 335, states that al-Firyābī resided in Jerusalem and that his father studied with him. One of his authorities was Ḍamrah b. Rabīʿah (above, n. 90). Al-Firyābī appears in *Tafsīr*, VII, 193, l. 3 (*ad* Qur. 6:98), IX, 143, l. 9 (*ad* Qur.8:24), XV, 148, l. 14 (*ad* Qur. 18:19), XXI, 20, l. 1 (*ad* Qur. 30:15); *Ṣarīḥ*, 196.

96. See Ibn Abī Ḥātim, I,1, 148 f.; Dhahabī, *Mīzān*, I, 75 f.; Ibn Ḥajar, *Tahdhīb*, I, 181-3; Yāqūt, *Muʿjam*, II, 149 f.; Rosenthal, *Muslim Historiography*[2], 278. He is cited in *Tahdhīb*, *Musnad Ibn ʿAbbās*, index, 1050, *Musnad ʿAlī*, index, 424; *Tafsīr*, XII, 24, l. 3 (*ad* Qur. 11:38), XIV, 197, l. 25 (*ad* Qur. 16:88), XVI, 161, l. 4 (*ad* Qur. 20:115). He may be meant in *Ṣarīḥ*, 196, where Yaʿqūb b. Ibrāhīm al-Jūzajānī is mentioned (?).

pursued their "quest of knowledge."

The year Ṭabarī came to Egypt is indicated in one passage as 253/867, and in another as 256/870.[97] It is tempting to consider the former date as referring to his first arrival in the country, and the second as the date of his return after the excursion to Syria and Palestine. This may have been so, in particular, since both dates appear to go back to one authority, Ibn Kāmil. The context in which the dates are embedded seems to confirm the first date as quite certain. It depicts Ṭabarī as comparatively unknown when he reached Egypt, and willing to have his scholarly competence tested by someone about his own age, a certain Abū al-Ḥasan ʿAlī b. Sirāj. In this connection, Ibn Sirāj is rather strangely described as a sort of arbiter of the Egyptian intellectual establishment whose word was taken as the ultimate endorsement of someone's standing as a scholar and man of general culture.[98] The second date, 256/870, is connected with an anecdote that shows Ṭabarī as a newcomer unfamiliar with life in Egypt and indicates a great scholar as his host. Taking all these small indicia into account, it seems that while the year 253 can be taken as correctly dating his first arrival in Egypt, the date of 256 for his return visit to the country is much less certain.

Yūnus b. ʿAbd al-Aʿlā (170–264/787–877)[99] was Egypt's leading scholar in the fields of *ḥadīth* and Qur'ān reading. Ṭabarī profited from Ibn ʿAbd al-Aʿlā's knowledge in these disciplines, as he certainly did from other competent Egyptian scholars. But no doubt the greatest boon which Ṭabarī reaped from his sojourn in Egypt was an increased understanding of the legal systems of Mālik and al-Shāfiʿī. His host, al-Rabīʿ b. Sulaymān (174-270/790[1]-884),[100] who welcomed him to Egypt and who made a living as muezzin of

97. See *Irshād*, VI, 432, l. 7, and 434, l. 4, ed. Rifāʿī, XVIII, 52 and 55. Ibn ʿAsākir, LXXII, quoting Ibn Yūnus, *Ghurabā'*, has 263. This is no doubt a mistake (in the Ibn ʿAsākir manuscript?) and should be corrected to 253.

98. Since Ibn Sirāj is supposed to have died in 308/920, shortly before Ṭabarī's death, he could at best have been ten years older. See *TB*, XI, 431–3 (where he is described as a resident of Baghdad); Dhahabī, *Nubalā'*, XIV, 283; Ibn al-ʿImād, *Shadharāt*, II, 252. The wrong date of death (358/968[9]) appears in Dhahabī, *Mīzān*, III, 131, and Ibn Ḥajar, *Lisān*, IV, 320 f. The information we have about him does not support the role he is assigned in connection with Ṭabarī's stay in Egypt.

99. See, for instance, below, translation, n. 220; *Dhayl*, III, 2372, ed. Cairo, XI, 551, and elsewhere; Ibn al-Jazarī, *Ghāyah*, II, 406 f.; Subkī, *Ṭabaqāt*, II, 170–80.

100. See below, translation, n. 736.

the Mosque of ʿAmr, had been connected with al-Shāfiʿī and was a transmitter of his works. It is very likely that Ṭabarī also met the other leading exponent of Shāfiʿism, al-Muzanī (175-264/791[2]-878), and discussed with him matters such as general consensus *(ijmāʿ)*, which came to constitute an important element in Ṭabarī's legal thought; his biographers, however, do not seem to have been quite clear about whether there was a meeting and what was discussed at it.[101]

Among his many contacts in Egypt, the most important was probably the one with the eminent Ibn ʿAbd al-Ḥakam family.[102] Its members had been intimately connected with the imām al-Shāfiʿī, next to whose grave they found their final resting places.[103] They also were outstanding representatives of Mālik's legal school. Muḥammad b. ʿAbdallāh b. ʿAbd al-Ḥakam, who headed the family in those years,[104] attracted scholars from all over the world to come and study with him. He had the distinction of being both a student of al-Shāfiʿī and a Mālikite jurist, and he possessed the reputation of being the outstanding expert on law and *ḥadīth* among contemporary Egyptians.[105] Years before, he had traveled to Baghdad in connection with the infamous inquisition concerning the createdness or uncreatedness of the Qurʾān. Like Ibn Ḥanbal, he had shown himself to be a stout defender of its uncreatedness. We do not know whether he ever went back to Baghdad in his later years, but this is highly unlikely. His brother ʿAbd al-Raḥmān is best known as a historian. He contributed information to the *History* as well as *Tahdhīb* and *Tafsīr.*[106] A third brother, Saʿd, did not do much, if any, publishing. He is known to have taught in Mecca for some time, presumably in connection with his pilgrimage, but this seems to have been a brief interlude

101. See *Irshād*, VI, 432, l. 16, 433, ll. 15, 17, ed. Rifāʿī, XVIII, 53 f., and below, 67 f. For al-Muzanī, see Sezgin, *GAS*, I, 492 f. Ṭabarī's friend Ibn Khuzaymah, who was in Egypt at the same time, studied with al-Muzanī, see Subkī, *Ṭabaqāt*, II, 93.

102. See *EI*², III, 674 f., s. v. Ibn ʿAbd al-Ḥakam.

103. See *Irshād*, VI, 395, ed. Rifāʿī, XVII, 323, in the biography of al-Shāfiʿī.

104. See below, translation, n. 93. He is mentioned often (I have noted more than twenty-five references) in *Tafsīr*, where his authorities are his father and other Egyptian scholars. See also *Tahdhīb, Musnad Ibn ʿAbbās*, index, 1072.

105. See Ibn Taghrībirdī, *Nujūm*, III, 44.

106. See below, translation, n. 712. As he was to die in 257/871, Ṭabarī may have still been in Egypt at the time of his death.

in his teaching career in Egypt.[107] It was no doubt in Egypt that Ṭabarī received from him the information which he incorporated in *Tafsīr* and *Tahdhīb.*[108]

We hear little about Ṭabarī's contemporaries who were his friends rather than merely colleagues or teachers. This makes an anecdote concerning his experiences in Egypts valuable as a source of information, even if it is of doubtful historicity. Four scholars, all named Muḥammad, were together in Egypt when they ran out of money and had to go hungry. The four Muḥammads were, in addition to Ṭabarī, Muḥammad b. Naṣr al-Marwazī, Abū Bakr Muḥammad b. Hārūn al-Rūyānī (from Ṭabaristān), and Muḥammad b. Isḥāq b. Khuzaymah al-Nīsābūrī—all, it may be noted, men of Persian origin. They cast lots in order to determine who would go out and beg for food. Ibn Khuzaymah was chosen, but before he could leave, a messenger from the governor (? *wālī*) of al-Fusṭāṭ came with fifty dīnārs for each of the four. The governor was sending them the money because he had just had a dream about hungry Muḥammads and, pious as he was, wished to alleviate their plight.[109] There is much

107. See Ibn Abī Ḥātim, II,1, 92.

108. His transmission in *Tafsīr* (and, with one exception, in *Tahdhīb*) is always on the authority of Ḥafs b. 'Umar or Abū Zur'ah Wahballāh b. Rāshid. See *Dhayl*, III, 2391, ed. Cairo, XI, 565, and elsewhere; *Tahdhīb, Musnad Ibn 'Abbās*, index, 1058; Ibn 'Abd al-Ḥakam, *Futūḥ Miṣr*, 24, l. 14; *Tafsīr*, VIII, 102, l. 25 (*ad* Qur. 7:17), XII, 79, l. 30, 86, l. 34 (*ad* Qur. 11:114, 118), XV, 166, l. 4 (*ad* Qur. 18:46), XVIII, 96, l. 29 (*ad* Qur. 24:31), XX, 16, l. 12 (*ad* Qur. 27:90), XXII, 38, l. 6 (*ad* Qur. 33:70 f.), XXIV, 60, l. 16 (*ad* Qur. 41:6 f.).

The reference to a certain Yūnus b. 'Abdallāh b. 'Abd al-Ḥakam in *Tafsīr*, VII, 199, l. 18 (*ad* Qur. 6:103) is apparently a mistake. The source of Yūnus there, Khālid b. 'Abd al-Raḥmān, is listed as an authority of Muḥammad and Sa'd (b. 'Abdallāh b. 'Abd al-Ḥakam); see Ibn Ḥajar, *Tahdhīb*, III, 103.

109. See *TB*, II, 164 f.; Ibn 'Asākir, LXXIV f.; *Irshād*, VI, 427 f., ed. Rifā'ī, XVIII, 46 f.; Subkī, *Ṭabaqāt*, II, 250 f. Yāqūt states that he did not use *TB* for this story, but the work of al-Sam'ānī; however, Sam'ānī, *Ansāb*, IX, 40 ff., does not contain it. For al-Marwazī (202–94/817[8]–906[7]), see Sezgin, *GAS*, I, 494; for al-Rūyānī (d. 307/919[20]), see *GAS*, I, 171; and for Ibn Khuzaymah, see *GAS*, I, 601. In a different context, Subkī, *Ṭabaqāt*, III, 102, speaks of "four Muḥammads." Al-Rūyānī is replaced by Muḥammad b. Ibrāhīm b. al-Mundhir al-Nīsābūrī, who, according to Subkī, died in 309 or 310/921–2, but possibly a few years later; see Sezgin, *GAS*, I 495 f. The existence of a motif of "four Muḥammads"casts further doubt on the historicity of the story. The large amount of money involved and the premise of extreme financial hardship experienced by scholars as well-connected and welcomed to Egypt as Ṭabarī is described as having been make it appear a legend. It was, however, a common occurrence for traveling students to run out of money,

in the story that hardly permits it to be taken literally. Its basic assumption, however, appears to be factual. The four had come to Egypt on research trips and knew each other and probably roomed together. Muḥammad b. Naṣr al-Marwazī was about twenty years older than the other three and was clearly an established scholar and jurist in his fifties. Although already esteemed as scholars, the others fell hardly into the same category, being in their late twenties or early thirties. Among them, Ibn Khuzaymah, born a year earlier than Ṭabarī and outliving him by one year, qualified well as a personal friend. His path may have crossed with that of Ṭabarī before, as he had studied with the same teachers, such as Ibn Bashshār and Bishr b. Muʿādh in al-Baṣrah and Abū Kurayb and Ismāʿīl b. Mūsā al-Fazārī in al-Kūfah.[110] Ibn Khuzaymah became a very productive scholar in the same fields as Ṭabarī. He spent his life in his hometown of Nīsābūr; but he showed lasting loyalty to his former fellow student. On every possible occasion, he strongly defended Ṭabarī against Ḥanbalite attacks, and he missed no opportunity to praise his scholarship. A student returning from Baghdad who reported that he had not dared to study with Ṭabarī because of a Ḥanbalite boycott was told by Ibn Khuzaymah that he would have profited more from attending a lecture of Ṭabarī than he did from all his study with the other teachers in Baghdad.[111] And when Ibn Khuzaymah found out that a certain Ibn Bālawayh had written down the entire *Tafsīr* on Ṭabarī's dictation between 283/896 and 290/903, he asked him to lend him his copy. He returned it after a long time[112] with the comment: "I perused it from beginning to end. I know of nobody upon the face of the earth who is more learned than Muḥammad b. Jarīr. He has been wronged by the Ḥanbalites."[113] This is as much in-

even if, as in the case of Abū Bakr b. Abī Dāwūd, they were sons of prominent scholars; see *TB*, IX, 466 f.

110. Ibn Khuzaymah also studied with Aḥmad b. Manīʿ in Baghdad. Ibn Manīʿ was an authority of Ṭabarī in *Tafsīr* and *Tahdhīb*. As he died in his eighties in 244/859 (see *TB*, V, 160 f.), Ṭabarī might have met Ibn Khuzaymah in his early period in Baghdad. Ibn Khuzaymah further studied with Ṭulayq b. Muḥammad al-Wāsiṭī in al-Baṣrah (see Ibn Khuzaymah, 179). Ṭulayq also occurs in *Tafsīr* and *Tahdhīb*, but his date of death is not known.

111. See *TB*, V, 164; Ibn ʿAsākir, LXXVIII; Dhahabī, *Nubalāʾ*, XIV, 272.

112. The proposed reading "two years" in Ibn ʿAsākir, as against the attested "several years," may or may not be correct.

113. See above, n. 111, and *Irshād*, VI, 425, ed. Rifāʿī, XVIII, 42 f. Ibn Khuzay-

formation about a lifelong friendship between fellow students as we can expect to gather from sources that usually tended to disregard personal aspects of scholarship.

His Fifty Years of Scholarly Activity in Baghdad

The person

It is not known how much time Ṭabarī spent in Egypt after 256/870 before returning to Baghdad.[113a] It is tempting to assume that during his western journey, and before his return, he performed the pilgrimage to Mecca, either during his sidetrip to Syria and Palestine or on the way back to Baghdad. The date of 256/870, which appears in the *Story of the Belt* (see below, 99), seems to be more than just a lucky guess and may well have preserved a true fact from Ṭabarī's biography. Scholarly pilgrims often remained in the Sacred Territory for considerable periods of time. However, since nothing is known about his having studied with resident scholars in the Ḥijāz,[114] any time he might have spent there for the performance of the pilgrimage would not have been very long.

With his return to Baghdad, his formal education was completed and his student days were over. The time had come for him to devote himself entirely to teaching and publication. The tremen-

---

mah shared Ṭabarī's negative view of Ibn Ḥanbal as a jurist. A young scholar, who later became famous, Abū Bakr al-Qaffāl (291–365/ 903[4]–975[6], see Sezgin, *GAS*, I, 497 f.), visited Ibn Khuzaymah and told him that he was on his way to study with a Ḥanbalite jurist, whereupon Ibn Khuzaymah exclaimed: "Say, a Shāfiʿite, for Aḥmad b. Ḥanbal was just one of al-Shāfiʿī's young men." See *Irshād*, VI, 379, ed. Rifāʿī, XVII, 298, in the biography of al-Shāfiʿī. Al-Qaffāl is said to have studied with Ṭabarī, see Ṣafadī, *Wāfī*, IV, 112, l. 16; Subkī, *Ṭabaqāt*, III, 201, l. 1. This must have been in the last years of the lives of Ṭabarī and Ibn Khuzaymah, when al-Qaffāl was still in his teens.

Only the last two sentences of Ibn Khuzaymah's statement appear in Samʿānī, *Ansāb*, IX, 42; Ṣafadī, *Wāfī*, II, 16 f.

113a. Ferré, "Vie de Jesus," 8, is convinced that Ṭabarī returned in 258/871[2].

114. The statement of Samʿānī, *Ansāb*, IX, 41, l. 1, that Ṭabarī's travels took him to the Ḥijāz, seems to be offhand and cannot be relied on. A reference to the various nationalities of his teachers makes no mention of the Ḥijāz; see *TB*, II, 165, ll. 5 f., quoted in Ibn ʿAsākir, LXXIII, l. 3; Ibn al-Jawzī, *Muntaẓam*, VI, 170, l. 21. I have so far not succeeded in identifying any authority of Ṭabarī whom he could have met only in Mecca and Medina. See also below, n. 344a.

dous volume of work he accomplished evoked the admiration of his contemporaries as well as later generations. Some attempts at quantification were undertaken. Necessarily they were crude. In his continuation of Ṭabarī's *History,* al-Farghānī stated that some unnamed disciples of Ṭabarī had figured out that if one took the number of folios of his works and divided it by the number of days from his puberty to his death at the age of eighty-six, one would find that he wrote fourteen (!) folios every single day (which would amount to roughly 350,000 folios).[115] And the grammarian 'Alī b. 'Ubaydallāh al-Simsimī (d. 415/1024) told his student, al-Khaṭīb al-Baghdādī, that Ṭabarī used to write forty (!) folios each day for forty years (which rather shortens the time of his publishing career for the sake of round figures).[116] Such statistics were of course not needed to convince anyone that Ṭabarī was unusually prolific in an age that boasted of many prolific authors.

Productivity on such a scale required not only a rarely gifted type of personality but also the existence of material conditions that were conducive to sustained work. Before discussing Ṭabarī's scholarship, it might be well to pause and review what is known of his life as a mature individual in the complex and sophisticated society of a large Muslim city.

Apparently soon after his return to Baghdad, although the only date we have indicates that it was after 290/903, he took up residence in East Baghdad's Shammāsiyyah district to live there until he died.[117] It was, we are told, a neighborhood which had been home to many grammarians in the past.[118] His house was located at the Baradān Bridge.[119] It presumably was identical with the house in Ya'qūb Square, in which he is said to have died and which is described as being in the neighborhood of the Khurāsān Gate—not, of course, the Khurāsān Gate in the Round City but the one through which the Khurāsān Road leaves al-Shammāsiyyah

115. See *Irshād,* VI, 426, ed. Rifā'ī, XVIII, 44.

116. See *TB,* II, 163, quoted by Ibn 'Asākir, LXXVII. For al-Simsimī, see Sezgin, *GAS,* IX, 184.

117. See *Irshād,* VI, 435, ll. 3 f., 438, ll. 11 f., ed. Rifā'ī, XVIII, 56, 60 f.

118. For the grammarians mentioned in this connection, see below, 107.

119. Marked no. 53 on map V in Le Strange, *Baghdad.* The map is reproduced in Lassner, *Topography,* 203.

and the city.[120] Ya'qūb Square is not listed in the topographical descriptions of Baghdad, but Baradān Bridge and Khurāsān Road might easily have been used for indicating the same location. Ṭabarī's mosque—that is, the neighborhood mosque where he regularly worshiped—was situated at some distance from his house in Sūq al-'Aṭash (presumably, "Thirst Bazaar") of the adjacent Mukharrim district. It is mentioned in a report by Abū 'Alī al-Ṭūmārī.[121] One night during the last third of the month of Ramaḍān, al-Ṭūmārī served as lantern *(qindīl)* bearer for Abū Bakr b. Mujāhid when he headed toward his mosque for the nightly services (*tarāwīḥ*). Ibn Mujāhid passed his mosque and went on to the mosque in Sūq al-'Aṭash, where Ṭabarī could be heard reciting sūrah 55 (al-Raḥmān). To the question of the astonished al-Ṭūmārī of why he was keeping the people in his mosque waiting for him while he listened to the Qur'ān recitation of someone else in another mosque, Ibn Mujāhid replied that he did not think that there was any other human being in the world who could read the Qur'ān as well as Ṭabarī.[122] House and mosque no doubt circumscribed much of Ṭabarī's daily life. At home, he did his research and writing. He taught, it seems, mainly in his mosque.

Ṭabarī appears never to have married. A Spanish scholar, Maslamah b. (al-)Qāsim al-Qurṭubī (d. 353/964) traveled in the Near East in the decade after Ṭabarī's death, when he was in his twenties. Probably in his *Ṣilah,* a biographical dictionary, he has the following information, evidently obtained from someone who knew Ṭabarī: "He was celibate *(ḥaṣūr)* and did not know women.

---

120. See Ibn al-Jawzī, *Muntaẓam,* VI, 172; Dhahabī, *Nubalā',* XIV, 282. The Khurāsān Gate is marked no. 58 on map V, and no. 17 on Le Strange's map VIII. See also Lassner, *Topography,* 263, n. 13. A Ya'qūb Road (*darb*) is mentioned in the biography of Aḥmad b. 'Alī (Ibn) al-Bādā (see below, 100) in *TB,* IV, 322.

121. Abū 'Alī 'Īsā b. Mūsā b. Aḥmad al-Ṭūmārī was born in 262/875 and died in 360/970, see *TB,* XI, 176 f. Abū Bakr Aḥmad b. Mūsā b. al-'Abbās b. Mujāhid, the great authority on Qur'ān reading, was born in 245/859 and died in 324/936. He was born and buried in Sūq al-'Aṭash, more precisely, near al-Khursī (al-Ḥarashī) Square (*TB,* V, 145, 1. 7). See Ibn al-Nadīm, *Fihrist,* 31; *TB* V, 144–8; Sezgin, *GAS,* I, 14; Shawqī Ḍayf's introduction to his edition of Ibn Mujāhid's *Sab'ah*; and also below, 67 and nn. 293, 337.

122. See *TB,* II, 164, quoted by Ibn 'Asākir, LXXXV.

The approximate location of Sūq al-'Aṭash is marked no. 66 on map V of Le Strange.

Ṭabarī's reputation for excellence in Qur'ān reading and recitation was well-attested; see below, n. 337.

In (2)36, when he was twelve, he left his town to travel in quest of knowledge. He never ceased to pursue knowledge eagerly until he died."[123] There is no reason to doubt this information, even if there is little to either confirm or refute it. He was not married when he went to Egypt. This we learn from one of those innocent dialect jokes, so greatly enjoyed by Egyptians, that was played on him when he came there. He was looking for furniture for his domicile and was told to buy certain necessary items, including, among other puzzling objects, something as strange as "two donkeys." He replied that not only had he no use for two donkeys and the other things mentioned to him, but his stipend did not allow such heavy expenditures and should not be wasted on something that was of no value for his studies. It turned out that the entire purchase did not cost more than two and one-third dirhams, a very affordable small sum. The "two donkeys" in reality referred to a wooden bed frame, with a mattress of woven palm leaves *(suddah)*. The raised bed was needed for protection against vermin which bothered those who had to sleep on the ground; fleas in the clothes, in particular, were a terrible plague, and clothes had to be hung up before going to bed. The Egyptians had mentioned a *zīr* as a needed item. To Ṭabarī, *zīr* recalled something connected with music, and piety forbade him to have anything to do with it. In fact, it meant a receptacle for water. And the *qaṣriyyah* which they considered indispensable was a bread bowl. Ṭabarī apparently had understood *qaṣriyyah* in its ordinary meaning of (chamber) pot, and possibly he thought of small children whom he did not have or expected, for he indignantly exclaimed that he "had not let down his pants for either a forbidden or a permitted (sexual activity)."[124] It was not unusual for an ambitious young scholar under thirty to stay unmarried for a while. Ibn Ḥanbal, for instance, got married only after he had passed forty.[125] Thus, the one apparently true element in the amusing story—that is, that Ṭabarī was not married during his visit to Egypt—gives no indication of what was the situation later in his life.

There is, however, a possible reference to a son of his from his

123. See Ibn Ḥajar, *Lisān*, V, 102. For Maslamah, see Ibn Ḥajar, *Lisān*, VI, 35 f.; Rosenthal, *Muslim Historiography*², 437, n. 2.
124. See *Irshād*, VI, 434, ed. Rifāʿī, XVIII, 55 f.
125. See Ibn al-Jawzī, *Manāqib*, 373.

old age. It is an incidental remark in another anecdote illustrating Ṭabarī's scrupulousness with respect to gifts. A certain Abū al-Faraj b. Abī al-'Abbās al-Iṣfahānī al-Kātib was studying ("reading") Ṭabarī's works with him. He found out that Ṭabarī was interested in a mat for a small sofa,[126] so he went and took the measurements of the sofa and had a mat made that fitted it. He thought that a small gift of the sort would endear him to his revered teacher. He put it in its place and presented it to him, but "when he left, he called his son and gave him four dīnārs"—quite a large sum—"but he did not want to take them and Ṭabarī wanted to accept the mat only if (his countergift of four dīnārs was accepted)."[127] This intentionally literal translation seems to imply that it was Ṭabarī's son to whom his father gave the money to act as messenger, but this

---

126. For *ṣuffah*, see, for instance, Sadan, *Mobilier*, 124 n.

127. See *Irshād*, VI, 457, ed. Rifā'ī, XVIII, 87. It seems an open question whether this Abū al-Faraj al-Iṣfahānī can be identified with the famous author of *Aghānī*. The latter was born in 284/897 and began his scholarly studies at an early age. If the year of his birth is correctly stated, he could have had a child old enough near the end of Ṭabarī's life to play the role indicated in the story. Abū al-Faraj often mentions Ṭabarī as his authority for historical information in *Aghānī* as well as *Maqātil al-Ṭālibiyyīn*. He indicates that Ṭabarī "told" him a certain story or that he "read" it in his presence. Once he states that Ṭabarī told him a story "from memory" (*Aghānī*, IV, 138, *Agh.*3, V, 28) Some of his Ṭabarī quotations cannot be traced in *History*. He may not have derived all of them from Ṭabarī *viva voce* or may not accurately have remembered what he had learned; and, on occasion, he may have used Ṭabarī's published work in order to supplement his information. However, the basic fact that he studied with Ṭabarī cannot be denied. His contact with Ṭabarī may have fallen any time after 299/911–2 when Ṭabarī can be assumed to have lectured on his *History* in preparation for its forthcoming publication.

In his magisterial biography of Abū al-Faraj, 108, Muḥammad A. Khalafallāh mentions the story but does not comment on the identity of the Abū al-Faraj mentioned in it, evidently, because he ruled out the possibility that he could be the author of *Aghānī*. In fact, the patronymic of his father (here Abū al-'Abbās) is, it seems, not attested anywhere. In contrast to other family members of the famous litterateur, his father remained completely in the shadows; he may have died young and left no record of any noteworthy activities. Still, our lack of knowledge about his *kunyah* is no decisive argument against the identification. For the lively discussion about the dates of birth and death of the author of *Aghānī*, see Khalafallāh's work and the introduction by Ṣalāḥ al-dīn al-Munajjid of his edition of Abū al-Faraj's *Adab al-ghurabā'*. On p. 88 of the edition, Abū al-Faraj indicates that he was still alive in 362; this year gives a *terminus post quem* for his death. To add to the confusion, a story placed by him in the time of his youth is dated in the late 350s. While this may seem to cast doubt on the indicated date of his birth, it would seem that he cannot have been born much later and could have had a son able to walk in Ṭabarī's lifetime. See also *Encyclopaedia Iranica*, I, 282 f., s. v. Abu'l-Faraj Eṣfahānī.

is not certain. It could be the donor's son to whom Ṭabarī gave the money for handing over to his father, who then refused acceptance. Thus, the evidence for a son of Ṭabarī (possibly the son of a slave girl) remains inconclusive. His *kunyah* Abū Jaʿfar, of course, does not require the existence of a son called Jaʿfar. If he had surviving children, our sources might very well have had occasion to mention them. As it is, the evidence clearly favors the assumption that Ṭabarī never married throughout his life.

His financial status was no impediment to founding a family. Scholars less fortunately situated often saw having many children as detrimental to their scholarly activities. Ṭabarī, as we have seen, had a private income, and all the opportunities for a religious scholar with the right connections to earn money were open to him. He had no difficulty in his youth finding a position as tutor to the son of a high official.[128] But he apparently never accepted a position in the government or, as would have been natural for him, in the judiciary. There is an anecdote that reflects his attitude toward official employment. It fits Ṭabarī's personal situation; therefore, it is presumably not just another illustration of the common motif that scholars ought to be reluctant to enter public service. When al-Khāqānī, the son of his former employer just referred to, was appointed to the wazirate in 299/312,[129] he sent him a large sum of money as a gift. Ṭabarī refused to accept it. The new wazīr then offered him a judgeship, only to meet with another refusal, and then a third refusal when he offered to appoint him to the *maẓālim* jurisdiction.[130] His friends and students urged him to accept the *maẓālim* position, since it was in need of the prestige of a renowned jurist at the head of it. He angrily rebuked them and said that they more than anybody else should not encourage him to accept the position but rather discourage him from accepting it.[131] The determining element in his attitude was not, it seems, a general objection to service in government and the judiciary but his total immersion in scholarly activity. The students

128. See above, 16 ff.

129. See *EI*², III, 824, s. v. Ibn Khāḳān (3). We have no information on his personal relations with his (half-)brother Abū Yaḥyā.

130. The *maẓālim* court dealt with cases outside the competence of the qāḍīs of the sharīʿah jurisdiction.

131. See Ibn ʿAsākir, LXXXV; Dhahabī, *Nubalāʾ*, XIV, 275. The source was al-Farghānī.

should have recognized the importance for themselves of having him available for teaching unencumbered by official duties. The thought of an office as a sinecure would, of course, not have occurred to someone like Ṭabarī.

Teaching could have been a source of income for him. He hardly belonged to those who refused compensation for all teaching as a matter of unbending principle. The number of students who attended his lectures seems to have varied greatly. There were very many at certain times, and a few carefully selected ones at others. The former was probably the rule. Especially in his later years, young students flocked to him to hear the famous man and to be able to say that they had studied with him.[132] He probably neither wanted nor needed to derive any appreciable income from his students. Another potential source of income was legal advice of some kind or other. The only reported instance of such activity, solicited by the government of al-Muktafī, tells of a gift in lieu of a fee and rather relates to the stories of stipends and gifts which in his later years appear to have been showered upon him and which frequently involved substantial sums. As stated before, those stories were meant to be illustrative of Ṭabarī's attitude toward the giving of gifts and the legal and moral propriety of accepting them.[133]

In the case of al-Muktafī, protocol required that the Caliph deal not personally with Ṭabarī. Al-Muktafī told his wazīr, al-ʿAbbās b. al-Ḥasan,[134] that he wished to hear Ṭabarī's views on a planned endowment, so that it would be set up in a way that could not be contested. A meeting was arranged to be conducted by two officials,

---

132. See, for instance, al-Qaffāl, above, n. 113. Many who claimed to have studied with Ṭabarī are known to have died in the second half of the fourth century and thus were probably born not much before 290. Yāqūt mentions ʿAlī (b. Muḥammad) b. ʿAllān al-Ḥarrānī, who died in 355/966 (*Muʿjam*, II, 232), Sahl (Suhayl) b. Aḥmad b. Sahl al-Rīwandī, who died as early as 350/961–2 (*Muʿjam*, II, 891), and Abū Bakr Yūsuf b. al-Qāsim b. Yūsuf al-Mayānajī, who supposedly died as late as 375/end of 985 (*Muʿjam*, IV, 708). Like Ibrāhīm b. Aḥmad al-Mīmadhī (*Muʿjam*, IV, 718), for whom no dates are available, all these men are rarely mentioned in the sources, and nothing is known about their relationship, if any, to Ṭabarī.

133. See above, n. 38.

134. Al-ʿAbbās b. al-Ḥasan was al-Muktafī's wazīr from 291/904 to the caliph's death four years later; see below, translation, Vol. XXXVIII, 149, 189. On his sponsorship of Ṭabarī's *Khafīf*, see below, 112.

Ṣāfī al-Ḥuramī (d. 298/911) and Ibn al-Ḥawārī (d. 311/923).[135] The Caliph listened from behind the curtain to Ṭabarī's lengthy disquisition on the subject at hand, and when Ṭabarī was on the point of leaving, he had a splendid gift brought out and presented to him. Ṭabarī did not want to accept it, but the two officials warned him that this was unseemly behavior. A caliphal gift was not to be rejected. It was customary to reward those who had rendered a service to a caliph with presents or the fulfilment of a wish expressed by them. The idea of expressing a wish appealed to Ṭabarī since, presumably depending on the nature of the wish, it was unobjectionable. Ṭabarī's wish was that the police be ordered to see to it that petitioners not be admitted to the prayer enclosure *(maqṣūrah)* in the mosque until the Friday sermon was finished, so that there was no disturbance and interruption of it. The wish was fulfilled, and Ṭabarī gained great admiration all around.[136] For Ṭabarī, the acceptance of a gift was conditioned upon the recipient's making, or at least having the ability to make, a countergift of equivalent or greater value. As an aspiring politician, Abū al-Hayjā', the founder of the Ḥamdānid dynasty, sent Ṭabarī a gift of three thousand dīnārs. Ṭabarī refused to accept the magnificent present on the ground that he could not afford a return gift of similar value. He was confronted with the argument that no countergift was required in this case, since Abū al-Hayjā' meant his gift to be a good deed that was pleasing to God and would secure for him a heavenly reward *(al-taqarrub ilā allāh)*. It proved of no avail.[137] We cannot help feeling that under the circumstances, the gift may have had some political purpose, such as obligating Ṭabarī to the donor and assuring support for him in the legal community and civilian administration. Ṭabarī may have sensed that and, therefore, shied away from a gift which could become embarrassing at some time in the future.

The same Khāqānī who had offered Ṭabarī a high position in the judiciary made Ṭabarī a present of pomegranates at some other time. Ṭabarī accepted the pomegranates and distributed them

135. For Ṣāfī, see below, translation, Vol. XXXVIII, 103, n. 516. For Ibn al-Ḥawārī, see 'Arīb, 113; Hamadhānī, *Takmilah*, 42; Miskawayh, in *Eclipse*, index; Bowen, index, s. v. Ibn al-Ḥawwārí

136. See Ibn 'Asākir, LXXVI; Dhahabī, *Nubalā'*, XIV, 270, from al-Farghānī.

137. See *Irshād*, VI, 457, ed. Rifā'ī, XVIII, 87, For Abū al-Hayjā', see *EI*², III, 126 f., s. v. Ḥamdānids.

among his neighbors. Hearing about it, al-Khāqānī, either because he was touched by Ṭabarī's generous spirit or because he thought that his gift was considered too insignificant, sent Ṭabarī a basket with a purse which was filled with ten thousand dirhams. An accompanying note asked Ṭabarī either to accept the money for himself or distribute it among deserving friends, as he had done with the pomegranates. The messenger was probably unaware of the contents of al-Khāqānī's note, but as it came from a high-ranking personality, he thought that it was important, and he insisted upon being admitted into Ṭabarī's house. He was not aware or did not care that he was disturbing Ṭabarī during hours that he was reserving for writing and during which he had given strict orders that nobody was to bother him. Ṭabarī read the note and told the messenger that it was alright to accept the gift of pomegranates, but he could not accept the money. When it was pointed out to him that he was given the option of distributing the money among his needy friends *(aṣḥāb)*, he remained unpersuaded and replied that the wazīr himself should distribute the money since he knew better who needed money and could make the best use of it.[138] A very similar remark is ascribed to Ṭabarī on another occasion.[139]

Ṭabarī had good relations with humbler folks in the neighborhood, where he was certainly looked up to as one of its most distinguished residents. When a neighbor called Abū al-Muḥassin al-Muḥarrir (thus, presumably, a professional scribe) made him a present of two chickens, he gave him a garment in return, something obviously more expensive,[140] thereby following the principles that governed his attitude toward gifts. In spite of his eminence, Ṭabarī was in general easy for his neighbors, be they scholars or ordinary people, to get along with. He went with them on picnics[141] and gave them advice for their children.[142]

Certain remarkable traits and attitudes that guided his daily life apart from his scholarly pursuits were fortunately recorded for posterity. His physical appearance showed a darkish brown

138. See *Irshād*, VI, 457 f., ed. Rifāʿī, XVIII, 87 f. For al-Khaqānī, see above, nn. 128 and 129.

139. In connection with the composition of *Khafīf*, see below, 112.

140. See *Irshād*, VI, 457, ed. Rifāʿī, XVIII, 87.

141. See below, 41.

142. See below, 50.

complexion and large eyes, as well as a long beard—hardly very characteristic features. Equally commonplace was the statement that he was well-spoken and eloquent. It was more noteworthy that his hair and beard stayed quite black until he was in his eighties. He was tall and lean.[143] His leanness may have contributed to his vigor and good health throughout his long life. As far as our knowledge goes, he was seriously ill only during his last ten years when he suffered from attacks by an illness diagnosed as pleurisy *(dhāt al-janb).*[144] It may have been illness or old age that caused him to stop lecturing some time before his death.[145]

His leanness may not exclusively have been an accident of heredity. He was very diet-conscious. The noteworthy feature of the diet favored by him is that it was one that would find qualified approval among today's dietitians.[146] He avoided fat and ate red meat plainly prepared *(al-ṣirf),* cooked with nothing but raisins (raisin juice *zabīb).* He ate only white bread *(samīdh),* because it was baked with refined wheat flour *(ghasl al-qamḥ).*[147] He liked *rāziqī* grapes, *wazīrī* figs,[148] fresh dates *(ruṭab),* and *ḥiṣrim* ("unripe fruit")[149] in season to go with his meals. He counseled

143. See *TB,* II, 166, quoted by *Irshād,* VI, 423, ed. Rifāʿī, XVIII, 40; Ibn al-Jawzī, *Muntaẓam,* VI, 170; Dhahabī, *Nubalāʾ,* XIV, 282. Ibn ʿAsākir, XCI, considered the little-changed hair color noteworthy.

144. See *Irshād,* VI, 461, ed. Rifāʿī, XVIII, 94. "Pleurisy" is a conventional translation. It is impossible to guess what illness was really meant according to modern terminology.

145. See below, 83 and 120.

146. All the information on Ṭabarī's diet discussed here appears in *Irshād,* VI, 459 f., ed. Rifāʿī, XVIII, 90 ff.

147. *Samīdh,* an ancient Semitic word, is connected with Greek *semidalis* and, possibly, also with semolina. See Fraenkel, *Fremdwörter,* 32, and, for instance, Brockelmann, *Lex. Syr.*[2], 479b, and von Soden, *Akkadisches Handwörterbuch,* (II), 1018a. For the suggested relation of Latin *simila* (from which semolina is derived) with the Semitic word, see, for instance, *Oxford Latin Dictionary,* 1763a.

148. For the *rāziqī* grape, see Lane, 1077a; Heine, *Weinstudien,* 121; and, for instance, Ibn al-Rūmī, *Dīwān,* III, 987 f.; Ibn Abī ʿAwn, *al-Ajwibah al-muskitah,* 166. The *wazīrī* fig remains to be identified. Both the *wazīrī* fig and the *rāziqī* grape are mentioned as noteworthy ʿIrāqī products by Abū Bakr al-Khuwārizmī, *Rasāʾil,* 49. Cf. also Jāḥiẓ, *Ḥayawān,* VIII, 8; al-Ḥuṣrī, *Jamʿ,* 291 (Cairo 1372/1953).

149. *Ḥiṣrim* is mentioned, for instance, by Rāzī, *Ḥāwī,* XX, 300, XXIII,1, 44. For a potion *(sharāb)* made from it, see *Ḥāwī,* XXI, 1, 118; it is possibly identical with the thickened juice *(rubb)* of *ḥiṣrim* mentioned by Ṭabarī, *Firdaws,* 483. For the dish called *ḥiṣrimiyyah,* see Rosenthal, "Hidden illness," 59, n. 89. The reference to *ḥiṣrim* is continued with the remark that "in the summer, he often did not go without *ḥays* (date meal mixed with butter and curd), basil, and nenuphar."

against the consumption of sesame, honey, and dried dates *(tamr)*, to which he ascribed unpleasant side effects, such as overloading *(l-ṭ-kh*, lit. soiling) the stomach, weakening one's eyesight, and ruining the teeth;[150] and in the case of sesame and honey, also causing bad mouth odor. His favorite food was a special milk dish cooked until the milk was condensed, with bread crumbs added, and then eaten cold with milk, seasoned with marjoram/thyme *(ṣ/sa'tar)*, *ḥabb al-sawdā'*,[151] and olive oil. He also enjoyed *isfīdhbāj* and *zīrbāj*, kinds of pies made with meat or chicken and gruel.[152] When he overindulged occasionally, as he had to in order to be good company during a picnic with his neighbors in the countryside, and ate too much of a bean dish,[153] he later treated himself at home with a variety of medicines including electuaries.[154]

His diet was clearly based upon the views and practices of contemporary medicine, in which he considered himself well-versed. It owed little, if anything, to the delight in high cuisine widespread among the upper crust of society and the intellectuals moving among them, or the squeamishness affected by the *ẓurafā'*, the refined dandies.[155] On the other hand, his insistence on good table manners, while certainly in keeping with prevailing fashions, derived mainly from the religious law which paid much attention to the subject. His appearance projected the cleanliness demanded by religion and society, just as it reflected his inner purity.[156] He

---

150. See below, n. 237.

151. Unidentified.

152. *Zīrbāj(ah)*, approximately "underlaid gruel," appears, for instance, in Ṭabarī, *Firdaws* 476; *Arabian Nights*, ed. Mahdi, 304; Dozy, I, 618b; Steingass, 633b *(zīrbā)*; Rodinson, "Recherchess," 134, n. 3, 137, 149 ("poulet en gelée"). *Isfīdhbāj* "white gruel " is listed in Dozy, I, 22b; Steingass, 58b; *Ṭabīkh*, ed. al-Bārūdī, 31 f., trans. Arberry, "A Baghdad cookery book," 46. Dishes in Ṭabarī's time commonly had Persian names; Ṭabarī's Persian origin had nothing to do with their use by him.

153. *Qarāḥ al-bāqillā*, approximately "clear bean broth," may be identical with *mā' al-baqillā* described in *Ṭabīkh*, ed. al-Bārūdī, 33, trans. Arberry, "A Baghdad cookery book," 47.

154. "Electuaries *(juwārishnāt)*" have a long chapter in Ṭabarī, *Firdaws*, 474–81. See also *Wörterbuch*, *K*, 365b, s. v. *kammūnī*; Steingass, 1100b *(guwārish, guwārisht* [!]).

155. For the social stratum of *ẓurafā'*, see, for instance, Washshā', *Muwashshā*, 129 ff.; Ghazi, "Raffinés," 39 ff. In connection with Ṭabarī's leanness mentioned before, see *Muwashshā*, 50, where the Arab ideal of leanness is discussed.

156. See *Irshād*, VI, 456, l. 18, ed. Rifā'ī, XVIII, 86.

would put his hand into the bowl and take a morsel, then, when coming back for a second time, he would wipe clean the part of the bowl that had become besmeared the first time, so that only one side of the bowl would be soiled.[157] He took a bite of food with his right hand as was proper, but he simultaneously also covered his beard with his left, lest it be soiled by dripping sauce or the like. He daintily used his napkin to wipe his mouth, and he did not spit in public. Such spitting was hardly less of a social sin than was frequently swearing by God. He studiously avoided both.[158]

Less commendable, it seems to us, was his attitude toward another guest at a banquet who noticed how longingly a waiter looked at one of the dishes and sneaked him a morsel from it. Ṭabarī shamed the man by asking pointedly who had given him permission to do that.[159] And again, his general fastidiousness provoked him to gossipy criticism of a great scholar, Abū Ḥātim al-Sijistānī. He told others that he had seen Abū Ḥātim applying stibium *(kuḥl)* to his eyes so clumsily that some of it ran down on his beard and from there on his clothes in front. In a way, for Ṭabarī, that seemed to disqualify Abū Ḥātim from being considered a respectable scholar.[160]

All these small details are no doubt to be taken as factual. It is hard to imagine that anyone would have bothered to invent them. It was more perfunctory to describe Ṭabarī as living the true religious life, as someone who was abstemious and observed the religious law punctiliously. Even if it was perfunctory, it is not difficult to believe that it described him accurately. His daily routine is also described in an interesting manner. As customary, it began with the preceding night. He slept in (a room cooled with dampened?) felt in a short-sleeved shirt perfumed with sandal oil and rose water.[161] He rose early for the morning prayer at home, then did research and writing until afternoon. He prayed the afternoon

157. Ibn Kāmil has the following introductory remark: "I have never seen anyone eat in a more refined manner (*aẓraf aklan*)."

158. See *Irshād*, VI, 459, ed. Rifāʿī, XVIII, 90, from Ibn Kāmil. For the use of the napkin, see the forthcoming article "mandīl" in *EI*^{2}.

159. See *Irshād*, VI, 458 f., ed. Rifāʿī, XVIII, 89.

160. See Zubaydī, *Ṭabaqāt*, 101, from Ibn Kāmil. Zubaydī, 65, seems to quote the year of Ṭabarī's death from al-Farghānī.

161. For the manifold uses of *ṣandal* and *māʾ al-ward* in perfumes, see, for instance, Kindī (pseudo-), *Kīmiyāʾ*, 342, ff., 268 f.

prayer in public, presumably in his mosque in Sūq al-ʿAṭash. He recited the Qur'ān and taught Qur'ān reading there until evening. Finally, before returning home, he taught jurisprudence and studied (having students study jurisprudence and other subjects) until the time of the late night prayer.[162] The details here appear a bit schematic and hardly characteristic of Ṭabarī as an individual. But the description of his daily routine makes the obvious point that he led a highly disciplined life.

Urbanity and wit combined in Ṭabarī with a sense of humor. Along with the ability to write occasional verse with reflections on man and society—for Ṭabarī's poetical efforts, see below, 48—all this was very much part of the picture of the good Muslim. Meeting the nine-year-old son of Ibn Kāmil, he would playfully comment on his names and their auspicious omen.[163] A witty remark might express his strong conviction that religious scholarship deserved precedence over political prominence. A person whose turn had come to read the Qur'ān hesitated when he noticed that the great wazīr al-Faḍl b. Jaʿfar b. al-Furāt had just entered the room. "Your turn is now," Ṭabarī told him, "so don't be disturbed by either the Tigris or the Euphrates *(Furāt)*!"[164] A conversation with Abū al-Faraj b. al-Thallāj[165] was on a less elevated level. It was about cooking and involved the preparation of a dish called *ṭabāhajah.* Abū al-Faraj pronounced it *ṭabāhaqah* and defended his pronunciation with the (quite correct) observation that Persian *g* appeared in Arabic as either *j* or *q*. Ṭabarī rejoined that in this case, his name should be Abū al-Faraq b. al-Thallāq. This was meant as light banter and not in any way as indicative of Ṭabarī as a stickler for philological accuracy.[166] In fact, he was not above making fun, as philologians were wont to do, of the pedantry of many of their colleagues. He complained that a certain Abū Bakr b. al-Jawālīqī overdid things to the point of nausea *(bughḍah* "ha-

162. See *Irshād*, VI, 460, ed. Rifāʿī, XVIII, 92.

163. See above, 15.

164. See Ibn ʿAsākir, LXXXVI, ll. 13 f. For the Ibn al-Furāt family of officials, see *EI²*, III, 767 f., s. v.

165. See below, n. 195.

166. See *Irshād*, VI, 461, ed. Rifāʿī, XVIII, 93. For *ṭabāhajah*, see *Ṭabīkh*, ed. al-Bārūdī, 16 f., trans. Arberry, "A Baghdad cookery book," 37. Ṭabarī cannot have been ignorant of the equivalence of *j* and *q* in Arabicized Persian words. The well-known sweet dish *fālūdhaj* was no doubt known to him in this form, but he writes *fālūdhaq* in *Ikhtilāf*, ed. Kern, I, 105.

tred"). The unfortunate fellow became known as Baghīḍ al-Ṭabarī, approximately "Ṭabarī's pet hatred."[167] Yet, Ṭabarī's friendly joking in company was never permitted by him to degenerate into conflicting with the seriousness required of scholars.[168]

Ṭabarī's life as a human being is presented as that of an individual living up to the best ideals of his society. Major flaws, if there were any,[169] are not indicated in our biographical sources. The picture before our eyes may indeed have been composed of real, historically true fragments from the life of an exceptional man.

The scholar

Even as a child, Ṭabarī used to say in later life, he had wanted to write a Qur'ān commentary along the lines of his great *Tafsīr.*[170] His scholarly productivity, indeed, constituted an uninterrupted continuum from his early youth to his death. Publication of his principal legal works came first and never stopped, followed by that of his Qur'ān Commentary and, finally, the *History.* His primary focus was jurisprudence. Like other scholars of the time,[171] he specialized in three fields, which had to be mastered by every legal scholar to some degree: legal theory as such and as it applied to legal practice, Qur'ānic science, and history in the restricted sense of a few dates of the lives of individuals. An understanding of the science of *ḥadīth* was basic to all three subjects. Ṭabarī's contribution to all of them was gigantic. It was his particular merit that he eventually went beyond the religious and legal interest of his colleagues in biographical data and expanded it into a historical work that dealt with the entire sweep of history known to him.[172]

---

167. See *Irshād,* VI, 461, ed. Rifāʿī, XVIII, 93 f. The source (Ibn Kāmil ?) continues with an anecdote about the foolishness of the man.

168. See *Irshād,* VI, 456 f., ed. Rifāʿī, XVIII, 86.

169. On questionable character traits, see below, 58 f. They are rare and doubtful.

170. See *Irshād,* VI, 429, ll. 11 f., ed. Rifāʿī, XVIII, 62.

171. The works of Ibn Ḥanbal, who was averse to publishing, included a *Tafsīr* and a *Ta'rīkh* (at least according to his biographer Ibn al-Jawzī, *Manāqib,* 248 f.) Ibn al-Nadīm, *Fihrist,* 229, makes no mention of a *Ta'rīkh.*

172. Earlier or contemporary histories that were written by jurists are apparently not preserved.

The central position of the law in Muslim society required its theoreticians and practitioners to possess a certain familiarity with most aspects of Muslim civilization. As a genius whose accomplishments allowed viewing him as the perfect scholar, Ṭabarī was credited with exceptional learning in a variety of disciplines. It could easily be deduced from his *Tafsīr* that he was well-versed in grammar and lexicography.[173] Excellence was claimed for him also in other fields of philology classified among the Arab linguistic sciences. His personal contacts with philologists of all descriptions were quite numerous, if much less so than his contacts with traditionists and legal scholars. For instance, he visited the philologist Abū Ḥātim al-Sijistānī, possibly in those early years when he studied in al-Baṣrah. He appears to have been repelled by his disregard for cleanliness,[174] and, in addition to a few *ḥadīth*s, he did not learn much more from him than a far-fetched etymology for his native Ṭabaristān as derived from "land of the axe (Persian *tabar=ṭabar)*" so named because the early Muslim settlers there were forced to clear the woods with axes.[175]

His interest in foreign languages deserves notice, in particular, because it is connected with his attitude toward the intensely debated question of the occurrence of non-Arabic words in the Qur'ān. He naturally knew Persian, even if sporadic quotation of Persian verses does not mean very much in this respect.[176] In *Tafsīr,* he discussed the relationship of Persian and Arabic (I, 7) and the Ethiopic loan words (I, 6–8). From al-Farrā', he learned that *fātiḥ* or *fattāḥ* apparently meant "judge" in the language of ʿUmān (IX, 3, l. 12, *ad* Qur. 8:89), clearly a South Arabian (South Semitic) term. Mūsā could be derived from Coptic "water" and "tree" (*moou* and *sei* [?])[176a] (I, 222, l. 2, *ad* Qur. 2:51).

173. See *Irshād*, VI, 437, l. 14, ed. Rifāʿī, XVIII, 60. *Tahdhīb* is mentioned there as providing additional evidence, as, in fact, it does by its regular sections on strange words in the traditions under discussion.

174. See above, n. 160.

175. See *Irshād*, VI, 429, ll. 5–11, ed. Rifāʿī, XVIII, 48. The etymology is repeated with some modifications by Samʿānī, *Ansāb*, 39, and Yāqūt, *Muʿjam*, III, 503.

176. See *History*, text below, II, 193, 1494, 1602, f., and von Grünebaum, "Bemerkung," 224; Rosenthal, *Muslim Historiography*², 135, n. 1.

176a. Bentley Layton calls my attention to *šēn* as the common Coptic word for "tree," and to *še/ē/i*, meaning "wood." The word meant here may, in fact, be *šēn*. It would render the second part of the name of Moses according to its Hebrew/Aramaic form and point to a Jewish or, more likely, Christian origin of the

He was aware of the fanciful suggestion that *ṭāhā* is "O man" in Nabataean/Syriac (XVI, 102 f., *ad* Qur. 20:2), but he apparently rejected the (Byzantine) Greek derivation of *firdaws* (XVI, 29, l. 22, *ad* Qur. 18:107). All this is traditional material long at home in Qur'ān commentaries,[177] yet, it underlines Ṭabarī's concern with language.

He is said to have studied poetry with the great philologist Tha'lab (200–91/815[6]–904) and to have been one of his early students. Tha'lab had a reputation for severity in his judgment of other scholars and was considered to be a difficult person to deal with, but he called Ṭabarī one of the most sagacious Kūfan (grammarians). He lived to see him achieve great fame with his *Tafsīr.*[178] Ṭabarī was also acquainted with Tha'lab's disciple, Abū 'Umar al-Zāhid, known as Ghulām Tha'lab (261–345/874[5]–957), who praised the *Tafsīr*'s accuracy in grammar and language.[179] While still in his youth, Ṭabarī acquired an expert knowledge of Arabic poetry. It stood him in good stead in Egypt when Ibn Sirāj asked him about the seventh-century poet al-Ṭirimmāḥ, whose poetry was no longer known in Egypt. Ṭabarī knew al-Ṭirimmāḥ's poems by heart and was able to recite and explain them in public.[180]

Another anecdote, however, tries to belittle Ṭabarī's knowledge of poetry and related subjects. The Ḥanafite judge and litterateur Aḥmad b. Isḥāq b. al-Buhlūl (231–317 or 318/845–929 or 930) entered into an animated conversation on many subjects with a person he did not recognize who was sitting next to him at a funeral. Ibn al-Buhlūl's son, Abū Ṭālib Muḥammad (d. 348/959), told him that his conversation partner was the famous Ṭabarī. Then, on an-

---

etymology taken over by the Qur'ān commentators. The neglect of the final *n* of *šēn* may have been triggered originally by thinking of the accusative ending of the name in Greek. See Crum, 317a *(sei)*, 568b *(šēn)*, and 546a *(še/ē/i)*.

177. As are phonetic observations such as the exchangeability of *th* and *f* (*Tafsīr*, I, 247, l. 9, *ad* Qur. 2:61 XXX, 47, l. 7, *ad* Qur. 81:11), *s* and *z* (VIII, 157, ll. 8 f., *ad* Qur. 7:71), and *k* and *q* (XXX, 47, l. 5, *ad* Qur. 81:11).

178. See *Irshād*, VI, 438, ll. 1–6, 439, l. 6, ed. Rifā'ī, XVIII, 60, 62, l. 4. For Tha'lab, see Sezgin, *GAS*, IX, 140–2. Since Tha'lab had finished his studies already in 225/240 and was by then a popular teacher (see *TB*, V, 205, l. 6, 209, l. 21), it seems rather implausible that Ṭabarī studied with him before he had many students.

179. See *Irshād*, VI, 439, ll. 12–15, ed. Rifā'ī, XVIII, 62. For Ghulām Tha'lab, see Sezgin, *GAS*, IX, 147 f.

180. See *Irshād*, VI, 432, ll. 14–16, ed. Rifā'ī, XVIII, 53. *Tahdhīb* repeatedly quotes his poetry.

other similar occassion, he engaged Ṭabarī in reciting poetry and biographical data (*siyar*, connected with poetry). Ṭabarī frequently faltered, but Ibn al-Buhlūl was able to recite all the verses without a hitch and give all the answers.[180a]

The theory of versification as embodied in the science of prosody (*ʿarūḍ*) was known to Ṭabarī. How solid his knowledge was, is another question. He was asked about prosody in Egypt and supposedly learned all there was to know about it overnight from a borrowed copy of al-Khalīl's fundamental work on the subject.[181] Someone of his intellectual caliber could probably become proficient in any subject by just reading one book about it.

Ṭabarī seems to have enjoyed discussing evidential verses in *Tafsīr* and, especially, in *Tahdhīb* for the explanation of rare words in traditions. He inserted poetical quotations in *History* when they served to enliven the narrative or to support the historical argument, whether he chose the verses himself or, which is much more likely in most cases, quoted them from the sources used by him. He was fond of reciting verses and composing some of his own, and he engaged in occasional poetic exchanges with friends and acquaintances; this, of course, was the custom of all educated persons in medieval Islam.[182]

He often recited verses that al-Awzāʿī had earlier been fond of; they dealt with the advisability of decent persons remaining aloof and keeping concealed what they knew and could do, when conditions in the world were topsy-turvy and stupidity and meanness prevailed.[183] He is credited with verses extolling *ḥadīth* and *ḥadīth* scholars. For him, they represented all that is of true value for Muslims; he incidentally used the opportunity to excoriate any interest in "innovations" (*bidaʿ*).[184]

The verses most generally ascribed to him speak of his con-

180a. See *TB*, IV, 32 f.; ʿAbd al-Qādir al-Qurashī, I, 58 f.

181. See *Irshād*, VI, 434 f., ed. Rifāʿī, XVIII, 56. Another reference to Ṭabarī's competence in prosody is found in *Irshād*, VI, 427, l. 6, ed. Rifāʿī, XVIII, 45, l. 9, in a quotation from *al-Iqnāʿ fī iḥdā ʿashrata qirāʾah* by al-Ḥasan b. ʿAlī al-Ahwāzī (362–446/972[3]–1054; see Brockelmann, *GAL*, Suppl. I, 720).

182. See above, 43.

183. See Muʿāfā, *Jalīs*, I, 168 f.

184. See Ibn ʿAsākir, LXXXVI f. Although the verses are introduced as "by" Ṭabarī, he may have merely quoted them. This is even more likely with four verses addressed to Mayyās, which are a satire on an irrelevant (person?); see Ibn ʿAsākir, LXXXVIII. On Ṭabarī's attitude toward "innovations," see below, 61.

tempt for worldly riches and the negative qualities commonly associated with wealth and poverty:

When I am in financial difficulties, my companion won't know it.
When I am wealthy, my friend will be wealthy.

My sense of shame preserves me my decency
as well as my gentility *(rifqī)* in making demands on my companion *(rafīqī)*.

Were I willing to squander my decency,
it would be easy for me to become rich.

Perhaps they also reflect the middle-class circumstances in which he grew up and spent his entire life:

I do not like two character qualities and what they represent:
the arrogance of wealth and the humility of poverty.

When you get wealthy, don't get arrogant,
and when you get poor, show your disrespect for fate![185]

To a high ranking 'Alid who had written him complaining about the difficulty of finding reliable friends and distinguishing between good and bad ones, Ṭabarī—apparently assuming that the writer could possibly have meant him by "someone," although he eagerly desired to be esteemed by him—replied:

My amīr has a bad opinion of someone seriously concerned.
Would there were a way to obtain his good opinion!

(Re)consider, my amīr, what you have thought and said,
for a good opinion from you is something beautiful.[186]

185. These verses are found in all major biographical notices, all of which depend on *TB*, II, 165, so that the occasional variant readings they contain are of no significance. The exception is Subkī, *Ṭabaqāt*, who does not mention the verses. In this context, it may be meaningful that the Prophetic tradition quoted by Ṭabarī to the author of *Aghānī* (see above, n. 75) condemns the arrogant treatment of others as inferiors by expecting them to rise (for the *ḥadīth*, see Ibn Ḥanbal, IV, 91, 95).

186. See *TB*, II, 166, quoted by Ibn 'Asākir, LXXXVIII; *Irshād*, VI, 426, ed. Rifā'ī, XVIII, 43. The circumstances of the poetical exchange were apparently unknown to the author of *TB*. The writer, Aḥmad b. 'Īsā al-'Alawī, remains unidentified. Others named Aḥmad b. 'Īsā, such as the one who died in 323/935 *(TB*, IV, 280 f.)

All these verses are pleasant enough, but they are nothing out of the ordinary. Al-Qifṭī exaggerated more than a little when he described Ṭabarī's poetry as "above the poetry of scholars,"[187] even if scholarly poetry, it must be said, never enjoyed any critical acclaim to begin with. The last word on Ṭabarī as a poet or critic of poetry belonged to the prominent litterateur al-Ṣūlī. He moved in court circles and may well have caught at least occasional glimpses of Ṭabarī in his old age. Confronted with a variant reading in a verse as quoted in *History* (text below, I, 759), he ruled out the possibility that Ṭabarī's text might be correct. He remarked tartly that Ṭabarī was not as great an authority on rare words in poetry as he was on other subjects.[188]

Ṭabarī's acquaintance with the exact sciences such as arithmetic and algebra was hardly intimate. He can be assumed to have had some knowledge, such as was needed by jurists.[189] A mastery of logic, dialectics, and, indeed, *falsafah* ("Greek philosophy")[190] was attributed to him. Contemporary speculative theology was saturated with philosophical thought, and Ṭabarī had to know and make use of the various techniques of philosophy as tools for the refutation of sectarian (Muʿtazilah) views and the defense of his beliefs.

Medicine was one of his great interests. As many other learned men were accustomed to do, he sometimes dabbled in the practice of it. A fellow Ṭabarī, ʿAlī b. Rabban, was the author of an important medical encyclopaedia entitled *Firdaws al-ḥikmah.* This work became Ṭabarī's medical bible. Ibn Rabban, we hear, considered the study of medicine (as well as some knowledge of moral philosophy) indispensable for a maturing boy of fourteen.[191] Little is known about his biography, except that he was a government

---

or the one mentioned below, n. 352, are no doubt not the same person. The place where he wrote to Ṭabarī may be identical with al-Balad near Mosul.

187. See Qifṭī, *Muḥammadūn*, 264.

188. See Ṣūlī, *Akhbār al-Rāḍī wa-al-Muttaqī*, 39, trans. Canard, I, 84; Rosenthal, *Muslim Historiography*², 53.

189. See *Irshād*, VI, 438 f., ed. Rifāʿī, XVIII, 61.

190. For logic and dialectics, see *Irshād, loc. cit.* (n. 189), and, for dialectics, *Irshād*, VI, 437, ll. 15 f., ed. Rifāʿī, XVIII, 60. According to Ibn ʿAsākir, XC, Ṭabarī studied "the theories of the philosophers and physicists."

191. See Ṭabarī, *Firdaws*, 99. It may be noted that Ṭabarī was well aware of al-Shāfiʿī's position with regard to (Greek) books on medicine taken as booty; see *Ikhtilāf*, ed. Schacht, 179; Rosenthal, *Muslim Historiography*², 75, n. 5.

official in his native country in earlier years and that he remained a Christian for much of his life before he converted to Islam during the reign of al-Mutawakkil.[192] Ṭabarī may in fact have known him personally, possibly during his early years in Baghdad, not long before Ibn Rabban's death. The *Firdaws* had been completed a few years before. There is a report, which cannot be verified, that Ṭabarī studied with him the entire work and wrote it down. According to Ibn Kāmil, he had a copy of it in six parts in his possession. He even kept it under his prayer carpet.[193]

Ṭabarī occasionally gave medical advice to his friends and students when one of their children became sick. When Abū al-Faraj b. al-Thallāj, who later was a jurist of Ṭabarī's legal school, fell ill, Ṭabarī suggested a cure to his father Abū al-ʿAbbās. The worried father was only too willing to give it a try, for he reasoned that coming from a man like Ṭabarī, it no doubt enjoyed divine blessing. Ṭabarī described his suggested remedy and the way it was to be applied in these words: "Shave his head and prepare very greasy cakes smothered in (chicken) fat.[194] Let him eat them until he is full, then take the rest and put it on his pate and let him sleep in this condition. If God wills, he will be all right."[195] The remedy proved effective—and certainly could not have done any harm—and Abū al-Faraj recovered, but Ṭabarī outlived him, and Abū al-Faraj died a short while before him. Ṭabarī also treated himself when he was ill. He described to a Christian physician sent to him by the wazīr ʿAlī b. ʿĪsā what he had done to cure himself. The physician had to admit that he himself could not have done better. With rather heavy flattery, he added that if Ṭabarī were a Christian, his coreligionists would consider him one of the apostles.[196]

---

192. See Ullmann, *Medizin*, 119–22; Sezgin, *GAS*, III, 236–40.

193. See *Irshād*, VI, 429, ed. Rifāʿī, XVIII, 48.

194. For *jūdhābah* (Persian *gūdhāb*), see, for instance, *Ṭabīkh*, ed. al-Bārūdī, 71 f. (ch. 8), trans. Arberry, "A Baghdad cookery book," 208 f. and 28 f. where Arberry translates a couple of poems on *jūdhābah*. See also Rodinson, "Recherches," 103, 133.

195. See *Irshād*, VI, 460, f., ed. Rifāʿī, XVIII, 93. On Ibn al-Thallāj, see above, n. 165.

196. See *Irshād*, VI, 461 f., ed. Rifāʿī, XVIII, 94. On Ṭabarī's illness, see above, n. 144. The story is remarkable for showing Ṭabarī in direct contact with a non-Muslim. It is hard to say how much other contact with Christians and, perhaps, Jews he might have had. His familiarity with Jewish and Christian historical/religious material does not imply any sort of personal acquaintance. For this

There was a religious side to Ṭabarī's concern with medicine. A quotation from *al-Ādāb al-ḥamīdah* (see *Ādāb al-nufūs*, below, 82) recommends the effectiveness of a procedure for relief in unpleasant situations. It had been suggested by an early Muslim and consisted of reciting sūrahs 91 and 92, each seven times, and asking God for help. Relief would come in the first, third, fifth, or, maybe, seventh night. The recipe was tried by someone who felt great pain and did not know what to do about it. He said the prescribed prayer before going to bed. Falling asleep, he immediately dreamed that two men came and sat down, one at his head and the other at his feet. The one told the other to feel his body. When he came to a certain place of his head, he ordered him not to shave the spot but wash it with *khaṭmiyyah* and then draw blood there by means of cupping, with the added suggestion that he ought also to recite sūrah 95. In the morning, he tried to find out why he was told to use *khaṭmiyya*, and he was told that it was for stopping the flow of blood from the wound caused by the bloodletting.[197]

As a man of general education, Ṭabarī was thus interested in numerous aspects of contemporary intellectual life. Even those aspects which were viewed with growing suspicion by the legal and religious scholarship, of which Ṭabarī was a foremost representative, were not excluded. He did not contribute actively to them but restricted his serious scholarly efforts to his prime concerns, law and *ḥadīth*, Qur'ānic science, and history. He was conscious of the fact that each of these large fields had its own vocabulary and technique of exposition, but it can be observed that his treatment of them always shows the same general traits characteristic of his approach to scholarship.

His large literary output required considerable discipline in his daily routine and scholarly habits.[198] He paid attention to such comparatively minor details as the best way of reading books in connection with his research. As reported by one of his students,

---

material, see *History*, translation, Vols. I and II, and Abdalmajid Charfi, "Christianisme."

197. See Tanūkhī, *Faraj*, I, 19, f. For *khaṭmī (khiṭmī)* "marshmallow," see, for instance, Lane, 768a; Rosenthal, "Hippocratic Oath," 68 ff.; and, in particular, Rāzī, *Ḥāwī*, XX, 398–401. *Khaṭmiyyah* is presumably the salve for wounds made from it alone or a concoction with honey water *(melikraton)* mentioned by al-Rāzī in the first place, quoting Dioscurides, III, 146, 1, ed. Wellmann, II, 155, ll. 4 f.

198. See above, 39 and 42 f.

Ibn al-Mughallis, he would systematically go twice through the works he wished to consult, carrying them from one corner of his house to another and then, when he had finished with them, returning them to their original place.[199] He appears to have done all his research by himself without assistants. Only once do we hear that he asked for help in his research. It was near the end of his life that he requested from a bookseller named Abū al-Qāsim al-Ḥusayn b. Ḥubaysh that he assemble for him the available titles on *qiyās.* They were more than thirty books. When he returned them to the bookseller, it was discovered that he had marked them with red ink,[200] apparently his way of locating suitable references to be used by him at some later date.[201] His lecturing, when a large audience was present, required the customary use of repetitors *(mustamlī),* but the name of only one of them is preserved, Abū Saʿīd ʿAmr b. Muḥammad b. Yaḥyā al-Dīnawarī.[202]

Like other students and scholars, Ṭabarī kept his notebooks and occasionally made reference to them. Quoting an interpretation of Qur. 79:3 by Mujāhid, he indicates that he found it "in my book," presumably a notebook dating back to the time when he studied with Abū Kurayb.[203] A reference to his notebooks is also found in connection with information derived from al-Ḥasan b. al-Ṣabbāḥ.[204] When there was a question whether ʿAbdallah b. ʿUmar or ʿAbdallāh b. ʿAmr (b. al-ʿĀṣ) was meant, he called attention to

199. See *Irshād,* VI, 444, ll. 1–6, ed. Rifāʿī, XVIII, 68 f. For a translation of the passage in context, see below, 110. Abū al-Ḥasan ʿAbdallāh b. Aḥmad b. Muḥammad b. al-Mughallis died in 324/936. He was a follower of the school of the Ẓāhirite Dāwūd b. ʿAlī, for whose relations with Ṭabarī see below, 132. For Ibn al-Mughallis, see Ibn al-Nadīm, *Fihrist,* 218, ll. 4–9; Dhahabī, *ʿIbar,* II, 201. He provided Ibn Kāmil with much information.

200. See *Irshād,* VI, 453, ll. 5–8, ed. Rifāʿī, XVIII, 81, and the translation of the passage below, 120. Booksellers customarily served as lending libraries.

201. Possibly, the statement might refer to annotations made by Ṭabarī.

202. He was the transmitter of *Ṣarīḥ,* see text, 193, trans., 186. He is the Abū Saʿīd al-Dīnawarī who is said to be Ṭabarī's *mustamlī* in Dhahabī, *Nubalāʾ,* XIV, 280, and *ʿUluww,* 150. It does not seem impossible that he is identical with Abū Saʿīd ʿUmar b. Aḥmad al-Dīnawarī who played an unhappy role in connection with *Ādāb al-nufūs*; see below, n. 308. Another Dīnawarī, Abū Saʿīd ʿUthmān b. Aḥmad, who reported the anecdote involving Ibn al-Furāt (above, n. 164), is certainly a different person.

203. See *Tafsīr,* XXX, 20, ll. 6 f. The published recension of Mujāhid's commentary does not mention the quotation.

204. See *Tafsīr,* XV, 166, ll. 31 f. (*ad* Qur. 18:46). Al-Ḥasan b. al-Ṣabbāḥ died in 249/863; see *TB,* VII, 330–2; Ibn Ḥajar, *Tahdhīb,* II, 289 f.

the fact that it was Ibn ʿUmar that was found "in my book."[205]

Ṭabarī derived the materials for his major publications almost exclusively from written works, despite the pretense of oral transmission which obscures the picture to some degree by preventing more specific reference. In *History,* the written sources used by him are usually transparent, even though they are not preserved,[206] but it is very rare indeed that title and author are expressly mentioned, as in the case of the *History of the Baṣrans (Kitāb Akhbār ahl al-Baṣrah)* by ʿUmar b. Shabbah.[207] It was also unusual for him to quote his prime source, in this case, Sayf b. ʿUmar, with express reference to "his book."[208] He was, of course, aware of the intermediate written stages through which his material reached him, but he only exceptionally mentioned them in the way he did with a book of Abū Qilābah which Ayyūb al-Sakhtiyānī said he had read.[209] The "books" of contemporaries he made use of naturally remained mostly unmentioned, but he tells us how he received information from Ziyād b. Ayyūb. Dallawayh, as Ziyād was called, was a very old man when Ṭabarī met him in Baghdad. He produced for him *(akhraja ilayya)* "a book containing traditions on the authority of several shaykhs who, he said, had been his direct authorities. Some of it he taught me *viva voce,* some he did not. The latter (material) I copied from it (or him, *katabtuhū minhu)."*[210] A prophetical *ḥadīth* transmitted through Sufyān al-Thawrī described the coming of the Sufyānī at the end of time. It had found much attention in Syria, and Ṭabarī, who obviously did not like it, discussed it there with Muḥammad b. Khalaf al-ʿAsqalānī. In this connection, Ṭabarī mentions that he also saw

205. See *Dhayl,* III, 2490, ed. Cairo, XI, 638.

206. Ṭabarī's use of them helps to reconstruct them. For recent works on the Ṭabarī sources Abū Mikhnaf and al-Madāʾinī, with a thorough discussion of the problems involved, see U. Sezgin, *Abū Mikhnaf,* and Rotter, "Überlieferung." Noth, "Charakter," takes issue (principally on Sayf b. ʿUmar) with J. Wellhausen who is reputed to have been among the first to deal with Ṭabarī's sources.

207. See *History,* text below, II, 168.

208. See *History,* text below, I, 2391.

209. See *Tafsīr,* XXX, 174, l. 2 (*ad* Qur. 99:7); Sezgin, *GAS,* I, 68. See also U. Sezgin, *Abū Mikhnaf,* 83, in connection with *History,* II, 881 f.

210. See *History,* text below, I, 3159. Ziyād b Ayyūb, who was born in 166/782[3], had begun already his serious study of *ḥadīth* at the age of fifteen. He died in 252/866. See Bukhārī, *Taʾrīkh,* II, 1, 315; *TB,* VIII, 479–81; Ibn Ḥajar, *Tahdhīb,* III, 355.

it in "the book of al-Ṣudā'ī."[211] As in the case of Ziyād b. Ayyūb, al-Ṣudā'ī's book appears to have been an unpublished notebook.

Since quotations make up the bulk of the contents of Ṭabarī's major works, the question of his accuracy in quoting arises constantly. It cannot be satisfactorily answered in a general way, since most of his sources are not preserved. Even where they are, it is always possible that Ṭabarī used another text or recension than the one preserved. Small changes in the wording or carefully chosen omissions or the deliberate failure to take account of all available sources can make a big difference and even alter the entire picture, particularly in the interpretation of historical data. It is a safe assumption that Ṭabarī used such procedures on occasion intentionally (and, presumably, most frequently when contemporary 'Abbāsid interests were involved), or it just happened to him without his being fully aware of the consequences. Modern historians, for whom this is a crucial question, have mostly restricted themselves to raising it in connection with certain points of historical information. This is probably the most that can be done at present.[212] The assumption that Ṭabarī's quotations can in general be relied upon as being accurate has not been disproved and, as matters stand, remains valid.

At the core, his honest and solid attitude toward scholarship is indisputable. His reverence for scholarship, often stressed by his biographers, is obvious, and so is his desire to present what he considered factual information, hard facts, to his students and to contemporary and future readers. He wished to be concise and to disregard irrelevant data. A cherished anecdote tells of his initial concept of the size of *History* and *Tafsīr*. It was to produce much larger works than he finally did. But when he asked his students whether they possessed the energy to study such enormous works, he found to his dismay that they thought they would not be able to read them in a lifetime. He concluded that their attitude showed a general lack of noble ambition. So he cut the size of the works

211. See *Tafsīr*, XXII, 72 f. (*ad* Qur. 34:51). On al-'Asqalānī, see above, n. 92, and on al-Ṣudā'ī, see below, translation, n. 168. Ṭabarī's attitude toward the belief in the expected Sufyānī is attested, for instance, below, translation, Vol. XXXVIII, 181. On notebooks, see also above, 17 and 21.

212. For individual studies, see above, n. 206, and, for a general judgment, see Cahen, "L'historiographie arabe," 149 and 160.

down to what it eventually became.[213] The anecdote is almost certain to be an invention without any basis in fact, but it shows a true understanding not only of Ṭabarī's tremendous capacity but also of his concern with the essentials in all his publications. He continually stressed that he wanted to be brief or that he did not want to repeat himself.[214] Statements of this sort take the place of accurate cross-referencing, for which there existed no practical methods in the manuscript age.[215] Their frequency also reveals his realization of the need for economy in dealing effectively with a body of knowledge which already in his time had grown to almost unmanageable proportions.

The most remarkable aspect of Ṭabarī's approach is his constant and courageous expression of "independent judgment *(ijtihād).*" After having quoted his sources and the views represented by them, he states what he considered the most acceptable view. With respect to legal and dogmatic differences, Ṭabarī is not reluctant to make his preference known, as is clear from *Ṭabṣīr* and the preserved parts of *Ikhtilāf* and *Tahdhīb*. Expectedly, this feature is much more prominent in *Tafsīr* than it is in *History* . His own views are consistently introduced by "Abū Jaʿfar says". He carefully argues and documents what he believes to be the "most likely" report or opinion.[216] His conclusions, it may be added, usu-

213. See *TB*, II, 163, quoted by Ibn ʿAsākir, LXXXVIII; Samʿānī, *Ansāb*, IX, 42; *Irshād*, VI, 424 f., ed. Rifāʿī, XVIII, 42; Dhahabī, *Nubalāʾ*, XIV, 274 f.; and *Tadhkirat al-ḥuffāẓ*, II, 252.

214. All of Ṭabarī's major works, but particularly *Tafsīr*, state more frequently that there is no need for repetition *(iʿādah)* than that making the work unnecessarily long is to be avoided *(iṭālah)*. For *History*, see text below, I, 251, (translation, Vol. II, 46), and I, 671.

215. Such cross-referencing as there is was not very convenient even for learned Qur'ān scholars. See *Tafsīr*, VI, 29, l. 21 (*ad* Qur. 4:175), referring back to the verse on inheritance (Qur. 4:12) earlier in sūrah 4, or *Tafsīr*, XIII, 155, l. 1 (*ad* Qur. 14:37), referring back to sūrah 2 (verses 125 ff.).

216. In *Tafsīr*, the most commonly used term is "the correct view *(al-ṣawāb)* in my/our opinion." Elsewhere, the expression "the truth in my opinion *(al-ḥaqq ʿindī)*" is also found. *Tabṣīr* uses both indiscriminately. The situation in *Ikhtilāf* is slightly puzzling. In Schacht's text, Ṭabarī does not explicitly indicate his preferences. Kern's text, on the other hand, has at first a number of instances of *al-ḥaqq ʿindī* (I, 13, 19, 22, 24, 29); later, it is quite regularly *al-ṣawāb ʿindī* (over twenty-five occurrences) or simply "our opinion." There are two possible explanations: The books of *Ikhtilāf* were written at different times or what is preserved represents different (perhaps also abridged) recensions. Either explanation is applicable, it would seem, according to the various parts of the preserved text.

ally deserve respect to this day. It is, of course, clear that he was a "compiler," in the sense that he reported the evidence derived from his sources without immediate comment or basic distortion. Most scholarly works in Muslim civilization followed this highly recommendable method. It was, however, an unfortunate misjudgment on the part of Brockelmann (*GAL*, I, 142, *GAL*,[2] I, 148) to speak of him as unoriginal ("kein selbständiger Kopf"), when he was undeniably concerned above all with seeing things his way, that is, being original and independent in his approach.

His own views often leaned toward moderation and compromise. He stated innumerable times that two of the suggested readings of a Qur'ānic passage were both possible and can be accepted and used as correct.[217] It was not only readings but also interpretations that challenged his tendency toward compromise. Two examples may be mentioned.

A particularly knotty problem presented itself in Qur. 5:6, the verse which somehow gave rise to one of the famous distinctions between Shī'ites and Sunnīs—the Shī'ah practice of "wiping" (the boots, although neither *khuffayn* nor any other footgear is mentioned in the Qur'ān) as against the sunnī practice of "washing" the feet in the ritual ablution before prayer.[218] It hinges on whether one reads the word "feet" as either a genitive or an accusative. Both readings, Ṭabarī argues, yield the same meaning as far as the legal requirement is concerned. However, he gives preference to the genitive on the basis of his interpretation of the meaning of "wiping" in the verse and for syntactic reasons. The philological

---

While the occurrences in *Tafsīr* are legion, there are fewer occasions for them in *History*; but they are not entirely absent, if in rather different forms. Thus *History*, text below, I, 416, speaks of one statement as more likely true *(ashbah bi-al-ḥaqq)* than another. Or Ṭabarī's opinion is given conditionally : "If this version is correct, then the first statement is wrong" (*History*, text below, I, 1367). *Wa-al-ṣawāb 'indī* appears in *History*, III, 1436.

217. On the expression of preference with respect to Qur'ān readings *(ikhtiyār)*, see Nöldeke-Schwally-Bergsträsser-Pretzl, III, 132 ff. There may be more than two readings involved, as, for instance, *Tafsīr*, XXVII, 16, ll. 27 f. (*ad* Qur. 52:21). Occasionally, Ṭabarī expressly states his own preference for one reading as the only one that is acceptable to him as correct, as, for instance, *Tafsīr*, V, 209, ll. 13 f. (*ad* Qur. 4:135 end).

218. See *Tafsīr*, VI, 81, l. 3–87, l. 22. Ṭabarī's conclusion appears on pp. 83, l. 19–84, l. 13. For a concise exposition of the problem in relation to Qur'ānic data, see Paret, *Der Koran. Kommentar und Konkordanz*, 115 f. See also Nöldeke-Schwally-Bergsträsser-Pretzl, III, 141.

point he makes in favor of the genitive is absolutely correct. Yet, the accusative became the Kūfī reading adopted in the canonic text, so as to leave no doubt about the "washing" of the feet. Ṭabarī's interpretation of "wiping" amounts to wiping the feet in their entirety *with water* (not mentioned in the Qur'ānic verse but somehow deducible from the sand ablution *[tayammum]* in Qur. 4:43) by using one's hand or its equivalent; thus wiping *and* washing are one process (which makes for more problems, such as whether washing without wiping is in compliance with the law). The discussion of this legal point of ritual is extraordinarily long, given Ṭabarī's concept of what his Qur'ān commentary should legitimately deal with.[219] He takes great pains to weaken or reinterpret traditions that would favor the Shī'ah practice, and pleads for the correctness of the sunnī view. His plea fell on deaf ears in certain circles prejudiced against him. He was accused of sympathy with the Shī'ah on this point. His expressed preference for the genitive reading could easily be seen as tilting toward the Shī'ah, no matter how consistently he argued for the sunnī practice, which he clearly accepted as the proper one.[220] The balancing feat he performs gives the impression of being a compromise between his scholarly instincts and the religious practices which he felt it necessary to uphold at all costs.

Another similar example is the way in which he argues both sides of a sensitive issue of a dogmatic nature that had arisen in

219. The subject of *aḥkām*, the legal data furnished by the Qur'ān, was a well-established subdiscipline of Qur'ānic science by the time of Ṭabarī. It was treated apart from general commentaries. Ṭabarī considered legal excursuses not appropriate in *Tafsīr.* Thus, he declared a detailed discussion of unintentional *(khaṭa')* killing to be out of place, since "our intention in this work *(Tafsīr)* is the explanation of the Revelation, and *khaṭa'* is not mentioned in it." He referred the reader to *Laṭīf* instead. See *Tafsīr*, VII, 28, ll. 30 ff. (*ad* Qur. 5:95); similarly, VII, 203, ll. 9 ff. (*ad* Qur. 6:103). Nevertheless, Ṭabarī was inevitably drawn into legal discussions on subjects such as retaliation *(qiṣāṣ)* (II, 60, *ad* Qur. 2:178), inheritance law (II, 74, *ad* Qur. 2:182), fasting (II, 103, *ad* Qur. 2:187), pilgrimage (II, 153, *ad* Qur. 2:193), divorce (II, 270 ff., *ad* Qur. 2:228 f.), prayer (II, 352, *ad* Qur. 2:238), abrogation (III, 12, *ad* Qur. 2:256, and elsewhere), entering the shops of merchants (XVIII, 90 f., *ad* Qur. 24:29). See also the preceding note and the discussion of *Laṭīf*, below, 113 ff.

220. See Ibn al-Jawzī, *Muntaẓam*, VI, 172. Ibn al-Jawzī seems to express here his own view (see also below, n. 233). Ibn Ḥajar, *Lisān*, V, 103, makes the hardly plausible suggestion that the statement that Ṭabarī was satisfied with wiping the feet in the ritual ablution might refer to the Shī'ite Muḥammad b. Jarīr al-Ṭabarī (see below, 118 f.).

connection with *maqāman maḥmūdan* in Qur. 17:79.[221] While the ablution problem concerned the entire Muslim community, his compromise in the case of *maqāman maḥmūdan* was dictated by the need to defend himself against personal attacks. Compromise by Ṭabarī, however, must never be confused with an absence of firm conviction.

The preoccupation with legal issues and the religious problems inextricably connected with them dominated the course of his life as a scholar. His stance was moderate to some degree, at least in minor matters. He might use the harsh word "obtuse" for someone who, he thought, did not understand him correctly;[222] but he also expressed himself in speaking about other scholars with a certain politeness ("I fear that shaykh erred").[223] On occasion, he was ready with sharp remarks, such as the observation that he had seen al-ʿAbbās b. Muḥammad al-Dūrī so intoxicated that "the walls were hitting him".[224] On his part, his reputation protected him from criticism in later centuries, but not entirely. His alleged attacks on Ibn ʿĀmir, one of the seven early Qur'ān readers, were criticized.[225] The historian Ibn al-Athīr would frankly object to some aspect of Ṭabarī's appproach to history,[226] and there is an intriguing statement that "various criticisms were made of him (*takallamū fīh bi-anwāʿ*)," which originated in circles with strong ties to Ṣūfism.[227] These criticisms may very well have been of an

---

221. See below, 71 ff. and Appendix B.

222. See *Tafsīr*, II, 269, l. 5 (*ad* Qur. 2:227).

223. See *Tafsīr*, II, 91, l. 5 (*ad* Qur. 2:185).

224. See *TB*, XII, 145, ll. 12–14, from Ibn Kāmil. Al-Dūrī (185–271/801–84) is mentioned quite frequently as an authority of Ṭabarī. It may be noted that he was an authority of Muḥammad b. Dāwūd al-Ẓāhirī (see *TB*, V, 256, l. 2). He was also one of those who supported the authenticity of the attribution to Mujāhid of the disputed interpretation of *maqāman maḥmūdan*, and was repeatedly cited in this connection by Khallāl, *Musnad*; see also Dhahabī, *'Uluww*, 143. For Ṭabarī on Abū Ḥātim al-Sijistānī, see above, n. 160, and on Abū Bakr b. Abī Dāwūd, below, n. 229.

225. See Ibn al-Jazarī, *Ghāyah*, I, 424, ll. 19 f.

226. See below, translation, introduction, n. 3.

227. See Ibn 'Asākir, LXXVIII f. Ibn 'Asākir had the remark from Abū al-Muẓaffar 'Abd al-Mun'im b. 'Abd al-Karīm b. Hawāzin al-Qushayrī (445–532/1053–1137[8]), a son of the author of the *Risālah*, the famous handbook on Ṣūfism. It went back to al-Sulamī (d. 412/1021) who collected Ṣūfī biographies in his *Ṭabaqāt al-Ṣūfiyya*. Not much is known so far about Ṭabarī's attitude toward Ṣūfism. He used Ṣūfī material in *Ādāb al-nufūs*; see below, 82. He certainly was opposed to the ecstatic mysticism which spread rapidly during his lifetime; see *History*, text below, III,

objective nature, but already his contemporaries felt that he was the innocent target of harmful and malicious slander "by enviers, ignoramuses, and heretics."[228]

Some fragments of a bitter controversy tell us of an occasion where Ṭabarī had to defend himself against such harmful and malicious backbiting. He was denounced by Abū Bakr b. Abī Dāwūd[229] to the influential chamberlain of al-Muqtadir, Naṣr al-Qushūrī. He was accused of Jahmite inclinations[230] and extremist pro-ʿAlid views and was forced to issue a denial.

> Abū Bakr b. Abī Dāwūd had sent a memorandum *(qiṣṣah)* concerning Ṭabarī to Naṣr, the Chamberlain. It contained several things, which he (Ṭabarī) denied. Thus he attributed to him Jahmite opinions in interpreting Qur. 5:64 ("and His two hands are both stretched out"), in that he gave to "His two hands" the (metaphoric meaning) of "His two favors *(niʿmatāh)*." (Ṭabarī) denied that and said, "I did not say that."[231] Another of those things was that (according to

2289, translation, Vol. XXXVIII, 199 f. It must be left an open question whether the Ṣūfīs' religious and ethical outlook appealed to him. It might very well have impressed him favorably to a certain degree. For a possible personal Ṣūfī contact, see below, n. 298.

228. See Ibn ʿAsākir, LXXXII.

229. Abū Bakr b. Abī Dāwūd, ʿAbdallāh b. Sulaymān b. al-Ashʿath, lived from 230/844[5] to 316/929 and thus was about six years older than Ṭabarī and survived him by six years. See *TB*, IX, 464 ff., in particular, 467 f. On him and his father, see also above, n. 74. He competed with Ṭabarī in writing a Qur'ān commentary; see Ibn al-Nadīm, *Fihrist*, 232, l. 28 (see below, 110).

TB, loc. cit., has a statement which is interesting in connection with the history of the composition of *Faḍā'il* (below, 91). Abū Bakr is said to have always stressed that he was willing to forgive every critic except one who accused him of hatred for ʿAlī (using the same expression as was used by Ṭabarī with respect to *bidʿah*; see below, n. 237). The reason for his remark was his awareness of being suspected of a well-concealed but deep aversion for ʿAlī and his partisans. Ṭabarī shared this suspicion. When he learned that Abū Bakr was lecturing on the virtues *(faḍā'il)* of ʿAlī, he made the snide remark: "Praise of God (a call to prayer) from a watchman *(takbīrah min ḥāris)*!" This would seem to be a proverbial statement for someone who does not practice what he preaches. *Ḥāris* might mean here "thief" (see Lane, 546b).

The first appearance in *History* of Naṣr al-Qushūrī is text below, III, 2144, translation, Vol. XXXVIII, 20, n. 114.

230. On Jahm and the Jahmiyyah, see *EI²*, II, 388, s.v. Djahm, Djahmiyya.

231. Ṭabarī refers to this interpretation in *Tafsīr*, VI, 194, l. 25, mentioning no names but including it among interpretations of the dialecticians (*ahl al-jadal*, see below, n. 416). His long discussion suggests that he does not accept it. The decisive

Abū Bakr b. Abī Dāwūd, Ṭabarī) transmitted the statement that the spirit of the messenger of God, when it left (him at death?), flowed into the palm of ʿAlī who then covered (slowly swallowed?)[232] it. He (Ṭabarī, or rather Abū Bakr?) said that the *ḥadīth* says only that he wiped his face with it, and does not contain "covered (slowly swallowed?) it".

This author[233] said: This is also absurd. However, Ibn Jarīr (Ṭabarī) wrote in reply to Naṣr, the Chamberlain: "There is no group in Islam like that contemptible group."[234] This is an ugly remark for him to make. For while it is necessary for him to counter an adversary, it is ugly in the extreme to blame his entire sect *(ṭā'ifah)* when he knew[235] who deserved to be blamed.[236]

The report is, unfortunately, not as clear and detailed as one might wish, but it illustrates Ṭabarī's dogmatic difficulties better than the general accusations of dogmatic heresy and extremist Shīʿah sympathies which we hear about mainly in connection with quarrels with the Ḥanbalites (who, in this case, presumably

element for Ṭabarī apparently was the use of the dual in "two hands," as against the immediately preceding "hand of God" in the singular. God's benefactions are innumerable, and this could be expressed by either the singular or the plural of *niʿmah*, but not by the dual. In *Tabṣīr*, fol. 88b, Ṭabarī explains the two hands as "stretched out with favors *(bi-al-niʿam)* for the creation, not withdrawn from the good."

232. The word is *ḥ-s-w* in the Hyderabad edition of Ibn al-Jawzī and *j-'-y*, according to the introduction of *Ikhtilāf*, ed. Kern, I, 10, nn. 3 and 4; see Ṭabarī, *Introductio etc.*, XCIX. The lexicographers, who tried hard to establish the meaning of *j-'-y*, thought of "to conceal" as the principal meaning of the root; see, for instance, Azharī, *Tahdhīb*, XI, 132 f.; Ibn Manẓūr, *Lisān*, XVIII, 138 f. They apparently do not list the tradition. De Goeje gives the impression that they did; he may have had a reference to it. Until it is located elsewhere, it will be difficult to decide what is really involved here.

233. The historian Thābit b. Sinān, who continued Ṭabarī's *History* to a few years before his death in 365/976, is mentioned by Ibn al-Jawzī in the context; but the speaker here may rather be Ibn al-Jawzī himself. However, the criticism of Ṭabarī's unfairness in blaming the entire group for the error of one of its members is difficult to ascribe to Ibn al-Jawzī. Only the rejection of the tradition as "absurd" may go back to Ibn al-Jawzī, while the rest comes from his unidentified source(?).

234. The "group *('iṣābah)*" is not named. Possibly, the students and sympathizers of Abū Bakr b. Abī Dāwūd are meant(?).

235. Thus the Hyderabad edition of Ibn al-Jawzī. The text in Ṭabarī, *Introductio etc.*, has "did not know," which is hardly correct.

236. See Ibn al-Jawzī, *Muntaẓam*, VI, 172. The text in Ṭabarī, *Introductio etc.*, XCVIII f., is taken from the Paris manuscript of the *Muntaẓam*.

cannot be held responsible).

There is every reason to assume that his dogmatic beliefs were basically those of the mainstream of "orthodox" Islam, as it was conceived, for instance, in the environment of Ibn Ḥanbal. Nothing to the contrary can be observed in his preserved dogmatic writings such as *Ṣarīḥ* and *Tabṣīr.* He appears as an implacable foe of "innovations *(bid'ah,* pl. *bida').*" When he was close to death and Ibn Kāmil asked him to pardon his enemies, he supposedly said that he would forgive them all except one individual who had accused him of "innovation". The person who had run afoul of him was his colleague Abū 'Alī al-Ḥasan b. al-Ḥusayn b. 'Alī al-Ṣawwāf (d. 310/December 925). He had objected to the praise which Ṭabarī showered on Abū Ḥanīfah, when he lectured on *Dhayl.*[237] In general, Ṭabarī is described as unswerving in his faithful adherence to the orthodox views of the ancient Muslim scholars in "most of his dogmatic views (*jull madhāhibihī*)." The qualifying "most" implies that there were exceptions. Regrettably, they are not mentioned. Only the fundamental points of dogma championed by the Mu'tazilah, with which Ṭabarī firmly disagreed, are enumerated in this connection.[238]

The politically most explosive aspect of Muslim dogmatics always was the imāmate, the leadership of the Muslim state and community. In the time of Ṭabarī, the focus was on the claims made for 'Alī, his descendants, and the Shī'ah as the legitimate rulers of Islam.[239] It is a moot question whether or not Shī'ism was numerically the majority party in the Muslim world at the time. It was the party that was out of power in most regions and, as far as the central government in Baghdad was concerned, it constituted a threat of subversion that had to be kept under control. Thus, the accusation of pro-Shī'ah sympathies was an easy

237. See *Irshād,* VI, 455, ll. 1–8, ed. Rifā'ī, XVIII, 84. For al-Ṣawwāf, see *TB,* VII, 297 f. He was the one who boasted that he had been eating dried dates all his life, when Ṭabarī expounded upon their harmfulness (above, n. 150). Ṭabarī was vindicated when al-Ṣawwāf's teeth fell out, and he lost much weight; see *Irshād,* VI, 459 f., ed. Rifā'ī, XVIII, 91.

238. See *Irshād,* VI, 453 f., ed. Rifā'ī, XVIII, 81 f.

239. Other sectarians, such as Khārijites and the pro-Umayyad Shī'ah, played a less important role, although they were by no means insignificant; see, for instance, below, translation, Vol. XXXVIII, 48 ff., for the pro-Umayyads, and passim for the Khārijites.

weapon against personal adversaries. Its effects probably varied greatly according to prevailing circumstances in each individual case. Sometimes, it could do permanent damage to the reputation of the accused. One of Ṭabarī's students, for example, Ibn Ayyūb (Abū Bakr Muḥammad b. ʿAbdallāh b. Muḥammad b. Ayyūb al-Qaṭṭān) was described to al-Khaṭīb al-Baghdādī as a sound transmitter of material from Ṭabarī but also as an extremist Shīʿite who held highly objectionable views. The Khaṭīb discussed the matter with another of his authorities who had studied with Ibn Ayyūb and was told by that person that he had never heard Ibn Ayyūb make unacceptable statements with pro-Shīʿah bias. His only crime was that he expressed himself in favor of recognizing ʿAlī superior position *(tafḍīl ʿAlī).*[240] This shows that Shīʿite tendencies could be deduced from open admiration of Alī. They could also be invented as malicious slender. In most cases, it is not possible for us to determine reasons and motivations. Old Ṭabarī appears to have been the victim of a campaign of slander by certain Ḥanbalites. They propagated the idea that he was a Shīʿah extremist and, ultimately, a heretic.[241] How successful they were, it is hard to say; quite a few people no doubt believed what they were told, although their numbers seem to have been inflated by rumor and tendentious reports. At any rate, there is not the slightest evidence for Ṭabarī's alleged Shīʿism. His roots in Ṭabaristān seem to have been in no way intertwined with local Shīʿism. His family rather belonged to the opposite camp.[242] If by any chance he harbored a deep down, secret animus against the ʿAbbāsid caliphate, he concealed it from his contemporaries as well as posterity. His works certainly do not support the accusation of Shīʿism or worse, though it must admitted that Ṭabarī would have avoided to mention things that might give reason to believe that the accusation was justified, even if it was. Opinions of his, such as the one ex-

240. See *TB*, V, 465. The Khaṭīb's informant on Ibn Ayyūb's alleged Shīʿism was his frequently cited authority Abū al-Qāsim al-Azharī (see Lassner, *Topography*, 234, n. 12, and index). The lenient view was taken by Judge Abū Bakr Muḥammad b. ʿUmar al-Dāwūdī (353–429/964–1038; see *TB*, III, 38).

241. As Miskawayh (see *Eclipse*, I, 84) states, this was the belief of the Ḥanbalite crowd *(al-ʿāmmah)* who caused the riot at the time of this death. Strangely, he makes no comment on the matter. See also *Irshād*, VI, 423, l. 17, ed. Rifāʿī, XVIII, 40, ll. 11 f. (see below, n. 292).

242. See also above, 13.

pressed in connection with wiping and washing in the ritual ablution, required considerable twisting in order to provide minimal support for it.[243]

The biographical sources depict him as a stout defender of the preeminence of all the first four caliphs. He felt compelled to defend ʿAlī against attacks and took every opportunity to profess his veneration of Abū Bakr and ʿUmar. In a discussion with a certain Ibn Ṣāliḥ al-Aʿlam about ʿAlī, Ṭabarī asked him what he thought about those who claimed that Abū Bakr and ʿUmar were not legitimate caliphs *(imāmā hudā)*. Al-Aʿlam replied that such claim was an "innovation." Considering Ṭabarī's rejection of any thought of *bidʿah*, that should perhaps have pleased him, but he was outraged by the reply and empathically insisted that it was not strong enough. Anyone who did not acknowledge the exalted status of the first two caliphs ought to be killed.[244] Reports of this sort could have been invented as a reaction to Ḥanbalite attacks, but Ṭabarī's orthodoxy with respect to the imāmate and Shīʿah beliefs seems to be beyond doubt.

Ṭabarī's struggle with the Ḥanbalites might be seen as a consequence of his independent judgment in matters of law. Just as pronouncements on points of Qur'ān interpretation must have made enemies for him among those who differed from his conclusions—and the competition was strong, as there were numerous Qur'ān scholars around and numerous laymen who had their own opinions on everything connected with the Qur'ān—anyone who insisted upon his own juridical and dogmatic views could expect to encounter determined hostility. Two such hostile encounters, the vicious Ḥanbalite attacks and the less grave conflict with the Ẓāhirites, will be discussed later in some detail.

Ṭabarī at first considered himself a Shāfiʿite, and many later Shāfiʿites were proud to claim him as one of their own.[245] For a

243. See above, 56 f.

244. See Ibn ʿAsākir, LXXXVI, quoted in a slightly shortened form by Dhahabī, *Nubalā'*, XIV, 275. Dhahabī's dependence on Ibn ʿAsākir can hardly be doubted, but it remains to be explained why he replaced Abū al-Fatḥ Muḥammad b. Aḥmad al-Ḥāfiẓ in the *isnād* by the equally correct form Abū al-Fatḥ b. Abī al-Fawāris (see *TB*, I, 352 f.). Dhahabī might have used an intermediate source, unless our text of Ibn ʿAsākir is faulty(?).

245. See Subkī, *Ṭabaqāt*, II, 251. The opinions of al-Rāfiʿī and Abū ʿĀṣim al-ʿAbbādī on Ṭabarī's position among Shāfiʿites were reported by Nawawī, *Tahdhīb*,

period of ten years, he functioned as a Shāfiʿite.[246] This may have been after his return from Egypt, and thus in the decade that ended about 267/880(1). By then, his own legal production had became extensive. His *Laṭīf* was a comprehensive exposition of both the basic principles *(uṣūl)* and the case law *(furūʿ)* of presumably the entire sharīʿah; at least parts of the work were then already in existence. Given his *ijtihād,* the legal views expressed in it must have included many which, not by themselves but in the aggregate, set Ṭabarī's legal thought apart from the other legal schools of his time. It was therefore a natural development for him and his circle of students to constitute themselves into a special legal school, the "Jarīrī *madhhab.*" The phrase "our *madhhab*"used in *Ikhtilāf*[247] in one place apparently does not understand *madhhab* as the view under discussion but refers to his "school"; however, because of the uncertainties connected with the dating of *Ikhtilāf,* the passage does not provide us with a *terminus ante quem* for the formal birth of the Jarīrī *madhhab.* Naming a sect or school after the father of the founder was a common practice. With respect to "Jarīrī", it is clear that neither Ṭabarī's given name nor the name of his country of origin would have made a distinctive designation for the school. It is not known, however, when the name "Jarīrī" was introduced, nor is there any precise information as to when the outside world began to look at Ṭabarī as the founder of his *madhhab.*

During his later years, his students were considered Jarīrīs or considered themselves as followers of Ṭabarī's legal views. Some wrote works on the Jarīrī *madhhab* or in defense of it. One of these Jarīrīs was considerably older than Ṭabarī, which is a testimony to Ṭabarī's reputation and, perhaps, his personal magnetism. He was Abū Muslim al-Kajjī, who was born in 200/815[6] and died in 292/904[5]. An authority on Qur'ān interpretation, he was an extraordinarily successful teacher. He had large numbers of students and is said to have employed no less than seven *mustamlīs.* Many of the students were standing with their inkpots in their hands during his lectures, because they could not be accommodated in

---

I, 70. See ʿAbbādī, *Ṭabaqāt,* 52. Al-ʿAbbādī has even less biographical information than Abū Isḥāq al-Shīrāzī, *Ṭabaqāt,* 76.

246. See Ibn ʿAsākir, LXXXIV, from al-Farghānī.

247. Ed. Kern, II, 61.

the normal manner.[248] It probably was important for Ṭabarī to have a man of this stature as a follower of his *madhhab*. Others identifiable as belonging to the early core of Jarīrīs during their master's lifetime were the government official *(kātib)* Ibn Abī al-Thalj (238-322/852[3]-934)[249] and Abū al-Ḥasan Aḥmad b. Yaḥyā b. 'Alī b. Yaḥyā b. Abī Manṣūr, who died in his early seventies in the year 327/938[9]. He was a member of the Ibn Munajjim family, and his pedigree clarifies his position in it. The Ibn Munajjims had produced several generations of courtiers and litterateurs. Some were also well-known as speculative theologians. Abū al-Ḥasan wrote *An Introduction to and support of Ṭabarī's school* as well as other works on his *madhhab*.[250]

Aḥmad b. Kāmil, Ṭabarī's biographer, also belonged to the original group of Jarīrīs. As a judge in al-Kūfah under the jurisdiction of the chief judge in Baghdad, Ibn Kāmil was in the position to promote the legal school to which he belonged. It seems, however, that he was a somewhat self-important and difficult personality. His juridical views were said to have been eclectic and in a way probably produced yet another legal school.[251]

The best known Jarīrī of the next generation who no longer had personal contact with Ṭabarī was al-Mu'āfā b. Zakariyyā' al-Nahrawānī, also referred to as Ibn Ṭarrār al-Jarīrī. Among other works, al-Mu'āfā wrote a large commentary on the Qur'ān; but his fame among posterity derived mainly from a literary work,

---

248. Also Kashshī or Kachchī, Abū Muslim Ibrāhīm b. 'Abdallāh b. Muslim has an entry in *TB*, VI, 120–4. He appears as Ṭabarī's authority in *Tafsīr*, II, 152 f., 233, l. 22, and 234, l. 6 (*ad* Qur. 2:197, 233); IV, 15, l. 12 (*ad* Qur. 3:97). Another scholar older than Ṭabarī but a transmitter of material from him was Abū Shu'ayb 'Abdallāh b. al-Ḥasan (206–95/821[2]–907[8]). See Ibn 'Asākir, LXIX f.; *TB*, IX, 435–7. However, he does not appear to have been a Jarīrī.

249. See *TB*, I, 338.

250. See Ibn al-Nadīm, *Fihrist*, 143 f.; Ṣafadī, *Wāfī*, VIII, 246 f.; Brockelmann, *GAL*, Suppl. I, 164; Sezgin, *GAS*, II, 439; Stern, "Abū 'Īsā," 438. Ibn al-Nadīm also listed him among the Mu'tazilah; see Fück, "Neue Materialien," 307, and Dodge's translation of the *Fihrist*, I, 428 f.

One wonders whether Ṭabarī's interest in "time" (see below, translation, 159 and 169 ff.) was in any way connected with the *Kitāb al-Awqāt* written by Abū al-Ḥasan b. al-Munajjim or with the *Kitāb al-Zamān* of Ibn Kāmil (see *Irshād*, II, 17, ed. Rifā'ī, IV, 105. *Irshād* cites *Fihrist*, where, however, this title and some other titles of Ibn Kāmil's publications do not appear on p. 32).

251. For Ibn Kāmil as a Jarīrī, see also below, 67. For another old Jarīrī, see above, n. 14.

entitled *al-Jalīs al-ṣāliḥ al-kāfī wa-al-anīs al-nāṣiḥ al-shāfī* (cited here as Mu'āfā, *Jalīs*). He served as judge for Bāb al-Ṭāq, a section of Baghdad which enjoyed long-standing fame as a center of literary and scholarly activity. In Yāqūt's words, al-Mu'āfā attempted to promote the Jarīrī *madhhab* by supporting (as Abū al-Ḥasan b. al-Munajjim had done), calling attention to, and defending it.[252]

The Jarīrī *madhhab* never gained a foothold strong enough to guarantee its survival in the harshly competitive world of politics dominated by the large and powerful legal sector of society. As Ibn Kāmil's career exemplifies, there were many persons practicing *ijtihād* and acting as potential founders of schools. Understandably, the competition was particularly brutal in the capital of the Empire, but even a powerful provincial base, such as had been enjoyed by al-Awzā'ī, often failed to ensure success. From all we know, it appears that Jarīrism was not distinctive enough to make it on purely intellectual grounds, and its followers were not sufficiently aggressive, or lacked political opportunity, to infiltrate the judiciary on a large scale so as to acquire the momentum necessary for gaining and perpetuating power,

By the time of Ṭabarī, certain legal schools, such as the Ḥanafites, Mālikites, and Shāfi'ites, had become firmly entrenched and, as history was to show, could no longer be displaced. Wherever there was acute rivalry for political control through the judiciary, the atmosphere was easily poisoned, and often lasting division resulted that affected even personal relations.[253] Normally, however, a certain harmony appears at least outwardly to have been prevalent. A debate about whether the formula "In the name of God, the Merciful, the Compassionate *(basmalah)*" was

---

252. On al-Mu'āfā, see Ibn al-Nadīm, *Fihrist*, 236; *Irshād*, VII, 162–4, ed. Rifā'ī, XIX, 151–4; Sezgin, *GAS*, I, 522 f.

Makhlad b. Ja'far al-Bāqarjī (d. 370/981) supposedly studied with Ṭabarī and, at the end of his life, claimed the right to (the transmission of?) Ṭabarī's *History*. Nothing is said about his having been a Jarīrī, but his son Abū Isḥāq Ibrāhīm (325–410/937–1020) was so described. See *TB*, XIII, 176 f., and VI, 189–91, in particular, 190, l. 3. For their role in the transmission of *al-Radd 'alā al-Ḥurqūṣiyyah*, see below, 123 f. Further Jarīrīs mentioned by Ibn al-Nadīm, 135, cannot be traced elsewhere. Lists of Jarīrīs compiled by modern scholars may be found, for instance, in the introduction to the edition of Mu'āfā, *Jalīs*, I, 44.

253. An example on the large scale is the apparent gradual development of bad relations between Ḥanafites and Shāfi'ites in Nīsābūr during the fourth/tenth century, see Bulliet, *Patricians*, 31 ff.

to be counted as part of the first sūrah of the Qur'ān that took place not long after Ṭabarī's death, is a good illustration of the generally peaceful state of affairs.

> Abū Bakr b. Kāmil said: One night, Abū Bakr Aḥmad b. Mūsā b. al-ʿAbbās b. Mujāhid came to us, while we were studying with him the large work on the Qur'ān reading of Abū ʿAmr b. al-ʿAlā'.[254] He found us engaged in a debate with some Shāfiʿite colleagues as to whether the *basmalah* belonged to the Book or did not belong to it. The meeting room was crowded with Shāfiʿites, Mālikites, Ḥanafites, and our colleagues (that is, Jarīrīs). Because of my studying (Qur'ān reading) with him, Ibn Mujāhid occasionally called me Kisā'ī.[255] So now he said to me: What is it that all of you here are engaged in? I told him, and he said: To which juridical school do you belong? I replied: That of Abū Jaʿfar al-Ṭabarī. He said: May God show mercy to (the late) Abū Jaʿfar! He told us the *ḥadīth* of Nūḥ b. Abī Bilāl—Saʿīd al-Maqburī—Abū Hurayrah about the *basmalah.*[256]
>
> Abū Bakr b. Mujāhid then started to praise Abū Jaʿfar al-Ṭabarī. He said: We have heard that he met with al-Muzanī, but don't ask how he bested him with all those Shāfiʿites present who were listening to him! (Ibn Mujāhid) did not mention anything that happened between the two.

---

254. Abū 'Amr b. al-'Alā', one of the seven Qur'ān readers, lived roughly from the 60s/684–9 to about 154/770. See, for instance, *EI*², I, 105 f., s. v.; Brockelmann, *GAL*, Suppl. I, 158; Sezgin, *GAS*, I, 5 f., 17; Ibn al-Jazarī, *Ghāyah*, I, 288–92. According to Ibn al-Nadīm, *Fihrist*, 31, Ibn Mujāhid (see above, n. 121) wrote a large and a small work on Qur'ān reading, as well as a work on the Qur'ān reading of Abū 'Amr. This work is probably the one meant here. The scene described is a meeting of some of those who were students of Ibn Mujāhid in Qur'ān reading, at which Ibn Mujāhid dropped in. He should have known, however, that Ibn Kāmil was a Jarīrī without having to ask him on that particular occasion. Perhaps the plural is meant, so that the question was about others in the gathering.

255. Ibn Mujāhid, who was known for his friendly banter *(mudā'abah)*, is comparing his gifted student Ibn Kāmil with the famous second/eighth-century Qur'ān reader and philologist, see *EI*², V, 174 f., s. v. al-Kisā'ī. Ibn Mujāhid's authority Muḥammad b. Yaḥyā known as the younger Kisā'ī (see Ibn al-Jazarī, *Ghāyah*, II, 279) is hardly meant.

256. For Ṭabarī on the *basmalah*, see *Tafsīr*, I, 37, where he refers back to *Laṭīf* and promises an exhaustive treatment for a later major work; see below, 113. The Prophet's *ḥadīth* on the various names of the first sūrah (*Tafsīr*, I, 36, ll. 22 ff.) may not be the one meant here.

Abū Bakr b. Kāmil said: I (had earlier?) asked Abū Ja'far about the problem he had debated with al-Muzanī, but he did not mention it. He was not the person to boast about having gained the better of an adversary[257] in a discussion. Abū Ja'far used to stress al-Muzanī's excellence; he praised him and always said what a good Muslim he was.[258]

Ṭabarī's altercation with Abū Bakr Muḥammad b. Dāwūd b. 'Alī (255–97/869–910), the son of the founder of the Ẓāhirite school, was potentially troublesome, but ended peaceably. Basically, it reflects an amicable environment in which scholars of different outlooks in the fields of law and *ḥadīth* lived and worked together. Dāwūd b. 'Alī (200[2]–70/815[8]–84) did not, we are told, measure up to Ṭabarī's all encompassing scholarship. He was an excellent, highly skilled debater. He also tended toward exhibiting a certain playfulness. Ṭabarī found it totally out of place whenever serious scholarly problems were under discussion. He studied with Dāwūd for some time and copied many of his works and lectures. After his death, as many as eighty fascicles of Dāwūd's treatises were found, written in Ṭabarī's fine hand.[259] Among them was a discussion of a subject that continued to be hotly debated, that of the createdness or uncreatedness of the Qur'ān. It had taken place between Dāwūd and the Muṭazilite Abū Mujālid al-Ḍarīr in the time of al-Muwaffaq, that is, in the last decade of Dāwūd's life.[260] Once, apparently near the end of Dāwūd's life, Ṭabarī got the better of him in a debate held in the presence of Dāwūd's followers. One of them, provoked by seeing his master being defeated, made some acerbic remarks against Ṭabarī who left in a huff and wrote a treatise against Dāwūd. Dāwūd's son Abū Bakr came to his father's aid, apparently shortly after the latter's death. Like Ṭabarī,

257. Following the emendation in *Irshād*, ed. Rifā'ī.

258. See *Irshād*, VI, 433, ed. Rifā'ī, XVIII, 53 f. See also above, n. 101.

259. It is conceivable, as suggested by the paragraphing of the text in *Irshād*, ed. Rifā'ī, XVIII, 78, that the reference is to Dāwūd and his library and fine hand, but this seems unlikely.

260. Abū Mujālid Aḥmad b. al-Ḥusayn, an active Mu'tazilite and a client of the caliph al-Mu'taṣim, died in 268/862, according to Ibn Kāmil, rather than in the following year. See *TB*, IV, 95 f.; Ṣafadī, *Wāfī*, VI, 33 (where 270 is indicated as the date of death); 'Abd al-Jabbār, *Sharḥ al-uṣūl al-khamsah*, 294 (with further references). For Ṭabarī's views on the subject, see, in particular, *Tabṣīr*, fols. 101a–102a, and *Ṣarīḥ*, passim.

Abū Bakr had been a precocious child. At the age of sixteen, he took over his deceased father's teaching *(ḥalqah)* and issued legal opinions *(fatwā)*.[261] He often seems to have done so in the same lighthearted spirit which led to the composition of his most famous work, an anthology of love poetry entitled *Kitāb al-Zahrah*. It is possible that his *Kitāb al-Intiṣār ʿalā Abū Jaʿfar al-Ṭabarī* was the work in defense of his father.[262] Abū Bakr also attacked Ṭabarī in a work of his on the principles of jurisprudence *(al-Wuṣūl ilā maʿrifat al-uṣūl)*. The issue was the interpretation of consensus (*ijmāʿ*). In *Ikhtilāf*, he alleged, Ṭabarī defined consensus as the agreement only of those legal authorities whose views he discussed in that work. Abū Bakr, insisting on *ijmāʿ* as the consensus of all legal authorities, seems to have taken this definition as Ṭabarī's general view on *ijmāʿ* beyond that particular work.[263] The controversy went on for a long time. Then one day, when Abū Bakr by chance visited a common acquaintance named Abū Bakr b. Abī Ḥāmid, Ṭabarī happened to be there, too. He was Abū Bakr b. Dāwūd's elder by thirty years, but he treated him with the greatest courtesy and remembered his father with high praise. This put an end to their hostility.[264]

Ṭabarī's relationship with the Ḥanbalites was of a totally different character. It is pictured as having had an important and disturbing impact on his life. This seems, in fact, to have been the case in some respect. The reports we have about it are all close to his time, but they are confused and contradictory. Their historicity has been denied.[265] However, while they reflect propaganda and appear to have been put into circulation by Ṭabarī's Ḥanbalite opponents, there is no good reason to go quite that far.

What caused the enmity of contemporary Ḥanbalites toward

261. See *TB*, V, 256, l. 13.

262. See Masʿūdī, *Murūj*, VIII, 255, ed. Pellat, V, 196; Ibn al-Nadīm, *Fihrist*, 217, l. 28. The suggestion, made *ad* Ibn ʿAsākir, LXXVII, n. g, that the author of *Intiṣār* was Abū Bakr b. Abī Dāwūd is unsupportable.

263. The Ẓāhirite view of *ijmāʿ* is discussed in Goldziher, *Ẓāhiriten*, 32 ff.

264. For a translation of the report on the episode, see below, 121 ff. It may be noted that there was bitter animosity between Ibn Ḥanbal and Dāwūd which was started by the former, see *TB*, VIII, 373 f., quoted by Samʿānī, *Ansāb*, IX, 130; Goldziher, *Ẓāhiriten*, 134.

265. See Kern's introduction to his edition of *Ikhtilāf*, 8 f. Kern's biographical sketch of Ṭabarī there and in his article on *Ikhtilāf* was an astonishing accomplishment in its time.

Ṭabarī? He was originally attracted to Baghdad by the fame of Ibn Ḥanbal,[266] and he continued to express the greatest respect for him.[267] His authorities and older contemporaries were students of Ibn Ḥanbal. Ibn Ḥanbal's younger son 'Abdallāh (213–90/828[9]–903),[268] who was the chief transmitter of his father's large collection of traditions, was only ten years older than Ṭabarī, and there was a constant overlap between 'Abdallāh's and Ṭabarī's teachers. Direct contact between Ṭabarī and Ibn Ḥanbal's family appears not to be attested, but they must have known one another. The final break between him and the Ḥanbalites is likely to have occurred with the publication of *Ikhtilāf,* which completely disregards Ibn Ḥanbal.[269] Ṭabarī is alleged to have expressed the opinion that he did not think of Ibn Ḥanbal as a jurist whose work in the field of jurisprudence compared with that of other great authorities but rather as an important *ḥadīth* scholar.[270] This observation is quite accurate and was endorsed by posterity as well as shared by some Ḥanbalites. It is, however, understandable that it could have led to riots if it was ever expressed *ex cathedra.* Another statement to the effect that he had not seen anyone transmitting legal opinions from Ibn Ḥanbal or any followers of his that were considered authoritative[271] was a slap in the face of contemporary Ḥanbalites. Ṭabarī may not have been so imprudent as to make these remarks in public in the form in which they are preserved; they may have surfaced in Ḥanbalite attacks against him and reflect Ḥanbalite suspicion as to how he felt about their school.

Another, and possibly decisive, factor was the situation in

266. See above, n. 44.

267. See *Ṣarīḥ,* text, 198, trans., 191. For the strange report on an apology full of praise for Ibn Ḥanbal and his school, see below, 104.

268. One of the authorities for the dates of 'Abdallāh's birth and death was al-Ṣawwāf, on whom see above, n. 237. Like Ibn Kāmil, al-Ṣawwāf was a student of 'Abdallāh. See *TB,* IX, 376, ll. 14 f.

269. The only reference to Ibn Ḥanbal ("Abū 'Abdallāh") traced so far in *Ikhtilāf* is an indirect one; see ed. Schacht, 139, l. 14, and Schacht's introduction, XV.

270. Since the basic sources do not seem to mention this remark, its historicity is slightly suspect. According to Kern, "Ṭabarī's Ihtilāf," 66, l. 1, the authorities mentioning it are Ibn al-Athīr, *Kāmil;* Abū al-Fidā', *Annales;* Ibn al-Shiḥnah (in the margin of Ibn al-Athīr, *Kāmil,* ed. Būlāq, 1290, VIII, 110), all under the year 310, and Ḥājjī Khalīfah, ed. Yaltkaya, I, 33. When it came to enumerate the fields in which Ibn Ḥanbal was a leading authority, mention of him as *imām al-ḥadīth* came first; see Ibn Abī Ya'lā, *Ṭabaqāt,* I, 5.

271. See *Irshād,* VI, 436, ll. 5 f., ed Rifā'ī, XVIII, 58.

which Ḥanbalism found itself in Ṭabarī's time. It was the latest of the then prominent and active legal schools[272] and was still struggling to become securely established when Ṭabarī, along with others, was a potential rival. The Ḥanbalites, moreover, counted in their ranks fighters determined to the point of fanaticism to promote themselves and their *madhhab.* Their readiness to use violence was effective as a deterrent to many scholars; they may have been less courageous than Ṭabarī, who refused to be intimidated.[273]

The Ḥanbalite struggle for ultimate success required a rallying point in the form of a slogan that could serve as a touchstone for true belief. A strange interpretation of the "praiseworthy position *(maqāman maḥmūdan)*" promised to the Prophet in Qur. 17:79 was chosen. It should be remembered that in Ibn Ḥanbal's life, the issue of the createdness or uncreatedness of the Holy Book had played a similar role. That issue was, of course, vastly more important, but it may not be quite as farfetched as it seems that his followers unconsciously felt that they, too, needed a dramatic issue to make themselves heard in the rough-and-tumble of religio-legal politics.

Qur'ān 17:79 was generally explained as eschatological[274] and the "praiseworthy position" as referring to Muḥammad's role as intercessor with the Deity on the Last Day. There was, however, a tradition reported from Mujāhid (but not found in the preserved recension of his commentary on Qur. 17:79) which reached Ṭabarī by way of 'Abbād b. Ya'qūb al-Asadī—Muḥammad b. Fuḍayl—Layth b. Abī Sulaym. It states that the "praiseworthy position" means that Muḥammad will be seated by God on his divine Throne.[275] Ḥanbalite championship of the tradi-

272. The latest authority frequently quoted in *Ikhtilāf* is the Shāfi'ite Abū Thawr (Ibrāhīm b. Khālid), who died in 240/854, see Sezgin, *GAS*, I, 491.

273. A number of contemporaries who did not want to tangle with Mujāhid's tradition are named in Dhahabī, *'Uluww*, 124–6; see also 75, 94, 99. It seems they did not offer resistance as Ṭabarī did eventually, even if, as was his nature, he too compromised on the issue for some time. The father of Abū Bakr, Abū Dāwūd al-Sijistānī, is mentioned as an advocate of the permissibility of transmitting Mujāhid's tradition in Khallāl, *Musnad*, and Qurṭubī, *Jāmi'*, X, 311.

274. In fact, the eschatological meaning of the verse does not seem certain and appears to be based solely on the use of the root *b-'-th.*

275. For the transmitters, see below, translation, nn. 1139, 239, and 54. Al-Layth is described as the son of Abū Sulaym in Khallāl, *Musnad*, and Dhahabī, *'Uluww*,

tion produced vehement outpourings of hatred against those who opposed it, allegedly with equal immoderation. They were called by every conceivable epithet; they were branded as innovators, liars, ignoramuses, heretics *(zindīq)*, and unbelievers. Above all, they were seen as Jahmīs, that is, speculative theologians (Muʿtazilites). Their nefarious intent—or, at any rate, the result of their attitude—was to deny a singular distinction to the Prophet, and, in the process, they defamed the exemplary Muslim that was Mujāhid. Already Ibn Ḥanbal's principal successor as spokesman for his legal school, Abū Bakr al-Marrūdhī (d. 275/888),[276] was strongly partial to Mujāhid's tradition and appears to have employed the "praiseworthy position" question as a sort of shibboleth. Abū Bakr al-Marrūdhī's student and successor as the principal Ḥanbalite scholar of his time, Abū Bakr al-Khallāl (d. 311/923), took up the subject. He reproduced his teacher's arguments at length and thus preserved them for posterity.[277] His younger contemporary, al-Barbahārī (d. 329/941),[278] then made the most of it. He missed no opportunity to proclaim Qur. 17:79 as referring to the Prophet's being seated on the divine Throne. Although al-Barbahārī's name is not mentioned in connection with Ṭabarī's Ḥanbalite trouble, he probably must be seen as the person behind much of it.

125, l. 3. He was a transmitter of Mujāhid; the better-known al-Layth b. Saʿd was born too late for that.

This interpretation is, of course, not incompatible with Muḥammad's position as chief intercessor. See Khallāl, *Musnad*, 83.

276. For Abū Bakr Aḥmad b. Muḥammad b. al-Ḥajjāj al-Marrūdhī, see Ibn Abī Yaʿlā, *Ṭabaqāt*, I, 56–63; Samʿānī, *Ansāb*, XII, 201 f.; Yāqūt, *Muʿjam*, IV, 506, s. v. Marw al-Rūdh. According to Dhahabī, *ʿUluww*, 125, l. 2, he wrote in defense of Mujāhid's tradition (see below, n. 277). Ibn Abī Yaʿlā, *Ṭabaqāt*, 60, states that al-Marrūdhī was asked about the Jahmiyyah's rejection of the "story of the Throne." This may refer to alleged Muʿtazilah views on the location of the Throne, rather than, specifically, to the tradition of Mujāhid.

277. For Abū Bakr al-Khallāl, see Sezgin, *GAS*, I, 511 f. I wish to thank J. van Ess for providing me with a xerox copy of Khallāl, *Musnad*, 75–99.

278. For al-Ḥasan b. ʿAlī b. Khalaf al-Barbahārī, see Sezgin, *GAS*, I, 512; Laoust, in *Mélanges Massignon*, III, 22–5. Ibn Abī Yaʿlā, *Ṭabaqāt*, II, 18–45, gives a good picture of his generally extremist positions. "Whenever al-Barbahārī attended a meeting, he would mention that God seats Muḥammad with Himself on the Throne." In 323/935, he was in hiding and his followers were strictly forbidden to assemble. One of them was accused of having set a disastrous fire in al-Karkh, see Hamadhānī, *Takmilah*, 79 f., ed. Cairo, XI, 294–6. See further Brockelmann, *GAL*, Suppl. I, 344, and the indexes of *Eclipse* and Massignon, *Passion*², as well as Allard, *Attributs*, 103 f.

The actual course of the events affecting Ṭabarī can be reconstructed only with difficulty, because supporters on both sides apparently circulated conflicting reports. Matters appear to have come to a head after the year 290/903. In that year, Ṭabarī returned to his home town in Ṭabaristān on a second, and apparently last, visit. He no doubt used the Khurāsān Road that took him through such large cities as Dīnawar and Hamadhān. In Dīnawar, he stopped to meet with scholars there and to give lectures; he may very well have done the same in other towns along the road, thus making his journey profitable intellectually and, possibly, economically. On his return to Baghdad, three Ḥanbalites, who do not seem further identifiable,[279] asked Ṭabarī about his views on Mujāhid's tradition. Ṭabarī is said to have declared bluntly that it was absurd. Moreover, he added a flippant jingle ridiculing it:

Praised be the One Who has no confidant
 and has no one to sit on His Throne.

Enraged Ḥanbalites thereupon stoned his residence and caused a serious disturbance which had to be subdued by force.

Trouble with the Ḥanbalites that took a similar form is also reported at the time of Ṭabarī's death. In connection with it, Nāzūk is mentioned as chief of police. He was appointed to this position only in 310/922[3], the year Ṭabarī died, but he appears to have held high positions in the police before and may already have been in charge of Ṭabarī's protection against potential Ḥanbalite violence. In 309/921[2], the wazīr ʿAlī b. ʿĪsā had offered Ṭabarī the opportunity to debate the matter with the Ḥanbalites in his residence. Ṭabarī agreed, but the Ḥanbalites did not show up.[280] However, shortly before his death, Ḥanbalite rioters supposedly

---

279. The three were Abū ʿAbdallāh al-Jaṣṣāṣ, Jaʿfar b. ʿArafah, and al-Bayāḍī. The identification of al-Bayāḍī with Abū ʿAlī Muḥammad b. ʿĪsā al-Bayāḍī was proposed by the editor of *Irshād*, VI, 436, n. 1, but requires confirmation. This individual, whose family claimed ʿAbbāsid descent, wrote on Qurʾān reading. He was killed by the Qarmaṭians in 294/906 on his return from the pilgrimage, see *TB*, II, 401; Samʿānī, *Ansāb*, 384.

On the incident, see also Goldziher, *Muslim Studies*, II, 158 (II, 168, of the original German). Goldziher's reference was to Suyūṭī, *Taḥdhīr*, 161, whose source scurrilously attributes this information to a storyteller in the streets of Baghdad.

280. See Ibn al-Jawzī, *Muntaẓam*, VI, 159, also Ṭabarī, *Introductio etc.*, XCVIII; Bowen, 187 f.

pelted his house with stones so numerous that they formed a large wall in front of it. The verse just quoted was discovered written on the wall of Ṭabarī's house. After the riot subsided, someone wrote underneath it:

Aḥmad[281] will no doubt have a high position
when he comes to the Merciful One,

Who will draw him near and seat him nobly
to spite an(y) envier,

Upon a throne enveloping him[282] with perfume
to make livid an(y) obnoxious liar.

(He has) truly this unique position *(al-maqām).*
This has been transmitted by Layth from Mujāhid.

Inscriptions in verse or prose on the walls of houses are a standard device of the Arabic literary imagination. It seems most unlikely that a man in Ṭabarī's position and at his advanced age would have been so childish as to write inflammatory verses on the walls of his house. Someone else might have done it in order to provoke the Ḥanbalite mob. Presumably, however, the mural poetry was a literary embellishment invented by Ḥanbalites which crept into the vague reports about the event.[283] The fact that historians report another bloody incident about *maqāman maḥmūdan* involving followers of the late Abū Bakr al-Marrūdhī for the year 317/929[284] neither confirms nor invalidates the historicity of the

281. "Aḥmad" apparently is meant to refer to the Prophet, but Ibn Ḥanbal's name was also Aḥmad. The undetermined singular of envier and liar in the following verses might be a veiled reference to a specific person, namely, Ṭabarī.

282. The translation "upon a throne enveloped with perfume" is possible, but the text in Ibn Abī al-Ḥadīd, *Sharḥ,* I, 656, ll. 4 f. (Beirut, 1963) = III, 224, ll. 15 f. (Cairo, 1379/1959), speaks against it.

283. The entire preceding account is not in *TB* and Ibn ʿAsākir. It appears in *Irshād,* VI, 436, ed. Rifāʿī, XVIII, 57-9, and (quoted by?) Ṣafadī, *Wāfī,* II, 286 f. See also Kern's introduction to his edition of *Ikhtilāf,* 8 f.

284. See Ibn al-Athīr, *Kāmil,* ed. Tornberg, VIII, 157 f., and, with only minor differences, a Berlin manuscript described as al-Birzālī's *History* and quoted in the introduction of *Ikhtilāf,* ed. Kern, 9. The incident is, however, unreported in the other sources consulted by me. Schreiner, *Gesammelte Schriften,* 436 f (= *ZDMG* 52 [1898], 535 f.), refers to a ninth/fifteenth-century author.

event involving Ṭabarī.

The circumstances surrounding the debate about the "praiseworthy position" deserve some more clarification. In his *Musnad,* Ibn Ḥanbal includes no traditions that support the interpretation of the phrase as referring to the Prophet's being seated on the divine Throne.[285] One might argue that the very fact that Ibn Ḥanbal has nothing to say about the impossibility of Mujāhid's interpretation could indicate that it could not be ruled out, using a type of argument employed by Ṭabarī in his discussion of the matter. This, however, is very unlikely. Ibn Ḥanbal may have simply disregarded Mujāhid's tradition as irrelevant or objectionable. After all, it had no *isnād* going back to more ancient authorities or the Prophet, while there were traditions having the Prophet's seal of approval that referred to intercession. Clearly, this made it necessary to invent an appropriate Prophetical tradition for Muḥammad's place on the divine Throne, and this was done. Ibn Battah (d. 387/997) listed one such tradition with the *isnād* Nāfi'— 'Abdallāh b. 'Umar—the Prophet.[286] He is certain not to have invented it himself. When it made its first appearance is hard to say; evidently, Abū Bakr al-Khallāl in the early years of the century did not yet know it.

In *Tafsīr,* Ṭabarī has a long and interesting discussion of the "praiseworthy position."[287] It again shows him to be the great compromiser. He admits that intercession is the interpretation that is solidly documented and which therefore has the best claim to being correct. However, he says, the other interpretation cannot entirely be ruled out. As the composition of *Tafsīr* antedates

285. See Ibn Ḥanbal, *Musnad,* I, 375 f., 398 f., III, 354, for traditions on intercession. For the tradition of Gabriel sitting "on a footstool" or "on the throne," presumably the divine Throne, between heaven and earth, see Ibn Ḥanbal, *Musnad,* III, 306: Ibn Ḥajar, *Fatḥ,* X, 305.

286. See Laoust, *Profession de foi d'Ibn Batta,* text, 61, trans., 112 f., especially note 1. In addition to Mujāhid, al-Wāḥidī (d. 468/1075) refers to a tradition of Ibn Mas'ūd, see Rāzī, *Tafsīr,* XXI, 32. He may have the same tradition in mind, mixing up, as it sometimes happens, 'Abdallāh b. 'Umar and 'Abdallah b. Mas'ūd. A tradition of 'Ā'ishah on the subject is discussed in Ibn al-Jawzī, *Daf',* 81, *ḥadīth* no. 39.

287. See *Tafsīr,* XV, 97, l. 10–100, l. 22. See the translation below, Appendix A, below, pp. 149–51. For another partial translation, see Andrae, *Person,* 270–2. For Ṭabarī's real feelings about Mujāhid and his tradition, it may be indicative that he rejects a view expressed by him with unusual harshness in connection with his commentary on the same verse of the Qur'ān, see *Tafsīr,* XV, 96, ll. 26–31.

the events described, it might be argued that Ṭabarī interpolated the discussion in *Tafsīr* after publication when Ḥanbalite hostility took such a truly ugly turn.[288] This cannot be proved. It might be assumed that he took at first a conciliatory attitude such as is displayed in *Tafsīr* and renounced it at some later date when he got disgusted with Ḥanbalite violence. This seems more likely, but again there is no hard evidence for it. Whatever it was, the view expressed in *Tafsīr* did nothing to assuage Ḥanbalite opposition to him which appears to have had deeper roots than merely disagreement about a catchy slogan.

The arguments marshalled by Ṭabarī for the purpose of making Mujāhid's tradition admissible were derived from speculative theology and show him adept in its ways of thinking and debating. The basic issue, as he sees it, is the problem of contiguity *(mumāssah)*. It had its proper place in physics but was transferred to theology by religious thinkers.[289] Al-Ashʿarī (ca 260–324/873[4]–935[6]), who lived most of his life in al-Baṣrah and was but a generation removed from Ṭabarī, considered the matter important enough to refer to it in his discussion of anthropomorphism *(tajsīm)*. God is not upon the Throne, except in the sense that He is above it but does not touch it. According to Hishām b. al-Ḥakam, God's location is in one specific place *(fī makān dūn makān)*. His place is the Throne, and He is in touch with it. The Throne encompasses and delimits Him. Another view holds that the Creator fills the Throne and is in touch with it. At this point, al-Ashʿarī adds that some *ḥadīth* scholars hold that the Throne is not filled by Him and that He (is thus able to) seat His Prophet with Himself on the Throne.[290] Ṭabarī considers the problem of God completely filling the Throne. He remarks on His contiguity and finds that only three possibilities apply to it. For him, however, the crucial point that must be made is that God's seating of Muḥammad on the Throne, with or without Himself, does not imply divinity ("lordship" *rubūbiyyah)* for the Prophet or deny his status as a human being ("servantship" *ʿubūdiyyah)*. In fact,

288. The information that he went even a step farther and apologized to the Ḥanbalites is suspect, see below, 104 f.

289. See Pines, *Atomenlehre*, 8 f., and, for instance, Juwaynī, *Shāmil*, 455 ff.

290. See Ashʿarī, *Maqālāt*, 210 f., and, in different connections, 35, 155, 221, 301–4.

the implied hint at Muḥammadan divinity would appear to be the most objectionable feature of Mujāhid's tradition. In touching upon this aspect, Ṭabarī comes close to the possible reason why Mujāhid might have made this seemingly un-Islamic statement. Christianity speaks of the Son not only as sitting on a throne but also of some mysterious being as sitting together with the Father in His Throne (Rev. 3:21). Even in remote Mecca, Mujāhid could have heard about these views or seen one of the many representations of the Trinity or the enthroned Christ.[291] He may very well have felt that Muḥammad should be similarly distinguished as was the prophet of Christianity.

The Ḥanbalites were probably to be blamed for occasional difficulties Ṭabarī experienced in scheduling his lectures and for deterring a few out-of-town students from attending them or otherwise receiving instruction from him. Those who knew Ṭabarī best always played down the inconveniences he suffered from the Ḥanbalites. Considerable uncertainty attaches to the reports of what went on at the time of his death. Ṭabarī is said to have been virtually prevented from leaving his house. When he died, some questionable sources report that it was necessary to bury him "at night"[292] in his courtyard, apparently in order to forestall any untoward incidents at the funeral. It was not unusual for individuals to be buried in their houses,[293] but it would not have been done ordinarily under the cover of darkness. If there was in-

291. Not much can be made in this connection of the allegation that Mujāhid used material provided by Christians and Jews in his Qur'ān commentary. See Ibn Sa'd, *Ṭabaqāt*, V, 344, l. 7, and the remark transmitted through Abū Bakr b. 'Ayyāsh (below, translation, n. 72) in Dhahabī, *Mīzān*, III, 439; Ibn Ḥajar, *Tahdhīb*, X, 43; Sezgin, *GAS*, I, 29. As one would expect, Dhahabī refers to Mujāhid's view of *maqāman maḥmūdan* with disapproval.

On Mujāhid and the vibrating of the divine Throne, see Goldziher, *Richtungen*, 108 f.

A similar but different idea was already expressed in Khallāl, *Musnad*, 82. The Muslims would be the laughing stock of Christians if they denied to Muḥammad the honor of sitting on the divine Throne, while granting semidivine status to Jesus.

292. This key element appears in Miskawayh, *Eclipse*, I, 84; Ibn al-Jawzī, *Muntaẓam*, VI, 172; Ibn al-Athīr, *Kāmil*, ed. Tornberg, VIII, 98; *Irshād*, VI, 423, l. 17, ed. Rifā'ī, XVIII, 40, ll. 11 f. Yāqūt remarks that he had this information from an unspecified source. The principal sources agree that Ṭabarī was buried on the morning after his death.

293. For instance, Abū Bakr b. Mujāhid was buried in a *turbah* in the harem of his house in Sūq al-'Aṭash. See above, n. 121.

deed noisy picketing of his home by Ḥanbalites which posed a threat of violence, it would have been taken care of expeditiously, and "tens of thousands soldiers" (used figuratively for enormously many) would hardly have been required. It is virtually unthinkable that someone of Ṭabarī's prominence and social standing would have been left without a well-attended funeral, unless he himself wanted it that way, and that anyone could have stopped such a funeral from taking place. Half a century earlier, something seemingly similar had happened, possibly also as the result of Ḥanbalite machinations. The great mystical writer al-Muḥāsibī was prevented from teaching, and, when he died, only four persons dared to attend his funeral.[294] There is no proof that the events supposedly surrounding Ṭabarī's death and funeral were merely a calque on what was believed to have happened earlier to al-Muḥāsibī. At any rate, the latter was not as important a public figure as was Ṭabarī, whose death reverberated through all the leading and influential circles in Baghdad. It is more likely that if there were not very many people present when he was buried, it was because he himself had expressed the wish that it should be that way. The role of Ḥanbalite hostility, though real, seems to have been exaggerated in connection with his death as it was in his life.

His Death

Death came to Ṭabarī on Monday, Shawwāl 27, 310/February 17, 923.[295] He was buried in his house the following morning. People prayed at his grave night and day for some time after his

294. See van Ess, *Gedankenwelt*, 10 f.

295. The complete dates found in *TB*, II, 166, were the only ones known to later biographers. The slight divergences between them can be interpreted in favor of the Monday date accepted here. Ibn Kāmil, who was present when Ṭabarī died, has Sunday evening, at two nights remaining of the month of Shawwāl. Converting the date to Shawwāl 27, this would be Monday, February 17. Another of Ṭabarī's students, who presumably was also there at the time, was ʿĪsā b. Ḥāmid b. Bishr al-qāḍī (d. 368/979; see *TB*, XI, 178 f.). He has Saturday evening, at four nights remaining. This would be Shawwāl 25, corresponding to Saturday, February 15. Ṣafadī, *Wāfī*, II, 284 f., understands this date to refer to Shawwāl 26, which, however, would correspond to Sunday, February 16. The decisive factor in favor of the Monday date is the incidental reference by al-Farghānī to the fact that Ṭabarī died on a Monday. See below, n. 300.

death.[296] As was customary, many eulogies were composed. One by the famous philologist Ibn Durayd, with whom Ṭabarī was acquainted,[297] is preserved in its entirety. A few verses are quoted of the eulogy of Abū Sa'īd b. al-A'rābī, apparently the mystic Abū Sa'īd Aḥmad b. Muḥammad b. Ziyād.[298]

Legends, as they were commonly invented to glorify the last moments of life of great men, were also reported about Ṭabarī. He was told in his dying hours about a particular prayer unknown to him. He called for ink and paper to record it. Asked why he did that in his hopeless condition, he replied: "Everybody should use any opportunity to acquire new knowledge until he is dead."[299] On the Monday on which he died, al-Farghānī reports, he asked for water to make the ablution for the noon prayer. When it was suggested to him that, weak as he was, he should combine the noon prayer with the afternoon prayer, he refused.[300]

He had a last word for his assembled students and friends, among them Ibn Kāmil, who asked for advice that would be beneficial for them to achieve salvation. His answer was worthy of the single-minded scholar he had been all his life: "My advice for you is to follow my religious practice and to act in accordance with what I have explained in my books—or something like it," the reporter rather lamely adds. "Then he repeated the confession of faith and mentioned God many times. He wiped his face with his hand and used it to close his eyes. When he let go, his spirit had left his body."[301]

---

296. This fact is always stressed, apparently on the authority of Ibn Kāmil. See *TB*, II, 166, l. 19.

297. On Ibn Durayd (223–321/838–933), see *EI*² III, 757 f., s. v. He reported Ṭabarī's remark on Abū Ḥātim al-Sijistānī; see above, n. 160.

298. See *TB*, II, 166–9; Ibn 'Asākir, XCI–XCVI, and the other biographers for his and Ibn Durayd's eulogies. For Ibn al-A'rābī (246–341/860–953), see Sezgin, *GAS*, I, 660 f. The addition of "Abū Sa'īd" in Ibn 'Asākir and Dhahabī, *Nubalā'*, XIV, 282, makes the identification virtually certain. It would seem unexpected to find a writer on mystical topics among the mourners of Ṭabarī (see above, n. 227). Moreover, as far as we know, Ibn al-A'rābī had no ties to Baghdad. Ibn 'Asākir, XCII, further quotes verses by a certain Muḥammad b. al-Rūmī, apparently a *mawlā* of the Ṭāhirid family.

299. See Ibn 'Asākir, LXXXIV. The transmission of the report involved al-Mu'āfā and a member of the Ibn al-Furāt family.

300. See Ibn 'Asākir, LXXXVIII f. Al-Farghānī had the information from Abū Bakr (b. Sahl) al-Dīnawarī

301. See Ibn 'Asākir, LXXXIX, continuing the preceding report. For another

There were always dreams conveying messages from the other world. Ṭabarī, too, had his message for a dreamer. Everything that had happened to him, and which others would have to face when they died, was really and truly good, he insisted. The dreamer then asked him whether he had been welcomed by God and would be willing to remember him to God. Ṭabarī took his wrist into his hand and pressed it to his breast, exclaiming: "You ask *me* to remember you to God, when we are taking you to the Messenger of God to give you his support?"[302] The Prophet, he meant to say, was more effective than he could be, and entry to the Prophet was assured to someone like him who had devoted more than seventy years to Islam with his immortal labors as a jurist and expert in traditions, Qur'ān interpreter, and historian.

His Works

The major works of Ṭabarī were first "dictated" in lectures. He worked on them at various times throughout his life. Their subject matter allowed for separate treatment of parts dealing with self-contained subjects. There is a considerable difference between the dates of final publication and the earlier dates when substantial portions of a given work got into circulation. This is the main reason why what seem to be the same works are referred to under different titles and what seem to be different titles are really books forming part of the final publication of one and the same work.

Ṭabarī's method of citing his own works is not uniform and raises at times some doubt as to whether the same work is meant. He prefers reference to subject matter. Formal titles were usually disregarded by him, if, in fact, they ever existed. Some works are described as having been incomplete at the time of his death. In his eighties, he had many incompleted large-scale projects; he must have worked on them for a long time and presumably used them in his lecturing. Their titles were naturally never fixed.

Another complicating factor affecting earlier bibliographers as

---

deathbed story involving Ibn Kāmil, see above, n. 237.

302. See Ibn 'Asākir, XCVI. The dreamer was a Hāshimite, al-Ḥasan b. 'Abd al-'Azīz. He was in charge of public prayers (*ṣāḥib al-ṣalāh*) at the mosque of al-Ruṣāfah, and he died seventy-five years old in 333/945. See *TB*, VI, 339.

well as us is the loss of the lists of Ṭabarī's works in their original forms. Those who preserved extracts from the bibliographies also had no longer any knowledge of many of the works listed. They also could not check the fate of supposedly unfinished books.

We have a certain amount of external and internal evidence for the order of his works as to the time of composition or publication. Our information is, however, incomplete. Thus, it is not advisable to arrange the following bibliography chronologically. The safe procedure chosen here is to follow an alphabetical arrangement according to the first words of known or presumptive titles and to provide ample cross-references.

Listings in square brackets are to titles which appear to be parts of other works, or to works wrongly attributed to Ṭabarī. The alphabetization disregards *kitāb, risālah,* and the preposition *fī.* For an attempt to present the works according to chronological order and to subject matter, see Appendix B, below, pp. 152–54.

[*Al-Ādāb al-ḥamīdah wa-al-akhlāq al-nafīsah* and slightly different forms: See *Ādāb al-nufūs*]

[*Ādāb al-ḥukkām* "The proper ways of procedure for judges": See *Basīṭ*]

Ādāb al-manāsik "The proper ways of performing the ritual of the pilgrimage"

Ibn ʿAsākir, LXXXI f.[303]:

> *Kitāb Ādāb al-manāsik.* The work deals with what a pilgrim needs from the day he leaves (for the pilgrimage) and what he should choose to take care of[304] for the beginning of his journey, what he should say and what prayers he should say upon mounting and descending, and the noteworthy sacred places *(al-manāzil wa-al-mashāhid)* he should see, and so on, during his entire pilgrimage.

Irshād VI, 453, l. 1, ed. Rifāʿī, XVIII, 81, l. 3, mentions only

303. Ibn ʿAsākir seems to have been quoted by Maqrīzī, *Muqaffā.*

304. This translates *al-itmām,* but the reading is dubious. De Goeje's correction to *al-ayyām* "the days he should select" may be preferable.

the title which he states to be *Mukhtaṣar manāsik al-ḥajj*. Dhahabī, *Nubalā'*, XIV, l. 4, shortens Ibn 'Asākir's title to *Kitāb al-Manāsik*.[305]

Ādāb al-nufūs "The proper ways of spiritual behavior"

The work is quoted under the title of *Kitāb al-Ādāb al-ḥamīdah wa-al-akhlāq al-nafīsah* by al-Tanūkhī (see above, n. 197) and *Kitāb al-Ādāb al-nafīsah wa-al-akhlāq al-ḥamīdah* by Dhahabī, *Nubalā'*, XIV, 277, ll. 12 f. There are other variants, but there can be no doubt as to their referring to *Ādāb al-nufūs*. The use of the title in quotations may indicate that manuscripts bearing it were in circulation. The former title also appears in Ḥājjī Khalīfah, ed. Yaltkaya, I, 42, from which it was derived by d'Herbelot, *Bibliothèque*, 52b.

Ibn 'Asākir, LXXXI:

> He started on the *Ādāb al-nufūs*. It is another of his precious works. He structured in it man's religious duties according to all parts of the human body beginning with the heart, the tongue, the eyes, the ears, and so on. It includes the traditions on the subject from the Prophet, the Companions, the Followers, and all those who can be used as evidence. In the work, he also mentions and refers to as evidence the discussions of Ṣūfīs and pious men, including their reported deeds and all that is clearly correct there. He did not complete the work.

Irshād, VI, 449, l. 18–450, l. 14, ed. Rifā'ī, XVIII, 76, l. 14–77, l. 15:

> One of his fine works is the one entitled *Adab*[306] *al-nufūs al-jayyidah wa-al-akhlāq al-nafīsah*, often called by him *Adab al-nafs al-sharīfah wa-al-akhlāq al-ḥamīdah*. In its introduction *(tarjamah)*, he went into great detail with respect to the religious sciences, excellence, asceticism, sincere de-

305. A passage in Murtaḍā al-Zabīdī, *Itḥāf*, V, 352, l. 1, cites Ṭabarī as reporting *fī al-manāsik* a tradition from Mujāhid's Qur'ān commentary. It may refer to this work, but the subject matter dealt with has no explicit connection to the pilgrimage and the reference could be to any of Ṭabarī's legal works.

306. The singular *adab* is used in the passage, instead of the usual plural *ādāb*.

votion, gratitude, and the discussion of hypocrisy, haughtiness, submissiveness, humility, and patience[307] as well as the command to do good and the prohibition to do evil. He began with a discussion of Satanic inspiration *(waswasah)* and psychologically motivated human actions *(aʿmāl al-qulūb)*. Then he mentioned a good deal about prayer *(duʿā')*, the excellence of the Qur'ān, and the moments and indications as to when prayer is heard. He included the traditions on the subject transmitted from the Prophet's practice *(sunan)* and the statements of the Companions and the Followers. He discontinued lecturing (on the work, *imlā')* at some point in the discussion of the command to do good and the prohibition to do evil. About five hundred folios were made public by him.

He had done four parts which had not yet been made public in lectures. (Those four parts) were in the hands of the copyist/bookseller *(al-warrāq)* Abū Saʿīd ʿUmar b. Aḥmad al-Dīnawarī[308] when (the latter) left for Syria with them. He was waylaid on the road. Only two parts remained in his possession. They contained the discussion of man's duties to God in connection with his senses of seeing and hearing. He had begun (those four parts) in 310/922. He died a short while after having discontinued lecturing. He used to say: "If this book is made public, it will be a beauty." For after the discussion of man's rights and duties, he wanted to continue it to (indicating) the protection thereby offered against the dangers of the Day of Resurrection and the conditions governing it and the circumstances and happenings in the other world and mention Paradise and the Fire.

Irshād, VI, 437, ll. 16–18, ed. Rifāʿī, XVIII, 60, ll. 4–6, and similarly VI, 456, ll. 14 f., ed. Rifāʿī, XVIII, 86, ll. 5–7, refers to *Ādāb al-nufūs* as indicative of Ṭabarī's asceticism, abstinence, humility, integrity, purity of action, sincerity of intent, and propriety in whatever he died.

The title *Ādāb al-nufūs* appears again in Ṣafadī, *Wāfī*, II, 286, l. 4, with no further information.

Dhahabī, *Nubalā'*, XIV, 274, ll. 2 f., was confused by Ibn

307. It may be noted that all these topics were treated in Ṣūfī handbooks.
308. See above, n. 202.

ʿAsākir's text, on which he drew, and considered *Tartīb al-ʿulamāʾ* mentioned immediately before as an independent work, while it is presumably a part of *Basīṭ*. This results in his stating that "the *Tartīb al-ʿulamāʾ* is one of his precious works. He started out in it with the *Ādāb al-nufūs* and Ṣūfī statements. He did not complete the work."

For al-Tanūkhī's quotation from the work, see above, n. 197. The passage preserved in Dhahabī, *Nubalāʾ*, 277, was quoted as an example of Ṭabarī's stylistic elegance. It reflects the pietistic tone of the work. It consists of a chapter heading and the beginning words of the chapter, apparently taken from the work's opening pages:

> The explanation of [the state] which makes it necessary[309]
> for a human being to check his state with respect
> to his psychologically motivated activity
> for God
>
> There is no state of the believer where his enemy (Satan) who is in charge of him does not try to entice him to his own way and to lie in wait for him, so as to block his (progress along) the straight roads of his Lord. Thus Satan said to his Lord, as he was made by Him one of those hoping for "postponement": "I shall lie (in wait) for them along Your straight path. Then I shall approach them from in front and from behind."[310] He was hoping to make his hostile expectation come true, as expressed in what he said to his Lord: "If You grant me postponement to the Day of Resurrection, I shall indeed take over control of (Adam's) progeny with few exceptions."[311] It is therefore every intelligent person's duty to train himself strenuously to make (Satan's) expectations not come true, to frustrate his hope, and to make every effort to humiliate him. Nothing in human activity is more detested by Satan than man's obedience to his Lord and disobedience to his own (Satan's) command, and nothing gives him greater joy than (man's) disobedience to his Lord and his

309. Read *yūjibu* for *yajibu*.
310. Qur. 7:14–17.
311. Qur. 17:62.

following his own (Satan's) command.

[*Ādāb al-quḍāh* or *Adab al-qāḍī* "The proper ways of procedure for judges": See *Basīṭ*]

Al-Ādar (?) *fī al-uṣūl* "? on the principles"

Irshād, VI, 453, l. 4, ed. Rifāʿī, XVIII, 81, ll. 6 f.:

He promised the *Kitāb al-'-d-r fī al-uṣūl* but made nothing of it public.

The "principles" are presumably those of jurisprudence, here to be treated in monograph form. Neither editor of *Irshād* indicates what *'-l-'-d-r* could possibly mean. Assuming some slight corruption in the text, *fī al-uṣūl* may not be part of a title, and something totally different may be concealed under the reading *'-l-'-d-r*.

[*Aḥkām sharā'iʿ al-Islām* "The laws of the Muslim religion"

This was the working title for a comprehensive exposition of the sharīʿah that Ṭabarī had apparently planned but never executed as intended. See *Tafsīr*, I, 37 (translated below, 113), and II, 352, l. 16 (*ad* Qur. 2:238).]

[*Fī ahl al-baghy* "On wrongdoers (rebels)": See *Laṭīf*]

[*Risālat al-Akhlāq* "On moral behavior": See *Mūjaz*]

[*Amthilat al-ʿudūl* "Forms for attorneys"

This is said to be the title of a book on document forms *(shurūṭ)*, a part of *Laṭīf*.]

[*al-ʿAqīdah* "(Ṭabarī's) Creed": See *Ṣarīḥ*

Listed as a separate title in Sezgin, *GAS*, I, 328, no. 8, the "Creed" is identical with *Ṣarīḥ*. A quotation from it in Dhahabī, *Nubalā'*, XIV, 280, and *ʿUluww*, 150, corresponds to *Ṣarīḥ*, text,

198, trans., 192.]

[Al-Aṭʿimah "Dietary laws": See *Laṭīf]*

[Al-Baṣīr fī maʿālim al-dīn: See *Tabṣīr]*

Basīṭ al-qawl fī aḥkām sharāʾiʿ al-Islām "A plain and simple exposition of the laws of the Muslim religion"

This title was used by Ṭabarī in *History*, I, 1455. He says there with reference to divergent statements as to how the Prophet performed the "prayer of fear" upon meeting with potential enemies during the raid of Dhāt al-riqāʿ: "God willing, I shall mention the different statements in our book entitled *Basīṭ al-qawl fī aḥkām sharāʾiʿ al-Islām* in the book on the prayer of fear."[312]

Ibn al-Nadīm, *Fihrist*, 234, ll. 22–24:

> *Kitāb al-Basīṭ fī al-fiqh.* He did not complete it. The following books of it have been made public: The large book on document forms *(shurūṭ)*, records and documents *(al-mahāḍir wa-al-sijillāt)*, last wills *(al-waṣāyā)*, the procedure for judges *(adab al-qāḍī)*, ritual purity, prayer, and charity taxes.

Ibn ʿAsākir, LXXXI:

> He started on his book *al-Basīṭ*. He made public its book on ritual purity in something like 1,500 folios. (The size was that large) because in each chapter, he mentioned the disagreements of the Companions, the Followers, and others according to their ways of transmission (that is, the various recensions in which their statements were transmitted). He also mentioned their reasons for the views chosen by them

312. *History*, I, 1453 ff., places the raid of Dhāt al-riqāʿ in the year 4/626. The circumstances were very much debated, and no agreement appears to have been achieved about the date of the raid and about the prayer of fear *(ṣalāt al-khawf)* connected with it. See the long exposition in Ibn Ḥajar, *Fatḥ*, VIII, 420–33. See also, for instance, Ibn Hishām, *Sīrah*, ed. Wüstenfeld, 661 ff., trans. Guillaume, 445–57. Ibn Ḥajar, 426 f., refers to the passage in *History*, I, 1455, in a rather unclear manner; his reference to *Tafsīr* may refer to *Tafsīr*, VI, 94 (*ad* Qur. 5:11).

as their *madhhab* and added his own preference and the arguments for it at the end of each chapter. He made public most of the *Basīṭ's* book on prayer and the entire *Ādāb al-ḥukkām,*[313] as well as the book on records and documents and the classification of scholars *(Tartīb al-ʿulamāʾ).*[314]

Irshād, VI, 448, l. 18–449, l. 17, ed. Rifāʿī, XVIII, 75, l. 7–76, l. 13:

One of his excellent works is the one entitled *Basīṭ al-qawl fī aḥkām sharāʾiʿ al-Islām*. He prefaced it with an interesting book entitled *Marātib al-ʿulamāʾ.*[315] He included in it the invocation *(khuṭbah)* of the work and urged the reader to acquire religious and legal knowledge. He strongly criticized those of his colleagues[316] who restricted themselves to transmitting it without using its contents in their juridical activities. Then he mentioned the scholars among the Companions of the Messenger of God who held legal views like himself *(tafaqqaha ʿalā madhhabihī),*[317] and the jurists of the major centers of the following four (generations) who successively transmitted that material. He started with Medina as the place to which the Prophet emigrated as well as his successors Abū Bakr, ʿUmar, and ʿUthmān, and those after them.[318] (He continued with) Mecca, the Noble Sanctuary, followed by the two Iraqs al-Kufāh and al-Baṣrah, and then Syria and Khurāsān. After discussing ritual purity, he worked on the book on prayer. In this work (that is, the entire *Basīṭ),* he mentioned the disagreements and agreements among scholars exhaustively with clear explanations of (the views expressed by them) and the indication of who held a particular view, and then he stated what was correct (in his

---

313. The correct reading *al-ḥukkām,* as against the text's *al-aḥkām,* is attested by Subkī, *Ṭabaqāt,* and Maqrīzī, *Muqaffā.* The work is identical with *Adab al-qāḍī/Ādāb al-quḍāh.*

314. Dhahabī, *Nubalāʾ,* XIV, 273, l. 21–274, l. 2, has an abridged version, as does Subkī, *Ṭabaqāt,* III, 122. Ṣafadī, *Wāfī,* II, 286, l. 4, merely has *Basīṭ al-qawl.*

315. *Tartīb al-ʿulamāʾ.*

316. The pronominal suffix refers to his own colleagues and students (see also n. 317). His criticism was no doubt held in general terms without naming names.

317. The pronominal suffix does not refer to the Prophet but to his own legal school.

318. Note that ʿAlī is not mentioned.

opinion in each case).[319] He made public about two thousand folios.

He (also) published the *Basīṭ*'s *Kitāb Ādāb al-quḍāh*, an outstanding accomplishment that is highly esteemed among his (publications, *al-ma'dūdah lahū)* because, after the invocation *(khuṭbah)*, he mentioned in it the praiseworthy character of judges and their secretaries. (He discussed) how judges must act after being appointed, what they must accept and what they must look at critically and then reverse earlier legal judgments. (He also included) a discussion of records *(sijillāt)*, legal testimony (by experts, *shahādāt)*, claims (of litigants, *da'āwī)*, and evidence *(bayyināt)*.[320] It was to include a discussion of all the legal knowledge needed by judges *(al-ḥākim)*, until he would finally be through with it. It is one thousand folios.

Ṭabarī used to recommend to his colleagues and students to devote serious study to *Basīṭ* and *Tahdhīb* in preference to any other of his works.

[Al-Bayān fī uṣūl al-aḥkām "A clear exposition of the legal principles": See *Laṭīf]*

[Al-Dalālah 'alā nubuwwat (Rasūl Allāh) "Evidence for the Prophethood of the Messenger of God"

Brockelmann, *GAL*, Suppl., I, 218, lists this title with reference to *History*, I, 1146:

> Abū Ja'far says: Reports on the Prophethood (of Muḥammad) are innumerable. Therefore, if God wills, a monograph should by devoted to them.

Such a monograph may actually have been written by Ṭabarī and become part of one of his other publications, or he may have intended to write one and never did, but *al-Dalālah...* was cer-

---

319. See above, n. 216.

320. These are the ordinary elements of court proceedings. If the rest of the paragraph is correctly translated, it means that the entire work was to include much more legal material of interest to jurists and judges, but only a thousand folios were so far available of the chapter on judges.

tainly never meant to be an actual title and was merely a description of the contents.]

Dhayl al-Mudhayyal "The Appendix (with historical information on religious scholars, needed in connection with *History*)"

The public presentation of *Dhayl* started after 300/912–3; see below.

The skimpy selection *(muntakhab)* from the work that is preserved and was published with *History,* III, 2295–2561, ed. Cairo, XI, 492–705, repeatedly refers to "*al-Mudhayyal*" as if this were another work (and *Dhayl al-Mudhayyal* a supplement to it), but presumably, the complete text of the work, now lost, entitled *Dhayl al-Mudhayyal,* was meant.[321]

Al-Farghānī's *Ijāzah* refers to "*Kitāb Ta'rīkh al-rijāl* 'History of personalities (= religious scholars)', entitled *Dhayl al-Mudhayyal.*"[322] In fact, the work is often listed as *Ta'rīkh al-rijāl*; see Ibn ʿAsākir (below); Dhahabī, *Nubalā',* XIV, 273, ll. 8–10; Ṣafadī, *Wāfī,* II, 285, ll. 20 f.; Subkī, *Ṭabaqāt,* III, 121, l. 9.

Ibn ʿAsākir, LXXIX:

> Also complete is *Ta'rīkh al-rijāl,* dealing with the Companions, the Followers, and their successors down to his own authorities from whom he wrote down *(kataba)* information.

Irshād, VI, 445, ll. 6–17, ed. Rifāʿī, XVIII, 70, l. 9–71, l. 3:

> His book entitled *Kitāb Dhayl al-mudhayyal.* It includes the history (dates, *ta'rīkh)* of the Companions of the Messenger of God who were killed or died during his life or after his death, in order of their relative closeness to him and to the Quraysh with respect to tribal affiliation. He then mentioned (the dates of) death of the Followers and the ancient Muslims after them, then their successors and down to his own teachers with whom he studied *(samiʿa).* He in-

321. For the references, see *Dhayl,* III, 2321, 2335, 2358, 2476, ed. Cairo, XI, 512, 523, 540, 628.

322. See *Irshād,* VI, 426, l. 18, ed. Rifāʿī, XVIII, 44, l. 18.

> cluded a number *(jumalan)* of their traditions and opinions *(akhbārihim wa-madhāhibihim)*, speaking up in defense of the outstanding scholars among them who were accused of holding opinions they did not, as, for instance, al-Ḥasan al-Baṣrī, Qatādah, 'Ikrimah,[323] and others. (On the other hand,) he also mentioned the weakness[324] and softness of transmitters who were considered weak and soft. At the end, the work contains fine chapters on those whose brothers transmitted traditions from them, fathers and sons (who transmitted from one another), and those who were not known by their names but by their patronymics, and vice versa. It is a truly excellent work which *ḥadīth* students and historians are eager to have. He made it public in lectures after the year 300/912–3. It is about one thousand folios.

In another context, *Irshād*, VI, 454, l. 15, ed. Rifāʿī, XVIII, 83, l. 10, adds that the beginning of *Dhayl* dealt with objectionable sectarian views, presumably, if the statement is correct, those falsely ascribed to early Muslims (?). In its lecture form, the work contained high praise for Abū Ḥanīfah; see above, n. 237.

Al-Faḍā'il "The virtues (and remarkable accomplishments and statements of certain ancient Muslims)"

Ṭabarī worked at different times on a project to collect comprehensive information on the "virtues" of the first four caliphs[325] as well as al-ʿAbbās, the ancestor of the ruling ʿAbbāsids. The formal titles of these works, if there were any, are in doubt.

The *Faḍā'il Abī Bakr wa-ʿUmar* are listed as an unfinished work in *Irshād*, VI, 452, l. 18, ed. Rifāʿī, XVIII, 80 f. According to *Irshād*, VI, 455 f., ed. Rifāʿī, XVIII, 85, ll. 5 f., Ṭabarī wrote his work in response to extremist Shīʿah slander of the Prophet's Companions and began with Abū Bakr and 'Umar. The *Faḍā'il al-ʿAbbās* are

---

323. For these ancient Muslims, see below, translation, nn. 642, 64, and 161. The preserved excerpt of *Dhayl* appears to contain the accusations leveled against 'Ikrimah, see III, 2483–85, ed. Cairo, XI, 633–5.

324. *Irshād*, ed. Rifāʿī, has a meaningless *ṣirf* for *ḍaʿf*.

325. 'Uthmān is only mentioned in Ibn ʿAsākir in a rather perfunctory fashion. It is impossible to be sure, but he may have been intentionally excluded from the *Faḍā'il* series, despite Ṭabarī's ordinary view of the first four caliphs.

listed in the immediately following lines. In the second passage, *Irshād* adds: "He began with a fine invocation *(khuṭbah)* and lectured on some of it. He discontinued all lecturing before his death, because he considered it too bothersome a task." It is not entirely clear whether this refers to the *Faḍā'il* of Abū Bakr and 'Umar or those of al-'Abbās, or both. Most likely it refers to all of Ṭabarī's lecturing activity.

The *Faḍā'il 'Alī b. Abī Ṭālib,* which also remained incomplete, constitute a special case, as intimated in the sources.

Ibn 'Asākir, LXXXII, used by Dhahabī, *Nubalā',* XIV, 274, ll. 6–9:

> When Ṭabarī learned that Abū Bakr b. Abī Dāwūd al-Sijistānī[326] spoke critically about the tradition of Ghadīr Khumm,[327] he composed the *Kitāb al-Faḍā'il.* He started with the virtues of Abū Bakr, 'Umar, 'Uthmān, and 'Alī and critically discussed and argued in favor of the soundness of the tradition of Ghadīr Khumm. His work came to an end with what he mentioned of the virtues of the Commander of the Faithful 'Alī.

Irshād, VI, 452, ll. 16 f., ed. Rifā'ī, XVIII, 80, ll. 15–17, briefly states that "in the beginning of the *Kitāb Faḍā'il 'Alī b. Abī Ṭālib,* he critically (and favorably) discussed the soundness of the traditions *(akhbār)* on Ghadīr Khumm and had this discussion followed by the virtues (of 'Alī). He did not finish the work."

Ibn Kāmil's report as reproduced in *Irshād,* VI, 455, l. 11–456, l. 1, ed. Rifā'ī, XVIII, 84, l. 13–85, l. 7, is more detailed:

> One of the scholars in Baghdad[328] had declared the Ghadīr Khumm (episode) to be untrue because, he said, 'Alī b. Abī Ṭālib was in the Yemen at the time when the Messenger of God was at Ghadīr Khumm. In a *muzdawwij* poem contain-

326. See above, n. 229.

327. On the celebrated and controversial designation by Muḥammad of 'Alī as his putative successor at the Pool of Khumm, see EI^2, II, 993 f., s. v. Ghadīr Khumm.

328. His identity as indicated in Ibn 'Asākir is no doubt correct. It would be interesting to know whether the omission of the name was due to Ibn Kāmil and, if so, why he might have omitted it.

ing descriptions of each place and station (in Arabia, connected with the Prophet's biography [?]), that man inserted the following lines alluding to the significance of the tradition of Ghadīr Khumm:

> Then we passed by Ghadīr Khumm,
> Subject to a large number of fraudulent statements
> About ʿAlī and the illiterate Prophet *(al-umm[i])*.

When Abū Jaʿfar learned about it, he started on a discussion of the virtues of ʿAlī b. Abī Ṭālib and mentioned the various recensions of the tradition of Khumm. Many people flocked to listen to (his lectures on) the subject.

Some extremist Shīʿites, who unseemingly slandered the Companions, came together. So Ṭabarī started (to write) on the virtues of Abū Bakr and ʿUmar. Then the ʿAbbāsids asked him about the *faḍāʾil* of al-ʿAbbās. He began.... (see above)."

In view of the importance of the subject for Shīʿah history, notice was occasionally taken of Ṭabarī's work among Shīʿites. The Shīʿah bibliographer al-Ṭūsī commented on it as follows:

> The historian Ṭabarī, not (his) Shīʿah (namesake), composed a *Kitāb Ghadīr Khumm*, commenting on the subject. We were informed about it by Aḥmad b. ʿAbdūn—Abū Bakr al-Dūrī—Ibn Kāmil—Ṭabarī.[329]

Later sunnī discomfort with Ṭabarī's effort was expressed by the fourteenth-century Ibn Kathīr.

> (Ṭabarī) concerned himself with the tradition of Ghadīr Khumm and composed two volumes[330] on the subject. In those volumes, he reported the various recensions as they were transmitted and by whom. His discussion is a mixed bag of valuable and worthless, sound and unsound information. This is in keeping with the custom of many *ḥadīth*

329. See Ṭūsī, *Fihrist*, 178. The only individual in the *isnād* not commonly connected with Ṭabarī is Aḥmad b. ʿAbdūn. He is said to have been known as Ibn Ḥāshir; see the editor's introduction of Ṭūsī, *Fihrist*, 11.

330. See Kern's introduction of his edition of *Ikhtilāf*, 12, where the manuscript said to contain the history of al-Birzālī is quoted as referring to two substantial volumes.

> scholars who (merely) report the information they have on a subject and make no distinction between what is sound and what is weak.[331]

The tentative conclusion which we may draw from all these statements would seem to be as follows: Ṭabarī occasionally lectured on the "virtues" (as he did on the traditions; see *Tahdhīb)* of some of the famous Companions. When an attack on the reliability of the report on the famous Shīʿah episode of Ghadīr Khumm was published, he felt impelled to discuss the subject and could not avoid continuing with a substantial account of ʿAlī's "virtues." The caliphal court then naturally suggested that equal time be given to their side and the virtues of al-ʿAbbās be properly extolled. Much politics of some sort or other was clearly involved in Ṭabarī's dealing with all those matters important alike to the Shīʿah, the sunnī orthodoxy, and the government authorities. While Ṭabarī's personal identification with "orthodox" attitudes cannot be doubted, he appears to have tried to be evenhanded in an objective scholarly manner, much to the embarrassment of later sunnī authors. He may have thought of putting all his lectures together in one major work on the "virtues" of the leading early Muslims. If he did, he did not live long enough to execute the project. Individual installments circulated for a while. It apparently did not take very long for them to become generally unavailable. Religio-political rancor and rivalry no doubt again played a role in their gradual disappearance.

[*Kitāb al-Fatwā* "On legal decisions": See below, n. 343]

Al-Faṣl bayn al-qirāʾah "The (schools of) variant readings of the Qurʾān presented in separate detail"

This seems to be an approximately correct rendering of the rather strange title. In this form, it occurs only in *Irshād.* It appears to have figured in Ibn Kāmil's bibliography. Everywhere else,

331. See Ibn Kathīr, *Bidāyah,* V, 208. Ibn Kathīr continues with a reference to Ibn ʿAsākir who, he says, also reported many recensions of the Prophet's speech at Ghadīr Khumm. The entire statement may go back to an older source, perhaps Ibn ʿAsākir. It is rather unlikely that Ibn Kathīr would have known Ṭabarī's work.

the work is simply described as dealing with the variant readings of the Qur'ān *(Kitāb fī al-qirā'āt).*

For a manuscript of the work preserved in al-Azhar, which has not yet been published, see Sezgin, *GAS,* I, 328, no. 9, and Gilliot, "Les sept lectures."

Al-Jāmiʿ is also mentioned as a title. Quoting al-Dānī, Ibn al-Jazarī states that Ṭabarī's "fine work on *qirā'āt*" was entitled *al-Jāmiʿ*.[332] Maqrīzī, *Muqaffā,* who also relied on al-Dānī, does not mention the title. It may derive from a confusion with *Jāmiʿ al-bayān,* the title of *Tafsīr* which, of course, was concerned with variant readings. In fact, Ḥājjī Khalīfah, ed. Yaltkaya, 1319a, lists Ṭabarī's *Jāmiʿ al-bayān* (!) among works on *qirā'āt,* although elsewhere (see n. 332), he has *al-Jāmiʿ* on *qirā'ah.* From the sources available to him, Pretzl also concluded that *al-Jāmiʿ* was not a different work.[333] It is, however, not entirely impossible, if unlikely, that a monograph on variant readings entitled *al-Jāmiʿ*, as distinct from the work on *qirā'āt,* was produced by Ṭabarī, perhaps based on *Tafsīr,* or circulated under his name.

Ibn al-Nadīm, *Fihrist,* 235, 1. 4, has *Kitāb al-Qirā'āt* and lists no further title on Qur'ān readings.

Among Ṭabarī's completed works, Ibn ʿAsākir, LXXIX, mentions *Kitāb al-Qirā'āt wa-al-tanzīl wa-al-ʿadad,* apparently one and the same work. This means that it also dealt with subjects such as the dates of the revelation of various sūrahs and statistical data such as the number of their verses.[334]

Irshād, VI, 441, l. 17–443, l. 17, ed. Rifāʿī, XVIII, 65, l. 13–68, l. 7, has much detail. Most of it derives from Ibn Kāmil. It is however, unclear what was found in his bibliography or went back to some other Ibn Kāmil tradition unconnected with the discus-

---

332. See Ibn al-Jazarī, *Ghāyah,* II, 107, ll. 5 f.; also idem, *Nashr,* I, 33: "a very substantial book containing over twenty (schools of) variants readings." The passage from *Nashr* was reproduced (directly or from a common source) by Ḥājjī Khalīfah, ed. Yaltkaya, I, 576, under *al-Jāmiʿ fī al-qirā'āt al-ʿashr.*

333. See Nöldeke-Schwally-Bergsträsser-Pretzl, 208, n. 7. From their work, Brockelmann, *GAL*², I, 149, derived the title *Jāmiʿ al-qirā'āt min al-mashhūr wa-al-shawādhdh wa-ʿilal dhālika wa-sharḥuhū.*

334. Ṣafadī, *Wāfī,* II, 285, ll. 5 f., states that Ṭabarī "wrote a work on *qirā'āt*" and lists it on 285, l. 20, as *al-Qirā'āt wa-al-ʿadad wa-al-tanzīl wa-ikhtilāf al-ʿulamā'.* He apparently understood *ikhtilāf al-ʿulamā'* as referring to differences with respect to Qur'ān readings, and not as a reference to *Ikhtilāf.*

sion of the work on Qur'ān readings. An obvious intrusion is a quotation from al-Farghānī. The repeated reference to Abū ʿUbayd al-Qāsim b. Sallām also speaks for different sources. With the exception of the Farghānī passage, the following translation renders the entire text of *Irshād*, which is instructive in many important respects:

> *Kitāb al-Faṣl bayn al-qirā'ah*. He mentioned in it the differences of the Qur'ān readers with respect to the variant readings *(ḥurūf)* of the Qur'ān. It is a very good work. He specified in it the names of the Qur'ān readers in Medina, Mecca, al-Kūfah, al-Baṣrah, Syria, and elsewhere. He gives separate details on each reading. He mentions it as is *(wajh)*, its interpretation *(ta'wīl)*,[335] the views expressed on it by each reader, and his own preference for what is correct on the basis of clear proof for the soundness of his preferred reading. It clearly shows his ability to interpret *(tafsīr)* and establish the correct linguistic form *(iʿrāb)*, an ability which nobody would deny is unmatched by other Qur'ān readers, even though they were excellent scholars and enjoyed priority. He introduced the work with an appropriate invocation *(khuṭbah)*. Such was his custom in his books. He started a given work with an invocation outlining its topic *(maʿnā)* and then constructed its contents in accordance with (the outline presented in) the invocation.[336]
>
> Abū Jaʿfar was famous for his Qur'ān recitation. Qur'ān readers from afar and other people came to pray behind him in order to hear him read and recite the Qur'ān.[337]
>
> When Abū Bakr b. Mujāhid, says Ibn Kāmil, mentioned Ṭabarī, he praised him highly: "Nothing like his book on the subject (of *qirā'āt*) has ever been written," and he said to us: "I have never heard anyone who was a better Qur'ān reader in the prayer niche *(miḥrāb)* than Abū Jaʿfar," or words to this effect.

335. In *Tafsīr*, Ṭabarī refers to Qur'ān interpreters commonly as *ahl al-ta'wīl*, and much less frequently as *ahl al-tafsīr*.

336. A good example is the *khuṭbah* "invocation/introduction" of *History*. See below, n. 445, and translation, n. 6.

337. The proximity to the mention of Abū Bakr b. Mujāhid (see above, n. 121) in the following paragraph makes it likely that this paragraph also goes back to him.

Ibn Kāmil continued: Abū Ja'far originally followed the Qur'ān reading of Ḥamzah,[338] before he settled on his own reading.

(A more detailed description of the development of Ṭabarī's work in the field of Qur'ān reading is inserted here following al-Farghānī.)

Ibn Kāmil continued quoting Abū Bakr b. Mujāhid: After having highly praised his work on variant readings *(kitābahū fī al-qirā'āt),* (Ibn Mujāhid) said: But I have found an error in it. He mentioned it to me, and I was astonished, since Ṭabarī followed the reading and recitation of Ḥamzah. It was because Ṭabarī based his work upon that of Abū 'Ubayd al-Qāsim b. Sallām.[339] Abū 'Ubayd had neglected that particular variant reading, and Ṭabarī copied it that way.

Ibn Kāmil continued: Abū Ja'far told us the following: I heard about a Qur'ān reader in Sūq Yaḥyā.[340] I went and read the Qur'ān to him from the beginning to Qur. 2:26: "God is not ashamed *(yastaḥyī)* to coin a simile." I repeatedly tried to make it clear to him that there were two *yā*'s (in *yastaḥyī).* He objected, and eventually I said: Do you want still more of an explanation for the two *yā*'s with an *i* vowel after the first?[341] He did not know what I was talking about. So I got up and never went back to him.

He continued: Ṭabarī had in his possession the recension of Warsh—Nāfi' as transmitted to him by Yūnus b. 'Abd al-

---

338. Ḥamzah, one of the seven Qur'ān readers, lived during the first three-quarters of the second/eighth century. See *EI*², III, 155, s. v. Ḥamzah b. Ḥabīb.

339. The remark is repeated at the end of the quotation. For the important author Abū 'Ubayd al-Qāsim b. Sallām, see Brockelmann, *GAL,* Suppl. I, 166 f. (many of his works have meanwhile been published). Ṭabarī often cites him in *Tafsīr* as an indirect source ("I was told on the authority of . . ."). Aḥmad b. Yūsuf al-Tha'labī (d. 273/886, see *TB,* V, 218 f.), mentioned below, appears repeatedly as the intermediate transmitter. His *nisbah* is also given, probably incorrectly, as Taghlibī.

340. The Yaḥyā Bazaar was located in al-Shammāsiyyah near the Tigris Bridge, according to Le Strange, *Baghdad,* 199 ff. and Map V (marked no. 45); Lassner, *Topography,* index.

341. The Egyptian edition of the Qur'ān spells *yastaḥyī* with one *yā'* and indicates that the following *i* vowel is to be read as a long *ī* (thus avoiding the implication that the alternate form *yastaḥī* may be meant). This appears to be the situation which Ṭabarī wished to explain to the man who proved to be inordinately obtuse.

Aʿlā from Warsh.[342] (Students) came to Ṭabarī on account of it. As I was told, Abū Bakr b. Mujāhid wanted to have private instruction in that recension from Ṭabarī. Although (Ibn Mujāhid) was a recognized scholar and esteemed by Ṭabarī, the latter refused. (He told him) that he would teach it only, if others were present together with him. This did not sit well with Abū Bakr (b. Mujāhid). Ṭabarī's reasons for the refusal was that he disliked to let anyone have any knowledge that he did not (equally) impart also to others. This was his moral stance. When a number of students studied a book with him, and one of them was unable to be present, he would not permit only some (of the students in class to continue) to study. And if someone wanted to study a book (with him) in absentia, he would not teach him the book until he presented himself in person. An exception was the book on legal decisions *(Kitāb al-Fatwā)*.[343]

His work on variant readings comprises the work of Abū ʿUbayd al-Qāsim b. Sallām. It was in his possession as transmitted by Aḥmad b. Yūsuf al-Thaʿlabī on Abū ʿUbayd's authority. He based his own work on it.

Irshād, VI, 427, ll. 6–9, ed. Rifāʿī, XVIII, 45, ll. 10–14, quotes from a work on Qur'ān reading entitled *al-Iqnāʿ* by Abū ʿAlī al-Ḥasan b. ʿAlī al-Ahwāzī (d. 446/1054[5]):

> (Ṭabarī's work) on *qirā'āt*, a truly great work (or a massive, large work?). The copy I have seen was in eighteen volumes, albeit written in a large script. He mentioned in it all the readings, both those generally accepted *(mashhūr)* and those that are unusual, with the reasons for each reading and comments on it. He did not diverge from what was generally known with respect to any reading he preferred (as being acceptable to him).

342. For ʿUthman b. Saʿīd, nicknamed Warsh (110–97/728[9]–812[3]), see Sezgin, *GAS*, I, 11; Ibn al-Jazarī, *Ghāyah*, I, 502 f. Nāfiʿ b. (ʿAbd al-Raḥmān b.) Abī Nuʿaym, one of the seven Qur'ān readers, lived in and beyond the first half of the second/eighth century, see Sezgin, *GAS*, I, 9 f. Yūnus b. ʿAbd al-Aʿlā has been mentioned above, n. 99, as one of Ṭabarī's authorities during his visit to Egypt.

343. No such title is mentioned among Ṭabarī's works. It could be part of one of his other legal works, or it may not be a specific work but a file of legal decisions kept by him, in case he was asked to render a decision on a problem.

[Ghadīr Khumm: See *Faḍā 'il]*

[*Ḥadīth al-himyān*: "The story of the Khurāsānian whose belt was lost in Mecca"

In the biography of Ibn al-Maḥāmilī (368-415/978[9]-1024), a Shāfi'ite jurist and an early teacher of al-Khaṭīb al-Baghdādī, this item is mentioned as a report *(khabar)* of Ṭabarī.[344] It was, the Khaṭīb says, the only bit of information he was ever able to elicit from Ibn al-Maḥāmilī. Subkī, *Ṭabaqāt*, IV, 49, merely quotes *TB* without adding anything to it. Sezgin, *GAS*, I, 328, no. 10, refers to a manuscript of the treatise in Cairo. Through the good services of Dr. Elise Crosby, I am in the possession of a microfilm enlargement of the text (Ms. 1558 [ḥadīth], pp. 439-45, dating from the ninth/sixteenth century). It turns out not to be a work by Ṭabarī, but it presents itself as a reminiscence from Ṭabarī's younger years told by him to Abū Khāzim al-Mu'allā b. Sa'īd al-Baghdādī al-Bazzār, who died about 353/964 (see *TB*, XIII, 190 f.). It was in Egypt in 346/964 that al-Mu'allā reported that he had heard Ṭabarī tell him the story in 300/912[3]. The gist of the story is as follows:

Ṭabarī was in Mecca in 240/855 (the pilgrimage in that year took place around the end of April). There he heard a Khurāsānian advertise the loss of a belt containing one thousand dīnārs. As we learn later, these thousand dīnārs were one-third of the amount of money his father had left him with the admonition that he give them to the most worthy person he might encounter on the pilgrimage. An old man, whose name was Abū Ghiyāth al-Ja'farī (being a client of Ja'far b. Muḥammad, apparently the sixth imām of the Shī'ah, Ja'far al-Ṣādiq), approached the Khurāsānian and suggested that a reward of ten percent be given to the finder if he came forward. When the Khurāsānian refused, he came down in the following two days to, at first, one percent and, then, a single dīnār. Ṭabarī suspected that the old man himself was the finder of the belt. He followed him to his house the first time, but he stayed at home the next day, as he was occupied with copying the famous work on Qurashite genealogy *(Kitāb al-Nasab)* by al-Zubayr b. Bakkār (d. 256/870).[344a] Ṭabarī had been right. The old man had

344. See *TB*, IV, 372 f.; Sezgin, *GAS*, I, 328, no. 10.

344a. I have no decisive information that Ṭabarī studied personally with al-the belt. His wife asked him to keep it, but he did not want to bring disgrace upon himself in his old age, no matter how grinding the poverty in which he lived together with his household consisting of his wife, his mother-in-law, two sisters, and four daughters. Thus, on the third day, when the Khurāsānian again refused to offer a monetary reward, he took him to his house, with the two of them being followed by Ṭabarī. The Khurāsānian identified the belt and its contents as his and was about to leave with it when he remembered his father's deathbed admonition. He realized that the honest old man was, among all the people he had met on his journey, the one most deserving of the money. So he gave the money to him and left. Ṭabarī also wanted to leave but was called back by the old man, who then distributed the money coin by coin to his family of nine, including Ṭabarī as the tenth person to receive a share of a hundred dīnārs. Ṭabarī lived on the money for a number of years and used it to defray all his study expenses. When he was in Mecca again after 256/870, he learned that the old man had died a few months after the episode with the belt. The four daughters and her husbands and offspring were still alive, but, as Ṭabarī was told, they were all gone in 290/903.

In the biography of al-Muʿallā, Dhahabī, *Mīzān,* IV, 148, and Ibn Ḥajar, *Lisān,* VI, 63 (both quoted in the margin of the Cairo manuscript), expressed themselves convinced that the story was invented by al-Muʿallā but gave no proof except claiming that al-Muʿallā was an untrustworthy transmitter. They may have a point. The story is of the type of the "four Muḥammads" (above, 29 f.) and even more unbelievable. The way in which Ṭabarī came into the possession of his share seems fanciful and hardly reflects credit on him. There are pro-Shīʿah overtones, which may point to Ḥanbalite propaganda directed against him. On the other hand, it might just be possible that the two visits to Mecca, the one in 240 when Ṭabarī was about sixteen, and the other after 256, during or after his stay in Egypt, have a basis in fact and supply us with an otherwise missing bit of biographical information. There is, of course, nothing unusual with a young student undertaking

Zubayr b. Bakkār. In *History,* he is mostly introduced as an indirect, possibly written, source. *Ḥaddathanā,* in I, 1314 and 3072, may reflect a misuse of the term. On the other hand, Ṭabarī may very well have met al-Zubayr in Baghdad or in Mecca where, however, he became judge only in 242 (according to Sezgin, *GAS,* I, 317).

the pilgrimage, perhaps in the company of fellow students and teachers.

According to the sources, the story came into circulation during the fourth/tenth century. Beyond al-Mu'allā, the chain of transmitters, as indicated in the manuscript, is flawless: Ṭabarī—al-Mu'allā—Abū Bakr Aḥmad b. Ibrāhīm Ibn Shādhān al-Bazzār (298-383/910-93, see *TB*, IV, 18-20)—Aḥmad b. 'Alī (Ibn) al-Bādā (d. 420/1029, see *TB*, IV, 322; he taught the story in Rabī' II, 417/May-June 1026. Al-Bādā, of uncertain origin, looks rather like al-Bārā in the manuscript)—Abū Muḥammad Rizqallāh b. 'Abd al-Wahhāb al-Tamīmī *al-wā'iẓ* (d., eighty-eight years old, in 488/1095, see Dhahabī, *'Ibar*, III, 320 f.)—Abū al-Faḍl Muḥammad b. Nāṣir b. Muḥammad (467-550/1074[5]-1155, see Rosenthal, *Muslim Historiography*², 524, n. 2; Eche, *Les Bibliothèques arabes*, 180 f.), who received permission to transmit the story from Rizqallāh but also copied it from a manuscript by a certain Abū al-Ḥasan al-...[344b]—Ibn al-Jawzī, the famous Ḥanbalite scholar and historian (510-97/1116[7]-1201)—Abū al-Faraj 'Abd al-Laṭīf b. 'Abd al-Mun'im al-Ḥarrānī (587-672/1191-1273, see Ibn al-'Imād, *Shadharāt*, V, 336)—Ṣadr al-dīn Muḥammad b. Muḥammad b. Ibrāhīm al-Maydūmī (664-754/1266-1353, see Ibn Ḥajar, *Durar*, IV, 157 f.)—Aḥmad b. Muḥammad b. Abī Bakr al-Wāsiṭī (745-836/1344[5]-1433, see Sakhāwī, *Ḍaw'*, II, 106 f.). Some of the individuals mentioned were very young when they received permission to transmit the story. This agrees with its edifying moral character which was thought particularly suitable for young children.]

'Ibārat al-ru'yā "On dream interpretation"

Irshād, VI, 452 f., ed. Rifā'ī, XVIII, 81, ll. 2 f., states that Ṭabarī worked on "a book on dream interpretation containing traditions

344b. The manuscript has al-..ādhānī, which I have so far been unable to identify. There was an Abū al-Ḥasan al-Baradānī who died in 469/1077 (and was possibly born in 388/998, if 308 in the *Muntaẓam* is to be corrected to 388). See Sam'ānī, *Ansāb*, II, 144, and Ibn al-Jawzī, *Muntaẓam*, VIII, 311. However, the correction of Barādhānī to Baradānī is not self-evident, and the first two consonants can be read in a large variety of ways.

(on the subject) but died before he could produce it." It was another of those projects on which Ṭabarī was still working at the time of his death. As indicated, it was a work on *ḥadīth.*

Ikhtilāf 'ulamā' al-amṣār fī aḥkām sharā'i' al-Islām "The disagreements of the scholars in the major centers with respect to the laws of the Muslim religion"

This is the full title of the celebrated work, which is partly preserved (see below). It is often referred to in an abridged form, such as *Ikhtilāf 'ulamā' al-amṣār,*[345] *Ikhtilāf al-'ulamā',*[346] or simply *al-Ikhtilāf.* The title *Ikhtilāf al-fuqahā'* is found, notably in Ibn al-Nadīm but also elsewhere.[347] It is the title used in the printed editions of the preserved parts of the work. See also Kern, "Ṭabarī's Ikhtilāf," 65.

A report in *Irshād* (see below, 85) apparently is of Ḥanbalite inspiration. It speaks of the publication of the work after Ṭabarī's death, if this is what the rather strange report really means. Probably, the reference to *Ikhtilāf* figured in it only by some sort of obfuscation. *Ikhtilāf* was also considered Ṭabarī's first literary production. In view of the fact that *Laṭīf* is cited in it and was considered by Ṭabarī in the choice of its contents,[348] this may also seem a strange statement. It is well possible, however, that parts of *Ikhtilāf* came out before the publication of any part of *Laṭīf* and that quotations from *Laṭīf* occurred only in later parts of *Ikhtilāf* or were subsequently added by Ṭabarī in those earlier parts already published. No absolute publication dates are mentioned in the sources.

As in the case of *Laṭīf,* Ṭabarī also wrote, or started on, an introductory *risālah* to *Ikhtilāf* dealing with the basic principles (see below, n. 356).

Irshād, VI, 445, l. 17–447, l. 18, ed. Rifā'ī, XVIII, 71, l. 4–73, l. 5, presents a full discussion of the history of the work:

345. See al-Farghānī, *Ijāzah,* in *Irshād,* VI, 427, l. 2, ed. Rifā'ī, XVIII, 45, ll. 4 f.; Ibn 'Asākir, LXXIX; Dhahabī, *Nubalā',* XIV, 273, l. 12; Ṣafadī, *Wāfī,* II, 286, l. 2.

346. See 'Abbādī, *Ṭabaqāt,* 52.

347. See Ibn al-Nadīm, *Fihrist,* 235, l. 5; *Irshād* (see below); Murtaḍā al-Zabīdī, *Itḥāf* (see below, n. 361).

348. See below, 116.

His work famed for excellence in East and West entitled *Kitāb Ikhtilāf ʿulamāʾ al-amṣār fī aḥkām sharāʾiʿ al-Islām.* His intention was to mention in it the statements of the following jurists: (1) Mālik b. Anas, the leading Medinese jurist, according to two recensions, (2) ʿAbd al-Raḥmān b. ʿAmr al-Awzāʿī, the leading Syrian jurist, (3) the Kūfan Sufyān al-Thawrī, according to two recensions, (4) Muḥammad b. Idrīs al-Shāfiʿī, according to the transmission of al-Rabīʿ b. Sulaymān[349] on al-Shāfiʿī's authority, the Kūfans (5) Abū Ḥanīfah al-Nuʿmān b. Thābit, (6) Abū Yūsuf Yaʿqūb b. Muḥammad al-Anṣārī, and (7) Abū ʿAbdallāh Muḥammad b. al-Ḥasan al-Shaybānī, a *mawlā* of the Shaybān, and (8) Abū Naṣr Ibrāhīm b. Khālid al-Kalbī.[350]

In his work, Ṭabarī had originally included one of the Muʿtazilites *(ahl al-naẓar),* namely, ʿAbd al-Raḥmān b. Kaysān, because at the time when (Ṭabarī) was working on *(Ikhtilāf),* (Ibn Kaysān's) views were not used as the basis for a(n unacceptable) legal school.[351] After some time, however, (Ibn Kaysān's) colleagues and students expressed poorly informed legal views, and Ṭabarī excluded him from his work.

I heard Ṭabarī respond to a question (about the history of *Ikhtilāf)* he was asked by Abū ʿAbdallāh Aḥmad b. ʿĪsā al-Rāzī.[352] He said that he had first undertaken to work on it in order to mention the views of those opposed to his (own views). The work then gained wider circulation, and he was asked by his colleagues and students (who were adherents of his school) to lecture on it.

When Muḥammad b. Dāwūd al-Iṣbahānī[353] published his book known under the title of *al-Wuṣūl ilā maʿrifat al-uṣūl,*

---

349. Ṭabarī studied with him in Egypt; see above, n. 100.

350. He must be Abū Thawr, although Abū Thawr's *kunyah* was doubtful and is sometimes said to have been Abū 'Abdallāh, while Abū Thawr was a nickname; see Subkī, *Ṭabaqāt,* II, 74; Ibn Ḥajar, *Tahdhīb,* I, 118. For Abū Thawr, see above, n. 272. The numbering has been added in the translation.

351. Possibly the famous Abū Bakr 'Abd al-Raḥmān b. Kaysān al-Aṣamm, who died long before Ṭabarī was born, is meant. See Sezgin, *GAS,* I, 624 f.; Ritter, in his edition of Ash'arī, *Maqālāt,* 617.

352. He is certainly not identical with the 'Alid mentioned above, n. 186, and remains unidentified. This is particularly regrettable, since knowing about him might have clarified who the speaker here was.

353. See above, 68 f.

he mentioned in the chapter on general consensus *(ijmāʿ)* as the view of Ṭabarī that *ijmāʿ* meant the consensus of the afore-mentioned eight jurists to the exclusion of everybody else. He based himself on Ṭabarī's statement: "They agreed *(ajmaʿū)*, and thereby agreement was reached on the point being argued." (Ṭabarī) then said in the introduction of the chapter on disagreement *(khilāf)*: "Then they disagreed. Mālik held one view, al-Awzāʿī another, and so-and-so still another." (Combining the two statements, Muḥammad b. Dāwūd concluded) that those for whom Ṭabarī reported consensus were identical with those for whom he reported disagreement.[354] This is an error on the part of Ibn Dāwūd. Had he considered what Ṭabarī had written in the *Risālah* of *Laṭīf* and the *Risālah* of *Ikhtilāf* (and) in many of his works, namely, that *ijmāʿ* is the uninterrupted transmission of traditions agreed upon by the Companions of the Messenger of God, and not something based on opinion or deduced by analogical reasoning, he would have realized that the view expressed by him (as to Ṭabarī's understanding of *ijmāʿ*) was a grievous error and obvious mistake.

Abū Jaʿfar thought highly of his *Ikhtilāf*, which was the first of his works (to be put in publishable form, *ṣunnifa*). He often said to me: "I have written two books that are indispensable for jurists, *Ikhtilāf* and *Laṭīf*."

Ikhtilāf is about three thousand folios. In order not to repeat himself, he did not deal in it with his own preferences (as to what he considered the correct view in each case),[355] because he had done a good job in this respect in *Laṭīf*.

He had written for *Ikhtilāf* an introductory *risālah*, which he later dropped.[356] In it, he discussed general consensus and traditions originating with single authorities of recognized probity *(al-āḥād al-ʿudūl)*, additions[357] not in *Laṭīf*, as

354. Ergo, the jurists considered in *Ikhtilāf* represented consensus in every sense.
355. But see above, n. 216.
356. Or: "which he later stopped lecturing on," which is the same thing. It does not mean: "which he separated (from *Ikhtilāf* and treated as a separate work)."
357. This translation seems possible and has therefore been preferred to the text in ed. Rifāʿī. Supplying the preposition *ʿinda*, it yields the rather different sense: "discussing consensus and traditions . . ., he mentioned additions not in *Laṭīf* . . ."

well as *marāsīl* traditions[358] and abrogation *(al-nāsikh wa-al-mansūkh).*

Irshād, VI, 437, ll. 1–6, ed. Rifāʿī, XVIII, 59, ll. 2–8, also reports the following dubious statement in connection with the Ḥanbalite affair discussed above, 73 ff.:

> Ṭabarī secluded himself in his house and produced his well-known book containing his apology *(iʿtidhār)* to the (Ḥanbalites). He mentioned his own legal views *(madhhab)* and dogmatic beliefs. He declared unreliable those who thought differently about him with respect to these matters. He lectured to them *(qara'a ʿalā)* on the book. He extolled Aḥmad b. Ḥanbal and mentioned his legal views *(madhhab)* and dogmatic beliefs as being correct. He continued to refer to him constantly until he died. His book on *ikhtilāf* was not made public by him before he died. It was buried in the ground and made public and copied *(n-s-kh,* by the Ḥanbalites) — I mean *Ikhtilāf al-fuqahā'*. I heard this from a number of people, including my father.[359]

Ikhtilāf is listed in Brockelmann, *GAL,* I, 143, Suppl. I, 218, and Sezgin, *GAS,* I, 328. For the editions of Kern and Schacht, see below, Bibliography, under *Ikhtilāf.* The reprints of Kern's edition mentioned by C. Gilliot, in *Studia Islamica,* 63 (1986): 189–92, were not available. The title of the manuscript published by Schacht is *Mukhtaṣar Ikhtilāf ʿulamā' al-amṣār* (see p. IX); there may be at least some truth to the statement that it was indeed an abridgment (see also above, n. 216).

In *Tabṣīr,* fol. 92b, Ṭabarī refers to his *Kitāb Ahl al-baghy* "On wrongdoers (rebels)." Since *Tabṣīr* is greatly concerned with differences of opinion and *Ikhtilāf* had a book on the subject (see ed. Schacht, X), it stands to reason that the reference is to *Ikhtilāf* and not to another of Ṭabarī's legal writings.

358. A *mursal* tradition is one with an *isnād* that does not lead back all the way to the Prophet.

359. Perhaps, ʿAbd al-ʿAzīz b. Hārūn(?), mentioned *Irshād,* VI, 435, l. 5, ed. Rifāʿī, XVIII, 56, l. 14, is meant as the son of Hārūn b. ʿAbd al-ʿAzīz mentioned in *Irshād* a few lines later. Abū ʿAlī Hārūn b. ʿAbd al-ʿAzīz appears as a transmitter of information from Ṭabarī in Ibn ʿAsākir, LXXXII, l. 17, and LXXXIV, l. 16 (see below, 106 f.). All this is more than uncertain. The suspicion remains that the narrator was perhaps an unidentified Ḥanbalite.

Irshād, VI, 435, ll. 12 f., ed. Rifāʿī, XVIII, 57, l. 5, refers to the *Kitāb al-Janā'iz* "On funerals" of *Ikhtilāf*. A few possible cross-references to non-preserved parts of *Ikhtilāf* are listed by Kern, "Ṭabarī's Ikhtilāf," 65. In his edition, I, 50, Kern includes a reference to *Kitāb al-Aymān wa-al-nudhūr* "On oaths and vows."[360] He also reproduced (II, 123–5) the text of two quotations found in Murtaḍā al-Zabīdī, *Itḥāf*, dealing with Ṭabarī's discussion of masturbation and anal intercourse in *Ikhtilāf*.[361] Murtaḍā al-Zabīdī wrote this section of his large work in 1168/1755. Thus, as late as the middle of the twelfth/eighteenth century, Ṭabarī's *Ikhtilāf* was used, apparently directly. See further Muranyi, "*Kitāb al-Siyar*," 84 f.

[*al-Iʿtidhār* "Apology (to the Ḥanbalites)": See *Ikhtilāf*

This is obviously not a formal title. It was not a work published by Ṭabarī and may have existed only in Ḥanbalite wishful thinking.]

Jāmiʿ al-bayān ʿan ta'wīl āy al-Qur'ān "The complete clarification of the interpretation of the verses of the Qur'ān"

This official title of Ṭabarī's great Qur'ān commentary *(Tafsīr)* is mentioned in *History:* see below, text, I, 87, translation, n. 562. It never gained much popularity and was almost always replaced by the simple *Tafsīr*.[362] The work is mentioned in all Ṭabarī biographies, large and small, and usually praised very highly. During his lifetime, it probably was considered his outstanding scholarly achievement, even more so than his great works on law and *ḥadīth*. It has retained its outstanding importance to this day. It says much for the general esteem accorded to the work that the Christian philosopher and theologian Yaḥyā b. ʿAdī, who died

360. Other similar references are believed by Kern to be derived from *Laṭīf* (see below, 116). He concluded, it seems, that this was so from the phrase "in our book, the book on . . .". In contrast, Ṭabarī here does not have "in our book" but only "*Kitāb al-Aymān* . . . ."

361. See Murtaḍā al-Zabīdī, *Itḥāf*, V, 306 and 375. He introduces the quotation as coming from *Ikhtilāf al-fuqahā'*.

362. *Irshād* omits *āy* in one instance (misprint?). The work is quoted exceptionally as *al-Bayān* in Zarkashī, *Burhān*, I, 214.

in his eighties in 363/974, reportedly copied it twice for sale to provincial rulers.[363]

The work took many years to complete. In 270/883[4],[364] a substantial portion was made public by Ṭabarī in the form of public lectures. Between 283/896 and 290/903, if not earlier, the entire work was ready for publication.

Al-Farghānī's *ijāzah* was written on a volume of *Tafsīr.* He referred to the work as "*Kitāb al-Tafsīr,* entitled *Jāmiʿ al-bayān ʿan taʾwīl āy al-Qurʾān.*"[365] Al-Farghānī also provided the information to be found in Ibn ʿAsākir, LXXIX:[366]

> Among his completed works is his excellent *Kitāb Tafsīr al-Qurʾān.* He explained in it the legal data derived from the Qurʾān, its abrogating and abrogated verses, its difficult passages, and its rare words. (He also discussed) the disagreements between commentators and religious scholars with respect to the Qurʾān's legal data and its interpretation together with an indication of what he considered the correct view in each case, its proper vocalization *(iʿrāb ḥurūfihī),* the condemnation of heretics in it, the (biblical and other) stories, the reports on the nations (of the world), the Resurrection, and other wise statements and marvelous matters. He did that word by word, verse by verse, from the beginning where the formula "I take refuge in God" is used, to the letters of the alphabet.[367] If a scholar claimed that he could write ten books based on it, of which each would deal with a special remarkable subject that is exhaustively presented, he could do it.

Al-Farghānī, at least in part through Hārūn b. ʿAbd al-ʿAzīz,[368] also told the following anecdotes, as reported in Ibn ʿAsākir,

363. See Ibn al-Nadīm, *Fihrist,* 264, ll. 9 f.

364. It is tempting to think of a mistake for 290, but this common error seems to be most unlikely in this case; see below, n. 371.

365. See *Irshād,* VI, 426, l. 16, ed. Rifāʿī, XVIII, 44, ll. 15 f.

366. Dhahabī, *Nubalāʾ,* XIV, 373, ll. 6–8, depends on Ibn ʿAsākir.

For a succinct survey of the numerous publications on the various topics of Qurʾānic science, which existed in the fourth/tenth century, see Ibn al-Nadīm, *Fihrist.*

367. The formula *aʿūdhu bi-Allāh* used before the recitation of the Qurʾān is discussed in *Tafsīr,* I, 37 f. For the letters of "*abū jād,*" see below, n. 379.

368. See above, n. 359.

LXXXII, ll. 17–9, and l. 19–LXXXIII, l. 2:

For three years before I went to work on the *Kitāb al-Tafsīr,* I asked God for permission to produce the work and for His help in doing what I had in mind, and He did help me.

Al-Farghānī (through Hārūn b. ʿAbd al-ʿAzīz ?) said: A chaste neighbor[369] of Abū Jaʿfar told me: I had a dream in which I saw myself in the classroom *(majlis)* of Abū Jaʿfar al-Ṭabarī when his *Tafsīr* was studied with him. I heard a voice coming from in between heaven and earth say: He who wants to study the Qur'ān as it was revealed should study this work.

Irshād, VI, 439, l. 3– 441, l. 17, ed. Rifāʿī, XVIII, 61, l. 17–65, l. 13, is an obvious composite of sources, but most of the factual information appears to come from ʿAbd al-ʿAzīz b. Muḥammad al-Ṭabarī's monograph, through Ibn Kāmil:

His book entitled *Jāmiʿ al-bayān ʿan ta'wīl al-Qur'ān.*[370] Abū Bakr b. Kāmil says: He dictated *(amlā)* to us one hundred and ninety verses of the *Kitāb al-Tafsīr.* Thereafter, he continued to the end of the Qur'ān and read (the entire work?) to us. This was in 270/883[4].[371] The work (soon) became very famous. Abū al-ʿAbbās Aḥmad b. Yaḥyā Thaʿlab and Abū al-ʿAbbās Muḥammad b. Yazīd al-Mubarrad, the great authorities on grammar and semantics *(iʿrāb* and *maʿānī),* were still alive at the time, as were other expert Arab grammarians such as Abū Jaʿfar al-Rustamī, Abū Ḥasan b. Kaysān, al-Mufaḍḍal b. Salamah, al-Jaʿd, and Abū Isḥāq al-Zajjāj.[372] The *Tafsīr* achieved wide distribution in East and West. All contemporary scholars read it, and all considered

---

369. This is the hardly credible meaning of the text. *Irshād,* VI, 439, ll. 17 f., ed. Rifāʿī, XVIII, 63, l. 2, has "a shaykh from the Bridge of Ibn ʿAfīf" (= "chaste"). To my knowledge, no such bridge occurs in the topographical works, but it it likely to be the correct reading. Ibn ʿAsākir may have miscopied the same source, or the corruption may have occurred in the textual tradition of his work. Though missing in *Irshād,* "neighbor" may be original, thus placing the man in al-Mukharrim or nearby in East Baghdad.

370. See above, n. 362.

371. While the preceding sentence seems to speak of the entire work, the date appears to be intended for those lectures on the first sūrah and part of the second sūrah.

372. All the authors named in this and the following paragraphs of the quotation

it truly excellent.

Abū Jaʿfar said: I felt the inner urge to write the work when I was still a child.

ʿAbd al-ʿAzīz b. Muḥammad al-Ṭabarī quoted Abū ʿUmar al-Zāhid[373] as saying: For a long time, I made my living collating books with people. (Once) I asked Abū Jaʿfar about the interpretation of a verse. He said: Collate *(qābil)* this work *(Tafsīr)* from beginning to end! (I did) and could not find a single wrong reading *(ḥarf)* with respect to grammar and lexicography.

Abū Jaʿfar said: (This and the next paragraph have been translated above from Ibn ʿAsākir.)

Abū Bakr Muḥammad b. Mujāhid said: I heard Abū Jaʿfar say: I wonder how anyone who reads the Qur'ān and does not know its interpretation can enjoy reading it.[374]

He started the *Kitāb al-Tafsīr* with an invocation *(khuṭbah).* The introductory essay *(risālah)* of *Tafsīr* proves the eloquence, inimitability *(iʿjāz),* and clarity of expression *(faṣāḥah),* not matched anywhere else, with which God has distinguished the Qur'ān. Among introductory topics *(muqaddamātin),* he discussed commenting on *(tafsīr)* and ways of interpreting *(wujūh al-ta'wīl)* the Qur'ān, the interpretation *(ta'wīl)* of what is known[375] and what has been indicated as permitted to comment on *(tafsīr)* as well as what is forbidden (see *Tafsīr,* I, 25-27, 31 f.). He discussed the Prophet's statement that "the Qur'ān was revealed in seven letters" (see *Tafsīr,* I, 9–25),[376] further, in which tongues the

---

are so well-known that it would be superfluous to comment on them. For chronological purposes, it is interesting to notice that Thaʿlab died in 291/904 (above, n. 178), and al-Mubarrad in 285–6/898–9. For Abū Jaʿfar Aḥmad b. Muḥammad b. Rustam (d. about 310/922), see Sezgin, *GAS,* IX, 160 f.; for Abū (al-)Ḥasan Muḥammad b. Aḥmad b. Kaysān (d. about 299/911 or later?), see Brockelmann, *GAL,* Suppl. I, 170, Sezgin, *GAS,* IX, 158–60; for al-Mufaḍḍal b. Salamah (d. about 290/903), see *GAL,* Suppl. I, 191, *GAS,* IX, 139 f.; for Muḥammad b. ʿUthmān al-Jaʿd (d. about 320/932), see *GAS,* IX, 163; and for Abū Isḥāq Ibrāhīm b. al-Sarī al-Zajjāj (d. 310/922 or later), see *GAL,* Supp. I, 170; *GAS,* IX, 81 f.

373. See above, n. 179.

374. A rather similar remark is ascribed to Saʿīd b. Jubayr in *Tafsīr,* I, 28, ll. 12 f.: "He who reads the Qur'ān and then does not interpret it is like a blind man or a Bedouin." "Muḥammad" is a mistake for Aḥmad.

375. Or "can be known, is knowable" by human beings, and not only by God.

376. See *Concordance,* I, 448b, and Gilliot, "Les sept lectures."

Qur'ān was revealed, and he refuted those who said that it contains non-Arabic words (see *Tafsīr,* I, 6 ff.).[377] He mentioned the interpretation of the names of the Qur'ān and the sūrahs (see *Tafsīr,* I, 32-35), and other such introductory matters. He had this followed by the interpretation of the Qur'ān letter by letter. He mentioned the statements of the Companions, the Followers, and those who followed the Followers, the discussions of the Kūfan and Baṣran grammarians *(ahl al-i'rāb),* and a number *(jumal)* of Qur'ān readings and the variant readings of (the schools of) Qur'ān reading concerning root forms *(maṣādir),* lexicography/dialectology *(lughāt),* plurals, and duals. He discussed the abrogating and abrogated verses of the Qur'ān, its legal data, and differences in this respect. He mentioned some of the statements of the speculative theologians *(ahl al-naẓar)*[378] as made by some innovators, and he refuted them according to the views *(madhāhib)* of the affirmers *(ahl al-ithbāt,* the "orthodox") and as required by the traditions *(sunan),* all the way to the end of the Qur'ān. He had this followed by the interpretation of the alphabet and its letters, the different opinions of people concerning them, and how he himself preferred to interpret them.[379] Nobody could add anything to it, nor would he find the subject treated as completely by anybody else.

He used in it the (earlier) commentaries by Ibn 'Abbās in five recensions, Sa'īd b. Jubayr in two recensions, Mujāhid b. Jabr in three, and often more, recensions, Qatādah b. Di'āmah in three recensions, al-Ḥasan al-Baṣrī in three recensions, 'Ikrimah in three recensions, al-Ḍaḥḥāk b. Muzāḥim in two recensions, and 'Abdallāh b. Mas'ūd in one recension. He further used the commentaries of 'Abd al-Raḥmān b. Zayd b. Aslam, Ibn Jurayj, and Muqātil b. Ḥayyān. Moreover, *(Tafsīr)* contains well known traditions on the authority of the Qur'ān commentators and others. It includes all that is needed of traditions transmitted with an

377. See, however, above, 45 f.

378. See, for instance, Appendix A, below, 149–51.

379. The discussion of phonetics and orthography is not included in the introduction of *Tafsīr.* As indicated here, it supposedly appeared at the end of the entire work. The text as published does not contain it.

uninterrupted chain of transmitters mainly from the Prophet *(musnad al-ḥadīth)*.

He paid no attention to unreliable (commentators). Thus, the work contains no (traditions) from the works of Muḥammad b. al-Sā'ib al-Kalbī, Muqātil b. Ḥayyān, or Muḥammad b. 'Umar al-Wāqidī, because he considered them suspect (as Qur'ān and *ḥadīth* scholars). But when he referred to history, biography, or Arab stories, he did include reports from Muḥammad b. Sā'ib al-Kalbī, his son Hishām, Muḥammad b. 'Umar al-Wāqidī, and others, whatever was needed and could be found only in their works.[380]

In *Tafsīr,* he mentioned numerous discussions and suggested meanings *(ma'ānī)* from the books of 'Alī b. Ḥamzah al-Kisā'ī, Yaḥyā b. Ziyād al-Farrā', Abū al-Ḥasan al-Akhfash, Abū 'Alī Quṭrub, and others, whenever needed as required by the discussion. These (famous grammarians and lexicographers) were the ones who discussed the meanings and provided (explanations for Qur'ānic) meanings and grammar *(ma'ānī al-i'rāb)*. When he quoted from them, he often did not mention them by name.

This work comprises ten thousand folios, or fewer, depending on the size of the script. 'Abd al-'Azīz b. Muḥammad al-Ṭabarī said: I have seen a manuscript in Baghdad which comprised four thousand folios.

The task of commenting on *Tafsīr* and condensing it started early. A Mu'tazilite of Turkish origin, Abū Bakr Aḥmad b. 'Alī b. Bayghjūr, known as Ibn al-Ikhshēd, who lived in Sūq al-'Aṭash and died in 326/938, wrote an abridgment.[381] A commentary written by Abū Bakr b. Abī Dāwūd al-Sijistānī in competition with Ṭabarī was judged by history to have been a failure.[382] Among Abū Bakr's authorities, we find Ibn Bashshār and Ibn al-Muthannā who figure so prominently in Ṭabarī's works.

380. The sharp distinction made by Ṭabarī between historians and specialists in other fields is noteworthy.

381. See Ibn al-Nadīm, *Fihrist,* 173 (also 34, l. 14, and 235, l. 3); *TB,* IV, 309. *M-'-j-w-r,* as his ancestor's name is spelled in *Fihrist,* is an implausible form. The reading *B-y-gh-j-w-r* of *TB* is more likely as a Turkish-Persian name. See, for instance, Bakjūr (*Eclipse,* index, s. v. Bekjūr).

382. See above, n. 229.

See Brockelmann, *GAL*, I, 143, Suppl., I, 218, and Sezgin, *GAS*, I, 327, for literature and editions. *Tafsīr* became known in Europe only about the time that the publication of *History* started.[383] It was first printed in Cairo 1321/1903 and 1323/1905, reprinted in Beirut, 1400/1980. The edition Cairo 1323 is considered the better of the two.[384] Modern printings, such as one edited by Maḥmūd M. Shākir and A. M. Shākir (Cairo, 1961), regrettably fail to indicate the paginations of the earlier editions.

An abridged French translation by Pierre Godé has been appearing in Paris since 1983. An English translation by J. Cooper has been announced for 1986. The first volumes of Godé's work have been seen by me.

[Al-Jāmiʿ fī al-qirā'āt "The complete collection of variant readings in the Qur'ān": See *Faṣl]*

[Al-Janā'iz "On funerals": See *Ikhtilāf]*

[Al-Jirāḥ "On wounds": See *Laṭīf]*

Al-Khafīf fī aḥkām sharā'iʿ al-Islām "The light work on the laws of the Muslim religion"

This full title of what was a condensed version of *Laṭīf* appears in Ibn ʿAsākir, LXXX, ll. 2 f.,[385] and *Irshād*; see below. Ibn al-Nadīm, *Fihrist*, 235, l. 4, has *al-Khafīf fī al-fiqh*, followed somewhat incongruously by the word *laṭīf*. Ibn ʿAsākir similarly states that the work, which was completed by Ṭabarī, was "a slim abridgment *(mukhtaṣar laṭīf)*." A law book of four hundred folios could indeed be called "slender,"[386] but it is tempting to assume with Goldziher, "Die literarische Thätigkeit, " 364, n. 11, that in the *Fihrist* as well as Ibn ʿAsākir, the intended meaning was "an abridgment of *Laṭīf*." Subkī, *Ṭabaqāt*, III, 121, ll. 10 f., describes the work merely as "a short work *(mukhtaṣar)* on jurisprudence." The reference to *Laṭīf* in Qifṭī, *Inbāh*, III, 90, is followed by one to

383. See Loth, "Ṭabarī's Korancommentar."
384. See Nöldeke-Schwally-Bergsträsser-Pretzl, III, 240.
385. Reproduced by Dhahabī, *Nubalā'*, XIV, 273, l. 13.
386. On the double meaning of *laṭīf*, see below, 113 and 115.

another work described as "a treatise *(maqālah)* on jurisprudence used by scholars (in their legal work)." *Khafīf* is presumably meant here.

The composition of *Khafīf* must be dated between 291/904 when al-ʿAbbās b. al-Ḥasan was appointed wazīr, and 296/908 when he lost his life. One might assume that al-ʿAbbās may not yet have been wazīr (and al-Muktafī not yet caliph) at the time Ṭabarī wrote *Khafīf*; this, however, seems unlikely. It should be noted that the *nisbah* al-ʿAzīzī indicated in *Irshād* is not attested elsewhere for the wazīr, nor is any other *nisbah*, as far as I know. On the other hand, the *kunyah* Abū Aḥmad seems confirmed by the existence of a son of his named Aḥmad.[387]

Following al-Farghānī, Ibn ʿAsākir, LXXXVI, l. 18–LXXVII, l. 2, combines the anecdote of Ṭabarī's refusal of al-Muktafī's gift (see above, 37 f.), in which the wazīr al-ʿAbbās b. al-Ḥasan played a role, with a similar anecdote involving the reason for the composition of *Khafīf*:

> Al-ʿAbbās b. al-Ḥasan[388] sent a message to Ṭabarī telling him that he wished to study jurisprudence, and asked him to produce a short work *(mukhtaṣar)* according to his legal school for him. Ṭabarī wrote for him the *Kitāb al-Khafīf* and dispatched it to him. When al-ʿAbbās sent him a thousand dīnārs, he did not accept the money but returned it to him. He was told to use it for charity. He did not want to do that. He said: You (using the plural addressing al-ʿAbbās) know better how to use your money and to whom to give charity.

The fullest information is found in *Irshād*, VI, 448, ll. 8–12, ed. Rifāʿī, XVIII, 74, ll. 11–18:

> One of his excellent works is the book entitled *Kitāb al-Khafīf fī aḥkām sharāʾiʿ al-Islām*, an abridgment of the *Kitāb al-Laṭīf*. Abū Aḥmad al-ʿAbbās b. al-Ḥasan al-ʿAzīzī wanted to look into some legal matters and corresponded with Ṭabarī concerning an abridgment of one of his works. Ṭabarī produced this book in order to facilitate the under-

387. See ʿArīb, 63.

388. In Dhahabī's very abridged quotation (*Nubalāʾ*, XIV, 270, ll. 14 f.), *al-wazīr* replaces the proper name. In the similar anecdote, above, 39, the wazīr is al-Khāqānī.

> standing of the subject. It is about four hundred folios. It is a book that makes the subject easy for the person who studies it. It contains (the discussion of) many problems which both scholars and beginning students would do well to memorize.

According to Ibn al-Nadīm, *Fihrist*, 235, l. 4, al-Muʿāfā wrote a commentary on *Khafīf*.

Al-Laṭīf fī aḥkām sharā'iʿ al-Islām "The slim[389] work on the laws of the Muslim religion" or, more commonly, *Laṭīf al-qawl....* "The slim discussion of ...".

The second form of the title appears *Ikhtilāf*, ed. Kern (II, 29, 79, 83, 90 f.) with the substitution of the synonymous *al-dīn* for *al-Islām*. The first form is found in the introduction of *Tafsīr* (I, 37, ll. 13 ff.):

> We have explained briefly what we considered the correct statement here in our book *al-Laṭīf fī aḥkām sharā'iʿ al-Islām*. God willing, we shall give an exhaustive explanation and report the statements of the Companions, the Followers, and ancient and recent scholars in our great work on the laws of the Muslim religion *(kitābunā al-akbar fī aḥkām sharā'iʿ al-Islām)*.[390]

In *Tafsīr*, the work is constantly cited under slightly different titles, such as *Laṭīf al-qawl fī sharā'iʿ al-Islām* (XVIII, 68, l. 12), or *...aḥkām sharā'iʿ al-dīn* (VIII, 16, l. 7) as in *Ikhtilāf*, or *Laṭīf al-qawl fī aḥkām al-sharā'iʿ* (VIII, 28, l. 31), or simply *al-Laṭīf* (II, 252, l. 17, 289, l. 11).[391] But the work is also referred to by the title or contents of its individual "books," with no reference to the overall designation.

---

389. The source of *Irshād* (below, 115) claims that Ṭabarī himself did not intend *laṭīf* in its physical meaning but in its metaphorical meaning of "subtle." However, Ṭabarī, in fact, meant to imply that in comparison to the enormous mass of data to be discussed, *Laṭīf* was, in spite of its considerable size, a slim and concise work. The flattering interpretation was no doubt owing to a student and admirer.

390. See also above, under *Aḥkām sharā'iʿ al-Islām*.

391. *Tafsīr*, VI, 44, l. 16, has a dubious *al-Laṭīf (!) al-qawl fī al-aḥkām* (misprint?). Subkī, *Ṭabaqāt*, III, 121, l. 10, lists *Laṭīf* as "*Kitāb Aḥkām sharā'iʿ al-Islām*, composed in accordance with the results of his independent judgment." The form of the title possibly results from a confusion with the larger planned work.

The title *al-Laṭīf min al-bayān ʿan aḥkām sharāʾiʿ al-Islām* (*Tafsīr*, II, 264, ll. 11 f.) includes *al-bayān*, which properly belongs to the title of the introductory *risālah* on legal principles (see II, 269, l. 10, where, in the same context, *uṣūl* is included). The *risālah* was no doubt at times published separately and then carried the title of *al-Bayān ʿan uṣūl al-aḥkām* (I, 404, l. 4, II, 31, ll. 1 f., V, 7, l. 16, VI, 159, l. 19, XV, 59, l. 21, XVIII, 99, l. 15). Here the operative word is *uṣūl* "principles." It is also combined with *laṭīf* to yield such hybrids as *Laṭīf al-qawl min al-bayān ʿan uṣūl al-aḥkām* (I, 276, l. 24, II, 269, l. 10, also *Tahdhīb, Musnad Ibn ʿAbbās*, 770, where *fī* replaces *min*), or *Laṭīf al-bayān ʿan uṣūl al-aḥkām* (III, 12, l. 14, VII, 200, ll. 15 f., X, 29, l. 27), or even *al-Laṭīf ʿan uṣūl aḥkām* (VIII, 79, l. 11). The short title *al-Laṭīf min al-bayān* (II, 222, l. 15) clearly refers to the *risālah*.

The work is widely listed in Ṭabarī biographies. Ibn al-Nadīm, *Fihrist*, has two references. On p. 234, l. 24, we read: "*Kitāb al-Laṭīf* on jurisprudence. It comprises...," while ll. 20 f., states:

> *Kitāb al-Laṭīf* on jurisprudence. It comprises a number of books on the order of juridical works *fī al-mabsūṭ*.[392] The number of books of *Laṭīf* is....

The missing number is supplied by Ibn ʿAsākir, LXXIX f., from al-Farghānī:

> Also complete is *Laṭīf al-qawl fī aḥkām sharāʾiʿ al-Islām.* It represents his legal school with his own preferred views well presented[393] and argued. It consists of eighty-three books, including *Kitāb al-Bayān ʿan uṣūl al-Islām*, which is the (general introductory) essay *(risālah)* of *Laṭīf.*

Al-Farghānī's *ijāzah*, as quoted in *Irshād*, VI, 429, ll. 19 f., ed. Rifāʿī, XVIII, 43, ll. 1 f., has *Kitāb Laṭīf al-qawl wa-khafīfihī fī sharāʾiʿ al-Islām.* This may possibly refer to *Laṭīf* and its condensation *Khafīf.* A translation "A slender and light discussion

392. In the context, this hardly refers to a specific work entitled *al-Mabsūṭ* (such as the one by the Ḥanafite al-Shaybānī). It is probably to be understood as a work on laws well-organized and easily understandable, such as was the case with works given *Mabsūṭ* as a title.

393. Read *jawwadahū*, as is found in Ṣafadī, *Wāfī*, II, 285 f., and Dhahabī, *Nubalāʾ*, XIV, 273, ll. 10 f., who both depend on Ibn ʿAsākir.

of Muslim laws" makes little sense, even if *Irshād* in the passage to be quoted associates the two descriptive terms with the work.

Irshād, VI, 447, l. 11–448, l. 7, ed. Rifāʿī, XVIII, 73, l. 8–74, l. 10, describes *Laṭīf* as follows:

> His book entitled *Kitāb Laṭīf al-qawl fī aḥkām sharāʾiʿ al-Islām.* It is the sum total of his legal school and is relied upon by all its followers. It is among the most valuable of his own books and those of other jurists as well, because it is the best and most instructive of any textbook of a legal school. God willing, this will be obvious to everybody who reads it carefully.
>
> Abū Bakr b. Rāmīk[394] used to say: No better book on a legal school has ever been produced than the *Laṭīf* of Abū Jaʿfar on his legal school.
>
> In the beginning of the work, Ṭabarī much apologized for its brevity. The books of *Laṭīf* exceed those of *Ikhtilāf* by (!) three, namely, *Kitāb al-Libās* "on clothing," *Kitāb Ummahāt al-awlād* "on slave girls giving birth to children by their masters," and *Kitāb al-Shurb* "on drink."[395] *Laṭīf* is one of the very best books. Ṭabarī is unique with respect to it. Nobody should think that by calling it *al-Laṭīf* ("slim" or "subtle"), he meant to imply that it was of small size and its content of light weight. He wished the title to be understood as referring to the subtlety of the ideas expressed in it and the numerous critical discussions *(naẓar)* and indications of reasons (for points of law) it contains. It is about 2,500 folios. It includes a good book on *shurūṭ* (document forms) entitled *Amthilat al-ʿudūl* from *Laṭīf.*[396] The work has

394. Ibn Rāmīk remains to be identified.

395. It is understandable that Ṣafadī, *Wāfī*, 286, ll. 3 f., thought of independent treatises.

396. See above, under *Amthılat al-ʿudūl.* Ḥājjī Khalīfah, ed. Yaltkaya, II, 1046, refers to Ṭabarī's "exhaustive treatment of *shurūṭ* in a book according to the legal principles of al-Shāfiʿī," which was "plagiarized" by Abū Jaʿfar al-Ṭaḥāwī (see Sezgin, *GAS*, I, 441) when he wrote on the subject. Al-Ṭaḥāwī outlived Ṭabarī by only a few years. Wakin, *Documents*, 23, n. 6, doubts the correctness of Ḥājjī Khalīfah's statement. It may be noted that Ibn Kāmil also wrote on *shurūṭ* (see Ibn al-Nadīm, *Fihrist*, 32, l. 14). He would seem to be a more likely candidate for dependence on Ṭabarī. It was, of course, a common topic.

> a *risālah* in which there are discussed the principles of jurisprudence, consensus *(ijmā')*, traditions going back to only one transmitter *(āḥād)*,[397] *marāsīl* traditions,[398] abrogations as they affect the legal situation, and traditions *(akhbār)* and commands and prohibitions which are summary and require explanation *(mujmal)* and which are interpreted *(mufassar)*, the actions of the messengers, (passages with) general and specific (application, *al-khuṣūṣ wa-al-'umūm)*, and independent judgment, the invalidity of expressing unsupported legal opinions *(istiḥsān)*, and other debated matters.

Some information on *Laṭīf* is provided by cross-references in other works of Ṭabarī. It is, however, not always clear which section of *Laṭīf* is precisely aimed at. All the references in *Ikhtilāf* (ed. Kern, II, 29, 79, 83, 90 f., 103, 115) concern certain aspects of *kafālah* "surety bond, bail." This, however, need not mean that they all go back to the same book of *Laṭīf*. The discussion of surety bond in cases of contractual manumission *(mukātabah*, ed. Kern, II, 79, 83) may have had its place in that context. In fact, a *Kitāb al-Rahn* "On surety deposits" and a *Kitāb al-Ghuṣūb (?)* "On laws concerning robbery/rape by force" (ed. Kern, II, 103, 115) are indicated as sources in connection with problems of *kafālah*.[399] The situation with regard to the remaining citations is more ambiguous.

Tafsīr often refers to the introductory *risālah* of *Laṭīf* for problems of the general and specific (*al-khuṣūṣ wa-al-'umūm*),[400] abrogation (*al-nāsikh wa-al-mansūkh*),[401] command and prohibi-

397. See *Tahdhīb, Musnad Ibn 'Abbās*, 770.

398. See above, n. 358.

399. See above, n. 360.

400. *Tafsīr*, I, 276, ll. 24 f., *ad* Qur. 2:69, expressly refers to the subject of *al-'umūm wa-al-khuṣūṣ*. Further references in *Tafsīr*, I, 404, l. 4. *ad* Qur. 2:116, II, 269, l. 10, *ad* Qur. 2:228, V, 7, l. 16, *ad* Qur. 4:24.

401. See *Tafsīr*, II, 222, l. 15, *ad* Qur. 2:221, III, 12, l. 14, *ad* Qur. 2:256 (possibly referring to *al-'umūm wa-al-khuṣūṣ*), VI, 159, l. 19, *ad* Qur. 5:142, VIII, 79, l. 11, *ad* Qur. 6:159. The passage *Tafsīr*, VII, 200, l. 15, *ad* Qur. 75:22 f., referring to the beatific vision, may also have to do with abrogation. Discussions of abrogation, such as, for instance, *Tafsīr*, IX, 135, l. 17, *ad* Qur. 8:16, or X, 58, l. 5, *ad* Qur. 9:6, are quite likely to belong to the introductory *risālah*, even though they occur unassigned.

tion *(al-amr wa-al-nahy)*,[402] and, possibly, consensus *(ijmāʿ)*[403] and analogical reasoning *(qiyās)*.[404] The reference in *Tahdhīb, Musnad Ibn ʿAbbās*, II, 770, concerns the permissibility of acting on the basis of a tradition transmitted from a single authority (see above, n. 397) and thus goes back to the *risālah*.

References to other parts of *Laṭīf* are usually more difficult to assign: *Tafsīr*, I, 37, ll. 13 f., on the "seven verses" of the first sūrah and the inclusion of the *basmalah* in the count (possibly from the *risālah* ?), II, 252, l. 17, *ad* Qur. 2:226, on oaths (or on intercourse), II, 264, ll. 11 f., 289, l. 11, *ad* Qur. 2:228 and 229, on divorce, [II, 352, l. 16, *ad* Qur. 2:238, on prayer, to be dealt with in the planned larger work, above, n. 390], V, 134, l. 13, *ad* Qur. 4:94, on blood money, VI, 44, l. 16, *ad* Qur. 5:3, on the meat of dead animals, VII, 28, l. 31, *ad* Qur. 5:95, on hunting (in the Sacred Territory), VIII, 16, l. 7, *ad* Qur. 6:121, on the meat of properly slaughtered animals (see above, n. 404), XIV, 93, l. 8, *ad* Qur. 16:67, on intoxication, thus probably from *Kitāb al-Shurb*, and XVIII, 68, l. 12, *ad* Qur. 24:9, mentioning *bāb al-liʿān* "the chapter on the *liʿān*[405] formula of divorce."

[*Al-Libās* "On clothing": See *Laṭīf*]

[*Al-Maḥāḍir wa-al-sijillāt* "On records and documents": See *Basīṭ*]

[*Al-Manāsik* "On the pilgrimage ritual": See *Ādāb al-manāsik*]

[*Marātib al-ʿulamāʾ* "On the classification of scholars": See *Basīṭ*]

Al-Mūjaz fī al-uṣūl "A concise treatment of the (legal) principles"

Irshād, VI, 453, l. 3, ed. Rifāʿī, XVIII, 81, ll. 5 f.:

Kitāb al-Mūjaz fī al-uṣūl. He began it with a treatise on

---

402. See *Tafsīr*, X, 29, l. 27, *ad* Qur. 8:66, XVIII, 99, l. 15, *ad* Qur. 24:33 (dealing with contractual manumission). A connection with *al-ʿumūm wa-al-khuṣūṣ* may exist in *Tafsīr*, XV, 59, l. 21, *ad* Qur. 17:33.

403. See *Tafsīr*, II, 31, ll. 1 f., *ad* Qur. 2:158.

404. See *Tafsīr*, VIII, 16, l. 7, *ad* Qur. 6:121, listed in the following paragraph.

405. See *EI*², V, 730–2, s.v. liʿān.

moral behavior *(risālat al-akhlāq)*, but then discontinued (lecturing on it).

The title is also listed in Ṣafadī, *Wāfī*, II, 286, ll. 6 f. We do not know whether Ṭabarī stopped work on it because of old age or because he had other projects to which he gave priority. See also above, *al-Ādar (?) fī al-uṣūl.*

Mukhtaṣar al-farā'iḍ "A short work on the religious duties"

No more than the title is known about this presumptive monograph mentioned in *Irshād*, VI, 453, ll. 1 f., ed. Rifā'ī, XVIII, 81, ll. 3 f.

[*Mukhtaṣar Manāsik al-ḥajj* "A short work (abridgment of the work ?) on the ritual of the pilgrimage": See *Ādāb al-Manāsik*]

[*Mukhtaṣar Ta'rīkh* ... "The short work on the history of...": See *Ta'rīkh*]

[*Musnad Ibn 'Abbās* "The Prophetical traditions transmitted by Ibn 'Abbās": See *Tahdhīb*]

[*Al-Musnad al-mukharraj* "The Prophetical traditions made public".

Ibn 'Asākir mentions *Tahdhīb* but also refers in another place (Ibn 'Asākir, LXXXII) to this title and describes the work as "unfinished and containing all the traditions, sound or unsound, transmitted by the Companions on the authority of the Messenger of God." It is, however, reasonable to assume that the work is identical with *Tahdhīb*, and the title derives from another bibliographical tradition.]

[*Al-Mustarshid* "The seeker of guidance"

Ibn al-Nadīm, *Fihrist*, 235, l. 4, has this title among the works of Ṭabarī. However, as discovered by Goldziher, "Die literarische Thätigkeit," 359, Ṭūsī, *Fihrist*, 187, states that the author of *Mustarshid* was, in fact, not the historian but a certain Abū Ja'far

Muḥammad b. Jarīr b. Rustam al-Ṭabarī.[406]

Sezgin, *GAS*, I, 540, lists *Kitāb al-Mustarshid* on the imāmate of ʿAlī b. Abī Ṭālib as existing in manuscripts and having been printed in al-Najaf (not available to me). He further lists as works of the same Ibn Rustam two more titles, *Dalāʾil al-imāmah* and *Bishārat al-Murtaḍā*. According to Sezgin, the author of all three works probably died in the first quarter of the fourth/tenth century. However, the published text of *Dalāʾil al-imāmah* dealing with the twelve imāms (al-Najaf, 1369/1949) cites al-Muʿāfā among its authorities. This precludes a composition of the work in its present form before the end of the century at the earliest. On the other hand, the text also refers to its supposed author (?) Abū Jaʿfar as having, among his authorities, Sufyān b. Wakīʿ (d. 247/861)[407] — his father, an *isnād* much used by Ṭabarī. Our admittedly defective knowledge of *Dalāʾil al-imāmah* suggests that it was a compilation of post-Ṭabarian date.

The situation with respect to *Bishārat al-Muṣṭafā li-Shīʿat al-Murtaḍā* is equally uncertain. The title was listed erroneously by Brockelmann among Ṭabarī's works (see *GAL*, Suppl. I, 218, no. 7). Modern scholars ascribe its authorship to various unknown individuals. In the edition al-Najaf, 1383/1963, the name of Muḥammad b. Abī al-Qāsim b. Muḥammad b. ʿAlī is found. Ibrāhīm, in the introduction to his Ṭabarī edition (ed. Cairo, I, 20)(see also Ḥūfī, 253) refers to *al-Dharīʿah ilā muṣannafāt al-Shīʿah*, III, 117, for the information that the author's name was Abū Jaʿfar Muḥammad b. ʿAlī b. Muslim al-Ṭabarī al-Āmulī. Aghā Buzurg al-Ṭihrānī, *Ṭabaqāt aʿlām al-Shīʿah*, 242, names Muḥammad b. al-Qāsim b. Muḥammad b. ʿAlī ʿImād al-dīn al-Ṭabarī al-Āmulī. Only one thing is clear: Ṭabarī had nothing to do with the work.

Reference to the present title, *al-Mustarshid fī al-imāmah*, was also made by Najāshī, *Rijāl*, 266. Najāshī informs us that he received the *Mustarshid*, as well as other works by Ibn Rustam, through Aḥmad b. ʿAlī b. Nūḥ—al-Ḥasan b. Ḥamzah al-Ṭabarī, who died in 358/968[9].[408] This *isnād* would seem to confirm that

406. See above, 13.
407. See below, translation, n. 66.
408. See Najāshī, *Rijāl*, 48. Aḥmad b. ʿAlī b. Nūḥ is mentioned in *Rijāl*, 63, but without a date.

Mustarshid was, in fact, written early in the fourth/tenth century. Ibn al-Nadīm might have seen the work and, perhaps, considered it a work of Ṭabarī, provided he had not read it or had mixed up his notes.[409]

See, further, the discussion of *al-Radd ʿalā al-Ḥurqūṣiyyah,* below.]

[Fī al-Qirā'āt "On Qur'ān readings": See *Faṣl]*

[Al-Qiṭ ʿān "The two sections (of *History,* dealing with the dynasties of the Umayyads and ʿAbbāsids)": See *Ta'rīkh]*

Fī al-Qiyās "On analogical reasoning"

This is not a title but a description of the contents of a work on the principle of analogical reasoning which Ṭabarī thought of writing but never did. See *Irshād,* VI, 453, ll. 4–8, ed. Rifāʿī, XVIII, 81, ll. 7–13:

> He wanted to produce a book on analogical reasoning but did not do it. Abū al-Qāsim al-Ḥusayn b. Ḥubaysh, the copyist/bookseller *(al-warrāq),* said: Abū Jaʿfar had asked me to collect for him scholarly works on analogical reasoning, and I collected some thirty books. They remained with him for a short while. As is known, he then discontinued lecturing on traditions, several months before his death. When he returned the books to me, I found red markings he had made in them.[410]

Al-Radd ʿalā dhī al-asfār "A refutation of the one with the tomes (?)"[411]

This is the work which Ṭabarī wrote against the founder of the

409. Old uncertainty as to the authenticity of the one or other title ascribed to Ṭabarī will come up in connection with *Ramy,* below.

410. See above, n. 200.

411. *Asfār* here means presumably "books," and not "travels". It is not clear whether this is an allusion to donkeys carrying books (Qur. 62:5), or what else may be behind it, except that it obviously refers to Dāwūd, perhaps, as the author of the many fascicles mentioned(?).

Ẓāhirite school, Dāwūd b. ʿAlī al-Iṣbahānī (see above, 68 f.). The only circumstantial report available is that preserved in *Irshād*, VI, 450, l. 16–452, l. 11, ed. Rifāʿī, XVIII, 78, l. 1–80, l. 9.[412] It goes back, in part or in its entirety, to Ibn Kāmil:

His book entitled *al-Radd ʿalā dhī al-asfār,* his refutation of Dāwūd b. ʿAlī al-Iṣbahānī. The reason why he wrote this book was as follows: Abū Jaʿfar had been in close contact with Dāwūd b. ʿAlī for a while and had written down many of his books. In his inheritance, we found eighty fascicles from his books in his[413] fine hand. (This material) included the problem debated between Dāwūd b. ʿAlī and the Muʿtazilite Abū Mujālid al-Ḍarīr in Wāsiṭ on going out to al-Muwaffaq when there was dissension about the createdness of the Qurʾān.[414]

Dāwūd b. ʿAlī possessed some knowledge of speculative theology *(naẓar),* traditions, disagreement (among jurists?), and (religious) laws (?, *sunan)* but not very much. He was eloquent and well-spoken and in full control of himself. He had colleagues and students who were strongly inclined to levity and developed a certain approach to employ in discussions *(naẓar),* so as to cut off their adversaries. It sometimes happened that Dāwūd b. ʿAlī debated (with someone about) definite proofs for a legal problem. When he saw that (his adversary)[415] was deficient in traditions, he would steer (the discussion) to it. Or, when he would discuss traditions with him, he would steer him to jurisprudence. Or, when he saw that he was (not?) deficient in both (traditions and jurisprudence, he would steer him) to logical disputation *(jadal).*[416] He himself was deficient in grammar and lexicography, even

412. The title is mentioned in Ṣafadī, *Wāfī,* II, 286, l. 5.

413. See above, n. 259. I understand the pronoun to refer to Ṭabarī, here and in connection with "his inheritance."

414. See above, n. 260. " Going out" could be "switching to the side of, " but this is hardly meant. Probably, on one of his frequent stays in Wāsiṭ, al-Muwaffaq convoked a disputation on the subject.

415. According to a footnote in Rifāʿī's edition, the meaning would be: "saw himself deficient." It seems, however, that Dāwūd was the one who cleverly did the switching to another subject when he noticed that his adversary had a weakness in it.

416. The science of *jadal* is Aristotle's topics.

though he had some acquaintance with these subjects. Abū Jaʿfar, on the other hand, was well informed in every discipline that came up in a debate. To his dying days, he disliked and refrained from behavior that was unbecoming for scholars. He preferred seriousness under all circumstances.

One day, a problem was discussed by Dāwūd b. ʿAlī with Abū Jaʿfar, and the discussion stopped Dāwūd b. ʿAlī (short, so that he was unable to make a retort). His colleagues and students were chagrined, and one of them made acerbic remarks to Abū Jaʿfar. The latter left the meeting and produced the book under discussion. He made public successive portions of it, amounting eventually to a fragment of about one hundred folios. He started with an invocation *(khuṭbah)*, which, however, he did not lecture on *(min ghayr imlā')*. It is among the best and most eloquent of Abū Jaʿfar's works, containing....[417]

After the death of Dāwūd b. ʿAlī, he discontinued (working and lecturing on) the subject. Only as much of the work as was written down by his outstanding *(muqaddamūn)* colleagues and students got into the hands of his[418] colleagues and students, and (the material) was not passed on (to others). Among those who wrote down this book were Abū Isḥāq b. al-Faḍl b. Ḥayyān al-Ḥulwānī — Abū Bakr b. Kāmil said that we studied *(samiʿnāh)* it with him —, Abū al-Ṭayyib al-Jurjānī, Abū ʿAlī al-Ḥasan b. al-Ḥusayn al-Ṣawwāf,[419] Abū al-Faḍl al-ʿAbbās b. Muḥammad (b.?) al-Muḥassin, and others. Al-Ru'āsī, one of Dāwūd b. ʿAlī's outstanding colleagues, said that Dāwūd forbade that man who had made the (offensive) remarks to Abū Jaʿfar to participate in discussions for one year as a punishment for the incident he had caused.

Then, Dāwūd b. ʿAlī's son Muḥammad undertook to respond to Abū Jaʿfar's refutation of his father. He did so in a particularly harsh manner with respect to three problems and took to slandering Abū Jaʿfar. This was the book of his

417. The text as printed defies grammar and sense and requires correction.

418. Possibly, the pronoun refers to (Abū Bakr b.) Dāwūd b. ʿAlī's people, but it seems rather Ṭabarī who is meant.

419. With the exception of al-Ṣawwāf (se above, n. 237), the individuals mentioned still await identification.

addressed to the refutation of Abū Ja'far b. Jarīr.

Abū al-Ḥasan b. al-Mughallis[420] said: Abū Bakr (Muḥammad) b. Dāwūd b. 'Alī said to me: Abū Ja'far's attack on my father was always on my mind. When I came one day to Abū Bakr b. Abī Ḥāmid,[421] Abū Ja'far was there, and Abū Bakr b. Abī Ḥāmid said to him: This is Abū Bakr Muḥammad b. Dāwūd b. 'Alī al-Iṣbahānī. Being aware of my position (in scholarship), Abū Ja'far welcomed me cordially when he saw me. He started to heap praise upon my father and complimented me in a manner that completely disarmed me.

[*Al-Radd 'alā al-Ḥurqūṣiyyah* "A refutation of the Ḥurqūṣiyyah"

This title was brought to the attention of scholars by L. Massignon in a particularly impenetrable footnote of his immortal *Passion*.[422] Massignon's source appears to have been *Tabṣirat al-'awāmm* of Abū Turāb Murtaḍā b. al-Dā'ī,[423] which unfortunately has remained inaccessible to me. Without further specifying his sources, Massignon assumed that Ḥurqūṣiyyah referred to a certain tribal group, Zuhayr b. Ḥurqūṣ, as ancestors of Ibn Ḥanbal. According to Sezgin, *GAS*, I, 328, n. 2, the prominent early Khārijite Ḥurqūṣ b. Zuhayr[424] might be meant. Brockelmann, *GAL*, Suppl. I, 218, furthered the discussion by adducing Najāshī, *Rijāl*.[425] There, it is stated expressly that a non-Shī'ah (*'āmmī*) Abū Ja'far Muḥammad b. Jarīr al-Ṭabarī was the author of *al-Radd 'alā al-Ḥurqūṣiyyah*, in which he mentioned the recensions (of the reports) on the Day of the Pool (= Ghadīr Khumm). Al-Najāshī's authorities were Abū Isḥāq Ibrāhīm b. Makhlad (al-Bāqarjī) — his father (Makhlad b. Ja'far). Both belonged, it seems, to Ṭabarī's circle (see above, n. 252). Thus, the work could indeed have been by Ṭabarī. It may, however, be noted that Makhlad became "confused" in his later years. His son persuaded him to claim (being

420. See above, n. 199.

421. Unidentified.

422. See Massignon, *Passion*², III, 154, n. 5, English trans., III, 142 n. 140.

423. See Brockelmann, *GAL*, Suppl. I, 711.

424. See *EI*², III, 582 f., s. v.

425. See Najāshī, *Rijāl*, 225 (= 246 in the later edition cited by Sezgin, I, 328, n.2).

an authorized transmitter of?) a number of works, among them Ṭabarī's *History*, while, in reality, he just relied upon purchased copies. This casts doubt also on his reliability with respect to *al-Radd ʿalā al-Ḥurqūṣiyyah* but not sufficiently so as to justify rejecting the attribution to Ṭabarī out of hand.

The connection with Ghadīr Khumm suggests that Ḥurqūṣiyyah could have served as a nickname for Abū Bakr b. Abī Dāwūd al-Sijistānī (above, nn. 229 and, especially, 326), but no evidence for this assumption is available. For the time being, it is not implausible to suggest that *al-Radd ʿalā al-Ḥurqūṣiyyah* was part of *Faḍāʾil.]*

Fī al-Radd ʿalā Ibn ʿAbd al-Ḥakam ʿalā Mālik "A refutation of Ibn ʿAbd al-Ḥakam('s statement on certain views of) Mālik"[426]

Irshād, VI, 453, ll. 2 f., ed. Rifāʿī, XVIII, 55, ll. 3–5, lists this title (which, however, was not a real title), adding that the work "did not reach his students and colleagues." *Irshād*, VI, 434, ll. 1–4, ed. Rifāʿī, XVIII, 55, ll. 1–4, explains further, apparently relying on Ibn Kāmil:

> We have heard that he was asked in al-Fusṭāṭ to refute Mālik on some point, and he did so in connection with something that Ibn ʿAbd al-Ḥakam had discussed. (Ṭabarī's) work has not come into our hands. Perhaps it was one of the things that the adversaries *(al-khuṣūm)* prevented from being circulated *(nashr)*.

It is not quite clear who the "adversaries" were and why there was opposition to the work. The Mālikites may have objected to it, even though Ibn ʿAbd al-Ḥakam would not have attacked Mālik in an unseemly manner, and Ṭabarī himself is unlikely to have attacked Ibn ʿAbd al-Ḥakam (but may have been critical of Mālik).[427]

Since the work originated during Ṭabarī's stay in Egypt and presumably was made public at the time, it can claim to be his earliest publication of which we have notice, seeing that the earliest publication dates of *Laṭīf* and *Ikhtilāf* cannot be

426. The member of the Ibn ʿAbd al-Ḥakam family meant here is no doubt Muḥammad b. ʿAbdallāh (above, n. 104).

427. The Ḥanbalites are certainly not meant in this context.

precisely established.

[Al-Ramy bi-al-nushshāb "On arrow shooting"

Irshād, VI, 453, ll. 8–11, ed. Rifāʿī, XVIII, 81, ll. 14–18, declared the work to be supposititious:

> ʿAbd al-ʿAzīz b. Muḥammad said: A small book on arrow shooting has come into my possession. I know of nobody who studied it with him, nor of anybody to record and confirm his authorship or attribute it to him. I am afraid that it is wrongly ascribed to him.

If it was a legal treatise, Ṭabarī might have been the author, since the subject of shooting was of great concern to jurists.[428] However, Ṭabarī's biographer ʿAbd al-ʿAzīz b. Muḥammad knew the contents of the work, and we do not. Thus, we ought to accept his opinion. If it was a technical treatise on archery, Ṭabarī's authorship is indeed most unlikely. The assumption of a confusion with *Kitāb al-Wāḍiḥ fī al-ramy bi-al-nushshāb* by a certain ʿAbd al-Raḥmān b. Aḥmad al-Ṭabarī seems farfetched, even if this author did not live in the seventh/thirteenth century but in or before the historian's time.[429]

[Ṣalāt al-khawf "The prayer of fear": See *Basīṭ]*

Ṣarīḥ al-sunnah "The essence of orthodox Muslim belief"

The work was also known as Ṭabarī's "Creed" *(al-ʿAqīdah,* see above, 85) and, it seems mistakenly, as *Sharḥ al-sunnah* "Explanation of...." Ibn ʿAsākir, LXXXII, refers to it as "a slender *(laṭīf)* book, in which Ṭabarī explained his (theological) views *(madhhabahū)* and religious theory and practice in the service of God

---

428. Among others, Muḥammad b. ʿAbdallāh b. ʿAbd al- Ḥakam wrote a book on (horse) racing and shooting; see Ibn Farḥūn, *Dībāj*, 232. Ṭabarī himself paid attention to the prowess in archery of some early Muslims; see *Dhayl*, III, 2301, 2312, 2362, ed. Cairo, XI, 497, 506, 543.

429. See Brockelmann, GAL^2, I, 149, no. 8, Suppl. I, 906. The work is preserved in a number of manuscripts. It was quoted extensively by Ibn Qayyim al-Jawziyyah, *Furūsiyyah*, 110 ff.; its authorities, as quoted in Ibn Qayyim al-Jawziyyah, cannot easily be identified for dating purposes.

(*wa-mā yadīnu Allāha bihī*)."[430] *Irshād*, VI, 452, ll. 14–16, ed. Rifāʿī, XVIII, 80, ll. 13–15, echoes this description with only slight differences: "Also, his treatise known as *Kitāb Ṣarīḥ al-sunnah* in several folios. He mentioned in it his (theological) views, religious theory and practice, and beliefs."

See Brockelmann, *GAL*, Suppl. I, 218, no. 6, and Sezgin, *GAS*, I, 328, nos. 6 and 8. *Ṣarīḥ* was edited on the basis of an Istanbul manuscript and translated by D. Sourdel (see Bibliography, under *Ṣarīḥ*).

[*Al-Ṣalāh* "On prayer": See *Basīṭ*]

[*Al-Sariqah* "On theft": See *Laṭif*]

[*Sharḥ al-sunnah* "An explanation of orthodox Muslim belief": See *Ṣarīḥ*]

[*Al-Shudhūr* is a title listed by Ḥājjī Khalīfah, ed. Yaltkaya, 1429, who ascribed it to the historian whom he calls a Ḥanbalite (!), no doubt a meaningless misattribution]

[*Al-Shurb* "On drink": See *Laṭīf*]

[*Al-Shurūṭ* "On document forms": See *Basīṭ* and *Laṭīf* (above, n. 396)]

Tabṣīr ulī al-nuhā wa-maʿālim al-hudā "An instruction for the intelligent and directions toward right guidance"

This is the title as it appears in the Escorial manuscript, 1514, fols. 81a–104b. Elsewhere, it is plain *Tabṣīr*, at times enlarged with *fī uṣūl al-dīn* or *fī maʿālim al-dīn*.

Ibn ʿAsākir, LXXX, quotes al-Farghānī:

430. "*Allāha*" also appears in the manuscript used for the edition of *Ṣarīḥ*, text, 199, n. 1. *Irshād* may have omitted it for simplification. Note further that Dhahabī, *Nubalāʾ*, XIV, 274, l. 4, reads *Sharḥ al-sunnah* following Ibn ʿAsākir. Ṣafadī, *Wāfī*, II, 286, l. 6, has *Ṣarīḥ al-sunnah*.

> Also completed is his book entitled *al-Tabṣīr,* a treatise *(risālah)* addressed to the inhabitants of Āmul in Ṭabaristān. He comments in it on the principles of the religion of Islam *(uṣūl al-dīn),* which he has been following *(yataqallad).*[431]

Irshād, VI, 452, ll. 10–14, ed. Rifāʿī, XVIII, 80, ll. 10–13, shows an obviously incorrect *al-Baṣīr:*

> Among Abū Jaʿfar's writings is his treatise entitled *al-Baṣīr fī maʿālim al-dīn* addressed to the people of Ṭabaristān concerning the disagreement that had arisen among them on (matters such as the identity or non-identity of) name and thing named *(al-ism wa-al-musammā)*[432] and the doctrines *(madhāhib)* of innovators.[433] It is about thirty folios.

The work is partly preserved in the mentioned Escorial manuscript;[434] see Brockelmann, *GAL,* I, 143, no. 2, Suppl. I, 218, no. 5, and Sezgin, *GAS,* I, 328, no. 5. Attention was first drawn to it in 1901 by Becker, "Ṭabarī's sogenannte Catechesis Mahometana." In the introduction, Ṭabarī says that the people of Ṭabaristān had asked him to write such a treatise because of the large number of confusing, sectarian, and divisive views that were causing trouble among them.

Without indicating a title, Ibn Ḥazm quotes *Tabṣīr,* fol. 85b, for

431. *Yataqallad* is doing the opposite of what innovators do. Dhahabī, *Nubalāʾ,* XIV, 273, ll. 14 f., has a shortened version of Ibn ʿAsākir. Both Ṣafadī, *Wāfī,* II, 286, l. 7, and Subkī, *Ṭabaqāt,* III, 121, l. 11, list the title of the work as *Kitāb al-Tabṣīr fī uṣūl al-dīn.*

432. This intensively discussed problem of speculative theology was considered a sort of touchstone showing whether religious scholars had the correct attitude. They were strongly warned against paying attention to it. Ṭabarī's Egyptian authority Yūnus b. ʿAbd al-Aʿlā, for instance, is supposed to have said: "I heard al-Shāfiʿī say: When you hear someone say that the name is different from the thing named or the name is identical with the thing named, testify against him (and say) that he is a Mutakallim and has no religion ...." See Subkī, *Ṭabaqāt,* II, 174. Ṭabarī himself refers to the *ism-musammā* problem in the introduction of *Tabṣīr* (fol. 82b) among the abominable indications of unbelief current at the time in Ṭabaristān. See also *Ṣarīḥ,* text, 198, trans., 192.

433. The "innovators" were mainly the speculative theologians, the Qadariyyah/Jahmiyyah. Their scandalous heretical views were gaining the upper hand in the region, which also suffered under the dominance of incompetent troublemakers (*tara"us al-ruwaybiḍah,* "dregs of the population" [see trans., Vol. XXXII, 55, n. 177], an allusion to the Shīʿite sectarian rulers?); see *Tabṣīr,* fol. 82b.

434. I wish to thank the authorities of the Biblioteca de El Escorial for providing me with a microfilm of the work.

the need of Muslims at an early age to know about names and attributes in order to avoid being branded as unbelievers.[435]

Dhahabī, *Nubalā'*, XIV, 279, l. 6–280, l. 4, and *'Uluww*, 150 f., has a somewhat shortened and mangled quotation from the chapter on divine attributes known through statements of the Qur'ān and the *ḥadīth*. It appears on fol. 87b of the Escorial manuscript.

[*Al-Tafsīr* "Qur'ān commentary": See *Jāmi' al-bayān*]

[*Al-Ṭahārah* "On ritual purity ": See *Basīṭ*]

Tahdhīb al-āthār wa-tafṣīl ma'ānī al-thābit 'an Rasūl Allāh min al-akhbār"An improved treatment and detailed discussion of the traditions established as going back to the Messenger of God"

Ṭabarī's most ambitious work on traditions is more commonly referred to as *Tahdhīb al-āthār* or, simply, *al-Tahdhīb*.[436] It is mentioned by all Ṭabarī biographers. It remained unfinished but apparently began to circulate rather early in Ṭabarī's career. The fact that *Laṭīf* is quoted in it does not help very much to fix the time of the first appearance of parts of it.[437] *Tahdhīb* was possibly meant to rival Ibn Ḥanbal's *Musnad*. In fact, though, it was much more than a mere collection of traditions. Its singular conception was to provide an exhaustive and penetrating analysis of the philological and legal implications of each *ḥadīth* mentioned and to discuss its meaning as well as its significance for religious practice and theory. Thus, it contains what amounts to monographs on a number of important topics.

Al-Farghānī's *ijāzah* as quoted in *Irshād*, VI, 426, l. 20–427, l. 1, ed. Rifā'ī, XVIII, 45, ll. 2 f., mentions that he studied the Prophetical traditions transmitted *(musnad)* by the Ten[438] and by Ibn 'Abbās down to the traditions on the Prophet's heavenly journey *(mi'rāj)* from the *Kitāb al-Tahdhīb*.

It was presumably Ibn Kāmil who used the long title of the

---

435. See Ibn Ḥazm, *Fisal*, IV, 35, as mentioned by van Ess, *Erkenntnislehre*, 49.
436. See also above, *al-Musnad al-mukharraj*.
437. See above, 117.
438. For the Blessed Ten, the ten old Muslims who were assured of Paradise, see EI^2, I, 693, s. v. al-'ashara al-mubashshara.

work. According to *Irshād*, VI, 448, ll. 12–18, ed. Rifāʿī, XVIII, 74, l. 17–75, l. 6, he said:

> *Kitāb Tahdhīb al-āthār wa-tafṣīl al-thābit ʿan Rasūl Allāh min al-akhbār.* It is a work, the like of which it would be difficult for any other scholar to produce and complete. Abū Bakr b. Kāmil said: After Abū Jaʿfar's death, I have not seen anyone who possessed more religious knowledge, knew more about the works of religious scholars and the disagreements of jurists, and had a greater command of all scholarly disciplines. (I know) because I tried hard to produce a work on the Prophetical traditions transmitted (*musnad*) by ʿAbdallāh b. Masʿūd in the way Abū Jaʿfar had done (with the *musnads*) of others. I was unable to do a good job, and it did not come out right.

Ibn al-Nadīm, *Fihrist*, 235, ll. 4 f., states his intention to mention the published parts of the unfinished *Tahdhīb*, but the text contains a blank space.

TB, II, 163, ll. 10 f., called Ṭabarī's unfinished work entitled *Tahdhīb al-āthār* unequaled in the treatment of its subject, as far as he knew. His remark was quoted by nearly all later biographers.[439]

Ibn ʿAsākir, LXXX f., quotes al-Farghānī at length to bring out the importance of the work:

> He started on the composition of *Tahdhīb al-āthār*. It is one of his most remarkable works. He began with the traditions of Abū Bakr al-Ṣiddīq that in his opinion[440] were transmitted with sound chains of transmitters. He discussed each one of them with their weaknesses (*ʿilal*),[441] their recensions, and their contents as to law, the practice of the Prophet

439. For instance, Samʿānī, *Ansāb*, IX, 41; Ibn al-Jawzī, *Muntaẓam*, VI, 171; *Irshād*, VI, 424, l. 12, ed. Rifāʿī, XVIII, 41, ll. 14 f.; Safadī, *Wāfī*, II, 285; Ibn al-Jazarī, *Ghāya*, II, 107; Dhahabī, *Nubalāʾ*, XIV, 270, ll. 1 f.; Subkī, *Ṭabaqāt*, III, 22, ll. 9 f.; Ibn Kathīr, *Bidāyah*, XI, 145; Ibn Taghrībirdī, *Nujūm*, III, 205, ll. 13 f.

440. Read *ʿindahū*, as in the quotation from Ibn ʿAsākir in Subkī, *Ṭabaqāt*, III, 121, ll. 12–16.

441. As understood in *Tahdhīb*, *ʿilal* are the illnesses, affecting practically exclusively the chains of transmitters, which are potential reasons for considering a given tradition as "sick (*saqīm*)."

(sunan), and the disagreements and arguments of scholars. (He also discussed) their contents with respect to meanings *(maʿānī)* and their rare words, and (he reported) the attacks of heretics on them and refuted them and explained the corruptness of their attacks. He made public of the work the Prophetical traditions transmitted by the Blessed Ten, the people of the House, and the *mawlā*s as well as a large fragment of Prophetical traditions transmitted by Ibn ʿAbbās. It was his intention to report every last sound tradition of the Messenger of God and discuss them all in the way he had started, so that nobody would ever be able to attack any part of the knowledge of the Messenger of God. He also intended to report all that is needed by religious scholars, as he had done in *Tafsīr.* Thus, (if he had been able to complete the work), he would have dealt with the (entire) science of the religious law *(al-sharīʿah)* on the basis of the Qurʾān and the traditions and practice of the Prophet *(sunan)*. He died before the completion of the work. Thereafter, there was nobody to interpret and discuss a single one of those traditions the way he had done.

After repeating most of this information, Dhahabī, *Nubalāʾ*, XIV, 273, ll. 15–20, expressed what appears to be his personal opinion: "If the work had been completed as planned, it would have to come to a hundred volumes." This, of course, was an offhand guess, but it is hardly an exaggeration.

See Brockelmann, *GAL*, I, 143, Suppl. I, 217 f., and Sezgin, *GAS*, I, 327. The preserved fragments of the *Musnads* of ʿAlī and ʿAbdallāh b. al-ʿAbbās were published in three volumes in 1982 by Maḥmūd M. Shākir. The *Musnad* of ʿUmar b. al-Khaṭṭāb remains to be published.

Al-Taʾrīkh "The History"

Because of its fame, the work was commonly referred to simply as Ṭabarī's *History.* Its most authentic title is the one indicated by Ṭabarī himself in the colophon of one of the manuscripts. It is *Mukhtaṣar taʾrīkh al-rusul wa-al-mulūk wa-al-khulafāʾ* "The short work on the history of messengers, kings, and caliphs."[442] Similarly, Ṭabarī refers to it as *Mukhtaṣar ta'rīkh al-rusul wa-al-mulūk.*[443] It seems that Ṭabarī had a predilection for "short work" as an expression of modesty and an indication that a subject required a much longer treatment than the one it was receiving from him.

We also find titles such as "History of the messengers, prophets, kings, and caliphs" (al-Farghānī) or "History of nations and kings" *(TB)*, as well as "History of the messengers and kings" expanded to "and their historical record and all those who lived in the time of each one of them" (Ibn Kāmil).[444] Scribes who copied the work for a patron presumably often preferred some impressive title to put on the title page, but the simple *Ta'rīkh* really needed no amplification. There could never be any doubt as to which work was meant.

According to *Irshād*, VI, 427, ll. 17 f., ed. Rifā'ī, XVIII, 44, ll. 16–18, al-Farghānī referred in his *ijāzah* to:

> *Kitāb al-Rusul wa-al-anbiyā' wa-al-mulūk wa-al-khulafā'* and the two sections *(al–qiṭ'ān,* on the Umayyads and 'Abbāsids) of the work. However, I did not study it (with Ṭabarī directly) but used it by (written) permission *(ijāzah).*

Ibn Kāmil's full and perceptive description of the work appears in *Irshād*, VI, 443, l. 17–445, l. 6, ed. Rifā'ī, XVIII, 68, l. 6–70, l. 9:

> Among his works is his great *History* entitled *Ta'rīkh al-rusul wa-al-mulūk wa-akhbāruhum wa-man kān fī zaman kull wāḥid minhum.* He began with an invocation *(khuṭbah)* that (briefly) summarizes the significant aspects of its contents *(ma'ānī).*[445] He then discussed what time is and the du-

442. See translation below, Vol. XXXVIII, p. xvii.

443. See *Dhayl*, III, 2358, ed. Cairo, XI, 540.

444. A rather similar title appears in a Leiden manuscript and seemed to Kosegarten, the first editor of large portions of *History*, who used a Berlin manuscript, to be the authoritative title of the work: *Ta'rīkh al-mulūk wa-akhbāruhum* (Kosegarten: *a'māruhum!) wa-mawālid* (K. *wa-mawālīd) al-rusul wa-anbā'uhum wa-al-kā'in alladhī* (K. deest) *kān fī zaman kull wāḥid minhum.* See Hamaker, *Specimen*, 19, and Kosegarten, I, IV and 3.

445. See above, n. 336. The general accuracy of Ibn Kāmil's analysis of the con-

ration in time (of the world) according to the divergent opinions of the Companions and others and the nations opposed to our view on the subject. A chapter like this can be found only in his work.[446]

Abū al-Ḥasan ʿAbdallāh b. Aḥmad b. Muḥammad b. al-Mughallis, the jurist,[447] said: Of all the scholars we have ever seen, he possessed the best understanding and had the greatest concern for knowledge and research. Because of his concern with scholarly research, he had his books all laid out on one side of his residence,[448] then went through them for the first (time) one by one, in the process carrying them to the other side, until he was through with them; then he studied them again and returned them to their original place.[449] (Ibn al-Mughallis) said one day: Nobody has ever done what Abū Jaʿfar did with respect to writing and giving a full presentation of history *(ta'rīkh al-zamān)*. (Ibn Kāmil) continued: Abū al-Ḥasan b. al-Mughallis said to me one day while we were talking about scholarship and the excellence of scholars: By God! I do think that Abū Jaʿfar al-Ṭabarī forgot as much of what he knew by heart till his death as so-and-so—naming an important scholar—ever knew by heart all his life.

Abū Jaʿfar continued in *History* with the discussion of the creation of time as days and nights and (argued) that God alone created them. He mentioned the first (thing) that was created, namely, the Pen, as well as everything (created) thereafter one by one according to the traditions *(āthār)* on the subject and the different opinions of scholars about it. He then mentioned Adam and Eve and the accursed Iblīs as well as Adam's descent (fall to earth). He continued with brief histories of each prophet, messenger, and king, down to

tents of *History* can easily be verified by the reader of this translation.

446. The correct wording of the text cannot easily be established, but there is no doubt about its meaning.

447. On Ibn Mughallis, see above, n. 199. Although this paragraph refers to *History* only in the second of its three statements, it is obvious that all of it goes back to Ibn Kāmil and, presumably, his Ṭabarī bibliography.

448. Ed. Rifāʿī suggests to read *ḥā'ir* with the putative meaning of "quiet (corner)," but this seems dubious. *Ḥāratihī* in the text may have its ordinary meaning of "residential quarter of a town" (and hence, residence ?).

449. See above, n. 199.

(the time of) our Prophet, including also the history of minor successor kings *(mulūk al-ṭawā'if)* and the kings of the Persians and the Rūm. He then mentioned the birth of the Messenger of God, his genealogy, his male and female ancestors, his children, his wives, (the origin of) his Prophetical mission, his raids and expeditions, and the situation of his Companions. Then he mentioned the rightly guided caliphs after (the Prophet's death). He continued with the history of the Umayyads and the ʿAbbāsids in two sections, one devoted to the Umayyads, and the other to the ʿAbbāsids, with the historical comments he made in *History (wa-mā sharaḥahū fī Kitāb al-Ta'rīkh)*. This (portion of *History)* was made public by way of *ijāzah* down to the year 294/906[7]. He did not continue with the subsequent years, because the reign of al-Muqtadir (which extended throughout Ṭabarī's remaining years) fell into them. He had been asked to comment on the two sections (dealing with the Umayyads and the ʿAbbāsids), and he complied and called (this portion of *History*) the "two sections (*at-qiṭʿān*)."

This work is of unique excellence and distinction in the world. It brings together many religious and worldly disciplines. It is about five thousand folios.

Ibn al-Nadīm, *Fihrist*, 234, l. 24–235, l. 2, adds information on continuations of *History* and ends with a remarkable statement on the necessary qualifications for writing history:

Kitāb al-Ta'rīkh, with the two sections (on the Umayyads and the ʿAbbāsids). He finished dictating it in 302/915 and stopped there.

A number of people have abridged the work and omitted the *isnāds*, among them a man known as Muḥammad b. Sulaymān al-Hāshimī,[450] and another one, a secretary known as.... Among Mosulites, Abū al-Ḥusayn al-Shimshāṭī al-Muʿallim[451] and a man known as al-Salīl b. Aḥmad.[452] A

---

450. Unidentified.

451. Possibly, Abū al-Ḥasan ʿAlī b. Muḥammad al-ʿAdawī al-Shimshāṭī, a teacher of Nāṣir al-dawlah's son Abū Taghlib? See Ibn al-Nadīm, *Fihrist*, 154, ll. 22–28, and the index of Dodge's translation, II, 1099 f.

452. Possibly, the informant of the Ibn Jinnī mentioned in Yāqūt, *Muʿjam*, II,

> number of people have made additions covering the period from where it ends to our time. Their additions are not reliable, because (the men who wrote them) were not connected with the government *(dawlah)*, nor did they have knowledge.[453]

Since the work was so well known, many biographers felt no need to say much about it. *TB*, II, 163, l. 9, merely mentions Ṭabarī's famous work, *Ta'rīkh al-umam wa-al-mulūk*. As in the case of *Tahdhīb*, *TB* was quoted by most later biographers. This was also the title cited by Ḥājjī Khalīfah, ed. Yaltkaya, I, 297, and from there, it became known in seventeenth-century Europe through d'Herbelot, *Bibliothèque*, 866b, s. v. Tarikh AlThabari; see below, 138 f.

Ibn 'Asākir, LXXIX, used as usual by Dhahabī, *Nubalā'*, XIV, 273, l. 8, merely mentions as completed his "*Ta'rīkh* that extends down to Ṭabarī's own age." And Qifṭī, *Inbāh*, III, 89, l. 6, described the *Kitāb al-Ta'rīkh* as the greatest work in its field. In another work, al-Qifṭī has a passage on the continuators of Ṭabarī. It was inserted in his biography of Thābit b. Sinān and was, perhaps, derived from al-Qifṭī's monograph on Ṭabarī.[454]

More information on *History* will be found in the following pages and, of course, in all the volumes of this translation.

[*Ta'rīkh al-rijāl* "The history of personalities": See *Dhayl*]

[*Tartīb al-'ulamā'* "The classification of scholars": See *Ādāb al-nufūs* and *Basīṭ*]

[*Ummahāt al-awlād* "On slave girls giving birth to children by their masters": See *Laṭīf*]

[*Al-Waṣāyā* "On last wills": See *Basīṭ*]

[*Al-Zakāh* "On charity taxes": See *Basīṭ*]

490, l. 3, as suggested in the index of Dodge's translation of *Fihrist*.

453. In other words, they were neither government officials nor scholars (of religion and law) and thus had no access to important historical information and no understanding of the processes of history. See also below, n. 455.

454. See Rosenthal, *Muslim Historiography*², 81–83.

The *History* and Its English Translation

The History *in Islam and the West*

The preceding long list of Ṭabarī's writings contains very few titles devoted predominantly to historical or biographical research, and a perusal of the biographical sketch presented here makes it quite clear that the outward course of his life was comparatively little influenced by his occupation with history. These are incontrovertible facts. Even the availability of more bibliographical information than we have is unlikely to refute them. Ṭabarī's importance as a scholar in his time and his role as a participant in contemporary affairs were the result of his scholarly activities in the legal and religious sphere. Yet, the outstanding significance of *History* was realized while he was still alive. It was welcomed by the students who heard Ṭabarī lecture on it or received his *ijāzah* to study and transmit it. They went on to use it in their own works, as was done, for instance, by the author of *Aghānī* (see above, n. 127). Its uniqueness was praised by a contemporary such as Ibn al-Mughallis (see above, p. 132). A writer on world history writing in a rather different tradition, al-Mas'ūdī, was acquainted with Ṭabarī as an important historian. About a generation after Ṭabarī's death, he spoke of *History* as "a work superior to all other historical works because of the abundant information it contains" and declared it "an extremely useful work," for, he reasoned, Ṭabarī's position as the leading jurist and religious scholar of his time made it possible for him to know all there was to know about history.[455]

455. See Mas'ūdī, *Murūj*, I, 15 f., ed. Pellat, I, 15; Rosenthal, *Muslim Historiography*^{2}, 508. For government experience as a necessity for the historian, see

Ṭabarī became known primarily by his *History.* It was, as M. J. de Goeje put it, the great work "whose fame has never faded from his own day to ours."[456] His biographers would, of course, not fail to praise his other accomplishments, and they mention those in the field of history as merely one aspect of his work and not the first and foremost;[457] but for Muslims, he was the historian of Islam. When it was necessary to distinguish him from other Ṭabarīs, it was as Ṭabarī the historian.

As was already suggested by O. Loth,[458] the explanation for this development is not far to seek. Ṭabarī's works on jurisprudence and *ḥadīth* continued to be admired, and his Qur'ānic scholarship set an enduring and always respected standard of excellence. Yet, works on law and religion always were at the center of an enormous literary activity, and no matter how traditional much of it was or seemed to be, new tendencies and concerns constantly left their changing imprint on them. *History,* on the other hand, was, in accordance with the basic character of Muslim historiography, never really superseded. It remained the unique source for the period it covered, even when other sources for it were still available. Later historians constantly used Ṭabarī's work, at first directly, but then, in the course of time, usually indirectly through other histories such as the one of Ibn al-Athīr. The new works offered much of Ṭabarī's information in a shortened form and, naturally, added much subsequent history. Thus, they were easier to handle and had the advantage of being of greater interest for the ma-

---

above, n. 453. Al-Mas'ūdī's relationship with Ṭabarī is problematic. He once mentioned Ṭabarī as his oral authority (Mas'ūdī, *Tanbīh,* 267). Thus, it would seem that he knew him personally(?). See also Khalidi, *Islamic Historiography,* 148. *Murūj* (IV, 145, ed. Pellat, II, 145) expressly refers to *History* and elsewhere mentions Ṭabarī as a source of historical information *(Murūj,* V, 8, 40, ed. Pellat, II, 184, 202). None of the references can, however, be traced to *History.* Could al-Mas'ūdī have quoted from memory what he had heard long ago in Ṭabarī's lectures?

456. See de Goeje in the ninth edition of the *Encyclopaedia Britannica,* XXIII, 3b (Edinburgh, 1888). I owe this reference to Muth's work.

457. *Irshād,* VI, 423, ed. Rifā'ī, XVIII, 40, introduces Ṭabarī as "a *ḥadīth* scholar, jurist, Qur'ān reader, and historian" (in this order). Dhahabī, *'Ibar,* II, 146, mentions *Tafsīr* first, and then *Ta'rīkh.* On the other hand, Qifṭī, *Muḥammadūn,* 263 f., speaks of "the author of the famous *History* and *Tafsīr."* Of course, not much can be made of this.

458. See Loth, "Ṭabarī's Korancommentar," 590. Loth says that (in contrast to *Tafsīr*), *History* had no competitors. This, however, rather oversimplifies the situation.

jority of readers who wanted to learn about events close to their own times. Some, if not many, later historians continued to use Ṭabarī and even seek out earlier sources, but manuscripts became increasingly difficult to find. Ibn Khaldūn copied a document at first from Ibn al-Athīr and was only later able to collate the text as it appears in Ṭabarī.[459] This was more like the exception that confirmed the general rule. Ṭabarī always remained the historian of Islam, but his original work receded from general view.

Early translations into Persian and Turkish languages further attest to the fame of *History*. They show, however, a similar tendency toward adaptations of the original text. According to our philological understanding of the term, they could hardly be called translations. A Turkish translation, incidentally, was published already in 1844 and served as a source for some studies by contemporary Western scholars.

The history of the European acquaintance with Ṭabarī's *History* in a way constituted a reversal of the chronological process. The Arabic and Muslim works which attracted the curiosity of early Orientalists were generally those of more recent dates and, in particular, those of current use in the Near East. The historians whose works were introduced in seventeenth-century Europe, such as the histories of al-Makīn and Abū al-Fidā', were acquainted with Ṭabarī's work as a rule only at second or third hand.[460] Only later did the search for the original text start. It was a slow process, and it began in earnest only at the end of the eighteenth century. After the publication of the Leiden edition in the last quarter of the nineteenth century, the stage was reached where the later excerptors and adapters of Ṭabarī in Arabic as well as Persian and Turkish were disregarded by modern historians, except, of course, for whatever information not found in Ṭabarī they were able to contribute.

The name of Ṭabarī the historian had, however, been long familiar in the West. B. d'Herbelot (1625–95), whose *Bibliothèque Orientale* was published posthumously in 1697, featured a substantial article on "Thabari" (*Bibliothèque*, 1014). He started out by describing him as "the most famous of all Ṭabarīs on account

459. See Ibn Khaldūn, *Muqaddimah*, II, 139, n. 751.
460. For instance, L. Marracci knew *History* through al-Makīn. See Nallino, "Le fonti arabe," II, 96, n. 1. Marracci did not know *Tafsīr*, of course.

of the general *History* from the creation of the world to the time in which he lived that was published by him." The special article he devoted to *History* (*Bibliothèque,* 866 f.) gives as good a summary of the work's history as could be found in the West until more than a century had passed. It deserves to be quoted here in full on account of its historical interest. Practically all of its contents was derived by d'Herbelot from the great bibliographical work of Ḥājjī Khalīfah (1609–57), whose lifetime overlapped with his own.[461]

> TARIKH AlThabari. C'est le titre d'une Histoire fort celebre, qui passe pour le fondement des autres Histoires Musulmannes. Elle a été composée par Abou Giafar Mohammed Ben Gioraïr, natif du Thabarestan, qui mourut l'an 310. de l'hegire. Elle commence à la Creation du Monde, & finit en l'an 300.[462] de l'hegire. Elle porte encore le titre particulier de ,Tarikh alomam v almolouk. Elle est aussi souvent citée sous le titre de ,Tarikh Giafari, & les Persans la nomment aussi ,Tarikh pesser Gioraïr, l'Histoire du fils de Gioraïr.
>
> Ebn AlGiouzi écrit, que cette Histoire dans son Original contient plusieurs volumes, & que l'Edition que nous avons entre les mains n'en est qu'un Abbregé, & Ebn AlSobki rapporte dans ses Thabacat, que Thabari ayant demandé à ses amis, s'ils prendroient plaisir à lire une Histoire de tous ce qui étoit arrivé dans le Monde jusqu'à son temps, ils luy répondirent, qu'ils la liroient volontiers s'il étoit possible de la trouver, & que cet Auteur leur ayant dit, qu'il avoit compilé trente mille feüilles sur cette matière, ses amis luy repliquerent, que tout le temps de leur vie ne suffiroit pas pour les lire. Sur cecy, Thabari leur dit, qu'il l'abbregeroit autant qu'il pourroit, & c'est cet Abbregé, dit ,Sobki, qui nous est resté entre les mains.
>
> Cet Abbregé a été traduit en Langue Persienne par Abou A'li Mohammed AlIâli,[463] Vizir des Sultans Samanides, du

461. D'Herbelot used Galland's manuscript of Ḥājjī Khalīfah. See Laurens, *Barthélemi d'Herbelot,* 17. For his indirect use of Ṭabarī, see Laurens, 58. Ḥājjī Khalīfah's lengthiest Ṭabarī entry is in connection with *History;* that on *Tafsīr* is much briefer. See Ḥājjī Khalīfah, ed. Yaltkaya, 297 f.

462. Ḥājjī Khalīfah has 309 (for the latter date, see below, translation, Vol. XXXVIII, xv).

463. I. e., a misreading of al-Bal'amī.

temps de Mansour Ben Nouh, l'an 352. de l'hegire.

Cette même Histoire a été traduite en Langue Turquesque par un Auteur incertain, & c'est celle que l'on trouve communément entre les mains des Turcs.

Abou Mohammed A'bdallah Ben Mohammed AlFargani a fait la continuation de l'Histoire de Thabari, & l'a publiée sous le titre de ,Selat.

Abou Hassan Mohammed Ben A'bdalmalek AlHamadhani, mort l'an 521. de l'hegire, y a fait un autre Supplement.

In the nineteenth-century West, "history" was about to replace "philosophy" as the fundamental culture symbol of the age. With it came a long period of the avid study of everything that could be understood as "history." The occupation with Ṭabarī's historical work gained in intensity, as is chronicled in F.-C. Muth's very useful survey of Ṭabarī's *History* as mirrored in European scholarship published in 1983. Ṭabarī's other works meanwhile continued to be all but unknown to Western scholars. It was only near the end of the century that O. Loth called attention to *Tafsīr,* when a manuscript of the work had become known (see above, n. 383).

Not surprisingly, if quite inaccurately, Ṭabarī was described—shades of Herodotus!—as "Vater der arabischen Geschichte" by A. D. Mordtmann, who in 1848, relying on the recently published Turkish translation, collected *History*'s information on Ṭabaristān (see Bibliography, below, under Mordtmann). After the publication of the Leiden edition, the interest of scholars soon turned to the challenging task of disentangling the source situation in the original text of *History.* This was a promising undertaking, owing to the fact that Ṭabarī himself, in his way, was careful to hint at the sources employed by him throughout his work. The name of J. Wellhausen should be mentioned here as that of the highly regarded pioneer in this field (see above, n. 206). The work has been continued with a good measure of success, but much more remains to be done.

It was, and has remained, more difficult to gain an insight into the manner in which Ṭabarī used his sources. In other words, what was his approach to the writing of history and his view of history in general and the historical data he surveyed in his work? What considerations determined his choice of a given source in preference to other sources that might have been available to him? What, if anything, did he omit, thereby altering trends and historical interpretation, be it consciously or unconsciously ? Beyond a general Baghdad-centrism that was indicated by his own residence in the capital and by the audience for which he was writing, what were his views on historical events and personalities? We hear, for example, that he predicted the failure of Ibn al-Muʿtazz's revolt as soon as it happened. When he was informed about it, he inquired about the new wazīr and chief judge. Hearing their names, he expressed the view that the choice of such accomplished men who were ahead of their times in a period of general retrogression was wrong and Ibn al-Muʿtazz would not last.[464] If this is the correct understanding of the reported remark, he seems to have meant that the course of historical events depended upon prevailing trends and the government must conform to the trends of the times in order to master them. Such express statements are rare in Ṭabarī's case. They are also often, as in the given example, of dubious historicity. The answers to the questions raised must be sought by means of internal evidence.

The present translation has as one of its purposes that of furthering this discussion. Whatever might come of it, the fact remains that Ṭabarī's *History* is our greatest single source of information for much of the early centuries of Muslim history. The existence of a standard work of this kind is apt to exercise a certain restrictive influence and to promote the tendency to rely on it unduly. Such was arguably the case with Ṭabarī's *History* for quite some time. It hardly is any longer. His *History* is now ready to take its proper place in Muslim historiography—not at the head, but at the very center.

464. The report goes back to al-Muʿāfā, with a suspiciously vague *isnād* connecting it to Ṭabarī. See Muʿāfā, *Jalīs*, I, 472, quoted in *TB*, X, 98 f. (above, n. 18). The name of the chief judge is al-Ḥasan b. al-Muthannā; he must be the same individual as Abū al-Muthannā Aḥmad b. Yaʿqūb, mentioned below, translation, Vol. XXXVIII, 189–91. It may be noted that Ṭabarī figures among the transmitters of the story of ʿĀʾishah that promotes the idea of a steady deterioration in history; see Rosenthal, "*Sweeter than Hope*," 25.

The Text

Scholars interested in the history of libraries in Islam usually cite the Egyptian historians al-Musabbiḥī and Ibn Abī Ṭayyi', who lived, respectively, around the turn of the fourth/tenth and sixth/twelfth centuries. Brief remarks from the works of these historians illustrate the large size of Muslim libraries in general as well as, in particular, the high esteem in which Ṭabarī's *History* was held. According to al-Musabbiḥī, the Fāṭimid caliph al-ʿAzīz, who reigned from 975 to 996, spent one hundred dīnārs for a copy of *History* that was offered to him. He then found out that his library already contained more than twenty copies of the work, including one in Ṭabarī's own hand. According to Ibn Abī Ṭayyi', 1,220 copies of *History* were in the library of the Fāṭimid palace complex when Saladin took over in 567/1171.[465] We are not told whether these were complete sets or individual volumes. Whatever it was, the figure of 1,220 seems to be a somewhat exaggerated guess. It is, however, quite possible that an autograph of Ṭabarī found its way into the possession of royal bibliophiles and that the Fāṭimid rulers, conscious of their position in history, collected as many volumes as they could of a work that reflected the past glory of Islam to which they themselves aspired in vain. At a much later date, the Ottoman sultans had the same abundant means and the same motivation for acquiring choice copies of *History*. It is thus not by chance that today, the best of the preserved manuscripts are found in Istanbul and complete sets can be reconstructed from the library holdings there. While Ṭabarī manuscripts are preserved in numerous European and Middle Eastern libraries, it is usually only individual volumes and not the entire work.

For modern scholars trained in the proper technique of text edition, it was natural to look especially to Istanbul for manuscripts to be used in the planned edition of *History*. In the second half of the nineteenth century, this was no simple task; but M. J. de Goeje and his co-workers succeeded admirably in obtain-

465. See Maqrīzī, *Khiṭaṭ*, I, 408 f., cited, for instance, by Mez, *Renaissance*, 164 f.; Pedersen, *Arabic Book*, 118 f. Al-Maqrīzī has 1,200 but the correct 1,220 is preserved in Abū Shāmah, *Rawḍatayn*, I, 200, l. 4, ed. Cairo, 1956, I, 507, l. 7, and Ibn Kathīr, *Bidāyah*, XII, 266, year 567. See Rosenthal, *Muslim Historiography*², 50. One may wonder whether 20 in 1,220 has something to do with the figure of "more than twenty" in al-Musabbiḥī.

ing the necessary manuscript material and preparing an edition which presented an accurate text with a full critical apparatus and a good deal of additional information. In addition to the chief mover of the project, de Goeje (1836–1909), the honor roll of famous Orientalists of the past century who participated in the enterprise included J. Barth (1851–1914), S. Fraenkel (1855–1909), I. Guidi (1844–1935), S. Guyard (1846–84), M. Th. Houtsma (1851–1943), P. De Jong (1832–1890), D. H. Müller (1846–1912), Th. Nöldeke (1836–1930), E. Prym (1843–1913), V. Rosen (1849–1908), and H. Thorbecke (1837–90).[466] The publisher was the great house of E. J. Brill, which accomplished the difficult task of printing between the years 1879 and 1901. All editorial material, such as the brief summaries of the contents accompanying the individual volumes, the introduction, the glossary of noteworthy terms, and the model index, was written in Latin, as was fitting at the time for an inter-European enterprise. The full Latin title of the edition, which chose *Kitāb Ta'rīkh al-rusul wa-al-mulūk* for the Arabic title page (see above, 131), was *Annales quos scripsit Abu Djafar Mohammed Ibn Djarir at-Tabari,* which led scholars often to refer to it as *Annales.*

The Leiden edition had practically nothing in the way of predecessors,[467] and it has as yet not been replaced. Manuscripts in the collections of the Topkapısarayı in Istanbul were not accessible at the time. As far as our present knowledge goes, they are the only significant manuscript material not used in the Leiden edition, although the chance of making new discoveries remains. It would seem that the oldest portion of a manuscript of *History* is a number of folios bound into Ms. Köprülü, I, 1047, covering the years 64–66.[468]

The Istanbul material was largely used by the editor of the Cairo edition, Muḥammad Abū al-Faḍl Ibrāhīm, who had made himself a respected name as the editor of many important texts. His edition began to appear in 1969 and was reprinted repeatedly. Ibrāhīm omitted the critical apparatus of the Leiden edition. He basically

---

466. See Fück, *Arabische Studien,* in particular, 212 ff.

467. See Muth, passim.

468. The Istanbul manuscripts have been studied by R. Stephen Humphreys, who presented a preliminary report on his findings at the meeting of the American Oriental Society in Ann Arbor, Michigan, in April 1985.

restricted himself to indicating the variant readings of the Topkapısarayı manuscripts, with the exception of Ms. Revanköşk, no. 1555 (Karatay, *Catalogue*, no. 5735, see below, translation, Vol. XXXVIII, xv f.). He also used some manuscript material from Egypt and India. It seems that he mainly listed variants he considered significant. He adopted the sound principle of showing the pagination of the standard Leiden edition in the margin of his text and thereby established the proper manner of reference for all who work on *History.* This procedure must be continued in any future edition, including the new scientific edition which it is hoped will some day be published and supersede the Leiden edition.

In connection with establishing the Arabic text, there was no pressing need to consult the Persian and Turkish versions. No case has as yet been made that these reworkings of the original could be of any real help, except, perhaps, with respect to additions not appearing in the available manuscripts. Even less useful are all the abridgments of the Arabic, the retranslations of the Persian version into Arabic, and the like. However, the difficult task of a bibliographical description of all this material remains to be undertaken, even if the results promise to be meager, at least as far as Ṭabarī's original text is concerned.

A work such as *History* allows the incorporation in the text of additions at certain stages of the manuscript tradition. Such additions might have entered the text during Ṭabarī's lifetime, coming from his own hand or that of others who might or might not have acted with his knowledge and approval. Later authors who used *History* show some such additions or corrections to the accepted text. There is a strong likelihood that they were not responsible for them but followed some manuscript authority. The chronological arrangement, in particular, facilitated insertions. Professional copyists would not normally have tampered with the text they copied, but scholarly readers might have made marginal additions which eventually entered the text. Usually, additions that came about in this manner cannot be expected to have left an express indication of their origin in the text; but *History*, II, 1368–72, contains what is specifically stated to be " an addition in the biography of ʿUmar b. ʿAbd al-ʿAzīz *not from the work of Abū Jaʿfar,* to the beginning of the caliphate of Yazīd b. ʿAbd al-Malik b. Marwān." The situation is less clear in *History,* II, 835–43. The passage which raised doubts already in the mind of its editor is poorly attested in the manuscript tradition. It is also not found in the Topkapısarayı manuscript. It is thus difficult to accept it as a Ṭabarian addition, although this is not entirely precluded; the passage may go back to notations which Ṭabarī had made for himself and which he had intended to insert in the appropriate places. In all the minor instances of additions or omissions, the decision as to whether they go back to Ṭabarī must be made in each case individually. Probably, very many can indeed be considered as somehow connected to Ṭabarī (see below, translation, Vol. XXXVIII, xvii ff.). Such small problems remain to be solved, before a definitive text of *History* is in our hands. Nothing of the sort, however, can be assumed to affect the understanding of the historical contents as Ṭabarī meant it to be understood.

Previous Translations

Arabists are fond of recalling that the various editors of *History* were supposed to provide translations of the volumes edited by them, but only Theodor Nöldeke took up the idea and published his justly celebrated *Geschichte der Perser und Araber zur Zeit der Sasaniden* (E. J. Brill, Leiden, 1879, reprinted Graz, 1973). His translation covered *History*, I, 813–1067; he omitted some brief portions as having no immediate bearing upon Persian history (I, 890, l. 4–892, l. 13, 901, l. 1–917, l. 17, 966, l. 15–981, l. 2).[469] It is regrettable that the other editors did not follow Nöldeke's example. Their long and intimate occupation with the text uniquely qualified them for the task. Their translations, had they been published, would have been most helpful to subsequent translators and might have stimulated translations into other languages. Above all, the existence of *History* in translation would have constituted a strong incentive for historians who were not Near Eastern specialists to make use of it in their work.

Under the direction of G. E. von Grunebaum, Elma Marin trans-

469. When Nöldeke was urged to prepare a second edition of his Ṭabarī translation, he spoke of it as "perhaps the best I have ever done" (letter to Goldziher, dated September 11, 1910; see Róbert Simon, *Ignác Goldzıher*, 340).

Ṭabarī's much less detailed and scattered treatment of ancient Iranian mythological history was translated by Christensen (see below, translation, n. 151).

lated Ṭabarī's treatment of the caliphate of al-Muʿtaṣim from *History*, II, 1164–1329. Her work was published by the American Oriental Society in New Haven in 1951. Individual passages of some lines to a number of pages in length have, of course, been translated in many publications, as was dictated by their particular subject matter.

It can be assumed that quite a few Arabists dreamed of preparing a complete translation, but their names went unrecorded, or, at least, are unknown to this writer.[470] J. A. Williams contemplated the task, and D. M. Dunlop tried to organize a collaborative effort while being a professor at Columbia University. A translation of the whole by one person has certain advantages. It makes for much greater uniformity in approach and execution. As it demands a total long-term immersion in the text, it holds the promise of yielding unexpected insights. However, the chances of bringing such a major enterprise to final fruition are small. Collaboration by a number of scholars offers a better chance for success. Upon the initiative of Ehsan Yarshater of Columbia University, such a collaborative effort was initiated in 1971. It proved possible for Michael G. Morony, a participant in the project, to arrange for a division of the entire text into portions of about two hundred pages each, distributed over thirty-eight volumes. Thus, the chore of finding capable and willing translators could begin. It was thought impractical to postpone publication until all volumes were completed. The first three volumes (XXVII, XXXV, and XXXVIII) appeared in 1985 under the aegis of the State University of New York Press, which, like E. J. Brill before, had voluntarily declared itself ready to undertake the difficult work of publication in the service of scholarship. The present hope is that the entire task will be completed by 1995.* As was the case with the Leiden edition, financial support had to be found. Strenuous efforts on the part of Ehsan Yarshater succeeded in surmounting this hurdle, but the search for funds has to continue in order to keep the enterprise going.

Toward the end of achieving a desirable degree of uniformity in presentation and format, some directions were deemed necessary

---

470. See also Muth, I.

*As of December 1987, nine volumes of the English translation have been published.

to be given to the translators. At the same time, it was realized that the quality of the work might be enhanced if each translator relied primarily on his own judgment and expertise. A generous allowance of space was set aside for annotation, but again, it was left to the individual translator to make the difficult choice of what required annotation and how much information the footnotes should contain. General introductory remarks for each volume were suggested in order to provide all the necessary observations to be made in connection with a given volume, while keeping in mind the quite different character of the various sections of *History.*

The system of transliteration employed in the translation follows by and large a practice that has by now become standard in the scholarly publications of Arabists and Islamicists. This writer wishes, however, to express disagreement with the choice of *-iyy- [-uww-]* for *-īy- [-ūw-].* Under the influence of the *Encyclopaedia of Islam,* this transliteration is widely used. It is plainly wrong, and not just a simple matter of convention. For the rendering of names of localities, exact transliteration was recommended as the norm, except for a very few place names that have accepted English forms of long standing; thus al-Kūfah (with the retention of the definite article), but Mecca, and not Makkah. Doubts as to what constitutes an accepted form are many. With the growing Western familiarity with Near Eastern geography, these doubts have not diminished but rather have increased. Accurate transliteration thus seemed preferable. The definite article in the names of frequently mentioned and quoted authors has often been omitted, especially in bibliographical references, and it is (almost) always Ṭabarī, instead of al-Ṭabarī.

A special concern has been how to best serve those readers who might not know Arabic. In fact, it is hoped that specialists will find the translation useful; but a translation primarily addresses itself to those not fully familiar with the original language. This regard for non-Arabists has led, for instance, to the insistence upon an unambiguous rendering of dates and upon providing chapter headings. It has also influenced the choice of the secondary literature in the footnotes, with the understanding that Arabic and Islamic studies have not yet progressed to the state where the secondary literature is sufficiently developed to make possible reliance on it exclusively. For Qur'ān quotations, the translation of

A. J. Arberry was suggested with some hesitation, but again, it was left to the individual translator to decide upon the most suitable renditions.

There was never any doubt as to which edition should constitute the basis for the translation, as the Leiden text is the only scientific edition in existence. Translators were, however, aware of the Cairo edition and the need to consult it wherever it was thought to contain a superior text. No priority was assigned to consulting manuscripts. Translators who had the opportunity were encouraged to do so. The gain to be obtained from the consultation of manuscripts did not loom large as a rule, but it is undeniable that in any occupation with ancient texts, no matter how carefully edited, recourse to manuscripts is of value, if only for the purpose of ascertaining that the available printed editions are indeed reliable.

The hope was expressed that the translations should be accurate and faithful to the original and, at the same time, idiomatic and fluent in English. This great ideal, if constantly invoked, is rarely achieved anywhere. Editorial and stylistic help has been provided to the extent possible. The translator's individuality could never be entirely suppressed nor, indeed, should it be.

The only liberty that the translators were asked to take with the Arabic text affects the presentation of *isnād*s, the chains of transmitters that served Ṭabarī as an indication of his sources. A literal translation would typically run like this: "*A* told me that *B* told us: *C* told us on the authority of *D*, on the authority of *E* that *F* said...." A less clumsy rendering was chosen to take its place, to wit: "According to *A* — *B* — *C* — *D* — *E* — *F* ...." Occasional exceptions as required by the flow of the narrative were permitted. The simplification is fully justified in view of the less cluttered text page resulting from it and the amount of space saved. It conceals, however, the numerous variations in the form of the *isnād*s indicated by Ṭabarī. These variations are important for a more precise understanding of the source situation. Scholars concerned with source problems must have recourse to the Arabic text.

At this time, the halfway mark in the project is not far off. When the entire work is completed, a retrospective on its genesis and execution will improve and enlarge upon the present brief and preliminary remarks.

Appendix A

A Partial Translation of Tafsīr *on Qur. 17:79 (Above, pp. 75 f.)*

Tafsīr, XV, 99, l. 21–100, l. 22:

"Even though the traditions we have mentioned on the authority of the Prophet and his Companions and the Followers indicate the correct interpretation of *maqāman maḥmūdan* in Qur. 17:79 (as referring to Muḥammad's role as intercessor on the Day of Resurrection), Mujāhid's statement that God will seat Muḥammad on His Throne remains one whose soundness cannot be rejected either on the basis of tradition *(khabar)* or on the basis of speculation *(naẓar)*. This is so because there is no tradition from the Messenger of God or anyone of his Companions or the Followers that declares it to be impossible.

With respect to speculation, all adherents of Islam differ on the implication of (such seating) in only three ways:

One group *(firqah)* says: God is separate from His creation. He was so before He created the things. Then He created the things but was not contiguous with them. He Himself remained as He had always been, except that being not contiguous with the things He created, He is necessarily separate from them, since any maker of the things must be either contiguous with the material substances *(ajsām)* or separate from them. So they said. As this is so, and God is the maker *(fāʿil)* of the things and, according to their statement, He is not permitted to be described as being contiguous with the things, their line of thought makes it necessary to assume that He is separate from them. According to their theory *(madhhab)*, it is the same whether he seats Muḥammad on His Throne or upon earth, since their statement implies that His separateness from His Throne and His separateness from His earth mean the same, since He is (equally) separate from both and is not contiguous with either.

A second group says: Before God created the things, there was no thing for Him to be contiguous with or separate from. Then He created the things. He set them up by His power, remaining Himself as He had always been before His creation of the things, not being contiguous with nor separate from any thing. According to their statement, too, it is the same whether He seats Muḥammad on His Throne or upon His earth, since according to their statement, His Throne and His earth are the same with respect to His being neither contiguous with nor separate from the one or the other.

A third group says: Before God created the things, there was no thing for him to be contiguous with or separate from. Then He created *(aḥdatha* and *khalaqa)* the things. He created for Himself a throne, upon which He sat straight and with which He became contiguous. Correspondingly, before He created the things, there was no thing for which He would provide sustenance or which He would deprive of it. Having created the things, He provided sustenance for one thing and deprived another of it, gave to one and withheld from another. So they said. Thus likewise, before He created the things, there was no thing for Him to be contiguous with or separate from. He created the things and then He was contiguous with the Throne by sitting on it but no other creature. He may be contiguous with or separate from any of His creatures He wants. According to their theory, too, it is the same whether He seated Muḥammad on His Throne or seated him on a pulpit of light, since their statement implies that God's sitting on His Throne is not by way of occupying the entire Throne, nor is seating Muḥammad (on it) necessitating the attribute of divinity (for Muḥammad) or depriving him of the attribute of humanity *(rubūbiyyah-ʿubūdiyyah)*, just like Muḥammad's being kept separate from the things he is kept separate from does not necessitate for him the attribute of divinity or deprive him of the attribute of humanity (merely) because he is described as being kept separate from them as, according to those who make this statement, God is described as being separate from them. So they say. If the meaning of being separate *(mubāyin)* and being kept separate *(mubāyan)* does not necessitate for Muḥammad to be deprived of the attribute of humanity and to enter into the conceptual realm *(ma'nā)* of divinity, then his sitting on the Throne of the Merciful One does not necessitate that.

From what we have said, it has become clear that it is not impossible for an adherent of Islam to say what Mujāhid has said, namely, that God will seat Muḥammad on His Throne. If someone says: We do not disapprove of God's seating Muḥammad on His Throne (in view of the following tradition transmitted by) 'Abbās b. 'Abd al-'Aẓīm—Yaḥyā b. Kathīr—al-Jurayrī—Sayf al-Sadūsī—'Abdallāh b. Salām:[471] 'On the Day of Resurrection, Muḥammad will be on the Lord's footstool *(kursī),*' but we disapprove of God's seating him *together with Him,* it should be said: Is it then permissible in your opinion that He seat him on it but not together with him? If he permits this, he is led to affirming that either he is together with Him, or God seats him (on the Throne) while being Himself either separate from it or neither contiguous with nor separate from it. Whatever alternative he chooses, he thereby enters into something that he disapproves. If he says that it is not permissible, he deviates from the statements of all the groups we have reported. This means diverging from the views of all adherents of Islam, since there is no other possible statement than those three, according to each of which Mujāhid's statement in this sense is not impossible."

---

471. (Al-)'Abbās b. 'Abd al-'Aẓīm al-'Anbarī died before 250/864 (see *TB,* XII, 127 f.; Ibn Ḥajar, *Tahdhīb,* V, 121 f.). His authority, Yaḥyā b. Kathīr (al-'Anbarī), died after 200/816 (see Ibn Ḥajar, *Tahdhīb,* XI, 266, no. 536). Yaḥyā's authority was Salm b. Ja'far (see Ibn Ḥajar, *Tahdhīb,* IV, 127 f.), omitted in *Tafsīr.* Abū Mas'ūd Sa'īd b. Iyās al-Jurayrī died in 144/761[2] (see Ibn Ḥajar, *Tahdhīb,* IV, 5–7). The unidentified Sayf al-Sadūsī and the famous 'Abdallāh b. Salām (see below, translation, n. 178) are suspect. The tradition appears in Khallāl, *Musnad,* 76, 86, 92 f.

Appendix B

A Classification and Chronology of Ṭabarī's Literary Production

The following classification of Ṭabarī's work according to subject matter is slightly uncertain where it deals with works that are not preserved.

Law:	*Ādāb al-manāsik*
	Al-Ādar (?) fī al-uṣūl
	Basīṭ
	Ikhtilāf
	Khafīf
	Laṭīf
	Mūjaz
	Radd ʿalā Ibn ʿAbd al-Ḥakam
Qurʾān:	*Faṣl (fī al-qirāʾāt)*
	Jāmiʿ al-bayān (Tafsīr)
Ḥadīth:	*ʿIbārat al-ruʾyā*
	Tahdhīb
	See also *Faḍāʾil*
Theology:	*Dalālah*
	Faḍāʾil
	Radd ʿalā dhī al-asfār

	Ṣarīḥ *Tabṣīr*
Religious Ethics:	*Ādāb al-nufūs* See also *Faḍā'il* and *Mūjaz*
History:	*Dhayl* *Ta'rīkh*

Any attempt to establish a relative chronological order must reckon with the fact that Ṭabarī worked on his large works throughout his career. He also started on projects, worked and lectured on them sporadically, and maybe never published them. In a number of cases, no sufficient data are ascertainable.

Works that can be dated with reasonable certainty:

1. *Radd 'alā Ibn 'Abd al-Ḥakam* (about 255)
2. *Laṭīf* (quoted in *Tafsīr, Ikhtilāf, Tahdhīb)*
3. *Ikhtilāf*
4. *Radd 'alā dhī al-asfār* (before 270, left incomplete ?)
5. *Tafsīr* (270–90) (cited in *Ta'rīkh*)
6. *Tabṣīr* (about 290)
7. *Khafīf* (291–96)
8. *Ta'rīkh* (294, 302) (cited in *Dhayl*)
9. *Dhayl* (after 300)

Incomplete at the time of Ṭabarī's death:

Ādāb al-nufūs
Basīṭ (quoted in *History* as forthcoming, but presumably to be placed between 4 and 5 as regards its starting time)
Faḍā'il
Mūjaz
Radd 'alā dhī al-asfār (above 4)
Tahdhīb (to be placed between 2 and 3)

Projects that were not executed:

Al-Ādar (?) fī al-uṣūl
Aḥkām sharā'i' al-Islām
Dalālah (mentioned in *History*)
'Ibārat al-ru'yā
al-Qiyās (planned at the end of his life)

As yet unclassifiable:

Ādāb al-manāsik
Ādāb al-nufūs
Faṣl (fī al-qirā'āt) (after *Ta'rīkh* ?)
Ṣarīḥ (before or after 6 ?)

From the Creation to the Flood

Translator's Foreword

The monotheistic environment of the Near East provided a powerful model for the idea that history must be written as beginning with the creation of the world. In Islam, the tradition continued, and history was presented as a continuum stretching seamlessly from the six days of creation to contemporary times, although neither before nor after Ṭabarī were histories so commonly composed in this manner as is often assumed. The material for primeval pre-Islamic history which was abundantly available to Ṭabarī was determined by the Qur'ān. A vast explanatory mythology developed in connection with it at an early stage. Some of the legends that were inherited or invented were occasionally ascribed to the Prophet directly. Much more frequently, they were credited to certain early Muslim authorities. Qur'ān commentaries drawing on this information were composed in unpublished, and soon also in published, form at least since the early eighth century. Ṭabarī, as the author of what in all likelihood was the most voluminous Qur'ān commentary ever assembled down to his time, was thoroughly familiar with most, if not all, of these works.

His basic task in the first part of his *History* was to make historical sense out of the material collected by earlier scholars and largely taken over into his own commentary, to which he refers by its proper title (below, n. 562)—here it is referred to simply as *Tafsīr*. In rearranging and presenting the material as sequential history, he used throughout the same literary method as *Tafsīr*, providing first a summary of the topic to be discussed, then quoting the sources, and, finally, wherever he considered it necessary, giving a critical evaluation of them (frequently an effort to reach a compromise between divergent views). He succeeded in his effort to historicize legend as well as was possible in his time and age. Later Muslim historians who used Ṭabarī's *History* were considerably more skeptical than he as to the compatibility of all that legendary material with what they had come to consider history. Miskawayh, for instance, dared to dismiss all antediluvian accounts as being too poorly documented for consideration by historians. Ibn al-Athīr criticized Ṭabarī for bad historical and literary judgement with respect to some of the material the latter had thought worthy of consideration.[1]

In keeping with the methods developed by the traditional religious science of his day, Ṭabarī rightly stressed the traditional nature of *all* historical knowledge. What happened in the past can be known only by reports originating with an eyewitness, or at least a contemporary, and handed down from one individual to another in successive stages. It was beyond his ken to realize that in dealing with what we call prehistorical happenings, "history" can be approached only by means of intellectual (or, nowadays, scientific) speculation. Ṭabarī did have a certain inkling of the problem involved. Repeatedly, he asserts that only traditional information can be counted on to prove the soundness of historical data and that the usefulness of intellectual speculation in this connection must be discounted. With respect to the former, his statement was apologetic; with respect to the latter, it was polemical. The stress on the supremacy of intellect and reason *(ʿaql)* was the hallmark of the Mutakallimūn, the philosophical theologians of his age, who tried with considerable success at the time to assert themselves, and it is their introduction of *ʿaql* into the Muslim view of the world that Ṭabarī attempted to reject while defending the supremacy of tradition.

In one respect, however, he clearly shows how deeply he was influenced by the new thought system. It cannot be decided whether he himself fully realized it—this may indeed have been the case—but he admitted (text below, I, 6) that his historical research did include a small measure of rational argumentation. At the begin-

---

1. See below, n. 3 of the Foreword and nn. 436 and 1029 to the translation.

ning of the *History,* he raises the question of the nature and definition of time as being fundamental to all history. His answer remains traditional, but the question could be raised in this form only after the Aristotelian analysis of the physical world in which human history evolves had become familiar in Muslim civilization. Ṭabarī argues that all history is a function of time and that, therefore, a definition of time that clearly establishes its meaning is the crucial starting point for historical investigation. This was an important insight, and there appears to be a strong possibility that Ṭabarī was in fact the first to introduce it prominently into historiography (as apparently suggested by one of his early biographers, see above, General Intro., n. 446). It is unfortunately true that most of the Arabic historical literature that could serve for comparison is yet to be recovered. The *History* of al-Yaʿqūbī (d. 284/897–98 or later) is incomplete in the beginning, where the same argument regarding time might have been made. A century earlier, Khalīfah b. Khayyāṭ (d. 204/819–20) had begun his *History* with no more than a brief note on the term *ta'rīkh,* understood by him not as "history," but as the means for dating events—a note that is not at all informed by philosophical reflection.[2] Thus, Ṭabarī's approach to time in history may very well have been absent in earlier histories. It can be assumed, at any rate, to have developed at the earliest in the course of the third/ninth century. If it is indeed original with Ṭabarī, it is another truly remarkable testimony to his intellectual alertness. It may be added that Ibn al-Athīr was fully aware of the origin of Ṭabarī's speculation on the concept of time. It belonged, he states, in the discussion of the (theological) principles of the Mutakallimūn and had no place in a historical work.[3]

A particularly difficult challenge to the historian's critical acumen were views known in ninth-century Baghdad on the origin and early history of the world which competed and often were in conflict with the monotheistic tradition shared by Judaism, Christianity, and Islam. This had given pause to historians before Ṭabarī and had led to crude attempts at finding some common ground between the disparate traditions. Ṭabarī, like many of the leading scholars in Iraq, a man with ties to Iran, restricted himself to the

2. See also Rosenthal, *Muslim Historiography,*[2] 287, *n* 4.
3. See Ibn al-Athīr, *Kāmil,* ed. Tornberg, I, 12.

Magian (Zoroastrian) material and inserted rather brief reports on it in what he felt were appropriate places. He gives the impression of doing that with some reluctance and an apparent unwillingness to take those alien beliefs too seriously. Indeed, the very existence of competing mythological histories may have severely tested Ṭabarī as an historian and as a faithful Muslim.

The basis for the following translation has been the Leiden text as edited by the Semitist Jakob Barth in Leiden, 1879–81. It is, however, obvious that the Istanbul manuscript Topkapısarayı Ahmet III 2929/1,[4] which was consulted by M. Abū al-Faḍl Ibrāhīm for the Cairo edition, has a text that, in general, is superior to that of the manuscripts used in Leiden. At the very beginning, Ms. Ahmet III provides the only reliable text, but its superiority is evident nearly everywhere. In most cases, its readings therefore have been adopted from the Cairo edition with no further comment. The reader of this translation should, however, rest assured that while noteworthy, the variants hold no substantive implications for the understanding of the text.

No manuscripts have been consulted directly for the present translation. There are passages here and there where the manuscript situation remains slightly uncertain, and a look at the manuscripts might have been helpful. A great merit of the Cairo edition that deserves to be mentioned is its occasional use of *Tafsīr*, from which Ṭabarī drew much of his material for this volume.

For all practical purposes, the following pages are a commentary on Genesis, chapters 1–10, from the creation of the world to Noah and the Flood—a mirror reflecting centuries of thought and a new Muslim way of looking at the ancient story. This being the case, the greatest selectivity in the number and kind of notes to be included was required. The scholarly literature deserving attention is nearly unlimited, and the problems are numerous. Much that could and should have been said has been passed over in silence. The following considerations have guided the choice of notes:

1. Qur'ānic quotations have, of course, been always noted. How-

4. See Karatay, *Catalogue*, III, 339 f., no. 5730.

ever, the artful weaving together of quotations from and allusions to the Qur'ān, which is evident to anyone reading the Arabic text, could not always be brought out in translation.

2. The chains of transmitters *(isnād)* are a most important key to the early history of Muslim historiogaphy. At least some information had to be provided for each individual occurring in them. All transmitters therefore have been briefly annotated at their first mention in the text. In order to facilitate their location through the Index, short forms of their names appearing in the text have often, but not consistently, been completed by additions in parentheses.

The identification of individual transmitters has been restricted here to basically two works, the *History of Baghdad (Ta'rīkh Baghdād,* cited as *TB)* of al-Khaṭīb al-Baghdādī and Ibn Ḥajar's *Tahdhīb. TB* brings us quite close to Ṭabarī's time and environment. *Tahdhīb* was compiled in the first half of the ninth/fifteenth century and constitutes the culmination of the labors of *ḥadīth* scholars in the field of biography. The information it contains is a summary of all the earlier literature. The significant dates for the life and death of the transmitters are all faithfully reported. Where Ibn Ḥajar fails to indicate such dates, it is almost certain that none ever existed in any earlier source. As a matter of fact, early biographical collections were much more chary with dates than later ones. This is proof that scholarly research and speculation, as against direct attestation, were responsible for providing many of the dates. Scholarship is never infallible, and, in certain cases, the very identification of an individual may have depended upon a kind of circular reasoning that reconstructed relationships on the basis of the *isnād*s as found in the *ḥadīth* collections and the *tafsīr* literature. Ibn Ḥajar often leaves us with a number of alternative dates to choose from. Usually no decision has been made here as to which of the divergent dates may be correct, even where this could possibly have been done. When references to the one or other biographical work in addition to *TB* and *Tahdhīb* have been given, this has been done for some reason, which, however, has been left unstated.

The role of *isnād*s as indications of Ṭabarī's sources has been somewhat obscured by the schematic representation adopted here, in which simple dashes separate individual transmitters.

However convenient, this scheme removes valuable if ambiguous hints at the various stages of the process of written transmission.

The material quoted here by Ṭabarī from *Tafsīr* was no doubt taken from earlier Qur'ān commentaries, most of them still lost or imperfectly known. Recensions of some of those commentaries have recently been published, such as the works of Sufyān al-Thawrī, Mujāhid, and Muqātil.[5] It should be noted that the corresponding information provided by Ṭabarī in traditions with *isnād*s including these men can be only very rarely traced back to them. In view of the complex history of the compilation of those recensions, as discussed by G. Schoeler and others (below, n. 503), this is hardly surprising. It does not, however, cast doubt on the genuineness of the attribution.

Among the secondary literature on the transmitters, Fuat Sezgin's *Geschichte des arabischen Schrifttums (GAS)* has been cited as consistently as possible. It allows for checking the literary activities of a given scholar and, in particular, finding out whether he is known as the author of a Qur'ān commentary. The short article by Heribert Horst, "Zur Überlieferung im Korankommentar aṭ-Ṭabarīs," has been systematically referred to, not so much for its occasional additional information as for its concise discussion of the configurations of Ṭabarī's *isnād*s. The important study of G. H. A. Juynboll, *Muslim Tradition. Studies in Chronology, Provenance and Authorship of Early Ḥadīth* (Cambridge University Press, 1983), goes, as its title indicates, far beyond the elementary data of concern to us here.

3. Among the sources of the *History*, Ṭabarī's own *Tafsīr* has always been consulted and usually cited. Close parallels from earlier or contemporary works have occasionally been mentioned. As is the case with much of the earlier *ḥadīth* literature, his primary historical sources, such as the works of Ibn Isḥāq and the Kalbī family, are also lost. Little use has been made of the *ḥadīth* literature. Works by later authors have been referred to only in exceptional cases. This also includes the literature on the prophetical stories *(qiṣaṣ al-anbiyā')*. W. M. Brinner's forthcoming translation of the closely related work by al-Tha'labī and W. M. Thackston's translation of the very different *Tales of the Prophets of al-Kisā'ī*

---

5. For the situation with respect to the *Tafsīr* of Mujāhid, however, see the introduction of the *Tafsīr*'s editor, 25–27.

(Boston, 1978) show the difference between their approach and that of the historian.

4. With respect to the sources of Ṭabarī's sources—that is, the comparative data to be found in Christian, Jewish, and Middle-Persian literature (including the later Firdawsī)—only a few references have been given in the notes. The relationship of Ṭabarī's material to the Book of Genesis requires many more references and discussions than appear in the notes here. The Jewish midrashic literature and secondary works, such as Speyer's *Biblische Erzählungen,* should have been referred to more frequently than is actually the case. A detailed analysis, for instance, of the role of the *Schatzhöhle* tradition was, of course, not possible here.[6] The references given to non-Muslim sources can do no more than serve as a stimulus for further investigation.

In his review of E. Marin's translation of Ṭabarī's section dealing with the caliphate of al-Muʿtaṣim, Helmut Ritter remarked that translations of difficult Arabic texts such as Ṭabarī's *History* should preferably be undertaken as collaborative efforts of more than one translator, for, Ritter said, "someone who translates by himself falls all too easily into the unavoidable vicious traps waiting for translators from this harmfully deceptive ("heimtückisch") language. The collaboration of two or more scholars gives at least some protection against getting lost in the Arabian desert."[7] My own lifetime experience has convinced me more and more of the truth of Ritter's impishly phrased remark. True collaboration in Ritter's sense has not been possible here, and mistakes can probably be found with comparative ease. But I have at least enjoyed and profited from the help of fellow scholars. I may mention G. Böwering, who gave me access to printed editions and manuscripts of early Qur'ān commentaries in his pos-

6. A. Goetze discusses the influence of the work on the histories of al-Ya'qūbī and Ṭabarī in *Zeitschrift für Semitistik* 3 (1924): 60–71, 153–55.

7. See *Oriens* 6 (1953): 157.

session, and J. Lassner, whose editorial work has gone far beyond the ordinary duty of an editor. Infelicities of style that will be encountered are the result of my having occasionally failed to accept my editor's suggestions.[8]

Franz Rosenthal

8. I may mention the frequent "He continued (said)" interrupting the narrative. I have retained it, although it will no doubt puzzle the reader. It can mean that the preceding statement is completed or, more commonly, that it is being continued. It can also indicate that there is a break in the narrative as compared to the source from which the statement is quoted. Often no decision is possible, and I have refrained from speculating about its meaning in a given context, or from simply omitting it.

In the Name of God, the Merciful, the Compassionate

(Invocation)

PRAISED BE GOD, first before any first and last after any last, enduring without cease and persevering in everything without moving away, Creator of His creation from no original or model! He is singular and unique without number. He remains after everyone infinitely without term. His are glory and greatness, splendor and might, authority and power. He is above having a partner in His authority, or in His uniqueness having one like Him, or in His administration an aid or helper, or having a child or spouse or "any equal."[1] He cannot be fully imagined and encompassed by the regions[2] and "reached by the eyes while He reaches them. He is subtle and knowledgeable."[3] [I, 1]

I praise Him for His benefits and am grateful to Him for His favors in the manner befitting one who singles Him out for praise and who hopes to receive more (favors) from Him for having been grateful. I ask Him to grant me to say and do what will bring me close to Him and please Him. I believe in Him as one who declares [2] oneness belonging exclusively to Him and who reserves glorification for Him alone.

I confess that there is no God but God, being one and having no partner. I confess that Muḥammad is His noble servant and His trustworthy Messenger whom He chose for transmitting His message and sent with His revelation to call His creation to worship Him. He manifested His command,[4] labored strenuously in His path, advised His nation *(ummah)*, and worshiped Him until death came to him from God, never flagging in his effort and never relaxing in his strenuous labor. May God bless him with the most excellent and purest prayer and give him peace!

---

1. Qur. 112:4.
2. Cf. Qur. 55:33, referring to "regions of heaven and earth."
3. Qur. 6:103. Ms. Ahmet III supplies "while...them." Its omission in the Leiden edition may constitute Ṭabarī's more original text.
4. Cf. Qur. 15:94.

(Introduction)

And now: God—great is His majesty and His names are sanctified—created His creation without any necessity for Him to create them, and He brought them forth without any need for Him to bring them forth. Rather, He created those whom He singled out by His command and His prohibition and whom He tested by His worship, so that they would worship Him and He would in turn bestow generous favors upon them. They would thus praise Him for His favors and He in turn would give them more of His generosity and bounty and add to His superiority and power for their benefit, as He says: "I have created jinn and men only to worship me. I do not want any sustenance from them, and I do not want them to provide food for Me. God is the Sustainer, potent and firm."[5]

In creating them as He did, He did not increase His authority by as much as the weight of a speck of dust beyond what it had always been before He created them. Nor does His annihilating them and making them nonexistent diminish Him by as much as
[3] the weight of a hair. For circumstances do not change Him, fatigue does not affect Him, and (the passing of) days and nights does not diminish His authority because He is the Creator of all eternal and temporal time.[6]

In this fleeting world, His many manifestations of generosity and bounty include and encompass all human beings. He gave them ears, eyes, and hearts and singled them out for possessing reason which makes it possible for them to distinguish between truth and falsehood and to recognize what is useful and what is harmful. He made the earth for them a carpet, so that they would have there passable roads to walk on,[7] and "the heaven a well-guarded roof"[8] and a lofty construction. From it He brought down for them plentiful rain and sizable sustenance. He made the moon of the night and the sun of the day run constantly one after the

---

5. Qur. 51:56–58.

6. *Al-duhūr wa-al-azmān.* For the various aspects of "time," see text below. What follows here is the customary summary of the contents usually provided by the author of a medieval Muslim book.

7. Cf. Qur. 71:19 f., quoted literally except for the substitution of the third person for the second of the Qur'ānic text.

8. Qur. 21:32.

other for their welfare. He made for them "the night a garment" and "the day the time for a livelihood."[9] In His benevolent concern for them, He made an alternation between the moon of the night and the sun of the day, blotting out the sign of the night and making the sign of the day something to see by, as He—great is His majesty and His names are sanctified—says: "And We have made the night and the day two signs. We have blotted out the sign of the night, and We have made the sign of the day something to see by, so that you may seek bounty from your Lord and so that you may know the number of years and the reckoning. For everything, We have made clear distinctions."[10] And so that they may achieve knowledge of the times—the hours of night and day, the months and the years—when the religious duties God has imposed upon them are to be fulfilled, such as prayer, charity, pilgrimage, fasting, and their other religious duties, as well as the time for settling [4]
their debts and their claims, as He says: "They will ask you about the new moons. Say: They are fixed times for mankind and the pilgrimage."[11] He further says: "He is the one who made the sun a luminosity and the moon a light, setting up fixed stations for it so that you may know the number of years and the reckoning. God created that only because it is right, distinguishing the signs for people who know. In the alternating of night and day and whatever God has created in the heavens and on earth, there are signs for people who fear God"[12] —all this being kindness shown by Him to His creation and an expression of His favor and concern for them.

A large number of His creatures were grateful to Him for the favors which He bestowed upon them. Thus, He gave many of them more benefits and gifts in addition to the generous favors He had bestowed upon them earlier, as God promised them, saying: "Your Lord announced: If your are grateful, We shall give you more, and if you are ungrateful, the punishment meted out by Me will be great."[13] He combined for them more (benefits) in this fleeting life of theirs with success in achieving bliss and eternal residence in blissful Paradise in their life to come in the other world. For many

9. Qur. 78:10 f.
10. Qur. 17:12.
11. Qur. 2:189.
12. Qur. 10:5 f.
13. Qur. 14:7.

of them, He postponed the promised increase to the time of their coming to Him, so as to show them more bounteous generosity on "the day when the innermost hearts are tested."[14] A large number of them were ungrateful for His favors, denying His benefits and worshiping someone else. Therefore He deprived many of them of the generous kindness He had shown them earlier. He unleashed upon them destructive vengeance in this fleeting world and stored up for them shameful punishment in the life to come in the other world. He let many of them enjoy His favors while they were alive by way of deception, thus making their load heavier so that they would be deserving of the punishment prepared by Him for them in the life to come in the other world.

[5] We take refuge in God against any activity that might bring (us) close to His wrath, and we ask Him for success with respect to everything that might lead (us) to His acceptance and love.

Abū Ja'far (al-Ṭabarī) says: In this book of mine, I shall mention whatever information has reached us about kings throughout the ages from when our Lord began the creation of His creation to its annihilation. There were messengers sent by God, kings placed in authority, or caliphs established in the caliphal succession. God had early on bestowed His benefits and favors upon some of them. They were grateful for His favors, and He thus gave them more favors and bounty in addition to those bestowed by Him upon them in their fleeting life, or He postponed the increase and stored it up for them with Himself. There were others who were not grateful for His favors, and so He deprived them of the favors He had bestowed upon them early on and hastened for them His revenge. There were also others who were not grateful for His favors; He let them enjoy them until the time of their death and perdition. Every one of them whom I shall mention in this book of mine will be mentioned in conjunction with his time but (only) summaries of the events in his day and age will be added, since an exhaustive treatment is not possible in a lifetime and makes books too

14. Qur. 86:9.

long.[15] This will be combined with references to the length of their natural life and the time of their death.

First, however, I shall begin with what for us comes properly and logically first, namely, the explanation of

What is time?
How long is its total extent?
Its first beginning and final end.
Whether before God's creation of (time) there was anything else.
Whether it will suffer annihilation and whether after its annihilation there will be something other than the face *(wajh)* of the Highly praised, the Exalted Creator.[16]
What was it that was before God's creation of time and what will be after its final annihilation?
How did God's creation of it begin and how will its annihilation take place?
Proof that there is nothing eternal *(a parte ante)* except God unique and powerful, to Whom belongs the kingdom of the heavens and the earth and what is between them and what is underneath the soil.[17] [6]

This must be done briefly and concisely, for in this book of ours we do not intend to present the arguments concerning time but rather the dates of past kings mentioned by us and summaries of their history, the times of the messengers and prophets and how long they lived, the days of the early[18] caliphs and some of their biographical data, and the extent of the territories under their control,[19] as well as the events that took place in their age. There-

15. The conventional fear of long-windedness is expressed repeatedly by Ṭabarī, even in connection with his massive *Tafsīr.* See above, General Introduction, n. 214.

16. *Wajh* ("face") with reference to God in the Qur'ān is *pars pro toto* and means "person." The translation "face" has been retained here, because the word was a theological issue in the Muslim debate of anthropomorphism.

17. Cf. Qur. 20:6, combined with 3:189, 5:18, etc.

18. *Sālif* refers here to the early caliphs, presumably the first four. It should be noted that this introduction makes no reference to Umayyad or 'Abbāsid history. It is concerned only with the companions of the Prophet, the Followers, and later transmitters as in the works on personality criticism of *ḥadīth* scholars. It would appear to have been written before Ṭabarī himself was clear about the form his work would eventually take.

19. Or, perhaps: "the extent of time of their holding office" ?

fore, if God wills and gives me strength through help and power from Him, I shall continue and mention the companions of our Prophet, their names, their patronymics, the extent of their pedigrees, and how long they lived and when and where they died. I shall then mention those who followed them doing good, in accordance with the conditions we have set down for mentioning them. Then, in addition to them, I shall likewise mention those who came after them, giving additional data about them. I do this for the purpose of clarifying whose transmission (of traditions) is praised and whose information is accepted,[20] whose transmission is rejected and whose transmission is disregarded, and whose tradition is considered feeble and whose information is considered weak. In addition, I give the reason why someone's information is disregarded and the cause for someone's tradition being considered feeble.

I wish to God that He may help me in my intentions and aims and give me success in my purposes and desires, for He possesses might and strength. May God pray for His Prophet Muḥammad and give him peace!

The reader should know that with respect to all I have mentioned and made it a condition to set down in this book of ours, I rely upon traditions and reports[21] which I have transmitted and which I attribute to their transmitters. I rely only very exceptionally upon what is learned through rational arguments and produced by internal thought processes. For no knowledge of the history of men of the past and of recent men and events is attain-
[7] able by those who were not able to observe them and did not live in their time, except through information and transmission provided by informants and transmitters. This knowledge cannot be brought out by reason or produced by internal thought processes. This book of mine may (be found to) contain some information,

20. Leiden: "is transmitted."

21. *Akhbār* and *āthār*, it seems, is used throughout with no clearcut distinction in meaning.

For this passage, see text below, I, 56. Cf. also the colophon of the entire *History*, Vol. XXXVIII, p. xvii.

mentioned by us on the authority of certain men of the past, which the reader may disapprove of and the listener may find detestable, because he can find nothing sound and no real meaning in it. In such cases, he should know that it is not our fault that such information comes to him, but the fault of someone who transmitted it to us. We have merely reported it as it was reported to us.

What Is Time?

(Abū Ja'far al-Ṭabarī) says: Time[22] is the hours of night and day. This may be said of both long and short extents of time.

The Arabs say: "I came to you at the time— *zamāna* or *zamana* —of al-Ḥajjāj[23] (being) amīr." By this, they mean: during the period when *(idh)* al-Ḥajjāj (was) amīr.

They say: "I came to you in the time– *zamāna* or *zamana* –of cutting off (the dates from the palms)." By this, they mean: at the moment *(waqt)* of cutting (them) off.

They also say: "I came to you in the times—using the plural *azmān* —of al-Ḥajjāj (being) amīr." They intend thereby to make each moment *(waqt)* of his amīrate a certain period of time *(zamān)*. Thus the *rajaz* poet says:

Winter has come, and my shirt is worn out,
tatters, being laughed at by al-Tawwāq.[24]

22. Arabic possesses a number of words expressing the concept of time. Ṭabarī here distinguishes between the two most important of them, *zamān/zaman* and *waqt*, the former indicating extended time and the latter indicating moment of time. This basic distinction is made in the theoretical discussion of the concept of time. It is very often disregarded in actual linguistic usage. In this translation, the translation "moment" for *waqt* has often been used. It should be noted that *waqt* occurs in the Qur'ān, but *z-m-n* does not. In "night and day," the Arabic word for "daytime" *(nahār)* is used here. *Yawm* ("day") technically indicates the twenty-hour period, but in Ṭabarī as elsewhere it is also commonly used for daytime.

23. The famous Umayyad governor (d. 85/704). Cf. *EI*², III, 39-43, s. v. al-Ḥadjdjādj.

24. For this verse in the *rajaz* meter, see Ibn Manẓūr, *Lisān*, XI, 315, 376, XV, 215, where al-Tawwāq is said to be the name of the son of (the poet ?). The form of the name appears to be uncertain; it is also read al-Nawwāq. The verse is ascribed to some unnamed bedouin in Dīnawarī, *Nabāt*, 239 f. The reading there is *minhā* (referring to the tatters as being laughed at) for *minhu* (referring, in general, to shirt) or *minnī* (referring to the poet). Attention to the passage in al-Dīnawarī has been called by 'Abd al-Qādir al-Baghdādī, *Khizānah*, I, 114. The verse is quoted in

The poet uses here the plural of "worn out" in connection with "shirt." He intends thereby to describe each piece of the shirt as being worn out. Similarly, one says: "a vast barren (pl. *sabāsib)* land, "and the like.

For the use of *zaman* for *zamān*, there is the verse of al-Aʿshā of the Banū Maymūn b. Qays:

For a time *(zamanan)*, I was a man in the Iraq
modest in (my) camping place, long in contentedly doing
[8] without.[25]

By *zamanan* he intends *zamānan*.

Thus, as mentioned by me and as I have described and explained it, *zamān* is a noun designating the hours of night and day.

How Long Is the Total Extent of Time from Beginning to End, First to Last?

The early scholars before us differed in this respect. Some said that the total extent of time is seven thousand years.

Those who said this

According to Ibn Ḥumayd[26] —Yaḥyā b. Wāḍiḥ[27] —Yaḥyā b.

Tafsīr, XIX, 47 *(ad* Qur. 26:53-56).

25. See al-Aʿshā, *Dīwān*, 22, no. 2, verse 77. The difficult last word appears in various forms. *Al-taghann*, for *al-taghannī*, as in the edition of al-Aʿshā and the Cairo edition of Ṭabarī, is explained as *istighnā'* in Ibn Manẓūr, *Lisān*, XIX, 373.

26. Muḥammad b. Ḥumayd, Abū 'Abdallāh al-Rāzī, died in 248/862, apparently more than eighty years old. See *TB*, II, 259-64; *Tahdhīb*, IX, 127-31; Horst, 296, n. 3. He was one of Ṭabarī's most important authorities, in particular as a second-generation transmitter from the historian Ibn Isḥāq. Ibn Isḥāq's work on the *Beginnings (al-Mubtada'*, see Sezgin, *GAS*, I, 289) can be assumed to be the source of much of the material reported by Ṭabarī. On Ibn Ḥumayd in connection with *isnāds* in Ṭabarī's *Tafsīr* and *History*, see also Sezgin, *GAS*, I, 29 f., 79, 242, 253. Relevant information on Ibn Isḥāq's *Mubtada'* can be expected from G. D. Newby, see *Jerusalem Studies in Arabic and Islam* 7 (1986) : 123. See also above, General Introduction, 17f.

27. No dates are provided in either *TB*, XIV, 126–28, or *Tahdhīb*, XI, 293 f.

Ya'qūb[28] —Ḥammād[29] —Sa'īd b. Jubayr[30] —Ibn 'Abbās[31] : This world is one of the weeks of the other world—seven thousand years. Six thousand two hundred[32] years have already passed. (The world) will surely experience hundreds of years, during which there will be no believer in the oneness of God there.

Others said that the total extent of time is six thousand years.

Those who said this

According to Abū Hishām[33] —Mu'āwiyah b. Hishām[34] —Sufyān[35] —al-A'mash[36] —Abū Ṣāliḥ[37] —Ka'b[38] : This world is six thousand years.

According to Muḥammad b. Sahl b. 'Askar[39] —Ismā'īl b. 'Abd

---

28. Abū Ṭālib Yaḥyā b. Ya'qūb appears as an authority of Yaḥyā b. Wāḍiḥ in text below, I, 1284, as well as Bukhārī, *Ta'rīkh*, IV, 2, 312. His pedigree is given as Yaḥyā b. Ya'qūb b. Mudrik b. Sa'd b. Habtah (Khaythamah) al-Anṣārī. He is listed in Ibn Ḥajar, *Lisān*, VI, 282 f. There, as in Dhahabī, *Mīzān*, IV, 415, he is said to have been the maternal uncle of the famous Ḥanafite judge Abū Yūsuf, whose great-grandfather was Sa'd b. Habtah. Habtah was the name of Sa'd's mother.

29. Ḥammād b. Abī Sulaymān Muslim died in 119 or 120/737–38. See *Tahdhīb*, III, 1–18; Ibn Ḥajar, *Fatḥ*, XIV, 136.

30. Ibn Jubayr died about fifty years old in 95/714. See *Tahdhīb*, IV, 11–14; Sezgin, *GAS*, I, 28 f.; Horst, 303, n. 8.

31. 'Abdallāh b. 'Abbās, the Prophet's cousin and reputedly the greatest early authority on Qur'ān interpretation, died in 68/687[8]. See *EI*², I, 40 f., s. v. 'Abdallāh b. al-'Abbās.

32. Ed. Leiden: six thousand and (several) hundred years. Quoting Ṭabarī, Ibn Ḥajar, *Fatḥ*, XIV, 136, has 6,100.

33. Abū Hishām al-Rifā'ī, Muḥammad b. Yazīd b. Muḥammad b. Kathīr b. Rifā'ah, died in 248/862. He was a judge in al-Madā'in and wrote on Qur'ān reading. See *TB*, III, 375–77; *Tahdhīb*, IX, 256, f.; Ibn al-Jazarī, *Ghāyah*, II, 280 f.

34. Died 204 or 205/819–20. See *Tahdhīb*, X, 218 f., where he is described as a transmitter from Sufyān al-Thawrī.

35. Sufyān al-Thawrī, ca. 96/714[5] to 161/778. See *Tahdhīb*, IV, 111–15; Sezgin, *GAS*, I, 518 f.; Horst, 296, n. 20. He and his younger contemporary and namesake Sufyān b. 'Uyaynah (below, n. 67) shared the same authorities and students and are often listed as "the two Sufyāns." Thus, it is sometimes difficult to know which "Sufyān" is meant.

36. Sulaymān b. Mihrān al-A'mash lived from ca. 60 or 61/679–80 to ca. 148/765. See *Tahdhīb*, IV, 222-26; *EI*², I, 431, s. v. al-A'mash.

37. Presumably, Abū Ṣāliḥ Dhakwān al-Sammān who died in 101/719[20]. See *Tahdhīb*, III, 219 f. Another of the many Abū Ṣāliḥs, Bādhām/Bādhān, a *mawlā* of 'Alī's sister Umm Hāni', was an authority of al-A'mash. See *Tahdhīb*, I, 416 f.

38. For the legendary transmitter Ka'b al-aḥbār, who is said to have died between 32 and 35/652–56, see *Tahdhīb*, VIII, 438–40; *EI*², IV, 316 f., s. v.; Sezgin, *GAS*, I, 304f.

39. Died 251/865. See *TB*, V, 313 f.; *Tahdhīb*, IX, 207.

al-Karīm[40] —ʿAbd al-Ṣamad b. Maʿqil[41] —Wahb[42] : Five thousand six hundred years of this world have elapsed. I do not know which kings and prophets lived in every period *(zaman)* of those years. I asked Wahb b. Munabbih: How long is (the total duration of) this world? He replied: Six thousand years.

[9] Abū Jaʿfar (al-Ṭabarī) says: The correct statement here is the one whose soundness is proved by information having come down from the Messenger of God.[43] It is what we were told by Muḥammad b. Bashshār[44] and ʿAlī b. Sahl[45] —Mu'ammal[46] — Sufyān—ʿAbdallāh b. Dīnār[47] —Ibn ʿUmar[48] : I heard the Messenger of God say: As compared to the term of those before you, your term is (like the time) from afternoon prayer to sunset.

According to Ibn Ḥumayd—Salamah[49] —Muḥammad b. Isḥāq[50] —Nāfiʿ[51] —Ibn ʿUmar: I heard the Prophet say: As compared to the term of the nations of the past, your term is just like (the time)

40. For Ismāʿīl b. ʿAbd al-Karīm b. Maʿqil b. Munabbih b. Kāmil, see *Tahdhīb,* I, 315 f. He was a nephew of ʿAbd al-Ṣamad b. Maʿqil and a grandnephew of Wahb b. Munabbih.

41. A nephew of Wahb b. Munabbih, ʿAbd al-Ṣamad died in the first decade of the eighth century. See *Tahdhīb,* VI, 328.

42. The celebrated Wahb b. Munabbih lived from ca. 655 to around 750, see, for instance, *Tahdhīb,* XI, 166–68; Sezgin, *GAS,* I, 305–7; Horst, 303, n. 7.

43. Ṭabarī often argues in the same manner in his *Tafsīr.*

44. Ibn Bashshār lived from 167/783[4] to 252/866. See *TB,* II, 101–5; *Tahdhīb,* IX, 70–73; Horst, 296, n. 4.

45. ʿAlī b. Sahl al-Ramlī often occurs as an authority in *Tafsīr,* but he apparently is not listed in either *TB* or *Tahdhīb.* He is mentioned as a student of Mu'ammal in *Tahdhīb,* X, 380. He apparently was the author of a letter in strong support of the Mujāhid tradition (see above, General Introduction, 71 ff.) quoted in Khallāl, *Musnad,* 91 f.

46. Mu'ammal b. Ismāʿīl died in 205 or 206/820–21. See *Tahdhīb,* X, 380 f. He has both Sufyāns as his authorities, and both of them are listed as students of ʿAbdallāh b. Dīnār.

47. Died in 127/744[5]. See *Tahdhīb,* V, 201–3.

48. ʿAbdallāh, a son of the caliph ʿUmar, died in 73/692[3]. See *Tahdhīb,* V, 228 f.; *EI*², I, 53 f., s. v. ʿAbdallāh b. ʿUmar.

49. Abū ʿAbdallāh Salamah b. al-Faḍl al-Azraq died after 190/805[6], suppposedly 110 years old. See *Tahdhīb,* IV, 153 f.; Horst, 303, n. 3. He was entrusted with *(ṣāḥib)* Ibn Isḥāq's *Maghāzī* and transmitted both the *Maghāzī* and the *Mubtada'.*

50. The famous historian, author of the biography *(Sīrah)* of the Prophet and other historical works, was born ca. 85/704 and died in 150/767 or shortly thereafter. See *TB,* I, 214–34; *Tahdhīb,* IX, 38-46; *EI*², III, 810 f., s. v. Ibn Isḥāḳ; Sezgin, *GAS,* I, 288–90; Horst, 303, n. 4.

51. Apparently, Nāfiʿ, the *mawlā* of Ibn ʿUmar, who died in 119 or 120/737–38. See *Tahdhīb,* X, 412–15.

between the afternoon prayer to sunset.

According to al-Ḥasan b. ʿArafah[52] —Abū al-Yaqẓān ʿAmmār b. Muḥammad, a son of the sister of Sufyān al-Thawrī[53] —Layth b. Abī Sulaym[54] —Mughīrah b. Ḥakīm[55] —ʿAbdallāh b. ʿUmar: The Messenger of God said: Only as much of this world remains for my nation as the extent (of time that remains) for the sun when the afternoon prayer has been performed.

According to Muḥammad b. ʿAwf[56] —Abū Nuʿaym[57] —Sharīk[58] —Salamah b. Kuhayl[59] —Mujāhid[60] —Ibn ʿUmar: We were sitting together with the Prophet when the sun was over Quʿayqiʿān[61] after the afternoon prayer. He said to us: As compared to the lives of those who have passed, your lives are like what remains of this day as compared to what has passed of it.

According to Ibn Bashshār and Muḥammad b. al-Muthannā[62] —Khalaf b. Mūsā[63] —his father—Qatādah[64] —Anas b. Mālik[65] : One

---

52. He was supposedly 100 or 110 years old when he died in Sāmarrā in 257/870[1]. See *TB*, VII, 394–96; *Tahdhīb*, II, 293.

53. Died 182/798. See *TB*, XII, 252 f.; *Tahdhīb*, VIII, 305.

54. Layth supposedly died in 143/760–61 or 148/765. See *Tahdhīb*, VIII, 465–68; Ibn al-Jazarī, *Ghāyah*, II, 34. For his role in the transmission of the Mujāhid tradition, see above, General Introduction, n. 275.

55. See *Tahdhīb*, X, 258.

56. Died 272 or 273/885–86. See *Tahdhīb*, IX, 383 f.

57. Abū Nuʿaym al-Faḍl b. Dukayn lived from 130/747[8] to 219/834. See *TB*, XII, 346–57; *Tahdhīb*, VIII, 270–76; *EI*², I, 143, s. v. Abū Nuʿaym; Sezgin, *GAS*, I, 101.

58. Sharīk b. ʿAbdallāh al-Nakhaʿī was born in 95/713[4] and died in 177 or 178/793–94. See *TB*, IX, 279-95; *Tahdhīb*, IV, 333–37.

59. Died 122 or 123/739–41. See *Tahdhīb*, IV, 155–57.

60. Abū al-Ḥajjāj Mujāhid b. Jabr was born in 21/642. He died in 104/722[3] or possibly four years earlier. He was the author of a Qurʾān commentary much used by Ṭabarī. See *Tahdhīb*, X, 42–44; Sezgin, *GAS*, I, 29; Horst, 295, n. 9. See above, General Introduction, 71.

61. A mountain about twelve *mīl* (24 km) south of Mecca. See Yāqūt, *Muʿjam*, IV, 146.

62. Ibn al-Muthannā, Abū Mūsā al-Zamin, lived from 167/783[4] to between 250 and 252/864–66. See *TB*, III, 283–86; *Tahdhīb*, IX, 425–27. The Arabic text makes the following distinction: Ibn Bashshār said: *I* was told by Khalaf, whereas Ibn al-Muthannā said: *We* were told....

63. Khalaf b. Mūsā b. Khalaf al-ʿAmmī died between 220 and 222/835–37. See *Tahdhīb*, III, 155. His father Mūsā b. Khalaf is listed in *Tahdhīb*, X, 341 f.

64. Qatādah b. Diʿāmah lived from ca. 60/680 to 117/735. See *Tahdhīb*, VIII, 351–56; *EI*², IV, 748, s. v. Ḳatāda b. Diʿāma; Sezgin, I, 31 f.; Horst, 300, n. 6. An edition of his *Kitāb al-Nāsikh* appears to have been published in Beirut, 1984 (not seen).

65. The famous transmitter from the Prophet died very old, between 710 and 715. See *Tahdhīb*, I, 376–79; *EI*², 482, s. v. Anas b. Mālik.

day the Messenger of God addressed his companions when the sun had almost set and only a small sliver of it remained visible. He
[10] said: By the One Who holds the soul of Muḥammad in His hand! As compared to what remains of our (life in this) world, that which has passed is like what remains of this day as compared to what has passed of it, and you will see only a little (more) of the sun.

According to Ibn Wakīʿ[66] —Ibn ʿUyaynah[67] —ʿAlī b. Zayd[68] — Abū Naḍrah[69] —Abū Saʿīd[70] : The Prophet said at sunset: What remains of this world as compared to what has passed of it is just like the rest of this day as compared to what has passed of it.

According to Hannād b. al-Sarī[71] and Abū Hishām al-Rifāʿī—Abū Bakr b. ʿAyyāsh[72] —Abū Ḥaṣīn[73] —Abū Ṣāliḥ[74] —Abū Hurayrah[75] : The Messenger of God said: When I was sent (to transmit the divine message), I and the Hour were like these two, pointing at his index and middle fingers.[76]

We were told about the same by Abū Kurayb[77] —Yaḥyā b.

---

66. Sufyān b. Wakīʿ b. al-Jarrāḥ appears to have been very old when he died in 247/861. See *Tahdhīb*, IV, 123–25; Horst, 296, n. 7.

67. Sufyān b. ʿUyaynah lived from 107/725 to 196/812. See *TB*, IX, 174–84; *Tahdhīb*, IV, 117–22; Sezgin, *GAS*, I, 96. See above, n. 35.

68. ʿAlī b. Zayd b. ʿAbdallāh b. Abī Mulaykah Zuhayr b. Judʿān died between 129 and 131/746–49. See *Tahdhīb*, VII, 322–24.

69. Abū Naḍrah al-Mundhir b. Mālik al-ʿAbdī al-ʿAwqī died before al-Ḥasan al-Baṣrī, presumably in 108 or 109/726–28. See *Tahdhīb*, X, 302 f.

70. I am not sure which of the many companions of the Prophet called Abū Saʿīd may be meant here. The *Tahdhīb* reference to him in connection with Abū Naḍrah (n. 69) also has no further qualification.

71. Hannād b. al-Sarī b. Muṣʿab b. Abī Bakr lived from 152/769 to 243/857. See *Tahdhīb*, XI, 70 f.

72. For Ibn ʿAyyāsh (b. 95–96/713–15, d. 193–94/808–10), see *Tahdhīb*, XII, 34–37; Ibn al-Jazarī, *Ghāyah*, I, 325–27.

73. Abū Ḥaṣīn ʿUthmān b. ʿĀṣim died between 127 and 132/744–50. See *Tahdhīb*, VII, 126–28.

74. He is to be identified with Dhakwān (above, n. 37). See Ibn Ḥajar, *Fatḥ*, XIV, 137, reporting the tradition from Ṭabarī and others with the same *isnād* to Ibn ʿAyyāsh.

75. Abū Hurayrah's death is placed in 58–59/677–79. See *Tahdhīb*, XII, 262-67; EI^2 , I, 129, s. v.; H. Hemgesberg, *Abu Huraira* (Diss. Frankfurt am Main, 1965).

76. See *Concordance*, III, 29b47–53. See also Ibn Ḥajar, *Fatḥ*, XIV, 134–38, which is largely a commentary on Ṭabarī with much additional information and various interpretations. It would seem obvious that the original meaning is the closeness of the index and middle fingers for pointing (in contrast to any other combination of two fingers). However, there is another interpretation, see below, n. 88.

77. Abū Kurayb Muḥammad b. al-ʿAlāʾ, one of Ṭabarī's most frequently quoted immediate authorities here as well as in the *Tafsīr*, died in 248/862 or the year

Ādam[78] —Abū Bakr—Abū Ḥaṣīn—Abū Ṣāliḥ—Abū Hurayrah—the Prophet.

According to Hannād—Abū al-Aḥwaṣ[79] and Abū Mu'āwiyah[80] —al-A'mash—Abū Khālid al-Wālibī[81] —Jābir b. Samurah[82] : The Messenger of God said: When I was sent, I and the Hour were like these two.

According to Abū Kūrayb—'Aththām b. 'Alī[83] —al-A'mash — Abū Khālid al-Wālibī—Jābir b. Samurah: (I feel) as if I were looking at the two fingers of the Messenger of God—pointing to the forefinger and the one next to it—while he was saying: When I was sent, I and the Hour were like this one is in relation to that one.

According to Ibn Ḥumayd—Yaḥyā b. Wāḍiḥ—Fiṭr[84] —Abū Khālid al-Wālibī—Jābir b. Samurah: The Messenger of God said: When I was sent, I and the Hour were like these two—holding his index and middle fingers together.

According to Ibn al-Muthannā—Muḥammad b. Ja'far[85] — [11]
Shu'bah[86] —Qatādah—Anas b. Mālik: The Messenger of God said: When I was sent, I and the Hour were like these two. Shu'bah said: I heard Qatādah say in his stories *(qiṣaṣihī?)*:[87] like the excess length of the one over the other.[88] (Shu'bah) added: I do not know whether (Qatādah) mentioned it on the authority of Anas or reported it on his own.

---

before, at the age of eighty-seven. See *Tahdhīb*, IX, 385 f.

78. A Qur'ān reader who studied with Ibn 'Ayyāsh for three years, he died in 203/818. See *Tahdhīb*, XI, 175 f.; Ibn al-Jazarī, *Ghāyah*, II, 363 f.

79. Not identified.

80. Abū Mu'āwiyah Muḥammad b. Khāzim al-Ḍarīr was born in 113 or 114/731–32. He died in 195/810[1]. See *Tahdhīb*, IX, 137–39.

81. Died 100/718[9]. See *Tahdhīb*, XII, 83 f.; Bukhārī, *Ta'rīkh*, IV, 2, 251; Ibn Abī Ḥātim, IV, 2, 120 f. See below, n. 577.

82. Died in the middle forties/692–95. See *Tahdhīb*, II, 39 f.

83. 'Aththām died in 195/810[1] or the year before. See *Tahdhīb*, VII, 105 f.

84. Fiṭr b. Khalīfah died between 153 and 155/770–72. See *Tahdhīb*, VIII, 300–2.

85. Apparently, Muḥammad b. Ja'far Ghundar who died between 192–94/807–10 at the age of ninety-three. See *Tahdhīb*, IX, 96–98.

86. The famous scholarly authority Shu'bah b. al-Ḥajjāj lived from 82 or 83/701–2 to 160/776[7]. See *TB*, IX, 255–66; *Tahdhīb*, IV, 338–46.

87. This might be the title of a work, or part of a work, by Qatādah (?).

88. Here we have one of the traditions that understand the reference to the two fingers not as indicating closeness *(mujāwarah* in Ibn Ḥajar, *Fatḥ*, see above, n. 76) but as indicating length *(ṭūl)*. The length of the time remaining was indicated by the difference in length between the two fingers. See below, 181 f.

According to Khallād b. Aslam[89] —al-Naḍr b. Shumayl[90] —Shu'bah—Qatādah—Anas b. Mālik: The Messenger of God said: When I was sent, I and the Hour were like these two.

We were told the same by Mujāhid b. Mūsa[91] —Yazīd[92] —Shu'bah—Qatādah—Anas b. Mālik—the Prophet, with the addition in his *ḥadīth*: and he pointed with the middle and index fingers.

According to Muḥammad b. 'Abdallāh b. 'Abd al-Ḥakam[93] —Ayyūb b. Suwayd[94] —al-Awzā'ī[95] —Ismā'īl b. 'Ubaydallāh[96]: When Anas b. Mālik came to al-Walīd b. 'Abd al-Malik,[97] al-Walīd asked him: What have you heard the Messenger of God mention about the Hour? Anas replied: I heard the Messenger of God say: You (pl.) and the Hour are like these two—pointing with his two fingers.

According to al-'Abbās b. al-Walīd[98] —his father—al-Awzā'ī—Ismā'īl b. 'Ubaydallāh: When Anas b. Mālik came to al-Walīd b. 'Abd al-Malik, al-Walīd asked him: What have you heard the Messenger of God mention about the Hour? Anas replied: I heard the

---

89. Khallād died ca. 249/863 in Sāmarrā. See *TB*, VIII, 342 f.; *Tahdhīb*, III, 171 f.

90. Died 203 or 204/818–20. See *Tahdhīb*, X, 437 f.; Yāqūt, *Irshād*, ed. Margoliouth, VII, 123 ff., ed. Rifā'ī, XIX, 238–43; Brockelmann, *GAL*, I, 102, *Suppl.*, I, 161; Sezgin, *GAS*, I, 262.

91. Mujāhid b. Mūsā lived from 158/775 to 244/858. See *TB*, XIII, 265 f.; *Tahdhīb*, X, 44 f.

92. Yazīd b. Hārūn b. Zādī b. Thābit was born in 118/736 or the year before. He died in 206/821. See *TB*, XIV, 337–47; *Tahdhīb*, XI, 366-69.

93. A member of the well-known Egyptian family of traditionists and historians, the source also of many traditions in Ṭabarī's *Tafsīr*, he lived from 182/799 to 268 or 269/882–83. See *Tahdhīb*, IX, 260–62; *EI*^{2}, III, 674 f., s. v. Ibn 'Abd al-Ḥakam; Sezgin, *GAS*, I, 474.; above, General Introduction, 28 f.

94. The dates of death indicated in *Tahdhīb*, I, 405 f., are hard to reconcile with this chain of transmitters. If Ayyūb b. Suwayd drowned in 193/808[9], Ibn 'Abd al-Ḥakam would then have been only ten or eleven years old. 201 or 202/816–18 also seems unlikely. However, as a transmitter from al-Awzā'ī, he probably could not have died much later.

95. The jurist and founder of a short-lived legal school, al-Awzā'ī died in 157/773[4] at the age of seventy, according to Ṭabarī, *Dhayl al-Mudhayyal*, ed. Leiden, III, 2514, ed. Cairo, XI, 656. Slightly different dates appear in *Tahdhīb*, VI, 238–42. See also *EI*^{2}, I, 772 f., s. v.

96. Born in 61/680[1], Ismā'īl b. 'Ubaydallāh died in 131 or 132/748–50. See *Tahdhīb*, I, 317 f.

97. The two Umayyad caliphs reigned, respectively, in 685–705 and 705–15.

98. Al-'Abbās b. al-Walīd b. Mazyad lived from around 169/785[6] to 270/883[4]. Ṭabarī studied with him in Bayrūt. According to al-'Abbās, his father died in 203/818[9] at the age of seventy-seven. See *Tahdhīb*, V, 131–133, XI, 150 f.; Ibn 'Asākir, *Tahdhīb*, VII, 272; Ṣafadī, *Wāfī*, XVI, 658.

Messenger of God say: All of you and the Hour are like these two.

According to Ibn ʿAbd al-Raḥīm al-Barqī[99] —ʿAmr b. Abī Salamah[100] —al-Awzāʿī—Ismāʿīl b. ʿUbaydallāh: When Anas b. Mālik came to al-Walīd b. ʿAbd al-Malik, and so on.

According to Muḥammad b. ʿAbd al-Aʿlā[101] —al-Muʿtamir b. Su- [12]
laymān[102] —his father—Maʿbad[103] —Anas: The Messenger of God said: When I was sent, I and the Hour were like these two. He added: With his two fingers, thus!

According to Ibn al-Muthannā—Wahb b. Jarīr[104] —Shuʿbah—Abū al-Tayyāḥ[105] —Anas: The Messenger of God said: When I was sent, I and the Hour were like these two—the index and middle fingers. Said Abū Mūsā (Ibn al-Muthannā): Wahb pointed with the index and middle fingers.

According to ʿAbdallāh b. Abī Ziyād[106] —Wahb b. Jarīr—Shuʿbah—Abū al-Tayyāḥ and Qatādah—Anas: The Messenger of God said: When I was sent, I and the Hour were like these two—joining his two fingers.

According to Muḥammad b. ʿAbdallāh b. Bazīʿ[107] —al-Fuḍayl b. Sulaymān[108] —Abū Ḥāzim[109] —Sahl b. Saʿd[110] : I saw the Messenger of God, holding his two fingers, the middle finger and the one

---

99. The two brothers Aḥmad and Muḥammad, the sons of ʿAbdallāh b. ʿAbd al-Raḥīm, are often referred to as (Ibn) al-Barqī and can then not be distinguished. Aḥmad is listed in Ibn Abī Ḥātim, I,1, 61, Muḥammad in III,2, 301. The latter supposedly died in 249/863. See *Tahdhīb*, IX, 263.

100. ʿAmr b. Abī Salamah, Abū Ḥafṣ al-Tinnīsī, died between 212 and 214/827–29. See *Tahdhīb*, VIII, 43 f.

101. Muḥammad b. ʿAbd al-Aʿlā al-Ṣanʿānī died in 245/859[60] in al-Baṣrah. See *Tahdhīb*, IX, 289; Horst, 296, n. 1. Al-Muʿtamir b. Sulaymān is named as his authority in Bukhārī, *Taʾrīkh*, II,1, 174; Rosenthal, *Muslim Historiography*[2], 395.

102. Born in or before 100/718[9]. al-Muʿtamir died in 187/802[3]. See *Tahdhīb*, X, 227 f. For his father Abū al-Muʿtamir Sulaymān b. Ṭarkhān (ca. 46–143/666–760), see *Tahdhīb*, IV, 201–3; Sezgin, *GAS*, I, 285 f.

103. For Maʿbad b. Hilāl, see *Tahdhīb*, X, 225.

104. Wahb b. Jarīr died in 206 or 207/821–23. See *Tahdhīb*, XI, 161 f.

105. Abū al-Tayyāḥ Yazīd b. Ḥumayd died between 128 and 130/745–48. See *Tahdhīb*, XI, 320 f.; Ibn Ḥajar, *Fatḥ*, XIV, 134.

106. ʿAbdallāh b. Abī Ziyād al-Ḥakam al-Qaṭawānī died in 255/869. See *Tahdhīb*, V, 190.

107. Ibn Bazīʿ died in 247/861[2]. See *Tahdhīb*, IX, 248 f.

108. Died around the middle of the 180s/799–802. See *Tahdhīb*, VIII, 291 f.

109. Abū Ḥāzim Salamah b. Dīnār died between 130 and 140/747–57. See *Tahdhīb*, IV, 143 f.

110. Sahl b. Saʿd al-Sāʿidī was supposedly born in 617 and may have lived until 88/707 or even longer. See *Tahdhīb*, IV, 252 f.; Ibn ʿAbd al-Barr, *Istīʿāb*, II, 664 f.

next to the thumb, thus! He said: When I was sent, I and the Hour were like these two.

According to Muḥammad b. Yazīd al-Adamī[111] —Abū Ḍamrah[112] —Abū Ḥāzim—Sahl b. Sa'd al-Sā'idī: The Messenger of God said: I was sent with the Hour like these two—pressing the middle finger and the one next to the thumb together. He said: I and the Hour are just like two race horses (in a closely contested race).[113] Then he said: I and the Hour are just like a man sent by people in advance as a scout. When he is afraid that he will be overtaken, he signals with his cloth: They have reached you! They have reached you! It is me! It is me!

According to Abū Kurayb—Khālid[114] —Muḥammad b. Ja'far—Abū Ḥāzim—Sahl b. Sa'd: The Messenger of God said: When I was sent, I and the Hour were like these two—holding his two fingers together.

[13] According to Abū Kurayb—Khālid—Sulaymān b. Bilāl[115] —Abū Ḥāzim[116] —Sahl b. Sa'd: The Messenger of God said: When I was sent, I and the Hour were thus—joining his two fingers, the middle finger and the one next to the thumb.

According to Ibn 'Abd al-Raḥīm al-Barqī—Ibn Abī Maryam[117] —Muḥammad b. Ja'far—Abū Ḥāzim—Sahl b. Sa'd: The Messenger of God said: When I was sent, I and the Hour were like these two—holding his two fingers together.

According to Abū Kurayb—Abū Nu'aym—Bashīr b. al-Muhājir[118] —'Abdallāh b. Buraydah[119] —his father: I heard the Messenger of God say: I and the Hour were sent together. It almost preceded me.

---

111. Died 245/860. See *TB*, III, 374; *Tahdhīb*, IX, 530.

112. Abū Ḍamrah Anas b. 'Iyāḍ was born around 104/722[3] and died in 200/815. See *Tahdhīb*, I, 375.

113. Cf. Rosenthal, *Gambling*, 117.

114. Khālid b. Makhlad died in the early 210s/825–30. See *Tahdhīb*, III, 116–18.

115. Died in the 170s/ca. 788–93 in Medina. See *Tahdhīb*, IV, 175 f.

116. Abū Sālim in the Leiden edition seems a simple mistake.

117. Sa'īd b. al-Ḥakam b. Abī Maryam lived from 144/761[2] to 224/838[9]. See *Tahdhīb*, IV, 17 f.

118. See *Tahdhīb*, I, 468 f.

119. Supposedly born in 637, 'Abdallāh b. Buraydah b. al-Ḥuṣayb al-Aslamī died as judge of Marw, possibly as late as 115/733 (?). His father died between 60 and 64/679–84. See *Tahdhīb*, V, 157 f., and I, 432 f.

According to Muḥammad b. ʿUmar b. Hayyāj[120]—Yaḥyā b. ʿAbd al-Raḥmān[121]—ʿUbaydah b. al-Aswad[122]—Mujālid[123]—Qays b. Abī Ḥāzim[124]—al-Mustawrid b. Shaddād al-Fihrī[125]: The Prophet said: I was sent immediately before the coming of the Hour. I preceded it like this one preceding that one—(referring) to his two fingers, the index finger and the middle finger. Abū ʿAbdallāh[126] described (it) to us by holding the two fingers together.

According to Aḥmad b. Muḥammad b. Ḥabīb[127]—Abū Naṣr[128]—al-Masʿūdī[129]—Ismāʿīl b. Abī Khālid[130]—al-Shaʿbī[131]—Abū Jabīrah:[132] The Messenger of God said: I was sent together with the Hour like these two—pointing with his two fingers, the middle finger and the index finger—like the excess length of this one over that one.

According to Tamīm b. al-Muntaṣir[133]—Yazīd (b. Hārūn)—Ismāʿīl (b. Abī Khālid)—Shubayl b. ʿAwf[134]—Abū Jabīrah—some elders of the Anṣār: We heard the Messenger of God say: When I [14]
came, I and the Hour were thus! Al-Ṭabarī says: Tamīm demonstrated it to us. He pressed the index finger and the middle finger

120. Died 255/869. See *Tahdhīb*, IX, 362 f.

121. See *Tahdhīb*, XI, 250.

122. See *Tahdhīb*, VII, 86.

123. Mujālid b. Saʿīd b. ʿUmayr died in 144/762. See *Tahdhīb*, X, 39–41.

124. Qays b. Abī Ḥāzim seems to have died in the late 90s/712–17. See *Tahdhīb*, VIII, 386–89.

125. Al-Mustawrid died in 45/665[6] in Alexandria. See *Tahdhīb*, X, 106 f.

126. According to *Tahdhīb*, only Qays b. Abī Ḥāzim, among those mentioned in the chain of transmitters, had the patronymic Abū ʿAbdallāh. Ibn Hayyāj's patronymic supposedly was Abū ʿUbaydallāh.

127. Unidentified. His *nisbah* was al-Ṭūsī. See below, n. 226.

128. Unidentified. See below, n. 551.

129. ʿAbd al-Raḥmān b. ʿAbdallāh al-Masʿūdī died in 165/781[2]. See *Tahdhīb*, VI, 210–12. His descendant Yaḥyā b. Ibrāhīm b. Muḥammad b. Abī ʿUbaydah b. Maʿn (see *Tahdhīb*, XI, 174 f.) provided Ṭabarī with information through a family *isnād*. See, for instance, *Tafsīr*, V, 81, VII, 57, XIV, 20, XXIII, 91, XXVI, 17, XXVII, 117.

130. Died 146/763[4]. See *Tahdhīb*, I, 291 f.

131. The famous ʿAmr b. Sharaḥīl al-Shaʿbī was born in 640 and died sometime during the third decade of the eighth century. See *TB*, XII, 227–34; *Tahdhīb*, V, 65–69; Sezgin, *GAS*, I, 277.

132. See *Tahdhīb*, XII, 52 f. According to Ibn ʿAbd al-Barr, *Istīʿāb*, IV, 1619, three companions of the Prophet bore the patronymic Abū Jabīrah.

133. Born in 169/785[6] or later, Tamīm died in 244/858[9], according to his grandson Baḥshal, the author of the *History of Wāsiṭ*, 233 f. See also *Tahdhīb*, I, 514 f.

134. See *Tahdhīb*, IV, 311; Bukhārī, *Taʾrīkh*, II, 2, 259.

together and said to us: Yazīd pointed with his two fingers, the index finger and the middle finger, pressing them together. He continued. I preceded the Hour like this one precedes that one, immediately before the coming of the Hour, using the expression *nafas min al-sāʿah* or *nafas al-sāʿah.*

Thus, (the evidence permitting) a conclusion is as follows: The beginning of the day is the rise of dawn, and its end is the setting of the sun. Further, the reported tradition on the authority of the Prophet is sound. As we have mentioned earlier, he said after having prayed the afternoon prayer: What remains of this world as compared to what has passed of it is just like what remains of this day as compared to what has passed of it. He also said: When I was sent, I and the Hour were like these two—holding index finger and middle finger together; I preceded it to the same extent as this one—meaning the middle finger—preceded that one—meaning the index finger. Further, the extent (of time) between the mean time of the afternoon prayer—that is, when the shadow of every thing is twice its size, according to the best assumption (*ʿalā al-taḥarrī)* —(to sunset) is the extent of time of one-half of one-seventh of the day, give or take a little. Likewise, the excess of the length of the middle finger over that of the index finger is something about that or close to it.[135] There is also a sound tradition on the authority of the Messenger of God, as I was told by Aḥmad b. ʿAbd al-Raḥmān b. Wahb[136] —his paternal uncle ʿAbdallāh b. Wahb[137] —Muʿāwiyah b. Ṣāliḥ[138] —ʿAbd al-Raḥmān b. Jubayr b. Nufayr[139] —his father Jubayr b. Nufayr—the companion of the Prophet, Abū Thaʿlabah al-Khushanī[140] : The Messenger of

135. Rough measuring of my middle and index fingers shows the proportion to be about 9 cm to 8.3 cm. Seven-tenths is slightly more than one-fourteenth of nine. The time of the afternoon prayer is mostly defined as beginning when an object's shadow is one-third of its size (in addition to what it was at noon), and extending to the time of the sunset prayer. One-fourteenth of a day apparently refers to one-fourteenth of a twenty-four hour period.

136. Died 264/877. See *Tahdhīb*, I, 54–56.

137. Born in 125/742[3], he died in 197/813. See *Tahdhīb*, VI, 71–74; Sezgin, *GAS*, I, 466; Horst, 305, n. 2.

138. Muʿāwiyah b. Ṣāliḥ died in the 170s/around 790, or in the 150s/around 770 (?). See *Tahdhīb*, X, 209–12; Horst, 293, n. 4.

139. He died in 118/736, and his father, who was born in pre-Islamic times, died ca. 80/699. See *Tahdhīb*, VI, 154, and II, 64 f.; Ibn ʿAbd al-Barr, *Istīʿāb*, I, 234.

140. Abū Thaʿlabah died in or before 75/694. See *Tahdhīb*, XII, 49-51; Ibn ʿAbd

God said: Indeed, God will not make this nation incapable of (lasting) half a day—referring to the day of a thousand years. [15]

All these facts taken together make it clear that of the two statements I have mentioned concerning the total extent of time, the one from Ibn ʿAbbās, and the other from Kaʿb,[141] the one more likely to be correct in accordance with the information coming from the Messenger of God is that of Ibn ʿAbbās transmitted here by us on his authority: The world is one of the weeks of the other world—seven thousand years.[142]

Consequently, because this is so and the report on the authority of the Messenger of God is sound—namely, that he reported that what remained of the time of this world during his life was half a day, or five hundred years, since five hundred years are half a day of the days, of which one is a thousand years—the conclusion is that the time of this world that had elapsed to the moment of the Prophet's statement corresponds to what we have transmitted on the authority of Abū Thaʿlabah al-Khushanī from the Prophet, and is 6,500 years or approximately 6,500 years. God knows best!

Our statement about the duration of the periods *(azmān)* of this world from its very beginning to its very end is the most firmly established of all the statements we have, on account of the testimony to its soundness as explained by us. Information has (also) been transmitted on the authority of the Messenger of God to prove the soundness of the statement that all of this world is six thousand years. If its chain of transmitters were sound, we would have to go no further. It is Muḥammad b. Sinān al-Qazzāz[143] —ʿAbd al-Ṣamad b. ʿAbd al-Wārith[144] —Zabbān[145] —ʿĀṣim[146] —

al-Barr, *Istīʿāb*, IV, 1618.

141. See text above, I, 8.

142. According to the Prophet, five hundred years remain, and they are one-fourteenth of the total duration of the world.

143. Muḥammad b. Sinān died in 271/884[5] at an advanced age, since some of his authorities died in the early years of the second century. See *Tahdhīb*, IX, 206 f.

144. Died 206 or 207/821–22. See *Tahdhīb*, VI, 327 f. His son ʿAbd al-Wārith (d. 252/866) transmitted information to Ṭabarī, see, for instance, *Tafsīr*, II, 28.

145. If Zabbān is correct, he would be Zabbān b. Fāʾid (text below, I, 318), who died in 155/771[2]. See *Tahdhīb*, III, 308. But note that *Tahdhīb*, VI, 327, lists Abān (below, n. 823) as one of the authorities of ʿAbd al-Ṣamad.

146. ʿĀṣim b. Bahdalah, the great Kūfan Qurʾān reader, is said to have died in 127 or 128/744–46, although earlier dates in the 120s were also suggested. See *Tahdhīb*, V, 38–40; Ibn al-Jazarī, *Ghāyah*, 346–49; EI^2, I, 706 f., s. v.; Sezgin, *GAS*, I, 7. The

Abū Ṣāliḥ—Abū Hurayrah: The Messenger of God said: *Al-ḥuqb* is eighty years. The day of them is one-sixth of this world.[147] According to this tradition, it is clear that all of this world is six thousand years. That is because, if one day of the other world equals one
[16] thousand years and a single such day is one-sixth of this world, the conclusion would be that the total is six of the days of the other world, and that is six thousand years.

The Jews assume that they can consider the total (age of the world) from God's creation of Adam to the time of the hijrah as firmly established at 4,642 years according to what is clearly stated in their Torah—the one they possess today.[148] They have made a detailed count by indicating the birth and death of each man and prophet from the time of Adam to the hijrah of our prophet Muḥammad. I hope to mention those details and other detailed counts made by scholars from among the people of the Scriptures and other scholars expert in biography and history when I get to it, if God wills.

The Greek Christians assume that the Jewish claim in this re-

---

identification of 'Āṣim with 'Āṣim (b. Bahdalah) b. Abī al-Najjūd is indicated in *Tafsīr* (see the following note).

147. *Ḥuqb*, pl. *aḥqāb*, occurs in Qur. 18:60 and 78:23. The meaning appears to be something like "long time." In his *Tafsīr*, Ṭabarī is very detailed in connection with Qur. 78:23 *(Tafsīr*, XXX, 8 f.). The tradition there, with the *isnād* from Abū Hurayrah to 'Āṣim, defines *ḥuqb* as being eighty years of 360 days, of which each day is a thousand years. Most of the other traditions cited are similar, but none of them speaks of the duration of the world, as is the case here. In "(The day of) them," the antecedent of "them" could only be "years." Unless the text was corrupt already in Ṭabarī's original, his reasoning might be: Each day of those eighty years is like a thousand years, and a thousand years is one-sixth of the duration of this world. However, in the context, this seems to explain nothing.

148. Ibn al-Athīr, *Kāmil*, ed. Tornberg, I, 11, has 4,343. This is closer to the figure of 4,381–82 which is given by Ḥamzah al-Iṣfahānī, *Annales*, 85 (cf. Bīrūnī, *Chronology*, text, 14 f., trans., 17 f.) and which corresponds to traditional Jewish usage. The figure 4,042 in Ḥamzah,11, appears to be a simple mistake, with the three (six ?) hundred missing (?).

The Christian figure of 5,992 is close to that of 5,990 in Ḥamzah and that of 5,969 of the Antiochian era, to which Ginzel, III, 288, refers. Bīrūnī has 6,122–3.

The Persian figure of 3,139 years seems to have no counterpart elsewhere. It is always much higher, such as 4,182 or 4,409 in Ḥamzah, 11 and 29, and 4,287–8 in Bīrūnī. It is somewhat closer to the 3,725 or 3,735 years from the Flood to Yazdjard mentioned in the *zīj*es. However, if the number of years from Adam to the Flood is added to that figure, the difference between the resulting figure and 3,139 is even greater. See Pingree, *Thousands*, 39 f., 130; Hāshimī, *'Ilal*, 246.

The source for Ṭabarī's precise figures remains to be found. See also text, below, I, 1068 ff., and, for instance, Stern, "Abū 'Īsā."

spect is false. According to their view of the sequence in the Torah that they possess, the duration of the days of this world from the creation of Adam to the time of the hijrah of our Prophet Muḥammad is properly stated at 5,992 years and some months. They have made a detailed count to support their claim by indicating the birth and death of each prophet and ruler from the age of Adam to the hijrah of the Messenger of God. They assume that the smaller number of years in the Jewish chronology as against that of the Christians results from the fact that the Jews rejected the prophethood of Jesus, the son of Mary, since (for them) his description and the time of his being sent (as a prophet) are firmly established in the Torah.[149] They say: The time that is fixed for us in the Torah for the person whose description is that of Jesus has not yet come. They believe that they are waiting for his appear- [17]
ance and his time.

I think that the person whom they are waiting for, claiming that his description is firmly established in the Torah, is the Antichrist *(al-Dajjāl),* whom the Messenger of God has described to his nation. He mentioned to them that most of the Antichrist's followers will be Jews. If the Antichrist is ʿAbdallāh b. Ṣayyād,[150] he is a person of Jewish origin.

The Magians[151] assume that the duration of time from King Jayūmart to the time of the hijrah of our Prophet is 3,139 years. They do not combine that with a known genealogy beyond Jayūmart, assuming that Jayūmart is Adam, the father of mankind–May God pray for and give peace to him and all the prophets and messengers of God![152] Historians continue to hold

149. According to Bīrūnī, *Chronology,* text, 15, trans., 18, the shorter chronology of the Jews resulted from their desire to have the appearance of Jesus occur in the fourth millennium, in the middle of the seven thousand years corresponding to their expectation for the world's duration.

150. For the legendary Ibn Ṣayyād, who is supposed to have contact with the Prophet and to have died in 63/682–83, see Wensinck, *Handbook,* 103b; Ibn Khaldūn, *Muqaddimah,* I, 205; D. J. Halperin, "The Ibn Ṣayyād traditions."

151. See *EI*[2], V, 1110–18, s. v. Madjūs. The Zoroastrian mythology covered by Ṭabarī in this volume extends from Gayōmart to Jamshēd. It has been treated in considerable detail by A. Christensen in the two volumes of *Les types du Premier Homme et du Premier Roi.* Christensen includes translations of the relevant material from Ṭabarī and the later Muslim literature. The translation of the above passage appears in Christensen, I, 66 f.

152. See, further, text below, I, 147 f.

different opinions about him. Some say the same as the Magians. Others say that he took the name of Adam after he became ruler of the seven climes, and that he was none other than Gomer b. Japheth b. Noah.[153] He was pious, kind, and affectionate to Noah and attached to his service. Because of his piety and service to him, Noah prayed for him and his progeny to God to give him a long life, to have him firmly settled in the land, to grant him victory over those who opposed him and them, and to provide for him and his progeny royal authority that would last uninterruptedly. His prayer was heard. Jayūmart and his children were granted all of that. He is the father of the Persians. He and his children continued to rule until their royal authority came to an end when the Muslims entered Madā'in Kisrā[154] and took it away from them. Others say others things. We hope to mention the statements that have reached us, when we mention the chronology of the (Persian) rulers, how long they lived, their genealogy and the circumstances
[18] of[155] their royal authority.

The Proofs for the Origination of Momentary and Extended Time and Night and Day

We have said earlier that time is but a noun designating the hours of night and day.[156] The hours of night and day are but measurements indicated by the running of the sun and the moon in the sphere, as God says: "And a sign for them is the night. We strip the day from it. So they are in darkness. And the sun: It runs to a place where it is to reside (at night). This is decreed by the One Mighty and Knowing. And the moon: We have decreed for it stations, until it becomes again (slender) and curved) like an ancient raceme of a palm tree (which has been left on the tree stripped of the dates). The sun must not reach the moon, nor does night precede day. All swim in a sphere."[157]

Since time has to do with the hours of night and day as we have

---

153. Gomer (see Genesis 10:2), whose name evoked that of Gayōmart, appears as Jāmir in Arabic. See also text below, I, 216, etc.

154. "The cities of Khusraw (Chosroes)" refers to ancient Ctesiphon. See *EI*², V, 945 f., s. v. al-Madā'in.

155. This may be meant rather than "the reasons for."

156. See text above, I, 8.

157. Qur. 36:37–40.

mentioned, and the hours of night and day are but the traversal by the sun and the moon of the degrees of the sphere, the conclusion is certain that time as well as night and day are originated and that the One Who originated that is God Who alone by Himself originated His entire creation. "He is the One Who created night and day, the sun and the moon. All swim in a sphere."[158] Even one not knowing that that originates from God's creation can indeed not be ignorant of the difference in the conditions of night and day, namely that one of them—the night—brings down blackness and darkness upon creation, and the other—the day—brings down light and luminosity upon them and the removal of the night's blackness and darkness.

Now if this so, and it is impossible that the two with their different conditions come together at any one moment anywhere, the certain conclusion is that one of them must be before the other, and whichever is before its companion has the other no doubt come after it. This is explanation and proof for their origination [19]
and for their being creatures of their Creator.

A further proof for the origination of days and nights is that each day comes after a day that was before it, and before a day that will come after it. Now, it is known that what was not and came into being was originated and created and has a creator and originator. Still another proof is that days and nights are countable. Anything that can be counted must have either an even or an odd number. If it is an even number, it begins with two. This shows the soundness of the statement that it has a beginning and a start. If it is an odd number, then it starts with one. This proves that it has a beginning and a start. Now, whatever has a beginning must have one who begins (it), and that is its creator.

Whether God, before He Created Time and Night and Day, Created Any Other of the Created Things

We have stated before that time is but the hours of night and day and that the hours are but the traversal by the sun and the moon of the degrees of the sphere.

Now then, this being so, there is (also) a sound tradition from

158. Qur. 21:33.

the Messenger of God told us by Hannād b. al-Sarī, who also said that he read all of the *ḥadīth* (to Abū Bakr)[159] —Abū Bakr b. ʿAyyāsh—Abū Saʿd al-Baqqāl[160] —ʿIkrimah[161] —Ibn ʿAbbās: The Jews came to the Prophet and asked him about the creation of the heavens and the earth. He said: God created the earth on Sunday and Monday. He created the mountains and the uses they possess on Tuesday. On Wednesday, He created trees, water, cities and the cultivated and barren land. These are four (days). He continued (citing the Qur'ān): "Say: Do you really not believe in the One Who created the earth in two days, and set up others like Him?
[20] That is the Lord of the worlds. He made in it firmly anchored (mountains) above it and blessed it and decreed that it contain the amount of food it provides, (all) in four days, equally for those asking"[162] —for those who ask.[163] He continued: On Thursday, He created heaven. On Friday, He created the stars, the sun, the moon, and the angels, until three hours remained. In the first of these three hours, He created the terms (of human life), who would live and who would die. In the second, He cast harm upon everything that is useful for mankind. And in the third, (He created) Adam and had him dwell in Paradise. He commanded Iblīs to prostrate himself before Adam,[164] and He drove Adam out of Paradise at the end of the hour. When the Jews asked: What then, Muḥammad? he said: "Then He sat straight upon the Throne."[165] The Jews said: You would be right, if you had finished, they said, with: Then He rested. Whereupon the Prophet got very angry, and it was revealed: "We have created the heavens and the earth and what is between them in six days, and fatigue did not touch Us. Thus be patient with what you say!"[166]

---

159. The clarifying "to Abū Bakr" appears only in *Tafsīr,* XXIV, 61, as stated in the Cairo edition, but not in Ṭabarī's text here or below, I, 42 and 54.

160. Died in the 140s/757–66. See *Tahdhīb,* IV, 79 f.

161. ʿIkrimah, a *mawlā* of Ibn ʿAbbās and one of the most distinguished transmitters, is supposed to have died around 104–7/722–25 at the age of eighty. See *Tahdhīb,* VII, 263–73; *EI*², III, 1081 f., s. v. ʿIkrima; Horst, 295, n. 6.

162. Qur. 41:9 f.

163. For this paraphrase, see *Tafsīr,* XXIV, 61, l. 12; text below, I, 51.

164. See *EI*², III, 668 f., s. v. For a more detailed study of the controversial Iblīs figure in Islam, see Awn, *Satan's Tragedy and Redemption.*

165. Qur. 7:54, etc.

166. Qur. 50:38 f. For the entire tradition, see *Tafsīr,* XXVI, 61.

According to al-Qāsim b. Bishr b. Ma'rūf[167] and al-Ḥusayn b. 'Alī al-Ṣudā'ī[168] —Ḥajjāj[169] —Ibn Jurayj[170] —Ismā'īl b. Umayyah[171] —Ayyūb b. Khālid[172] —'Abdallāh b. Rāfi', the *mawlā* of Umm Salamah[173] —Abū Hurayrah: The Messenger of God took me by the hand. Then he said: God created the soil on Saturday. Upon it, He created the mountains on Sunday. He created the trees on Monday. He created evil[174] on Tuesday. He created light on Wednesday. He scattered the animals on the earth on Thursday, and He created Adam as the last of His creatures after (the time of) the afternoon prayer in the last hour of Friday, in the time between the afternoon prayer and night(fall).[175]

According to Muḥammad b. 'Abdallāh b. Bazī'—al-Fuḍayl b. Sulaymān—Muḥammad b. Zayd[176] —Abū Salamah b. 'Abd al- [21]
Raḥmān b. 'Awf[177] —Ibn Salām[178] and Abū Hurayrah who men-

167. Al-Qāsim b. Bishr b. Aḥmad (or Aḥmad b. Bishr) b. Ma'rūf appears to be the individual meant here. See *TB*, XII, 427; *Tahdhīb*, VIII, 308. For the common *isnād* starting with al-Qāsim—al-Ḥusayn, see below, nn. 185 and 186. This is, in fact, the form in which the *isnād* appears in connection with the tradition in *Tafsīr*, XII, 3 (*ad* Qur. 11:7).

168. Al-Ṣudā'ī died in 246 or 248/860–62. See *Tahdhīb*, II, 359; Sam 'ānī, *Ansāb*, VIII, 283.

169. Ḥajjāj (or al-Ḥajjāj) b. Muḥammad, the transmitter of Ibn Jurayj's Qur'ān commentary, died in 206/821[2]. See *TB*, VIII, 236–39; *Tahdhīb*, II, 205 f.; Horst, 295, n. 3. The same chain of transmitters is found in connection with the *ḥadīth* in Muslim, *Ṣaḥīḥ*, II, 640; Ibn Ḥanbal, II, 327; *Concordance*, I, 268a23, VI, 5b42.

170. Ibn Jurayj, 'Abd al-Malik b. 'Abd al-'Azīz, died seventy years old between 149 and 151/766–68. See *Tahdhīb*, VI, 402–6; Sezgin, *GAS*, I, 91; Horst, 295, n. 4.

171. Ismā'īl b. Umayyah died between 139 and 144/756–61. See *Tahdhīb*, I, 283 f.

172. See *Tahdhīb*, I, 401, no. 739; Bukhārī, *Ta'rīkh*, I, 1, 413 f., where reference is made to the *ḥadīth* above.

173. For this *mawlā* of the Prophet's wife Umm Salamah, see *Tahdhīb*, V, 206.

174. *Al-makrūh* is explained as "evil," because it is considered as contrasting with the following "light," which is good. See Ibn al-Athīr, *Nihāyah*, IV, 18. *Wörterbuch*, letter K, 158a, refers further to a late work translated by Rescher, *Orientalische Miszellen*, I, 173, which characterizes the days of the week and states that Tuesday is the most unlucky day of all. See also below, n. 369. However, the "evil" contrasted with "light" could conceivably be darkness. "Darkness" does appear, if rarely, as a separate creation, see text below, I, 36.

175. See *Tafsīr*, XII, 3 (*ad* Qur. 11:7).

176. Muḥammad b. Zayd b. al-Muhājir b. Qunfudh is stated to have lived a hundred years. See *Tahdhīb*, IX, 173 f.

177. For this son of the powerful member of the electoral council at the death of the caliph 'Umar, see *Tahdhīb*, XII, 115–18.

178. 'Abdallāh b. Salām supposedly died in 43/663[4] in Medīna. See *Tahdhīb*, V, 249; *EI*², 52, s. v.; Sezgin, *GAS*, I, 304.

tioned the hour (of Adam's creation) on Friday on the authority of the Prophet as he stated it. 'Abdallāh b. Salām said: I know which hour it is. God began the creation of the heavens and the earth on Sunday, and He finished in the last hour of Friday. Thus, it is the last hour of Friday (in which Adam was created).

According to al-Muthannā[179] —al-Ḥajjāj—Ḥammād[180] —'Aṭā' b. al-Sā'ib[181] —'Ikrimah: The Jews asked the Prophet: What about Sunday? The Messenger of God replied: On it, God created the earth and spread it out. They asked about Monday, and he replied: On it, He created Adam. They asked about Tuesday, and he replied: On it, He created the mountains, water, and so on. They asked about Wednesday, and he replied: Food. They asked about Thursday, and he replied: He created the heavens. They asked about Friday, and he replied: God created night and day. Then, when they asked about Saturday and mentioned God's rest(ing on it), he exclaimed: God be praised! God then revealed: "We have created the heavens and the earth and what is between them in six days, and fatigue did not touch Us."[182]

The two reports transmitted by us from the Messenger of God have made it clear that the sun and the moon were created after God had created many things of His creation. That is because the *ḥadīth* of Ibn 'Abbās on the authority of the Messenger of God indicates that God created the sun and the moon on Friday. If this is so, earth and heaven and what is in them, except the angels and Adam, had been created before God created the sun and the moon. All this (thus) existed while there was no light and no day, since night and day are but nouns designating hours known through the traversal by the sun and the moon of the course of
[22] the sphere. Now, if it is correct that the earth and the heaven and what is between them, except what we have mentioned, were in existence when there was no sun and no moon, the conclusion is that all that existed when there was no night and no day. The

---

179. For Ṭabarī's compatriot and early teacher al-Muthannā b. Ibrāhīm al-Āmulī, one of his most often quoted authorities in the *Tafsīr*, see Horst, 293, n. 2; above, General Introduction, n. 48. For al-Ḥajjāj, see below, n. 319.

180. Since 'Aṭā' had both Ḥammāds as his students, the one here could be either Ḥammād b. Abī Sulaymān (above, n. 29) or Ḥammād b. Salamah b. Dīnār. The latter died in 167/784. See *Tahdhīb*, III, 11–16. See also *TB*, III, 284, l. 16.

181. 'Aṭā' died in the 130s/750–55. See *Tahdhīb*, VII, 203–7.

182. Qur. 50:38.

same (conclusion results from) the following *ḥadīth* of Abū Hurayrah reported on the authority of the Messenger of God: God created light on Wednesday—meaning by "light" the sun, if God wills.

Someone might ask: You have assumed that "day" is just a noun designating a period of time (*mīqāt*) between the rising of dawn and the setting of the sun, and now, you assume that God created the sun and the moon days after He began creating the things He did. Thus, you have established periods of time and called them "days" while there was no sun and no moon. If you have no proof for the soundness of this, it is a contradictory statement.

The answer is: God called what I have mentioned "days." Thus, I have used for them the same designation He did. The use of "days" when there was no sun and no moon may be compared to (the use of "morning" and "evening" in) God's word: "They have their sustenance in (Paradise) in the morning and in the evening"[183] —(using "morning" and "evening" in spite of the fact that) there is no morning or evening there, because there is no night in the other world and no sun and no moon, as God says: "Those who do not believe are in doubt about it, until the Hour comes upon them suddenly, or the punishment of a barren day comes upon them."[184] God called the Day of Resurrection a "barren day", because it is a day with no night after its coming. Speaking of the "days" before the creation of the sun and the moon was intended to refer to a period of a thousand of the years of this world, each of which has twelve of the months of the people of this world. Their hours and days are counted by the traversal by the sun and the moon of the course of the spheres. Likewise, "morning" and "evening" in connection with the sustenance provided for the inhabitants of Paradise were used for a period of duration with which they were familiar in this connection as "time" in this world. That is, "time" as indicated by the sun and its running in
the sphere, although, for the inhabitants of Paradise, there is no [23]
sun and no night.

Similar statements have been made by early scholars, such as, for instance

183. Qur. 19:62.

184. Qur. 22:55. "Barren" is "childless," because the Day of Resurrection produces no night to follow upon it.

According to al-Qāsim[185] —al-Ḥusayn[186] —Ḥajjāj—Ibn Jurayj—Mujāhid: God entrusts the management of everything to the angels for a thousand years, and then again until another thousand years have elapsed, repeating the process forever. He said: "(In) a day whose measure is a thousand years".[187] "Day" is His saying to what He entrusts to the angels for a thousand years: "Be! And it is."[188] But He called it "day", calling it just as He pleased. All this is on the authority of Mujāhid. He continued. God's word: "A day with your Lord is like a thousand years of your counting,"[189] is entirely the same thing.[190]

Reports similar to the one that has come down on the Prophet's authority, namely, that God created the sun and the moon after His creation of the heavens and the earth and other things, have come down from a number of early (scholars), as follows:

According to Abū Hishām al-Rifāʿī—Ibn Yamān[191] —Sufyān—Ibn Jurayj—Sulaymān b. Mūsā[192] —Mujāhid—Ibn ʿAbbās, commenting on: "And He said to (the heaven) and the earth: Come willingly or unwillingly! They said: We come willingly,"[193] as follows: God said to the heavens: Cause My sun and My moon to rise and cause My stars to rise, and to the earth He said: Split your rivers[194] and bring forth your fruit. Both replied: "We come willingly."[195]

185. Al-Qāsim always appears in Ṭabarī as the transmitter from al-Ḥusayn b. Dāwūd. Horst, 295, n. 1, identifies him with al-Qāsim b. al-Ḥasan b. Yazīd al-Hamadhānī, who died in 272/885. See *TB*, XII, 432. *TB* mentions as one of his authorities Mūsā b. Ismāʿīl al-Tabūdhakī who, like al-Ḥusayn b. Dāwūd, died in the 220s (see below, n. 270).

186. Al-Ḥusayn b. Dāwūd, who died in 226/840[1] was known as Sunayd. He studied Ibn Jurayj's collection of traditions, entitled *al-Jāmiʿ*, with Ḥajjāj. See *TB*, 42–44; *Tahdhīb*, IV, 244 f.; Horst, 295, n. 2.

187. Qur. 32:5.

188. Qur. 2:117, etc.

189. Qur. 22:47.

190. See *Tafsīr*, XXI, 59.

191. Yaḥyā b. Yamān transmitted from Sufyān al-Thawrī and died in 188–89/803–5. See *Tahdhīb*, XI, 306 f.

192. Died between 109 and 115/727–33. See *Tahdhīb*, IV, 226 f.

193. Qur. 41:11.

194. That is, splitting the surface of the earth so as to create river beds. For the association of "river" with "splitting," cf. Ethiopic *falag* ("river").

195. For the comment of Ibn ʿAbbās, see also *Tafsīr*, XXIV, 64.

According to Bishr b. Mu'ādh[196] —Yazīd[197] —Sa'īd[198] — Qatādah, commenting on: "And He revealed in every heaven its command"[199] : He created in it its sun, its moon, and its stars, and what is good for it.[200] [24]

These reports, mentioned by us on the authority of the Messenger of God and those who mentioned them on his authority, have made it clear that God created the heavens and the earth before He created time, day and night, and the sun and the moon. God knows best!

Explaining the Annihilation of Time and Night and Day and That Nothing Remains Except God

Proof of the soundness of this statement is the words of God: "Everyone on it is annihilated, but the face of your Lord, Majestic and Venerable, remains,"[201] and: "There is no God but He. Everything perishes but His face."[202]

If everything perishes but His face, as God says, and night and day are darkness and light created by Him for the well-being of His creation, there can be no doubt that they will perish and be annihilated. Thus, God informs (us) and says: "When the sun shall be rolled up,"[203] meaning that it shall be obscured, so that its light will be gone. That will take place at the Coming of the Hour. No further elaboration is needed, since it is acknowledged by all those who confess God's oneness, the Muslims, the people of the Torah and the Gospel, and the Magians. It is denied only by others who do not confess the oneness of God. We do not intend to explain the erroneousness of their statements in this book. All those whom

---

196. Bishr died in or before 245/859. See *Tahdhīb*, I, 458; Horst, 301, n. 16.

197. Abū Mu'āwiyah Yazīd b. Zuray' lived from 101/719[20] to ca. 798. See *Tahdhīb*, XI, 325–28; Horst, 301, n. 17.

198. Sa'īd b. Abī 'Arūbah was "confused" for a number of years before his death in the 150s/ca. 772. See *Tahdhīb*, IV, 63–66; Horst, 301, n. 18.

199. Qur. 41:12. The meaning of "its command" is debatable. It seems to be "what was going to happen there" (R. Paret) or "what God commanded to happen there."

200. The suffix in *wa-ṣalāḥahā* could hardly be intended to mean "them (their well-being)." For the tradition, see *Tafsīr*, XXIV, 64.

201. Qur. 55:26 f.

202. Qur. 28:88. See above, n. 16.

203. Qur. 81:1.

we have mentioned as acknowledging the annihilation of the entire world until there remains only the One Eternal and Unique,
[25] acknowledge that God revives and resurrects them after they have perished, except idol worshipers, for they acknowledge annihilation but do not acknowledge resurrection.

The Proof for God Being Eternal and First before Everything and for His Originating Everything by His Power

The proof for this statement (is as follows): There is nothing in this world that is observable except a body or something subsisting in a body.[204] There is no body that is not either separate or connected. There is no separate body that cannot be imagined as becoming joined to some other like forms, and there is no connected body that cannot be imagined as becoming separated. When one of the two is deprived of existence, so, too, is the other. If two parts of it become connected after having been separate, one concludes that the connection of the two originated in them after it did not exist, and if separation originates in them after connection, one concludes that the separation in them originated after it did not exist.

Now, this is so with everything in the world. What is not observable is to be judged as being of the same kind[205] as what we do observe in the sense of body or subsisting in a body. What cannot be free from having origination is no doubt originated through composition by someone composing it if it is connected, or through separation by someone separating it if it is separated; the conclusion is that the one who connects it if it is connected, and separates it if it is separated, is someone not similar to it and for whom being connected or being separated is not permissible. This is the One Unique and Powerful, the One Who establishes connections between different things, the One to Whom nothing is similar. He "has power over everything."[206]

204. On *jism* "body, material substance," see *EI*², II, 553–55, s. v. djism.

205. Read *mim-mā*, as in two manuscripts. *Jins* "kind, genus," is hardly the proper term here. Ṭabarī means that there is no other way to observe the supernatural (which cannot really be done) except by analogy with the physical world which we can observe by means of the senses.

206. Qur. 2:20, etc.

Thus, our description has made it clear that the Creator and Originator of all things was before everything, that night and day and time and hours are originated, and that their Originator Who administers and manages them exists before them, since it is impossible for something to originate something unless its originator exists before it. (It is also clear that) God's word: "Don't (the unbelievers) look at the camels (and reflect) how they were created, and at the heaven how it was raised, and at the mountains how they were set up, and at the earth how it was spread out flat?"[207] contains the most eloquent evidence and the most effective proofs for those who use reason to reflect and the mind to be instructed, that the Creator of all those things is eternal and that everything of their kind is originated and has a Creator that is not similar to them. That is because everything mentioned by our Lord in this verse, the mountains, the earth, the camels, is dealt with and administered by man, who may move it around and manage it, who may dig, cut, and tear down, none of which he is prevented from doing. Yet, beyond that, man is not able to bring anything of that into existence without a basis (to work from). The conclusion is that the one who is incapable of originating those things could not have originated himself and that the one who is not prevented from managing and organizing whatever he wishes could not have been brought into existence by someone like himself and he did not bring himself into existence. Further, the One Who brought (man) up and gave him substantial *('ayn)* existence is the One Who is not incapable of (doing) anything He wishes, and He is not prevented from originating anything He wants. He is "God Unique and Forceful."[208] [26]

Someone might ask: Why should it be disapprovable to assume that the things you have mentioned result from the action of two eternal (beings)?[209] The reply would be: We disapprove of that because we find that the administration is continuous and the creation perfect. We say: If the administrators were two, they would necessarily either agree or disagree. If they agree, the two would conceptually be one, and the one would be made two merely by [27]

207. Qur. 88:17–20.
208. Qur. 12:39, etc.
209. Dualism was probably very much on Ṭabarī's mind, but what is meant here is not dualism as such but polytheism.

positing two. If they differ, it would be impossible to find the existence of the creation perfect and (its) administration continuous. For each one of two who differ does what is different from what his fellow does. If one gives life, the other causes death. If one of them produces existence, the other produces annihilation. It would thus be impossible for anything in creation to exist in the perfection and continuity it does. God's words: "If there were other gods except God in (heaven and earth), both would be ruined. Praised be God, Lord of the Throne, (who is above) what they describe";[210] and: "God has not taken to Himself a child, and there has been no god together with Him. Otherwise, each god would have gone off with what he created and risen over the others. Praised be God (who is above) what they describe. He knows what is unseen and what is observable, and He is exalted above their associating (other gods with Him)"[211] —these words of God are the most eloquent evidence and the most concise explanation as well as the most effective proof for the falsehood of those falsehood-mongers who associate (other gods) with God. That is because, if there were another god except God in the heavens and the earth, the condition of the two as to agreement and disagreement would necessarily be the one I have described. Saying that there may be agreement implies that saying they are two is wrong. It confirms the oneness of God and is an absurd statement in as much as the one who makes it calls the one two. Saying that there may be disagreement indicates ruin for the heavens and the earth, as our Lord says: "If there were other gods except God in them, both would be ruined."[212] For if one originates and creates something, it would be the other's business to put it out of existence and invalidate it. That is because the actions of two who differ are different, just as fire that warms and snow that cools what fire has warmed.

Another argument (would be this): If it were (true) as those who
[28] associate other gods with God say, each one of the two whom they consider as eternal would necessarily be either strong or incapable. If both were incapable, each one, being incapable, would be defeatable and not be a god. If both were strong, each one of them, by virtue of being incapable of subduing the other, would

210. Qur. 21:22.
211. Qur. 23:91 f.
212. Qur. 21:22.

be incapable and being incapable would not be a god. If each one of them were strong enough to subdue the other, he, by virtue of the strength of the other to subdue him in turn, would be incapable. God is above the association of other gods with Him!

It has thus become clear that the Eternal One, the Creator and Maker of all things is the One Who existed before everything and Who will be after everything, the First before everything and the Last after everything. He existed when there was no momentary and extended time, no night and no day, no darkness and no light except the light of His noble face, no heaven and no earth, no sun and no moon and no stars. Everything but He is originated, administered and made. He alone by Himself created everything without an associate, helper, and assistant. Praised be He as powerful and forceful!

According to ʿAlī b. Sahl al-Ramlī—Zayd b. Abī al-Zarqāʾ[213] —Jaʿfar[214] —Yazīd b. al-Aṣamm[215] —Abū Hurayrah: The Prophet said: After my death, you all will be asked about everything, to the extent that someone might even say: God there created everything, but who created Him?[216]

According to ʿAlī—Zayd—Jaʿfar—Yazīd b. al-Aṣamm—Najabah b. Ṣabīgh[217] : I was with Abū Hurayrah when he was asked about that. He exclaimed: God is great!, and said: My friend did not tell me anything unless I saw him and was looking at him.[218] Jaʿfar said: I have also heard that (Abū Hurayrah) said: If people ask you

213. He resided for some time in al-Ramlah and died there in 140/757[8]. See *Tahdhīb*, III, 413 f.

214. Jaʿfar b. Burqān died before or in 154/771. See *Tahdhīb*, II, 84–86; Bukhārī, *Taʾrīkh*, I, 2, 186.

215. Yazīd b. al-Aṣamm died seventy-three years old between 101 and 104/719–23. His maternal aunt was Maymūnah, a wife of the Prophet. See *Tahdhīb*, XI, 313 f.

216. The tradition appears with the same chain of transmitters (Jaʿfar b. Burqān to Abū Hurayrah) in Muslim, *Ṣaḥīḥ*, I, 97. See *Concordance*, II, 71a34 f.–b2.

217. See Bukhārī, *Taʾrīkh*, IV, 2, 133, no. 2462.

218. That is, Abū Hurayrah claims that his contact with the Prophet was always strictly personal and direct, implying that he never heard the Prophet make such an awful statement, which is usually considered to go back to the machinations of Satan. A close version in Ibn Ḥanbal, II, 539, seems to confirm the reading *wa-anā* of the Leiden text against *aw anā* of the Cairo edition. A connection is made with the Jahmiyyah in Abū Dāwūd, *Sunan*, IV, 319.

about that, say: God "is the Creator of everything."[219] God is the One Who was before everything, and God will be after everything.

[29] Thus, the conclusion is that the Creator of all things existed while there was nothing but He. He originated all things and then administered them. He had created various kinds of beings before the creation of extended and momentary times and before the creation of the sun and the moon which He causes to run in their spheres. It is through them that moments and hours are known, eras are established, and night is separated from day.

Let us now discuss what that prior creation was and what was created first.

The Beginning of Creation: What Was Created First?

Sound indeed is the following report on the authority of the Messenger of God which I have received from Yūnus b. ʿAbd al-Aʿlā[220]—(ʿAbdallāh) b. Wahb (and also from ʿUbayd b. Ādam b. Abī Iyās al-ʿAsqalānī[221] —his father—al-Layth b. Saʿd[222])—Muʿāwiyah b. Ṣāliḥ—Ayyūb b. Ziyād[223] —ʿUbādah b. al-Walīd b. ʿUbādah b. al-Ṣāmit[224] —his father: My father ʿUbādah b. al-Ṣāmit said: My dear son! I heard the Messenger of God say: The first (thing) created by God is the Pen. God said to it: Write!, and it proceeded at that very hour to (write) whatever is going to be.[225]

According to Aḥmad b. Muḥammad b. Ḥabīb[226] —ʿAlī b.

219. Qur. 6:102, etc.

220. Born in 170/787, Yūnus died in 264/877. See *Tahdhīb*, XI, 440 f.; Horst, 305, n. 1.

221. ʿUbayd died in 258/872. See *Tahdhīb*, VII, 58. His father Ādam died in 220 or 221/835–36 at the age of eighty-eight or ninety. See *TB*, VII, 27-30; *Tahdhīb*, I, 196.

222. Al-Layth was born in 93 or 94/711–13. He died in 175/December, 791. See *TB*, XIII, 3-14; *Tahdhīb*, VIII, 459-65; *EI*², V, 711, s.v.; Sezgin, *GAS*, I, 520.

223. See Bukhārī, *Taʾrīkh*, I, 1, 414 f.; Ibn Ḥajar, *Lisān*, I, 481.

224. For ʿUbādah, see *Tahdhīb*, V, 114. For his father, al-Walīd, who died during the caliphate of ʿAbd al-Malik, see *Tahdhīb*, XI, 137. And for his famous grandfather, ʿUbādah b. al-Ṣāmit, who was present at Badr and died, seventy-two years old, in 34/654–5 in al-Ramlah, or perhaps later during the caliphate of Muʿāwiyah (?), and was buried in Jerusalem, see *Tahdhīb*, V, 111 f.

225. In *Tafsīr*, XXIX, 11 f., the tradition quoted here does not seem to have been accorded the prominence it has here. Much of the information quoted above also appears in *Tafsīr*, XXIX, 10–12.

226. See above, n. 127. The quotation of the tradition in *Tafsīr*, XXIX, 11, replaces

al-Ḥasan b. Shaqīq[227] —'Abdallāh b. al-Mubārak[228] —Rabāḥ b. Zayd[229] —'Umar b. Ḥabīb[230] —al-Qāsim b. Abī Bazzah[231] —Sa'īd b. Jubayr—Ibn 'Abbās who used to tell that the Messenger of God said: The first thing created by God is the Pen. God commanded it to write everything.

I was told the same by Mūsā b. Sahl al-Ramlī[232] —Nu'aym b. Ḥammād[233] —Ibn al-Mubārak—Rabāḥ b. Zayd—'Umar b. Ḥabīb—al-Qāsim b. Abī Bazzah—Sa'īd b. Jubayr—Ibn 'Abbās—the Messenger of God. [30]

According to Muḥammad b. Mu'āwiyah al-Anmāṭī[234] —'Abbād b. al-'Awwām[235] —'Abd al-Wāḥid b. Sulaym[236] —'Aṭā'[237] : I asked al-Walīd b. 'Ubādah b. al-Ṣāmit: What was your father's last exhortation to you when he was at the point of death? Al-Walīd replied: He called me and said: My dear son! Fear God, knowing that you shall not truly fear God and attain (religious) knowledge until you believe in God Unique and in predestination both good and bad. I heard the Messenger of God say: The first (thing) created by God was the Pen. God said to it: Write! The Pen asked: What shall I write? God replied: Write what is predestined *(al-qadar)* ! He con-

---

him with a certain Muḥammad b. 'Abdallāh al-Ṭūsī who also appears unidentifiable.

227. Born in 137/754[5], Ibn Shaqīq died in the first half of the 210s/826–30. See *TB*, XI, 370–72; *Tahdhīb*, VII, 298 f. His son Muḥammad (below, n. 758) was a direct informant of Ṭabarī.

228. Ibn al-Mubārak lived from 118 or 119/736–37 to 181/797. See *TB*, X, 152-69; *Tahdhīb*, V, 382-87; *EI*[2] , III, 879, s. v. Ibn al-Mubārak; Sezgin, *GAS*, I, 95.

229. Rabāḥ b. Zayd, as read correctly in the Cairo edition, died in 187/803 at the age of eighty-one. See *Tahdhīb*, III, 233 f.

230. See *Tahdhīb*, VII, 431.

231. Ibn Abī Bazzah died around 120/737[8]. See *Tahdhīb*, VIII, 310.

232. Died in 260 or 261/874–75. See *Tahdhīb*, X, 347; Sezgin, *GAS*, I, 347.

233. Nu'aym b. Ḥammād died in 228/843, or, perhaps. in 227 or 229. See *TB*, XIII, 306–14; *Tahdhīb*, X, 458–63; Sezgin, *GAS*, I, 104 f. A Tübingen dissertation of 1979 by Jorge Aguade deals with one of his works (not seen).

234. See *Tahdhīb*, IX, 463 f. *Tafsīr*, XXIX, 11, has Muḥammad b. Ṣāliḥ, presumably by mistake.

235. 'Abbād lived from 118/736 to ca. 185/801. See *TB*, XI, 104–6; *Tahdhīb*, V, 99 f.

236. See *Tahdhīb*, VI, 435 f.

237. Presumably, 'Aṭā' b. al-Sā'ib (above, n. 181).

The two versions in Ibn Ḥanbal, V, 317, make it abundantly clear that the thrust of the tradition is directed toward the inclusiveness of divine predestination with respect to both good and evil. See L. Gardet, in *EI*[2] , IV, 365b, s. v. al-Ḳaḍā' wa 'l-ḳadar.

tinued: And the Pen proceeded at that very hour to (write) whatever was and whatever is going to be for all times.

The early (scholars) before us differed in this matter. We shall mention their statements and have that then followed by the (correct) explanation of it, if God wills.

Some of them said about the same as what has been transmitted on the authority of the Messenger of God.

Those who said this

According to Wāṣil b. ʿAbd al-Aʿlā al-Asadī[238] —Muḥammad b. Fuḍayl[239] —al-Aʿmash—Abū Ẓabyān[240] —Ibn ʿAbbās: The first thing created by God is the Pen. God said to it: Write!, whereupon the Pen asked: What shall I write, my Lord? God replied: Write what is predestined! He continued. And the Pen proceeded to (write) whatever is predestined and going to be to the Coming of the Hour. Then, (God) lifted up the water vapor and split the heavens off from it.[241]

We were told about the same by Wāṣil b. ʿAbd al-Aʿlā—Wakīʿ[242] —al-Aʿmash—Abū Ẓabyān—Ibn ʿAbbās.

[31] According to Muḥammad b. al-Muthannā—Ibn Abī ʿAdī[243] —Shuʿbah—Sulaymān[244] —Abū Ẓabyān—Ibn ʿAbbās: The first thing created by God is the Pen. It proceeded to (write) whatever is going to be.

We were told about the same by Tamīm b. al-Muntaṣir—Isḥāq[245] —Sharīk—al-Aʿmash—Abū Ẓabyān or Mujāhid—Ibn ʿAbbās.

---

238. Died in 244/858[9]. See *Tahdhīb,* XI, 104.

239. Muḥammad b. Fuḍayl b. Ghazwān died in 194–95/809–11. See *Tahdhīb,* IX, 405 f.

240. Abū Ẓabyān Ḥusayn b. Jundub died in 89 or 90/707–9. See *Tahdhīb,* II, 379 f.

241. Text below, I, 48, has an expanded text, which appears also in *Tafsīr,* XXIX, 10.

242. Wakīʿ b. al-Jarrāḥ b. Malīḥ, who was born in 128–29/745–47, died in 197/812[3] or the following year on the return from the pilgrimage. See *TB,* XIII, 496–512; *Tahdhīb,* XI, 123–31; Sezgin, *GAS,* I, 96 f.

243. Muḥammad b. Ibrāhīm b. Abī ʿAdī al-Qasmalī died between 192 and 194/807–10. See *Tahdhīb,* IX, 12 f.; Bukhārī, *Taʾrīkh,* I, 1, 23.

244. Al-Aʿmash?

245. Isḥāq b. Yūsuf al-Azraq died in 194 or 195/809–11 during the caliphate of al-Amīn. See Ibn Saʿd, *Ṭabaqāt,* VII, 2, 62; Bukhārī, *Taʾrīkh,* I, 1, 406; Ibn Abī Ḥātim, I, 1, 238. He is named among the authorities of Tamīm and among the transmitters from Sharīk *(Tahdhīb),* IV, 334), but one of his authorities is also said to be al-Aʿmash, and not Sharīk, who was an authority of Isḥāq b. ʿĪsā b. al-Ṭabbāʿ (d. 214–15/829–30).

According to Muḥammad b. ʿAbd al-Aʿlā—Ibn Thawr[246] —Maʿmar[247] —al-Aʿmash—Ibn ʿAbbās: The first thing created is the Pen.

According to Ibn Ḥumayd—Jarīr[248] —ʿAṭāʾ—Abū al-Ḍuḥā Muslim b. Ṣubayḥ[249] —Ibn ʿAbbās: The first thing created by my Lord is the Pen. God said to it: Write!, and it wrote whatever is going to be to the Coming of the Hour.[250]

Others said: Rather, the first of the created things created by God is light and darkness.

Those who said this

According to Ibn Ḥumayd—Salamah b. al-Faḍl—Ibn Isḥāq: The first (thing) created by God was light and darkness. He then distinguished between the two and made the darkness a night that is black and dark (so that one cannot see) and the light a day that illuminates and enables one to see.[251]

Abū Jaʿfar (al-Ṭabarī) says: In my opinion, of the two statements the one most likely to be correct is that of Ibn ʿAbbās. That is because of the report, mentioned by me earlier, from the Messenger of God who said: The first thing created by God is the Pen.

Someone might say: You say that of the two statements—the one that the first of the created things created by God is the Pen, and the other that it is light and darkness—the statement most likely to be correct is: The first of the created things created by God is the Pen. What, then, is the patent meaning of the tradition transmitted from Ibn ʿAbbās which you were told [32]
by Ibn Bashshār—ʿAbd al-Raḥmān[252] —Sufyān—Abū Hāshim[253] —Mujāhid: I said to Ibn ʿAbbās: There are people who consider

246. Muḥammad b. Thawr al-Ṣanʿānī died around 190/805[6]. See *Tahdhīb*, IX, 87; Horst, 296, n. 10. See also *Tafsīr*, XXIX, 10.

247. The important early historian Maʿmar b. Rāshid lived from ca. 96/714[5] to between 152 and 154/769–71. See *Tahdhīb*, X, 243–46; Sezgin, *GAS*, I, 290 f.; Horst, 296, n. 19.

248. Born in 107/725[6], Jarīr b. ʿAbd al-Ḥamīd (b. Jarīr) b. Qurṭ al-Rāzī died in 188/804. See *TB*, VII, 253–61; *Tahdhīb*, II, 75–77.

249. Abū al-Ḍuḥā died ca. 100/718[9] during the caliphate of ʿUmar b. ʿAbd al-ʿAzīz. See *Tahdhīb*, X, 132 f.

250. See *Tafsīr*, XXIX, 10.

251. See *Tafsīr*, I, 151 (*ad* Qur. 2:29).

252. ʿAbd al-Raḥmān b. Mahdī lived from 135/752[3] to 198/814. See *TB*, X, 240–48; *Tahdhīb*, VI, 279–81; Horst, 296, n. 13.

253. The Cairo edition identifies him with Abū Hāshim Ismāʿīl b. Kathīr. See *Tahdhīb*, I, 326.

predestination untrue? He said: (Then), they consider the Book of God untrue! I shall seize one of them by the hair and shake him up. God was on His Throne before He created anything. The first (thing) created by God was the Pen. It proceeded to (write) whatever is going to be to the Day of Resurrection. People will proceed merely in accordance with what is a foregone conclusion (decided by predestination and written down by the Pen). And (what then is the meaning of the tradition reported) on the authority of Ibn Isḥāq and transmitted to all of you by Ibn Ḥumayd—Salamah—Ibn Isḥāq? He continued (quoting) God's word: "It is He Who created the heavens and the earth in six days, while His Throne was upon the water."[254] It was as He describes Himself. There was nothing except the water upon which was the Throne, and upon the Throne was God, Majestic and Venerable. And the first (thing) created by God was light and darkness.

The answer would be: The statement of Ibn ʿAbbās that God was on His Throne upon the water before He created anything, and the first (thing) created by God was the Pen—if it is a sound (report) on his authority that he actually said that—would provide information that God created the Pen after He created His Throne. Shuʿbah transmitted this report on the authority of Abū Hāshim but did not say what Sufyān said, namely, that God was on His Throne, and the first (thing) created by Him was the Pen. Rather, he transmitted this (report) as did all the other transmitters on the authority of Ibn ʿAbbās mentioned by us, namely, that Ibn ʿAbbās said: The first (thing) created by God is the Pen.

Those who said this

[33] According to al-Muthannā—ʿAbd al-Ṣamad—Shuʿbah—Abū Hāshim—Mujāhid[255] —ʿAbdallāh (whether Ibn ʿUmar or Ibn ʿAbbās is not known): The first (thing) created by God is the Pen. God said to it: Proceed (to write)!, and the Pen proceeded to (write) whatever is going to be. People today merely carry out what is a foregone conclusion.

The same applies to the statement of Ibn Isḥāq mentioned by us which implies that God created light and darkness after He created His Throne and the water upon which the Throne was.

254. Qur. 11:7. *Tafsīr*, XII, 3–5, deals with much of the traditional material on creation.

255. See Mujāhid, *Tafsīr*, I, 687, which, however, is rather different.

The statement of the Messenger of God on the subject which we have transmitted from him is the one most likely to be correct, because he was most knowledgeable of the truth and soundness of any statement he would make on the subject. We have transmitted on the Prophet's authority that he said: The first thing created by God is the Pen—making no exception for anything whose creation might have preceded God's creation of the Pen. Rather, the Prophet's statement: The first thing created by God is the Pen, includes generally everything and indicates that the Pen was created before everything without making any exception for the Throne or water or anything else.

The tradition we have transmitted on the authority of Abū Ẓabyān and Abū al-Ḍuḥā—Ibn ʿAbbās, is more likely to be sound on the authority of Ibn ʿAbbās than the report of Mujāhid on (the latter's) authority which Abū Hāshim transmitted, since Shuʿbah and Sufyān differed with respect to this transmission on (Ibn ʿAbbās') authority, as I have already mentioned.

Ibn Isḥāq's statement indicates no authority from whom he transmitted it.

Here we have one of the things that cannot be known except through information from God or from the Messenger of God. I have already mentioned the tradition(s) with respect to this subject on the authority of the Messenger of God.

Those Who Put the Creation of the Pen in Second Place

After the Pen, and after God had commanded it to write whatever is going to be to the Coming of the Hour, God created fine clouds *(saḥāb)*. It is the *ghamām* which God mentions in the unambiguous parts of His Book, saying: "Do they have (anything) to look for but that God will come to them under a cover of clouds *(al-ghamām)* ?"[256] That was before He created His Throne. This appears in reports from the Messenger of God: [34]

According to Ibn Wakīʿ and Muḥammad b. Hārūn al-Qaṭṭān[257]

256. Qur. 2:210. "Unambiguous" *(muḥkam)*, in contrast to *mutashābih*, refers to Qur'ānic passages assumed to be not susceptible to divergent interpretations.

257. He is further called al-Rāziqī (?) in *Tafsīr*, XII, 4, 1. 14, but apparently cannot be identified with any certainty. He is hardly identical with Abū Nashīṭ Muḥammad b. Hārūn al-Bazzāz who died ca. 258/872. See *TB*, III, 352 f.; *Tahdhīb*,

—Yazīd b. Hārūn—Ḥammād b. Salamah—Ya'lā b. 'Aṭā'[258] —Wakī' b. Ḥudus[259] —his paternal uncle Abū Razīn[260] : I asked the Messenger of God: Where was our Lord before He created His creation? The Prophet replied: He was in a cloud (*'amā'*) with no air underneath or above it. Then He created His Throne upon the water.[261]

According to al-Muthannā b. Ibrāhīm—al-Ḥajjāj—Ḥammād—Ya'lā b. 'Aṭā'—Wakī' b. Ḥudus—his paternal uncle Abū Razīn al-'Aqīlī: I asked the Messenger of God: Where was our Lord before He created the heavens and the earth? The Prophet replied: In a cloud with air above and underneath it.[262] Then He created His Throne upon the water.

According to Khallād b. Aslam—al-Naḍr b. Shumayl—al-Mas'ūdī—Jāmi' b. Shaddād[263] —Ṣafwān b. Muḥriz[264] —Ibn Ḥuṣayn,[265] one of the companions of the Messenger of God: Some people came to the Messenger of God. They entered into his presence, and he began to give them glad tidings,[266] while they kept saying: Give us (gifts)! This continued until it annoyed the Messenger of God. Then they left. Some other people came in and said: We have come to greet the Messenger of God and become knowledgeable about the religion and ask about the beginning of this matter (the world). He said: So, accept the glad tidings, since
[35] those who have (just) left did not accept them. They said: We have done so. Whereupon the Messenger of God said: God existed while there was nothing else. His Throne was upon the water, and (all

IX, 493 f.

258. According to *Tahdhīb*, XI, 403 f., Ya'lā b. 'Aṭā' died in 120/737[8] in Wāsiṭ.

259. See *Tahdhīb*, XI, 131. His father's name is also given as 'Udu/as.

260. See *Tahdhīb*, VIII, 456 f.; Ibn 'Abd al-Barr, *Istī'āb*, IV, 1657. Abū Razīn's name supposedly was Laqīṭ. For the vocalization 'Aqīlī, instead of 'Uqaylī, see *Tahdhīb*, XI, 131 (editor's footnote).

261. See *Concordance*, IV, 388a11–13, and *Tafsīr*, XII, 4 (*ad* Qur. 11:7).

262. This statement is hardly correct. In *Tafsīr*, XII, 4, the negations are found as in the preceding tradition. In this case, the only difference between this and the preceding tradition is the two links of the chain of transmitters between Ṭabarī and Ḥammād b. Salamah.

263. Died, apparently, in the 120s/738–747. See *Tahdhīb*, II, 56 f.

264. Ṣafwān died in 74/693[4]. See *Tahdhīb*, IV, 430 f.

265. 'Imrān b. Ḥuṣayn died in 52 or 53/672–73 in al-Baṣrah. See *Tahdhīb*, VIII, 125 f.

266. According to *Tafsīr*, XII, 4, the glad tidings are that Muslims would not stay in Hell eternally. A mixture of the two traditions mentioned here is to be found in Bukhārī's *Ṣaḥīḥ*, see Ibn Ḥajar, *Fatḥ*, VII, 96 ff., and XVII, 179 ff.

that was going to be) was written on the memorial (Tablet) before anything (else was created).[267] Then God created seven heavens. Just then, someone came to me (Ibn Ḥuṣayn) and said: That camel of yours is gone. I went out (and found that) she was out of sight. I surely wish that I would have let her go (so that I would not have missed the rest of the Prophet's remarks).[268]

According to Abū Kurayb—Abū Mu'āwiyah—al-A'mash—Jāmi' b. Shaddād—Ṣafwān b. Muḥriz—'Imrān b. al-Ḥuṣayn: The Messenger of God said: Accept the glad tidings, Banū Tamīm! They replied: You gave the glad tidings to us. So now give us (gifts)! The Prophet said: Accept the glad tidings, Yemenites! They said: We did so. Now inform us how that matter was! Whereupon the Messenger of God said: God was upon the Throne. He was before everything, and He wrote everything that was going to be on the Tablet. ('Imrān) continued: Someone came to me and said: 'Imrān, that camel of yours has become untethered. I got up and found that she was out of sight. Therefore, I do not know what took place afterwards.

Then, there were differences about what God created after the cloud. Some said: Thereafter He created His Throne.[269]

Those who said this

According to Muḥammad b. Sinān—Abū Salamah[270]—Ḥayyān b. 'Ubaydallāh[271]—al-Ḍaḥḥāk b. Muzāḥim[272]—Ibn 'Abbās: God created the Throne as the first thing He created. Then He sat straight on it.

Others said: God created the water before the Throne. Then He created His Throne and placed it upon the water.

267. The construction is simplified in Bukhārī's *Ṣaḥīḥ* where the preposition "before" is omitted.

268. See *Tafsīr*, XII, 4.

269. On the preexistent divine throne, see, for instance, Speyer, *Biblische Erzählungen*, 21 ff.

270. He may be identical with Abū Salamah Mūsā b. Ismā'īl al-Minqarī al-Tabūdhakī who died in 223/838. He appears elsewhere as an authority of Muḥammad b. Sinān. See *Tahdhīb*, X, 333–35.

271. Not Ḥayyān—'Ubaydallāh, as in the Leiden edition. The correct text is found in the Cairo edition. See Ibn Ḥajar, *Lisān*, II, 370; Ibn Abī Ḥātim, I, 2, 246.

272. Al-Ḍaḥḥāk died between 102 and 106/720–25. See *Tahdhīb*, IV, 453 f.; Sezgin, *GAS*, I, 29 f.; Horst, 304, n. 10.

Those who said this

According to Mūsā b. Hārūn al-Hamdānī[273]—ʿAmr b. Ḥammād[274]
[36] —Asbāṭ b. Naṣr[275] —al-Suddī[276] —Abū Mālik[277] and Abū Ṣāliḥ[278] —Ibn ʿAbbās. Also (al-Suddī)—Murrah al-Hamdānī[279] —ʿAbdallāh b. Masʿūd[280] and some (other) companions of the Messenger of God: God's Throne was upon the water. He had created nothing except that which He created before the water.[281]

According to Muḥammad b. Sahl b. ʿAskar—Ismāʿīl b. ʿAbd al-Karīm—ʿAbd al-Ṣamad b. Maʿqil—Wahb b. Munabbih: Before He created the heavens and the earth, the Throne was upon the water. When He wanted to create the heavens and the earth, He grabbed a fistful of small rocks[282] in the water. He then opened the fist (with the rocks), and they rose in (the form of) smoke. Then he fashioned (the heavens into) seven heavens[283] and extended[284] the earth in two days. He finished the creation on the seventh day.

According to another statement, it was the Footstool *(kursī)* that our Lord created after the Pen. After the Footstool, He created the Throne. Thereafter He created the air and darkness. He then created the water and placed His Throne upon it.

Abū Jaʿfar (al-Ṭabarī) says: In my opinion, of the two statements the one most likely to be correct is that God created the water before the Throne, because of the soundness of the report mentioned by me earlier from Abū Razīn al-ʿAqīlī: When the Messenger of God was asked: Where was our Lord before He created His cre-

---

273. He appears to be unidentifiable; see Horst, 302, n. 3.

274. Died in 222/837. See *Tahdhīb*, VIII, 22 f.; Horst, 302, n. 6.

275. For Asbāṭ, see *Tahdhīb*, I, 211 f.; Horst, 302, n. 7.

276. Ismāʿīl b. ʿAbd al-Raḥmān al-Suddī died in 127/744[5]. See *Tahdhīb*, I, 313 f.; Horst, 302, n. 8.

277. For Abū Mālik Ghazwān al-Ghifārī, see *Tahdhīb*, VIII, 254 f.; Horst, 302, n. 10.

278. For Abū Ṣāliḥ Bādhām/n, known as *mawlā* of Umm Hāniʾ, see *Tahdhīb*, I, 416; Horst, 302, n. 9.

279. Murrah b. Sharaḥīl died in 76/695[6] or after the battle of Dayr al-Jamājim (82/701). See *Tahdhīb*, X, 88 f.; Ibn Abī Ḥātim, IV, 1, 366; Horst, 302, n. 11.

280. The famous Qurʾān reader Ibn Masʿūd died in 32/652[3]. See *Tahdhīb*, VI, 27 f.; *EI*², III, 873–75, s. v. Ibn Masʿūd; Horst, 202, n. 13.

281. For the full text of the tradition, see text below, I, 49, and *Tafsīr*, I, 152 (*ad* Qur. 2:29).

282. The plural seems indicated here, but see also text below, I, 50.

283. Cf. Qur. 41:12.

284. Cf. Qur. 79:30.

ation? he said: He was in a cloud with no air underneath or above it. Then He created His Throne upon the water. Thus, the Messenger of God reported that God created His Throne upon the water. It is impossible to assume that, seeing that He created it upon the water, He would have done so upon something nonexistent either before or simultaneously with it. If this is so, the Throne must [37] necessarily have been created either after God created the water or simultaneously with it. That its creation should have been before the creation of the water cannot possibly be sound according to the tradition transmitted on the authority of Abū Razīn—the Prophet.

It has been said that the water was upon the back of the wind when God created His Throne upon it. If this is so, the water and the wind were created before the Throne.

Those who say that the water was upon the back of the wind

According to Ibn Wakī'—his father—Sufyān—al-A'mash—al-Minhāl b. 'Amr[285] —Sa'īd b. Jubayr: When Ibn 'Abbās was asked in connection with God's word: "His Throne was upon the water":[286] Upon what was the water? he replied: Upon the back of the wind.[287]

According to Muḥammad b. 'Abd al-A'lā—Muḥammad b. Thawr—Ma'mar—al-A'mash—Sa'īd b. Jubayr: When Ibn 'Abbās was asked in connection with God's word: "His Throne was upon the water": Upon what was the water? he replied: Upon the back of the wind.

We were told the same by al-Qāsim b. al-Ḥasan—al-Ḥusayn b. Dāwūd—Ḥajjāj—Ibn Jurayj—Sa'īd b. Jubayr—Ibn 'Abbās.

He said[288] : The heavens and the earth and everything in them are encompassed by the oceans, and all of that is encompassed by the *haykal*,[289] and the *haykal* reportedly is encompassed by the Footstool.

Those who said this

According to Muḥammad b. Sahl b. 'Askar—Ismā'īl b. 'Abd al- [38]

285. See *Tahdhīb*, X, 319–21.
286. Qur. 11:7.
287. For this and the two following traditions, see *Tafsīr*, XII, 4.
288. The subject is hardly Ṭabarī, but it seems not clear who might be meant.
289. The meaning of *haykal* assumed here cannot easily be explained from the ordinary meanings of the word (anything stout, body, temple). It could be "gigantic body."

Karīm—'Abd al-Ṣamad—Wahb, mentioning some of His majesty (as being describable as follows): The heavens and the earth and the oceans are in the *haykal*, and the *haykal* is in the Footstool. God's feet are upon the Footstool. He carries the Footstool. It became like a sandal on His feet. When Wahb was asked: What is the *haykal*? he replied: Something on the heavens' extremities that surrounds the earth and the oceans like the ropes that are used to fasten a tent. And when Wahb was asked how the earths are (constituted), he replied: They are seven earths that are flat and islands. Between each two earths, there is an ocean. All that is surrounded by the (surrounding) ocean,[290] and the *haykal* is behind the ocean.

It has been said that there are a thousand years between God's creation of the Pen and His creation of all the rest.

Those who said this

According to al-Qāsim b. al-Ḥasan—al-Ḥusayn b. Dāwūd—Mubashshir al-Ḥalabī[291] —Arṭāh b. al-Mundhir[292] —Ḍamrah[293] : God created the Pen and then wrote down with it whatever He was creating and all His creation that was going to be. This writing then praised and glorified God for a thousand years before He created anything else in His creation. Then, when God wanted to create the heavens and the earth, He reportedly created six days and called everyone of them by a different name. The name of one of those days reportedly is *a-b-j-d*, that of another *h-w-z*, that of the third *ḥ-ṭ-y*, that of the fourth *k-l-m-n*, that of the fifth *s-'-f-ṣ*, and that of the sixth *q-r-sh-t*.[294]

Those who said this

According to al-Ḥaḍramī[295] —Muṣarrif b. 'Amr al-Yāmī[296] —

---

290. "Surrounding" *(muḥīṭ)* is the name of the ocean that surrounds the earth in the world view of medieval Muslim geographers.

291. Mubashshir b. Ismā'īl al-Ḥalabī died in 200/815[6]. See *Tahdhīb*, X, 31 f.

292. Arṭāh died in 162 or 163/778–80. See *Tahdhīb*, I, 198.

293. Ḍamrah b. Ḥabīb al-Ḥimṣī died in 130/747[8]. See *Tahdhīb*, IV, 459 f.

294. That is, the letters of the alphabet as they are arranged in the old Jewish/Christian order. The last two sentences do not appear in the quotation of this tradition in *Tafsīr*, XII, 4.

295. Unidentified.

296. Muṣarrif al-Yāmī died in 240/854[5]. See *Tahdhīb*, X, 158.

Ḥafṣ b. Ghiyāth[297] —al-ʿAlāʾ b. al-Musayyab[298] —a man from the Kindah—al-Ḍaḥḥāk b. Muzāḥim: God created the heavens and the [39] earth in six days. There is no day that does not have a name: *a-b-j-z, h-w-z, ḥ-ṭ-y, k-l-m-n, s-ʿ-f-ṣ,* and *q-r-sh-t.*

According to (al-Ḥaḍramī), omitting Muṣarrif—Ḥafṣ—al-ʿAlāʾ b. al-Musayyab—a shaykh of the Kindah—al-Ḍaḥḥāk b. Muzāḥim—Zayd b. Arqam[299] : God created the heavens and the earth in six days. Each day has a name: *a-b-j-d, h-w-z, ḥ-ṭ-y, k-l-m-n, s-ʿ-f-ṣ,* and *q-r-sh-t.*

Others say: Rather, God created one (day) and called it "Sunday," a second and called it "Monday," a third and called it "Tuesday," a fourth and called it "Wednesday," and a fifth and called it "Thursday."[300]

Those who said this

According to Tamīm b. al-Muntaṣir—Isḥāq (b. Yūsuf)—Sharīk (b. ʿAbdallāh al-Nakhaʿī)—Ghālib b. Ghallāb[301] —ʿAṭāʾ b. Abī Rabāḥ[302] —Ibn ʿAbbās: God created one day and called it "Sunday." Then He created a second and called it "Monday." Then He created a third and called it "Tuesday." Then He created a fourth and called it "Wednesday." Then He created a fifth and called it "Thursday."[303]

These two statements are not contradictory, since it is possible that the names of those days were in the language of the Arabs as stated by ʿAṭāʾ, and in the language of others as stated by al-Ḍaḥḥāk b. Muzāḥim.

It has been said that the days were seven, not six.

Those who said this

---

297. Born in 117/735, Ḥafṣ b. Ghiyāth died between 194 and 196/809–12. See *TB*, VIII, 188–200; *Tahdhīb*, II, 415–18.

298. See *Tahdhīb*, VIII, 192 f.

299. Zayd b. Arqam died in the second half of the sixties/684–88. See *Tahdhīb*, III, 394 f.

300. The inventor of this idea played on the fact that the days of the week from Sunday to Thursday are expressed in Arabic, as well as in Aramaic, by special numerals for one to five. This places Friday and Saturday in a category apart, since they are not expressed numerically.

301. Apparently not identifiable.

302. Born in the second year of the caliphate of ʿUthmān or in 27/647[8], ʿAṭāʾ b. Abī Rabāḥ died ca. 115/733. See *Tahdhīb*, VII, 199-203; *EI*², I, 730, s. v.; Horst, 295, n. 8.

303. See *Tafsīr*, XXIV, 61.

According to Muḥammad b. Sahl b. ʿAskar—Ismāʿīl b. ʿAbd al-
[40] Karīm—ʿAbd al-Ṣamad b. Maʿqil—Wahb b. Munabbih: The days are seven.

Both statements—the one, transmitted by us from al-Ḍaḥḥāk and ʿAṭāʾ, that God created six days, and the other from Wahb b. Munabbih that the days are seven—are sound and can be combined and are not contradictory. That is because the statement here by ʿAṭāʾ and al-Ḍaḥḥāk means that the days on which God created the creation from the time *(ḥīn)* He began the creation of heaven and earth and everything in them until He finished are six days, as God says: "It is He Who created the heavens and the earth in six days."[304] The statement of Wahb b. Munabbih, on the other hand, means that the number of days constituting a week is seven, not six.

The early (scholars) differed with respect to the day on which God created the heavens and the earth. Some of them said: He began with it on Sunday.

Those who said this

According to Isḥāq b. Shāhīn[305] —Khālid b. ʿAbdallāh[306] —al-Shaybānī[307] —ʿAwn b. ʿAbdallāh b. ʿUtbah[308] —his brother ʿUbaydallāh b. ʿAbdallāh b. ʿUtbah[309] —ʿAbdallāh b. Salām: God began the creation by creating the earth on Sunday and Monday.

According to al-Muthannā b. Ibrāhīm—ʿAbdallāh b. Ṣāliḥ[310] —Abū Maʿshar[311] —Saʿīd b. Abī Saʿīd[312] —ʿAbdallāh b. Salām: God

---

304. Qur. 11:7.

305. See *Tahdhīb,* I, 236 f.

306. Khālid b. ʿAbdallāh al-Ṭaḥḥān lived from about 110/728[9] (or 115/733[4]) to about 179–82/795–98. See *TB,* VIII, 294 f.; *Tahdhīb,* III, 100 f.

307. Abū Isḥāq Sulaymān b. Abī Sulaymān al-Shaybānī died ca. 140/757[8]. See *Tahdhīb,* IV, 197 f.

308. See *Tahdhīb,* VIII, 171–73.

309. Died in the nineties/708–18. See *Tahdhīb,* VII, 23 f. *Tahdhīb* quotes Ṭabarī's highly favorable opinion of him.

310. Presumably, Abū Ṣāliḥ ʿAbdallāh b. Ṣāliḥ, the secretary of al-Layth, who was born in 137 or 139/754–56 and died in 222 or 223/836–38. See *TB,* IX, 478–91; *Tahdhīb,* V, 256–61; Horst, 293, n. 3.

311. The author of a work on *maghāzī* ("raids"), Abū Maʿshar Najīḥ b. ʿAbd al-Raḥmān died in 170/787. See *TB,* XIII, 457–62; *Tahdhīb,* X, 419–22; *EI*², I, 140, s. v. Abū Maʿshar; Sezgin, *GAS,* I, 191 f. Ṭabarī still knew his son Muḥammad who died, ninety-nine years old, in 244 or 247/858–62. See *Tafsīr,* II, 182 *(ad* Qur. 2:204); *TB,* III, 326 f.; *Tahdhīb,* IX, 487 f.

312. Saʿīd b. Abī Saʿīd al-Maqburī appears to have died in the 120s/740–44. See *Tahdhīb,* IV, 38–40.

began the creation by creating the earth on Sunday and Monday.[313]

According to Ibn Ḥumayd—Jarīr (b. ʿAbd al-Ḥamīd)—al-A'mash—Abū Ṣāliḥ—Ka'b: God began with the creation of the heavens and the earth on Sunday and Monday. [41]

According to Muḥammad b. Abī Manṣūr al-Āmulī[314] —ʿAlī b. al-Haytham[315] —al-Musayyab b. Sharīk[316] —Abū Rawq[317] —al-Ḍaḥḥāk, commenting on God's word: "It is He Who created the heavens and the earth in six days"[318] —of the other world where the extent of each day is a thousand years. He began the creation on Sunday.

According to al-Muthannā—al-Ḥajjāj[319] —Abū ʿAwānah[320] —Abū Bishr[321] —Mujāhid: He began the creation on Sunday.

Others said: The day on which God began with the creation is Saturday.

Those who said this

According to Ibn Ḥumayd—Salamah b. al-Faḍl—Muḥammad b. Isḥāq: The people of the Torah say: God began the creation on Sunday, while the people of the Gospel say: God began the creation on Monday. We Muslims say, in accordance with what has come down to us from the Messenger of God: God began the creation on Saturday.

The statements of each of these two groups—the one saying that God began the creation on Sunday, and the other that God began the creation on Saturday—have been transmitted on the authority of the Messenger of God. We have mentioned both reports before

---

313. For the complete text of the tradition, see text below, I, 44, and *Tafsīr,* I, 153 (*ad* Qur. 2:29).

314. Unidentified.

315. None of the ʿAlī b. al-Haytham listed in *TB,* XII, 118 f. and *Tahdhīb,* VII, 394, can be identified as the one meant here.

316. Al-Musayyab b. Sharīk died during the caliphate of Hārūn al-Rashīd, in 185 or 186/801–2. See *TB,* XIII, 137–41; Ibn Ḥajar, *Lisān,* VI, 38 f.

317. For Abū Rawq ʿAṭiyyah b. al-Ḥārith, see *Tahdhīb,* VII, 224.

318. Qur. 11:7.

319. This is al-Ḥajjāj b. (al-)Minhāl who died in 216 or 217/831–32. See *Tahdhīb,* II, 206 f. He occurs, for instance, in *Tafsīr,* I, 168, l. 29, and XIV, 62, ll. 15 f. (*ad* Qur. 2:30 and 16:15).

320. Abū ʿAwānah al-Waḍḍāḥ died in 176/792. See *Tahdhīb,* XI, 116-20; Bukhārī, *Ta'rīkh,* IV, 2, 181.

321. Abū Bishr Ja'far b. Iyās died in the 120s/740–48. See *Tahdhīb,* II, 83 f.; Bukhārī, *Ta'rīkh,* I, 2, 186.

but shall repeat here some of the proofs for the soundness of the statements made by each of the two groups.

The report on the Prophet's authority verifying the statement [42] that the beginning of creation was on Sunday is what we were told by Hannād b. al-Sarī, who also said that he read all the *ḥadīth*[322]—Abū Bakr b. ʿAyyāsh—Abū Saʿd al-Baqqāl—ʿIkrimah—Ibn ʿAbbās: The Jews came to the Prophet and asked him about the creation of the heavens and the earth. He replied: God created the earth on Sunday and Monday.

The report on the Prophet's authority verifying the statement that the beginning of God's creation was on Saturday, is what I was told by al-Qāsim b. Bishr b. Maʿrūf and al-Ḥusayn b. ʿAlī al-Ṣudāʾī—Ḥajjāj—Ibn Jurayj—Ismāʿīl b. Umayyah—Ayyūb b. Khālid—ʿAbdallāh b. Rāfiʿ, the *mawlā* of Umm Salamah—Abū Hurayrah: The Messenger of God took me by the hand and said: God created the soil on Saturday. He created the mountains on Sunday.[323]

In my opinion, the statement here most likely to be correct is: The day on which God began the creation of the heavens and the earth is Sunday, because the early Muslim scholars agree on it.

In his statement, Ibn Isḥāq argued that it is as (he states, namely, that God began the creation on Saturday), on the basis of the assumption that God finished all His creation on Friday. It is the seventh day; on it, He sat straight on the Throne, and He made this day a festival for the Muslims. But as reported by us from him, Ibn Isḥāq's proof by which, he assumed, he argued for the soundness of his statement, proves precisely that he made a mistake here. That is because God informed His servants in more than one passage of His revelation[324] that He created the heavens and the earth and what is between them in six days. He says: "It is God Who created the heavens and the earth and what is between [43] them in six days. Then He sat straight on the Throne. You have no friend or intercessor apart from Him. Will you not be mindful?"[325] God also says: "Say: Do you really not believe in the One Who created the earth in two days, and set up others like him? That is the

322. See text above, I, 19, n. 159.
323. See text above, I, 20.
324. The Cairo edition reads: the unambiguous parts of His revelation.
325. Qur. 32:4.

Lord of the worlds. He made in it firmly anchored (mountains) above it and blessed it and decreed that it contain the amount of food it provides, (all) in four days, equally for those asking. Then He stretched out straight toward heaven, which was smoke, and said to it and to the earth: Come willingly or unwillingly! They said: We come willingly. He fashioned (heaven into) seven heavens in two days and revealed (in every heaven its command.[326] We adorned the lower heaven with lamps, and for guarding. This is the decree of the One Mighty and Knowing.)"[327]

There is no difference of opinion among all the scholars that the two days mentioned in God's word, "He fashioned it (into) seven heavens in two days," are included in the six days mentioned by Him before. Now then, God created the heavens and the earths and what is in them in six days. In addition, the reports on the authority of the Messenger of God that Adam was created last in God's creation and that He created him on Friday, clearly support each other. The conclusion is that Friday, on which God finished His creation, is included in the six days in which, God informs (us), He created His creation, for, if it were not included in the six days, He would have created His creation in seven days, and not in six. This is contrary to what is found in the divine revelation. Thus, since the matter is as we have described it, it is clear that the first day on which God began the creation of the heavens and the earth and what is in them was Sunday, since the last day was Friday. This makes six days as our Lord says. [44]

The reports coming down from the Messenger of God and his companions that the creation was finished on Friday will be mentioned by us in their proper places, if God wills.

What God Created on Each of the Six Days on Which, as He Mentions in His Book, He Created the Heavens and the Earth and What Is between Them

The early Muslim scholars differed in this respect. Some of them say, as I was told by al-Muthannā b. Ibrāhīm—ʿAbdallāh b. Ṣāliḥ—Abū Maʿshar—Saʿīd b. Abī Saʿīd—ʿAbdallāh b. Salām: God began

326. See above, n. 199. The text enclosed in parentheses is supplied in the Cairo edition.

327. Qur. 41:9–12.

with the creation on Sunday. He created the earths on Sunday and Monday. He created food and the firmly anchored (mountains) on Tuesday and Wednesday. He created the heavens on Thursday and Friday, and He finished in the last hour of Friday, in which He created Adam in haste.[328] That is the hour in which the Hour will come.[329]

According to Mūsā b. Hārūn—ʿAmr b. Ḥammād—Asbāṭ—al-Suddī—Abū Mālik and Abū Ṣāliḥ—Ibn ʿAbbās. Also (al-Suddī)—Murrah al-Hamdānī—Ibn Masʿūd and some (other) companions of the Prophet: He—meaning our Lord—made seven earths in two days, Sunday and Monday. He made on them "firmly anchored (mountains), lest (the earth) shake you up."[330] He created the mountains on the earth and the food to provide for its inhabitants and its trees and whatever is required for it, on two days, Tuesday and Wednesday. "Then He stretched out straight toward heaven, which was smoke,"[331] and made it into one heaven. Then He split (this one heaven) up into seven heavens on two days, Thursday and Friday.

[45] According to Tamīm b. al-Muntaṣir—Isḥāq (b. Yūsuf)—Sharīk (b. ʿAbdallāh al-Nakhaʿī)—Ghālib b. Ghallāb—ʿAṭāʾ b. Abī Rabāḥ—Ibn ʿAbbās: God created the earth on two days, Sunday and Monday.

According to these statements, the earth was created before heaven, because, in their opinion, it was created on Sunday and Monday.

Others said: God created the earth with the food it provides before heaven, without spreading it out. "Then He stretched out straight toward heaven and fashioned it into seven heavens."[332] Thereafter, He spread out the earth.

Those who said this

According to ʿAlī b. Dāwūd[333] —Abū Ṣāliḥ (ʿAbdallāh b. Ṣāliḥ)—

---

328. Cf. Qur. 21:37. See below, n. 607.

329. See text above, I, 40, and *Tafsīr*, I, 153 *(ad* Qur. 2:29).

330. Qur. 16:15 and 31:10.

331. Qur. 41:11.

332. Qur. 2:29. The use of the same word "fashioned" for *sawwāhunna* here and *qaḍāhunna* in Qur. 41:12 (above, n. 327, etc.) appears justified.

333. ʿAlī b. Dāwūd died in or before 272/885[6]. See *TB*, XI, 424 f.; *Tahdhīb*, VII, 317. In *Tafsīr*, I, 153 *(ad* Qur. 2:29), al-Muthannā takes his place in the *isnād*, but ʿAlī b. Dāwūd appears in *Tafsīr*, XXX, 29 *(ad* Qur. 79:29–32).

Mu'āwiyah (b. Ṣāliḥ)—'Alī b. Abī Ṭalḥah[334] —Ibn 'Abbās, commenting on God's word when He mentioned the creation of the earth before heaven and then mentioned heaven before earth: (It is explained by the fact that) He created the earth with the food it provides before heaven, without spreading it out. "Then He stretched out straight toward heaven and fashioned it into seven heavens."[335] Thereafter, He spread out the earth. This is (meant by) God's word: "And it was the earth that He spread out thereafter."[336]

According to Muḥammad b. Sa'd[337] —his father—his paternal uncle—his father—his father—Ibn 'Abbās, commenting on: "And it was the earth that He spread out thereafter. He brought forth from it its water and its pasture, and the mountains He anchored firmly."[338] It means that He created the heavens and the earth. When He had finished with heaven before creating food of the earth, He spread the food on it after creating heaven. And He firmly anchored the mountains. This is meant by "spreading it out." The food and the plants of the earth used to be good only on the night and the day.[339] This is (meant by) God's word: "And it was the earth that He spread out thereafter." Have you not heard that He continues: "He brought forth from it its water and its pasture"[340] ?

---

334. According to Khalīfah, *Ṭabaqāt*, 312, 'Alī b. Abī Ṭalḥah died in 120/737[8]. According to the lost History of Ḥimṣ by Abū Bakr Aḥmad b. Muḥammad b. 'Īsā (see Rosenthal, *Muslim Historiography*², 467), he died in 143/760[1]. *Tahdhīb*, VII, 339–41, prefers the latter date, but also refers to Khalīfah. Bukhārī, *Ta'rīkh*, III,2, 281 f., states that he visited the caliph Abū al-'Abbās (al-Saffāḥ), who died in 754. A plausible date for Ibn Abī Ṭalḥah's death would seemingly be ca. 750, if one also takes into account the surrounding authorities in the chain of transmitters. See also Horst, 293, n. 5.

335. Qur. 2:29.

336. Qur. 79:30. For the quotations in *Tafsīr*, see above, n. 333.

337. As indicated in *EI*², III, 922b, s. v. Ibn Sa'd, with reference to Horst, 294, this is not the author of the *Ṭabaqāt*. It is Muḥammad b. Sa'd b. Muḥammad b. al-Ḥasan b. 'Aṭiyyah b. Sa'd b. Junādah al-'Awfī, who died in 276/889 *(TB*, V, 322 f.). His father Sa'd b. Muḥammad is listed in *TB*, IX, 126. Sa'd's paternal uncle al-Ḥusayn b. al-Ḥasan died in 201 or 202/816–18 *(TB*, VIII, 29–32). Al-Ḥusayn's father al-Ḥasan b. 'Aṭiyyah died in 181/797 *(Tahdhīb*, II, 294), and 'Aṭiyyah b. Sa'd died in 111/729[30] *(Tahdhīb*, VII, 224–26). A family *isnād* as complete as this is most remarkable.

338. Qur. 79:30–32.

339. Only when the heaven and the sun and the moon were in existence could the food-producing plants really prosper.

340. Qur. 79:30 f. See *Tafsīr*, XXX, 29.

[46] Abū Ja'far (al-Ṭabarī) says: Regarding this, the correct statement, in our opinion, is the one of those who said: God created the earth on Sunday. He created the heaven on Thursday, and He created the stars and the sun and the moon on Friday. (We consider it correct) because of the soundness of the report mentioned by us earlier on the authority of Ibn 'Abbās from the Messenger of God. The tradition transmitted to us on the authority of Ibn 'Abbās is not impossible. It says that God created the earth but did not spread it out. Then He created the heavens "and fashioned them (into seven heavens),"[341] and thereafter "spread out" the earth. "He then brought forth from it its water and its pasture, and the mountains He anchored firmly." Indeed, in my opinion this is the correct statement. That is because the meaning of "spreading out" is different from that of "creating." God says: "Are you more difficult to create than the heaven He constructed? He raised high its roof and fashioned it. He darkened its night and brought forth its morning. And it was the earth He spread out thereafter. He brought forth from it its water and its pasture, and the mountains He anchored firmly."[342]

Someone might say: You realize that a number of interpreters have considered God's word: "And it was the earth that He spread out *thereafter,*" to mean: "He spread out *simultaneously*" (attributing to the preposition *ba'da* "after" the meaning of *ma'a* "together [simultaneous] with"). Now, what is your evidence for the soundness of your statement that we have here the meaning of "after," the opposite of "before"? The reply would be: The meaning of "after" generally known in Arab speech, as we have said, is that of the opposite of "before," and not "simultaneous with." Now, word meanings considered applicable are those that are preponderant and generally known among speakers (of a language), and no others are.[343]

It has been said that God created the Ancient House (the Ka'bah) upon the water on four pillars. He did this two thousand years

---

341. Qur. 2:29.

342. Qur. 79:27–32.

343. See *Tafsīr*, XXX, 30 (*ad* Qur. 79:30). It is one of Ṭabarī's exegetical principles that, unless there are reasons to the contrary, the most common and best-known meanings of words as used by the Arabs are applicable to the speech of God. See, for instance, *Tafsīr*, XII, 25 (*ad* Qur. 11:40). See also text below, I, 56.

before He created this world, and the earth was then spread out underneath it. [47]

Those who said this

According to Ibn Ḥumayd—Ya'qūb al-Qummī[344] —Ja'far[345] — 'Ikrimah—Ibn 'Abbās: The House was founded upon the water on four pillars two thousand years before (God) created this world. The earth was then spread out underneath the House.[346]

According to Ibn Ḥumayd—Mihrān[347] —Sufyān (al-Thawrī)—al-A'mash—Bukayr b. al-Akhnas[348] —Mujāhid—'Abdallāh b. 'Umar: God created the House two thousand years before the earth, and from it, the earth was spread out.

If this is so, the earth was created before the heavens were created, and the earth "spread out"—*d-ḥ-w* in the sense of *b-s-ṭ* — with its food, its pastures, and its plants after the creation of the heavens, as mentioned by us on the authority of Ibn 'Abbās.

According to Ibn Ḥumayd—Mihrān—Abū Sinān[349] —Abū Bakr[350] : The Jews came to the Prophet and said: Muḥammad, inform us about the creation created by God in these six days! The Prophet replied: He created the earth on Sunday and Monday. He created the mountains on Tuesday. He created the cities, food, the rivers, and the cultivated and barren land on Wednesday. He created the heavens and the angels on Thursday continuing to the last three hours of Friday. In the first of these three hours, He created the terms (of human life), in the second, harm, and in the

344. Ya'qūb b. 'Abdallāh al-Qummī died in 174/790–91. See *Tahdhīb*, XI, 390 f.; Bukhārī, *Ta'rīkh*, IV, 2, 391; Abū Nu'aym, *Akhbār Iṣbahān*, II, 351 f. Ya'qūb is mentioned as one of Ibn Ḥumayd's authorities in *TB*, II, 259, l. 3.

345. Ja'far b. Abī al-Mughīrah al-Qummī is listed *Tahdīb*, II, 108.

346. For this and the following tradition, see *Tafsīr*, XXX, 29 (*ad* Qur. 79:30–32). Cf. also *Tafsīr*, IV, 7 (*ad* Qur. 3:96).

347. For Abū 'Abdallāh Mihrān b. Abī 'Umar al-'Aṭṭār al-Rāzī, see *Tahdhīb*, X, 327; Bukhārī, *Ta'rīkh*, IV, 1, 429; Horst, 296, n. 12.

348. See *Tahdhīb*, I, 489 f.

349. Abū Sinān has the gentilic al-Shaybānī and is equated in the index of Ṭabarī with Abū Sinān Ḍirār b. Murrah al-Shaybānī, who died in 132/749[50]. See *Tahdhīb*, IV, 457; Khalīfah, *Ṭabaqāt*, 165.

350. The available data seem consistent with the possible equation of this person with Abū Bakr b. 'Abdallāh, who was a transmitter of 'Ikrimah and Shahr b. Ḥawshab. See text below, I, 1006, and I, 245 f. Abū Bakr b. 'Abdallāh could possibly be the best-known bearer of the name, Abū Bakr b. 'Abdallāh b. Abī Maryam, who died in 156/773. See Bukhārī, *Kunā*, 9, no. 55; *Tahdhīb*, XII, 28–30, who has 256. He may, however, be just another unidentified individual.

third, Adam. The Jews said: You speak the truth, if you finish (the statement). The Prophet realized what they had in mind. He got angry, and God revealed: "And fatigue did not touch Us. So be
[48] patient with what they say."[351]

Someone might say: If it is as you have described, namely, that God created the earth before heaven, then what is the meaning of the statement of Ibn 'Abbās told all of you by Wāṣil b. 'Abd al-A'lā al-Asadī—Muḥammad b. Fuḍayl—al-A'mash—Abū Ẓabyān—Ibn 'Abbās: The first thing created by God is the Pen. God then said to it: Write!, whereupon the Pen asked: What shall I write, my lord? God replied: Write what is predestined! He continued. And the Pen proceeded to (write) whatever is predestined and going to be to the Coming of the Hour. God then lifted up the water vapor and split the heavens off from it. Then God created the fish *(nūn)*, and the earth was spread out upon its back. The fish became agitated, with the result that the earth was shaken up. It was steadied by means of the mountains, for they indeed proudly (tower) over the earth.[352]

I was told about the same by Wāṣil—Wakī'—al-A'mash—Abū Ẓabyān—Ibn 'Abbās.

According to Ibn al-Muthannā—Ibn Abī 'Adī—Shu'bah—Sulaymān (al-A'mash ?)—Abū Ẓabyān—Ibn 'Abbās: The first (thing) created by God is the Pen. It proceeded to (write) whatever is going to be. (God) then lifted up the water vapor, and the heavens were created from it. Then He created the fish, and the earth was spread out on its back. The fish moved, with the result that the earth was shaken up. It was steadied by means of the mountains, for the mountains indeed proudly (tower) over the earth. So he said, and he recited: "*Nūn*. By the Pen and what they write."[353]

I was told the same by Tamīm b. al-Muntaṣir—Isḥāq (b. Yūsuf)—Sharīk (b. 'Abdallāh al-Nakha'ī)—al-A'mash—Abū Ẓabyān or Mujāhid[354] —Ibn 'Abbās, with the exception, however, that he

351. Qur. 50:38 f. See also text above, I, 19 ff.

352. For the first half of this tradition, see text above, I, 30, and n. 241, referring to *Tafsīr*, XXIX, 10 *(ad* Qur. 68:1-3), where this tradition as well as the following *isnād* occurs.

353. Qur. 68:1; *Tafsīr*, XXIX, 9. See also text above, I, 30 f.

354. For "or " the Leiden edition has "on the authority of," which may not be impossible, but the evidence seems to be against it. See text above, I, 31, and *Tafsīr*, XXIX, 9.

said: And the heavens were split off from it (instead of: were created).

According to Ibn Bashshār—Yaḥyā[355] —Sufyān—Sulaymān (al-A'mash ?)—Abū Ẓabyān—Ibn 'Abbās: The first (thing) created by [49]
God is the Pen. God said: Write!, whereupon the Pen asked: What shall I write? God replied: Write what is predestined! He continued. And (the Pen) proceeded to (write) whatever is predestined and going to be from that day on to the Coming of the Hour. Then God created the fish. He lifted up the water vapor, and heaven was split off from it, and the earth was spread out upon the back of the fish. The fish became agitated, and as a result, the earth was shaken up. It was steadied by means of the mountains, he continued, for they proudly (tower) over the the earth.

According to Ibn Ḥumayd—Jarīr (b. 'Abd al-Ḥamīd)—'Aṭā' b. al-Sā'ib—Abū al-Ḍuḥā Muslim b. Ṣubayḥ—Ibn 'Abbās: The first thing created by God is the Pen. God said to it: Write!, and it wrote whatever is going to be until the Coming of the Hour. Then God created the fish upon the water. Then he heaped up the earth upon it.[356]

This reportedly is a sound tradition as transmitted on the authority of Ibn 'Abbās and on the authority of others in the sense commented upon and explained and does not contradict anything transmitted by us from him on this subject.

Should someone[357] ask: What comment on his authority and that of others proves the soundness of what you have transmitted to us in this sense on his authority? he should be referred to what I have been told by Mūsā b. Hārūn al-Hamdānī and others—'Amr b. Ḥammād—Asbāṭ b. Naṣr—al-Suddī—Abū Mālik and Abū Ṣāliḥ—Ibn 'Abbās. Also (al-Suddī)—Murrah al-Hamdānī—'Abdallāh b. Mas'ūd and some (other) companions of the Messenger of God (commenting on): "He is the One Who created for you all that is on earth. Then He stretched out straight toward the heaven and fashioned it into seven heavens."[358] God's Throne was upon the water. He had not created anything except what He created before

355. Yaḥyā b. Sa'īd b. Farrūkh al-Qaṭṭān was born at the beginning of the year 120/Dec. 737–Jan.738. He died in 198/313. See *TB*, XIV, 135-44; *Tahdhīb*, XI, 216–20.

356. See text above, I, 31.

357. Lit.,"he," possibly referring to a particular individual (?).

358. Qur. 2:29.

the water.[359] When He wanted to create the creation, He brought forth smoke from the water. The smoke rose above the water and
[50] hovered loftily over it. He therefore called it "heaven."[360] Then He dried out the water, and thus made it one earth. He split it and made it into seven earths on Sunday and Monday. He created the earth upon a (big) fish (*ḥūt*), that being the fish (*nūn*) mentioned by God in the Qur'ān: "*Nūn*. By the Pen."[361] The fish was in the water. The water was upon the back of a (small) rock. The rock was upon the back of an angel. The angel was upon a (big) rock. The (big) rock—the one mentioned by Luqmān[362] —was in the wind, neither in heaven nor on earth. The fish moved and became agitated. As a result, the earth quaked, whereupon He firmly, anchored the mountains on it, and it was stable. The mountains proudly (tower) over the earth. This is stated in God's word that He made for the earth "firmly anchored (mountains), lest it shake you up."[363]

Abū Ja'far (al-Ṭabarī) says: The statement of those mentioned by me that God brought forth smoke from the water when He wanted to create the heavens and earth; that the smoke hovered loftily over it, by which is meant that it was high over the water, since everything that is high above another thing is its "heaven"; that He then dried out the water and made it one earth, indicates that God created heaven unfashioned before the earth and then created the earth. If it is as they say, it is not impossible that God stirred up smoke from the water and raised it high over the water, so that it became a heaven for it. Then He dried out the water, and the smoke that hovered loftily over it became an earth. But God did not spread it out and did not decree that it contain the food it provides, nor did He bring forth from it its water and its pasture, until He stretched out straight toward the heaven which was the smoke stirring from the water and rising high above it,

---

359. See text above, I, 36.

360. The verb *samā* means "to hover loftily," and the noun *samā'* means "heaven." If there is an etymological connection between them, it probably was in the opposite direction, that is, the verb was derived from the noun.

361. Qur. 68:1. *Ḥūt* appears in the Qur'ān also in connection with Jonah. There is no discernible distinction in meaning between *ḥūt* and *nūn*, the latter being the ancient Semitic word.

362. See Qur. 31:16 and *Tafsīr*, XXI, 46, on this verse.

363. Qur. 16:15. For the tradition in *Tafsīr*, see above, n. 281.

and He fashioned it into seven heavens. Then He spread out the earth which was water and dried the water out. Then He split the earth, making it into seven earths, and decreed that it contain the amount of food it provides and "brought forth from it its water [51] and its pasture, and the mountains He anchored firmly," as God says.[364] Thus, everything transmitted by us concerning this subject on the authority of Ibn ʿAbbās has a sound meaning.

Monday: We have mentioned before the difference of opinion among scholars as to what He created on it and what has been transmitted concerning the subject on the authority of the Messenger of God.[365]

What God created on Tuesday and Wednesday: We have also mentioned some of the information that has been transmitted concerning this subject. Here we shall mention some information not mentioned by us before. In our opinion, the sound report in this connection is what I was told by Mūsā b. Hārūn—ʿAmr b. Ḥammād—Asbāṭ—al-Suddī—Abū Mālik and Abū Ṣāliḥ—Ibn ʿAbbās. Also (al-Suddī)—Murrah al-Hamdānī—ʿAbdallāh b. Masʿūd and some (other) companions of the Messenger of God: God created the mountains on it—meaning the earth—and the food it provides for its inhabitants and its trees and whatever else is required for it on two days, Tuesday and Wednesday. That is when God says: "Say: Do you really not believe in the One Who created the earth in two days, and set up others like Him ? That is the Lord of the worlds. He made in it firmly anchored (mountains) above it and blessed it and decreed that it contain the amount of food it provides, all in four days, equally for those asking"—that is, those who ask (will find that) it is so.[366] "Then He stretched out straight toward heaven, which was smoke"[367] —that smoke came from the water's breathing—and made it into one heaven. Then He split (this one heaven) up into seven heavens on two days, Thursday and Friday.

According to al-Muthannā—Abū Ṣāliḥ—Abū Maʿshar—Saʿīd b. Abī Saʿīd—ʿAbdallāh b. Salām: God created food and the firmly

364. Qur. 79:31 f.
365. The reference may be to text above, I, 47.
366. See above, n. 163.
367. Qur. 41:9–11.

anchored (mountains) on Tuesday and Wednesday.[368]

[52] According to Tamīm b. al-Muntaṣir—Isḥāq (b. Yūsuf) —Sharīk (b. ʿAbdallāh al-Nakhaʿī)—Ghālib b. Ghallāb— ʿAṭāʾ b. Abī Rabāḥ—Ibn ʿAbbās: God created the mountains on Tuesday. That is why people say: It is a heavy day.[369]

Abū Jaʿfar (al-Ṭabarī) says: In our opinion, the sound statement concerning this subject is the tradition transmitted by us on the authority of the Prophet who said: God created the mountains and the uses they possess on Tuesday. On Wednesday, He created trees, water, cities, and the cultivated and barren land. We were told this by Hannād—Abū Bakr b. ʿAyyāsh—Abū Saʿd al-Baqqāl—ʿIkrimah—Ibn ʿAbbās—the Prophet.[370]

It has been transmitted on the authority of the Prophet that God created the mountains on Sunday. He created the trees on Monday. He created evil on Tuesday. He created the light on Wednesday. I was told this by al-Qāsim b. Bishr b. Maʿrūf and al-Ḥusayn b. ʿAlī al-Ṣudāʾī—Ḥajjāj—Ibn Surayj—Ismāʿīl b. Umayyah—Ayyūb b. Khālid—ʿAbdallāh b. Rāfiʿ, the *mawlā* of Umm Salamah—Abū Hurayrah—the Prophet.[371]

The first report[372] is sounder with respect to the source situation *(makhrajan)* and more likely to be true, because it is what most of the early (scholars) say.

Thursday: He created on it the heavens, which were compressed but then were split,[373] as I was told by Mūsā b. Hārūn—ʿAmr b. Ḥammād—Asbāṭ—al-Suddī—Abū Mālik and Abū Ṣāliḥ—Ibn ʿAbbās. Also (al-Suddī)—Murrah al-Hamdānī—ʿAbdallāh b. Masʿūd and some (other) companions of the Prophet (commenting on): "Then He stretched out straight toward heaven, which was smoke"[374] —that smoke came from the water's breathing—
[53] and made it into one heaven. Then He split (this one heaven) into seven heavens on two days, Thursday and Friday.

368. See text above, I, 44.

369. See *Tafsīr*, XXIV, 61, ll. 26 f. (*ad* Qur. 41:6), and above, n. 174. "Heavy" may not be intended to refer to the great weight of mountains but rather to the evil character of Tuesday.

370. See text above, I, 19.

371. See text above, I, 20.

372. That is, the one of Mūsā b. Hārūn; see text above, I, 51.

373. Cf. Qur. 21:30.

374. Qur. 41:11.

Friday—*yawm al-jum'ah* —is thus called because on it, God put together *(j-m-')* the creation of the heavens and the earth and "revealed in every heaven its command."[375] He continued: In every heaven, He created its (special) angels as well as its (special) oceans, the mountains with hail,[376] and what (man) does not know.[377] He then adorned the lower heaven with the stars and made them an ornament and guard to guard against the Satans.[378] When He completed creating whatever He pleased, He sat straight on the Throne. That is when He says: "He created the heavens and the earth in six days,"[379] and: "The two were compressed, and We split them apart."[380]

According to al-Muthannā—Abū Ṣāliḥ ('Abdallāh b. Ṣāliḥ) — Abū Ma'shar—Sa'īd b. Abī Sa'īd—'Abdallāh b. Salām: God created the heavens on Thursday and Friday, and He finished in the last hour of Friday, in which He created Adam in haste. This is the hour in which the Hour will come.[381]

According to Tamīm b. al-Muntaṣir—Isḥāq (b. Yūsuf)—Sharīk (b. 'Abdallāh al-Nakha'ī)—Ghālib b. Ghallāb—'Aṭā' b. Abī Rabāḥ—Ibn 'Abbās: God created the places for rivers and trees on Wednesday. He created the birds, the wild animals, reptiles, and beasts of prey on Thursday, and He created man on Friday. He finished creating everything on Friday.

In our opinion, the sound view is represented by the statement of those mentioned by us that God created the heavens, the angels, and Adam on Thursday and Friday. That is because of the report told us by Hannād b. al-Sarī, who also said that he read all of the *ḥadīth*[382] —Abū Bakr b. 'Ayyāsh—Abū Sa'īd (!) al-Baqqāl—'Ikrimah—Ibn 'Abbās—the Prophet: On Thursday He created [54]
heaven. On Friday He created the stars, the sun, the moon, and the angels, until three hours remained of it. In the first of these three hours, He created the terms (of human life), who would live

375. Qur. 41:12, see above, n. 199. For the etymology of "Friday" involved here, see text below, I, 113–15. Cf. also Mas'ūdī, *Murūj*, I, 48.

376. Cf. Qur. 24:43.

377. Cf. Qur. 96:5.

378. Cf. Qur. 37:6 f. and 41:12.

379. Qur. 11:7.

380. Qur. 21:30.

381. See text above, I, 44.

382. See above, n. 159.

and who would die. In the second, He cast harm upon everything that is useful for mankind. And in the third, He (created) Adam and had him dwell in Paradise. He commanded Iblīs to prostrate himself (before Adam), and He drove Adam out of Paradise at the end of the hour.[383]

According to al-Qāsim b. Bishr and al-Ḥusayn b. ʿAlī al-Ṣudāʾī—Ḥajjāj—Ibn Jurayj—Ismāʿīl b. Umayyah—Ayyūb b. Khālid—ʿAbdallāh b. Rāfiʿ, the *mawlā* of Umm Salamah—Abū Hurayrah: The Messenger of God took me by the hand and said: He scattered on it—meaning the earth—the animals on Thursday, and He created Adam after (the time of) the afternoon prayer of Friday as the last of His creatures in the last hour of Friday, in the time between the afternoon prayer and night(fall).[384]

Now then, God created the creation in six days, from the beginning of the creation of the heavens and the earth to the time He finished creating all creatures. Each day of the six in which He created them corresponds to a thousand of the years of this world. Between His beginning His creation of (all) that and the creation of the Pen, which He commanded to write whatever is going to be to the Coming of the Hour, there are a thousand years—one of the days of the other world, each of which corresponds to a thousand years of this world. The conclusion is that the time elapsed from when our Lord first began creating His creatures to when He fin-
[55] ished the last of them is seven thousand years, give, if God wills, or take a little. That is according to the traditions and reports transmitted by us which we have mentioned.[385] We have omitted many of them, because we do not like the book to become too long by mentioning (all this information).

If this is so, and if it is sound that, as proved by us earlier with the help of evidential statements, there is a duration of seven thousand years, give or take a little, from (the time) when our Lord finished His creation of all His creatures to the moment of the annihilation of all of them, the conclusion must be drawn that the time elapsed from when God first created His creation to the Coming of the Hour and the annihilation of the entire world extends over fourteen thousand of the years of this world, or fourteen of

383. See text above, I, 19 f.
384. See text above, I, 20.
385. See text above, I, 8 ff.

the days of the other world. Seven of these days—that is, seven thousand of the years of this world—represent the time elapsed from when God first began creating His first creatures to when He finished the creation of the last of them—namely, Adam, the father of mankind. The other seven days—that is, seven thousand of the years of this world—represent the period from when God finished the creation of His last creature—that is, Adam—to the annihilation of all His creatures and the Coming of the Hour and the return of everything to the state in which it was before there was anyone except the Eternal One, the Creator, Whose "are the creation and the command,"[386] Who was before everything, and there was nothing before Him, and Who will be after everything, and nothing will remain except His noble face.

Someone might say: What proof do you have for stating that each of the six days in which God created His creation corresponds to a thousand of the years of this world, and none (of those days) is like the days of the inhabitants of this world commonly known among them (as "days") ? God merely says: "The One Who created the heavens and the earth and what is between them in six [56]
days."[387] He gave us no information that it is as you say. Rather, He informed us that He created that in six days, and the days commonly known (as "days") among those addressed here are the days that begin with sunrise and last until sunset. You also say that whatever God says in addressing His servants in His revelation is meant to be understood according to its most common and preponderant meaning, but now you propose to understand the information given by God in His Book concerning the creation of the heavens and the earth and what is between them in six days according to a meaning of "day" that is not commonly known. When God wants to bring something into being, His command is completely effective, and thus it cannot be said that He created the heavens and the earth and what is between them in six days whose measure is six thousand of the years of this world. When He wants something to be, He commands it to be by just saying: "Be! And it is."[388] This is as our Lord says: "And Our command is

386. Qur. 7:54.
387. Qur. 25:59.
388. Qur. 2:117, etc.

but one[389] like a glance of the eye."[390]

The reply would be: Earlier in this book of ours we said that with respect to most of what we set down in it, we rely upon the traditions and reports on the authority of our Prophet and that of the righteous early Muslims before us, and we do not use reason and thinking for producing (the book), for most of its contents is information about past matters and events that are going to be. Knowledge of this sort cannot be produced and obtained by the use of reason.[391]

Should he ask whether there is proof from reported information *(khabar)* for the soundness of (the equation of "day" with a thousand years), the answer would be: It is something that according to our knowledge has not been contradicted by any leading religious authority.

Should he ask whether there is information transmitted on the authority of one of the leading scholars, the answer would be:
[57] Knowledge of it among early Muslim scholars is too common to require transmission attributed to one individual among them personally. It has been transmitted on the authority of a number of them mentioned personally by name. If he then asks to mention some of them, the answer is:

According to Ibn Ḥumayd—Ḥakkām[392] —ʿAnbasah[393] —Simāk[394] —ʿIkrimah—Ibn ʿAbbās, commenting on: God "created the heavens and the earth in six days"[395] —of which each day is like "one thousand years of your counting."[396]

According to Ibn Wakīʿ—his father—Isrāʾīl[397] —Simāk—ʿIkri-

---

389. The feminine *wāḥidah* ("one") has no explicit referent, but it seems fairly certain that the referent is intended to be *lamḥah* ("glance") in the singular, anticipating the following collective *lamḥ*. Thus, it means: (as quick) as a single glance of the eye. *Tafsīr*, XXVII, 66 *(ad* Qur. 54:50) explains: "a single irrefutable utterance *(qawlah)* as quick and immediate (as a glance of the eye)." Among the modern translators of the Qurʾān, A. J. Arberry follows Ṭabarī and translates "one word." R. Paret has "one action," and R. Bell offers the preferable "one flash."

390. Qur. 54:50.

391. See text above, I, 6 ff.

392. Abū ʿAbd al-Raḥmān Ḥakkām b. Salm al-Rāzī died after 190/805[6] in Mecca. See *TB*, VIII, 281 f.; *Tahdhīb*, II, 422, f.; Horst, 299, n. 7.

393. According to *Tahdhīb*, VIII, 155, he was ʿAnbasah b. Saʿīd b. al-Ḍurays.

394. Simāk b. Ḥarb died in 123/740[1]. See *Tahdhīb*, IV, 232–34.

395. Qur. 11:7.

396. See *Tafsīr*, XXI, 58 *(ad* Qur. 32:5).

397. Born in 100/718[9], Isrāʾīl b. Yūnus died in the early 160s/776–799. See *TB*, VII, 20–25; *Tahdhīb*, I, 261–63.

mah—Ibn 'Abbās, commenting on: "In a day whose measure is a thousand years of your counting,"[398] as follows: The six days on which God created the heavens and the earth.

According to 'Abdah[399] —al-Ḥusayn b. al-Faraj[400] —Abū Mu'ādh[401] —'Ubayd[402] —al-Ḍaḥḥāk concerning God's word: "In a day whose measure is a thousand years of your counting": He means the day of the six days in which God created the heavens and the earth and what is between them.

According to al-Muthannā—'Alī (b. al-Haytham)—al-Musayyab b. Sharīk—Abū Rawq—al-Ḍaḥḥāk, commenting on: "And He is the One Who created the heavens and the earth in six days"[403] —of the days of the other world. The measure of each day is a thousand years. He began with the creation on Sunday, and the creation was all together on Friday *(ijtama'a - jum'ah).*[404]

According to Ibn Ḥumayd—Jarīr (b. 'Abd al-Ḥamīd)—al-A'mash—Abū Ṣāliḥ—Ka'b: God began the creation of the heavens and the earth on Sunday, Monday, Tuesday, Wednesday, and Thursday. He finished on Friday. He continued: God made each day equal to a thousand years.

According to al-Muthannā—al-Ḥajjāj—Abū 'Awānah—Abū [58]
Bishr—Mujāhid: One of the six days is "like a thousand years of your counting."[405]

---

398. Qur. 32:5. See *Tafsīr,* XXI, 58.

399. *Tafsīr,* XXI, 58 starts the *isnād* with: "I was told by al-Ḥusayn b. al-Faraj," as is commonly found in *Tafsīr.* Elsewhere, we find 'Abdān al-Marwazī instead of 'Abdah (see text below, I, 80); further 'Abdah al-Marwazī (I, 96), 'Abdān b. Muḥammad al-Marwazī (I, 117), and 'Abdān al-Marwazī (I, 312), apparently all referring to the same individual. However, he appears unidentifiable under any form of the name. *TB,* XI, 135 f., has a certain 'Abdān b. Muḥammad al-Marwazī (b. 220/835, d. 293/906), a transmitter of Muqātil's *Tafsīr,* but he belonged to the generation of Ṭabarī and was himself a student of Abū Kurayb and an authority of the Ṭabarī biographer Ibn Kāmil. He could hardly be meant here. See also Horst, 304.

400. Al-Ḥusayn b. al-Faraj does not seem to be safely identifiable with al-Ḥusayn b. al-Faraj al-Khayyāṭ. See *TB,* VIII, 84–86; Ibn Abī Ḥātim, I, 2, 62; Ibn Ḥajar, *Lisān,* II, 307; Horst, 304, n. 7.

401. As indicated by Horst, 304, n. 8, Abū Mu'ādh al-Faḍl b. Khālid (see text below, I, 80) died around 211/826[?]. See Ibn al-Jazarī, *Ghāyah,* II, 9; Ibn Abī Ḥātim, III, 2, 61.

402. 'Ubayd (wrongly, it seems, 'Ubaydallāh, see text below, I, 80) b. Sulaymān is briefly listed in *Tahdhīb,* VII, 67; Ibn Abī Ḥātim, II, 2, 408; Horst, 304, n. 9.

403. Qur. 11:7.

404. *Tafsīr,* XII, 4 *(ad* Qur. 11:7) contains a version of the tradition whose *isnād* omits the first two links mentioned above.

405. Qur. 32:5.

So it is. There is no point to someone's asking: How can God be described as having created the heavens and the earth and what is between them in six days, seeing that when He wants something to be, He commands it to be just by saying: "Be! And it is." (The reason why such a question would be pointless is) because whatever can be imagined as covered by such a statement is also covered by a statement such as: He created all of that in six days whose duration corresponds to that of six days of this world, because when He wants something to be, He commands it to be just by saying: "Be! And it is."[406]

Night and Day: Which Was Created before the Other? The Beginning of the Creation of the Sun and the Moon and a Description of Them, as Time Is Known Through Them

Regarding God's creation, we have mentioned the things which He created before He created momentary and extended time. We have explained that momentary and created time is but the hours of night and day, and that is but the traversal by the sun and the moon of the degrees of the sphere.[407] Now, let us ask which came first, night or day? Differences of opinion exist among those who speculate on the subject. Some say that God created night before day, using as evidence for the truth of this statement that when the sun sets and its luminosity, which is identical with daytime, is gone, night comes suddenly with its darkness. It must be concluded that the luminosity (of the sun) is what descends upon the night and that, without the day descending upon the night and obliterating it, the night would be stable. This being the case with regard to night and day is proof that the night was created first and that the sun was created later. This is expressed in a statement transmitted on the authority of Ibn ʿAbbās. According to [59]

406. Qur. 2:117, etc. Ṭabarī argues here that the creation word of God is timeless and leaves open the question of how much time in human terms might be involved in any particular aspect of creation. Thus, if there is a tradition about "days" meaning thousands of years, it is not irreconcilable with God's immediacy of creation and is as acceptable as any other tradition or chronological framework may be.

407. See text above, I, 18.

Ibn Bashshār—'Abd al-Raḥmān (b. Mahdī)—Sufyān (al-Thawrī)—his father[408] —'Ikrimah—Ibn 'Abbās: Asked whether the night existed before the day, (Ibn 'Abbās?) replied: Don't you see! When the heavens and the earth were compressed,[409] was there anything but darkness between them? This is meant for you to realize that the night existed before the day.

According to al-Ḥasan b. Yaḥyā[410] —'Abd al-Razzāq[411] —(Sufyān) al-Thawrī—his father—'Ikrimah—Ibn 'Abbās: The night is before the day. Then he said: "The two were compressed, and We then split them apart."[412]

According to Muḥammad b. Bashshār—Wahb b. Jarīr—his father[413] —Yaḥyā b. Ayyūb[414] —Yazīd b. Abī Ḥabīb[415] —Marthad b. 'Abdallāh al-Yazanī[416] : Whenever 'Uqbah b. 'Āmir[417] saw the new moon, that is, the new moon of Ramaḍān, he did not spend that very night in prayer (but waited) until he had fasted the following day and thereafter spent the nights in prayer. When I mentioned this to Ibn Ḥujayrah,[418] he said: The night before the day or the day before the night?[419]

Others said: Day was before night. For the soundness of this statement of theirs they used as evidence (the argument) that God existed while there was neither night nor day and nothing at all except Him, and that it was His light with which He illuminated everything He created after having created it, until He created night.

---

408. Sa'īd b. Masrūq died between 126 and 128/743–746. See *Tahdhīb*, IV, 82.

409. Cf. Qur. 21:30. In commenting on this Qur'ānic passage, Ṭabarī decided in favor of another interpretation. See *Tafsīr*, XVII, 15.

410. Died in 263/877 in his eighties. See *Tahdhīb*, II, 324 f.; Horst, 296, n. 2.

411. 'Abd al-Razzāq b. Hammām lived from 126/743[4] to 211/827. See *Tahdhīb*, VI, 310–15; Sezgin, *GAS*, I, 99; Horst, 296, n. 11.

412. Qur. 21:30. The tradition appears in *Tafsīr*, XVII, 15.

413. Jarīr b. Ḥāzim died in 175/791[2] in his eighties. See *Tahdhīb*, II, 69–72.

414. Died in 168/784 [5]. See *Tahdhīb*, XI, 186-88.

415. Born in 53/672[3], Yazīd b. Abī Ḥabīb died in 128/745[6]. See *Tahdhīb*, XI, 318 f.

416. Died in 90/708[9]. See *Tahdhīb*, X, 82.

417. 'Uqbah died at the end of Mu'āwiyah's caliphate in 58/677[8]. See *Tahdhīb*, VIII, 242–44; Ibn 'Abd al-Barr, *Istī'āb*, III, 1073 f.

418. Apparently, 'Abd al-Raḥmān b. Ḥujayrah, who died in the early eighties/699–702, rather than his son 'Abdallāh. See *Tahdhīb*, VI, 160.

419. 'Uqbah's action with respect to the nightly prayers during Ramaḍān (*tarāwīḥ*) could be interpreted either way as to the question of precedence of night over day or vice versa.

Those who said this

According to ʿAlī b. Sahl—al-Ḥasan b. Bilāl[420] —Ḥammād b. Salamah —Abū ʿAbd al-Salām al-Zubayr[421] —Ayyūb b. ʿAbdallāh al-Fihrī[422] —Ibn Masʿūd: With your Lord there is neither night nor day. The light of the heavens comes from the light of His face. The measure of each of those days of yours is twelve hours with Him.

Abū Jaʿfar (al-Ṭabarī) says: Of the two statements on this subject the one which, in my opinion, is most likely to be correct is that
[60] night was before day. For day comes, as I have mentioned, from the luminosity of the sun, and God created the sun and made it run in the sphere only after He had spread the earth and laid it out, as He says: "Are you more difficult to create than the heaven He constructed? He raised high its roof and fashioned it. He darkened its night and brought forth its morning."[423] If the sun was created after the heaven was made a roof and its night darkened, it must be concluded that before the sun was created and before God brought forth morning from heaven, (the heaven) was dark and not luminous. Now, if our observation about night and day contains clear proof that day is what comes suddenly upon the night, because it is at night that the sun sets and its luminosity is gone,[424] so that the air becomes dark, then the day is what comes suddenly upon the night with its luminosity and light. God knows best!

The report(s) on the authority of the Messenger of God differ as to the moment when God's creation of the sun and the moon began. As transmitted on (Ibn ʿAbbās') authority, (the Prophet) said: God created the sun, the moon, the stars, and the angels on Friday, until three hours remained of it.[425] This we were told by Hannād b. al-Sarī—Abū Bakr b. ʿAyyāsh—Abū Saʿd al-Baqqāl—ʿIkrimah—Ibn ʿAbbās—the Prophet.

As transmitted by Abū Hurayrah, the Prophet said: God cre-

---

420. See *Tahdhīb*, II, 258, and below, n. 601.

421. In the sparse references to Abū ʿAbd al-Salām al-Zubayr, he is also connected with Ayyūb (b. ʿAbdallāh) b. Mu/ikraz. See Bukhārī, *Ta'rīkh*, II, 1, 378; Ibn Abī Ḥātim, I, 2, 584. Also *Tahdhīb*, I, 407.

422. See *Tahdhīb*, I, 407 f.; Bukhārī, *Ta'rīkh*, I, 1, 419, no. 1343; Ibn Abī Ḥātim, I, 1, 251, no. 898. It seems that he is nowhere given the gentilic al-Fihrī; *Tahdhīb* has al-ʿĀmirī.

423. Qur. 79:27–29.

424. The Cairo edition has: the sun sets and its luminosity is gone, be it at night or during the day.

425. See text above, I, 20.

ated light on Wednesday.[426] This I was told by al-Qāsim b. Bishr and al-Ḥusayn b. ʿAlī—Ḥajjāj b. Muḥammad—Ibn Jurayj—Ismāʿīl b. Umayyah—Ayyūb b. Khālid—ʿAbdallāh b. Rāfiʿ—Abū Hurayrah—the Prophet: God created light on Wednesday. [61]

However this may be, God created many other creatures before He created (the sun and the moon). He then created them in consequence of His superior knowledge of what is beneficial for His creation. He gave them constant movement. Then He distinguished between the two, making one of them the sign of night and the other the sign of day. He blotted out the sign of night and made the sign of day something to see by.[427]

Concerning the reason for the difference between the conditions of the sign of night and the sign of day, there are reports transmitted on the authority of the Messenger of God. I shall mention some of these reports which I have, as well as similar reports transmitted on the authority of a number of early (scholars).

Among the traditions transmitted from the Messenger of God on this subject is what I have been told by Muḥammad b. Abī Manṣūr al-Āmulī—Khalaf b. Wāṣil[428] —Abū Nuʿaym ʿUmar b. Ṣubḥ al-Balkhī[429] —Muqātil b. Ḥayyān[430] —ʿAbd al-Raḥmān b. Abzā[431] —Abū Dharr al-Ghifārī[432] : I walked hand in hand with the Prophet around evening when the sun was about to set. We did not stop looking at it until it had set. He continued. I asked the Messenger of God: Where does it set? He replied: It sets in the heaven and is then raised from heaven to heaven until it is raised to the highest, seventh heaven. Eventually, when it is underneath the Throne, it falls down and prostrates itself, and the angels who are in charge of it prostrate themselves together with it. The sun then says: My Lord, whence do You command me to rise, from where I set or from where I rise? He continued. This is

426. See text above, I, 20.

427. Cf. Qur. 17:12.

428. Unidentified. The *isnād* is considered dubious, see below, n. 436.

429. For ʿUmar b. (al-)Ṣubḥ, see *Tahdhīb*, VII, 463 f.

430. The Qur'ān commentator Muqātil b. Ḥayyān died ca. 150/767. See *Tahdhīb*, X, 277–79; Sezgin, *GAS*, I, 36.

431. See *Tahdhīb*, VI, 132 f.

432. Abū Dharr al-Ghifārī died in 31 or 32/651–53. See *Tahdhīb*, XII, 90 f.; *EI*², I, 114, f., s. v.; A. J. Cameron, *Abū Dharr al-Ghifārī* (London, 1973). A very different brief version of the tradition in Abū Dharr's name is mentioned in *Tafsīr*, XXIII, 5.

(meant by) God's word: "And the sun: It runs to a place where it is to reside (at night)"—where it is held underneath the Throne—"That is decreed by One Mighty and Knowing"[433] —by "this" is meant the procedure of the "mighty" Lord in His royal authority, the Lord Who is "knowing" about His creation. He continued.
[62] Gabriel brings to the sun a garment of luminosity from the light of the Throne, according to the measure of the hours of the day. It is longer in the summer and shorter in the winter, and of intermediate length in autumn and spring. He continued. The sun puts on that garment, as one of you here puts on his garment. Then, it is set free to roam in the air of heaven until it rises whence it does. The Prophet said: It is as if it had been held for three nights. Then it will not be covered with luminosity and will be commanded to rise from where it sets. This is (meant by) God's word: "When the sun shall be rolled up."[434] He continued. The same course is followed by the moon in its rising, its running on the horizon of the heaven, its setting, its rising to the highest, seventh heaven, its being held underneath the Throne, its prostration, and its asking for permission. But Gabriel brings it a garment from the light of the Footstool. He continued. This is (meant by) God's word: "He made the sun a luminosity and the moon a light."[435] Abū Dharr concluded: Then I went away together with the Messenger of God, and we prayed the evening prayer. This report from the Messenger of God indicates that the only difference between the condition of the sun and that of the moon is that the luminosity of the sun comes from the wrap of the luminosity of the Throne with which the sun was covered, while the light of the moon comes from a wrap of the light of the Footstool with which the moon was covered.

The other report,[436] referring to a different concept, is what I was told by Muḥammad b. Abī Manṣūr—Khalaf b. Wāṣil—

433. Qur. 36:38.
434. Qur. 81:1.
435. Qur. 10:5.
436. This tradition of Ibn 'Abbās extends to text below, I, 74. The Cairo edition refers to the noteworthy criticism of Ibn al-Athīr, *Kāmil*, ed. Tornberg, I, 17: The story contradicts reason, it is not a sound *ḥadīth*, and something of such importance should not be accepted into books if the *isnād* is so weak. It is, of course, understandable that writers on the stories of the prophets such as al-Tha'labī gave it prominent play.

Abū Nuʿaym—Muqātil b. Ḥayyān—ʿIkrimah: One day when Ibn ʿAbbās was sitting (at home or in the mosque), a man came to him and said: Ibn ʿAbbās, I heard Kaʿb, the Rabbi, tell a marvelous story about the sun and the moon. He continued. Ibn ʿAbbās who had been reclining sat up and asked what it was. The man said: He suggested that on the Day of Resurrection, the sun and the moon will be brought as if they were two hamstrung oxen, and flung into Hell. ʿIkrimah continued. Ibn ʿAbbās became contorted [63]
with anger and exclaimed three times: Kaʿb is lying! Kaʿb is lying! Kaʿb is lying! This is something Jewish he wants to inject into Islam. God is too majestic and noble to mete out punishment where there is obedience to Him. Have you not heard God's word: "And He subjected to you the sun and the moon, being constant"[437] —referring to their constant obedience. How would He punish two servants that are praised for constant obedience? May God curse that rabbi and his rabbinate! How insolent is he toward God and what a tremendous fabrication has he told about those two servants that are obedient to God! He continued. Then he said several times: We return to God.[438] He took a little piece of wood from the ground and started to hit the ground with it. He did that for some time, then lifting his head he threw away the little piece of wood and said: You want me to tell you what I heard the Messenger of God say about the sun and the moon and the beginning of their creation and how things went with them? We said: We would, indeed, May God show mercy unto you. He said: When the Messenger of God was asked about that, he replied: When God was done with His creation and only Adam remained to be created, He created two suns from the light of His Throne. His foreknowledge told Him that He would leave here one sun,[439] so He created it as (large as) this world is from east to west. His foreknowledge also told Him that He would efface it and change it to a moon; so the moon is smaller in size than the sun. But both are seen as small because of the sun's altitude and remoteness from the earth.

He continued: If God had left the two suns as He created them

437. Qur. 14:33.

438. Cf. Qur. 2:156. The use of the phrase here characterizes the statement as a sin and misfortune.

439. That is, not two suns but a sun and a moon derived from it. Possibly, it should be the dual: ... leave the two of them one sun.

in the beginning, night would not have been distinguishable from day. A hired man then would not know until when he should la-
[64] bor and when he should receive his wages. A person fasting would not know until when he must fast. A woman would not know how to reckon the period of her impurity.[440] The Muslims would not know the time of the pilgrimage. Debtors would not know when their debts become due. People in general would not know when to work for a livelihood and when to stop for resting their bodies. The Lord was too concerned with His servants and too merciful to them (to do such a thing). He thus sent Gabriel to drag his wing three times over the face of the moon, which at the time was a sun. He effaced its luminosity and left the light in it. This is (meant by) God's word: "And We have made the night and the day two signs. We have blotted out the sign of the night, and We have made the sign of the day something to see by."[441] He continued. The blackness you can see as lines on the moon is a trace of the blotting. God then created for the sun a chariot with 360 handholds from the luminosity of the light of the Throne and entrusted 360 of the angels inhabiting the lower heaven with the sun and its chariot, each of them gripping one of those handholds. He entrusted 360 of the angels inhabiting (the lower?) heaven with the moon and its chariot, each of them gripping one of those handholds.

Then he said: For the sun and the moon, He created easts and wests (positions to rise and set) on the two sides of the earth and the two rims of heaven, 180 springs in the west of black clay—this is (meant by) God's word: "He found it setting in a muddy spring,"[442] meaning by "muddy *(ḥami'ah)*" black clay—and 180 springs in the east likewise of black clay, bubbling and boiling like a pot when it boils furiously. He continued. Every day and night,
[65] the sun has a new place where it rises and a new place where it sets. The interval between them from beginning to end is longest for the day in summer and shortest in winter. This is (meant by) God's word: "The Lord of the two easts and the Lord of the two wests,"[443] meaning the last (position) of the sun here and the last

440. See *EI*², III, 1010–13, s. v. 'idda.

441. Qur. 17:12.

442. Qur. 18:86. See *Tafsīr*, XVI, 9 f., on this verse. Ṭabarī argues that either the interpretation of the adjective *ḥami'ah* as "black clay" favored by Ibn 'Abbās or its interpretation as *ḥāmiyah* "hot" is possible.

443. Qur. 55:17. See *Tafsīr*, XXVIX, 74 f., on this verse for much comparable

there. He omitted the positions in the east and the west (for the rising and setting of the sun) in between them. Then He referred to east and west in the plural, saying: "(By) the Lord of the easts and the wests."[444] He mentioned the number of all those springs (as above).

He continued. God created an ocean three *farsakhs* (18 kilometers) removed from heaven. Waves contained,[445] it stands in the air by the command of God. No drop of it is spilled. All the oceans are motionless, but that ocean flows at the rate of the speed of an arrow. It is set free to move in the air evenly, as if it were a rope stretched out in the area between east and west. The sun, the moon, and the retrograde stars[446] run in its deep swell. This is (meant by) God's word: "Each swims in a sphere."[447] "The sphere" is the circulation of the chariot in the deep swell of that ocean. By Him Who holds the soul of Muḥammad in His hand! If the sun were to emerge from that ocean, it would burn everything on earth, including even rocks and stones, and if the moon were to emerge from it, it would afflict (by its heat)[448] the inhabitants of the earth to such an extent that they would worship gods other than God. The exception would be those of God's friends whom He would want to keep free from sin.

Ibn 'Abbās said that 'Alī b. Abī Ṭālib said to the Messenger of God: You are like my father and my mother! You have mentioned the course of the retrograde stars *(al-khunnas)* by which God swears in the Qur'ān,[449] together with the sun and the moon, and the rest. Now, what are *al-khunnas*? The Prophet replied: 'Alī, they are five stars: Jupiter *(al-birjīs)*, Saturn *(zuḥal)*, Mercury *('uṭārid)*, Mars *(bahrām)*, and Venus *(al-zuhrah)*. These five stars [66]
rise and run like the sun and the moon and race[450] with them to-

material.

444. Qur. 70:40. *Tafsīr*, XXIX, 55, on this verse, refers to Ibn 'Abbās as reporting on the theory of 360 different "windows" *(kūwah)* for sunrises and sunsets.

445. *Saqfan maḥfūẓan* in Qur. 21:32 was explained by Qatādah as "waves contained" *(mawj makfūf)*, see *Tafsīr*, XVII, 17, on the verse. It is also used as an explanation of *falak* ("sphere").

446. For the problem of *al-khunnas* in Qur. 81:15, see below, n. 449.

447. Qur. 21:33 and 36:40. See *Tafsīr*, XVII, 16 ff., on the former verse.

448. For the transitive use of *f-t-n*, see Lane, 2334 f.

449. Qur. 81:15. For the various attempted explanations, see *Tafsīr*, XXX, 47 f., on the verse. Here, it is explained as referring to the five planets.

450. Cf. Qur. 100:1.

gether. All the other stars are suspended from heaven as lamps are from mosques, and circulate together with heaven praising and sanctifying God with prayer. The Prophet then said: If you wish to have this made clear, look to the circulation of the sphere alternately here and there. It is the circulation of heaven and the circulation of all the stars together with it except those five. Their[451] circulation today is what you see, and that is their prayer. Their circulation to the Day of Resurrection is as quick as the circulation of a mill[452] because of the dangers and tremors of the Day of Resurrection. This is (meant by) God's word: "On a day when the heaven sways to and fro and the mountains move. Woe on that day unto those who declare false (the Prophet's divine message)."[453]

He continued. When the sun rises, it rises upon its chariot from one of those springs accompanied by 360 angels with outspread wings. They draw it along the sphere, praising and sanctifying God with prayer, according to the extent of the hours of night and the hours of day, be it night or day. When God wishes to test the sun and the moon, showing His servants a sign and thereby asking them to stop disobeying Him and to start to obey, the sun tumbles from the chariot and falls into the deep of that ocean, which is the sphere. When God wants to increase the significance of the sign and frighten His servants severely, all of the sun falls, and nothing of it remains upon the chariot. That is a total eclipse of the sun, when the day darkens and the stars come out. When God wants
[67] to make a partial sign, half or a third or two-thirds of it fall into the water, while the rest remains upon the chariot, this being a partial eclipse. It is a misfortune for the sun or for the moon. It frightens His servants and constitutes a request from the Lord (for them to repent). However this may be, the angels entrusted with the chariot of the sun divide into two groups, one that goes to the sun and pulls it toward the chariot, and another that goes to the chariot and pulls it toward the sun, while at the same time they keep it steady in the sphere, praising and sanctifying God with prayer, according to the extent of the hours of day or the hours of night, be it night or day, summer or winter, autumn or spring

451. Referring, it seems, to heaven and the stars.

452. For a different combination of "mill" with "sphere," see *Tafsīr,* XVII, 17 f. (*ad* Qur. 21:33).

453. Qur. 52:9–11.

between summer and winter, lest the length of night and day be increased in any way. God has given them knowledge of that by inspiration and also the power for it. The gradual emergence of the sun or the moon from the deep of that ocean covering them which you observe after an eclipse (is accomplished by) all the angels together who, after having brought out all of it, carry it (back) and put it upon the chariot. They praise God that He gave them the power to do that. They grip the handholds of the chariot and draw it in the sphere, praising and sanctifying God with prayer. Finally, they bring the sun to the west. Having done so, they put it into the spring there, and the sun falls from the horizon of the sphere into the spring.

Then the Prophet said, expressing wonder at God's creation: How wonderful is the divine power with respect to something than which nothing more wonderful has ever been created![454] This is (meant by) what Gabriel said to Sarah: "Do you wonder about God's command?"[455] It is as follows: God created two cities, one in the east, and the other in the west. The inhabitants of the [68]
city in the east belong to the remnants of the ʿĀd and are descendants of those ʿĀd who were believers, while the inhabitants of the city in the west belong to the remnants of the Thamūd and are descendants of those who believed in Ṣāliḥ.[456] The name of the city in the east is Marqīsīyā in Syriac and Jābalq in Arabic, and the name of the city in the west is Barjīsīyā in Syriac and Jābars in Arabic.[457] Each city has ten thousand gates, each a *farsakh* (6 kilometers) distant from the other. Ten thousand guards equipped with weapons alternate each day as guards for each of these gates; after that (one day, those guards) will have no (more) guard duty until the day the Trumpet will be blown.[458] By Him Who holds the soul of Muḥammad in His hand! Were those people not so many

454. The Cairo edition has: we have never seen anything more wonderful.

455. Qur. 11:73. The names of Gabriel and Sarah are not mentioned in the Qur'ān in this connection.

456. On the pre-Islamic peoples of ʿĀd and the historically more tangible Thamūd mentioned in the Qur'ān as having been in conflict with the prophets Hūd and Ṣāliḥ, see, for instance, EI^2, I, 169, s.v. ʿĀd.

457. The Arabic names of the legendary cities are listed in Yāqūt, *Muʿjam*, II, 2 f. A historic Jābalq near Iṣfahān occurs in Ṭabarī, text below, III, 6. The Aramaic names appear to admit of no plausible Aramaic explanation, except for the final -ā imitating the Aramaic definite article.

458. Cf. Qur. 6:73, etc.

and so noisy, all the inhabitants of this world would hear the loud crash made by the sun falling when it rises and when it sets. Behind them are three nations, Mansak, Tāfīl, and Tārīs, and before them are Yājūj and Mājūj.[459] Gabriel took me to them during my night journey from the Sacred Mosque to the Farthest Mosque.[460] I called on Yājūj and Mājūj to worship God, but they refused to listen to me. Gabriel then took me to the inhabitants of the two cities. I called on them to follow the religion of God and to worship Him. They agreed and repented. They are our brothers in the (true) religion. Those of them who do good are together with those of you who do good, and those of them who do evil are together with those of you who do evil. Gabriel then took me to the three nations. I called on them to follow the religion of God and to wor-
[69] ship Him. They disapproved of my doing so. They did not believe in God and considered His messengers liars. They are in the Fire together with Yājūj and Mājūj and all those who were disobedient to God. Whenever the sun sets, it is raised from heaven to heaven by the angels' fast flight, until it is brought to the highest, seventh heaven, and eventually is underneath the Throne. It falls down in prostration, and the angels entrusted with it prostrate themselves together with it. Then it is brought down from heaven to heaven. When it reaches this heaven, dawn breaks. When it comes down from one of those springs, morning becomes luminous. And when it reaches this face of heaven, the day becomes luminous.

He continued. In the east, God places a veil of darkness on the seventh ocean according to the number of nights from the day God created this world until the day when this world will be cut off. At sunset, an angel entrusted with the night comes and grabs a handful of the veil's darkness. He then moves toward the west, all the time gradually releasing some of the darkness through the

459. While the role of Gog and Magog and their famous dam is derived from the Qur'ān and is well defined in the Islamic geographical view of the world, the "three nations" appear to be an insignificant embellishment, and the forms of their names are anything but certain. As indicated here, the two cities are located behind Gog and Magog, and the three nations behind the two cities. "Mansak" and "Tārīs" appear among the Japhetite successor nations, that is, seven brothers that also include the Turks, Khazars, Slavs, Kamārā, and Chinese. See Dīnawarī, *al-Akhbār al-ṭiwāl*, ed. Guirgass, 4; Yāqūt, *Mu'jam*, III, 53. Yāqūt, *Mu'jam*, IV, 304, describes Kamārā as a village near Bukhārā.

460. Cf. Qur. 17:1.

interstices of his fingers, watching out for the twilight. When the twilight has disappeared, the angel releases all the darkness. He then spreads out his two wings. They reach the two sides of the earth and the two rims of heaven and pass outside in the air as far as God wishes. The angel drives the darkness of the night with his wings, praising and sanctifying God with prayer, until he reaches the west. When he has reached the west, morning dawns from the east. The angel puts together his wings, then puts together the parts of the darkness one by one in his palms, then grabs in one palm as much of the darkness as he had taken from the veil (of darkness) in the east, and places it in the west on the seventh ocean. From there comes the darkness of the night.

When the veil is transported (completely) from east to west, [70]
the Trumpet is blown, and this world comes to its end. The luminosity of the day comes from the east, and the darkness of the night comes from that veil. The sun and the moon always continue this way from rising to setting, and on to their being raised to the highest, seventh heaven and their being held underneath the Throne. They will continue so until the moment comes that was fixed by God for the repentance of His servants. Sins will become more numerous on earth. Goodness will be gone, and nobody will command it (be done). That which is disapproved will spread, and nobody will prohibit it.

When this takes place, the sun will be held underneath the Throne for one night. Whenever it prostrates itself and asks for permission (to proceed to) whence it should rise, it is given no answer until the moon joins it and prostrates itself together with the sun and asks for permission (to proceed to) whence it should rise. The moon, too, is not given an answer. Finally, (the angel?) will hold the sun for three nights and the moon for two nights. The length of that night is known only to those who pray during the night while on earth. They will be a small group found in every Muslim locality. They are held in contempt by others while feeling humble themselves. Any (individual belonging to this select group) will sleep that night as he slept the nights before. He then will rise, perform the ritual ablutions, enter his place of prayer, and say his special prayer *(wird)* just as before. Then he will go outside but will not see the morning. He will dislike that and feel that something bad is about to happen. He will say: Perhaps I have

shortened my recitation (of the Qur'ān) too much, or cut short my prayer, or got up before my time. He continued. Then, during the second night, he will again say his *wird* prayer as before. Again, he will go outside but will not see the morning. This will add to his annoyance, which will become mixed with fear. Feeling that something bad is about to happen, he will say: Perhaps I have shortened my recitation, or cut short my prayer, or got up at the beginning of the night. Afraid and apprehensive of what he
[71] anticipates might be the terror of the third night, he will again say his *wird* prayer as before. Then he will go outside and lo and behold! there is the night (still) in its place, while the stars had completed their revolution and reached their place at the beginning of the night. At that, he will become very apprehensive and fearful in the knowledge of the anticipated terror of that night. Fear will close in on him, and he will cry and become flustered.

The people of the localities who were spending the nights in prayer used to know each other before and were in contact with one another. Now they will call out to one another. They will all come together in one of the mosques and implore God with tears and loud wailing for the rest of the night, while the negligent remain neglectful. Finally, when three nights are completed for the sun and two for the moon, Gabriel will go to the sun and the moon and say: The Lord commands you to return to your (positions in the) west and to rise there. We have no luminosity or light for you. He continued. At that, the sun and the moon will cry so loudly that the inhabitants of seven heavens below them and the inhabitants of the awnings of the Throne and the carriers of the Throne above them will hear it. They will cry because the sun and the moon are crying but also because they are pervaded by fear of death and fear of the Day of Resurrection.

He continued. While the people are waiting for the sun and the moon to rise from the east, they will notice that they had already risen from the west behind their necks, black and rolled up like sacks,[461] with the sun having no luminosity and the moon no light, as in the case of eclipses in earlier times. The inhabitants of this world will cry out loudly to one another. Mothers will neglect their children, and lovers the fruit of their hearts. Every soul will

461. "Two ravens" according to the Leiden edition.

be preoccupied with what is happening to it. He continued. The righteous and the pious will benefit from their crying on that day. It will be written down for them as an act of divine worship. The wicked and the immoral, on the other hand, will not benefit from their crying on that day. It will be written down against them as a loss. He continued. The sun and the moon will rise like two camels joined together.[462] Each of the two will compete and try to outrace the other. Eventually, when they have reached the navel—that is, the middle—of heaven, Gabriel will go to them and take hold of their horns and return them to the west. He will not permit them to set in those springs in the west where they used to set but [72]
will let them set in the Gate of Repentance.

'Umar b. al-Khaṭṭāb said (at this point): I and my family are your ransom,[463] O Messenger of God, but may I ask what is the Gate of Repentance? The Prophet replied: 'Umar, God created a gate for repentance behind the west with two doorleaves of gold encrusted with pearls and jewels, set apart a distance requiring a speeding rider forty years to traverse. That gate has been open since God created His creation (and will stay open) to the morning of that night when the sun and the moon rise from their (positions in the) west. The repentance of any human being that has repented sincerely, from Adam to the morning of that night, enters that gate and is then lifted up to God.

Mu'ādh b. Jabal[464] now said: You are like my father and my mother, O Messenger of God, but may I ask what is sincere repentance? The Prophet replied: It means that the sinner repents the sin he committed and apologizes to God and then never returns to it, just as milk does not return to the udder.

He continued. Gabriel will then put back the doorleaves and close them so tightly as if there had never been a cleft between them. Once the Gate of Repentance is closed, no repentance will

---

462. Cf. Ka'b's "two oxen," text above, I, 62 f. Here, racing animals are meant, and "camel" appears to be most likely as the intended meaning of *ba'īr*. No connection of "joined together" *(qarīn)* with the following "horns" *(qurūn)* needs to be assumed.

463. The formulas expressing devotion here and later have the purpose of mitigating the impertinence inherent in daring to address a question to the Prophet.

464. Among the young assistants of the Prophet the one closest to him, Mu'ādh b. Jabal was born around 600 and died in 18/639. See *Tahdhīb*, X, 186–88; Ibn 'Abd al-Barr, *Istī'āb*, III, 1402–7.

be accepted. If some Muslim does a good deed, he will no longer benefit from it, unless he used to do good deeds before, for all will receive the same credits and debits as before. He continued. This is (meant by) God's word: "On the day when one of the signs of your Lord comes, belief will not benefit a soul that did not believe before or acquired some good in his belief."[465]

Ubayy b. Ka'b[466] now said: Your are like my father and my mother, O Messenger of God, but may I ask how will it be thereafter with the sun and the moon, and how will it be with mankind and this world? The Prophet replied: Ubayy, the sun and the moon will thereafter be covered with light and luminosity.
[73] They will rise and set over mankind as before. As for mankind, having looked at the awesomeness of the sign as they did, they will beset this world so hard that they will cause rivers to flow, plant trees, and build buildings. As to this world, if a man had produced a colt in it, he would not be able to mount it from the time the sun rises from its (position in the) west to the day the Trumpet is blown.[467]

Ḥudhayfah b. al-Yamān[468] now said: I and my family are your ransom, O Messenger of God, but may I ask how will they be when the Trumpet is blown? The Prophet replied: Ḥudhayfah! By Him Who holds the soul of Muḥammad in His hand! Surely, the Hour will come and the Trumpet be blown while a man who just treated his water basin with clay will not (have time to) draw water from it. Surely, the Hour will come while two men holding a garment between them will not (have time to) fold it or sell it to one another. Surely, the Hour will come while a man, having lifted a morsel to his mouth, will not (have time to) eat it. Surely, the Hour will come while a man who leaves with the milk just

---

465. Qur. 6:158.

466. The early transmitter of a recension of the Qur'ān. Indications of Ubayy's date of death vary considerably, from the time of the caliphate of 'Umar to the later years of the caliphate of 'Uthmān, or even after 'Uthmān's death. See *Tahdhīb*, I, 187 f.; Ibn 'Abd al-Barr, *Istī'āb*, I, 65–70; Ibn al-Jazarī, *Ghāyah*, I, 31 f.; Jeffery, *Materials*, 114 ff.

467. The end of the world will come suddenly, and human beings, noticing its approach, will rush to do something.

468. Ḥudhayfah died in 36/656. He is known as a special confidant of the Prophet, although his early history as a Muslim appears somewhat clouded. See *Tahdhīb*, II, 219 f.; Ibn 'Abd al-Barr, *Istī'āb*, II, 334–36.

drawn from his camel will not (have time to) drink it. The Prophet then recited this verse of the Qur'ān: "Surely, it will come upon them suddenly when they are unaware."[469]

When the Trumpet is blown and the Hour comes and God distinguishes between the inhabitants of Paradise and the inhabitants of the Fire, who had not yet entered either, He will call for the sun and the moon. They are brought, black and rolled up, having fallen into quaking and confusion and being terribly afraid because of the terror of that day and their fear of the Merciful One. Finally, when they are around the Throne, they will fall down and prostrate themselves before God, saying: Our God! You know our obedience and our continuous worship of You. You know how quickly we executed Your command in the days of this world. Thus, do not punish us because the polytheists worshiped us. We did not call on them to worship us, nor did we neglect to worhip You. The Lord will say: You have spoken the truth. Now I have taken it upon Myself to begin and to restore.[470] I am restoring you to where I had you begin, Thus, return to what you were created from! The sun and the moon
said: Our God, what did You create us from? God said: I cre- [74]
ated you from the light of My Throne. Thus, return to it! He continued. There will come forth from each of the two a flash of lightning so brilliant that it almost blinds the eye with its light. It will mingle with the light of the Throne. This is (meant by) God's word: "He begins and He restores."[471]

ʿIkrimah said: I got up with the individuals who were told the story, and we went to Kaʿb and informed him about Ibn ʿAbbās' emotional outburst at (hearing) his story and about the story Ibn ʿAbbās had reported on the authority of the Messenger of God. Kaʿb got up with us, and we went to Ibn ʿAbbās. Kaʿb said: I have learned about your emotional outburst at my story. I am asking God for forgiveness and I repent. I have told the story on the basis of a well-worn book that has passed through many hands. I do not

469. Qur. 29:53.
470. Cf. Qur. 85:13, see the following note.
471. *Tafsīr*, XXX, 88 (*ad* Qur. 85:13), shows Ṭabarī as expressing himself in favor of Ibn ʿAbbās' interpretation that God originates and repeats punishment. Others refer the verse to God's creation and recreation of life in the other world.

know what alterations made by the Jews it may have contained. Now you have told a story on the basis of a new book recently revealed by the Merciful One and on the authority of the lord and best of the prophets. I would like you to tell it to me so that I can retain it in my memory as told on your authority. When I have been told it, it will replace my original story.

'Ikrimah said: Ibn 'Abbās repeated the story to Ka'b, while I followed it in my heart paragraph by paragraph. He neither added nor omitted anything, nor did he change the sequence in any way. This added to my desire (to learn from) Ibn 'Abbās and to retain the story in my memory.[472]

A tradition on the subject transmitted by the early (scholars) is what we were told by Ibn Ḥumayd—Jarīr (b. 'Abd al-Ḥamīd)—'Abd al-'Azīz b. Rufay'[473] —Abū al-Ṭufayl:[474] Ibn al-Kawwā'[475] asked 'Alī: O Commander of the Faithful! What is that smudge in the moon? 'Alī replied: Don't you read the Qur'ān? (It says): "We have blotted out the sign of the night."[476] That smudge is (a trace of) the blotting.[477]

According to Abū Kurayb—Ṭalq[478] —Zā'idah[479] —'Āṣim (b. Bahdalah)—'Alī b. Rabī'ah[480] : Ibn al-Kawwā' asked what that blackness in the moon was, and 'Alī replied: "We have blotted
[75] out the sign of the night, and We have made the sign of the day something to see by." That blackness is (a trace of) the blotting.

According to Ibn Bashshār—'Abd al-Raḥmān (b. Mahdī)—

---

472. The phrase translated "to retain ...memory" could mean but hardly does in the context: "to become a *ḥadīth* expert."

473. 'Abd al-'Azīz, the son of Abū Kathīrah Rufay' (below, n. 484), died around 130/747[8] in his nineties. See *Tahdhīb*, VI, 337 f.

474. Abū al-Ṭufayl 'Āmir b. Wāthilah was born in 622–23. He died as the last of the Prophet's companions in the first decade of the second century/719–28. See *Tahdhīb*, V, 82–84; Ibn 'Abd al-Barr, *Istī'āb*, II, 798 f.

475. Text below, II, 67 f. (ed. Cairo, V, 212) gives the full name of Ibn al-Kawwā' as 'Abdallāh b. Abī Awfā, who died in 86 or 87/705[6] in al-Kūfah. See *Tahdhīb*, V, 151; Ibn 'Abd al-Barr, *Istī'āb*, III, 870 f. Neither author refers to 'Abdallāh b. Abī Awfā as Ibn al-Kawwā'.

476. Qur. 17:12.

477. All the following traditions appear in the same order in *Tafsīr*, XV, 38 *(ad* Qur. 17:12).

478. Ṭalq b. Ghannām died in 211/826. See *Tahdhīb*, V, 33 f.

479. Zā'idah b. Qudāmah died around 160 or 161/776–78. See *Tahdhīb*, III, 306 f.

480. See *Tahdhīb*, VII, 320 f.

Isrā'īl—Abū Isḥāq[481] —'Ubayd b. 'Umayr:[482] I was with 'Alī when Ibn al-Kawwā' asked him about the blackness in the moon. 'Alī replied: That is the sign of the night blotted out.

According to Ibn Abī al-Shawārib[483] —Yazīd b. Zuray'—'Imrān b. Ḥudayr[483a] —Abū Kathīrah Rufay':[484] When 'Alī b. Abī Ṭālib told them to ask whatever they wished, Ibn al-Kawwā' got up and said: What is the darkness in the moon? 'Alī replied: Damn you! Why did you not ask about something concerning your religion and your (life in the) other world? But then he said: It is (a trace of) the blotting out of the night.

According to Zakariyyā' b. Yaḥyā b. Abān al-Miṣrī[485] —Ibn 'Ufayr[486] —Ibn Lahī'ah[487] —Ḥuyayy b. 'Abdallāh[488] —Abū 'Abd al-Raḥmān[489] —'Abdallāh b. 'Amr b. al-'Āṣ[490] : A man asked 'Alī what the blackness in the moon was. 'Alī replied: God says: "And We have made the night and the day two signs. We have blotted out the sign of the night, and We have made the sign of the day something to see by."[491]

---

481. Abū Isḥāq 'Amr b. 'Abdallāh al-Hamdānī, the grandfather of Isrā'īl b. Yūnus (above, n. 397), died between 126 and 129/743–47 at the age of ninety-six. See *Tahdhīb*, I, 261–63.

482. Died in 68/687[8]. See *Tahdhīb*, VII, 71. In *Tafsīr*, XV, 38, he is replaced by 'Abdallāh b. 'Umar.

483. Muḥammad b. 'Abd al-Malik b. Abī al-Shawārib died in 244/858 in al-Baṣrah. See *TB*, II, 344 f.; *Tahdhīb*, IX, 316 f. For his son 'Alī, see text below, III, 2159.

483a. 'Imrān b. Ḥudayr died in 149/766. See *Tahdhīb*, VIII, 125.

484. For Rufay', the father of 'Abd al-'Azīz (above, n. 473), see *Tahdhīb*, III, 286; Bukhārī, *Ta'rīkh*, II,1, 298 f.; Ibn Abī Ḥātim, I,2, 510 f.

485. Zakariyyā' b. Yaḥyā is not identifiable among his numerous namesakes. Since he was an Egyptian and the entire chain of transmitters concerns Egyptians, Ṭabarī may have received this information in Egypt.

486. The historian of Egypt Sa'īd b. Kathīr b. 'Ufayr lived from 146/763[4] to 226/840[1]. See *Tahdhīb*, IV, 174 f.; Sezgin, *GAS*, I, 361.

487. 'Abdallāh b. Lahī'ah lived from ca. 96/714[5] to 174/709[1]. See *Tahdhīb*, V, 373-79; *EI*², III, 853 f., s. v. Ibn Lahī'a; Sezgin, *GAS*, I, 94. The *isnād* of Ibn Lahī'ah is found in Ibn 'Abd al-Ḥakam, *Futūḥ Miṣr*, 257 f.

488. For Ḥuyayy, see *Tahdhīb*, III, 72.

489. Abū 'Abd al-Raḥmān 'Abdallāh b. Yazīd al-Ma'āfirī al-Ḥubulī was sent by 'Umar b. 'Abd al-'Azīz to Tunisia where he died and was buried in Tunis. See *Tahdhīb*, VI, 81 f.; Sam'ānī, *Ansāb*, IV, 52–54.

490. A son of the conqueror of Egypt, 'Abdallāh appears to have died in the later sixties/685–90. See *Tahdhīb*, V, 337 f. Like the other links in this chain of transmitters, he frequently occurs as a transmitter in Ibn 'Abd al-Ḥakam's *Futūḥ Miṣr*, see, especially, 253 f.

491. Qur. 17:12.

According to Muḥammad b. Sa'd—his father—his paternal uncle—his father—his father—Ibn 'Abbās, commenting on: "And We have made the night and the day two signs. We have blotted out the sign of the night": It is the blackness in the night.

According to al-Qāsim[492] —al-Ḥusayn—Ḥajjāj—Ibn Jurayj—Ibn 'Abbās: The moon used to give luminosity just as the sun does, with the moon being the sign of the night and the sun being the sign of the day. "We have blotted out the sign of the night." (That is) the blackness in the moon.

According to Abū Kurayb—Ibn Abī Zā'idah[493] —Ibn Jurayj—
[76] Mujāhid, commenting on God's word: "And We have made the night and the day two signs": The sun is the sign of the day, and the moon is the sign of the night. "We have blotted out the sign of the night": (That is) the blackness in the moon. Thus God created it.

According to al-Qāsim—al-Ḥusayn—Ḥajjāj—Ibn Jurayj—Mujāhid, commenting on: "And We have made the night and the day two signs": The night and the day. Thus God created the two. (Also) Ibn Jurayj—'Abdallāh b. Kathīr,[494] commenting on: "We have blotted out the sign of the night, and We have made the day something to see by": The darkness of the night and the brightness *(sadaf)*[495] of the day.

According to Bishr b. Mu'ādh—Yazīd b. Zuray'—Sa'īd (b. Abī 'Arūbah)—Qatādah, commenting on God's word: "And We have made the night and the day two signs. We have blotted out the sign of the night": We used to be told[496] that the blotting of the sign of the night is the blackness that is in the moon. "And We have made the sign of the day something to see by": Giving light. God created the sun having more light and being larger than the moon.

---

492. For this *isnād,* see text above, I, 23.

493. Yaḥyā b. Zakariyyā' Ibn Abī Zā'idah died between 182 and 184/798–800 at the age of sixty-three. See *TB*, XIV, 114–19; *Tahdhīb*, XI, 208–10.

494. The Qur'ān reader Ibn Kathīr lived from 45/665[6] to 120/738. See *Tahdhīb*, V, 367 f.; Ibn al-Jazarī, *Ghāyah*, II, 443-45; *EI*², III, 817b, s. v. Ibn Kathīr; Horst, 295, n. 11.

495. The lexicographers ascribe to *sadaf* the meanings "darkness of night" or something like "early twilight," but also "luminosity" and, in particular, "whiteness (light) of day." See Ibn Manẓūr, *Lisān*, XI, 48, l. 6.

496. These words are not in *Tafsīr*, XV, 38.

According to Muḥammad b. ʿAmr[497] —Abū ʿĀṣim[498] —ʿĪsā[499] — Ibn Abī Najīḥ[500] —Mujāhid (commenting on): "And We have made the night and the day two signs": The night and the day. Thus, God created the two. Also (al-Ṭabarī)—al-Ḥārith[501] —al-Ḥasan[502] —Warqāʾ[503] —Ibn Abī Najīḥ—Mujāhid.

Abū Jaʿfar (al-Ṭabarī) says: In our opinion, the correct statement on this subject is that God created the sun of the day and the moon of the night as two signs, then made the sign of the day, which is the sun, something to see by and blotted out the sign of the night, which is the moon, through the blackness in it.

It is permissible (to say) that God created them as two suns from the light of His Throne and then blotted out the light of the moon in the night, as stated by some we have mentioned. This was the reason for the difference of the condition of the sun and the moon. It is (also) permissible (to say) that the sun receives its luminosity [77] through the wrap of luminosity of the Throne, with which it is covered, and the moon receives its light from the wrap of light of the Footstool, with which it is covered.[504]

If the chain of transmitters of one of the two reports I have mentioned were sound, we would adopt that report, but the chains of transmitters of both reports are disputed. Thus, we have not con-

497. Muḥammad b. ʿAmr b. al-ʿAbbās al-Bāhilī died in 249/863. See *TB*, III, 127; Sezgin, *GAS*, I, 20, 29, 79; Horst, 297, n. 2.

498. Abū ʿĀṣim al-Nabīl, whose name was al-Ḍaḥḥāk b. Makhlad and who lived from 122/740 to between 212 and 214/827–29, see *Tahdhīb*, IV, 450-53; *EI*², *Suppl.*, I, 17 f., s. v. Abū ʿĀṣim al-Nabīl; Horst, 297, n. 4.

499. ʿĪsā b. Maymūn died around 170/786. See *Tahdhīb*, VIII, 235 f.; Sezgin, *GAS*, 820b (index); Horst, 297, n. 6.

500. ʿAbdallāh b. Abī Najīḥ died in 131 or 132/748–50. See *Tahdhīb*, VI, 54 f.; Bukhārī, *Taʾrīkh*, III,1, 233; Horst, 297, n. 8.

501. Al-Ḥārith b. Muḥammad b. Abī Usāmah lived from 180/end of 796 to 282/end of 895. See *TB*, VIII, 218 f.; Horst, 294, n. 4.

502. Al-Ḥasan b. Mūsā al-Ashyab died between 208 and 210/823–26. See *TB*, VII, 426–29; *Tahdhīb*, II, 323; Horst, 297, n. 5.

503. Warqāʾ b. ʿUmar b. Kulayb, reputedly the author of a Qurʾān commentary and, in any case, an important link in the transmission of Mujāhid's commentary, died ca. 160/776. See *TB*, III, 515–18; *Tahdhīb*, XI, 113–15; Horst, 297, n. 7. In the published recension of Mujāhid's *Tafsīr*, Warqāʾ to Mujāhid is the last three links of the six-link chain there, but the text contains no comment on Qur. 17:12. Cf. F. Leemhuis, "Ms. 1075 Tafsīr"; G. Schoeler, Überlieferung der Wissenschaften," 202, 210, referring to G. Stauth's dissertation on Mujāhid (1969) and further literature.

504. See text above, I, 61 f.

sidered it permissible to decide on the soundness of the contents of the reports as regards the difference of condition between the sun and the moon. We know for certain, however, that God differentiated between their capacities for giving light because He knew through His superior knowledge that the difference was best for the well-being of His creation. Thus, He made a distinction between them and made the one something that gives light to see by, and the other something that has its luminosity blotted out.

In this book, we have refrained from mentioning (too) many reports and things about the sun and the moon, as we have also done in describing the beginning of God's creation of the heavens and the earth and by omitting all the many other things connected with God's creation. We have mentioned as much as we have in this book of ours only because it is our intention to fulfil the condition laid down by us in its beginning that we would mention time[505] and the history of kings, prophets, and messengers. Dates and times are fixed as to their (precise) moments by the measurements of the hours indicated by the sun and the moon running in their spheres, as we have mentioned in the reports transmitted by us on the authority of the Messenger of God. Whatever took place before God created the sun and the moon, took place outside of moments and hours and night and day.

We have explained with testimony adduced by us from traditions and reports the duration, expressed in years and time periods, of this world from the first beginning of God's production of what He wanted to produce to the time He finished produc-
[78] ing all His creatures. For the period of time extending from God's completion of all creation to the annihilation of all of it, we have brought proofs from reports, used by us to prove the soundness of our statements, coming from the Messenger of God, his companions, and other scholars of the Muslim nation. The stated purpose of this book of ours is to mention the history of kings and tyrants, those who disobeyed their Lord and those who were obedient to Him, as well as the times of the prophets and messengers. We have discussed how chronological dates can be soundly established and how information about moments and hours can be ascertained. (Moments and hours are established by) the sun and the moon.

505. *Al-azminah* "the times" here may refer to Ṭabarī's discussion of the concept of time or to time periods, as it does in the following sentence.

One makes it possible to learn about the hours and moments of the night, and the other, the hours and moments of the day.

(The Story of Iblīs)

Now, let us speak about the one who was the first to be given royal authority and was shown favor by God but was ungrateful for it. Having denied God's divine Lordship, he was proud and overbearing toward his Lord and was therefore deprived by God of His divine favor and shamed and humiliated. We shall continue and mention those who adopted his ways and followed in his footsteps and were therefore subjected by God to His divine revenge. Counted among the partisans of Iblīs, they were made to share in his shame and humiliation. There were also their counterparts and successors[506] among kings and messengers and prophets who obeyed their Lord and left praiseworthy memories. God willing, we shall mention them, too.

First among the Ungrateful is Iblīs, Their Guide (Imām), *Their Leader, and Their Chief— May God Curse Him!*

God had created Iblīs beautiful. He had ennobled and honored him and reportedly made him ruler over the lower heaven and the earth. In addition, He had made him one of the keepers of Paradise. But he became overbearing toward his Lord and claimed divine lordship for himself and reportedly called on those under his control to worship him. Therefore, God transformed him into a stoned Satan.[507] He deformed him and deprived him of the benefits He had granted him. He cursed him and drove him out of His heavens in the fleeting present world and then gave to him and his [79]
followers and partisans the Fire of Hell as their place of residence in the other world. We take refuge in God for protection against His divine wrath and against whatever action brings a person close to His wrath and against getting into trouble.[508]

---

506. Hardly: his (Satan's) opponents and those after him.
507. Cf. Qur. 3:36 and 19:98.
508. The derivation of the idiom *al-ḥawr ba'd al-kawr* ("twisting after untwisting [?]") is debated by the lexicographers. The meaning adopted here is the most likely one, though it is by no means certain. It means approximately getting into a

We shall begin with a summary of the reports that have come down to us from the early (scholars) about the honors given Iblīs by God before he became overbearing toward Him and claimed what was not his to claim. We hope to continue with mentioning the events in the days of his rule and royal authority until all of that ceased to be his, and to mention the reason why the earlier favors and beautiful benefits and other things God had bestowed on him ceased to be his—all of this in an abridged form.

The Received Reports about the Control and Rule of Iblīs over the Lower Heaven and the Earth and All in Between

According to al-Qāsim b. al-Ḥasan—al-Ḥusayn b. Dāwūd—Ḥajjāj—Ibn Jurayj—Ibn 'Abbās: Iblīs was one of the noblest angels and belonged to the most honored tribe among them. He was a keeper of Paradise. He had the authority to rule over the lower heaven as well as the earth.[509]

According to al-Qāsim—al-Ḥusayn—Ḥajjāj—Ibn Jurayj—Ṣāliḥ, the *mawlā* of al-Taw'amah[510] and Sharīk b. Abī Namir,[511] either one or both of them—Ibn 'Abbās: There was an angelic tribe of jinn, and Iblīs belonged to it. He governed all in between the heaven and the earth.[512]

According to Mūsā b. Hārūn al-Hamdānī—'Amr b. Ḥammād—Asbāṭ—al-Suddī —Abū Mālik and Abū Ṣāliḥ—Ibn 'Abbās. Also (al-Suddī)—Murrah al-Hamdānī—Ibn Mas'ūd and some (other)
[80] companions of the Prophet: Iblīs was made ruler over the lower heaven. He belonged to a tribe of angels called jinn. They were called jinn because they were the keepers of Paradise *(al-jannah)*.

---

tight spot after having had it easy. See Lane, 665c, and the references in *Wörterbuch*, letter K, 428b.

509. See *Tafsīr*, I, 178 *(ad* Qur. 2:34), and XV, 169 f. *(ad* Qur. 18:50).

510. Ṣāliḥ b. Nabhān died around 125/791[2]. See *Tahdhīb*, IV, 405–7. Taw'amah ("Twin") was the daughter of Umayyah b. Khalaf, one of the Meccans killed at Badr.

511. Sharīk b. 'Abdallāh b. Abī Namir died ca. 140/757. His grandfather participated in the battle of Badr on the side of the Meccans. See *Tahdhīb*, IV, 337 f.; Bukhārī, *Ta'rīkh*, II, 2, 237 f.

512. This tradition, as well as the one at the end of this section, is part of a longer tradition quoted in *Tafsīr*, XV, 169 *(ad* Qur 18:50). Cf. also *Tafsīr*, I, 178 f. *(ad* Qur. 2:34).

In addition to being ruler, Iblīs was a keeper (of Paradise).[513]

According to ʿAbdān al-Marwazī[514] —al-Ḥusayn b. al-Faraj—Abū Muʿādh al-Faḍl b. Khālid—ʿUbaydallāh[515] b. Sulaymān—al-Ḍaḥḥāk b. Muzāḥim, commenting on God's word: "They prostrated themselves, except Iblīs. He was one of the jinn"[516] : Ibn ʿAbbās used to say: Iblīs was one of the noblest angels and belonged to their most honored tribe. He was a keeper of Paradise, and his was the rule over the lower heaven as well as the earth.

According to Ibn Ḥumayd—Salamah—Abū al-Azhar al-Mubārak b. Mujāhid[517] —Sharīk b. ʿAbdallāh b. Abī Namir—Ṣāliḥ, the *mawlā* of al-Taw'amah—Ibn ʿAbbās: There is an angelic tribe called jinn. Iblīs belonged to them. He used to rule all in between heaven and earth. Then he became disobedient, and God therefore transformed him into a stoned Satan.[518]

The Ingratitude of the Enemy of God for His Lord's Favor, His Overbearance Toward God, and His Claiming Divine Lordship

According to al-Qāsim—al-Ḥusayn—Ḥajjāj—Ibn Jurayj, commenting on: "And whoever among them says: I am a god besides Him"[519]: Whichever angel says: "I am a god besides Him" calls to worship of himself, and only Iblīs said that. Thus, this verse was revealed with reference to Iblīs.

According to Bishr b. Muʿādh—Yazīd (b. Zurayʿ)—Saʿīd (b. Abī ʿArūbah)—Qatādah, commenting on: "And whoever among them says: I am a god besides Him, will have Hell as his recompense from Us. So do We recompense the wrongdoers."[519] This verse [81]
(was revealed) specifically for Iblīs, the enemy of God, when he said what he said, may God curse him and have him stoned! He thus continued: "will have Hell as his recompense from Us. So do We recompense the wrongdoers."

---

513. See *Tafsīr*, I, 160 and 178 (*ad* Qur. 2:30 and 34).

514. See above, n. 399. In *Tafsīr*, I, 178, his name is omitted.

515. *Tafsīr*, I, 178, has ʿUbayd. See above, n. 402.

516. Qur. 18:50.

517. Died a year or two before al-Thawrī, thus in 776[7]. See Bukhārī, *Ta'rīkh*, IV,1, 427; Ibn Abī Ḥātim, IV,1, 340 f.; Ibn Ḥajar, *Lisān*, V, 12.

518. See above, n. 512.

519. Qur. 21:29.

According to Muḥammad b. ʿAbd al-Aʿlā—Muḥammad b. Thawr—Maʿmar—Qatādah, commenting on: "And whoever among them says: I am a god besides Him, will have Hell as his recompense from Us." This verse (was revealed) specifically for Iblīs.[520]

The Events That Took Place During the Days of the Royal Authority and Rule of the Accursed Iblīs and the Reason Why He claimed Divine Authority and Perished

One of the events that took place during the rule of the enemy of God while he was (still) obedient to God is what was mentioned to us on the authority of Ibn ʿAbbās in a report told us by Abū Kurayb—ʿUthmān b. Saʿīd[521] —Bishr b. ʿUmārah[522] —Abū Rawq—al-Ḍaḥḥāk—Ibn ʿAbbās: Iblīs belonged to a tribal group of angels called jinn. Among the angels it was they who were created from the fire of the simoom.[523] He continued. His name was al-Ḥārith.[524] He continued. He was one of the keepers of Paradise. He continued. All the angels except this tribal group were created from light. He continued. The jinn mentioned in the Qur'ān were created "from a bright flame *(mārij)* of fire"—*(mārij* being) a tongue of fire blazing on its side(s and top).[525] He continued. And He created man from clay. The first to dwell on earth were the jinn. They caused corruption on it and shed blood[526] and killed each other. He continued. God sent Iblīs to them with an army

520. The entire section consists of material from *Tafsīr,* XVII, 13 *(ad* Qur. 21:29).

521. Ibn Abī Ḥātim, III,1, 152, no. 832, lists a certain ʿUthmān b. Saʿīd al-Zayyāt as a transmitter from Bishr b. ʿUmārah and an authority of Abū Kurayb. He would seem to be the individual meant here. *Tahdhīb,* VII, 119, no. 255, indicates only that he is an authority of Abū Kurayb. A certain ʿUthmān b. Saʿīd al-Murrī appears in *Tahdhīb,* VII, 119, no. 256, and Bukhārī, *Ta'rīkh,* III,2, 224, also as an authority of Abū Kurayb.

522. Bishr b. ʿUmārah appears to have been known mainly as a transmitter from Abū Rawq. See *Tahdhīb,* I, 455; Bukhārī, *Ta'rīkh,* I,2, 81; Ibn Abī Ḥātim, I,1, 362.

523. The wind known as simoom presumably received its name from the Qur'ānic usage of *samūm* in connection with fire in Qur. 15:27. The passage appears in *Tafsīr,* XIV, 21, on this verse.

524. The preceding three sentences in *Tafsīr,* I, 178 *(ad* Qur. 2:34).

525. Qur. 55:15. The sentence appears in *Tafsīr,* XXVII, 74, on this verse. The tradition to this point is quoted in *Tafsīr,* I, 178.

526. Cf. Qur. 2:30.

of angels. They were that tribal group called jinn. Iblīs and those with him caused a bloodbath[527] among them and eventually banished them to the islands in the oceans and the mountainsides.[528] His success went to his head, and he said: I have done something nobody has ever done before. He continued. God was aware of how Iblīs felt, but the angels who were with him were not.[529] [82]

According to al-Muthannā—Isḥāq b. al-Ḥajjāj[530] —ʿAbdallāh b. Abī Jaʿfar[531] —his father—al-Rabīʿ b. Anas[532] : God created the angels on Wednesday. He created the jinn on Thursday, and He created Adam on Friday. He continued. Some jinn disbelieved, and the angels went down to them on earth to fight them. Thus, bloodshed and corruption came into being on earth.

The Reason Why the Enemy of God Was Enticed to be Overbearing Toward His Lord and Thereby Perished

The early (scholars) among the Companions and Followers differed on this subject. We just mentioned one of the statements transmitted on the authority of Ibn ʿAbbās by al-Ḍaḥḥāk, namely, that when Iblīs caused a bloodbath among the jinn who disobeyed God and caused corruption on earth, and expelled them, he was pleased with himself and on account of it considered himself more excellent than anybody else.

The second statement on the subject transmitted on the authority of Ibn ʿAbbās is that Iblīs was the ruler and governor of the lower heaven as well as the governor of all in between the lower heaven and the earth and the keeper of Paradise and also zealously worshiped God, but then he became pleased with himself and therefore thought that he was superior. So he became over-

---

527. According to the reading suggested in the Cairo edition.

528. From "The first to dwell" to this point in *Tafsīr*, I, 156 f. (*ad* Qur. 2:30).

529. The entire text of the tradition is to be found in *Tafsīr*, I, 155, where it continues commenting on Qur. 2:30.

530. He is mentioned as a transmitter of ʿAbdallāh b. Abī Jaʿfar in Ibn Abī Ḥātim, I,1, 217. His *nisbah* being al-Ṭāḥūnī, he is listed in Samʿānī, *Ansāb*, IX, 2 f. See also Horst, 298, n.6.

531. For ʿAbdallāh b. Abī Jaʿfar ʿĪsā b. Māhān, see *Tahdhīb*, V, 176 f., and for his father, *Tahdhīb*, XII, 56 f. See also Horst, 298, n. 7, and 299, n. 11.

532. Al-Rabīʿ b. Anas died in 139 or 140/756–58 during the caliphate of al-Manṣūr, See *Tahdhīb*, III, 238 f.; Sezgin, *GAS*, I, 34; Horst, 299, n. 12. For the tradition, see *Tafsīr*, I, 157 and 163 (*ad* Qur. 2:30).

bearing toward his Lord.

The transmission of the report on the authority of Ibn ʿAbbās

According to Mūsā b. Hārūn al-Hamdānī—ʿAmr b. Ḥammād—Asbāṭ—al-Suddī—Abū Mālik and Abū Ṣāliḥ—Ibn ʿAbbās. Also (al-
[83] Suddī)—Murrah al-Hamdānī—Ibn Masʿūd and some (other) companions of the Prophet: When God finished with the creation of whatever He liked, He sat straight upon the Throne. He made Iblīs ruler over the lower heaven. Iblīs belonged to a tribe of angels called jinn. They were called jinn because they were the keepers of Paradise. In addition to being ruler (of the lower heaven), Iblīs was a keeper (of Paradise). Then haughtiness affected him, and he said: God gave all that to me only because of some distinctive quality. So I was told by Mūsā b. Hārūn. I was (also) told this by Aḥmad b. Abī Khaythamah[533] —ʿAmr b. Ḥammād who commented: because of some distinctive quality of mine making me superior to the angels. When that haughtiness affected him, God was aware of it. He said to the angels: "I am placing on earth a vicegerent."[534]

According to Ibn Ḥumayd—Salamah b. al-Faḍl—Ibn Isḥāq—Khallād b. ʿAṭā'[535] —Ṭāwūs[536] —Ibn ʿAbbās: Before committing disobedience, Iblīs was one of the angels. His name was ʿAzāzīl. He was one of the dwellers on earth. He was one of the most zealous and knowledgeable of the angels. That led him to haughtiness. He belonged to a tribal group called jinn.[537]

Ibn Ḥumayd gave us about the same account again, reporting from Salamah—Ibn Isḥāq—Khallād b. ʿAṭā'—Ṭāwūs or Abū al-Ḥajjāj Mujāhid—Ibn ʿAbbās, and others. However, he said: (Iblīs) was an angel named ʿAzāzīl. He was one of the dwellers and cultivators on earth. The dwellers on earth from among the angels used to be called jinn.

According to Ibn al-Muthannā—Shaybān[538] —Sallām b. Mis-

533. The historian Aḥmad b. Abī Khaythamah died ninety-four years old in 279/872. See *EI*^{2}, III, 687, s.v. Ibn Abī Khaythama; Sezgin, *GAS*, I, 319 f.

534. Qur. 2:30. The tradition is quoted in *Tafsīr*, I, 160, on this verse.

535. See Bukhārī, *Ta'rīkh*, II, 1, 170 f.; Ibn Abī Ḥātim, I, 2, 366. *Tafsīr*, I, 178, has the apparent mistake Khallād — 'Aṭā'.

536. Died about 106/724[5]. See *Tahdhīb*, V, 8–10.

537. This and the following tradition are quoted in *Tafsīr*, I, 178 (*ad* Qur. 2:34).

538. Apparently, Shaybān b. Farrūkh b. Abī Shaybah who lived from ca. 140/757[8] to 235 or 236/849–51. See *Tahdhīb*, IV, 374 f.

kīn[539] —Qatādah—Sa'īd b. al-Musayyab[540] : Iblīs was the chief of the angels of the lower heaven.[541]

The third statement transmitted on the authority of Ibn 'Abbās is that he used to say: The reason for (what happened) is that [84]
Iblīs belonged to a remnant of creatures created by God. He commanded them to do something, but they refused to be obedient to Him.

The transmission of the report on the authority of Ibn 'Abbās

According to Muḥammad b. Sinān al-Qazzāz—Abū 'Āṣim (al-Nabīl)—Shabīb[542] —'Ikrimah—Ibn 'Abbās: God created some creatures and said: "Prostrate yourselves before Adam!"[543] They replied: We shall not do that. He continued. He sent a fire to consume them. He then created other creatures and said: "I am creating a human being from clay,"[544] so prostrate yourselves before Adam! They refused, and God sent a fire to consume them. Then He created these and said: Will you not prostrate yourselves before Adam? They replied: Yes! Iblīs belonged to those who refused to prostrate themselves before Adam.

Others said: Rather, the reason is that he belonged to the remnant of the jinn who were on earth. They shed blood and caused corruption on it. They were disobedient to their Lord. Therefore, the angels fought against them.

Those who said this

According to Ibn Ḥumayd—Yaḥyā b. Wāḍiḥ—Abū Sa'īd al-Yaḥmadī Ismā'īl b. Ibrāhīm[545] —Sawwār b. al-Ja'd al-Yaḥmadī[546] —Shahr b. Ḥawshab,[547] commenting on God's word: "He was one of the jinn"[548] : Iblīs was one of the jinn whom the angels drove

---

539. Died between 164 and 167/780–84. See *Tahdhīb*, IV, 286 f.

540. Depending on the age he is said to have reached, Ibn al-Musayyab was born between 634 and 639. He died about 93 or 94/711–13. See *Tahdhīb*, IV, 84-88; Khalīfah, *Ṭabaqāt*, 244; Bukhārī, *Ta'rīkh*, II, 1, 467 f.; Sezgin, *GAS*, I, 276.

541. See *Tafsīr*, I, 178 *(ad* Qur. 2:34).

542. For Shabīb b. Bishr, see *Tahdhīb*, IV, 306. *Tafsīr*, I, 180 *(ad* Qur. 2:34), has Sharīk(!)—someone—'Ikrimah.

543. Qur. 2:34, etc. The entire tradition appears in *Tafsīr*, I, 180.

544. Qur. 38:71.

545. *Tafsīr*, I, 179, has an unlikely Abū Sa'īd al-Yaḥmadī—Ismā'īl b. Ibrāhīm. However, no identification seems possible.

546. Briefly listed in Bukhārī, *Ta'rīkh*, II, 2, 170; Ibn Abī Ḥātim, II, 1, 270, without al-Yaḥmadī.

547. Died early in the second century/ca. 719–29. See *Tahdhīb*, IV, 369–72.

548. Qur. 18:50.

away. One of the angels captured him and took him to heaven.[549]

According to ʿAlī b. al-Ḥasan[550] —Abū Naṣr Muḥammad b. Aḥmad al-Khallāl[551] —Sunayd b. Dāwūd—Hushaym[552] —ʿAbd al-
[85] Raḥmān b. Yaḥyā[553] —Mūsā b. Numayr and ʿUthmān b. Saʿīd b. Kāmil[554] —Saʿd b. Masʿūd[555] : The angels used to fight the jinn, and Iblīs was taken captive. He was young and used to worship together with the angels. When they were commanded to prostrate themselves before Adam and Iblīs refused, God said: "Except Iblīs. He was one of the jinn."[556]

Abū Jaʿfar (al-Ṭabarī) says: In my opinion, the statement most likely to be correct is one that agrees with God's word: "We said to the angels: Prostrate yourselves before Adam!, and they did, except Iblīs. He was one of the jinn. He wickedly disobeyed the command of his Lord."[557] It is possible that his wickedness in disobeying the command of his Lord resulted from his being one of the jinn. It is (further) possible that it resulted from his being pleased with himself because he worshiped his Lord so zealously, possessed great knowledge, and had been entrusted with the rule over the lower heaven and the earth as well as the post of keeper of Paradise. (But) it is (also) possible that there was some other reason. Knowledge of this subject can be attained only through a report that provides valid proof, but we have no such report, and the differences with respect to the matter are as indicated by the reports transmitted by us.

It was (also) said that the reason why Iblīs perished was that before Adam, the jinn were on earth. God sent Iblīs to act among

---

549. See *Tafsīr*, I, 179 (*ad* Qur. 2:34).

550. His identity seems to be established by the fact that Muslim al-Jarmī is one of his authorities (see below, n. 632), and ʿAlī b. al-Ḥasan b. ʿAbdawayh al-Khazzāz appears among Muslim al-Jarmī's transmitters in *TB*, XIII, 100. According to *TB*, XI, 374 f., that ʿAlī b. al-Ḥasan died in 277/987[8]. *Tafsīr*, I, 179, has ʿAlī b. al-Ḥusayn.

551. He could possibly be identical with the Abū Naṣr mentioned above, n. 128.

552. Born in 104 or 105/722–24, Hushaym b. Bashīr died in 183/799. See *TB*, XIV, 85–94; *Tahdhīb*, XI, 59–64; Sezgin, *GAS*, I, 38.

553. It is doubtful whether he could be identified with the individual listed in *Tahdhīb*, IV, 294.

554. Both Mūsā and ʿUthmān are unidentified.

555. He may possibly be the obscure Saʿd b. Masʿūd briefly listed as a transmitter from Ibn ʿAbbās. See Bukhārī, *Taʾrīkh*, II, 2, 64; Ibn Abī Ḥātim, II,1, 94.

556. Qur. 18:50. The tradition is quoted in *Tafsīr*, I, 179 (*ad* Qur. 2:34).

557. Qur. 18:50.

them as judge. He did so conscientiously *(bi-al-ḥaqq)* for a thousand years, so that he eventually was called "arbiter" *(ḥakam)*. God called him thus and revealed to him his name. At that, he became filled with haughtiness. He became self-important and caused terror, hostility, and hatred among those to whom God had sent him as arbiter. This is assumed to have caused them to fight so bitterly on earth for two thousand years that their horses waded in the blood of (those killed). They continued. This is (meant by) God's word: "Were We wearied by the first creation? No! Rather they are in uncertainty about a new creation (at the end of the [86]
world),"[558] and (by) the statement of the angels: "Will You place on (earth) one who will cause corruption on it and shed blood?"[559] At that, God sent a fire that consumed them. They continued. When Iblīs saw the punishment that had descended upon his people, he ascended to heaven. He stayed with the angels worshiping God in heaven as zealously as did no other creature. He continued to do so, until God created Adam and that well-known episode of Iblīs' disobedience to his Lord occurred.

(The Story of Adam)

One of the events that took place in the days of the rule and royal authority of Iblīs was God's creation of our father Adam, the father of mankind. That was as follows: As the angels did not know about Iblīs' involvement with haughtiness, God wanted to make them aware of it and to show them what had gone wrong with Iblīs when he was about to be ruined and lose his royal authority and rule. In this connection, God said to the angels: "I am placing on earth a vicegerent." They replied: "Will You place on it one who will cause corruption on it and shed blood?"[560] It has been transmitted on the authority of Ibn ʿAbbās that the angels said exactly that, noticing what the jinn, who were dwellers on earth before, were doing. When their Lord said to the angels: "I am placing on earth a vicegerent," they asked: Will You place on it one who will behave like the jinn who, when on earth, shed blood there and caused corruption and were disobedient to You, "whereas we

558. Qur. 50:15.
559. Qur. 2:30.
560. Qur. 2:30.

praise and sanctify You"? The Lord now said to them: "I know what you do not know."[561] He (means to) say: I know about Iblīs' involvement with overbearance which you do not know. I know that he intends to oppose my command and that he has been enticed to wrongdoing and futile self-deception. I am going to show
[87] you this attitude of his, so that you can see it with your own eyes.

Many statements have been made on this subject. We have reported a number of them in our book entitled *The Complete Clarification of the Interpretation of the Verses of the Qur'ān.* [562] We hate to add to the length of our book by mentioning (all of) that here.

When God wanted to create Adam, He commanded that the soil from which Adam was to be made be taken from the earth, as we were told by Abū Kurayb—ʿUthmān b. Saʿīd—Bishr b. ʿUmārah—Abū Rawq—al-Ḍaḥḥāk—Ibn ʿAbbās: He—meaning the Lord—then commanded to lift up Adam's soil. God created Adam "from sticky *(lāzib)* clay"[563] —*lāzib* ("sticky") meaning viscous and sweet smelling— "from *masnūn* slime"[564] —*masnūn* being "stinking." He continued. It became stinking slime after (having been compact) soil.[565] He continued. God created Adam with His own hand.[566]

According to Mūsā b. Hārūn—ʿAmr b. Ḥammād—Asbāṭ—al-Suddī—Abū Mālik and Abū Ṣāliḥ—Ibn ʿAbbās. Also (al-Suddī)—Murrah al-Hamdānī—Ibn Masʿūd and some (other) companions of the Prophet, commenting on the angels saying: "Will You place on it one who will cause corruption on it and shed blood, whereas we praise and sanctify You ? and (God) replied: I know what you do not know"[567] —that is, of the affair of Iblīs. God then sent Gabriel to the earth to bring Him some of its clay. The earth said: I take refuge in God against your taking something away

561. Qur. 2:30.
562. This is the formal title of Ṭabarī's *Tafsīr,* which is the source for the material used here.
563. Qur. 17:11.
564. Qur. 15:26, 28, and 33.
565. The suggestion of the Leiden edition, here and text below, I, 90, l. 2, to read *iltizāb* "after having become sticky," for "after ... soil," is hardly possible, as one would expect the definite article and *l-z-b* VIII is not listed in the dictionaries. "After ... soil" is also the reading of *Tafsīr.*
566. See *Tafsīr,* I, 158 f. *(ad* Qur. 2:34).
567. Qur. 2:30.

from me and mutilating me. So Gabriel returned without having taken (any clay) and said: My Lord, the earth took refuge in You, and I granted it its wish. God then sent Michael, and exactly the same thing happened. Then He sent the angel of death. When the earth took refuge in God against him, he said: I take refuge in God against returning without having executed His command. So he took (some soil) from the face of the earth and made a mixture. [88]
He did not take the soil from a single place but took red, white, and black soil.[568] Therefore, the children of Adam came out different. He went up with the soil, then moistened it so it would become "sticky clay"—*lāzib* ("sticky") means something that adheres *(l-z-q)* to something else. Then (the moistened soil) was left to change and become stinking *(muntin).* That is where God says: "From *masnūn* slime." He commented: stinking.[569]

According to Ibn Ḥumayd—Yaʿqūb al-Qummī—Jaʿfar b. Abī al-Mughīrah—Saʿīd b. Jubayr—Ibn ʿAbbās: The Lord Almighty sent Iblīs[570] to take some skin *(adīm)* from the earth, both sweet and salty, and God created Adam from it. For this reason he was named Adam—that is, because he was created from the skin *(adīm)* of the earth. For the same reason Iblīs asked: "Shall I prostrate myself before one whom You have created from clay?"[571] —that is, that clay brought by myself.

According to Ibn al-Muthannā—Abū Dāwūd[572] —Shuʿbah—Abū Ḥaṣīn—Saʿīd b. Jubayr: He was named Adam just because he was created from the skin *(adīm)* of the earth.[573]

According to Aḥmad b. Isḥāq al-Ahwāzī[574] —Abū Aḥmad[575] —

---

568. Cf. Targum Pseudo-Jonathan *ad* Genesis 2:7, and, without reference to color, Babylonian Talmud, Sanhedrin, 38a-b. See also *Tafsīr,* I, 169 *(ad* Qur. 2:31).

569. The tradition is found in *Tafsīr,* I, 160, and, in part, I,169 *(ad* Qur. 2:29 and 31).

570. *Tafsīr,* I, 169, has "angel of death." According to the tradition's concluding words, this cannot be meant here.

571. Qur. 17:61.

572. Abū Dāwūd Sulaymān b. Dāwūd al-Tayālisī lived from 133/750[1] to 203 or 204/818–20. See *TB,* IX, 24-29; *Tahdhīb,* IV, 182–87; Brockelmann, *GAL, Suppl.,* I, 257; Speight, in *The Muslim World,* 63 (1973), 249–68.

573. This, and the following two traditions, appear in reverse order in *Tafsīr,* I, 169 *(ad* Qur. 2:31).

574. Died in 250/864. See *Tahdhīb,* I, 14 f.

575. Abū Aḥmad Muḥammad b. ʿAbdallāh al-Zubayrī died in 203/818. See *TB,* V, 402–4; *Tahdhīb,* IX, 254–56.

Mis'ar[576] —Abū Ḥaṣīn—Sa'īd b. Jubayr: Adam was created from the skin *(adīm)* of the earth and therefore called Adam.

According to Aḥmad b. Isḥāq—Abū Aḥmad—'Amr b. Thābit[577] —his father—his grandfather—'Alī: Adam was created from the skin *(adīm)* of the earth, containing something pleasant *(ṭayyib)* and something good and something bad. All this can be seen in Adam's children, (who are) good and bad.

According to Ya'qūb b. Ibrāhīm[578] —Ibn 'Ulayyah[579] —'Awf.[580] Also Muḥammad b. Bashshār and 'Umar b. Shabbah[581] —Yaḥyā b. Sa'īd—'Awf. Also Ibn Bashshār—Ibn Abī 'Adī and Muḥammad
[89] b. Ja'far (Ghundar) and 'Abd al-Wahhāb al-Thaqafī[582] —'Awf. Also Muḥammad b. 'Umārah al-Asadī[583] —Ismā'īl b. Abān[584] — 'Anbasah[585] —'Awf al-A'rābī— Qasāmah b. Zuhayr[586] —Abū Mūsā al-Ash'arī[587] —the Messenger of God: God created Adam from a handful (of soil) which He took from the entire earth. Thus, the children of Adam came to correspond to the earth in being red, black, white, or (colors) in between, and in being plain or rugged, unpleasant or pleasant.[588] The clay from which Adam was made

---

576. Mis'ar b. Kidām died between 153 and 155/770–72. See *Tahdhīb*, X, 113–15.

577. 'Amr b. Thābit b. Abī Khālid Hurmuz al-Wālibī died in 172/788[9]; his father is listed in *Tahdhīb*. See *Tahdhīb*, VIII, 9 f., and II, 16 f. For his grandfather Hurmuz, who is said to have transmitted from 'Alī indirectly, see above, n. 81.

578. Born in 166/782[3], Ya'qūb b. Ibrāhīm b. Kathīr al-Dawraqī died in 252/866. See *TB*, XIV, 277–80; *Tahdhīb*, XI, 381 f. For his brother Aḥmad, see Sezgin, *GAS*, I, 112.

579. Ibn 'Ulayyah Ismā'īl b. Ibrāhīm b. Miqsam lived from 110/728[9] to 193 or 194/808–10. See *TB*, VI, 229–40; *Tahdhīb*, I, 275–79; Rosenthal, *Muslim Historiography*², 366, n. 4.

580. 'Awf b. Abī Jamīlah al-A'rābī lived from 59/678[9] to 146 or 147/763–64. See *Tahdhīb*, VIII, 166 f.

581. The historian Abū Zayd 'Umar b. Shabbah was born in 173/789 and died in 262/876. See *TB*, XI, 208–10; *Tahdhīb*, VII, 460; Sezgin, *GAS*, I, 345.

582. Born about 108–10/726–29, 'Abd al-Wahhāb b. 'Abd al-Majīd al-Thaqafī died in 194/809–10. See *TB*, XI, 18-21; *Tahdhīb*, VI, 449 f.

583. He occurs frequently in *History* and *Tafsīr* as well as *Ikhtilāf*, ed. Schacht, 227.

584. He may be either al-Warrāq (d. 216/831) or al-Ghanawī (d. 210/825[6]) who are both mentioned in *Tahdhīb*, I, 269–71.

585. He is probably identical with 'Anbasah, mentioned above, n. 393.

586. Died around 700. See *Tahdhīb*, VIII, 378.

587. The famous Abū Mūsā al-Ash'arī supposedly died at the age of sixty-three between 42 and 53/662–73. See *Tahdhīb*, V, 362 f.; *EI*², I, 695 f., s. v. al-Ash'arī, Abū Mūsā.

588. The tradition is quoted to this point in *Tafsīr*, I, 169 f. (*ad* Qur. 2:31). Ibn Khuzaymah, 64, refers to Adam's creation from clay of various colors.

was moistened until it became "sticky clay," then was left to become stinking slime, and then *ṣalṣāl* ("dry clay" or "potter's clay"), as God says: "We created man from dry clay from stinking slime."[589]

According to Ibn Bashshār—Yaḥyā b. Sa'īd and 'Abd al-Raḥmān b. Mahdī—Sufyān—al-A'mash—Muslim al-Baṭīn[590] —Sa'īd b. Jubayr—Ibn 'Abbās: Adam was created from three (kinds of clay): dry clay *(ṣalṣāl)*, slime *(ḥama')*, and sticky clay. The "sticky" clay *(lāzib)* is the good clay. *Ḥama'* is *ḥami'ah*,[591] and *ṣalṣāl* is finely pounded soil. God means by "from *ṣalṣāl*" : from dry clay which has *ṣalṣalah*, that is, makes sounds.[592]

It has been mentioned that God caused Adam's clay to ferment. He left it lying around as a body *(jasad)* for forty nights, or, according to another statement, forty years.

Those who said this

According to Abū Kurayb—'Uthmān b. Sa'īd—Bishr b. 'Umārah —Abū Rawq—Ḍaḥḥāk—Ibn 'Abbās: God commanded to lift up [90]
the soil from which Adam was to be made. He created Adam from sticky clay from stinking slime. He continued. It became stinking slime only after (having been compact) soil.[593] He continued. He created Adam from it with His own hand. He continued. It remained lying around as a body *(jasad)* for forty nights. Iblīs used to come to it and kick it with his foot, whereupon it made sounds. He continued. This is (meant by) God's word: "From *ṣalṣāl* like potter's clay."[594] He means: like something separated that is not compact. He continued. Then (Iblīs) entered Adam's mouth and left from his posterior, and he entered his posterior and left from his mouth. Then he said: You are not something for making sounds *(ṣalṣalah)*. What, then, were you created for? If I am given authority over you, I shall ruin you, and if you are given authority over

589. Qur. 15:26, etc.

590. For Muslim b. (Abī) 'Imrān al-Baṭīn, see *Tahdhīb*, X, 134.

591. The reading in *Tafsīr* (see n. 592) of *ḥam'ah* makes it even clearer that the Qur'ānic word is considered by Ibn 'Abbās as belonging to the root *ḥ-m-'* and not, as suggested by others, to the root *ḥ-m-y*.

592. See the slightly different versions in *Tafsīr*, XIV, 19 *(ad* Qur. 15:26), and XXIV, 73 *(ad* Qur. 55:14–16).

593. See above, n. 565.

594. Qur. 15:26, etc.

me, I shall disobey you.[595]

According to Mūsā b. Hārūn—'Amr b. Ḥammād—Asbāṭ—al-Suddī—Abū Mālik and Abū Ṣāliḥ—Ibn 'Abbās. Also (al-Suddī)—Murrah al-Hamdānī—Ibn Mas'ūd and some (other) companions of the Prophet: God said to the angels: "I am creating a human being from clay. When I have fashioned him and blown some of My spirit into him, fall down in prostration before him!"[596] God created him with His own hands, lest Iblīs become overbearing toward (Adam), so that (God) could say to (Iblīs): You are overbearing toward something I have made with My own hand(s), which I Myself was not too haughty to make!? So God created Adam as a human being. He was a body of clay for forty years the extent of Friday(?).[597] When the angels passed by him, they were frightened by what they saw. The angel most frightened was Iblīs. He would pass by him, kick him, and thus make the body produce a sound as potter's clay does. That is (meant) where God says: "From *ṣalṣāl*
[91] like potter's clay."[598] Then he would say: What were you created for? He entered his mouth and left from his posterior. Then he said to the angels: Don't be afraid of that one, for your Lord is solid, whereas this one is hollow.[599] When I am given authority over him, I shall ruin him.[600]

We were told on the authority of al-Ḥasan b. Bilāl[601] —Ḥammād b. Salamah—Sulaymān al-Taymī[602] —Abū 'Uthmān al-Nahdī[603] —Salmān al-Fārisī[604] : God caused Adam's clay to ferment for forty

---

595. The tradition appears in *Tafsīr*, I, 158 f. (*ad* Qur. 2:30) and, in part, XXIV, 73 (*ad* Qur. 55:14–16).

596. Qur. 38:71 f.

597. That is, the forty years were no longer than the hour on Friday during which Adam was created?

598. Qur. 15:26, etc.

599. This refers to an interpretation given *al-ṣamad* in Qur. 112:2, which, incidentally, is not the one preferred by Ṭabarī in *Tafsīr*, XXX, 224, on this verse.

600. See *Tafsīr*, I, 160.

601. See *Tahdhīb* II, 258. Elsewhere, 'Alī b. Sahl is mentioned as the transmitter between al-Ḥasan b. Bilāl and Ṭabarī. Both 'Alī and al-Ḥasan were from al-Ramlah.

602. See above, n. 102.

603. One of the legendary longevous men of early Islamic times who was said to have lived 130 or 140 years, Abū 'Uthmān al-Nahdī supposedly died in 95/713[4] or, using a round figure suggesting a mere guess, in 100/718[9]. See *Tahdhīb*, VI, 277 f.; Sam'ānī, *Ansāb*, XIII, 217; Rosenthal, *Sweeter than Hope*, 82.

604. A famous legendary figure of early Islam, Salmān al-Fārisī may have died

days and then put him together with His own hands. His pleasant part came out in God's right hand, and his unpleasant part in God's left. God then wiped His hands one with the other and so mixed both (pleasant and unpleasant). That is why pleasant comes forth from unpleasant, and unpleasant from pleasant (in man's constitution).

According to Ibn Ḥumayd—Salamah—Ibn Isḥāq: Reportedly—God knows best!—God created Adam, then put him down and looked at him for forty days before blowing the spirit into him, until he became *ṣalṣāl* like potter's clay untouched by fire. He continued. When, after that period during which Adam was *ṣalṣāl* like potter's clay, God wanted to blow the spirit into him, He went to the angels and said to them: "When I ... have blown some of My spirit into him, fall down in prostration before him!"[605]

When God blew the spirit into him, the spirit came to Adam by way of his head, as the early (scholars) are reported to have said.

Those who said this

According to Mūsā b. Hārūn—ʿAmr b. Ḥammād—Asbāṭ—al-Suddī —Abū Mālik and Abū Ṣāliḥ—Ibn ʿAbbās. Also (al-Suddī)—Murrah al-Hamdānī—Ibn Masʿūd and some (other) companions of the Prophet: At the time God wanted to blow the spirit into Adam, He said to the angels: When I blow some of My spirit into him, prostrate yourselves before him! Now, when He blew the spirit [92]
into him and the spirit entered his head, Adam sneezed. The angels said: Say: "Praise be to God!,"[606] and he did. Whereupon God said to him: May your Lord show mercy into you! When the spirit entered his eyes, he looked at the fruits of Paradise, and when it entered his belly, he craved food. So he jumped up, before the spirit reached his feet, in his haste to get at the fruits of Paradise. This is (meant) where God says: "Man was created of haste."[607] So all the angels together prostrated themselves, "except Iblīs. He refused to be with those prostrating themselves."[608] "He refused and was

---

in the thirties/650s. See *Tahdhīb*, IV, 137–39; Massignon, *Salmān Pāk*.

605. Qur. 38:72.

606. Qur. 1:1.

607. Qur. 21:37. "*Of* haste" is one of the interpretations given by the commentators. See also the following tradition. "*In* haste" is also recognized as possible.

608. Qur. 15:30 f.

overbearing, being one of the unbelievers."[609] When God said to Iblīs: "What prevented you from prostrating yourself, as I commanded you?"—before what I have created with My own hands—"(Iblīs) said: I am better than he."[610] I am not one to prostrate myself before a human being You have created from clay. Whereupon God said to him: "Fall down[611] from (Paradise)! It is not yours to—meaning, you must not—be overbearing in it. So leave! You are one of the mean beings."[612] "Meanness" is humility.

According to Abū Kurayb—'Uthmān b. Sa'īd—Bishr b. 'Umārah—Abū Rawq—al-Ḍaḥḥāk—Ibn 'Abbās: When God blew some of His spirit into him—meaning into Adam—it was by way of his head. Wherever something of God's spirit began to move in Adam's body, it became flesh and blood. When the blown spirit reached his navel, he looked at his body and was pleased to see its beauty. He attempted to get up but could not. This is (meant by) God's word: "Man was created of haste."[613] He commented (on "of haste"): Distressed, with no patience for either fortunate or unfortunate (events). He continued. When the blown spirit had completely pervaded his body, he sneezed and said, by divine inspiration: "Praise be to God, the Lord of the worlds!"[614] God said: May God show mercy unto you, Adam! Then He said to the particular angels who were with Iblīs, not those who were in the
[93] heavens: Prostrate yourselves before Adam, and all of them did, "except Iblīs who refused and was overbearing,"[615] because of the haughtiness and self-importance inspired by his soul. Iblīs said: I shall not prostrate myself, as I am older and better than he is as well as physically stronger. "You created me from fire, and You created him from clay,"[616] meaning that fire is stronger than clay. He continued. When Iblīs refused to prostrate himself, God "be-

---

609. Qur. 2:34.

610. Qur. 7:12.

611. The Leiden edition has "Leave" as against the Qur'ānic text which may have been restored by the editor of the Cairo edition or some earlier copyist.

612. Qur. 7:13. The tradition appears in *Tafsīr*, I, 160 (*ad* Qur. 2:30), and also in part in *Tafsīr*, XVII, 19 (*ad* Qur. 21:37).

613. Qur. 21:37.

614. Qur. 1:1.

615. Qur. 2:34. This and the two following sentences are quoted in *Tafsīr*, VIII, 98 (*ad* Qur. 7:12).

616. Qur. 7:12 and 38:76.

deviled" him *(ablasahū)*,[617] that is, He eliminated any hope for him to attain some good and made him a stoned Satan as punishment for his disobedience.[618]

According to Ibn Ḥumayd—Salamah—Muḥammad b. Isḥāq: Reportedly–God knows best!—when the spirit reached his head, he sneezed. Then he said: "Praise be to God!"[619] He continued. The Lord then said to him: May your Lord show mercy unto you! When Adam straightened up, the angels fell down in prostration before him, in order to live up to the agreement God had made with them and to indicate obedience to the command He had given them. But Iblīs, the enemy of God, remained standing (alone) among them and did not prostrate himself out of haughtiness, self-importance, iniquity, and envy. God said to him: "Iblīs, what prevented you from prostrating yourself before what I have created with My own hands?" to:"I shall certainly fill Hell with you and all those of them who follow you."[620] He continued. When God was finished with censuring Iblīs, and Iblīs persisted in disobedience, God hurled a curse at him and drove him out of Paradise.

According to Muḥammad b. Khalaf[621] —Adam b. Abī Iyās—Abū Khālid Sulaymān b. Ḥayyān[622] —Muḥammad b. ʿAmr—Abū Salamah—Abū Hurayrah— the Prophet. Also Abū Khālid—al-Aʿmash—Abū Ṣāliḥ—Abū Hurayrah—the Prophet.[623] Also Abū Khālid—Dāwūd b. Abī Hind[624] —al-Shaʿbī—Abū Hurayrah—the Prophet. Also Abū Khālid—Ibn Abī Dhubāb al-Dawsī[625] —

617. Arab scholars naturally combined Iblīs with the root *b-l-s*. The meaning of *ablasa* is indicated to be "to make someone despair, to eliminate one's hope." See *Tafsīr*, I, 180 (*ad* Qur. 2:34). This root meaning may be genuine, but it could have originated from etymological speculation on the name Iblīs, cf. "bedevil." See also text below, I, 151.

618. The complete text is to be found in *Tafsīr*, I, 159 (*ad* Qur. 2:30). For the last sentence, see also *Tafsīr*, I, 180 (*ad* Qur 2:34).

619. Qur. 1:1.

620. Qur. 38:75–85.

621. Died in 260/873–74. See *Tahdhīb*, IX, 149.

622. Born in 114/732[3], Sulaymān b. Ḥayyān died in 189 or 190/804–6. See *TB*, IX, 21–24; *Tahdhīb*, IV, 181 f.

623. This *isnād* is found only in the Cairo edition.

624. Died between 139 and 141/757–59. See *Tahdhīb*, III, 204 f.

625. Al-Ḥārith b. ʿAbd al-Raḥmān Ibn Abī Dhubāb al-Dawsī died in 146/763[4]. See *Tahdhīb*, XI, 369 f.

[94] Sa'īd al-Maqburī and Yazīd b. Hurmuz[626] —Abū Hurayrah—the Prophet: God created Adam with His own hand and blew some of His spirit into him. He commanded the multitude of angels to prostrate themselves before Adam, and they did. Adam sat down, then sneezed and said: "Praise be to God!" His Lord said to him: May your Lord show mercy unto you! Go to that multitude of angels and say to them: Peace be upon you! He went and said to them: Peace be upon you! and they responded: And upon you be peace and the mercy of God! Adam then returned to his Lord Who said to him: This is your greeting and the greeting for your progeny to use among themselves. When Iblīs showed the haughtiness and disobedience to his Lord which he had kept concealed in his soul—(as indicated in the Qur'ān) when the angels asked their Lord Who told them: "I am placing on earth a vicegerent": "Will You place on it one who will cause corruption on it and shed blood, whereas we praise and sanctify You?" and the Lord replied: "I know what you do not know"[627] —the angels became fully aware of what had been concealed to them (about Iblīs), and they realized that among them there was one who was disobedient to God and opposed to His command.

(Adam Is Taught All the Names)

God then "taught Adam all the names."[628] The early Muslim scholars before us differed with respect to the names that He taught Adam, whether it was some specific names he was taught or the names in general. Some said: He was taught the name of everything.

Those who said this[629]

According to Abū Kurayb—'Uthmān b. Sa'īd—Bishr b. 'Umārah —Abū Rawq—al-Ḍaḥḥāk—Ibn 'Abbās: "God taught Adam all the names." They are the names commonly known and used among
[95] men, (such as) man, animal, earth, plain, ocean, mountain, donkey, and similarly (the names of) nations and others.

626. Yazīd b. Hurmuz died during the caliphate of 'Umar b. 'Abd al-'Azīz. See *Tahdhīb*, XI, 369 f.
627. Qur. 2:30.
628. Qur. 2:31.
629. All the following traditions are included in *Tafsīr*, I, 170 f. (*ad* Qur. 2:31).

According to Aḥmad b. Isḥāq al-Ahwāzī—Abū Aḥmad—Sharīk (b. ʿAbdallāh al-Nakhaʿī)—ʿĀṣim b. Kulayb[630]—al-Ḥasan b. Saʿd[631]—Ibn ʿAbbās,commenting on: "And He taught Adam all the names," as follows: He taught him the name of everything, down to fart and little fart.

According to ʿAlī b. al-Ḥasan—Muslim al-Jarmī[632]—Muḥammad b. Musʿab[633]—Qays b. al-Rabīʿ[634]—ʿĀṣim b. Kulayb—Saʿīd b. Maʿbad[635]—Ibn ʿAbbās, commenting on God's word: "And He taught Adam all the names," as follows: He taught him the name of everything, down to bit and little bit, fart and wind.

According to Muḥammad b. ʿAmr—Abū ʿAṣim (al-Nabīl)—ʿĪsā b. Maymūn—Ibn Abī Najīḥ—Mujāhid, commenting on God's word: "And He taught Adam all the names," as follows: (The names of) all that God has created.[636]

According to Ibn Wakīʿ—Sufyān—Khaṣīf[637]—Mujāhid, commenting on: "And He taught Adam all the names," as follows: He taught him the names of everything.

According to Sufyān (b. Wakīʿ)—his father—Sharīk (b. ʿAbdallāh al-Nakhaʿī)—Sālim al-Afṭas[638]—Saʿīd b. Jubayr: God taught him the name of everything down to camel *(baʿīr)*, cow, and sheep.

According to al-Ḥasan b. Yaḥyā—ʿAbd al-Razzāq—Maʿmar— [96]
Qatādah, commenting on God's word: "And He taught Adam all the names," as follows: He taught him the name of everything

630. Died in 137/754[5]. See *Tahdhīb*, V, 53 f.

631. See *Tahdhīb*, II, 279 f.

632. Muslim b. ʿAbd al-Raḥmān al-Jarmī died in 240/855 in Tarsus. See *TB*, XIII, 100. Cf. also above, n. 550.

633. Muḥammad b. Muṣʿab al-Qirqisānī apparently is the individual meant here. He is listed in *TB*, III, 276–79; *Tahdhīb*, IX, 458–60. The date of death indicated in *TB* and presumably copied from *TB* in *Tahdhīb* (280/893[4] or 288/901) is preposterous in view of his authorities. A date of 188/804 would fit into the chain of transmitters in text below, I, 2754.

634. Qays b. al-Rabīʿ died in the second half of the 160s/781–85. See *TB*, XII, 456–62; *Tahdhīb*, VIII, 391–95.

635. Saʿīd b. Maʿbad appears to be the individual briefly listed in Bukhārī, *Taʾrīkh*, II, 1, 468, and Ibn Abī Ḥātim, II, 1, 63, as having been in contact with Ibn ʿAbbās.

636. *Tafsīr*, I, 170, has two slightly different traditions with different *isnād*s which seem to have been combined here.

637. Khaṣīf b. ʿAbd al-Raḥmān died between 136 and 138/753–56. See *Tahdhīb*, III, 143 f.; Bukhārī, *Taʾrīkh*, II, 1, 208; Ibn Abī Ḥātim, I, 2, 403 f.; Dhahabī, *Mīzān*, I, 653 f. Khuṣayf seems to be the more commonly used vocalization, see, in particular, the footnote in the cited entry of *Tahdhīb*.

638. Sālim b. ʿAjlān al-Afṭas died in 132/749[50]. See *Tahdhīb*, III, 441 f.

(saying): This is a mountain, this is such-and-such, and that is such-and-such. "Then he presented" those names[639] "to the angels and said: Tell me the names of these, if you speak the truth!"

According to Bishr b. Muʿādh—Yazīd b. Zurayʿ—Saʿīd (b. Abī ʿArūbah)—Qatādah, quoting God's word: "And He taught Adam all the names" to "You are knowing and wise,"[640] and commenting: "Adam, tell them their names!" And Adam told each kind of creature about its name and referred it to its genus.

According to al-Qāsim b. al-Ḥasan—al-Ḥusayn b. Dāwūd—Ḥajjāj—Jarīr b. Ḥāzim and Mubārak[641] —al-Ḥasan.[642] And (Ḥajjāj)—Abū Bakr[643] —al-Ḥasan and Qatādah: He taught him the name of everything (saying): These are horses, these are mules, and camels, jinn, wild animals. And he began to call everything by its name.

Others said: Rather, he was taught some specific names. They said: What God taught him was the names of the angels.

Those who said this

According to ʿAbdah al-Marwazī—ʿAmmār b. al-Ḥasan[644] —ʿAbdallāh b. Abī Jaʿfar—his father—al-Rabīʿ (b. Anas), commenting on God's word: "He taught Adam all the names," as follows: The names of the angels.

Others said something similar, that the names He taught Adam were those for specific things. They said, however, that what he was taught was (not the names of the angels but) the names of his
[97] progeny.

---

639. Qur. 2:31 has "them," and this wording is reestablished in the editions of Ṭabarī. *Tafsīr*, I, 171, has "those names" (and also, incorrectly, "those things"). The pronoun "them" referring to persons caused problems for the commentators. Ṭabarī, in the *Tafsīr*, I, 171, expressed preference for the specific interpretation of "them" as angels or progeny.

640. Qur. 2:31 f. and 33.

641. Al-Mubārak b. Faḍālah, a transmitter from al-Ḥasan al-Baṣrī, died between 164 and 166/780–83. See *TB*, XIII, 211–16; *Tahdhīb*, X, 28–31.

642. The great al-Ḥasan b. Abī al-Ḥasan al-Baṣrī lived from ca. 21/642 to 110/728[9]. See *Tahdhīb*, II, 263–70; *EI*², III, 247 f., s. v. Ḥasan al-Baṣrī; Sezgin, *GAS*, I, 591–94; Horst, 301, n. 13.

643. The same *isnād* occurs in text below, I, 101, and appears to have to be understood as indicated. Ḥajjāj is mentioned elsewhere as an authority of Abū Bakr b. ʿAbdallāh, for whom see above, n. 350. Abū Bakr b. ʿAbdallāh b. Abī Maryam is, however, not listed as a transmitter from either al-Ḥasan al-Baṣrī or Qatādah.

644. ʿAmmār b. al-Ḥasan lived from 159/775[6] to 242/856[7]. See *Tahdhīb*, VII, 399; Sezgin, *GAS*, I, 34, 79, 243; Horst, 299, n. 5. *Tafsīr*, I, 171, has the *isnād* start: I was told by ʿAmmār... For Ạbdah al-Marwazī, see above, n. 399.

Those who said this

According to Yūnus—Ibn Wahb—Ibn Zayd,[645] commenting on God's word: "And He taught Adam all the names," as follows: The names of his progeny.[646]

When God taught Adam all the names, God presented those bearing names to the angels and said to them: "Tell Me the names of these, if you speak the truth." As mentioned, God said this to the angels only because, when He said to them: "I am placing on earth a vicegerent," they had said: "Will You place on it one who will cause corruption on it and shed blood, whereas we praise and sanctify You?" Thus, after having created Adam and having blown the spirit into him and having taught him the names of everything He had created, he presented (them) to the angels and said to them: "Tell Me the names of these, if you speak the truth," (which is) that if I place one of you as My vicegerent on earth, you will obey, praise, and sanctify Me and not be disobedient. If I place someone not belonging to you (as My vicegerent on earth), he will cause corruption and shed blood. Now, if you do not know their names, although you can observe and see them with your own eyes, it is more likely that you will not know what will happen with you, if I place one of you as My vicegerent on earth, or with others, if I place one of them as My vicegerent on earth, when they are out of your sight and you do not see them with your own eyes, and you have not been informed what you or they will do.

This is what a number of early Muslims have said, as transmitted on their authority. Some of them are [98]

According to Mūsā b. Hārūn—ʿAmr b. Ḥammād—Asbāṭ—al-Suddī—Abū Mālik and Abū Ṣāliḥ—Ibn ʿAbbās. Also (al-Suddī)—Murrah al-Hamdānī —ʿAbdallāh b. Masʿūd and some (other) companions of the Prophet commenting on: "If you speak the truth": The children of Adam will cause corruption on earth and shed blood.[647]

According to Abū Kurayb—ʿUthmān b. Saʿīd—Bishr b. ʿUmārah —Abū Rawq—al-Ḍaḥḥāk—Ibn ʿAbbās, commenting on: "If you

645. ʿAbd al-Raḥmān b. Zayd b. Aslam died in 182/798. See *Tahdhīb*, IV, 177-79; Sezgin, *GAS*, I, 38; Horst, 305, n. 3.

646. *Tafsīr*, I, 171 (*ad* Qur. 2:31), adds: all of them.

647. *Tafsīr*, I, 172 f. (*ad* Qur. 2:31).

speak the truth": If you know why I place on earth a vicegerent.[648]

It has also been said that God said that to the angels, because when He began to create Adam, they said among themselves: Let God create whatever He wants to, but whatever creature He may create, we are more knowledgeable and more honored by God than that creature. Thus, when God created Adam and taught him the names of everything, He presented the things whose names He had taught Adam to the angels and said to them: "Tell Me the names of these, if you speak the truth" in your claim that whatever creature God has created (before), you were more knowledgeable and more honored by God than that creature.

Those who said this

According to Bishr b. Muʿādh—Yazīd b. Zurayʿ—Saʿīd—Qatādah, commenting on God's word: "And when your Lord said to the angels: I am placing on earth a vicegerent"[649]: He thus asked the angels for advice concerning the creation of Adam, and they said: "Will You place on it one who will cause corruption on it and shed blood?" The angels knew from the knowledge of God (given to them) that nothing was more detestable to God than shedding
[99] blood and causing corruption on earth. "Whereas we praise and sanctify You. God said: I know what you do not know." It was in God's knowledge that from that vicegerent, there would come forth prophets, messengers, righteous people, and the inhabitants of Paradise. He continued. It has been mentioned to us that Ibn ʿAbbās used to say: When God began to create Adam, the angels said: God would not create a creature more honored by Him and more knowledgeable than we are. They were tested by the creation of Adam, just as were the heavens and the earth through obedience, when God said: "Come willingly or unwillingly! They said: We come willingly."[650]

According to al-Qāsim—al-Ḥusayn b. Dāwūd—Ḥajjāj—Jarīr b. Ḥāzim and Mubārak—al-Ḥasan. Also (Ḥajjāj)—Abū Bakr—al-Ḥasan and Qatādah:[651] God said to the angles: "I am placing on earth a vicegerent," (meaning that) He said to them: I am

648. *Tafsīr*, I, 172 (*ad* Qur. 2:31).
649. Qur. 2:30.
650. Qur. 41:11. See text above, I, 23.
651. See above, n. 643.

making ...[652] But they came forward with their opinion (as to the propriety of God's impending action). He had taught them some knowledge and withheld other knowledge that He knew but they did not. On the strength of the knowledge He had taught them, they asked: "Will you place on it one who will cause corruption on it and shed blood?" From the knowledge of God (given to them), the angels knew that no sin was greater in God's eyes than shedding blood. (Because of the knowledge they did not have, they continued:) "Whereas we praise and sanctify You. God said: I know what you do not know." Now, when God started to create Adam, the angels murmured among themselves saying: Let our Lord create whatever He wants, but whatever He may create, we are more knowledgeable and more honored by God than that creature. So when God created Adam and blew some of His spirit into him, He commanded the angels to prostrate themselves before Adam because of what they had said. He thus preferred Adam to them, and they realized that they were not better than he was. They then said: If we are not better than he is, we are (at least) more knowl- [100]
edgeable, because we existed before him, and the nations were created before him. When they thus boasted about their knowledge, they were tested. "God taught Adam all the names. Then He presented them to the angels and said: Tell Me the names of these, if you speak the truth"[653] (in saying) that you are more knowledgeable than whatever else I have created. Thus, inform Me about the names of these, if you speak the truth! They[654] continued. The angels hurriedly sought repentance, as is done by every believer. "They said: Glory be to You! We have no knowledge but what You have taught us. You are knowing and wise. He said: Adam, tell them their names! When he did, God said: Did I not say to you that I know the secret (things) of the heavens and the earth and that I know what you reveal and what you keep concealed."[655] (God said that) because they had said: Let our Lord create whatever He wants, but He shall not create a creature more honored by Him and more knowledgeable than we. He continued. He taught

652. One of the interpretations of *jāʿilun* in Qur. 2:30 is, as here, *fāʿilun*, see *Tafsīr*, I, 156, l. 10. The use of *fāʿilun*, it seems, was felt to convey God's determination to go through with the creation of Adam.

653. This and the following sentence occur in *Tafsīr*, I, 173 (*ad* Qur. 2:31).

654. The dual referring to al-Ḥasan and Qatādah is found in the Cairo edition.

655. Qur. 2:32 f.

him the names of everything (saying): These are horses, these are mules, and camels, jinn, wild animals. And he began to call everything by its name, and nation after nation was presented to Him. God says: "Did I not say to you that I know the secret (things) of the heavens and the earth and that I know what you reveal and what you keep concealed?" He continued. (The knowledge) they revealed (refers to) their saying: "Will you place on it one who will cause corruption on it and shed blood?" (The knowledge) they kept concealed (refers to) their saying to one another: We are better and more knowledgeable than he.[656]

We[657] were told on the authority of 'Ammār b. al-Ḥasan—'Abdallāh b. Abī Ja'far—his father—al-Rabī' b. Anas, commenting on: "Then He presented them to the angels and said: Tell Me the names of these, if you speak the truth" to "You are knowing and wise."[658] That was when they said: "Will You place on it one who will cause corruption on it and shed blood" to "sanctify You."[659] He continued. When they realized that He was placing on earth a
[101] vicegerent, they said among themselves: Whatever God may create, we are more knowledgeable and more honored by God than that creature. Now, God wanted to inform them that He preferred Adam to them. He taught him all the names and said to the angels: "Tell Me the names of these, if you speak the truth" to: "I know what you reveal and what you keep concealed."[660] (The knowledge) they revealed (refers to) their saying: "Will You place on it one who will cause corruption on it and shed blood?" The knowledge they kept concealed among themselves (refers to): Whatever God may create, we are more knowledgeable and honored than that creature. (Yet,) they realized that God preferred Adam to them with respect to knowledge and honor.[661]

When Iblīs' haughtiness and opposition to the command of his Lord which had been concealed from the angels became apparent to them, and[662] the Lord censured Iblīs for the disobedience he

656. For the entire tradition, see *Tafsīr*, I, 162 f. (*ad* Qur. 2:30).
657. *Tafsīr*, I, 163: I was told.
658. Qur. 2:31 f.
659. Qur. 2:30.
660. Qur. 2:31–33.
661. See *Tafsīr* I, 163 (*ad* Qur. 2:30).
662. The omission of "and" in the Cairo edition, which greatly changes the text, seems a mistake.

had shown to Him by not prostrating himself before Adam, but Iblīs persisted in his disobedience and continued in his error and perversion, God cursed him and expelled him from Paradise. He deprived him of the rule that had been his over the lower heaven and the earth, and deposed him from his post as keeper of Paradise. God said to him: "Leave it!"—meaning Paradise—"for you are stoned. The curse will be upon you to the Day of Judgement."[663] (God said this to Iblīs) while he was still in heaven and had not (yet) fallen to earth.

At the time, God had Adam dwell in His Paradise, as I was told by Mūsā b. Hārūn—'Amr b. Ḥammād—Asbāṭ—al-Suddī—Abū Mālik and Abū Ṣāliḥ—Ibn 'Abbās. Also (al-Suddī)—Murrah al-Hamdānī—Ibn Mas'ūd and some (other) companions of the Prophet: Iblīs was driven out of Paradise when he was cursed, [102]
and Adam was settled in Paradise. Adam used to go about there all alone, not having a spouse to dwell with.[664] He fell asleep, and when he woke up, he found sitting at his head a woman who had been created by God from his rib. He asked her what she was, and she replied: A woman. He asked for what purpose she had been created, and she replied: For you to dwell with me. The angels, looking (to find out) the extent of Adam's knowledge, asked him her name. He replied: Eve (Ḥawwā'). When the angels asked why she was called Eve, he replied: Because she was created from a living *(ḥayy)* thing. God said: "Adam, dwell you and your spouse in Paradise! Eat freely of its plenty wherever you wish!"[665]

According to Ibn Ḥumayd—Salamah—Ibn Isḥāq: When God finished with censuring Iblīs, He went to Adam, whom He had taught all the names, and said: "Adam, tell their names" to: "You are knowing and wise."[666] He continued. He then cast slumber upon Adam, as we have heard from the people of the Torah among the people of the Book and other scholars on the authority of 'Abd-

663. Qur. 15:34 f.

664. Cf. Qur. 7:189 (also 30:21). It should be kept in mind that *sakana ilā* is commonly used metaphorically, thus, in the Qur'ānic context, "supply his needs, be a comfort to him." See *sakan* in the following tradition.

665. *Tafsīr,* I, 182 *(ad* Qur. 2:35).

666. The mistake here, referring to Qur. 2:33–32 (!), may go back to Ṭabarī. The Leiden edition has "mighty" for "knowing." This compounds the error, as the combination "mighty and wise" first occurs in Qur. 2:129. *Tafsīr,* I, 182, has "knowing." The Cairo edition simply restores the text of Qur. 2:33.

allāh b. ʿAbbās and others. Then He took one of Adam's ribs from his left side and replaced it with flesh, while Adam was asleep and did not stir, until God had created his spouse Eve from that rib of his. He fashioned her to be a woman for him to dwell with. When slumber was lifted from him and he woke, he saw her at his side. It has been assumed—God knows best!—that Adam said: My flesh and blood and spouse, and he dwelled with her. When God gave him a spouse and made for him a comfort *(sakan)* from his own person, He said to him face to face[667] : Adam, dwell you and your spouse in Paradise! Eat freely of its plenty wherever you wish, but
[103] do not go near this tree, or you will be wrongdoers."[668]

According to Muḥammad b. ʿAmr—Abū ʿĀṣim (al-Nabīl)—ʿĪsā (b. Maymūn)—Ibn Abī Najīḥ—Mujāhid,[669] commenting on God's word: "And He created from him his spouse,"[670] as follows: Eve from Adam's lowest rib *(quṣayrā')*, while he was asleep. Then Adam woke up and said: *Attā!*, which is "woman" in Nabataean.[671]

We were told the same by al-Muthannā—Abū Ḥudhayfah[672] —Shibl[673] —Ibn Abī Najīḥ—Mujāhid.

According to Bishr b. Muʿādh—Yazīd b. Zurayʿ—Saʿīd (b. Abī ʿArūbah)—Qatādah, commenting on: "And He created from him his spouse": Meaning Eve who was created from one of Adam's ribs.

(God's Testing of Adam)

Now we shall discuss how God tested the obedience of our father

---

667. *Tafsīr*, I, 182, apparently incorrectly reads *fa-talā* "and recited." See again text below, I, 134, n. 841.

668. *Tafsīr*, I, 182 *(ad* Qur. 2:35).

669. See Mujāhid, *Tafsīr*, I, 143.

670. Qur. 4:1.

671. The aspirated *th* indicated in the Ṭabarī text seems unlikely, as the Eastern Aramaic pronunciation of the word for "woman" was *'attā ('ntt')*. However, the local origin of the Arabic tradition is, of course, uncertain. Modern Mandaic has *eththā*.

This and the following two traditions are to be found in *Tafsīr*, IV, 150 *(ad* Qur. 4:1).

672. Abū Ḥudhayfah Mūsā b. Masʿūd died in 220 or 221/835–36 at the age of ninety-two. See *Tahdhīb*, X, 370 f.; Horst, 296, n. 14.

673. Shibl b. ʿAbbād (ʿUbād ?) died in 148/765. See *Tahdhīb*, X, 370 f.; Horst, 296, n. 21 (where the wrong year is indicated).

Adam and afflicted him (for failing the test), how Adam was disobedient to his Lord after God had given him honor and high rank with Him and enabled him to enjoy wholesome plenty in God's Paradise, and how he lost all of that and went from the luxury and pleasurable and plentiful way of life in Paradise to the miserable way of life of the inhabitants of the earth: tilling, hoeing, and planting the soil.

When God settled Adam and his spouse in His Paradise, He permitted them to eat of whatever fruit they wished, except the fruit of one tree. This was to afflict them and have God's judgement on them and their progeny come to pass, as God says: "And (we said): Adam, dwell you and your spouse in Paradise! Eat freely of [104]
its plenty wherever you wish, but do not go near this tree, or you will be wrongdoers."[674] Satan whispered to them and eventually succeeded in making it appear good and desirable for them to eat of the fruit of the tree which their Lord had forbidden them to eat and thus to disobey God. They ate from it, and as a result, their secret parts that had been concealed from them became apparent to them.

How Iblīs, the enemy of God, managed to entice them to (eat of the fruit of the tree) is mentioned in the report I was told by Mūsā b. Hārūn al-Hamdānī—'Amr b. Ḥammād—Asbāṭ—al-Suddī—Abū Mālik and Abū Ṣāliḥ—Ibn 'Abbās. Also (al-Suddī)—Murrah al-Hamdānī—Ibn Mas'ūd and some (other) companions of the Prophet: When God said to Adam: "Dwell you and your spouse in Paradise! Eat freely of its plenty wherever you wish, but do not go near this tree, or you will be wrongdoers," Iblīs wanted to go and meet them in Paradise, but the keepers (of Paradise) prevented him from entering. He went to the snake, an animal with four feet as if it were a camel—it seemed like one of the most beautiful of animals. Iblīs talked to it (trying to persuade it) to let him enter its mouth and take him in to Adam. The snake let him do it, passed by the keepers, and entered without their knowledge, because that was God's plan. Now, Iblīs talked to Adam from the mouth of the snake, but Adam paid no attention to what he said. So Iblīs went out to him and said: "Adam, may I lead you to the tree of eternity

674. Qur. 2:35. The addition from the Qur'ānic text of "And we said" in the Cairo edition is unjustified. The Leiden edition has "and" before "Adam" from the parallel text Qur. 7:19.

and a rule that never decays?"[675] —meaning: May I lead you to a tree which, if you eat from it, you will be a ruler like God, or both you and (Eve) will have eternal life and will never die? Iblīs swore to them by God: "I am one of those who give you good advice."[676]
[105] But by tearing their clothes, Iblīs wanted to show them their secret parts, which had been concealed from them. From his reading of the books of the angels, he knew, what Adam did not, that they had secret parts. Their clothes were *al-ẓufr.*[677] Adam refused to eat from the tree, but Eve came forward and ate. Then she said: Eat, Adam! For I have, and it has done me no harm. But when Adam ate, "their secret parts became apparent to them, and they started to cover themselves with leaves of Paradise stitched together."[678]

According to Ibn Ḥumayd—Salamah—Ibn Isḥāq—Layth b. Abī Sulaym—Ṭāwūs al-Yamānī—Ibn ʿAbbās: Iblīs, the enemy of God, proposed to the animals on earth that they[679] should take him into Paradise, so that he could speak with Adam and his spouse, but every animal refused. Finally, he spoke to the snake and said to it: If you take me into Paradise, I shall shield you from the descendants of Adam, and you will be under my protection. The snake put him between two of its fangs and took him in. Iblīs talked to Adam and his spouse from the snake's mouth. The snake was dressed and walking on four feet, but God then undressed it and made it walk on its belly. He continued. Ibn ʿAbbās says: Kill it wherever you find it, and break the (covenant of) protection

675. Qur. 20:120. The following portion of the tradition is found in part in *Tafsīr,* XVI, 162, on this verse.

676. Qur. 7:21.

677. That is, fingernails. This is explained by reference to Jewish literature. *Berēshīt Rabbā,* 196 (*ad* Genesis 3:21) refers in this connection to clothing "smooth as a fingernail, beautiful as a pearl." Targum Pseudo-Jonathan (*ad* Genesis 3:7 and 21) describes Adam and Eve as created with clothing of fingernails (*ṭup̄rā),* and says that "their fingernails (*ṭup̄rayhōn)*" were later replaced. Thaʿlabī, *Qiṣaṣ,* 32, describes Adam's original skin as being like fingernails. The use of the word in the tradition is explained by Muslim scholars as referring to the whiteness, sheerness (*ṣafāʾ*), and thickness (*kathāfah*) of fingernails. See Ibn al-Athīr, *Nihāyah,* III, 61, cited in Ibn Manẓūr, *Lisān,* VI, 192; Ṭabarī, *Introduction etc.,* CCCXLVI. The description of the clothing of Adam and Eve in Paradise as a film of light or the like, which appears elsewhere in the Muslim sources, is also found in the quoted passages of the midrash.

678. Qur. 7:22. The entire tradition appears in *Tafsīr,* I, 187 (*ad* Qur. 2:36).

679. *Annahā,* according to *Tafsīr,* I, 188 (*ad* Qur. 2:36) and, it seems, some Ṭabarī manuscripts. The more difficult *ayyuhā* of the Ṭabarī editions would mean: ...made a proposition...and asked which one would....

granted it by the enemy of God![680]

According to al-Ḥasan b. Yaḥyā—'Abd al-Razzāq—'Umar b. 'Abd al-Raḥmān b. Muhrib[681] —Wahb b. Munabbih: When God settled Adam and his spouse in Paradise, He forbade him that tree. The tree's branches were intertwined, and it bore fruit which the [106] angels ate to live eternally. That was the fruit which God forbade Adam and his spouse to eat. Now, when Iblīs wanted to cause their downfall, he entered inside the snake. The snake had four feet as if it were a Bactrian camel and was one of the most beautiful animals created by God. When the snake had entered Paradise, Iblīs went out from inside of it. He picked some of (the fruit of) the tree which God had forbidden Adam and his spouse to eat, took it to Eve, and said: Look at this tree! How sweet does it smell! How good does it taste! How beautiful is its color! Eve took and ate of the (fruit offered to her). Then she went with it to Adam and said: Look at this tree! How sweet does it smell! How good does it taste! How beautiful is its color! Thus, Adam ate of it, and their secret parts became apparent to them. Adam went inside the tree (to hide). His Lord called out to him: Adam, where are you? Adam replied: I am here,[682] my Lord. God said: Will you not come out? Adam replied: I feel shame before You, my Lord. God said: Cursed is the earth from which you were created, with a curse which will change its fruits to thorns. He continued. Neither in Paradise nor on earth was there a tree more excellent than the acacia *(ṭalḥ)* and the lote-tree *(sidr)*.[683] Then God said: Eve, you are the one who inveigled My servant (Adam). Pregnancy will be difficult[684] for you, and when you want to give birth to what is in your womb, you will often be in mortal danger. To the snake He said: You are the one who let the accursed Iblīs enter your belly, so that he was able to inveigle My servant. You are cursed with a curse that will have

---

680. *Tafsīr*, I, 188 (*ad* Qur. 2:36).

681. The name is given in its correct form in the Cairo edition. See Bukhārī, *Ta'rīkh*, III, 2, 173; Ibn Abī Ḥātim, III, 1, 121.

682. Lit., I am it.

683. *Ṭalḥ* and *sidr* are two kinds of tree mentioned in Qur. 56:28 f. The reference to them here appears to identify them as the original "tree" of Paradise. There was much speculation as to what that tree was. Already before Islam, it was identified with wheat, the vine, etc. For corresponding Jewish identifications, see Speyer, *Biblische Erzählungen*, 65. On *sidr*, see also below, n. 969.

684. The meaning of *kurhan* is determined as usual by its opposite, which here is "easy" (text below, I, 109). But it also suggests unwillingness or disgust.

the effect that your feet will be retracted into your belly, and only the soil will be your sustenance. You will be the enemy of the children of Adam, and they will be your enemies. Wherever you encounter one of them, you will hold on to his heel, and wherever he encounters you, he will crush your head. Wahb was asked: And what did the angels use to eat? He replied: God does whatever He
[107] wants.[685]

According to al-Qāsim b. al-Ḥasan—al-Ḥusayn b. Dāwūd—Ḥajjāj—Abū Ma'shar—Muḥammad b. Qays[686]: God forbade Adam and Eve to eat from one tree in Paradise, but (otherwise) they could freely eat of its plenty wherever they wished. Satan came and entered inside the snake. He spoke to Eve and whispered to Adam. He said: "Your Lord has only forbidden you this tree, lest you become angels or live eternally. And (Iblīs) assured them with an oath: I am one of those who give you good advice."[687] He continued. Eve cut[688] the tree, and it bled. The feathers[689] that covered Adam and Eve dropped off, "and they started to cover themselves with leaves of Paradise stitched together. Their Lord called out to them: Did I not forbid you this tree, and did I not tell you that Satan is for you a clear enemy?"[690] Why did you eat of it, when I have forbidden it to you? Adam said: My Lord, Eve made me eat of it. When God asked Eve: Why did you make him eat of it? she replied: The snake commanded me to do it. So God asked the snake: Why did you command Eve to do it? and the snake replied: Iblīs commanded me to do it. God said: Cursed and banished (is Iblīs).[691] Now, you, Eve, as you caused the tree to bleed, you will bleed every new moon, and you, snake, I shall cut off your feet and you will walk slithering on your face. Whoever encounters you, will crush your head with stones. "Fall down being one another's

685. Cf. Qur. 3:40 or 22:18. *Tafsīr*, I, 186 f. (*ad* Qur. 2:36), has the entire tradition.

686. Muḥammad b. Qays supposedly died during the turbulent reign of al-Walīd b. Yazīd (743–44). See *Tahdhīb*, IX, 414; Khalīfah, *Ṭabaqāt*, 259. In Ibn Abī Ḥātim, IV,1, 63 (no. 282), and 64 (no. 286), he appears to have been split into two individuals; this might be correct.

687. Qur. 7:20 f.

688. *Tafsīr*, I, 189, 1, 3, reads "bit."

689. Cf. Qur. 7:26.

690. Qur. 7:22.

691. Cf. Qur. 7:18.

enemy!"[692]

According to ʿAmmār b. al-Ḥasan—ʿAbdallāh b. Abī Jaʿfar—his father—al-Rabīʿ (b. Anas): Someone told me that Satan entered Paradise in the form of an animal with feet, thought to be a camel. He continued. He was cursed. As a result, his feet fell off, and he became a snake.[693]

I was told on the authority of ʿAmmār—ʿAbdallāh b. Abī Jaʿfar—his father—al-Rabīʿ (b. Anas)—Abū al-ʿĀliyah[694]: Some camels [108]
were originally jinn. He continued. All of Paradise was allowed to him—meaning Adam—except the tree. He and Eve were told: "Do not go near this tree, or you will be wrongdoers."[695] He continued. Satan went to Eve to start with her. He said: Have you two been forbidden anything? Eve replied: Yes, this tree. Whereupon Satan said: "Your Lord has only forbidden you this tree, lest you become angels or live eternally."[696] He continued. Eve ate first[697] from the tree. She then commanded Adam to eat from it. He continued. It was a tree which made whoever ate from it defecate. He continued. But there must be no faeces in Paradise. He continued. "And Satan caused them to slip from Paradise and drove both of them out of what they were in."[698] He continued. So he drove Adam out of Paradise.[699]

According to Ibn Ḥumayd—Salamah—Muḥammad b. Isḥāq—some scholar(s): When Adam entered Paradise and saw the generous plenty there and the share of it given to him by God, he said: Would we could live eternally! When Satan heard him say that, he recognized it as Adam's weak spot, and he approached him by means of (the issue of) eternal life.[700]

According to Ibn Ḥumayd—Salamah—Ibn Isḥāq: I was told that

---

692. Qur. 2:36 and 7:24. The entire tradition in *Tafsīr*, I, 188 f. (*ad* Qur. 2:36).
693. *Tafsīr*, I, 187 (*ad* Qur. 2:36).
694. Abū al-ʿĀliyah Rufayʿ b. Mihrān died, according to Ibn Saʿd, *Ṭabaqāt*, VII, 1, 81–85, in 90/709, according to Bukhārī, *Taʾrīkh*, II,1, 298, in 93/712, and according to *Tahdhīb*, III, 284–86, in or before or later than any one of these years. See also Sezgin, *GAS*, I, 34; Horst, 299, n. 13.
695. Qur. 2:35.
696. Qur. 7:20.
697. Following the reading *badaʾat* of *Tafsīr*, I, 188, l. 1 (*ad* Qur. 2:36). The Ṭabarī editions have "came forth to eat"(?).
698. Qur. 2:36.
699. *Tafsīr*, I, 187 f.
700. *Tafsīr*, I, 188.

Satan made his first attempt to trick Adam and Eve by mourning for them in a way that saddened them when they heard it. When they asked him what it was that made him cry, he replied: I am crying for you. You will die and be forced to give up the luxury and generous plenty you are enjoying. This remark made a deep impression on them. Next, he went to them and whispered, saying: "Adam, may I lead you to the tree of eternity and a rule that never decays?"[701] He (also) said: "Your Lord has only forbidden
[109] you this tree, lest you become angels or live eternally. And (Iblīs) assured them with an oath: I am one of those who give you good advice."[702] That is, you may become angels or live eternally, and that (alternative) means: If you do not become angels in the luxury of Paradise, you will (at least) not die. God says: "And he thus hooked them with deceit."[703]

According to Yūnus—Ibn Wahb—Ibn Zayd (commenting on God's word: "And he whispered"[704]): Satan whispered to Eve about the tree and succeeded in taking her to it; then he made it seem good to Adam. He continued. When Adam felt a need for her and called her, she said: No! unless you go there. When he went, she said again: No! unless you eat from this tree. He continued. They both ate from it, and their secret parts became apparent to them. He continued. Adam then went about in Paradise in flight. His Lord called out to him: Adam, is it from Me that you are fleeing? Adam replied: No, my Lord, but I feel shame before You. When God asked what had caused his trouble, he replied: Eve, my Lord. Whereupon God said: Now it is My obligation to make her bleed once every month, as she made this tree bleed. I also must make her stupid, although I created her intelligent *(ḥalīmah)*, and must make her suffer pregnancy and birth with difficulty, although I made it easy for her to be pregnant and give birth. Ibn Zayd continued: Were it not for the affliction that af-

701. Qur. 20:120.
702. Qur. 7:20 f.
703. Qur. 7:22. The entire tradition is found in *Tafsīr*, I, 188 *(ad* Qur. 2:36).
704. This lemma from Qur. 7:20 and 20:120 is missing in some Ṭabarī manuscripts and *Tafsīr*, I, 188. It was no doubt supplied for the sake of clarity somewhere along the line of the textual tradition of the *History*.

fected Eve, the women of this world would not menstruate, and they would be intelligent and, when pregnant, give birth easily.

According to Ibn Ḥumayd—Salamah—Muḥammad b. Isḥāq—Yazīd b. ʿAbdallāh b. Qusayṭ[705]—Saʿīd b. al-Musayyab: I heard him swear by God unequivocally[706]: As long as Adam was in his right mind, he did not eat from the tree. Eve, however, gave him wine to drink, and when he was drunk, she led him to the tree, and he [110]
ate from it.[707]

When Adam and Eve committed the sin (of eating from the forbidden tree), God drove them out of Paradise and deprived them of the luxury and generous plenty they had enjoyed. He threw them, their enemy Iblīs, and the snake down to earth. The Lord said to them: "Fall down being one another's enemy!"[708]

What we have stated about the subject was also stated by the early Muslim scholars

According to Yūnus—Ibn Wahb—ʿAbd al-Raḥmān b. Mahdī—Isrāʾīl—Ismāʿīl al-Suddī—someone who heard Ibn ʿAbbās say commenting on: "Fall down being one another's enemy!" as follows: Adam, Eve, Iblīs, and the snake.[709]

According to Sufyān b. Wakīʿ and Mūsā b. Hārūn—ʿAmr b. Ḥammād—Asbāṭ—al-Suddī[710]—Abū Mālik and Abū Ṣāliḥ—Ibn ʿAbbās. Also (al-Suddī)—Murrah al-Hamdānī—Ibn Masʿūd and some (other) companions of the Messenger of God (in connection with): "Fall down being one another's enemy!": And He cursed the snake, cut off its legs, left it to walk upon its belly, and made the soil its sustenance. He threw Adam, Eve, Iblīs, and the snake down.

According to Muḥammad b. ʿAmr—Abū ʿĀṣim (al-Nabīl)—ʿĪsā b. Maymūn—Ibn Abī Najīḥ—Mujāhid, commenting on God's word: "Fall down being one another's enemy!": Adam, Eve, Iblīs, and the snake.[711]

705. Died in 122/740 at the age of ninety. See *Tahdhīb*, XI, 342 f.
706. Lit., without making allowance for an exception by saying, "if God wills."
707. *Tafsīr*, I, 188.
708. Mujāhid, *Tafsīr*, I, 73, mentions only Iblīs and Adam in this connection.
709. *Tafsīr*, I, 191 (*ad* Qur. 2:36).
710. *Tafsīr*, I, 190 f., and VIII, 107 (*ad* Qur. 7:24), omits the rest of the *isnād*.
711. *Tafsīr*, I, 191, omits Eve.

The Duration of Adam's Stay in Paradise. The Moment He Was Created by God and That of His Fall from Heaven to Earth Caused by God

Various reports on the authority of the Messenger of God have
[111] confirmed that it was on Friday that God created Adam, and on Friday that he drove him out of Paradise and cast him down to earth. On Friday, too, God accepted his repentance, and on Friday, he let him die.

The reports on the authority of the Messenger of God on this (subject)

According to ʿAbd al-Raḥmān b. ʿAbdallāh b. ʿAbd al-Ḥakam[712]—ʿAlī b. Maʿbad[713]—ʿUbaydallāh b. ʿAmr[714]—ʿAbdallāh b. Muḥammad b. ʿAqīl[715]—ʿAmr b. Shuraḥbīl b. Saʿīd b. Saʿd b. ʿUbādah[716]—Saʿd b. ʿUbādah[717]—the Messenger of God: There are five distinctions to Friday. On it, Adam was created, cast down to earth, and taken up by God. Also, there is an hour on Friday[718] during which God will give a human being everything he asks for, unless it be a crime or a severing (of family ties). And on Friday, the Hour will come. Every angel close to God, every heaven, mountain, earth, and wind—all are in awe of Friday.

According to Muḥammad b. Bashshār and Muḥammad b. Maʿmar[719]—Abū ʿĀmir[720]—Zuhayr b. Muḥammad[721]—ʿAbdallāh

---

712. The Egyptian historian, who lived from ca. 182/798[9] to 257/871. Their contact goes back to Ṭabarī's visit to Egypt. See *Tahdhīb*, VI, 208; *EI*², III, 674 f., s. v. Ibn ʿAbd al-Ḥakam; Sezgin, *GAS*, I, 355 f.

713. ʿAlī b. Maʿbad died in 218/833. See *Tahdhīb*, VII, 384 f. He appears as a transmitter from ʿUbaydallāh b. ʿAmr in Ibn ʿAbd al-Ḥakam, *Futūḥ Miṣr*, 231, 282, 293.

714. ʿUbaydallāh b. ʿAmr died in his late seventies in 180/796[7] in al-Raqqah. See *Tahdhīb*, VII, 42 f.

715. Died in the first half of the 140s/757-62 in Medina. See *Tahdhīb*, VI, 13–15.

716. For ʿAmr, his father Shuraḥbīl, and his grandfather Saʿīd, see *Tahdhīb*, VIII, 46, IV, 322, and IV, 37. As in text below, I, 112, both his father and his grandfather should probably figure in the chain of transmitters.

717. Saʿd b. ʿUbādah is said to have died in the 630s. See *Tahdhīb*, III, 475 f.; Ibn ʿAbd al-Barr, *Istīʿāb*, II, 594–99.

718. Muslim, *Ṣaḥīḥ*, I, 474 f., devotes a chapter to this special hour.

719. Muḥammad b. Maʿmar died after 250/864. See *Tahdhīb*, IX, 466 f.

720. Abū ʿĀmir ʿAbd al-Malik b. ʿAmr al-ʿAqadī died in 204 or 205/819–21. See *Tahdhīb*, VI, 409 f.

721. Died in or before 162/778. See *Tahdhīb*, III, 348–50.

b. Muḥammad b. ʿAqīl—ʿAbd al-Raḥmān b. Yazīd al-Anṣārī[722] —Abū Lubābah b. ʿAbd al-Mundhir[723] —the Prophet: The lord of the days (of the week) is Friday. It is the greatest of days and more [112]
revered in the eyes of God than the Day of Breaking the Fast and the Day of Slaughtering.[724] There are five distinctions to Friday. On it, God created Adam, cast him down to earth, and took him up. Moreover, there is an hour on Friday during which God will give a human being everything he asks for, unless it be something forbidden. And on Friday, the Hour will come. All angels close to God, every heaven and earth, all mountains and winds, and every ocean—all are in awe of Friday, expecting the Hour to come on it. The wording is that of Ibn Bashshār.[725]

According to Muḥammad b. Maʿmar—Abū ʿĀmir—Zuhayr b. Muḥammad—ʿAbdallāh b. Muḥammad b. ʿAqīl—ʿAmr b. Shuraḥbīl b. Saʿīd b. Saʿd b. ʿUbādah—his father—his grandfather—Saʿd b. ʿUbādah: A man came to the Prophet and said: O Messenger of God, tell us what good happened on Friday. The Prophet replied: On it, Adam was created, cast down, and taken up by God. Moreover, there is an hour on Friday during which God gives a human being everything he asks for, unless it be something criminal or a severing (of family ties). On it, too, the Hour will come. Every angel close to God, every heaven and earth, all mountains, every wind—all are in awe of Friday.[726]

According to ʿAbd al-Raḥmān b. ʿAbdallāh b. ʿAbd al-Ḥakam—Abū Zurʿah[727] —Yūnus[728] —Ibn Shihāb[729] —ʿAbd al-Raḥmān (b. Hurmuz) al-Aʿraj[730] —Abū Hurayrah—the Messenger of God: The best day ever to see the sun rise is Friday. On it, Adam was created, brought into Paradise, and driven out of it.[731]

---

722. Died between 93 and 98/711–17. See *Tahdhīb*, VI, 298 f.

723. See *Tahdhīb*, XII, 214; Ibn ʿAbd al-Barr, *Istīʿāb*, IV, 1740–42.

724. Shawwāl 1 and Dhū al-Ḥijjah 10.

725. For the tradition, see Ibn Mājah, I, 344; Ibn Ḥanbal, III, 430.

726. See Ibn Ḥanbal, V, 284.

727. Listed repeatedly as an authority in Ibn ʿAbd al-Ḥakam's *Futūḥ Miṣr*, Abū Zurʿah Wahballāh b. Rāshid died in 211/826. See Ibn Ḥajar, *Lisān*, VI, 235.

728. Yūnus b. Yazīd died in 159/775[6]. See *Tahdhīb*, XI, 450–52.

729. The prominent early historian Muḥammad b. Muslim b. Shihāb al-Zuhrī died between 123 and 125/740–43. See *Tahdhīb*, IX, 445–51; Sezgin, *GAS*, I, 280–83; Horst, 301, n. 12.

730. Died between 110 and 117/728–35 in Alexandria. See *Tahdhīb*, VI, 290 f.

731. See the chapter on the excellence of Friday in Muslim's *Ṣaḥīḥ*, I, 475, where

[113] According to Baḥr b. Naṣr[732] —Ibn Wahb—Ibn Abī al-Zinād[733] —his father—Mūsā b. Abī 'Uthmān[734] —Abū Hurayrah—the Messenger of God: The lord of the days is Friday. On it, Adam was created, brought into Paradise, and driven out of it. And the Hour will come precisely on Friday.[735]

According to al-Rabī' b. Sulaymān[736] —Shu'ayb b. al-Layth[737] —al-Layth b. Sa'd—Ja'far b. Rabī'ah[738] —'Abd al-Raḥmān b. Hurmuz (al-A'raj)—Abū Hurayrah—the Messenger of God: The sun has never risen over a day like Friday. On it, Adam was created, driven out of Paradise, and reestablished in it.

According to Ibn Ḥumayd—Jarīr (b. 'Abd al-Ḥamīd)—Manṣūr[739] and Mughīrah[740] —Abū Ma'shar Ziyād b. Kulayb[741] —Ibrāhīm[742] —al-Qartha' al-Ḍabbī, one of the first Qur'ān readers[743] —Salmān: The Messenger of God said to me: Salmān, do you know about Friday? I said: God and His messenger know better. (The Prophet) repeated (the question) three times: Salmān, do you know about Friday? (and always received the same answer. Then, he answered his own question): On it, your (sg.)—or your (pl.)—father was put together.[744]

---

the tradition is quoted.

732. Baḥr b. Naṣr lived from 180 or 181/796–97 to 267/881. See *Tahdhīb*, I, 420 f.

733. 'Abd al-Raḥmān b. Abī Zinād 'Abdallāh b. Dhakwān died in 174/790[1] at the age of seventy-four. See *TB*, X, 228–30; *Tahdhīb*, VI, 170–73. His father died sixty-six years old between 130 and 132/747–50. See *Tahdhīb*, V, 203–5.

734. See *Tahdhīb*, X, 360; Bukhārī, *Ta'rīkh*, IV,1, 290, no. 1237 or 1238; Ibn Abī Ḥātim, IV,1, 153, no. 689 or 690.

735. The tradition appears with a partly different *isnād* in Muslim, *Ṣaḥīḥ*, I, 475.

736. Al-Rabī' b. Sulaymān b. 'Abd al-Jabbār was born in 174/790[1] and died in 270/884. See *Tahdhīb*, III, 245 f.; Subkī, *Ṭabaqāt*, II, 132–39.

737. The son of al-Layth b. Sa'd (above, n. 222) lived from 135/752[3] to 199/814. See *Tahdhīb*, IV, 355 f.

738. Died in 136/753[4]. See *Tahdhīb*, II, 90.

739. Manṣūr b. al-Mu'tamir died at the end of 132 or in 133/750–51. See *Tahdhīb*, X, 312–15; Khalīfah, *Ṭabaqāt*, 164; Ibn Sa'd, *Ṭabaqāt*, VI, 235.

740. (al-)Mughīrah b. Miqsam died between 132 and 136/749–54. See *Tahdhīb*, X, 269–71.

741. Died in 119 or 120/737–38. See *Tahdhīb*, III, 182.

742. Ibrāhīm b. Yazīd al-Nakha'ī lived between 50/670 (?) and 96/714. See *Tahdhīb*, I, 177–79.

743. For al-Qartha', see *Tahdhīb*, VIII, 367 f.; Bukhārī, *Ta'rīkh*, IV,1, 199 f.

744. For the intended meaning of *jumi'a* (hardly *jummi'a*), see above, n. 375; also Ṭabarī, *Introductio etc.*, CLXVIII and DLXXVI. The ordinary meaning of *jamma'a* "to set up the Friday service" or the like, could hardly be interpreted in such a way that it would apply here.

According to Muḥammad b. 'Umārah al-Asadī—'Ubaydallāh b. Mūsā[745] —Shaybān[746] —Yaḥyā[747] —Abū Salamah[748] —Abū Hurayrah—Ka'b: The best day ever too see the sun rise is Friday. On it, Adam was created, entered Paradise, and was driven out of it. Moreover, the Hour will come on it. [114]

According to al-Ḥusayn b. Yazīd al-Adamī[749] —Rawḥ b. 'Ubādah[750] —Zakariyyā' b. Isḥāq[751] —'Amr b. Dīnār[752] —'Ubayd b. 'Umayr: The first day on which the sun rose is Friday. It is the most excellent of the days. On it, God created Adam in His likeness. When he finished, Adam sneezed. God inspired him to use (the formula of) praise, and then responded: May your Lord show mercy unto you![753]

According to Abū Kurayb—Isḥāq b. Manṣūr[754] —Abū Kudaynah[755] —Mughīrah—Ziyād—Ibrāhīm—'Alqamah[756] —al-Qartha'—Salmān: The Messenger of God said: Do you know about Friday? It is a day on which your (sg.)—or your (pl.)—father Adam was put together.

According to Abū Kurayb—'Uthmān b. Sa'īd—Abū al-Aḥwaṣ—Mughīrah—Ibrāhīm—'Alqamah—Salmān: The Messenger of God

---

745. 'Ubaydallāh b. Mūsā b. Bādhām/Bādhān was born in 128/745[6] and died in 213 or 214/828–29. See *Tahdhīb*, VII, 50–53.

746. Shaybān b. 'Abd al-Raḥmān al-Naḥwī died in 164/780[1]. See *TB*, IX, 271–74; *Tahdhīb*, IV, 373 f.

747. Yaḥyā b. Abī Kathīr died between 129 and 132/746–50. See *Tahdhīb*, XI, 268–70.

748. The son of 'Abd al-Raḥmān b. 'Awf (above, n. 177)?

749. The form of the name is uncertain. He could be identical with al-Ḥusayn b. Yazīd al-Sabī'ī who is mentioned as an authority of Ṭabarī in *Tafsīr*, II, 91, l. 2. Al-Ḥusayn b. Yazīd al-Anṣārī al-Qaṭṭān, who died in 244/Dec. 858–Jan. 859 (Ibn Abī Ḥātim, I, 2, 67; *Tahdhīb*, II, 376) would fit chronologically, but the identity is not certain. Al-Qaṭṭān is often mentioned in *Tafsīr*, as well as text below, I, 290.

750. Rawḥ b. 'Ubādah died between 205 and 207/820–23. See *TB*, VIII, 401-6; *Tahdhīb*, III, 293–96; Sezgin, *GAS*, I, 39 f.

751. See *Tahdhīb*, III, 328 f.

752. 'Amr b. Dīnār died in 125 or 126/742–44. See *Tahdhīb*, VIII, 28-30; Ibn Sa'd, *Ṭabaqāt*, V, 353 f.

753. See text above, I, 92 and 94.

754. Died in 204 or 205/819–21. See *Tahdhīb*, I, 250 f.

755. For Abū Kudaynah Yaḥyā b. al-Muhallab, see *Tahdhīb*, XI, 289.

756. 'Alqamah b. Qays al-Nakha'ī, an uncle of Ibrāhīm, was supposedly ninety years old when he died sometime between 61 and 63/680–83, although dates of death a decade later are also given. See *Tahdhīb*, VII, 276–78; Khalīfah, *Ṭabaqāt*, 147 f. Note that 'Alqamah does not appear in the almost identical *isnād* three traditions before.

said to me: Salmān, do you know about Friday? (repeating the question) two or three times (and then answering it himself): It is the day on which your (pl.) father Adam—or (simply) your (pl.) father—was put together.

According to Abū Kurayb—Ḥasan b. ʿAṭiyyah[757]—Qays (b. al-Rabīʿ)—Al-Aʿmash—Ibrāhīm—al-Qarthaʿ—Salmān: The Messenger of God said: Do you know about Friday? or something like that. On it, your (pl.) father Adam was put together.

[115] According to Muḥammad b. ʿAlī b. al-Ḥasan b. Shaqīq[758]—his father—Abū Ḥamzah[759]—Manṣūr—Ibrāhīm—al-Qarthaʿ—Salmān: The Messenger of God said to me: Do you know about Friday? I said: No, whereupon he said: On it, your (sg.) father was put together.

The Moment on Friday When God Created Adam and the One When Adam Was Cast Down to Earth

There are different opinions on this subject. A tradition transmitted on the authority of ʿAbdallāh b. Salām and others is the following which we were told by Abū Kurayb—Ibn Idrīs[760]—Muḥammad b. ʿAmr[761]—Abū Salamah—Abū Hurayrah—the Messenger of God: The best day ever to see the sun rise is Friday. On it, Adam was created, settled in Paradise, and cast down. On it, the Hour will come.[762] Moreover, on Friday there is an hour—indicating (by a gesture with his hand) that it would be a short one[763]—during which God will give a Muslim who happens (to

757. Died around 211/826[7]. See *Tahdhīb*, II, 294, no. 525.

758. Ibn Shaqīq died in 250 or 251/864–65. See *Tahdhīb*, IX, 349 f. For this father, see above, n. 227.

759. Abū Ḥamzah Muḥammad b. Maymūn al-Sukkarī died between 166 and 168/782–85. See *TB*, III, 266–69; *Tahdhīb*, IX, 486 f.

760. ʿAbdallāh b. Idrīs, judge of al-Kūfah, lived from ca. 115/733 to 192/807[8]. See *TB*, IX, 415–21; *Tahdhīb*, V, 144–46. This Ibn Idrīs is not to be confused with ʿAbd al-Munʿim b. Idrīs, a descendant of Wahb b. Munabbih and transmitter of his work, whose reputation for reliability was poor and who died ninety years old or older in 228/843, see *TB*, XI, 131–34; Ibn Ḥajar, *Lisān*, IV, 73 f.

761. Muḥammad b. ʿAmr b. ʿAlqamah died in 144 or 145/761–63. See *Tahdhīb*, IX, 375–77.

762. For the preceding portion of the tradition, see text above, I, 112 f. For the remainder, see *Tafsīr*, XVII, 21 (*ad* Qur. 21:37).

763. *Yuqalliluhā* appears to belong to Ṭabarī's original text and is not a later adjustment to the text as found in the *ḥadīth* collections and in *Tafsīr*. For the

pray) on it everything good he asks for. 'Abdallāh b. Salām said: I know which hour it is. It is the last hour of daytime on Friday. God says: "Man was created of haste. I shall show you My signs, but do not ask Me to make haste."[764]

We were told about the same, including the approximate wording of 'Abdallāh b. Salām, by Abū Kurayb—al-Muḥāribī,[765] — 'Abdah b. Sulaymān,[766] and Asad b. 'Amr[767] —Muḥammad b. 'Amr—Abū Salamah—Abū Hurayrah.[768]

According to Muḥammad b. 'Amr (al-Bāhilī)—Abū 'Āṣim (al-Nabīl)—'Īsā (b. Maymūn)—Ibn Abī Najīḥ—Mujāhid,[769] commenting on God's word: "Man was created of haste," as follows: (This refers to) Adam's statement when he was created after everything else at the end of daytime on the day of creation.[770] When the spirit gave life to his eyes, his tongue, and his head, but had not yet [116]
reached the lower part of his body, he said: O my Lord, make haste with my creation before sunset!

I was told the same by al-Ḥārith (b. Muḥammad b. Usāmah)—al-Ḥasan (b. Mūsā al-Ashyab)—Warqā'—Ibn Abī Najīḥ—Mujāhid.[771]

According to al-Qāsim (b. al-Ḥasan)—al-Ḥusayn (b. Dāwūd)—Ḥajjāj—Ibn Jurayj—Mujāhid, commenting on: "Man was created of haste," as follows: (This refers to) Adam when he was created after everything else. Then he mentioned about the same but said in his tradition: Make haste with my creation! The sun is already in the West.

According to Yūnus—Ibn Wahb—Ibn Zayd, commenting on God's word: "Man was created *of* haste," as follows: *In* haste. God created Adam at the end of that day of those two days—meaning Friday—and He created him hastily and made him hasty.

Some have assumed that God made Adam and his spouse dwell

---

explanation of the word, cf. Ibn Ḥajar, *Fatḥ*, III, 67–74.

764. Qur. 21:37.

765. 'Abd al-Raḥmān b. Muḥammad b. Ziyād al-Muḥāribī died in 195/810[1]. See *Tahdhīb*, VI, 265 f.

766. Died in 187 or 188/803–4. See *Tahdhīb*, VI, 458 f.

767. He is very possibly Asad b. 'Amr b. 'Āmir who died between 188 and 190/804–6. See *TB*, VII, 16-19; Ibn Abī Ḥātim, I, 1, 337 f.; Ibn Ḥajar, *Lisān*, I, 383–85.

768. See *Tafsīr*, XVII, 21 (*ad* Qur. 21:37).

769. See Mujāhid, *Tafsīr*, I, 410.

770. The addition of "Friday" in some manuscripts is not justified and is not found in *Tafsīr*, XVII, 20.

771. This and the following two paragraphs appear in *Tafsīr*, XVII, 20.

in Paradise after two hours had passed of Friday. It has also been said: After three hours. He cast him down to earth after seven hours had passed of that day. Thus, the duration of Adam and Eve's stay in Paradise was five hours of that day. It has also been said: Three hours.

Some said: Adam was driven out from Paradise in the ninth or tenth hour.

[117] *Those who said this*

Abū Ja'far (al-Ṭabarī) says: Reading to him, I studied (this report)[772] with 'Abdān b. Muḥammad al-Marwazī—'Ammār b. al-Ḥasan—'Abdallāh b. Abī Ja'far—his father—al-Rabī' b. Anas[773]—Abū al-'Āliyah: Adam was driven out of Paradise in the ninth or tenth hour. Then ('Abdān) said to me: Yes, after five days had passed of Nīsān.[774]

If someone making this statement means that God made Adam and his spouse dwell in Paradise after two hours of daytime had passed on Friday of the days of the inhabitants of this world, which are such that they constitute the (entire) day,[775] his statement in this respect is not far off the mark. Reports have come down on the authority of the early Muslim scholars to the effect that Adam was created in the last hour of the sixth day of the days of which each measures a thousand of our years. The conclusion is that a single hour of the hours of that day was eighty-three of our years.[776]

Now we have mentioned[777] that after our Lord caused Adam's clay to ferment, Adam remained forty years before God blew the spirit into him. "Of *our* years" is no doubt meant here. Then, the extent (of time) after the spirit was blown into him, until the entire process (of inspiriting) was completed and he was settled in Paradise and cast down to earth, can easily be assumed to have
[118] been thirty-five of our years. If, however, he means that Adam

---

772. Ṭabarī apparently studied with his authority the commentary of al-Rabī' b. Anas containing this tradition.

773. Al-Rabī' transmitted from both Anas b. Mālik and Abū al-'Āliyah, but the *isnād* is no doubt correct as given above, as against the Ṭabarī editions (see, however, Ṭabarī, *Introductio etc.*, DLXXVI).

774. This would be the sixth of April, a Friday, assuming that the first of the month was a Sunday.

775. The omission of *hiya,* as suggested in the Leiden edition, is unnecessary. The simpler translation: such as they are today, is unlikely.

776. In fact, eighty-three years and four months, as correctly stated below.

777. Text above, I, 89 ff.

was settled in Paradise after two hours of daytime had passed on Friday of the days of which a single day measures a thousand years of our years, then the statement he has made is not true. That is because all the preserved statements of scholars say that the spirit was blown into Adam at the end of daytime on Friday before sunset. Then, various reports on the authority of the Messenger of God have confirmed that God had Adam dwell in Paradise on Friday and cast him down to earth on it. If this is sound, the conclusion is that the last hour of daytime on one of the days of the other world and of the days each of which measures a thousand years of our years is an hour (remaining) after eleven hours have passed; thus, one of twelve hours equivalent to eighty-three years and four months of our years. Now, if this is so, Adam was created after eleven daytime hours had passed on Friday of the days each of which is a thousand years of our years. He then remained a body left lying around for forty of our years without having the spirit blown into him. Then the spirit was blown into him. His stay in heaven afterwards and his sojourn in Paradise, until he committed the sin (of eating from the forbidden tree) and was cast down to earth, was forty-three of our years and four months, this (together with the forty years of Adam's inanimate state) being one of the hours of one of the six days on which God created the creation.[778]

778. Ṭabarī is confronted here with contradictory data. They can, of course, not be reconciled, but he tries anyway. He assumes that Adam was created on Friday in the last of the twelve hours of daytime. Now, since Adam's entire existence until his expulsion from Paradise took place on the same Friday, it could at best have covered only one entire hour of Friday. According to the traditions that equate an otherworldly day (of twelve hours) with one thousand ordinary years, Adam's one-hour existence until his expulsion equaled eighty-three years and four months. Now, in his inanimate state, Adam lived forty years. Thus, forty-three years and four months remain to his expulsion. Assuming, as Ṭabarī had just stated, that Adam's stay in Paradise covered a number of hours on Friday, those hours could not be full-fledged years of eighty-three years and four months but had to be adjusted (as suggested in a footnote in the Leiden edition) to hours of a complete twelve-hour day constituting those eighty-three years and four months. Taking the number of five hours, as mentioned, this would lead to eighty-three (or eighty-three and one-third) divided by twelve and multiplied by five, that is, 34.588 (or 34.722), which is very close to the number thirty-five given in the text. Adding the forty years of Adam's inanimate existence, we obtain seventy-five years, which may have seemed to Ṭabarī to be reasonably close to eighty-three years and four months. The discussion of the second alternative, which is rejected by Ṭabarī, fails to make clear its point. The hours mentioned could not be full otherworldly hours,

[119] According to al-Ḥārith b. Muḥammad—Muḥammad b. Sa'd[779] —Hishām b. Muḥammad[780] —his father—Abū Ṣāliḥ—Ibn 'Abbās: Adam left Paradise (during the time) between two prayers, the noon prayer and the afternoon prayer. He was brought down to earth. His stay in Paradise was half a day of the days of the other world—that is, five hundred years—of a day that measures twelve hours and a thousand years as counted by the inhabitants of this world. This, too, is a statement contradicting what has been reported on the authority of the Messenger of God and our early scholars.

The Place on Earth to Which Adam and Eve Came When They Were Cast Down

Then, before sunset of the day—Friday—on which God had created Adam, He cast him down from heaven together with his spouse. According to the early scholars of our Prophet's nation, He brought him down in India.

This has been stated by some scholars, such as, for instance

According to al-Ḥasan b. Yaḥyā—'Abd al-Razzāq—Ma'mar—
[120] Qatādah: God cast Adam down to earth. The place where he fell down was the land of India.

According to 'Amr b. 'Alī[781] —'Imrān b. 'Uyaynah[782] —'Aṭā' b. al-Sā'ib—Sa'īd b. Jubayr—Ibn 'Abbās: When God first cast Adam down, it was in Dahnā(')[783] of the land of India.

---

because, at best, forty-three years and four months were available. It could, however, be that Ṭabarī in fact intended to argue that if seven or eight hours, as in the tradition quoted, were involved, the scheme would not work.

779. The author of the *Tabaqāt*, Ibn Sa'd, died in 230/845 at the age of sixty-two. See *TB*, V, 321 f.; *Tahdhīb*, IX, 182 f.; *EI*², III, 922 f., s. v. Ibn Sa'd; Sezgin, *GAS*, I, 300 f.

780. The famous historian Hishām b. Muḥammad b. al-Sā'ib al-Kalbī lived from ca. 120/738 to between 204 and 206/819–22. See *TB*, XIV, 45 f.; *EI*², IV, 495, s. v. al-Kalbī; Sezgin, *GAS*, I, 268–71. His equally important father, who was a historian but also the author of a Qur'ān commentary, died eighty-years old in 146/763–64. See *Tahdhīb*, IX, 178–81; *EI*², loc. cit.; Sezgin, *GAS*, I, 34.

781. 'Amr b. 'Alī b. Baḥr al-Fallās died in 249/January 864. See *TB*, XII, 207–12; *Tahdhīb*, VIII, 80–82.

782. For this brother of Sufyān b. 'Uyaynah, see *Tahdhīb*, VIII, 136 f.

783. Dahnā(') is apparently meant to be understood as identical with Dahnaj mentioned text below, I, 121. It seems to be intended here as a proper name; however, the Arabian desert Dahnā' might suggest the general sense of desert. In the

I was told on the authority of 'Ammār (b. al-Ḥasan)—'Abdallāh b. Abī Ja'far—his father—al-Rabī' b. Anas—Abū al-'Āliyah: Adam was cast down in India.

According to Ibn Sinān—al-Ḥajjāj—Ḥammād b. Salamah—'Alī b. Zayd—Yūsuf b. Mihrān[784] —Ibn 'Abbās—'Alī b. Abī Ṭālib: The land with the sweetest smell on earth is the land of India. When Adam was cast down there, some of the smell of Paradise clung to India's trees.[785]

According to al-Ḥārith (b. Muḥammad)—Ibn Sa'd—Hishām b. Muḥammad—his father—Abū Ṣāliḥ—Ibn 'Abbās: Adam was cast down in India, and Eve in Juddah.[786] He went in search of her, and eventually they were united. Eve drew near *(z-l-f)* him, hence al-Muzdalifah. They recognized *('-r-f)* each other, hence 'Arafāt. And they were united *(j-m-')* in Jam', hence Jam'.[787] He continued. Adam was cast down upon a mountain in India called Nūdh.[788]

According to Abū Hammām[789] —his father—Ziyād b. Khaytha-

fanciful geography of these traditions, a relationship with Daḥnā (see below, n. 858) is not entirely excluded in spite of the different consonant *(h/ḥ)*. In fact, in connection with the *Tafsīr's* commentary on Qur. 7:172 (*Tafsīr*, IX, 76, l.7), Daḥnā is described as a land in India.

784. See *Tahdhīb*, XI, 424 f.; Bukhārī, *Ta'rīkh*, IV, 2, 375 f.

785. See text below, I, 126. The above translation seems preferable to "and he made...cling."

786. The preferred vocalization today is Jiddah.

787. Like al-Muzdalifah and 'Arafāt, Jam' refers to some locality near Mecca connected with the pilgrimage. It is also sometimes considered as just another name for al-Muzdalifah.

788. The reference to the *mountain* of Nod on the eastern limits of Japheth's territory in *Schatzhöhle*, text, 136 f., trans., 30, a work which stands out among Ṭabarī's indirect sources, tips the scales in favor of reading the first letter *N*. Genesis 4:16 speaks of "the *land* of Nod, east of Eden." That Muslim scholars also often thought of Nūdh with *N*, is of no real consequence in this case. The Ṭabarī editions prefer Būdh/Bawdh. This sounds vaguely Indian because of the seeming resemblance to Buddha. Echoes of the mysterious Meru Mountain may come into play here, but they do not help with the form of the name. The mountain in Ceylon, mentioned later on in connection with Adam's habitat, appears as al-Ruhūn in Arabic literature. See Mas'ūdī, *Murūj*, I, 60; *Ḥudūd al-'ālam*, 194.

789. Abū Hammām (Humām?) al-Walīd b. Shujā' b. al-Walīd al-Sakūnī died presumably in 243/857, but the preceding year and even 239/853[4] are also mentioned as the year of his death. See *TB*, XIII, 473–76; *Tahdhīb*, XI, 135 f. His father Shujā' died between 203 and 205/818–21. See *TB*, IX, 247–50; *Tahdhīb*, IV, 313 f.

mah[790] —Abū Yaḥyā Bā'i' al-Qatt[791] —Mujāhid: We were told by Ibn 'Abbās that when Adam came down, it was in India.

[121] According to Ibn Ḥumayd—Salamah—Ibn Isḥāq: The people of the Torah on their part said: Adam was cast down in India upon a mountain called Wāsim on a river (valley) called Buhayl between two places in the land of India, al-Dahnaj and al-Mandal.[792] They continued. Eve was cast down in Juddah of the land of Mecca.

Others said: Rather, Adam was cast down in Sarandīb (Ceylon) upon a mountain called Nūdh, Eve in Juddah of the land of Mecca, Iblīs in Maysān,[793] and the snake in Iṣbahān. It has also been said that the snake was cast down in the desert *(al-barriyyah),* and Iblīs on the shore of the sea of al-Ubullah.

The soundness of this can be established only by a report serving as (conclusive) proof, but no such report on this subject is known to have been transmitted, except the report of Adam having been cast down in India. Its soundness is rejected neither by the Muslim scholars nor by the people of the Torah and the Gospel. Proof is firmly established by reports from some of them.

It has been mentioned that the summit of the mountain upon which Adam was cast down is one of those closest to heaven among the mountains of the earth and that, when Adam was cast down upon it, his feet were upon it while his head was in heaven and he heard the prayer and praise-giving of the angels. Adam became (too) familiar with that, and the angels were in awe of him. Therefore, Adam's size was reduced.

Those who said this

According to al-Ḥasan b. Yaḥyā—'Abd al-Razzāq—Hishām b.

790. According to Abū Hammām as reported by al-Bukhārī, Ziyād b. Khaythamah died two years before al-A'mash, which would be around 146/763. See *Tahdhīb*, III, 364, no. 668; Bukhārī, *Ta'rīkh*, II,1, 321; Ibn Abī Ḥātim, II,1, 530.

791. Probably, "the fodder seller," and identical with Abū Yaḥyā al-Qattāt, listed in *Tahdhīb*, XII, 277 f., but cf. Abū 'Ubayd, *Gharīb al-ḥadīth*, I, 339 (Hyd. 1384–87).

792. The entry Wāsim in Yāqūt, *Mu'jam*, IV, 891, is obviously derived from this Ṭabarī passage. Neither it nor Buhayl (the form is totally uncertain) can be identified. For Dahnaj, see above, n. 783. Al-Mandal is too general a term to allow identification, see *Ḥudūd al- 'ālam*, 87 and 240. The entry Wāshim in Bakrī, *Mu'jam*, IV, 1364, refers to Ibn Isḥāq, but may not have been taken from Ṭabarī. Bakrī, II, 539, has a separate entry Dahnaj, which is derived from the entry Wāshim.

793. Mesene, or Charakene, a province in southernmost Babylonia is slandered here as is Iṣbahān. In the case of Mesene, it certainly was because of its unhealthy climate. Al-Ubullah was the principal town of Maysān in Antiquity.

Ḥassān[794] —Sawwār, the son-in-law *(khatan)* of ʿAṭā'[795] —ʿAṭā' b. Abī Rabāḥ: When God cast Adam down from Paradise, Adam's feet were upon earth, while his head was in heaven and he heard [122] the speech and prayers of the inhabitants of heaven. He became (too) familiar with them, and the angels were in awe of him so much so that they eventually complained to God in their various prayers (*duʿā' and ṣalāh*). God, therefore, lowered Adam down to earth. Adam missed what he used to hear from the angels and felt lonely so much so that he eventually complained about it to God in his various prayers. He was therefore sent to Mecca. (On the way, every) place where he set foot became a village, and (the interval between) his steps became a desert, until he reached Mecca. God sent down a jewel *(yāqūt* ["ruby"]) of Paradise where the House is located today. (Adam) continued to circumambulate it, until God sent down the Flood. That jewel was lifted up, until God sent His friend Abraham to (re)build the House (in its later form). This is (meant by) God's word: "And We established for Abraham the place of the House as residence."[796]

According to al-Ḥasan b. Yaḥyā—ʿAbd al-Razzāq—Maʿmar—Qatādah: God founded the House together with Adam. Adam's head was in heaven, while his feet were upon earth. The angels were in awe of him. So his size was reduced to sixty cubits (30 meters). Adam was sad because he missed the voices and praise-giving of the angels. He complained about it to God, and God said: Adam, I have cast down a house for you to circumambulate, as one circumambulates My Throne, and to pray at it as one prays at My Throne. Adam left and went off. His steps were lengthened, and the interval between each (two) step(s) became a desert. These deserts continued to exist afterwards. Adam came to the House, and he and the prophets after him circumambulated it.[797]

According to al-Ḥārith—Ibn Saʿd—Hishām b. Muḥammad—his father—Abū Ṣāliḥ—Ibn ʿAbbās: When Adam's size was lowered to sixty cubits, he started to say: My lord! I was Your protege *(jār)*

794. Died between 146 and 148/763–65. See *Tahdhīb*, XI, 34–37; Bukhārī, *Ta'rīkh*, IV,2, 197 f.

795. For Sawwār b. Abī Ḥukaym, see Bukhārī, *Ta'rīkh*, II,2, 169.

796. Qur. 22:26. The tradition occurs in *Tafsīr*, I, 428 f. *(ad* Qur. 2:127). See text below, I, 131 and 193.

797. See *Tafsīr*, I, 429 *(ad* Qur. 2:127).

[123] in Your house,[798] having no Lord but You and no one to watch out for me except You. There I had plenty to eat and could dwell wherever I wanted. But then You cast me down to this holy mountain. (There,) I used to hear the voices of the angels and see them crowd around Your Throne and to enjoy the sweet smell of Paradise. Then You cast me down to earth and reduced me to sixty cubits. I was cut off from the voices and the sight (of the angels), and the smell of Paradise left me. God replied: Because of your disobedience have I done this to you, Adam. Then, when God saw the nakedness of Adam and Eve, He commanded Adam to slaughter a ram from the eight couples of small cattle He had sent down from Paradise. Adam took the ram and slaughtered it. Then he took its wool, and Eve spun it. He and Eve wove it. Adam made a coat for himself, and a shift and veil for Eve. They put on that clothing. Then God revealed to Adam: I have a sacred territory around My Throne. Go and build a house for Me there! Then crowd around it, as you have seen My angels crowd around My Throne. There I shall respond to you and all your children who are obedient to Me. Adam said: My Lord! How could I do that? I do not have the strength to do it and do not know how. So God chose an angel to assist him, and he went with him toward Mecca. Whenever Adam passed by a meadow or place that he liked, he would say to the angel: Let us stop here! and the angel would say to him: Please do! This went on until they reached Mecca. Every place where he stopped became cultivated land. and every place he bypassed became a desolate desert. He built the House with (materials from) five mountains: Mount Sinai, the Mount of Olives, (Mount) Lebanon, and al-Jūdī,[799] and he constructed its foundations with (materials from Mount) Ḥirā' (near Mecca). When he finished with its construction, the angel went out with him to 'Arafāt. He showed him all the rites (connected with the pilgrimage) that people perform today. Then he went with him to Mecca, and (Adam) circumambulated the House for a week. Returning to

798. *Dār* "mansion" is used because of the rhyming effect, and the entire phrase *jāruka fī dārika (jārak fī dārak)* may be understood as being under someone's protection without any specific reference to housing. If "house" is indeed intended, it might refer in the context to Paradise rather than the Ka'bah.

799. Al-Jūdī is the mountain where Noah's ark came to rest and which in later tradition was identified with Mount Ararat (see below, n. 1137). See *Tafsīr*, I, 428 (*ad* Qur. 2:127), and *EI*², II, 573 f., s. v. al-Djūdī.

the land of India, he died upon (Mount) Nūdh. [124]

According to Abū Hammām—his father—Ziyād b. Khaythamah —Abū Yaḥyā Bā'i' al-Qatt—Mujāhid—'Abdallāh b. 'Abbās: When Adam came down, it was in India. From there, he performed the pilgrimage to Mecca on foot forty times. I (Abū Yaḥyā) said: Abū al-Ḥajjāj,[800] could he not have ridden instead ? He replied: What could have carried him? Indeed, each of his steps covered the distance of a journey of three days, and his head reached heaven. (It led to) the angels complaining about his pride.[801] The Merciful One faulted him for that, and he was in a state of humbleness for forty years.

According to Abū Ma'mar Ṣāliḥ b. Ḥarb, the *mawlā* of the Hāshimites[802] —Thumāmah b. 'Abīdah ('Ubaydah) al-Sulamī[803] — Abū al-Zabīr[804] —Nāfi' (the *mawla* of Ibn 'Umar)—Ibn 'Umar: While Adam was in India, God revealed to him that he should perform the pilgrimage to this House. So Adam left India to go on the pilgrimage. Wherever he put down his foot on a place, that place became a village. Every interval between his steps became a desert. Eventually he reached the House. He circumambulated it and performed all the rites (of the pilgrimage). Then he wanted to return to India and went off. When he reached the two mountain passes of 'Arafāt, the angels met him and said: You have performed the pilgrimage faultlessly. This surprised him. When the angels noticed his surprise, they said: Adam! We have performed the pilgrimage to this House two thousand years before you were created.[805] He continued. And Adam felt properly chastised.

800. Mujāhid's patronymic.

801. In view of the idiom translated below "felt properly chastised" *(taqāṣarat ilā Ādam nafsuhū), nafsahū*, and not *nafasahū* ("his breath"), understood metaphorically, should be read also here.

802. See *TB*, IX, 316 f., where Ṣāliḥ b. Ḥarb is described as a *mawlā* of Sulaymān b. 'Alī b. 'Abdallāh b. al-'Abbās.

803. This Thumāmah was considered a "weak" transmitter. See Bukhārī, *Ta'rīkh*, I,2, 178; Ibn Ḥajar, *Lisān*, II, 94. Neither source mentions the *nisbah* al-Sulamī.

804. Abū al-Zabīr Muḥammad b. Muslim died in 126/743[4]. See *Tahdhīb*, IX, 440–43.

805. See Ya'qūbī, *Ta'rīkh*, I, 3.

(Perfumes, Fruits, and Other Things Adam Brought from Paradise)

It has been mentioned that when Adam was cast down to earth, he had upon his head a wreath made from (leaves of) the trees of Paradise. When he reached the earth and the wreath became dry,
[125] its leaves scattered, and the various kinds of perfume grew from them.

Some(one) said: Rather, this is what God has told about Adam and Eve, that they started to cover themselves with leaves of Paradise stitched together,[806] and when those leaves became dry, they scattered, and the various kinds of perfume grew from those leaves. God knows best!

Others said: Rather, when Adam realized that God would cast him down to earth, he started taking a branch of every tree he passed in Paradise and when he fell down to earth, those branches were with him. When the leaves on them became dry, they scattered. This was the origin of perfume.

Those who said this

According to Abū Hammām—his father—Ziyād b. Khaythamah—Abū Yaḥyā Bā'i' al-Qatt—Mujāhid—'Abdallāh b. 'Abbās: When Adam was leaving Paradise, he toyed with everything he passed. The angels were told: Let him do it! Let him take along whatever provisions from Paradise he wants to! When he came down, it was in India. The perfumes brought from India come from what Adam took out from Paradise.

Those who said: When Adam was cast down from Paradise, a wreath from the trees of Paradise was upon his head:

I was told on the authority of 'Ammār b. al-Ḥasan—'Abdallāh b. Abī Ja'far—his father—al-Rabī' b. Anas—Abū al-'Āliyah: Adam left Paradise, and when he did, he had with him a staff from the trees of Paradise, and upon his head there was a crown or wreath made from the trees of Paradise. He continued. He was cast down to India. From (that crown or wreath) comes every perfume in India.

According to Ibn Ḥumayd—Salamah—Ibn Isḥāq: Adam fell
[126] down upon it—meaning upon that mountain—having with him leaves of Paradise. He scattered them on that mountain. This was

806. Cf. Qur. 7:22.

the origin of all perfumes and fruits that are found only in India.

Other said: Rather, God provided him with some of the fruits of Paradise. Those fruits of ours come from them.

Those who said this

According to Ibn Bashshār—Ibn Abī ʿAdī, ʿAbd al-Wahhāb, and Muḥammad b. Jaʿfar—ʿAwf—Qasāmah b. Zuhayr—(Abū Mūsā) al-Ashʿarī: When God drove Adam out of Paradise, He provided him with some of the fruits there and taught him how to make everything. Those fruits of ours come from the fruits of Paradise, except that they change while the fruits of Paradise do not.

Others said: Adam's sweet smell clung to the trees of India.

Those who said: Perfume is found in India because, when Adam was cast down there, his sweet smell stuck to its trees

According to al-Ḥārith b. Muḥammad—Ibn Saʿd—Hishām b. Muḥammmad—his father—Abū Ṣāliḥ—Ibn ʿAbbās: When Adam came down, the smell of Paradise was with him. It clung to India's trees and river valleys, and everything there was filled with perfume. Therefore, perfume with the smell of Paradise is brought from there.

As it was said that some of the perfume of Paradise was brought down with Adam, so it was said that the Black Stone, which was (originally) whiter than snow, was brought down with him, as well as the staff of Moses made from the myrtle of Paradise, which, like Moses, was ten cubits (five meters) tall, and also myrrh and incense. Then, anvils, mallets, and tongs were revealed to him. When Adam was cast down upon the mountain, he looked at an [127]
iron rod growing on the mountain and said: This comes from that, and he began to break up trees that had grown old and dry with the mallet and heated that (iron) branch until it melted. The first thing (of iron) he hammered was a long knife, which he used for work. Then he hammered the oven, the one which Noah inherited and that boiled with the punishment in India.[807]

When Adam fell down, his head brushed against heaven. As a result, he became bald, and he passed on baldness to his children. Because he was so tall, the animals of the field fled (from him) and became wild animals from that day on. While Adam was standing

807. Cf. Qur. 11:40 and 23:27 and text below, I, 186 and 193 ff. In *Tafsīr*, XII, 25 (*ad* Qur. 11:40), Ṭabarī refers rather unenthusiastically to this interpretation of "the oven that boiled." See also Speyer, *Biblische Erzählungen*, 103.

on that mountain, he heard the voices of the angels and enjoyed the smell of Paradise. His size was (therefore) reduced to sixty cubits, which was his size until he died. All of Adam's beauty combined was not found in any of his children except Joseph.[807a]

It has been said that when Adam was cast down to earth, God provided him with thirty kinds of fruit—ten with shells, ten with stones, and ten with neither shells nor stones. The fruits with shells include walnuts, almonds, pistachio nuts, hazelnuts, poppy, acorns, chestnuts, coconuts, pomegranates, and bananas. Those with stones include peaches, apricots, plums, dates, sorbs, lotus fruit, medlar, jujubes, the fruit of the doom palm,[808] and *shahlūj* plums.[809] Those with neither shells nor stones include apples, quinces, pears, grapes, mulberries, figs, citrus fruit, breadfruit, ginger, and melon.[810]

It has been said that among the things Adam took out from Paradise, there was a bag with grains of wheat, but, according to another statement, Gabriel brought wheat to Adam when he became hungry and asked his Lord for food, whereupon God sent him seven grains of wheat with Gabriel. When Gabriel put
[128] them in Adam's hand, Adam asked him what it was, and Gabriel said to him: This is what drove you out of Paradise.[811] Each of those grains weighed 100,800 dirhams. When Adam asked Gabriel what he should do with them, Gabriel told him to spread them in the soil, and Adam did, whereupon God immediately made them grow. Thus, putting seeds into the soil became the custom among Adam's children. Then God commanded him to harvest the wheat, collect and husk it by hand, and winnow it. Then (Gabriel) brought two stones to him, and he placed one upon the other and ground the wheat. Then God commanded him to knead it and bake bread in the ashes. Gabriel gave Adam stones and iron, and (Adam) struck them together, producing fire. He was the first to bake bread in the ashes.

807a. The paragon of beauty in Islam.

808. For *muql*, see, for instance, Bīrūnī, *Ṣaydanah*, text, 350 f., trans., 307 f. See also Lane, 937b, s. v. *dawm*.

809. See Bīrūnī, *Ṣaydanah*, text, 24 f. and 388, trans., 17 f. and 347.

810. Mas'ūdī, *Murūj*, I, 61 f., has *quththā'* "cucumber" instead of "melon."

811. Because it is the fruit of the "tree" from which Adam and Eve had been forbidden to eat and which became such a nuisance for them on earth when they had to work hard to grow the wheat they needed for sustenance.

This statement just reported on the authority of the one who made it, contradicts transmissions on the authority of the early (scholars) of the nation of our Prophet. This is so in view of the report of al-Muthannā b. Ibrāhīm—Isḥāq (b. al-Ḥajjāj)—'Abd al-Razzāq—Sufyān b. 'Uyaynah and Ibn al-Mubārak—al-Ḥasan b. 'Umārah[812] —al-Minhāl b. 'Amr[813] —Sa'īd b. Jubayr—Ibn 'Abbās: The tree which God forbade Adam and his spouse to eat from was wheat.[814] When they ate from it, their secret parts became apparent to them. It was their (cover of) fingernails[815] that had kept their secret parts concealed from them. Now, they started to cover themselves with leaves of Paradise stitched together—fig leaves which they stuck together. Adam wandered about hiding in Paradise. A tree there took hold of his head. God called out to him: Adam, is it from Me that you are fleeing? Adam said: No, but I am ashamed of you, my Lord. God said: Was all that I granted and allowed you (to enjoy) in Paradise not enough to keep you from what I had forbidden? Adam replied: No, my Lord, but by Your [129] might!, I did not think that anyone would swear by You falsely (as was done by Iblīs). He continued. This is (meant by) God's word: "And (Iblīs) assured them with an oath: I am one of those who give you good advice."[816] God said: By My might! I shall cast you down to earth, and it will be only by toil that you will earn your living. He continued. Adam was cast down from Paradise, where both of them had freely eaten of its plenty, to where there was no longer plentiful food and drink. He was taught how to work iron, and he was commanded to plow. So he plowed, sowed,, and irrigated, and when (the crop) ripened, he harvested, thrashed, winnowed, ground, kneaded, baked bread, and ate. Adam did not learn about (all these matters) until all that God wanted to ripen did.[817]

Ibn Ḥumayd—Ya'qūb (al-Qummī)—Ja'far (b. Abī al-Mughīrah)—Sa'īd (b. Jubayr): A red ox was cast down for Adam to use for plow-

---

812. Died in 153/752[3]. See *Tahdhīb* II, 304–8.

813. The following "and" *(wa-'an)* seems to be a misprint in the Ṭabarī editions. It makes no sense and does not appear in *Tafsīr,* VIII, 105 f. *(ad* Qur. 7:22).

814. *Sunbulah* "ear of corn." See above, n. 683.

815. See above, n. 677.

816. Qur. 7:21.

817. Two different meanings of *balagha* appear to be involved here. Reading *b-l-'* in the first occurrence ("Adam did not eat...") simplifies matters but is hardly correct. For the tradition, see *Tafsīr,* VIII, 105 f. *(ad* Qur. 7:22).

ing while wiping the sweat from his brow. This is (meant by) God's word: "So let (Iblīs) not drive both of you out of Paradise, so that you will be miserable!"[818] That was Adam's misery.[819]

The statement made by these men is more likely to be correct and conforms more (than the earlier one) with the indications of the Book of our Lord. For, when God approached Adam and his spouse Eve and forbade them to obey their enemy, He said to Adam: "Adam! This (Iblīs) is an enemy to you and your spouse. So let him not drive both of you out of Paradise, so that you will be miserable! You do not have to go hungry or be naked in it, nor to be thirsty there or suffer from heat."[820] The conclusion is that the misery which God informed Adam would result from being obedient to his enemy Iblīs is the difficulty for him to obtain what would remove his hunger and his nakedness. It refers to the means by which his children obtain food, such as plowing, sowing, cultivating, irrigating and other such difficult and painful tasks. If
[130] Gabriel had brought him the food which he obtains by sowing without any more trouble, there would not be much to the misery here with which his Lord threatened him for obeying Satan and disobeying the Merciful One. But it was—God knows best!—as (reported in the tradition) we transmitted on the authority of Ibn ʿAbbās and others.

It has been said that anvils, tongs, mallets, and hammers came down together with Adam.

Those who said this

According to Ibn Ḥumayd—Yaḥyā b. Wāḍiḥ—al-Ḥusayn[821] —ʿIlbāʾ b. Aḥmar[822] —ʿIkrimah—Ibn ʿAbbās: Three things came down together with Adam: Anvils, tongs, mallets and hammers.

Then, as has been mentioned, God had Adam descend to the foot of the mountain upon which He had cast him, and made him ruler of all the earth and of all the jinn, dumb animals, beasts of burden, wild animals, birds and other (beings) upon it. Descending from the top of that mountain, Adam missed the speech of the

---

818. Qur. 20:117.
819. See *Tafsīr*, XVI, 161 *(ad* Qur. 20:117).
820. Qur. 20:117–19.
821. This is (al-) Ḥusayn b. Wāqid al-Marwazī, who died in 157 or 159/773–76. See *Tahdhīb*, II, 373 f.
822. For ʿIlbāʾ, see *Tahdhīb* VII, 273 f.

inhabitants of heaven, and he could no longer hear the voices of the angels. He looked at the vastness and expanse of the earth and saw no one but himself. He felt lonely and said: My Lord! Does this earth of Yours have no one but me to live there and praise You? The reply he received is what I was told by al-Muthannā b. Ibrāhīm—Isḥāq b. al-Ḥajjāj—Ismāʿīl b. ʿAbd al-Karīm—ʿAbd al-Ṣamad b. Maʿqil—Wahb: When Adam was cast down to earth and saw its vastness but did not see anyone but himself, he said: My Lord! Does this earth of Yours have no one but me to live there and praise and sanctify You? God said: I shall have some of your [131] children praise and sanctify Me on it. I shall have houses raised for mentioning Me on it, houses in which My creatures will give praise and mention My name. I shall have one of those houses singled out for my generosity and distinguish it from all others by My name and call it My House. I shall have it proclaim My greatness, and it is upon it that I have placed My majesty. Then, in addition, I, being in everything and together with everything, shall make that House a safe sanctuary whose sacredness will extend to those around, those underneath, and those above it. He who makes it sacred with My sacredness obligates Me to be generous to him. He who frightens its inhabitants there forfeits My protection and violates My sacredness. I shall have it be the first house to be founded as a blessing for mankind in the valley of Mecca. They will come to it disheveled and covered with dust upon all (kinds of) emaciated mounts from every deep ravine, shouting emotionally: At Your service *(labbayka)!* shedding copious tears and noisily proclaiming *Allāhu akbaru!* He whose exclusive intention it is to go there and nowhere else comes to Me as My visitor and becomes My guest. It befits a noble person to show generosity to those who come to him and are his guests, and to take care of everybody's need. You shall dwell there, Adam, as long as you live. Then the nations, generations, amd prophets of your children shall live there, one nation after the other, one generation after the other.

Then, as has been mentioned, He commanded Adam to go to the Sacred House which was cast down to earth for him, and to circumambulate it, just as he used to see the angels circumambulate God's Throne. (The Sacred House) was a single jewel (ruby) or pearl, as I was told by al-Ḥasan b. Yaḥyā—ʿAbd al-Razzāq—Maʿmar—

Abān[823] : The House was cast down being a single jewel (ruby) or pearl. Eventually, when God drowned the people of Noah, He lifted it up, but its foundation remained. God established it as a residence for Abraham, who (re)built it (in its later form). I have men-
[132] tioned earlier the reports that have come down on that subject.[824]

It has been mentioned that Adam wept bitterly because of his sin and repented it. He asked God to accept his repentance and forgive his sin. In asking God, Adam said, as we were told by Abū Kurayb—Ibn ʿAṭiyyah—Qays—Ibn Abī Laylā[825] —al-Minhāl —Saʿīd b. al-Jubayr—Ibn ʿAbbās, commenting on "And Adam received words from his Lord, and (God) forgave him"[826] : My Lord! Did you not create me with Your own hand? God replied: Yes. Adam said: My Lord! Did You not blow some of Your spirit into me? God replied: Yes. Adam said: My Lord! Did You not have me dwell in Your Paradise? God said: Yes. Adam said: My Lord! Did Your mercy not come before[827] Your wrath? God said: Yes. Adam said: Don't You think that, if I repent and improve, You might let me return to Paradise? God said: Yes. He continued. This is (meant by) God's word: "And Adam received words from his Lord."[828]

According to Bishr b. Muʿādh—Yazīd b. Zurayʿ—Saʿīd (b. Abī ʿArūbah)—Qatādah, commenting on: "And Adam received words from his Lord," as follows: My Lord! Don't You think, if I repent and improve, (everything will be all right)? God said: Then I shall let you return to Paradise. He continued. al-Ḥasan[829] said: "They (Adam and Eve) said: Our Lord! We have wronged ourselves, and if You do not forgive us and show mercy unto us, we shall be losers."[830]

---

823. This Abān is identified in the index of the Ṭabarī editions as Abān b. Ṣāliḥ, who, however, is mainly known as an authority of Ibn Isḥāq. He lived from 60/679[80] to the 110s/728–737. *Tahdhīb*, I, 97–101, lists Abān b. Abī ʿAyyāsh Fīrūz (died in or after 127/744[5]) as an authority of Maʿmar. He may be meant here, or, at least, Ibn Ḥajar thought so.

824. Text above, I, 122 (and below, I, 193). The tradition appears in *Tafsīr*, I, 429 (*ad* Qur. 2:127).

825. Muḥammad b. ʿAbd al-Raḥmān b. Abī Laylā died in 148/765. See *Tahdhīb*, IX, 301–3.

826. Qur. 2:37.

827. Probably not "precede," but "come in before" (in a race).

828. See *Tafsīr*, I, 193 f. (*ad* Qur. 2:37).

829. Al-Ḥasan al-Baṣrī?

830. Qur. 7:23.

According to Aḥmad b. Isḥāq al-Ahwāzī—Abū Aḥmad—Sufyān and Qays—Khaṣīf—Mujāhid, commenting on God's word: "And Adam received words from his Lord": This refers to "Our Lord! We have wronged ourselves, and if You do not forgive us and show mercy unto us, we shall be losers."

According to al-Ḥārith—Ibn Sa'd—Hishām b. Muḥammad—his father—Abū Ṣāliḥ—Ibn 'Abbās: When Adam was cast down from Paradise, he brought down with him the Black Stone, which was (originally) whiter than snow. Adam and Eve mourned for what [133] they had lost—that is, the luxury of Paradise—for two hundred years. They neither ate nor drank for forty days. Then they ate and drank, being at that time on (Mount) Nūdh, the mountain upon which Adam was cast down. He did not approach Eve for a hundred years.

According to Abū Hammām—his father—Ziyād b. Khaythamah—Abū Yaḥyā Bā'i' al-Qatt: When we were sitting in the mosque, Mujāhid said to me: Do you see this? I replied: Abū al-Ḥajjāj, (you mean) the Stone? He said: You call it a stone? I said: Is it not a stone? He said: Indeed, I was told by 'Abdallāh b. 'Abbās that it was a white jewel that Adam took out of Paradise and used to wipe his tears, for after he left Paradise, his tears did not stop for two thousand years, until he returned to it and Iblīs was no (longer) able to do anything to him. I said to him: Abū al-Ḥajjāj, why and how did it turn black? He replied: Menstruating women were touching it in the Jāhiliyyah.[831]

Adam left India for the House to which God had commanded him to go. When he finally came to it, he circumambulated it and performed the rites (of the pilgrimage). It has been mentioned that he and Eve met at 'Arafāt, where they recognized each other *('-r-f)*, and he drew near her *(z-l-f)* at al-Muzdalifah.[832] Then he returned with her to India. They took a cave as their shelter, repairing to it night and day.[833] God sent an angel to them to teach them what to wear and use for covering themselves. Supposedly, it was the skins of small cattle, (large) cattle, and beasts of prey. Some(one) said:

---

831. That is, the dark age before Islam.

832. See above, n. 787.

833. This cave somehow reflects the Cave of Treasure which plays such a large role in the *Book of Adam and Eve* as their residence, unless there is a connection here with the special cave of *Schatzhohle.*

It was only their children who wore that. Adam and Eve themselves used to wear leaves of Paradise stitched together to cover themselves.[834]

Then God rubbed Adam's back at Na'mān[835] of 'Arafah and
[134] brought forth his progeny *(dhurriyyah)*. He scattered them in front of him like tiny ants *(dharr)*.[836] He made covenants with them and "had them testify against[837] themselves: Am I not your Lord? and they said: Yes," as God says: "And your Lord took from the backs of the children of Adam their progeny and had them testify against themselves: Am I not your Lord? They said: Yes."[838]

According to Aḥmad b. Muḥammad al-Ṭūsī—al-Ḥusayn b. Muḥammad[839] —Jarīr b. Ḥāzim—Kulthūm b. Jabr[840] —Sa'īd b. Jubayr—Ibn 'Abbās—the Prophet: God took the covenant from Adam's back at Na'mān—meaning 'Arafah. He brought forth from his loin (his) progeny *(dhurriyyah)*, which He multiplied *(dh-r-')*. He scattered them in front of him like tiny ants *(dharr)*. Then He talked to them face to face[841] saying: "Am I not your Lord? They said: Yes. We (so) testify," to "for what those who were in the wrong did."[842]

According to 'Imrān b. Mūsā al-Qazzāz[843] —'Abd al-Wārith b. Sa'īd[844] —Kulthūm b. Jabr—Sa'īd b. Jubayr—Ibn 'Abbās, commenting on God's word: "And your Lord took from the backs of the children of Adam their progeny and had them testify against themselves: Am I not your Lord? They said: Yes," as follows: He

---

834. Cf. Qur. 7:22 and 20:121.

835. Na'mān was the name of the valley between 'Arafah and Minā. See Bakrī, *Mu'jam*, IV, 1316. It is here also identified with 'Arafah itself. *Tafsīr*, IX, 76,1. 30 *(ad* Qur 7:172), describes Na'mān as a valley beside 'Arafah.

836. *Dharr* refers to very small objects, specks of dust, (in modern Arabic) atom, but Ṭabarī decides in favor of "tiny ants" in *Tafsīr*, XI, 90, 1.29 *(ad* Qur. 10:61).

837. The translation "against" follows that of R. Paret in his translation of the Qur'ān.

838. Qur. 7:172.

839. Al-Ḥusayn b. Muḥammad b. Bahrām died between 213 and 215/828–30. See *TB*, VIII, 88-90; *Tahdhīb*, II, 366 f.

840. For Kulthūm, see *Tahdhīb*, VIII, 442.

841. See above, n. 667.

842. Qur. 7:172 f. See *Tafsīr*, IX, 75, on this verse; Ibn Ḥanbal, I, 272.

843. Died after 240/854[5]. See *Tahdhīb*, VIII, 141.

844. Died in 179 or 180/795–96 at the age of seventy-eight. See *Tahdhīb*, VI, 441–43.

rubbed Adam's back, and every living being to be created by God to the Day of Resurection came forth at Na'mān here—pointing with his hand. He took their covenants and "had them testify against themselves: Am I not your Lord? They said: Yes."[845]

According to Ibn Wakī' and Ya'qūb b. Ibrāhīm, the wording being that of the latter—Ibn 'Ulayyah—Kulthūm b. Jabr—Sa'īd b. Jubayr —Ibn 'Abbās, commenting on God's word: "And your Lord took from the backs of the children of Adam their progeny and had them testify against themselves: Am I not your Lord? They said: Yes." He rubbed Adam's back, and every living being to be [135] created by God to the Day of Resurrection came forth at Na'mān here which is behind 'Arafah. He took their covenant: "Am I not your Lord? They said: Yes. We (so) testify."[846]

According to Ibn Wakī'—'Imrān b. 'Uyaynah—'Aṭā' (b. al-Sā'ib)—Sa'īd b. Jubayr—Ibn 'Abbās: Adam was cast down as it happened, and God then rubbed his back and brought forth from it every living being to be created by Him to the Day of Resurrection. Then He said: "Am I not your Lord? They said: Yes." Then he recited: "And your Lord took from the backs of the children of Adam their progeny." And the Pen was dry with what is going to be from that day on to the Day of Resurrection.[847]

According to Abū Kurayb—Yaḥyā b. 'Īsā[848] —al-A'mash—Ḥabīb b. Abī Thābit[849] —Sa'īd b. Jubayr—Ibn 'Abbās, commenting on: "And your Lord took from the backs of the children of Adam their progeny," as follows: When God created Adam, He took his progeny from his back like tiny ants. He took two handfuls and said to those on the right: Enter Paradise in peace! And He said to the others: Enter the Fire! I do not care.[850]

According to Ibrāhīm b. Sa'īd al-Jawharī[851] —Rawḥ b. 'Ubādah

---

845. See *Tafsīr,* IX, 75 *(ad* Qur. 7:172).

846. See *Tafsīr,* IX, 75 f.

847. See *Tafsīr,* IX, 76.

848. Yaḥyā b. 'Īsā appears to be the individual listed in *Tahdhīb,* XI, 262 f., as having died about 201/816–17.

849. Ḥabīb b. Abī Thābit Qays (or Dīnār) died in 119/773. See *Tahdhīb,* II, 178–80; Khalīfah, *Ṭabaqāt,* 159.

850. See *Tafsīr,* IX, 76 *(ad* Qur. 7:172).

851. Originally from Ṭabaristān, Ibrāhīm b. Sa'īd al-Jawharī died ca. 250/864. See *TB,* VI, 93-96; *Tahdhīb,* I, 123–25.

and Sa'd b. 'Abd al-Ḥamīd b. Ja'far[852] —Mālik b. Anas[853] —Zayd b. Abī Unaysah[854] —'Abd al-Ḥamīd b. 'Abd al-Raḥmān b. Zayd b. al-Khaṭṭāb[855] —Muslim b. Yasār al-Juhanī[856] : When 'Umar b. al-Khaṭṭāb was asked about this verse: "And your Lord took from the backs of the children of Adam their progeny," he said: I heard the Messenger of God say: God created Adam, then rubbed his back with His right hand and brought forth from it (his) progeny. Then He said: I have created these for Paradise, and they will act
[136] as the inhabitants of Paradise. Then He rubbed his back with His left hand and said: I have created those for the Fire, and they will act as the inhabitants of the Fire. A man asked: O Messenger of God, how is that? Muḥammad replied: When God creates a human being for Paradise, He employs him to act as the inhabitants of Paradise, and he will enter Paradise. And when God creates a human being for the Fire, He will employ him to act as the inhabitants of the Fire, and will thus make him enter the Fire.[857]

It has also been said that God took Adam's progeny out of his back at Daḥnā.[858]

Those who said this

According to Ibn Ḥumayd—Ḥakkām—'Amr b. Abī Qays[859] —'Aṭā' (b. al-Sā'ib)—Sa'īd (b. Jubayr)—Ibn 'Abbās, commenting on: "And your Lord took from the backs of the children of Adam their progeny," as follows: When God created Adam, He rubbed his back at Daḥnā and brought forth from his back every living being to be created by Him to the Day of Resurrection. He said: "Am I not your Lord? They said: Yes." He continued: They will see. On that day, the Pen was dry with what is going to be to the Day of Resurrection.[860]

---

852. Died in 219/834. See *TB*, IX, 124–26; *Tahdhīb*, III, 477.

853. The author of the *Muwaṭṭa'* was born between 711 and 715. He died in 179/795[6]. See *Tahdhīb*, X, 5–9; Sezgin, *GAS*, I, 457–64.

854. Zayd b. Abī Unaysah died thirty-six years old between 119 and 125/737–43. See *Tahdhīb*, III, 397 f.; Sezgin, *GAS*, I, 87.

855. This grandson of a brother of the caliph 'Umar b. al-Khaṭṭāb died during the caliphate of Hishām b. 'Abd al-Malik. See *Tahdhīb*, VI, 119.

856. In his entry in *Tahdhīb*, X, 142, reference is made to this tradition.

857. See *Tafsīr*, IX, 77 (*ad* Qur. 7:172); Ibn Ḥanbal, I, 44 f.

858. See above, n. 783. Daḥnā is supposedly located near al-Ṭā'if. See text below, I, 1675, and the related entry in Yāqūt, *Mu'jam*, II, 557.

859. See *Tahdhīb*, VIII, 93 f.

860. See *Tafsīr*, IX, 76 (*ad* Qur. 7:172). The translation "they will see" is not

Some(one) said: God brought forth Adam's progeny from his loin in heaven before He cast him down to earth but after He had driven him out of Paradise.

Those who said this

According to Ibn Wakī'—'Amr b. Ḥammād—Asbāṭ—al-Suddī, commenting on: "And the Lord took from the backs of the children of Adam their progeny and had them testify against themselves: Am I not your Lord? They said: Yes," as follows: God drove Adam out of Paradise but did not cast him down from heaven. Then He rubbed the right side of Adam's back and somehow [137] brought forth from it progeny in the shape of tiny ants, white like pearls. He said to them: Enter Paradise by means of My mercy! Then He rubbed the left side of Adam's back and brought forth from it something in the shape of tiny black ants. He said to them: Enter the Fire! I do not care. This is meant where God speaks of "companions of the right" and "companions of the left."[861] Then He took the covenant and said: "Am I not your Lord? They said: Yes." And (God) gave (Adam) a willing group and a(n unwilling) group pretending piety (*'alā wajh al-taqiyyah?*).[862]

The Events That Took Place in Adam's Time after He Was Cast Down to Earth

The first of these events was the killing by Cain (Qābīl) b. Adam of his brother Abel (Hābīl).

Scholars disagree on the name of Qābīl. Some say that he was Qayn b. Adam. Others say that it was Qābīn[863] b. Adam. Others again say that it was Qāyin, and still others that it was Qābīl.

They also disagreed on the reason why he killed him:

On this subject, some say as I was told by Mūsā b. Hārūn al-Hamdānī—'Amr b. Ḥammād—Asbāṭ—al-Suddī—Abū Mālik and Abū Ṣāliḥ—Ibn 'Abbās. Also (al-Suddī)—Murrah al-Hamdānī—Ibn

---

entirely certain.

861. Qur. 56:27 and 41.

862. One of the versions of the tradition in *Tafsīr*, IX, 80 (*ad* Qur. 7:172) supplies the bracketed *kārihīn*. Cf. Qur. 41:11.

863. Possibly, a careful study of the manuscript evidence might tell us how Ṭabarī himself read these various forms. Ibn Ḥajar, *Fatḥ*, XV, 210, expressly states that there was a form Qābin with a short *i* and *n* for *l* (like the following Qāyin). The Cairo edition has Qāyīn instead of Qābīn.

Mas'ūd and some (other) companions of the Messenger of God: Every boy born to Adam was born together with a girl. Adam used to marry the boy of one pregnancy to the girl of another, and vice versa.[864] Eventually, two boys, called Cain and Abel, were born to him. Cain was a farmer and Abel a herdsman. Cain was the older of the two. He had a sister who was more beautiful than
[138] Abel's sister. Abel sought to marry Cain's sister, but Cain refused and said: She is my sister born together with me, and she is more beautiful than your sister. I deserve to marry her more (than you do). His father ordered Cain to marry her to Abel. However, he refused.

Cain and Abel offered a sacrifice to God (to find out) who was more deserving of the girl. On that day, Adam was absent, as he had gone to have a look at Mecca. God had said to Adam: Adam, do you know that I have a House on earth? Adam replied: Indeed, I do not. God said: I have a House in Mecca. So go there! Adam said to heaven: Guard my two children safely! But heaven refused. He addressed the earth (with the same request), but the earth refused. He addressed the mountains, and they also refused. He then spoke to Cain, who said: Yes! You shall go, and when you return, you will be happy with the state in which you will find your family. When Adam had left, Cain and Abel offered a sacrifice. Cain had always boasted of being better than Abel, saying: I am more deserving of her, because she is my sister, I am older than you, and I am the legatee *(waṣī)* of my father. For their sacrifices, Abel offered a fat young sheep, and Cain a sheaf of ears of corn. Finding a large ear, Cain husked and ate it. A fire came down from heaven. It consumed Abel's offering and left that of Cain. Whereupon Cain got angry and said: I shall kill you to prevent you from marrying my sister. Abel said: "God accepts only from those who fear Him. If you stretch out your hand to kill me, I shall not stretch out my hand to kill you" to: "And his soul suggested to him that he kill his brother."[865]

Cain now sought Abel in order to kill him, and young Abel tried

---

864. The "vice versa" statement is not found in the Leiden edition. The Cairo edition does not make it clear whether it derived it from *Tafsīr*, XXII, 40 *(ad* Qur. 33:72) or found it in the manuscripts of the *History*. The entire tradition appears in the cited passage of *Tafsīr*.

865. Qur. 5:27–30.

to escape from him on the mountain tops. But one day, Cain came upon him while he was herding his small cattle on a mountain and was asleep. He lifted a big rock and crushed Abel's head with it. So he died. Cain let him lie naked, not knowing about burials. God then sent two ravens that were brothers, and they fought with one another. When the one killed the other, it dug a hole for it and covered it with soil. When Cain saw that, he said: "Woe to me! Am I incapable of being like that raven, so as to conceal the secret parts of my brother?"[866] This is (meant by) God's word: "And God sent a raven to scratch a hole in the earth in order to show him [139]
how to conceal the secret parts of his brother...."[867] When Adam returned, he found that his son had killed his brother.

This story is (to be considered the explanation of) God's word where He says: "We have offered the (task of) safekeeping to the heavens and the earth and the mountains" to the end of the verse: "(Man) is unjust and ignorant"—meaning Cain when he took on the (task of) safekeeping for Adam and then did not guard his family.[868]

Others said: The reason for (Cain killing Abel) was that Eve bore two children to Adam in each pregnancy, one male and one female. When the male child reached puberty, Adam married him to the female child that had been born together with a brother of his in an earlier or later pregnancy. Cain, however, desired his twin sister and did not want Abel to have her, as I was told by al-Qāsim b. al-Ḥasan—al-Ḥusayn (b. Dāwūd)—Ḥajjāj—Ibn Jurayj—'Abdallāh b. 'Uthmān b. Khuthaym[869] : I went with Sa'īd b. Jubayr to do the (ritual) throwing of pebbles (at Minā). He was veiled and leaning on my arm. When we faced the mansion of Samurah al-Ṣawwāf[870] , he stopped and told me on the authority of Ibn 'Abbās: A woman was forbidden to marry her twin brother, and another

866. Qur. 5:31. The English translators of the Qur'ān paraphrase "secret (privy) parts" as vile body or naked corpse.

867. This precedes the just quoted statement of Qur. 5:31.

868. Qur. 33:72. The entire tradition appears in *Tafsīr,* XXII, 40 f., in connection with this verse. See above, n. 864, and *Tafsīr,* VI, 121 f. and 126 (*ad* Qur. 5:27 and 30).

869. The entry on 'Abdallāh b. 'Uthmān b. Khuthaym, who is supposed to have died about 754, in *Tahdhīb,* V, 314 f., is a particularly instructive example of the way in which dates of death were reconstructed through scholarly reasoning.

870. There may be a link between him and the Banū Ṣūfah mentioned in connection with Thabīr in Yāqūt, *Mu'jam,* I, 918(?).

of her brothers used to marry her. In each pregnancy, a man and a woman used to be born. (It happened that) a handsome woman was born, and an ugly woman was born. The brother of the ugly woman said (to the brother of the beautiful woman): Let me marry your sister, and I shall marry my sister to you. (The other brother) said: No! I am more deserving of my sister. So they offered a sacrifice. That of the one with the ram was accepted, while that of the farmer was not. So (the latter) killed (the former). That ram remained in custody with God until He let it go as Isaac's ransom. He slaughtered it upon this rock on Thabīr[871] at the mansion of Samurah al-Ṣawwāf, which is at your right hand when you throw the pebbles.[872]

According to Ibn Ḥumayd—Salamah—Muḥammad b. Isḥāq—
[140] some scholar(s) from the people of the first Book: Adam had intercourse with Eve before he committed the sin (of eating from the forbidden tree). She bore him his son Cain and Cain's twin sister. She had no craving or illness (when she was pregnant) with them nor pain in giving birth to them. She also saw no blood in connection with them because of the purity of Paradise. When, after committing disobedience by eating from the tree, Adam and Eve fell down to earth and felt secure there, Adam had intercourse with Eve, and she became pregnant with Abel and his twin sister. She had cravings and illness when she was pregnant with them, and pain in giving birth to them, and she saw blood in connection with them. Eve reportedly used to carry only twins, one male and one female, and in twenty pregnancies, she bore from Adam's loin forty children, male and female. Each man among them would marry any sister of his that he wanted, except his own twin sister that was born together with him; she was not permitted to marry him. Men could marry sisters at that time, because there were no women except their sisters and their mother, Eve.

According to Ibn Ḥumayd—Salamah—Muḥammad b. Isḥāq—some scholar(s) knowledgeable in the first Book[873] : Adam ordered his son Cain to marry his twin sister to Abel, and he ordered Abel

871. One of the hills of Mecca near Minā. For the rites associated with it, see *EI*², III, 32b, s. v. ḥadjdj.

872. See *Tafsīr*, VI, 126 (*ad* Qur. 5:30).

873. This follows the reading *bi-al-kitāb* adopted in the Cairo edition from *Tafsīr* (see n. 874). The reading of the manuscripts (*'an*) means: some scholar(s) on the authority of the first Book.

to marry his twin sister to Cain. Abel was pleased and agreed, but Cain refused, disliking (the idea), because he considered himself too good for Abel's sister. He desired his (own) sister and did not want Abel to have her. He said: We were born in Paradise, and they were born on earth. I am more deserving of my sister—Some scholar(s) of the people of the first Book say(s): Rather, the sister of Cain was one of the most beautiful human beings, and Cain begrudged her to his brother and wanted her for himself. God knows best what it was!—His father now said to him: Son, she is not permitted to you. Cain, however, refused to accept his father's word. So his father said to him: Then, son, offer a sacrifice, and let your [141] brother Abel offer one! The one whose offering is accepted by God deserves her the most. Cain was in charge of sowing, and Abel was in charge of shepherding. Cain therefore offered flour, while Abel offered some first-born sheep—Some say: He offered a cow—God sent down a white fire which consumed Abel's offering, leaving that of Cain.[874]

In this way, the acceptance of an offering to God used to be indicated. When God accepted Abel's offering, indicating the decision that Cain's sister was meant for Abel, Cain became angry. Haughtiness got the better of him, and Satan gained mastery over him. He followed his brother Abel who was with his herd, and killed him. The story of Cain and Abel was told by God to Muḥammad in the Qur'ān, saying: "And recite to them"—meaning the people of the Book—"the story of the two sons of Adam truthfully! They offered a sacrifice, and it was accepted for one of them" to the end of the story.[875]

He continued: When Cain had killed Abel, he was perplexed as he did not know how to conceal him, for this supposedly was the first killing among the children of Adam. "And God sent a raven to scratch a hole in the earth in order to show him how to conceal the secret parts of his brother. He said: Woe to me! Am I incapable of being like that raven, so as to conceal the secret parts of my brother?" to: "then many of them thereafter commit excesses on earth".[876]

874. See *Tafsīr*, VI, 121 (*ad* Qur. 5:27). For Cain's desire to marry his own twin sister, see *Schatzhöhle*, text, 34, trans., 8.

875. Qur. 5:27.

876. Qur. 5:31 f.

He continued: The people of the Torah[877] suppose that when Cain killed his brother Abel, God said to him: Where is your brother Abel? Cain replied: I do not know. I was not his keeper.[878] Whereupon God said to him: The voice of the blood of your brother calls out to Me from the earth. Now you are cursed from the earth which opened its mouth to accept the blood of your
[142] brother from your hand. If you work the earth, it will not again give you its produce,[879] and eventually, you will be an errant fugitive[880] on earth. Cain said: My sin is too great for You to forgive. Today, You have driven me from the face of the earth (and I shall keep concealed)[881] from before You and be an errant fugitive on earth. Everybody who meets me will kill me. God said: This is not so.[882] He who kills someone shall not be requited sevenfold, but he who kills Cain will be requited seven(fold). God put a sign upon Cain so that those who found him would not kill him, and Cain left from before God (and settled)[883] east of the Garden of Eden.[884]

Others have said concerning this subject: The one of them killed his brother because God commanded them to offer a sacrifice. The offering of one of them was accepted, but that of the other was not.

---

877. What follows is one of the rare instances of a quite literal translation from the Bible (Genesis 4:9–16). It is based not on the Hebrew Bible but on one of the early translations, most likely one into Aramaic/Syriac.

878. It would be possible to translate "am," but it was apparently understood to have reference to the time of the killing. The Biblical question is turned into a statement. This may be the result of an Aramaic original.

879. Arabic *ḥarth.* Hebrew "strength" was naturally understood this way, see, for instance, Targum Neofiti, I, 22 f. or Targum Pseudo-Jonathan *ad* Genesis 4:12. This explanation was so self-evident that it usually was not commented on.

880. *Fazi' tā'ih.* The first word includes the connotations of anxiety and flight.

881. The omission of the words in parentheses makes no sense and appears to be an oversight on the part of Ṭabarī. As mentioned in the Cairo edition, *Tafsīr,* VI, 128, has the correct text.

882. Hebrew *lkn* ("therefore") was interpreted in the relevant translations as *lō kēn* ("not so") (See also Speiser, *Genesis, ad* 4:15). This was taken to mean that the sevenfold vengeance applied only to the case of Cain. According to Aphrem, only Cain will be requited (and tortured) sevenfold, whereas later killers will be killed right away. See *Ephraem Syri in Genesim,* text, 51, trans., 39. Cf. also Ibn al-Ṭayyib, *Commentaire sur la Genèse,* text, 43, trans., 41. In the quoted edition of *Tafsīr,* the text is corrupt.

883. The omission of the verb, resulting in placing this scene east of the Garden of Eden, also occurs in *Tafsīr* and no doubt always existed in the Arabic translation of Genesis 4:16. See also the tradition in text below, I, 161.

884. See *Tafsīr,* VI, 128 *(ad* Qur. 5:31).

The latter loathed the other and killed him.

Those who said this

According to Ibn Bashshār—Muḥammad b. Ja'far—'Awf—Abū al-Mughīrah[885] —'Abdallāh b. 'Amr: Of the two sons of Adam who offered a sacrifice to God, of which one was accepted but not the other, one was a farmer, and the other the owner of small cattle. Both were commanded to offer a sacrifice. The owner of small cattle offered the noblest, fattest, and best of his small cattle, which he was fond of, while the farmer offered the worst of his agricultural produce, weeds and tares which he did not like. God accepted the sacrifice of the owner of small cattle but did not accept the sacrifice of the farmer. Their story has been told by God in His Book, saying: By God! The one killed was the stronger of the two, but the desire to avoid sin prevented him from proceeding[886] against [143]
his brother.

Others said what I was told by Muḥammad b. Sa'd—his father—his paternal uncle—his father—his father—Ibn 'Abbās: In connection with the affair of Cain and Abel, (it should be kept in mind that) there were no indigents to be given charity (from the sacrifice). Sacrifices were simply offered. While the sons of Adam were sitting (at leisure some day), they said: We should offer a sacrifice. When someone offered a sacrifice pleasing to God, God sent a fire to consume it. If it was not pleasing to Him, the fire went out. So they offered a sacrifice. One of them was a shepherd, and the other a farmer. The shepherd offered the best and fattest of his animals, while the other offered some of[887] his agricultural produce. The fire came down and consumed the sheep but left the agricultural produce. Adam's (one) son said to his brother: Should you (be allowed to) walk among men who have come to know that you offered a sacrifice that was accepted, while my sacrifice was rejected? Indeed not! The people must not look at me and at you (and think of) you as being better than I. And he said: "I shall kill you." His brother countered: What is my sin? "God accepts only

885. This Abū al-Mughīrah is listed in Bukhārī, *Kunā*, 70, no. 652, with no more information than provided by the chain of transmitters here.

886. The text in *Tafsīr*, VI, 120 (*ad* Qur. 5:27) has "stretching out his hand." This may be the meaning intended here.

887. *Tafsīr*, in quoting this tradition, has "the most odious of" *(abghaḍ)*. A pejorative adjective is needed and commonly found in other versions, but one or two also do not qualify the agricultural produce offered by Cain.

from those who fear Him."[888]

Others said: The story of those two men did not take place in Adam's time, and the sacrifice was not offered in his age. They said: The two belonged to the children of Israel. They added: The first person to die on earth was Adam. No one died before him.[889]

Those who said this

According to Sufyān b. Wakī'—Sahl b. Yūsuf[890] —'Amr—al-Ḥasan: The two men mentioned in God's word in the Qur'ān: "And recite to them the story of the two sons of Adam truthfully!"[891] belonged to the children of Israel. They were not sons from the loin of Adam. The sacrifice took place among the
[144] children of Israel. Adam was the first man to die.[892]

Some of them said: Adam had sexual intercourse with Eve one hundred years after their fall to earth. She bore him Cain and his twin sister Qalīmā[893] in one pregnancy, and then Abel and his sister in another. When they reached early manhood, Adam wanted to marry Cain's twin sister to Abel, but Cain refused. For this reason, the two offered a sacrifice. Abel's sacrifice was accepted, while that of Cain was not. Cain thus envied Abel and killed him on the mountain slope of Ḥirā'. He then descended from the mountain holding his sister Qalīmā by the hand and fled with her to 'Adan in the Yemen.[894]

According to al-Ḥārith (b. Muḥammad)—Ibn Sa'd—Hishām—his father—Abū Ṣāliḥ—Ibn 'Abbās: When Cain killed his brother Abel, he took his sister by the hand and brought her down to the

888. See *Tafsīr,* VI, 120 *(ad* Qur. 5:27).

889. See *Schatzhöhle,* text, 40, trans., 9. This helps to explain why Ṭabarī rejected the report later on (text below, I, 145 and 151) quite vehemently.

890. The index of the Ṭabarī editions appears to assume that he is identical with Sahl b. Yūsuf al-Sulamī who, however, was an authority of Sayf b. 'Umar. Thus at least two links in the chain would be missing between Sufyān and Sahl. If there is such an omission, 'Amr could be 'Amr b. Shu'ayb (d. 118/736), and al-Ḥasan, of course, al-Ḥasan al-Baṣrī. On the other hand, there was a Sahl b. Yūsuf al-Anmāṭī, who is supposed to have died in or after 190/805[6] (*Tahdhīb,* IV, 259 f.) and who might have been an authority of Sufyān b. Wakī'. In any case, the *isnād* would seem faulty.

891. Qur. 5:27.

892. See *Tafsīr,* VI, 122 *(ad* Qur. 5:27).

893. The name also appears in the form Iqlīmā. In *Schatzhöhle,* text, 34, trans., 8, it is Qlīmath. See also below, n. 903.

894. The name of the town of Aden in South Arabia and the identical Biblical Eden suggested the Yemenite location here.

foot of Mount Nūdh. Adam said to Cain: Go away! You will always be afraid and not safe from anyone you see. Everyone of (Cain's) children who passed by him shot at him. A blind son of Cain's came accompanied by one of his sons, who said to him: This is your father Cain. The blind man shot at his father Cain and killed him. The son of the blind man exclaimed: Oh, father! You have killed your father, whereupon the blind man raised his hand and slapped his son, and the son died. The blind man exclaimed: I have killed my father with a shot, and my son with a slap (of my hand).[895]

It has been mentioned in the Torah that Abel was twenty years old when he was killed, and Cain twenty-five when he killed Abel.

In our opinion, the sound statement is that the one of the two sons of Adam mentioned by God in His Book as having killed his brother is a son of Adam's loin, because proof has been transmitted that this is so:

According to Hannād b. al-Sarī—both Abū Mu'āwiyah and Wakī'—al-A'mash—'Abdallāh b. Murrah[896] —Masrūq[897] —'Abdallāh (b. Mas'ūd)—the Prophet. Also Ibn Ḥumayd—Jarīr (—al-A'mash, etc.). Also Ibn Wakī'—Jarīr and Abū Mu'āwiyah—al-A'mash (etc.): Adam's first son shares in the responsibility for every soul that is wrongfully killed. That is because he was the first to institute killing.[898] [145]

We were told about the same by Ibn Bashshār—'Abd al-Raḥmān b. Mahdī—Sufyān—al-A'mash—'Abdallāh b. Murrah—Masrūq—'Abdallāh (b. Mas'ūd)—the Prophet. Also Ibn Wakī'—his father (etc.)

This report from the Messenger of God makes clear the soundness of the statement that the two sons of Adam, whose story is told by God in His Book, were children of Adam's loin, because

---

895. In *Schatzhöhle*, text, 48–50, trans., 11 f., it is Lamech, the descendant of Cain (Genesis 4:18), who is the killer. The legend explains Lamech's verses in Genesis 4:28. For a comparison of the version in the *Schatzhöhle* with one of Aphrem, see Klijn, *Seth in Jewish, Christian and Gnostic Literature*, 69 and 73 f.

896. Died during the caliphate of 'Umar b. 'Abd al-'Azīz in 99 or 100/717–19. See *Tahdhīb*, VI, 24 f.

897. Masrūq b. al-Ajda' died in 62 or 63/681–83, at the age of sixty-three. See *Tahdhīb*, X, 109–11.

898. For this and the following paragraphs, see *Tafsīr*, VI, 125 *(ad* Qur. 5:29). See also *Concordance*, IV, 83b59–62, VI, 45a7–9; Ibn Ḥajar, *Fatḥ*, XV, 209 f. (where Ṭabarī is quoted), III, 394, VII, 179, and XVII, 65 f.

there can be no doubt that if they had been children of Israel, as transmitted on the authority of al-Ḥasan, the one of them described as having killed his brother would not have been the first to institute killing, since killing took place among the children of Adam before Israel and his children existed.

Someone might say: What is your proof that the two were children of Adam's loin and were not children of Israel? The reply would be: There is no disagreement about this among the early scholars of our nation, since the statement that they were children of Israel is corrupt (and thus can be disregarded).

It has been mentioned that when Cain killed his brother Abel, Adam mourned Abel, as we were told by Ibn Ḥumayd—Salamah—Ghiyāth b. Ibrāhīm[899] —Abū Isḥāq ('Amr b. 'Abdallāh) al-Hamdānī—'Alī b. Abī Ṭālib, may God ennoble his face!: When
[146] Adam's son killed his brother, Adam mourned the latter, saying:

The land and those upon it have changed.
The face of the earth is now ugly and dusty.
Everything tasty and colorful has changed.
The cheerfulness of a handsome face has become rare.

He continued. Adam received this reply:

Father of Abel! Both have been killed.
The one alive has become like the one slaughtered and dead.[900]
He brought evil of which he was
afraid. He brought it shouting.[901]

It has been mentioned that Eve bore Adam children in one hundred and twenty pregnancies. The first children were Cain and his twin sister Qalīmā, and the last 'Abd al-Mughīth and his twin sister Amat al-Mughīth.

---

899. Ghiyāth, whose reliability as a transmitter was greatly suspect, lived during the caliphate of al-Mahdī. See *TB*, XII, 323–27; Bukhārī, *Ta'rīkh*, IV,1, 109; Ibn Abī Ḥātim, III,2, 57; Ibn Ḥajar, *Lisān*, IV, 422. *Tafsīr*, VI, 122 (*ad* Qur. 5:27) does not give the name (at least in the edition used here).

900. Another reading is *bi-al-mawt/mayt:* "become through that death (dead one) the one slaughtered."

901. See *Tafsīr*, VI, 122 (*ad* Qur. 5:27). For the first three verses, cf. Mas'ūdi, *Murūj*, I, 65 (I, 39 Pellat); Rosenthal, *Sweeter than Hope*, 29, n. 121. The reply is supposed to have come from Iblīs.

As far as Ibn Isḥāq is concerned, it has been mentioned on his authority, as I have mentioned earlier,[902] that the total number of children born to Adam by Eve was forty; that is, male and female children born in twenty pregnancies. He added: We have the names of some of them, but not of others.

According to Ibn Ḥumayd—Salamah—Ibn Isḥāq: We have the names of fifteen men and four women, among them Cain and his twin sister, Abel, (Abel's twin sister) Labūdhā,[903] Adam's daughter Ashūth[904] and her twin brother, Seth and his twin sister,[905] Ḥazūrah and her twin brother, (born) when (Adam) was one hundred and thirty years old, Adam's son Ayād and his twin sister, Adam's son Bālagh and his twin sister, Adam's son Athātī and his twin sister, Adam's son Tawbah and his twin sister, Adam's son Banān and his twin sister, Adam's son Shabūbah and his twin sister, Adam's son Ḥayān and his twin sister, Adam's son Ḍarābīs and his twin sister, Adam's son Hadaz and his twin sister, Adam's son Yaḥūd and his twin sister, Adam's son Sandal and his twin [147] sister, and Adam's son Bāraq and his twin sister—every male of them born together with a female as twins.

902. Text above, I, 140.

903. Labūdhā is the form of the name as it appears in *Schatzhöhle*, text, 34, trans., 8, We have no way of knowing whether Ṭabarī himself thought it was Labūdhā or Layūdhā. For this name and some of the non-Biblical names mentioned later, reference was made to *Schatzhöhle* and Jubilees by Lidzbarski, *De propheticis...legendis*, 11 f. See also N. A. Stillman, "The Story of Cain and Abel," in *Journal of Semitic Studies* 19 (1974): 231–39.

Counting the name of Cain's sister not mentioned presumably because it was well known (above, n. 893), we have here indeed four females mentioned by name and fifteen males. The passage was no doubt quoted by Ṭabarī from Ibn Isḥāq's *Mubtada'*. Other authors were apparently suspicious and did not quote it. There were other lists, as, for instance, in Ibn Hishām, *Tījān*, 15. See also text below, I, 149.

In Ya'qūbī, *Ta'rīkh*, I, 4, Lūbadhā is the twin sister of Cain, and Iqlīmā that of Abel. See also Mas'ūdī, *Murūj*, I, 62; Tha'labī, *Qiṣaṣ*, 43.

All these names whose vocalization is not known to us have been vocalized here simply by supplying the vowel a. This has been done even where the names look suspiciously like Arabic names.

904. Said to be Cain's wife in text below, I, 167.

905. See text below, I, 152 f., where it is said first that Seth was born without a twin, and then that his twin was named 'Azūrā or Ḥazūrā, identical, no doubt, with Ḥazūrah mentioned here. It is also stated that it was Seth who was born when Adam had reached the age of one hundred and thirty (see also text below, I, 164). In the apocryphal literature, Seth's sister is repeatedly called 'Azūrā/Ḥazūrā. See Jubilees, IV, 8, and p. 30, note to IV, 1, in Charles' translation.

Most Persian scholars assume that Jayūmart is Adam.[906] Some assume that Jayūmart is the son of Adam's loins by Eve. Others have made many (diverse) statements on Jayūmart. It would make this book of ours too long to mention them (all). We have omitted reference to them, since our intention here is to mention the kings and their days and what we have made it a condition to mention in this book of ours.[907] The discussion of the different views on the pedigree of a given king is not the kind of subject for which we have undertaken the composition of the book. If we do mention something of the sort, it is to identify someone mentioned by us for those unacquainted with him. (I repeat:) The discussion of differing opinions on (a person's) pedigree is not something intended in this book of ours.

The statements of the Persian scholars on this subject have been disputed by other, non-Persian scholars who assume that he is (not ?) Adam. They agree with the Persian scholars as to his name but disagree with them[908] as to his personal identity *('ayn)* and description. They assume that the Jayūmart whom the Persians assume to be Adam is Gomer b. Japheth b. Noah.[909] He was a long-lived lord who settled on the mountain of Dunbāwand[910] of the Ṭabaristān mountains in the East and ruled there and in Fārs. His power grew, and he commanded his children to take control of Bābil. For various (brief) periods, they ruled over all the zones (of the earth). Jayūmart protected all the places to which he got (?). He built for himself cities and castles and populated them and made them prosperous. He also assembled weapons and established a cavalry. At the end of his life, he became a tyrant. He took the name of Adam and said: If someone calls me by any
[148] other name, I shall cut off his hand. He married thirty women who

906. See text above, I, 17 f., and below, I, 154. This and the following paragraphs were translated by Christensen, I, 67 f.

907. See text above, I, 6 f.

908. Read *khālafahum* or *khālafahā*. See Ṭabarī, *Introductio etc.*, DLXXVII.

909. See above, n. 153.

910. See EI^2, II, 106 f., s. v. Damāwand; Eilers, "Der Name Demawend." The vowel *u* in the first syllable is that prescribed by Yāqūt, *Mu'jam*, II, 606, but Ṭabarī might have used Danbāwand.

gave him many offspring. His son Mārī and daughter Māriyānah[911] were among those born at the end of his life. He liked them and promoted them, so that the (later) kings were their offspring. His realm expanded greatly.

I mention this information about Jayūmart in this place only because none of the scholars of the (various) nations disputes that Jayūmart is the father of the non-Arab Persians. They differ with respect to him only as to whether he is Adam, the father of mankind, as stated by those mentioned by us, or somebody else. In addition, (I refer to Jayūmart) because his rule and that of his children continued in the East and the mountains there uninterrupted in an orderly fashion, until Yazdjard b. Shahriyār, one of his descendants—May God curse him!—was killed in Marw in the days of ʿUthmān b. ʿAffān.[912] The history (or chronology) of the world's bygone years is more easily explained and more clearly seen based upon the lives of the Persian kings than upon those of the kings of any other nation. For no nation but theirs among those leading their pedigree back to Adam is known whose realm lasted and whose rule was continuous. No other nation had kings ruling all (their subjects) and chiefs protecting them against their adversaries, helping them to obtain the upper hand over their competitors, defending those wronged among them against those who did them wrong, and creating for them fortunate conditions that were continuous, lasting, and orderly, inherited by later generations from earlier ones. Thus, a history based upon the lives of the Persian kings has the soundest sources and the best and clearest data.

God willing, and there is no might and strength except in Him, I shall mention the information we have received about the lives of Adam and his descendants after him who succeeded him in prophethood and royal authority, both according to those who oppose the statement of the Persians who assume that he is [149] Jayūmart,and according to those who say that he is Jayūmart, the father of the Persians. And I shall discuss the history of the (Per-

911. These names are explainable as linguistic variants of those given in text below, I, 154. See Justi, *Iranisches Namenbuch,* 198 f. (under Maschyo); Christensen, I, 9 f.

912. On the death of the last Sassanian emperor Yazdjard in 31/651[2], see text below, I, 2872 ff.

sian kings), from differences expressed to unanimity achieved that someone who they agree ruled at a specific time was indeed the ruler at that time. I shall then continue in this manner down to this time of ours.

Let us now return (to our narrative) and provide further clarification concerning the error of those who said that the first to die on earth was Adam, and who denied that the two whose story is told by God in His word: "And recite to them the story of the two sons of Adam truthfully! They offered a sacrifice, "[913] came, as shown by this verse, from Adam's loin.

According to Muḥammad b. Bashshār—ʿAbd al-Ṣamad b. ʿAbd al-Wārith—ʿUmar b. Ibrāhīm[914] —Qatādah—al-Ḥasan—Samurah b. Jundub[915] —the Prophet: None of Eve's children survived. Therefore, she vowed that if one of her children were to survive, she would call him ʿAbd al-Ḥārith.[916] When a child of hers survived, she called him ʿAbd al-Ḥārith. That was due to Satan's inspiration.[917]

According to Ibn Ḥumayd—Salamah—Ibn Isḥāq—Dāwūd b. al-Ḥuṣayn[918] —ʿIkrimah—Ibn ʿAbbās: Eve would give birth to Adam's children and make them worship God, calling them ʿAbdallāh, ʿUbaydallāh ("Servant, or little Servant of God"), and the like. But then they would die. Now, Iblīs came to her and to Adam and said: Were you to give them other names, they would survive. So, when she gave birth to a male child for Adam, they called him ʿAbd al-Ḥārith. In this connection, God revealed His word: "It is

913. Qur. 5:27.

914. See *Tahdhīb*, VII, 425 f.

915. For Samurah b. Jundub, who died in 58 or 59/677–79, see *Tahdhīb*, IV, 236 f.; Ibn ʿAbd al-Barr, *Istīʿāb*, II, 653–55.

916. Al-Ḥārith, as explained in these traditions, was the original name of Iblīs. By naming the child "Servant of al-Ḥārith (Iblīs)," instead of "Servant of God," Adam and Eve associated Satan with God; they were thus exposed to the accusation of having introduced polytheism. Satan's opportunity came because during her first pregnancy, Eve was totally ignorant of the process of human reproduction and feared that she might produce a nonhuman animal. It was God's doing that the child was born without any defects, even if Satan tried to claim credit for it.

917. See *Tafsīr*, IX, 99 (*ad* Qur. 7:190).

918. Died in 135/752[3]. See *Tahdhīb*, III, 181 f.

He Who created you from a single soul" to "the two set up for Him associates in connection with what He had given them" to the end of the verse.[919]

According to Ibn Wakī' —Ibn Fuḍayl—Sālim b. Abī Ḥafṣah[920] —Sa'īd b. Jubayr, commenting on (the same verse): "When she became heavy (with child), they called on God, their Lord" to "And God is above your associating (others with Him)," as follows: When Eve became heavy with her first pregnancy, Satan came to her before she gave birth, and said: Eve, what is that in your womb? She said: I do not know. He asked: Where will it come out, from your nose, your eye, or your ear? She again replied: I do not know. He said: Don't you think, if it comes out healthy, you should obey me in whatever I command you? When she said: Yes, he said: Call him 'Abd al-Ḥārith! Iblīs—May God curse him!—was called al-Ḥārith. She agreed. Afterwards, she said to Adam: Someone came to me in my sleep and told me such-and such. Adam said: That is Satan. Beware of him, for he is our enemy who drove us out of Paradise. Then Iblīs—May God curse him!—came to her again and repeated what he had said before, and she agreed. When she gave birth to the child, God brought him out healthy. Yet, she called him 'Abd al-Ḥārith. This is (meant by) God's word: "They set up for Him associates in connection with what he had given them" to "And God is above your associating (others with Him)."[921] [150]

According to Ibn Wakī'—Jarīr and Ibn Fuḍayl—'Abd al-Malik[922] —Sa'īd b. Jubayr: When (Sa'īd) was asked whether Adam associated (others with God), he replied: God forbid that I should assume Adam did that! However, when Eve was heavy with child, Iblīs came and said to her: Where will this one come out, from your nose, your eye, or your mouth? He thereby caused her to despair (because she did not know and was afraid of what was going to happen). Then he said: Don't you think that, when it comes out perfectly formed—Ibn Wakī' said that Ibn Fuḍayl added: without harming or killing you—you should obey me? When she agreed, he said: Call him 'Abd al-Ḥārith, and she did. Jarīr added: So Adam's

919. Qur. 7:189 f. See *Tafsīr*, IX, 99 (*ad* Qur. 7:190).
920. Died about 140/757[8]. See *Tahdhīb*, III, 433 f.
921. See *Tafsīr*, IX, 100 (*ad* Qur. 7:190).
922. 'Abd al-Malik b. Abī Sulaymān died in 145/763. See *Tahdhīb*, VI, 396–98.

associating (others with God) was only in the name.[923]

[151] According to Mūsā b. Hārūn—'Amr b. Ḥammād—Asbāṭ—al-Suddī: So she—meaning Eve—gave birth to a boy. Iblīs came to her and said: Call (pl.) him my servant (*'abdī*)! If you don't, I shall kill him. Adam said to him: I obeyed you (once before), and you caused me to be driven out of Paradise. So he refused to obey him and called the child 'Abd al-Raḥmān "Servant of the Merciful One." Satan—May God curse him!—gained power over the boy and killed him. Eve bore another child, and when she gave birth to it, Satan said: Call him my servant! If you don't, I shall kill him. Adam said to him (again): I obeyed you (once before), and you caused me to be driven out of Paradise. So he refused and called the boy Ṣāliḥ,[924] and Satan killed him. The third time around, Iblīs said to Adam and Eve: If you (pl., want to) overcome me, call him 'Abd al-Ḥārith! Iblīs' name was al-Ḥārith. He was called Iblīs when he was bedeviled (*ublisa*)—became confused.[925] This (is meant by God's word) where He says: "They set up for him associates in connection with what He had given them"—meaning in connection with the names.[926]

Those who, as I have mentioned, have transmitted (reports) that some children of Adam and Eve died before them, and the even more numerous transmitters and statements not mentioned by us, contradict the statement of al-Ḥasan transmitted on his authority that the first person to die was Adam.[927]

In addition to giving Adam royal authority and rulership on earth, God made him a prophet and a messenger to his children. He revealed to Adam twenty-one scrolls. Adam was taught them by Gabriel and wrote them down with his own hand.

According to Aḥmad b. 'Abd al-Raḥmān b. Wahb—his paternal uncle[928]—al-Māḍī b. Muḥammad[929]—Abū Sulaymān[930]—al-

923. See *Tafsīr*, IX, 100 (*ad* Qur. 7:190).

924. The choice of the name results from the use of the adjective *ṣāliḥan* in Qur. 7:190.

925. See above, n. 617.

926. See *Tafsīr*, IX, 100 (*ad* Qur. 7:190). *Tafsīr* reads "giving a name."

927. See above, n. 889.

928. See above, nn. 136 and 137.

929. Al-Māḍī died in 183/799. See *Tahdhīb*, X, 2 f.

930. For 'Alī b. Sulaymān (?), see *Tahdhīb*, 328 f. The *kunyah* Abū Sulaymān does not appear in *Tahdhīb*, but the chain of transmitters is identical.

Qāsim b. Muḥammad[931] —Abū Idrīs al-Khawlānī[932] —Abū Dharr [152] al-Ghifārī: I entered the mosque and found the Messenger of God sitting there by himself. When I joined him, he said to me: Abū Dharr, there is a greeting for a mosque. It consists of praying two *rak'ahs*. So, get up and perform them! When I had done so, I sat with him and said: O Messenger of God! You have commanded me to pray. But what is prayer? He replied: The best of subjects, whether there is much or little of it. Then (Abū Dharr) mentioned a long story in which he said: I asked the Messenger of God how many prophets there are. He replied: 124,000. He continued: I asked him how many of those were messengers. He replied: Three hundred and thirteen, a large crowd (*jamman ghafīran*)—meaning a good many. He continued. I asked the Messenger of God who the first of them was, and he replied: Adam. He continued. I asked him whether Adam was a prophet sent as a messenger. He replied: Yes, God created him with His own hand and blew some of His spirit into him. Then He immediately fashioned him in perfect shape.[933]

According to Ibn Ḥumayd—Salamah—Muḥammad b. Isḥāq —Ja'far b. al-Zubayr[934] —al-Qāsim b. 'Abd al-Raḥmān[935] —Abū Umāmah[936] —Abū Dharr: I said: O Prophet of God! Was Adam

931. On the basis of this chain of transmitters, he is given a separate, questionable entry in *Tahdhīb*, VIII, 336 f.

932. Born supposedly in 8/630, Abū Idrīs died in 80/699. See *Tahdhīb*, V, 85-87; *EI*², IV, 1135, s. v. al-Khawlānī.

933. *Qubulan* "in perfect shape" is usually translated "face to face" (above, n. 667, and the next tradition). See Ṭabarī, *Introductio etc.*, CDXI. For a related tradition of Abū Dharr with a different chain of transmitters, see Ibn Ḥanbal, V, 178, 179, and 266. On the number of messengers (315), see Muqātil, *Tafsīr*, on Qur. 42:51.

934. *Tahdhīb*, II, 90–92, mentions a certain Ja'far b. al-Zubayr as a transmitter of al-Qāsim b. 'Abd al-Raḥmān, but he died in the 140s/757–67 and thus was a contemporary of Ibn Isḥāq. Ja'far b. al-Zubayr b. al-'Awwām (*Tahdhīb*, II, 92), the youngest brother of 'Abdallāh b. al-Zubayr, would fit chronologically. However, his son Muḥammad b. Ja'far b. al-Zubayr b. al-'Awwām, who died in the 110s/728–37 (*Tahdhīb*, IX, 93; Horst, 303, n. 6), usually appears as the authority of Ibn Isḥāq. He was a contemporary of al-Qāsim who here appears as his authority.

935. Al-Qāsim b. 'Abd al-Raḥmān died in the 110s/730–36. See *Tahdhīb*, VIII, 322–24.

936. The identification with the companion of the Prophet, Abū Umāmah Ṣudayy b. 'Ajlān al-Bāhilī, seems supported by the addition of the *nisbah* al-Bāhilī in text below, I, 2108, which has, however, a different *isnād*. It does not seem certain that he is meant here. He died in 81 or 86/700–5 at the age of ninety-one. See *Tahdhīb*, IV, 420 f.; Khalīfah, *Ṭabaqāt*, 46 and 303; Bukhārī, *Ta'rīkh*, II,2, 327 f.; Ibn 'Abd al-Barr, *Istī'āb*, II, 736.

a prophet? He replied: Yes, he was, and God spoke to him face to face.

Among the things God reportedly revealed to Adam was the prohibition against eating dead animals, blood, and pork. He also revealed to him the letters of the alphabet on twenty-one leaves.

Eve Giving Birth to Seth

When one hundred and thirty years of Adam's life had passed—that is, five years after Cain had killed Abel—Eve gave birth to Adam's son Seth. The people of the Torah have mentioned that Seth was born without a twin. They explain Seth as "Gift of God," meaning that he was a replacement[937] for Abel.

[153] According to al-Ḥārith b. Muḥammad—Ibn Sa'd—Hishām—his father—Abū Ṣāliḥ—Ibn 'Abbās: Eve bore Adam Seth and his sister 'Azūrah.[938] He was called "Gift of God," (a name) derived from Abel.[939] When Eve gave birth to him, Gabriel said to her: This is God's gift in place of Abel. (Seth's name) is Shith[940] in Arabic, Shāth in Syriac, and Shīth in Hebrew. He was Adam's legatee. On the day Seth was born to him, Adam was one hundred and thirty years old.

According to Ibn Ḥumayd—Salamah—Muḥammad b. Isḥāq: Reportedly—God knows best!—when Adam was about to die, he called his son Seth and appointed him his heir. He taught him the hours of night and day and indicated to him how the creatures should worship in each hour. He informed him that each hour had its special kind of creatures to worship in it. Then he said to him: Son, the Flood will be on earth and last seven years. He wrote his last will addressed to him. Seth reportedly was the legatee of his father Adam, so after Adam's death, political leadership fell to him. According to a tradition on the authority of the Messenger

937. The similarity of the word *khalaf* in the meaning of "replacement" to Aramaic *ḥlāp̄* translating Hebrew *taḥat* (Genesis 4:25) is hardly coincidental. For data on Seth in Arabic literature. cf. the unpublished Yale dissertation (1968) of Theodore Gluck, *The Arabic legend of Seth, the Father of Mankind.*

938. See above, n. 905.

939. Hebrew Hebel "Abel" is etymologized as composed of the Aramaic root *(y)-h-b* "to give" and *el* "God."

940. With a short vowel. The short vowel may represent the Hebrew *e*. Long *ā* in Shāth may indicate long *ē* . Long *ī* in the "Hebrew" form (which, in fact, is the accepted Arabic form of the name) could represent *ay* to *ē* (?).

of God, God revealed fifty scrolls to Seth.

According to Aḥmad b. 'Abd al-Raḥmān b. Wahb—his paternal uncle—al-Māḍī b. Muḥammad—Abū Sulaymān—al-Qāsim b. Muḥammad—Abū Idrīs al-Khawlānī—Abū Dharr al-Ghifārī: I said: O Messenger of God! How many books did God reveal? He replied: One hundred and four. God revealed fifty scrolls to Seth.

All the children of Adam today trace their pedigree back to Seth. That is because the offspring of all the other children of Adam except those of Seth have completely disappeared, and not one of [154] them remains. Thus, the pedigrees of all people today go back to Seth.

The Persians who say that Jayūmart is Adam say: Born to Jayūmart was his son Mashī, who married his sister Mashyānah.[941] She bore him his son Siyāmak and his daughter Siyāmī. Born to Siyāmak b. Mashī b. Jayūmart were his sons Afrawāk, Dīs, Barāsb, Ajwab (Ajrab), and Awrāsh, and his daughters Afrī, Dadhī, Barī, and Awrāshī. The mother of all of them was Siyāmī, the daughter of Mashī, their father's sister.

The Persians mention that the entire earth consists of seven climes. The land of Bābil and the regions reachable by people who go there by land or sea constitute a single clime. Its inhabitants are the offspring of the children of Afrawāk b. Siyāmak and their descendants. The remaining six climes not reachable today by land or sea are (inhabited by) the offspring of all the other sons and daughters of Siyāmak.

Siyāmak's daughter Afrī bore her brother Afrawāk King

941. The first three paragraphs are translated in Christensen, I, 116, and the rest of the chapter in Christensen, I, 147 f. The forms Mashī and Mashyānah may be the ones intended by Ṭabarī. The text of the Cairo edition has Mīshī (Mīshā) and Mīshānah. Among Iranian scholars, we find Mashia and Mashiana (Justi), Mashyaγ and Mashyānaγ (Christensen, II, 167), or Masya and Masyani (Anklesaria). For the variant forms Mārī and Māriyānah, see above, n. 911. For Fravāk as the son of Siyāmak, see *Bundahishn*, ed. Justi, ch. 32, and ed. Anklesaria, ch. 14, pp. 132 f., and ch. 35, pp. 292 f. The vocalization and etymology of the other names is quite uncertain. See the listings in Justi. Christensen, I, 116 and 121, attempts no explanation for the names which are attested only in Ṭabarī. For Afrī as an element in nomenclature, one may tentatively compare Naveh and Shaked, *Amulets*, 146 ff.

Hōshank Pēshdādh. It was he who succeeded his grandfather Jayūmart as ruler, and he was the first to rule over all the climes. God willing, we shall mention his history when we get to it.[942] It is assumed by some(one) that this Ōshahanj was the son of Adam's loin by Eve.

Hishām al-Kalbī, on his part said, as I was told on his authority: We have heard—God knows best!—that the first king to rule the earth was Ōshahanj b. Eber b. Shelah b. Arpachshad b. Shem b. Noah.[943] He continued. The Persians claim him and assume that he lived two hundred years after Adam's death. He continued. As we have heard, this king lived two hundred years after Noah, but the people of Fārs had him living two hundred years after Adam,
[155] with no indication of what was before Noah.

Hishām's statement deserves no consideration, because among the experts in Persian genealogy, King Hōshank is more famous than al-Ḥajjāj b. Yūsuf is among the Muslims.[944] Every people is more familiar than others with their own forefathers, pedigrees, and accomplishments. With respect to every complex matter, one must have reference to those people who were (directly) involved.

Some Persian genealogist(s) assume(s) that this King Ōshahanj Pēshdād is Mahalalel, that his father, Frawāk, is Mahalalel's father Kenan, that Siyāmak is Kenan's father Enosh, that Mashī is Enosh's father Seth, and that Jayūmart is Adam.[945] If this is so, there can be no doubt that Ōshahanj was a man in the time of Adam. This is because, as mentioned in the first Book,[946] Mahalalel's mother Dīnah, the daughter of Barākīl b. Mehujael b. Enoch b. Cain b. Adam,[947] gave birth to him after 395 years of Adam's life had passed. Thus, when Adam died, Mahalalel was 605 years old,

942. Ṭabarī seems to refer to text below, I, 170 ff., unless he has a more general reference in mind (perhaps, to text below, I, 201 ff.).

943. See Genesis 10:21–24 and 11:10–14.

944. The reference to the famous Umayyad governor (see *EI*^{2}, III, 39–43, s. v. al-Ḥadjdjāj b. Yūsuf) seems a bit strange until one realizes that it would have been unsuitable in the context to compare a secular and rather tyrannical ruler with the ancient rulers of Islam.

945. For the Biblical figures, see Genesis 5:1–12.

946. If the sg. "Book" as in the Cairo edition has the proper support in the manuscript tradition, it may be preferable to the pl. "Books" (Scriptures) found in the Leiden text.

947. See Genesis 4:17 f. Dīnah and Barākīl are, of course, not found in Genesis, but they appear as, respectively, wife and father-in-law of Kenan's son Mahalalel in Jubilees 4:15. See text below, I, 165.

since according to a tradition on the authority of the Messenger of God concerning Adam's life, Adam lived a thousand years.

The Persian scholars have assumed that the rule of this Ōshahanj lasted forty years. If the genealogists' statement concerning this king just mentioned by us is as indicated, it is not impossible to say that he became ruler two hundred years after Adam's death.

Adam's Death

There are differences of opinion as to the duration of Adam's life and how old he was when God took him unto Himself.

The received reports on the authority of the Messenger of God indicate what I was told by Muḥammad b. Khalaf al-ʿAsqalānī—Ādam b. Abī Iyās—Abū Khālid Sulaymān b. [156] Ḥayyān—Muḥammad b. ʿAmr—Abū Salamah—Abū Hurayrah—the Prophet. Also Abū Khālid—al-Aʿmash—Abū Ṣāliḥ—Abū Hurayrah—the Prophet. Also Abū Khālid—Dāwūd b. Abī Hind—al-Shaʿbī—Abū Hurayrah—the Prophet. Also Abū Khālid—Ibn Abī Dhubāb al-Dawsī—Saʿīd al-Maqburī and Yazīd b. Hurmuz—Abū Hurayrah—the Prophet: God created Adam with His own hand and blew some of His spirit into him. He commanded the angels to prostrate themselves before Adam, and they did. Adam sat down, then sneezed and said: Praise be to God! His Lord said to him: May your Lord show mercy unto you! Go to that multitude of angels and say to them: Peace be upon you! He went and said to them: Peace be upon you! and they responded: And upon you be peace and the mercy of God! Adam then returned to his Lord who said to him: This is your greeting and the greeting for your progeny to use among themselves.[948]

Then God closed His hand and said to Adam: Pick and choose! Adam said: I choose the right of my Lord. Both His hands are right hands. God opened His hand for him, and behold, there was the picture of Adam and all his progeny, and there was the term of each man written down with God. For Adam, a life of a thousand years had been written down. There were people there crowned by light. When Adam asked his Lord who they were, God replied:

948. The same tradition appears up to this point in text above, I, 93 f.

They are the prophets and messengers whom I shall send to My servants. Among them, there is a man who is the most luminous of them. However, a life of only forty years was written down for him. Adam asked: O my Lord! Why is a life of only forty years written down for this most luminous man among them? God said: That is what was written down for him. So Adam said: O my Lord! Shorten my life by sixty years for him! Now, the Messenger of God
[157] said: When God had settled Adam in Paradise and then had cast him down to earth, Adam used to count his days. So, when the Angel of Death came to seize him, Adam said to him: You have come too early, Angel of Death. The Angel of Death replied: I did not. Adam said: Sixty years of my life still remain. The Angel of Death replied: Nothing remains of your life. You asked your Lord to write (those sixty years) down for your son David. Adam replied: I did not. The Messenger of God continued: Adam forgot, and so did his progeny. Adam denied it, and so did his progeny. On that day, God established written documents and commanded (the use of) witnesses.[949]

According to Ibn Sinān—Mūsā b. Ismā'īl—Ḥammād b. Salamah —'Alī b. Zayd—Yūsuf b. Mihrān—Ibn 'Abbās: When the verse of the debt[950] was revealed, the Messenger of God said: The first to deny (an obligation) three times was Adam. When God created him, he rubbed his back and brought forth from it whatever He was going to multiply *(dh-r-y/dh-r-')*[951] to the Day of Resurrection. When He started to present them to Adam, Adam saw among them a man who shone. He said: O my Lord! Which prophet is this? God replied: This is your son David. Adam said: O my Lord! How long is his life? God replied: Sixty years, whereupon Adam said: O my Lord! Give him a longer life! God said: No, unless you take some years of your life and add them to his. Now, Adam's life was one thousand years, and he gave David forty of it. God wrote this down in a document and had the angels witness it. When Adam was about to die and the angels came to him to seize his spirit, he said: Forty years of my life still remain. The angels said:

949. This story argues the need in legal matters for agreements made in writing and duly witnessed because of human forgetfulness and the human propensity to renege on obligations.

950. That is, Qur. 2:282.

951. See text above, I, 134.

You gave them to your son David. Adam said: No, I did not give him anything. Whereupon God had the document brought down and had the angels produced as witnesses against him. Adam lived a full thousand years (despite the years he had given away), and David lived a full hundred years.[952]

According to Muḥammad b. Saʿd—his father—his paternal uncle—his father—his father—Ibn ʿAbbās, commenting on: "And your Lord took from the backs of the children of Adam their progeny" to "They said: Yes. We (so) testify,"[953] as follows: When God created Adam, he rubbed his back and brought forth all his progeny in the shape of tiny ants. He gave them speech, and they talked. "He had them testify against themselves."[954] He had light shine forth from one of them. He said to Adam: They are your progeny with whom the covenant has been made that I am their Lord, lest they associate something with Me, and I am obligated to provide for their sustenance. Adam said: Who is the one with the light? and God replied: David. Adam said: O my Lord! How long a term have You written down for him? God replied: Sixty years. Adam said: How long a life have You written down for me? and God replied: One thousand years. For every one of your progeny, I have written down how long he will live. Adam said: O my Lord! Give David a longer life! God said: The book here is all done, but, if you wish, give him some years from your own life! Adam agreed, although the Pen was dry for all the other of Adam's children. Thus, (God) wrote down for David (an additional) forty years for Adam's sake. so that David's term was a hundred years. When Adam had lived 960 years, the Angel of Death came to him. When Adam saw him, he said: Why (have you come)? He replied: You have completed your term. Adam said: I have lived 960 years. Forty still remain. When he said this to the Angel, the Angel replied: I have the information from my Lord. Adam now said: Then go back to your Lord and ask Him! The Angel went back to his Lord, who asked him why (he had come back). The Angel said: O my Lord! I have come back to You because I know You hold Adam in such high esteem. God said: Go back and in- [158]

952. See Ibn Ḥanbal, I, 251 f., 298 f., 371.
953. Qur. 7:172.
954. Qur. 7:172.

form him that he gave forty years to his son David.[955]

According to Ibn Bashshār—Muḥammad b. Ja'far—Shu'bah—Abū Bishr—Sa'īd b. Jubayr, commenting on this verse: "And God took from the backs of the children of Adam their progeny and
[159] had them testify against themselves: Am I not your Lord?"[956] as follows: He brought them forth from Adam's back and gave Adam a life of one thousand years. He continued. When Adam's progeny was presented to him, he saw among them one endowed with light. He wondered about him and asked who he was. God replied: He is David. His life has been set at sixty years. Adam thereupon made over to him forty years of his own life. When Adam was about to die, he started to argue with (the angels) about the forty years. He was told that he had given them to David. (A variant reading) is: *and* he started to argue with (the angels about the forty years, he was told...).[957]

According to Ibn Ḥumayd—Ya'qūb (al-Qummī)—Ja'far (b. Abī al-Mughīrah)—Sa'īd (b. Jubayr), commenting on God's word: "And your Lord took from the backs of the children of Adam their progeny," as follows: He brought forth his progeny from his back looking like tiny ants and presented them to Adam with their names and those of their fathers and their terms. He continued. He presented to Adam the spirit of David in a sparkling light, and Adam asked who he was. God replied: He is one of your progeny, a prophet I have created. Adam said: How long is his life? and God replied: Sixty years. Adam said: Add forty years of my life to his! He continued. (That was when) the pens were still moist and proceeding to write. The (additional) forty were thus set down for David. Adam's life was one thousand years. When he completed them except for the forty years, the Angel of Death was sent to him. He said: Adam, I have been commanded to seize you, whereupon Adam said: Do I not have forty more years to live? He continued. The Angel of Death thereupon went back to his Lord and said: Adam claims he has forty (more) years to live, and God said: Inform him that he made them over to his son David, while the pens were still moist, so they were set down for David.[958]

---

955. See *Tafsīr*, IX, 78 (*ad* Qur. 7:172).
956. Qur. 7:172.
957. See *Tafsīr*, IX, 79 (*ad* Qur. 7:172); Ibn Khuzaymah, 67.
958. This tradition as well as the following *isnād* is found in *Tafsīr*, IX, 79 (*ad*

We were told about the same by Ibn Wakīʿ—Abū Dāwūd—Yaʿqūb—Jaʿfar—Saʿīd.

It has been mentioned that Adam was ill for eleven days before his death. He made his son Seth his legatee and wrote his last will. Then he handed the document containing his last will to [160] Seth and commanded him to keep it concealed from Cain and his children, because Cain had killed Abel out of envy. That was when Adam singled Abel out for (receiving God's) knowledge. Seth and his children kept concealed the knowledge they possessed, and Cain and his children did not have any knowledge they could use.

The people of the Torah assume that Adam lived 930 years.[959]

According to al-Ḥārith—Ibn Saʿd—Hishām b. Muḥammad—his father—Abū Ṣāliḥ—Ibn ʿAbbās: Adam lived 936 years.[960] God knows best!

The reports received on the authority of the Messenger of God and our early scholars are as I have mentioned. The Messenger of God is the human being who knows best about it.

The reports received on his authority mention him as saying: Adam lived one thousand years, even after he made over those additional years from his own life to his son David. For God gave Adam the full number of years He had (originally) given him, before Adam gave David those (forty years). Perhaps, the years that Adam made over to David were not included in Adam's life in the Torah. So it was said that he lived 930 years.

Someone might say: Even if this so (that the Torah did not count those years), and Adam made over forty years of his life to his son David, it should be 960 years in the Torah, in order to be in agreement with the reports received on the authority of the Messenger of God. The reply would be: In connection with this subject, we have the tradition of the Messenger of God transmitted by us that it was sixty years of his own life that Adam made over to his son David—this is according to Abū Hurayrah's tradition on the Prophet's authority mentioned by us earlier.[961] If this is so, the [161] assumption made in the Torah about the duration of Adam's life

Qur. 7:172).

959. See Genesis 5:5.

960. Following Wahb b. Munabbih, Ibn Hishām, *Tījān*, 19, mentions 930 years in the text, but the manuscripts seem to have 937 (927).

961. See text above, I, 156 f. The discussion indicates serious concern with a Biblical statement, even if it does not quite work out.

agrees with what we have transmitted in this connection on the authority of the Messenger of God.

According to Ibn Ḥumayd—Salamah—Ibn Isḥāq: After writing his last will, Adam died. The angels assembled at his (place), because he was the chosen friend *(ṣafī)* of the Merciful One, and buried him. Seth and his brothers were in the regions east of Paradise at a village that was the first on earth. The sun and the moon were in eclipse for seven days and nights. When the angels assembled for (Adam's burial), and Seth collected the last will, he placed it upon a ladder (like that used for the ascent and descent of angels and souls)[962] in the company of the generation that our father Adam had brought out from Paradise, so that there would be no neglect with respect to mentioning God.

According to Ibn Ḥumayd—Salamah—Ibn Isḥāq—Yaḥyā b. ʿAbbād[963] —his father: I (Yaḥyā) heard him (ʿAbbād) say: I have heard that when Adam died, God sent him his shroud and embalming materials from Paradise. The angels then took charge of his grave and burial and hid him (from sight).

According to ʿAlī b. Ḥarb[964] —Rawḥ b. Aslam[965] —Ḥammād b. Salamah—Thābit al-Bunānī[966] —al-Ḥasan[967] —the Prophet: When Adam died, the angels washed him separately (several times) with water and prepared a burial site for him. They said: This (shall be) Adam's custom among his children.

According to Ibn Ḥumayd—Salamah—Ibn Isḥāq—al-Ḥasan b. Dhakwān[968] —al-Ḥasan b. Abī al-Ḥasan (al-Baṣrī)—Ubayy b. Kaʿb—the Messenger of God: Your father Adam was as tall as a very tall palm, that is, sixty cubits (30 meters). He had much hair,
[162] and his privy parts *(ʿawrah)* were concealed. When he committed

962. Doubts about the reading and interpretation of *miʿrāj* are, however, expressed in Ṭabarī, *Introductio etc.*, CCCLV.

963. For Yaḥyā b. ʿAbbād and his father ʿAbbād b. ʿAbdallāh b. al-Zubayr b. al-ʿAwwām, see *Tahdhib*, XI, 234 f. and V, 98.

964. Born in 175/December 791, ʿAlī b. Ḥarb died in 265/879. See *TB*, XI, 418–20; *Tahdhīb*, VII, 294–96.

965. Rawḥ b. Aslam is supposed to have died in the first decade of the third century/815–25. See *Tahdhīb*, III, 291 f.

966. Thābit b. Aslam al-Bunānī died eighty-six years old between 123 and 127/740–45. See *Tahdhīb*, II, 2-4; Khalīfah, *Ṭabaqāt*, 214; Samʿānī, *Ansāb*, II, 330.

967. Al-Ḥasan al-Baṣrī did not transmit directly from the Prophet.

968. See *Tahdhīb*, III, 276 f.

the sin (of eating from the forbidden tree), his secret parts became apparent to him. He fled about in Paradise, but a tree encountered him and seized him by his forelock. His Lord called out to him: (Are you) in flight from Me, Adam? Adam replied: No, by God, O my Lord, but I feel shame before You because of the crime I have committed. God cast him down to earth. When he was about to die, God sent him his embalming materials and shroud from Paradise. When Eve saw the angels, she went in to Adam in order to prevent them from entering *(dūnahum)*. Adam said: Leave me and the messengers of my Lord alone! It was you who caused the experience I suffered, and it was in connection with you that the misfortune befell me. When Adam was dead, the angels washed him separately (several times) with *sidr* and water and dressed him in separate layers of shrouds.[969] Then they prepared a grave and buried him. They then said: This (shall be) the custom of the children of Adam after him.

According to Aḥmad b. al-Miqdām[970] —al-Muʿtamir b. Sulaymān—his father, or supposedly Qatādah—a colleague of his—Ubayy b. Kaʿb—the Messenger of God: Adam was a man as tall as a very tall palm.

According to al-Ḥārith b. Muḥammad—Ibn Saʿd—Hishām—his father—Abū Ṣāliḥ—Ibn ʿAbbās: When Adam died, Seth said to Gabriel: Pray for Adam! Gabriel replied: You go and pray for your father and say *Allāhu akbaru* for him thirty times, five as (part of the prescribed) prayer and the other twenty-five as a special honor for Adam!

There are differences of opinion about the location of Adam's grave. What Ibn Isḥāq said, has already been mentioned.[971] Someone else said: He was buried in Mecca in the cave of Abū Qubays. It is a cave called Treasure Cave.[972]

---

969. *Sidr* is said to be crushed lotus leaves mixed with water to serve as a perfuming agent. The proper procedures of washing a corpse successively with water, *sidr*, and camphor and the use of several garments as shrouds are discussed at length in the Prophetic traditions. See also *EI*², II, 441 f., s. v. djanāza.

970. Aḥmad b. al-Miqdām died in 253/867. See *TB*, V, 162–66; *Tahdhīb*, I, 81 f. As is clear from the dates of his authorities, he lived into his nineties. He himself is credited with the statement that he was born two years before the death of Abū Jaʿfar, apparently the caliph al-Manṣūr, thus in 773.

971. See text above, I, 161?

972. Abū Qubays is one of the Meccan hills, see *EI*², I, 136, s. v. Abū Ḳubays. The Treasure Cave in Abū Qubays is mentioned in Yāqūt, *Muʿjam*, III, 769, s. v.

On this subject, there is a report transmitted on the authority
[163] of Ibn ʿAbbās that I was told by al-Ḥārith—Ibn Saʿd—Hishām—his father—Abū Ṣāliḥ—Ibn ʿAbbās: When Noah left the ark,[973] he (re)buried Adam in Jerusalem.

Adam's death took place on Friday. We have mentioned the relevant traditions earlier and would not like to repeat them here.[974]

On this subject, we have the following report transmitted on the authority of Ibn ʿAbbās which I was told by al-Ḥārith—Ibn Saʿd—Hishām b. Muḥammad—his father—Abū Ṣāliḥ—Ibn ʿAbbās: Adam died upon (Mount) Nūdh—Abū Jaʿfar (al-Ṭabarī) says: This refers to the mountain upon which he was cast down.[975]

It has been mentioned that Eve lived one year after Adam's death. Then she died. She was buried together with her spouse in the mentioned cave. That place remained the grave of Adam and Eve until the Flood. Noah then took them out, placed them in a coffin, and carried them along in the ark. When the earth had soaked up the water, he returned them to the place where they had been before the Flood. As mentioned, Eve spun, wove, kneaded, baked, and did all kinds of women's work.

(From Seth to Mahalalel)

We have mentioned the history of Adam and his enemy Iblīs and what God did with Iblīs when he became tyrannical and overbearing and rebelled against his Lord, then insolently spurned the favor shown him by God, persisted in his ignorance and perversity and asked his Lord for postponement, and He granted him postponement "to the day of the known moment."[976] (We have also mentioned) what God did with Adam, how He hastened His punishment of him for his sin and for having forgotten God's covenant,

---

ghār, as a place where Adam deposited his books. For the Treasure Cave of the holy mountain as the burial place of Adam and Eve and his early descendants, see *Schatzhöhle*, text, 38–42, trans., 9 f. In Yaʿqūbī's *Taʾrīkh*, I, 3–14, it plays a large role, as does the subsequent fate of Adam's corpse, presumably following some recension of the *Schatzhöhle* literature.

973. While "ark" is a special term which has been associated in our usage with Noah's ark, Arabic uses ordinary words for ship or boat. See below, n. 1071.

974. See text above, I, 111.

975. See above, n. 788.

976. Qur. 15:38 and 38:81 and the context of the verses.

and then covered him with His outstanding mercy, since Adam repented his slip, and forgave and guided him and saved him from error and perdition. Let us now return to the history of Cain and [164] the history of his children and that of Seth and his children. God willing, we shall mention both the followers of Adam's way and the party of Iblīs and imitators of his errors who proceeded along the path of either Adam or Iblīs, and (we shall mention) what God did with each group.

We already mentioned some matters pertaining to Seth, such as that he was the legatee of his father Adam among those left behind by Adam after his passing. We mentioned as well that a number of scrolls was revealed to him by God.[977]

Seth reportedly stayed in Mecca performing the pilgrimage *(ḥajj)* and the lesser pilgrimage *(ʿumrah)* until he died. He added the scrolls revealed by God to him to those of his father Adam and acted in accordance with their contents. He built the Kaʿbah with stones and clay.

Our early scholars, however, have said that the dome that God made for Adam where the House is located remained (as it was) to the days of the Flood. God lifted it up when He sent the Flood.[978]

When Seth fell ill, he reportedly appointed his son Enosh as his legatee. He then died and was buried together with his parents in the cave of Abū Qubays. He was born after 235 years of Adam's life had passed,[979] and he died at the age of 912 years.[980] As is assumed by the people of the Torah, Enosh was born to Seth after 605 years of his life had passed.[981]

Ibn Isḥāq, in turn, said as we were told by Ibn Ḥumayd—Salamah b. al-Faḍl—(Ibn Isḥāq): Adam's son Seth married his sister, Adam's daughter Ḥazūrah.[982] She bore him his son Yānish and his daughter Naʿmah.[983] Seth was 105 years old at the time.

---

977. See text above, I, 153.

978. See text above, I, 122. "Dome" (*qubbah*) is also "dome shaped tent."

979. As in the Bible, the figure is usually 130 years. See text above, I, 153.

980. Genesis 5:8.

981. Genesis 5:6 has 105, as in the next tradition; LXX has 205. The reference of "his" cannot be to Adam.

982. See above, n. 905.

983. In Jubilees 4:13, her name is Noam. See Fraade, *Enosh*, 18. Naamah appears as the name of Tubal-cain's sister in Genesis 4:22. Yānish for Enosh is unusual and possibly results from some misunderstood Aramaic spelling (the letter ' spelled *y* in Christian Palestinian Aramaic?).

[165] After the birth of Yānish, he lived another 807 years.[984]

After the passing of his father Seth, Enosh took over the political administration of the realm and the guidance of the subjects under his control in place of his father Seth. He reportedly continued his father's ways with no noticeable changes. As mentioned by the people of the Torah, Enosh lived altogether 905 years.[985]

According to al-Ḥārith—Ibn Sa'd—Hishām—his father—Abū Ṣāliḥ—Ibn 'Abbās: Seth begot Enosh and numerous other children. Enosh was Seth's legatee. Kenan was then born to Enosh b. Seth b. Adam by his sister, Seth's daughter Na'mah, after ninety years of the life of Enosh and 325 years of that of Adam had passed.[986]

Ibn Isḥāq, in turn, said as we were told by Ibn Ḥumayd—Salamah—Ibn Isḥāq: Seth's son Yānish married his sister, Seth's daughter Na'mah. When he was ninety years old, she bore him Kenan. After Kenan's birth, Yānish lived another 815 years. (Several) sons and daughters were born to him. The total length of Yānish's life was 905 years. At the age of seventy, Yānish's son Kenan married Dīnah, the daughter of Barākīl b. Mehujael b. Enoch b. Cain b. Adam.[987] She bore him his son Mahalalel. After the birth of Mahalalel, Kenan lived another 840 years. Thus the total length of Kenan's life was 910 years.[988]

[166] According to al-Ḥārith—Ibn Sa'd—Hishām—his father—Abū Ṣāliḥ—Ibn 'Abbās: Enosh begot Kenan and numerous other children. Kenan was his legatee. He begot Mahalalel and other children in addition. Mahalalel was his legatee. He begot Jared (Yarid)—that is, al-Yārid—and other children in addition. Jared was his legatee. He begot Enoch—that is, the prophet Idrīs[989] —and other children in addition. Enoch begot Methuselah and other children in addition. Methuselah was his legatee. He begot Lamech and other children in addition. Lamech was his legatee.[990]

---

984. Genesis 5:7.

985. Genesis 5:11.

986. Genesis 5:9. The figure of 325 agrees with the Biblical data.

987. See above, n. 947.

988. Genesis 5:13 f.

989. The Qur'ānic Idrīs was commonly identified with Enoch, probably on the basis of etymological speculation (*ḥ-n-k* and *d-r-s*), which may, or may not, be grounded in fact. See *EI*², III, 1030 f., s. v. Idrīs.

990. The statement on Lamech that is found in a manuscript used in the Cairo edition no doubt belonged to the original text. For the succession of "legatees," cf. the "commandments" *(p-q-d)* of *Schatzhöhle*, text, 112–14, trans., 27.

In the Torah, according to the people of the Book, it is mentioned that Mahalalel's birth took place after 395 years of Adam's life and seventy years of that of Kenan had passed.[991]

According to Ibn Ḥumayd—Salamah—Ibn Isḥāq: When Mahalalel b. Kenan was sixty-five years old, he married his maternal aunt Simʿan, the daughter of Barākīl b. Mehujael b. Enoch b. Cain b. Adam.[992] She bore him his son Jared. After Jared's birth, Mahalalel lived another 830 years. (Several other) sons and daughters were born to him. The total length of Mahalalel's life was 895 years.[993] Then he died.

According to the Torah, Jared reportedly was born to Mahalalel after 460 years of Adam's life had passed.[994] He followed the ways of his father Kenan, but (certain) events happened in his time.

The Events That Took Place in the Days of the Children of Adam from the Rule of Adam's Son to the Days of Jared[995]

It has been mentioned that when Cain killed Abel and fled from his father to the Yemen,[996] Iblīs came and said to him: Abel's of- [167]
fering was accepted and consumed by fire only because he used to serve and worship fire. So, you, too, set up a fire for yourself and your descendants! Cain thus built a fire temple. He was the first to set up and worship fire.

According to Ibn Ḥumayd—Salamah—Ibn Isḥāq: Cain married Adam's daughter Ashūt.[997] She bore him a male and a female, his son Enoch and his daughter ʿAdan.[998] Cain's son Enoch married his

991. Genesis 5:12.

992. Sim'an (vocalization?), who is mentioned again in text below, I, 172, thus was a sister of Dīnah (above, nn. 947 and 987). According to Jubilees, it was Dīnah who was married to Mahalalel.

993. Genesis 5:17.

994. Because Mahalalel was sixty-five when Jared was born (Genesis 5:15).

995. The chapter, in fact, extends to Noah. Jared's assumed crucial role in world history derives from the fact, stressed in *Schatzhöhle*, that the first millennium of the world came to an end during his lifetime.

996. See above, n. 894.

997. See above, n. 904.

998. The Ṭabarī manuscripts seem to have final *b*, but *n* is assured by Enoch 85:3. See also Milik, *The Books of Enoch*, 42. In Jubilees 4:20, Ednī is Methuselah's mother; in 4:27, Ednā is the name of the wife of Methuselah. See below, nn. 1031 and 1035.

sister, Cain's daughter 'Adan. She bore him three male children and one female, his sons Irad, Mehujael, and Abūshīl[999] and his daughter Mūlīth.[1000] Enoch's son Abūshīl married Enoch's daughter Mūlīth. She bore Abūshīl a male named Lamech. Lamech married two women, one named Adah and the other Zillah. Adah bore him Tūlīn (Jabal), who was the first to dwell in tents and to acquire property, and Tūbīsh (Jubal),[1001] who was the first to play string instruments and cymbals.[1002] Zillah bore him a male called Tubal-cain, who was the first to work copper and iron.[1003] Their children were godless tyrants *(jabābirah* and *farāʿinah* ["Pharaohs"]). They were given a large stature, supposedly thirty cubits (15 meters) tall. He continued. The children of Cain then disappeared, having left only a few descendants. Knowledge of the pedigrees of all the progeny of Adam was lost, and they no longer had offspring, except among the descendants of Adam's son Seth. They produced offspring, and the pedigrees of all men today go back to
[168] Seth rather than his father Adam, who is the father of mankind, except those children of his father and his brothers who left no (further) descendants.

He continued. The people of the Torah say: Rather, Cain married Ashūt. She bore him Enoch. To Enoch was born Irad, to Irad Mehujael, to Mehujael Abūshīl, and to Abūshīl Lamech. Lamech married Adah and Zillah, who bore him those mentioned by me.[1004] God knows best!

Ibn Isḥāq mentioned only what I have reported about Cain and his descendants.

Someone else knowledgeable in the Torah mentioned that the descendant of Cain who invented musical instruments was a man

---

999. Instead of b, it probably was originally (before Ṭabarī?) th, as the name apparently represents Methushael of Genesis 4:18. There Methushael is the son of Mehujael, who, in turn, is the son of Irad. A reading Anūshīl, an angelic name consisting of Enosh plus *il/el*, seems unlikely.

1000. Mūlīth no doubt corresponds to Mualeleth in Jubilees 4:14, where it is the name of Kenan's wife.

1001. The initial *t* in Tūlīn and Tūbīsh should probably be read *y*, since Jabal and Jubal of Genesis 4:20 f. are meant here.

1002. For *ṣanj* ("cymbal"), the meaning of some kind of string instrument is probably more common, so that Ṭabarī may have understood the instruments as representing two different string instruments.

1003. Genesis 4:19–22.

1004. This genealogy is, of course, more in line with Genesis 4:17.

called Tūbāl (Jubal). He invented musical instruments such as flutes, drums, lutes, pandores, and lyres in the time of Mahalalel b. Kenan. As a result, the descendants of Cain became very much engaged in amusement.[1005] Information about them reached the descendants of Seth in the mountain, and a hundred of them thought of going down to them, acting contrary to the exhortations of their forefathers. When Jared learned about it, he admonished them and forbade them (to go down), but they simply insisted and went down to the descendants of Cain. They liked what they saw there. When they wanted to go back, they were prevented by a previous call *(da'wah)*[1006] of their forefathers. When they tarried where they were, some misguided people in the mountain thought that they remained (down there) because they were happy there. They therefore slipped away and went down from the mountain. When they saw the amusement taking place there, they, too, liked it. They reached an accommodation with female descendants of Cain who rushed to them, and they stayed with them. They became very much engaged in iniquity. Wickedness and wine drinking spread.[1007]

Abū Ja'far (al-Ṭabarī) says: This statement is not far from the truth. That is so because about the same information has been transmitted on the authority of a number of the early scholars from the nation of our Prophet, even if they did not clearly indicate the time of the person during whose rule this event took [169]
place but mentioned only that it was in the period between Adam and Noah.

Those on whose authority this story has been transmitted

According to Aḥmad b. Zuhayr[1008]—Mūsā b. Ismā'īl—Dāwūd, meaning Ibn Abī al-Furāt[1009]—'Ilbā' b. Aḥmar—'Ikrimah—Ibn 'Abbās, reciting this verse of the Qur'ān (addressing women): "And do not display your finery as in the first Jāhiliyyah!"[1010] and

1005. *Lahw* "amusement" seems to be used here in this wider meaning; it is not merely musical entertainment.

1006. *Schatzhöhle* speaks of an "oath." The Arabic may be understood as prayer or curse.

1007. See *Schatzhöhle*, text, 64–68, trans., 15 f. This and the following story expand on Genesis 6:1–4.

1008. That is, the historian Ibn Abī Khaythamah (above, n. 533).

1009. According to *Tahdhīb*, III, 197, Dāwūd b. Abī al-Furāt died in 167/783–84, but this may not be correct.

1010. Qur. 33:33.

commenting on it as follows: It was the period between Noah and Idrīs(!) and it was a thousand years. There were two tribes *(baṭn)* of Adam's descendants. One of them dwelled in the plain, and the other in the mountain. The mountain men were handsome, and the mountain women ugly, while the women of the plain were beautiful, and the men ugly. Iblīs came to one of the inhabitants of the plain in the form of a young man and hired himself out as his servant. Iblīs invented something like the flutes used by shepherds but produced with it a sound, the likes of which people had not heard before. When those around them heard about it, they took turns going to them and listening to it. They established a yearly festival where they assembled, arranging for the women to display their finery to the men—he continued—and for the men to come down to them. One of the mountain people intruded upon them during that festival of theirs. He saw the beauty of the women and, going back to his companions, told them about it. They moved down to live with the women, with the result that wickedness appeared among the women. This is (meant by) God's word: "And do not display your finery as in the first Jāhiliyyah!"

[170] According to Ibn Wakī'—Ibn Abī Ghaniyyah[1011] —his father—al-Ḥakam,[1012] commenting on: "And do not display your finery as in the first Jāhiliyyah," as follows: There were eight hundred years between Adam and Noah. Their women were as ugly as could be, and their men were handsome. A woman always wanted a man for herself. Therefore, this verse was revealed: "And do not display your finery as in the first Jāhiliyyah!"

According to al-Ḥārith—Ibn Sa'd—Hishām—his father—Abū Ṣāliḥ—Ibn 'Abbās: Adam did not die before the number of his children on (Mount) Nūdh had reached forty thousand.

Adam noticed adultery, wine drinking, and corruption among them. He exhorted the children of Seth not to marry the children of Cain. The children of Seth placed Adam in a cave and appointed a guardian for him, so that none of the children of Cain would get near him. Those who came to him and for whom he

---

1011. Yaḥyā b. 'Abd al-Malik b. Ḥumayd b. Abī Ghaniyyah died between 186 and 188/802–4. See *Tahdhīb*, XI, 252. His father is listed in *Tahdhīb*, VI, 392 f.

1012. Al-Ḥakam b. 'Utaybah lived from around 47–50/667–70 to about 113–15/731–33. See *Tahdhīb*, II, 432 f.; Khalīfa, *Ṭabaqāt*, 162; Bukhārī, *Ta'rīkh*, I, 2 330 ff.

would ask for forgiveness belonged to the children of Seth. One hundred handsome children of Seth said: Would that we could look at what our cousins—meaning the children of Cain—are doing. So the hundred went down to the beautiful female children of Cain. The women detained the men, and they remained for a while. Then, another hundred said: Would that we could look at what our brothers are doing. They went down from the mountain, and the women detained them. Then all the children of Seth went down. The result was the coming of sin. They intermarried and mingled, and the children of Cain grew in numbers until they filled[1013] the earth. They are the ones who drowned in the days of Noah.[1014]

I have already mentioned what the Persian genealogists have said about Mahalalel b. Kenan. He was Ōshahanj who ruled over the seven climes. I have explained the statements of the Arab genealogists who oppose their (views).[1015]

If it was as stated by the Persian genealogists, I, in turn, was told on the authority of Hishām b. Muḥammad b. al-Sā'ib that (Ōshahanj) was the first to cut trees and build buildings and the [171]
first to produce minerals and make people understand their use. He commanded the people of his time to use mosques. He built two cities, the first to be built on earth. They are the city of Bābil in the southern region *(sawād)* of al-Kūfah and the city of al-Sūs (Susa). He ruled forty years.

Someone else said: It was during Ōshahanj's rule that iron was first produced. He made it into tools for the crafts. He assessed the available water in localities with a stagnant water supply.[1016] He urged people to till the soil, sow, harvest, and engage in all (kinds of agricultural) activity. He commanded people to kill beasts of prey and use clothing made from their skins as well as mats and to

1013. The Leiden edition has "ruled."
1014. The figure of one hundred occurs also in *Schatzhöhle*, see above, n. 1007. See also the version in Ya'qūbī, *Ta'rīkh*, I, 8.
1015. See text above, I, 154 f. The section is translated in Christensen, I, 148 f. (comments on I, 156 ff.).
1016. Christensen: Et il aménagea les eaux où elles étaient utiles.

slaughter cows, small cattle, and wild animals and eat their meat. He ruled forty years. He built the city of al-Rayy. Reportedly, it was the first city built after the city that was Jayūmart's residence, in Dunbāwand of Ṭabaristān.[1017]

The Persians say that this Ōshahanj was born a king. His way of life and the way he administered his subjects were outstandingly praiseworthy. That gave rise to his surname Fēshdādh, which in Persian means "the first to judge in justice," for *fāsh (pēsh)* means "first," and *dādh (dād)* means "justice and legal decision." They further mention that he went down to India and moved about in many places. When his situation was straightened out and his rule firmly established, he placed a crown *(tāj)* upon his head and gave an address in which he said that he had inherited the realm from his grandfather Jayūmart and that he meant (to inflict) punishment and revenge upon rebellious human beings and Satans. Again, they mention that he subdued Iblīs and his armies and forbade them to mix with human beings. Writing a document on a white sheet *(ṭirs)*, he imposed covenants upon them enjoining
[172] them not to confront any human being. He threatened them in case they did. He killed the rebels among them and a number of ghūls. Fearing him they fled into deserts, mountains, and (river) valleys. Ōshahanj ruled over all the climes. There were 236 years between the death of Jayūmart and the birth and rule of Ōshajanj. They further mention that Iblīs and his armies rejoiced at the death of Ōshahanj. That was because his death enabled them to enter the dwellings of the children of Adam and go down to them from the mountains and (river) valleys.

Let us now return to Jared (Yarid), also said to be Yārid. After 460 years of Adam's life had passed, Jared was born to Mahalalel and his maternal aunt Simʿan, the daughter of Barākīl b. Mehujael b. Enoch b. Cain.[1018] He was the legatee and successor of his father, according to what his father Mahalalel had set down in his last will addressed to him when he made him his successor after

1017. See text above, I, 147.
1018. See above, n. 992.

his death. His mother reportedly gave birth to him after sixty-five years of Mahalalel's life had passed. After his father perished, he acted in accordance with the last will of his ancestors and his forefathers, as they had done during the days of their lives.

As we were told by Ibn Ḥumayd—Salamah—Ibn Isḥāq, when Jared was 162 years old, he married Baraknā, the daughter of al-Darmasīl[1019] b. Mehujael b. Enoch b. Cain b. Adam. She bore him his son Enoch, who is the prophet Idrīs. He was the first of Adam's children to be given prophecy—as Ibn Isḥāq assumed—and the first to write with a pen. Jared lived 800 years after Enoch's birth. (Several) sons and daughters were born to him. The total length of Jared's life was 962 years. Then he died. [173]

Someone else among the people of the Torah said: Enoch—that is, Idrīs—was born to Jared. God granted him the gift of prophecy after 622 years of Adam's life had passed. He revealed thirty scrolls to him. He was the first after Adam to write and to exert himself in the path of God,[1020] as well as the first to cut and sew clothes. He also was the first to lead some of Cain's descendants into captivity and to enslave them. He was the legatee of his father Jared and exhorted to act in accordance with what his forefathers had stated in their last wills addressed to him and to each other. All this he did during Adam's lifetime.

He continued. Adam died after 308 years of the life of Enoch had passed, thus completing the 930 years we have mentioned as being the length of Adam's life.[1021] Enoch summoned his people and admonished them. He commanded them to be obedient to God and disobey Satan and not to mix with the descendants of Cain. However, they did not follow his command. Group after group of the descendants of Seth used to go down to the descendants of Cain.[1022]

He continued. It is (written) in the Torah that after 365 years of Idrīs' life and 527 years of the life of his father had passed, God raised up Idrīs. Thereafter, his father lived another 435 years to complete 962 years, as this was the length of Jared's life. Enoch

1019. The names in Jubilees 4:16 are Bāraka, the daughter of Rāsūyāl. Baraknā might originally have been Barakt(h)ā (?). The tradition reflects Genesis 5:18–20 quite literally.

1020. "Undertook the *jihād*." See also below, n. 1033.

1021. See text above, I, 160.

1022. See text above, I, 170.

was born after 162 years of Jared's life had passed.

According to al-Ḥārith—Ibn Sa'd—Hishām—his father—Abū Ṣāliḥ —Ibn 'Abbās: It was in Jared's time that idols were made,
[174] and some turned away from *islām*.

According to Aḥmad b. 'Abd al-Raḥmān b. Wahb—his paternal uncle—al-Māḍī b. Muḥammad—Abū Sulaymān—al-Qāsim b. Muḥammad—Abū Idrīs al-Khawlānī—Abū Dharr al-Ghifārī: The Messenger of God said to me: Abū Dharr! Four—that is, messengers—were Syrians: Adam, Seth, Noah, and Enoch who was the first to write with a pen. God revealed thirty scrolls to him.

Some(one) assumed that God sent Idrīs to all the people of the earth living in his time. He gave to him the combined knowledge of the men of the past, adding to it thirty scrolls. This is (meant by) God's word: "This is in the first scrolls, the scrolls of Abraham and Moses."[1023] He continued: By "first scrolls" are meant the scrolls that were revealed to Adam's son Hibat Allāh (Seth) and to Idrīs.

(Persian Kings after Ōshahanj: Ṭahmūrath)

Some(one) said: Bēwarāsb[1024] ruled in the time of Idrīs. Some of Adam's speeches had happened to reach him, and he used them to perform magic. Bēwarāsb practiced that magic.[1025] When he wanted something from anywhere in his realm, or when he liked a mount or a woman, he blew into a golden reed (pipe) he had, and everything he wished for would come to him. This is the origin of (the custom of) the Jews to blow (the shofar).

The Persians say: After Ōshahanj, Ṭahmūrath b. Wēwanjihān b.
[175] Khūbāndādh b. Khuyāydār b. Ōshahanj became ruler.[1026]

1023. Qur. 87:18 f.

1024. Bēwarāsb (meaning, as explained in Firdawsī, "ten thousand horses") is another name for al-Ḍaḥḥāk (Aždahāk). See *Bundahishn*, ed. Anklesaria, ch. 29, pp. 244 f., and ch. 34, pp. 282 f.; Firdawsī, *Shāhnāmah, Jamshīd*, verse 95 Mohl, verse 84 of the Russian ed.; text below, I, 181 and 201. See also Justi, *Iranisches Namenbuch*, 60 f., and Dīnawarī, *al-Akhbār al-ṭiwāl*, 6.

1025. See also Dīnawarī, *loc. cit.*

1026. Translated in Christensen, I, 193. Ibn al-Athīr, *Kāmil*, ed. Tornberg, I, 43, thought of *bih* and *jihān* "the best of the people of the earth" as a possible etymology of Wēwanjihān, but he is certainly wrong. The name of the father of Wēwanjihān is given as Vivangah in *Bundahishn*, ed. Anklesaria, ch. 35, pp. 292 f.

There are differences of opinion concerning the pedigree from Ṭahmūrath to Ōshahanj. Some give the pedigree just mentioned by me. Another Persian genealogist says, however, that it is Ṭahmūrath b. Ēwankihān b. Ankhad b. Askhad b. Ōshahanj.[1027]

As I was told on his authority, Hishām b. Muḥammad al-Kalbī said: Scholars have mentioned that the first ruler of Bābil was Ṭahmūrath. He continued. We have heard—God knows best!—that God gave him so much power that Iblīs and his Satans were submissive to him. He was obedient to God. He ruled forty years.

The Persians, in turn, assume that Ṭahmūrath ruled over all the climes. He placed a crown *(tāj)* upon his head and, on the day he became ruler, he said: With God's help, we shall remove the corrupt rebels from God's creation. His rule was praiseworthy, and [176] he was kind to his subjects. He built Sābūr in Fārs[1028] and resided there. He moved about in (various) countries. He jumped on Iblīs, mounted him, and rode around on him in the regions of the earth near and far.[1029] He frightened Iblīs and his rebellious companions until they scattered and dispersed. He was the first to use wool and hair for clothing and carpeting, and the first to use the horses, mules, and donkeys that are part of royal pomp. He ordered people to use dogs to guard and protect cattle from wild beasts and (to use) birds of prey *(jawāriḥ)* for hunting. He wrote in Persian. Bēwarāsb appeared in the first year of his rule and made propaganda for the religion of the Sabians.[1030]

We now return to Enoch—that is, Idrīs. As we were told by

Dīnawarī, *al-Akhbār al-ṭiwāl*, 4, has Īrān as his father. Justi, *Iranisches Namenbuch*, 374a, mentions Ayanhad as his father.

1027. For the genealogies, see Christensen, II, 110 ff.

1028. See Yāqūt, *Mu'jam*, III, 5 f. For Ṭahmūrath's inventions, cf. Firdawsī.

1029. Ibn al-Athīr, *Kāmil*, ed. Tornberg, I, 44, comments: "(The sources) must bear the responsibility (for this information). We have only reported what they have stated."

1030. Bēwarāsb is mentioned again in connection with the Sabians in text below, I, 184. There, the editor of the Leiden text indicates in a footnote that he withdraws his earlier suggestion that Būdāsb (Bodhisattva, see *EI*², I, 1215 f., s. v. Bilawhar wa-Yūdāsaf) might have been intended here. Ṭabarī almost certainly thought of Bēwarāsb, although Christensen, I, 206, strongly supports Būdāsb. See also Mas'ūdī, Murūj, II, 111.

Ibn Ḥumayd—Salamah—Ibn Isḥāq, when Jared's son Enoch was sixty-five years old, he married Hadānah, or Adānah, the daughter of Bāwīl[1031] b. Mehujael b. Enoch b. Cain b. Adam. She bore him his son Methuselah. He lived for 300 years after the birth of Methuselah. (Several) sons and daughters were born to him. The total length of Enoch's life was 365 years. Then he died.

Some(one) else among the people of the Torah said, referring to the authority of the Torah[1032] : Methuselah was born to Enoch after
[177] 687 years of Adam's life had elapsed. Enoch appointed him his successor to do God's command (*'alā amr Allāh*). Before Enoch was raised up (to God), he addressed his last will to Methuselah and his family, informing them that God would punish the descendants of Cain and those who mixed with them and were sympathetic to them, and he forbade them to mix with them. It has been mentioned that he was the first to ride horses, because he followed his father's prescribed practice with respect to the *jihād*.[1033] In his days, he went in the path of his forefathers and acted in obedience to God. Enoch had lived for 365 years when he was raised up (to God). Methuselah was born to him after sixty-five years of his life had passed.

As I was told by Ibn Ḥumayd—Salamah—Ibn Isḥāq, when Enoch's son Methuselah was 137 years old,[1034] he married 'Adnā (Ednā),[1035] the daughter of 'Azrā'īl b. Abūshīl b. Enoch b. Cain b. Adam. She bore him his son Lamech. Methuselah lived 700 years after the birth of Lamech. (Several) sons and daughters were born

1031. Notwithstanding the difference in the initial consonant, Hadānah/Adānah is no doubt originally identical with Ednā/Ednī (see also above, n. 998) in Jubilees 4:20. She is there the daughter of Dānēl who appears to be identical with Bāwīl, although the relationship of the forms Dānēl and Bāwīl is difficult to explain.

1032. The reading of the Cairo edition may be preferable to what is found in the Leiden edition: "as mentioned by the people of the Torah.

1033. See above, n. 1020.

1034. In the Old Testament tradition, the figures diverge more than usual in this case. The Hebrew text, for instance, has 187 (Genesis 5:25). The LXX has 167, and Targum Neofiti has 180. If the text is correct, the indicated 919 years of Methuselah's life would require that there was an interval of eighty-two years between his marriage and the birth of Lamech. Now, the Old Testament has 969, not 919, and so on.

1035. Jubilees 4:27 has Ednā, the daughter of Azrī'āl. Following Lidzbarski (above, n. 903), Ṭabarī, *Introductio etc.*, DLXXVI, suggests reading 'Adnā for 'Arbā and accordingly also corrects Qīnūsh (below, n. 1036) and 'Amzūrah (below, n. 1037). For Abūshīl, see above, n. 999.

to him. The total length of Methuselah's life was 919 years. Then he died. When Lamech b. Methuselah b. Enoch was 187 years old, he married Batanūs(h),[1036] the daughter of Barākīl b. Mehujael b. Enoch b. Cain b. Adam. She bore him Noah, the prophet—may God pray for him and give him peace! After Noah's birth, Lamech lived another 595 years. (Several) sons and daughters were born to him. The total length of his life was 780 years. Then he died. When Lamech's son Noah was 500 years old, he married ʿAmzūrah,[1037] the daughter of Barākīl b. Mehujael b. Enoch b. Cain b. Adam. She bore him his sons Shem, Ham, and Japheth. They were Noah's [178] children.[1038]

The people of the Torah say: Lamech was born to Methuselah after Adam had lived 874 years. He maintained his forefathers' obedience to God and their faithfulness to the agreements with Him. They continued. When Methuselah was about to die, he appointed Lamech as his successor and exhorted him in his last will addressed to him in the same way his forefathers had done. They continued. Lamech admonished his people and forbade them to go down to the descendants of Cain, but they did not allow themselves to be admonished, and eventually all those in the mountain went down to the descendants of Cain. Methuselah reportedly had another son besides Lamech, who was Ṣābi'. The Sabians are said to have been named Sabians after him. Methuselah was 960 old; Lamech was born after 187 years of his life had passed. Lamech then begot Noah, 126 years after the death of Adam, that is, after 1,056 years had elapsed from the day Adam was cast down by God to Noah's birth. When Noah reached maturity, Lamech said to him: You know that no one but us has remained in this place, but do not feel lonely and do not follow after the sinful nation! Noah would pray to his Lord and admonish his people, but they made light of him. God revealed to him that he had given his people a respite (from punishment) and would grant them a postponement for a certain period, so that they might retract (what they

1036. For Lamech's wife Bath Anōsh, see *Genesis Apocryphon*, col. II; Fitzmyer, *The Genesis Apocryphon*, 42 ff., 74, 77. Fitzmyer argues for the vocalization Bitenosh. Jubilees 4:28 has Bētēnōs. Ṭabarī's Qīnūsh is found in Tha'labī, *Qiṣaṣ*, 54. It is not quite clear whether the initial *b* in the Cairo edition is based upon manuscript evidence.

1037. Jubilees 4:33 has 'Emzārā, the daughter of Rākē'ēl.

1038. Genesis 5:32.

had done) and repent. That period, however, passed before they had expressed regret and repented.

Others than those whose statement(s) I have mentioned said: Noah lived in the time of Bēwarāsb. His people (worshiped idols).[1039] For 950 years,[1040] he called them to God. Whenever one generation passed away, another followed in this same religion of unbelief, until God sent (His) punishment down upon them and annihilated them.

[179] According to al-Ḥārith—Ibn Saʿd—Hishām—his father—Abū Ṣāliḥ—Ibn ʿAbbās: Methuselah begot Lamech and a number of other children in addition. Lamech was his legatee. He begot Noah. When Noah was born, Lamech was eighty-two years old.[1041] In that time, nobody was there to forbid evil. Therefore, God sent Noah to them—he was then 480 years old. Noah called them (to God) during his prophethood for 120 years. Then God commanded Noah to build the ark, and Noah did. He boarded it at the age of 600 years. All those people drowned. After (the building of) the ark, Noah lived on for another 350 years.

(Persian Kings from Ṭahmūrath to Jamshēd and al-Ḍaḥḥāk)

The Persian scholars, in turn, say[1042] : After Ṭahmūrath, Jam al-shīd (Jamshēd) became ruler. In their opinion, *al-shīdh* means "ray". He was supposedly given this nickname because of his beauty. He is Jam b. Wēwanjihān, a brother of Ṭahmūrath.[1043] He is said to have ruled over all the seven climes. He subjugated the jinn and humans living in them. He placed the crown *(tāj)* upon his head. When he was (securely) settled in his realm, he said: God has given us perfect splendor[1044] and great support. We shall

1039. It is not quite clear whether the restoration of the text as indicated in the Cairo edition is derived from a manuscript.

1040. See Qur. 29:14.

1041. The Hebrew text of Genesis 5:28 has 128 years, the LXX, 188 years. Lamech is said to have married Noah's mother at the age of 187 (text above, I, 177). This would indicate agreement with the LXX.

1042. Christensen, II, 85–88, contains a translation of this section.

1043. See above, n. 1026.

1044. No doubt, the *xvarᵉnah*, the eternal divine light of royalty, is meant here. See also below, n. 1054. The "golden crown" is expressly mentioned in the beginning of Firdawsī's chapter on Jamshēd.

do much good to our subjects. He originated the manufacture of swords and weaponry. He also showed (people) how to make brocade, silk, and other textile threads. He ordered garments woven and dyed and saddles with pommels carved to make the mounts more manageable.

As mentioned by some(one), he went into hiding after 616 years and six months of his rule had passed, and the country was without him for a year.[1045] After the first year to year five[1046] of his rule, he ordered the production of swords, coats of mail, *bīḍ* swords,[1047] and other kinds of weapons as well as iron tool(s) for craftsmen. From the year 50 to the year 100 of his rule, he ordered the spinning and weaving of brocade, silk, cotton, linen, and every other textile thread, the dyeing of material in various colors, cutting it [180]
into various patterns, and wearing it. From the year 100 to the year 150, he grouped people in four classes: warriors, jurists, government functionaries, craftsmen and farmers, and he reserved one class for himself as his servants.[1048] He ordered each class to do the work he had made obligatory for them. From the year 150 to the year 250, he fought the Satans and jinn, causing great slaughter among them and humiliating them. They were subjected (to doing forced labor) for him and had to follow his orders. From the year 250 to the year 316, he charged the Satans with cutting stones and rocks from the mountains and making marble, gypsum, and chalk. They also were directed to build buildings and baths with (these materials) and with clay. He also charged them with producing depilatories and with transporting, from the oceans, mountains, mines, and deserts, everything useful for mankind, such as gold, silver, and all other meltable precious metals, as well as differ-

1045. In the *Bundahishn*, trans. Justi, ch. 34, p. 46; ed. Anklesaria, ch. 36, pp. 306 f., the figures are 616 years and six months, plus one hundred years of hiding. For a flight of one hundred years, see Ḥamzah al-Iṣfahānī, *Annales*, 25, and Firdawsī, *Shāhnāmah, Jamshīd*, verse 203 Mohl, verse 179 of the Russian edition; text below, I, 181 and 183.

1046. The Leiden edition suggests a correction to "fifty."

1047. There seems to be no way of telling what distinguished "white" swords from others swords. The word is commonly used simply for "sword."

1048. Ṭabarī seems to suggest that the fourth of the four classes was that of the royal servants. However, the fourth class might rather be the craftsmen and farmers. They could hardly have been lumped together in the same class with civilian officials. Cf. the fourfold division in Thaʿālibī, *Ghurar*, 12. Thaʿālibī often relies on Ṭabarī, but apparently not in this instance.

ent kinds of perfumes and medicines. They carried out all those orders of his. Jamshēd then ordered the manufacture of a glass chariot.[1049] He harnessed[1050] the Satans to it, mounted it, and went on it through the air from his place, Dunbāwand, to Bābil in one day. That was the day Hurmuzrōz of Fawardīn Māh.[1051] Because of the miracle people saw him perform on that occasion, they established the day as New Year's Day *(nawrōz).* He ordered them to establish this day and the following five days as a festival and to celebrate it joyously. On the sixth day, Khurdādhrōz, he wrote to the people informing them that he had led a way of life pleasing to God among them. Part of God's reward to him for it was that God had removed from them (excessive) heat and cold, diseases,
[181] old age decay, and envy. For 300 years following the 316 years that had elapsed of his rule, people remained unaffected by any of the misfortunes that God had reportedly removed from them.[1052]

Thereafter, Jam became ungrateful for the favor shown him by God. He gathered the jinn and humans and informed them that he was in complete charge *(walī and mālik)* of them and that it was he who by his power was keeping diseases, old age decay, and death away from them. Denying God's benefactions to him, he persisted in his perversity, and nobody attending him (dared to) answer him.[1053] Immediately, he lost his splendor and might,[1054] and the angels whom God had commanded to administer his affairs withdrew from him. Bēwarāsb, who is called al-Ḍaḥḥāk, became aware of that.[1055] He hurried to Jam to chew him up, but Jam fled. Bēwarāsb got hold of him afterwards. He tore out his innards and swallowed them and sawed him apart with a saw.

Some Persian scholars say that Jam continued with his praiseworthy way of life until the last one hundred years of his rule. Then he became mentally confused and claimed divinity. Thereby

1049. Tha'ālibī, *Ghurar*, speaks of a coach made of ivory and teakwood (*al-'āj wa-l-sāj*), not glass (*zujāj*).

1050. Read *ṣafada* with the Cairo edition.

1051. That is, the first day of the month Fawardīn. See Bīrūnī, *Chronology*, text, 216, trans., 200.

1052. See Bīrūnī, *Chronology*, text, 217 f., trans., 202.

1053. See Firdawsī, *Shāhnāmah, Jamshīd*, verse 76 Mohl, verse 69 of the Russian edition.

1054. See above, n. 1044. For Jam's history as providing the prototype for being deprived of the *xvar^enah*, see *Yasht*, No. 19, in Lommel's translation.

1055. Namely, the fact that the *xvar^enah* had departed from Jam.

he and his government got into trouble. His brother Isfitūr (Spityura)[1056] attacked him and searched for him in order to kill him. Jam hid from him. During that period of hiding, he was an itinerant ruler. Bēwarāsb then went out against him, deprived him of his realm, and sawed him apart with a saw.

It is assumed by some(one) that Jam ruled 716 years, four months, and twenty days.

A story similar to that of King Jamshād[1057] has been mentioned on the authority of Wahb b. Munabbih from one of the kings of the past. If the chronology of that king did not differ from that of Jam, I would say that it is the story of Jam. This is what I was told by Muḥammad b. Sahl b. ʿAskar—Ismāʿīl b. ʿAbd al-Karīm—ʿAbd al-Ṣamad b. Maʿqil—Wahb b. Munabbih: A man became a [182] ruler as a young man. He said: I have a taste for ruling and find it pleasurable. I do not know whether all men (would find) it so, or I am alone among them in this respect. When told that ruling was like that, he asked: What will enable me (to remain a ruler a long time)? He was told: Obeying God rather than disobeying Him. So he summoned some of the best men in his realm and said to them: Attend to me at court, and whatever you think is an act of obedience to God, order me to do it, and whatever you think is an act of disobedience to God, warn me away, and I shall stay away from it! Both he and they did that. On account of it, his realm was in good shape for four hundred years, during which time he obeyed God. Then Iblīs got wind of it. He said: I have let a man who worships God be a ruler for four hundred years! He entered into the ruler's presence in the shape of a man, but the ruler was frightened of him and asked him who he was. Iblīs replied: There is no reason for you to be afraid. But inform me who you are! The ruler said: I am one of the children of Adam. Iblīs said to him: If you were one of Adam's children, you would have died as they do. Don't you see how many human beings have died and how many generations have passed ? If you were one of them, you would have died as they did. No, you are a god! Thus, summon the peo-

1056. Ṭabarī, *Introductio etc.*, DLXXVIII, refers to R. von Stackelberg as having made the identification in *Wiener Zeitschrift für die Kunde des Morgenlandes* 12 [1898]: 246. Spityura, considered a brother of Jamshēd, joined al-Ḍaḥḥāk in sawing him apart, see *Yasht*, trans. Lommel, 180, and *Bundahishn*, trans. Justi, ch. 2, p. 44; ed. Anklesaria, ch. 35, pp. 292 f.

1057. That is, Jamshēd.

ple to worship you! This idea entered the ruler's heart. He then ascended the pulpit and addressed the people saying: I have concealed something. Now, it has become clear to me that I should reveal it to you. You know that I have ruled you for four hundred years. Now, if I were one of the children of Adam, I would have died as they did. But I am a god! Therefore worship me! Immediately, he was seized by trembling. God revealed to one of those who were with the ruler: Inform him that I have been straightforward with him as long as he was straightforward with Me. Now that he has turned from obedience to Me to disobedience and is
[183] no (longer) straightforward with Me, I swear by My might that I shall give Bukht Nāṣir[1058] power over him. He shall cut off his head and seize all that is in his treasuries. At that time, whenever God was angry with someone, He gave Bukht Nāṣir power over him. The ruler did not stop saying, what he had been saying, and eventually, God gave Bukht Nāṣir power over him. Bukht Nāṣir cut off his head and loaded seventy ships with gold from his treasuries.

Abū Ja'far (al-Ṭabarī) says: However, there is a long time gap between Bukht Nāṣir and Jam, but al-Ḍaḥḥāk might have been called Bukht Nāṣir at that time.

Hishām b. al-Kalbī, as I was told on his authority, said: Jam became ruler after Ṭahmūrath. He had the most handsome face and the largest body among his contemporaries. He continued. It has been mentioned that Jam spent 619 years being obedient to God with his government flourishing and the country being securely his. Then he became an unjust tyrant. God therefore gave al-Ḍaḥḥāk power over him. Al-Ḍaḥḥāk marched against him with 200,000 men, and Jam kept fleeing from him for a hundred years. Al-Ḍaḥḥāk then got hold of him and sawed him apart with a saw. He continued. The total length of Jam's rule, from the time he became ruler to his death, was 719 years.

According to a report transmitted on the authority of a number of early (scholars), there were ten generations between Adam and

---

1058. Or, as in some manuscripts, Bukht Naṣṣar. See EI^2, I, 1297, s. v. Bukht-Naṣ(ṣ)ar.

Noah, all of them followers of the true religion. Unbelief originated only in the generation to whom Noah was sent. Reportedly Noah was the first prophet to be sent by God as a messenger to a people to warn them and call them to the recognition of the oneness of God.

Those who said this

According to Muḥammad b. Bashshār—Abū Dāwūd—Hammām[1059] —Qatādah—'Ikrimah—Ibn 'Abbās: There were ten generations between Noah and Adam, all of them followers of a true religious law. Then they had disagreements "and God sent [184] prophets as bringers of good tidings and warners."[1060] He continued. According to the reading of 'Abdallāh,[1061] (the Qur'ānic verse reads): "Mankind was one nation. Then they had disagreements."

According to al-Ḥasan b. Yaḥyā—'Abd al-Razzāq—Ma'mar—Qatādah, commenting on God's word: "Mankind was one nation," as follows: All of them were rightly guided. Then they had disagreements, "and God sent prophets as bringers of good tidings and warners." The first prophet to be sent was Noah.

1059. Hammām b. Yaḥyā died between 163 and 165/779–82. See *Tahdhīb*, XI, 67–70. *Tafsīr*, II, 194 (*ad* Qur. 2:213), has Hammām b. Munabbih (see Sezgin, *GAS*, I, 86) for Hammām—Qatādah, seemingly a mistake.

1060. Qur. 2:213. The verse is broken up here in nonconsecutive portions. This as well as the following tradition appear in *Tafsīr*, II, 194, on this verse.

1061. The addition of *fa-khtlafū* in the verse at this point is the reading of 'Abdallāh b. Mas'ūd. See Jeffery, *Materials*, 30.

The Events That Took Place in Noah's Time

We have already mentioned the disagreements in the religious outlook of the people to whom Noah was sent. Some say that Noah's people had agreed to do what God disapproves, committing wickedness, drinking wine, and letting their preoccupation with musical instruments divert them from obedience to God. Others say that they were people obedient to Bēwarāsb, who was the first to promulgate the views of the Sabians.[1062] His followers in this respect were those to whom Noah was sent. God willing, I shall mention the story of Bēwarāsb afterwards.[1063]

The Book of God reports that they had idols, for God says speaking about Noah: "Noah said: My Lord! They have been disobedient to me and have followed one whose property and children only add to his loss. They have devised a major plot and have said: Don't give up your gods! Don't give up Wadd, Suwāʿ, Yaghūth, Yaʿūq, and Nasr. They have led many astray."[1064] God sent Noah to them to make them afraid of His awesome power and to warn them of His assault. Noah was to call upon them to repent, to return to the
[185] truth, and to act in accordance with the commands given by God to His messengers and revealed by Him in the scrolls of Adam, Seth, and Enoch. When God sent Noah to them as a prophet, he reportedly was fifty years old.

1062. See above, n. 1030.
1063. Text below, I, 201, dealing with al-Ḍaḥḥāk/Aždahāk.
1064. Qur. 71:21-24.

Another (different) statement is what we were told by Naṣr b. ʿAlī al-Jahḍamī[1065] —Nūḥ b. Qays[1066] —ʿAwn b. Abī Shaddād:[1067] God sent Noah to his people when he was 350 years old. He stayed among them 950 years.[1068] Thereafter he lived for another 350 years.[1069]

According to al-Ḥārith—Ibn Saʿd—Hishām—his father—Abū Ṣāliḥ —Ibn ʿAbbās: God sent Noah to them when he was 480 years old. He then called them (to God) during his prophethood for 120 years. When he was 600 years old, he boarded the ark. He lived thereafter for another 350 years.

Abū Jaʿfar (al-Ṭabarī) says: As God says, Noah stayed among them 950 years, calling them to God secretly and openly. Generation after generation passed, and they did not respond to him, until three generations had passed with both him and them being in that condition. When God wanted to ruin them, Noah cursed them, saying: "My Lord! They have been disobedient to me and have followed one whose property and children only add to his loss."[1070] God commanded him to plant a tree, and he did. The tree grew and spread in all directions. Forty years after Noah had planted it, God commanded him to cut it down and use it for (building) an ark, as God says: "And make the boat under Our eyes and with Our inspiration!"[1071] Thus, he cut down the tree and began to work on it.

According to Ṣāliḥ b. Mismār al-Marwazī[1072] and al-Muthannā b. Ibrāhīm —Ibn Abī Maryam—Mūsā b. Yaʿqūb[1073] —Fā'id, the [186]
mawlā of ʿUbaydallāh b. ʿAlī b. Abī Rāfiʿ[1074] —Ibrāhīm b. ʿAbd al-Raḥmān b. Abī Rabīʿah[1075] : ʿĀ'ishah, the wife of the Prophet, told

1065. Naṣr al-Jahḍamī died in 250/864. See *TB*, XIII, 287–89; *Tahdhīb*, X, 430 f.
1066. Died in 183 or 184/800–1. See *Tahdhīb*, X, 485 f.
1067. See *Tahdhīb*, VIII, 171.
1068. See Qur. 29:14. *Tafsīr*, XX, 87, in the commentary on this verse, contains this tradition.
1069. See again text below, I, 198.
1070. Qur. 71:21.
1071. Qur. 11:37. In order to distinguish between Arabic *safīnah* used for "ark" and *fulk*, the translation "boat" has been used here for the latter.
1072. Ṣāliḥ b. Mismār died between 246 and 250/860–64. See *Tahdhīb*, IV, 403.
1073. See *Tahdhīb*, X, 378 f.
1074. For Fā'id, see *Tahdhīb*, VIII, 256 f. For ʿUbaydallāh, see *Tahdhīb*, VII, 37 f. His grandfather Abū Rāfiʿ was a *mawlā* of the Prophet, see Ibn ʿAbd al-Barr, *Istīʿāb*, IV, 1656 f.
1075. See *Tahdhīb*, I, 138; Bukhārī, *Ta'rīkh*, I, 1, 296 f.

(Ibn Abī Rabī'ah) that the Messenger of God had said: If God had shown mercy to anyone among Noah's people, it would have been the mother of the small child. The Messenger of God continued: Noah had stayed among his people for 950 years calling them to God. Then at the end of this time, he planted a tree which grew and spread in all directions. He then cut it down and began to build an ark. People who were passing by asked him (what he was doing). He replied: I am building an ark from (the tree). They made fun of him and said: You are building an ark on dry land!? How will it float? He replied: You will see. When he finished it "and the oven boiled,"[1076] and there was more and more water in the streets, the mother who loved her small child very much became fearful. She went out to the mountain and climbed one-third of it. When the water reached her there, she climbed two-thirds (on the way up). When the water reached her again, she went up to the summit. When the water was up to her neck, she lifted her child up with her hand[1077] until the water swept it away. If God had shown mercy to anyone of them, it would have been the mother of the small child.

According to (Muḥammad) b. Abī Manṣūr—'Alī b. al-Haytham —al-Musayyab b. Sharīk—Abū Rawq—al-Ḍaḥḥāk—Salmān al-Fārisī: Noah worked on the ark for four hundred years. He had let the teak tree grow for forty years until it grew to be 300 cubits tall—the cubit (being the length of the arm) to the shoulder.[1078]

[187] Noah worked on the ark with God's inspiration and under His instruction. Thus, God willing, it(s dimensions) were[1079] as we were told by Bishr b. Mu'ādh—Yazīd b. Zuray'—Sa'īd—Qatādah: It has been mentioned to us that the ark was 300 cubits long and fifty cubits wide, and its height in the sky was thirty cubits. Its entrance was on the wide side.[1080]

According to al-Ḥārith (b. Muḥammad)—'Abd al-'Azīz[1081] —

1076. Qur. 11:40 and 23:27. See above, n. 807.

1077. The story in *Tafsīr*, XII, 21 f. (*ad* Qur. 11:37-39) has "in front of her" (*bayn yadayhā*). Another version appears in Ibn Hishām, *Tījān*, 24.

1078. Apparently, another cubit than the ordinary one of 0.50 m is intended here. See below, n. 1088.

1079. Hardly, "it came into being."

1080. See Genesis 6:15 f. This, as well as the following tradition, appears in *Tafsīr*, XII, 22 (*ad* Qur. 11:37–39).

1081. On the basis of text below, I, 1721, he has been identified with 'Abd al-'Azīz

Mubārak (b. Faḍālah)—al-Ḥasan: The length of Noah's ark was 1,200 cubits, and its width was 600 cubits.

According to al-Qāsim (b. al-Ḥasan)—al-Ḥusayn (b. Dāwūd)—Ḥajjāj—Mufaḍḍal b. Faḍālah[1082] —'Alī b. Zayd b. Jud'ān—Yūsuf b. Mihrān—Ibn 'Abbās: The Apostles said to Jesus, the son of Mary: Would that you send us a man who saw the ark and could tell us about it. He went with them and came to an earthen hillock. There, he took a handful of the earth in his palm and asked: Do you know what this is? They replied: God and His prophet know best! Jesus said: This is the grave[1083] of Noah's son Ham. He continued. He struck the hill with his staff and said: Rise with God's permission! And behold there was Ham, with grey hair, shaking the earth from his head. Jesus asked him whether he had perished in that state (with grey hair). Ham replied: No, when I died, I was a young man, but I thought the Hour had come, and my hair turned grey. (Jesus) said: Tell us about Noah's ark! He said: It was 1,200 cubits long and 600 cubits wide. It had three stories, one for domestic and wild animals, another for human beings, and a third for birds. When the dung of the animals became excessive, God inspired Noah to tickle the elephant's tail. He did, and a male and a female hog fell down and attacked the dung. When the rat fell down into the seams (of the planks) of the ark and gnawed at them, God inspired Noah to strike the lion between its eyes, and a male [188]
and a female cat came out from its nose and attacked the rat. Jesus asked Ham: How did Noah learn that (all) the places had been under water (but were no longer)? He replied: He sent the raven to bring him information, but it found a corpse and pounced upon it,[1084] whereupon (Noah) cursed the raven that it should be fearful; therefore, the raven does not like houses. He continued. He then sent the dove. It came with an olive leaf in its beak and clay on its feet. Noah thus knew that (all) places had been under water (but were no longer). He continued. Therefore, the dove's necklace[1085] is the greyish-greenness on its neck. Noah blessed the dove that

---

b. Abān, who died in 207/822. See *TB*, X, 442–47; *Tahdhīb*, VI, 329–31.

1082. For this brother of Mubārak mentioned in the preceding *isnād*, see *Tahdhīb*, X, 273.

1083. *Tafsīr*, XII, 22 (*ad* Qur. 11:37–39), has *ka'b* "ankle-bone."

1084. See Ya'qūbī, *Ta'rīkh*, I, 12.

1085. The "necklace" is the ruff of feathers of the ring-dove which is said here to have originated under the circumstances indicated.

it should be tame and safe; therefore, the dove likes houses. He continued. The Apostles said: O Messenger of God, why do you not bring him to our people, so that he can sit down and talk with us? Jesus replied: How could one who has no sustenance follow you? He continued. Then Jesus said to Ham: Go back with God's permission! And Ham turned to dust again.[1086]

According to al-Ḥārith—Ibn Sa'd—Hishām—his father—Abū Ṣāliḥ —Ibn 'Abbās: Noah used carpentry to build the ark on Mount Nūdh,[1087] where the Flood made its appearance. He continued. The ark was 300 cubits long—the cubit being that of the grandfather of Noah's father[1088] —and it was fifty cubits wide. Its height in the sky was thirty cubits, six of which were above the water. It had a number of stories.[1089] He made three entrances for it, one beneath the other.

According to Ibn Ḥumayd—Salamah—Muḥammad b. Isḥāq—someone who is not suspect—'Ubayd b. 'Umayr al-Laythī who used to tell that he had heard that they—Noah's people—used to grab him—Noah—and choke him until he became unconscious. When he regained consciousness, he said: O God! Forgive my people for they do not know![1090] Ibn Isḥāq continued. They persisted in their disobedience (to God) and committed grave sins on earth. Noah had much trouble with them and they with him, and they
[189] caused him great tribulations. He waited for offspring after offspring, but each generation turned out worse than the one before, and eventually, the latest would say: That (Noah) was as crazy with our fathers and grandfathers who would accept nothing he said.[1091] Finally, Noah complained to God about their behavior and said, as told to us by God in His Book: "My Lord! I have called my people night and day, but my calling has only made them shun (me) more"[1092] to the part of the story where he finally says: "My Lord! Let no unbeliever stay on earth! If You do, they will lead Your servants astray and give birth only to wicked unbelievers,"

1086. The story appears in *Tafsīr,* see above, n. 1083.
1087. See above, n. 788.
1088. Apparently, Enoch.
1089. Genesis 6:16.
1090. This statement, with another chain of transmitters, is also found in *Tafsīr,* XXIX, 64 (*ad* Qur. 71:26–28). See Luke 23:34.
1091. Cf. Qur. 54:9.
1092. Qur. 71:5 f.

and on to the end of the story.[1093] When Noah thus complained about them to God and asked Him for help against them, God revealed to him: "And make the boat under Our eyes and with Our inspiration, and do not talk to Me about those who have done wrong. They will drown."[1094] Noah now proceeded to build the boat, because he feared[1095] his people. He began to cut wood and forge iron and prepared the materials for the boat, such as pitch and other material which only he knew to prepare well. While he was engaged in this work, his people who passed by made fun of him and scoffed at him. He would say: "If you make fun of us, we shall make fun of you, just as you do. In the end you will know to whom humiliating punishment will come and upon whom lasting punishment will descend."[1096] He continued. As I have heard it, they would say: Noah, you were a prophet, and now you have become a carpenter! He continued. God made women's wombs infertile, and no children were born to them.

He continued. The people of the Torah assume that God commanded Noah to build the boat from teak wood. He was to make it slanting, to cover it with pitch inside and out, and to make it [190]
eighty cubits long and fifty cubits wide, and its height in the sky thirty cubits. (God commanded him) to build it with three stories, a low, middle, and upper one, and to make windows in it. Noah did as he was commanded by God. Finally, he finished it. God had charged him as follows: "When Our command comes and the oven boils, then[1097] put on board a pair, two of each kind, and your family, except those against whom the decision has already been stated, also those who believed, but only few believed with him."[1098] He made the oven a sign between Himself and Noah and said: "When Our command comes and the oven boils," take in a pair, two of each kind, and board (the ark yourself)! When the oven boiled, Noah put on board those whom God had com-

1093. *Tafsīr*, XII, 22 f. (*ad* Qur. 71:26-28), adds here, and after "wrong" in the following Qur'ānic quotation, "that is, after today."

1094. Qur. 11:37.

1095. *Tafsīr*, XII, 22 f., reads, no doubt wrongly, *w-l-h-y* for *walahan*, yielding the quite plausible meaning: "and he gave up on his people."

1096. Qur. 11:38 f.

1097. The following "We said" of the Qur'ānic text has been restored in the Cairo edition, bur it is also missing in *Tafsīr*, XII, 22 f.

1098. Qur. 11:40.

manded him (to take)—they were few, as God says—and a pair, two of each kind, of any inspirited creature and tree(!), male and female. He brought in his three sons, Shem, Ham, and Japheth, and their wives, as well as six people who believed in him, thus altogether ten individuals, Noah, his sons, and their wives.[1099] Then he brought in the animals, as God had ordered him. His son Yām, who was an unbeliever, remained behind.[1100]

According to Ibn Ḥumayd—Salamah—Ibn Isḥāq—al-Ḥasan b. Dīnār[1101] —ʿAlī b. Zayd—Yūsuf b. Mihrān—Ibn ʿAbbās: I (Yūsuf b. Mihrān) heard him (Ibn ʿAbbās) say: The first animal to be put aboard was the ant, and the last the donkey. When Noah brought the donkey in and its front half was inside, Iblīs—may God curse him!—attached himself to its tail, so that it could not lift its legs. Noah started to say: Woe to you! Go in! The donkey rose but was unable (to proceed). Eventually, Noah said: Woe to you! Go in,
[191] even if Satan is with you! It was a slip of the tongue, but when Noah said it, Satan let the donkey proceed. It went in, and Satan went in with it. Noah said to him: How did you get in here with me, enemy of God? Satan replied: Did you not say: Go in, even if Satan is with you!? Noah said: Get out and leave me, enemy of God! Satan replied: You cannot escape from having me on board. Supposedly, Satan stayed in the rear *(ẓahr)* of the boat.

Now, Noah quietly settled down in the boat, having brought in all those who believed in him. That was on the seventeenth of the month[1102] of the year in which Noah entered (the ark) at the age of six hundred. When he, as well as all those brought aboard by him, had entered, the fountains of the great deep *(ghawṭ)* were set in motion and the gates of heaven opened,[1103] as God says to His prophet: "And We opened the gates of heaven for water to pour out and split the earth for springs (to gush forth). The water (from above and below) met for a matter (pre)determined."[1104] Noah and

---

1099. At first glance, the arithmetic here seems strange, but, as explained in text below, I, 195, the figure ten was reached by not counting the women.

1100. Yām is the name given by tradition to the unnamed son of Noah mentioned in Qur. 11:42 f.. See text below, I, 191. See *Tafsīr,* XII, 22 f. *(ad* Qur. 11:37-39).

1101. See *Tahdhīb,* II, 275 f.

1102. Genesis 7:11: "second month."

1103. See Genesis 7:11.

1104. Qur. 54:11 f. The meaning of the meeting of the waters is explained in text below, I, 192.

those with him entered inside the boat, which sheltered him and those with him on one (of the covered) stories. The time between God's sending down the water and the boat floating upon it was forty days and forty nights. As is assumed by the people of the Torah, the boat floated upon the water which kept rising higher and higher. God says to His Prophet Muḥammad: "And We carried him aboard (a ship) with planks and *dusur*"—meaning nails, iron nails—"which floated under Our eyes, as a reward for one who had been treated with ingratitude."[1105] The boat began to float with him and those with him "on mountainous waves."[1106] When Noah thus saw that the threat of his Lord had come true, "he called out to his son, who was standing apart," and who then perished
with all the others: "Son, come aboard with us, and do not be [192]
with the unbelievers!" He was an unfortunate person who had secretly been an unbeliever. (But he now) "said: I shall withdraw to a mountain which will protect me from the water." He had often taken refuge in the mountains from the rains that fell, and he thought that this would be so again.[1107] Noah "said: There is no one today to give protection against God's command, except for those to whom He shows mercy. Then the waves came between them, and he was among those drowned."[1108]

The water increased wildly and, as is assumed by the people of the Torah, rose fifteen cubits over the mountain tops.[1109] All creatures on the face of the earth, every inspirited being or tree, disappeared. No creature remained except Noah and those with him in the boat, as well as Og b. Anak,[1110] as is assumed by the people of the Book. The time between God's sending the Flood and the receding of the water was six months and ten nights.[1111]

1105. Qur. 54:13 f.

1106. Qur. 11:42.

1107. *Tafsīr*, XII, 23, l. 27 (*ad* Qur. 11:38), has *ya'had* for *yakūn*, with little change in meaning.

1108. Qur. 11:42 f.

1109. Genesis 7:20.

1110. The names are a combination of the Biblical giant king Og of Bashan and the giant Anakim, sons of Anak. Ṭabarī says that Og's height was 800 cubits, see text below, I, 501; according to *Tafsīr*, VI, 119 (*ad* Qur. 5:26), scholars of ancient history agreed that Og was killed by Moses. See, for instance, Ibn Khaldūn, *Muqaddimah*, I, 357 f. and II, 240.

1111. *Tafsīr*, XII, 23 (*ad* Qur. 11:37–39), contains the entire tradition beginning above, I, 190.

According to al-Ḥārith—Ibn Sa'd—Hishām—his father—Abū Ṣāliḥ —Ibn 'Abbās: God sent rain for forty days and forty nights. When the rain hit them, the wild animals, the (domestic) animals, and the birds all went to Noah and were subjected (to labor) for him. As commanded by God, he carried along "pair(s), two of each kind."[1112] He also carried along Adam's corpse, making it a barrier between the women and men.[1113] They boarded the ark on the tenth of Rajab, and they left it on the 'Āshūrā Day, (the tenth day) of al-Muḥarram; therefore, all those people fast on the 'Āshūrā Day.[1114] The water was brought forth in two equal parts. This is (meant by) God's word: "And We opened the gates of heaven for water *munhamirin*"—that is, *munṣabbin* pouring—"and We *fajjarnā*"— that is, *shaqqaqnā* split—"the earth for springs (to gush forth). The water (from above and below) met for a matter (pre)determined."[1115] Thus, (because of the word "meeting" that is used in the verse, it appears that) the water came in two equal
[193] parts, one from heaven, and the other from the earth. It rose fifteen cubits above the highest mountain on earth. The ark carried them around the entire earth in six months. It did not come to rest anywhere until it came to the Sacred Territory (of Mecca and Medina). However, it did not enter the Sacred Territory but circled around for a week. The House built by Adam was lifted up—lifted up, so as not to be submerged—"the inhabited House"[1116] with the Black Stone—on Abū Qubays. After the ark had circled around the Sacred Territory, it traveled with (those aboard) over the earth and eventually reached al-Jūdī—a mountain whose foot is in the land of Mosul—where it came to rest after six months at the completion of seven (nights), or, according to another statement, after

1112. Qur. 11:40.

1113. See text above, I, 163, and *Schatzhöhle*, text, 92, trans., 22; Ya'qūbī, *Ta'rīkh*, I, 10.

1114. See *EI*², I, 705, s. v. 'Āshūrā.

1115. Qur. 54:11 f.

1116. "The inhabited House" of Qur. 52:4 is usually explained as a heavenly counterpart of the Ka'bah. See *Tafsīr*, XXVII, 10 f., on that verse. For the raising of the Ka'bah, see text above, I, 122 and 131.

the six months[1117] —"a curse upon the wrongdoers!"[1118] When it had come to rest upon al-Jūdī, "it was said: Earth, swallow your water!"—meaning, absorb your water that came forth from you—"and Heaven, hold back!"—meaning, restrain your water—"and the water disappeared in the ground"—that is, the earth absorbed it. The water that had come down from heaven became the oceans that are seen on earth today. The last remnant of the Flood on earth was some water at Ḥismā.[1119] It remained on earth for forty years after the Deluge and then disappeared.

The "oven" with the water boiling that God made a sign between Himself and Noah was an oven of stone that belonged to Eve and came into Noah's possession.[1120]

According to Ya'qūb b. Ibrāhīm—Hushaym—Abū Muḥammad[1121] —al-Ḥasan: It was an oven of stone that belonged to Eve and eventually came into Noah's possession. He continued. Noah was told: When you see the water boil forth from the oven, go aboard, you and your companions!

There are differences of opinion concerning the location of the oven and the boiling water which was made by God a sign of what was between Himself and Noah. [194]

Some said: It was in India.

1117. The difference seems to be that on the one hand, there was a period of sixth months and seven (nights, *li-tamām al-sab'*) and, on the other, a period of exactly six months. In the latter case, the Cairo edition reads "seven" (months) without indicating any manuscript evidence. *Li-tamām al-sab'* could hardly refer to the seven circumnavigations of the Ka'bah, see text below, I,197. The correction to *al-sab'ah* suggested in Ṭabarī, *Introductio ect.*, DLXXVIII: "to the completion of seven months," while not impossible, is unlikely.

1118. Qur. 11:44, also the source of the following quotations.

1119. The location of Ḥismā has been sought in far northern Arabia, and even in Ḥarrān. See Yāqūt, *Mu'jam*, II, 367 f.

1120. See above, n. 807.

The following traditions on the provenience and location of the "oven" and the number of people in the ark can all be found in *Tafsīr*, XII, 25 f. (*ad* Qur. 11:40), except for the last tradition below, I, 195, by Hishām al-Kalbī referring to eighty persons.

1121. There are many Abū Muḥammads listed in the biographical dictionaries. The one mentioned as an authority of Hushaym may be meant here. See Bukhārī, *Kunā*, 67, no. 621; Ibn Abī Ḥātim, IV,2, 434, no. 2163; Ibn Ḥajar, *Lisān*, VI, 432, no.1079. See also Ṭabarī, *Introductio etc.*, DLXXVIII.

Those who said this

According to Abū Kurayb—'Abd al-Ḥamīd al-Ḥimmānī[1122] —Abū 'Amr al-Naḍr al-Khazzāz[1123] —'Ikrimah—Ibn 'Abbās, commenting on: "And the oven boiled," as follows: It boiled in India.

Others said: It was in the region of al-Kūfah.

Those who said this

According to al-Ḥārith (b. Muḥammad)—al-Ḥasan[1124] —Khalaf b. Khalīfah[1125] —Layth (b. Abī Sulaym)—Mujāhid: The water gushed forth in the oven. Noah's wife noticed it and told him about it. He continued. This was in the region of al-Kūfah.

According to al-Ḥārith—al-Qāsim[1126] —'Alī b. Thābit[1127] —al-Sarī b. Ismā'īl[1128] : Al-Sha'bī used to swear by God that the oven did not boil anywhere but around al-Kūfah.

There were differences of opinion about the number of the children of Adam who boarded the boat. Some said: They were eighty souls.

Those who said this

According to Mūsā b. 'Abd al-Raḥmān al-Masrūqī[1129] —Zayd b.
[195] al-Ḥubāb[1130] —Ḥusayn b. Wāqid al-Khurāsānī—Abū Nahīk[1131] : I heard Ibn 'Abbās say: In Noah's ark there were eighty men. One of them was Jurhum.[1132]

According to al-Qāsim (b. al-Ḥasan)—al-Ḥusayn (b. Dāwūd)—

1122. 'Abd al-Ḥamīd b. 'Abd al-Raḥmān al-Ḥimmānī died in 202/817[8]. See *Tahdhīb*, VI, 120; Sam'ānī, *Ansāb*, IV, 236 (with much information on his son Yaḥyā, who is listed in *TB*, XIV, 167–77).

1123. For al-Naḍr b. 'Abd al-Raḥmān, see *Tahdhīb*, X, 441 f.

1124. Presumably, al-Ḥasan b. 'Arafah (above, n. 52), listed as a transmitter from Khalaf b. Khalīfah. The reading "al-Qāsim" may have resulted from a mixup with al-Qāsim in the following tradition (n. 1126).

1125. Khalaf b. Khalīfah died at an advanced age ca. 180/796[7]. See *TB*, VIII, 318–20; *Tahdhīb*, III, 150–52.

1126. He is the well-known author Abū 'Ubayd al-Qāsim b. Sallām who died about 224/838[9] at the age of sixty-seven. See *TB*, XII, 403-16; *Tahdhīb*, VIII, 315–18; Brockelmann, *GAL*, Suppl., I, 166 f., *EI*², I, 157, s. v. Abū 'Ubayd.

1127. For 'Alī b. Thābit al- Jazarī, see *TB*, XI, 356–58; *Tahdhīb*, VII, 288 f.

1128. For this nephew of al-Sha'bī, see *Tahdhīb*, III, 459 f.

1129. For al-Masrūqī, who died in 258/871[2], see *Tahdhīb*, X, 355 f.

1130. Zayd b. al-Ḥubāb died in 203/818[9]. See *TB*, VIII, 442–44; *Tahdhīb*, III, 402–4.

1131. For Abū Nahīk 'Uthmān b. Nahīk, see *Tahdīb*, XII, 259.

1132. Jurhum was the supposed ancestor of an ancient Arabian tribe. See *EI*², II, 603 f., s. v. Djurhum. In the Biblical genealogies of Arabic tribes, the Jurhum figure among the descendants of Arpachshad.

Ḥajjāj—Ibn Jurayj—Ibn 'Abbās: Noah carried eighty persons aboard the ark.

According to al-Ḥārith—'Abd al-'Azīz (b. Abān)—Sufyān: Some(one) used to say: They were eighty, referring to "the few" in God's word: "But only a few believed with him."[1133]

According to al-Ḥārith—Ibn Sa'd—Hishām—his father—Abū Ṣāliḥ—Ibn 'Abbās: Noah carried in the ark his sons Shem, Ham, and Japheth, and his daughters-in-law, the wives of those sons of his, as well as seventy-three of the children of Seth who believed in him. Thus, there were eighty in the ark.

Some said: Rather, they were eight souls.

Those who said this

According to Bishr b. Mu'ādh—Yazīd b. Zuray'—Sa'īd—Qatādah: It was mentioned to us that only Noah, his wife, his three sons, and their wives, a total of eight, were all together in the ark.

According to Ibn Wakī' and al-Ḥasan b. 'Arafah—Yaḥyā b. 'Abd al-Malik b. Abī Ghaniyyah—his father—al-Ḥakam, commenting on: "But only a few believed with him," as follows: Noah, his three sons, and his four daughters-in-law.[1134]

According to al-Qāsim—al-Ḥusayn—Ḥajjāj—Ibn Jurayj: I was told that Noah carried along his three sons and three wives of his sons and his own wife; the men with their spouses thus numbered eight. The names of his sons were Shem, Ham, and Japheth. Ham [196]
attacked his wife (sexually) in the ark, so Noah prayed that his seed be altered, and he produced the blacks.[1135]

Others said: Rather, they were seven souls.

Those who said this

According to al-Ḥārith—'Abd al-'Azīz (b. Abān)—Sufyān—al-A'mash, commenting on: "And only a few believed with him," as follows: They were seven: Noah, three daughters-in-law, and three sons of his.

Others said: They were ten, not counting their wives.

1133. Qur. 11:40.

1134. Presumably, his three daughters-in-law and his wife, *kanā'in* here being understood as female relations through marriage.

1135. Ham's disregard of the prohibition of intercourse in the ark is mentioned in the Babylonian Talmud. See Sanhedrin 108b; Speyer, *Biblische Erzählungen*, 106; Lewis, *A study of the interpretation of Noah*, 144. See also above, n. 1113, and text below, I, 198.

Those who said this

According to Ibn Ḥumayd—Salamah—Ibn Isḥāq: He carried along his three sons, Shem, Ham, and Japheth, and their wives, as well as six men of those who believed in him. Thus, they were ten individuals, counting Noah, his sons, and (but not counting) their spouses.[1136]

As mentioned by the scholars among the people of the Book and others, God sent the Flood, after 600 years of Noah's life had passed and 2,256 years had elapsed since Adam was cast down to earth.

God reportedly sent the Flood on the 13th of Āb (August). Noah remained in the boat until the water had disappeared into the ground. The boat settled on Mount al-Jūdī in Qardā[1137] on the seventeenth day of the sixth month. Upon leaving the ark, Noah chose a place in the region of Qardā in the Jazīrah and built himself a village there which he called Thamānīn ("Eighty") because he had built a house there for each of the men who were with him; they were eighty. To this day, the village is called Sūq
[197] Thamānīn.[1138]

According to al-Ḥārith—Ibn Sa'd—Hishām b. Muḥammad—his father—Abū Ṣāliḥ—Ibn 'Abbās: Noah came down at a village, and each one of them built a house. Therefore, the village was called Sūq Thamānīn. All the children of Cain drowned. All the forefa-

---

1136. See above, n. 1099.

1137. Qardū (Qardō) is the targumic and Syriac rendering of Ararat in Genesis 8:4. See also *Schatzhöhle*, text, 98, trans., 23. The date there is given as the seventeenth day of the seventh month equated with Teshrīn I (October).

For the relationship of Qardō with Gordyaia, Gordyene, Kardouchoi, and Kurds, see *EI*², V, 447-49, s. v. Kurds, Kurdistān. For the Greek forms, see Pauly-Wissowa, especially, the entry Kardouchoi. For further Jewish and Christian references, see Kronholm, *Motifs*, 200 f.

For the Arabic form Qardā, see Yāqūt, *Mu'jam*, IV, 56, and the brief entry Ḳardā and Bāzabdā in *EI*², IV, 639a. The form Bāqardā (as well as al(!)-Thamanīn and 'Ayn Wardah [below, n. 1142]) appears already in Muqātil b. Sulaymān's *Tafsīr* in the commentary on Qur. 11:40.

The form al-Jūdī could very well have originated from a conflation of *Gurdī (Gordy-), slightly misread in its Syriac form, with some mountain in Arabia.

For al-Jazīrah, see *EI*², II, 523 f., s. v. al-Djazīra.

1138. For the Market of Thamānīn, see Yāqūt, *Mu'jam*, I, 934, and IV, 56; Sam'ānī, *Ansāb*, III, 149; Canard, *Ḥamdanides*, I, 112. *Schatzhöhle*, text, 102, trans., 24, states that eight persons left the ark and built the city called Thamānōn. See also Ya'qūbī, *Ta'rīkh*, I, 12; Mas'ūdī, *Murūj*, I, 75. [Thamānōn is hardly intended to be an Arabic form.]

thers between Noah and Adam were in the state of *islām*.

Abū Ja'far (al-Ṭabarī) says: (Noah) and his family became (muslims), whereupon God revealed to him that he would never bring another Flood to the earth.

According to 'Abbād b. Ya'qūb al-Asadī[1139] —al-Muḥāribī—'Uthmān b. Maṭar[1140] —'Abd al-'Azīz b. 'Abd al-Ghafūr[1141] —his father—the Messenger of God: Noah boarded the ark on the first day of Rajab. He and all those with him fasted. The ark floated with them for six months—thus, until al-Muḥarram. The ark anchored upon al-Jūdī on the 'Āshūrā Day, and Noah fasted and ordered all the wild and (domestic) animals with him to fast in gratitude to God.

According to al-Qāsim—al-Ḥusayn—Ḥajjāj—Ibn Jurayj: The upper story of the ark was occupied by the birds, the one in the middle by the human beings, and the lowest by the wild beasts. Its height in the sky was thirty cubits. The ark took off from 'Ayn Wardah[1142] on Friday, Rajab 10th. It anchored upon al-Jūdī on the 'Āshūrā Day. It passed by the House, which had been lifted up by God so it would not be submerged, and circumnavigated it seven times. It then went to the Yemen, and then returned.

According to al-Qāsim—al-Ḥusayn—Ḥajjāj—Abū Ja'far ('Īsā b. Māhān) al-Rāzī—Qatādah: When Noah went down from the ark on the tenth day of al-Muḥarram, he said to those with him: Those of you who have been fasting should complete their fast, and those of you who had been breaking the fast should fast. [198]

According to Bishr b. Mu'ādh—Yazīd (b. Zuray')—Sa'īd (b. Abī 'Arūbah)—Qatādah: It has been mentioned to us that it—meaning the boat—departed with them on the tenth of Rajab. It was in the water for 150 days and came to rest upon al-Jūdī for a month. They were brought down on the tenth of al-Muḥarram, the 'Āshūrā Day.

According to al-Qāsim—al-Ḥusayn—Ḥajjāj—Abū Ma'shar—Muḥammad b. Qays: In the time of Noah, every span of land on earth was claimed by some human being.

1139. 'Abbād b. Ya'qūb died in 250/end of 864. See *Tahdhīb*, V, 109 f.

1140. For 'Uthmān b. Maṭar, see *TB*, XI, 277–79; *Tahdhīb*, VII, 154 f.

1141. Ibn Abī Ḥātim, III, 1, 55, lists an Abū al-Ṣabāḥ 'Abd al-Ghafūr b. 'Abd al-'Azīz al-Wāsiṭī, who may have been a son of the individual mentioned here.

1142. See *EI*², I, 789a, s. v. 'Ayn al-Warda; Yāqūt, *Mu'jam*, III, 764; Bakrī, *Mu'jam*, IV, 1376, where it is described as the location of the "oven," as it is in Muqātil, *Tafsīr*, on Qur. 23:27.

As I was told by Naṣr b. ʿAlī al-Jahḍamī—Nūḥ b. Qays—ʿAwn b. Abī Shaddād: After the Flood, Noah lived another 350 years—that is, after the 950 years he had spent among his people.[1143]

Ibn Isḥāq, in turn, as we were told by Ibn Ḥumayd—Salamah (—Ibn Isḥāq), said: It is assumed by the people of the Torah that Noah lived for 348 years[1144] after coming down from the boat. He continued. The total length of Noah's life was 950 years. God then took him unto Himself.

Shem was reportedly born to Noah ninety-eight years before the Flood.[1145] Some of the people of the Torah say: There was no begetting (in the ark). (Additional) children were born to Noah only after the Flood and after he had left the boat.

They said: Those who were with him in the boat were people who believed in him and followed him. However, they disappeared and perished, and no descendants of theirs survived. In this world today, the children of Adam are the direct offspring of Noah and of no other descendants of Adam, as God says: "And We
[199] made his offspring the survivors."[1146]

Before the Flood, two sons were reportedly born to Noah who both perished. One of them was called Canaan. He continued. He was the one who drowned in the Flood. The other was called Eber. He died before the Flood.[1147]

According to al-Ḥārith—Ibn Saʿd—Hishām—his father—Abū Ṣāliḥ —Ibn ʿAbbās: Born to Noah were Shem, whose descendants were reddish-white; Ham, whose descendants were black with hardly any whiteness; and Japheth, whose descendants were reddish-brown. Canaan—the one who drowned—was called Yām by the Arabs. He occurs in the saying: Our paternal uncle Yām —he was balmy.[1148] They all had the same mother.

1143. See above, n. 1069.

1144. Since Genesis 8:13 says that Noah was 601 years old when he left the ark, 349 would have been a slightly more exact figure.

1145. According to *Schatzhöhle*, text, 76, trans., 18, Lamech died forty years before the Flood, and Shem was then in his sixty-eighth year. Thus, the birth of Shem took place 108 years before the Flood.

1146. Qur. 37:77.

1147. This statement appears to have been meant originally to indicate that the later Canaan (Genesis 10:6) and Eber (Genesis 10:21) had predeceased uncles after whom they were named. On the earlier Canaan, see Muqātil, *Tafsīr*, on Qur. 11:40.

1148. This, perhaps, is the approximate meaning of the ditty *Innamā hām—*

The Magians have no knowledge of the Flood.[1149] They say: Our rule continued uninterrupted since the age of Jayūmart—who they say is identical with Adam. It was inherited by consecutive rulers to the time of Fērōz b. Yazdjard b. Shahriyār.[1150] They (also) say: If (the story of the Flood) were sound, the pedigrees of the people would have been disrupted and their rule dissolved. Some of them acknowledge the Flood and assume that it took place in the clime of Bābil and nearby regions, whereas the descendants of Jayūmart had their dwellings in the East, and the Flood did not reach them.

Abū Ja'far (al-Ṭabarī) says: The information given by God concerning the Flood contradicts their statement, and what He says is the truth: "Noah called upon Us—and surely, good are those who respond![1151] We delivered him and his family from the great distress and made his offspring the survivors."[1152] God thus indicates that Noah's offspring are the survivors, and nobody else.

I have already mentioned the disagreement among people concerning Jayūmart. Some contradicted the Persians with respect to his identity and traced his pedigree to Noah.[1153]

According to Ibn Bashshār—Ibn 'Athmah[1154] —Sa'īd b. Bashīr[1155] —Qatādah—al-Ḥasan—Samurah b. Jundub—the Prophet, in connection with commenting on God's word: "And We made his offspring the survivors": Shem, Ham, and Japheth. [200]

According to Bishr (b. Mu'ādh)—Yazīd (b. Zuray')—Sa'īd (b. Abī

'ammunā Yām.

1149. See Mas'ūdī, *Murūj*, II, 105 f. For references to a limited flood allegedly from Persian tradition, see Pingree, *Thousands*, 5 ff., 39 f.

1150. See text above, I, 147 f. The insertion here of a son of Yazdjard III called Pērōz is probably not explainable.

1151. This is taken to refer to God as the One Who hears prayers.

1152. Qur. 37:75–77.

1153. See text above, I, 17 and 147.

1154. For Muḥammad b. Khālid, who was called Ibn 'Athmah after his mother 'Athmah, see *Tahdhīb*, IX, 142 f.

1155. Sa'īd b. Bashīr died eighty-nine years old between 168 and 170/784–87. See *Tahdhīb*, IV, 8–10.

ʿArūbah)—Qatādah, commenting on God's word: "And We made his offspring the survivors," as follows: All human beings are the offspring of Noah.

According to ʿAlī b. Dāwūd[1156] —Abū Ṣāliḥ (ʿAbdallāh b. Ṣāliḥ)—Muʿāwiyah (b. Ṣāliḥ)—ʿAlī (b. Abī Ṭalḥah)—Ibn ʿAbbās, commenting on God's word: "And We made his offspring the survivors," as follows: Only the offspring of Noah remained.[1157]

The Use of Eras

The following report of al-Zuhrī and al-Shaʿbī has been transmitted from ʿAlī b. Mujāhid[1158] —Ibn Isḥāq—al-Zuhrī. Also (Ibn Isḥāq—) Muḥammad b. Ṣāliḥ[1159] —al-Shaʿbī: When Adam fell down from Paradise and his descendants spread out, Adam's children established an era starting with his fall. This era continued, until God sent Noah. Then an era starting with Noah's mission (as prophet) was used, until the Drowning occurred and all those on the face of the earth perished. When Noah, his offspring, and all those in the ark came down to earth, he divided the earth among his sons into three parts.[1160] To Shem, he gave the middle of the earth where Jerusalem, the Nile, the Euphrates, the Tigris, the Sayḥān,[1161] the Jayḥān (Gihon), and the Fayshān (Pishon) are located. It extends from the Pishon to east of the Nile and from the region from where the southwind blows to the region from where the northwind blows. To Ham, he gave the part (of the earth) west of the Nile and regions beyond to the region from where the westwind blows. The part he gave to Japheth was located at the Pishon

---

1156. Died in 272/886. See *TB*, XI, 424 f.; *Tahdhīb*, VII, 317 (with probable misprints in the dates of death); Horst, 293, n. 1. See above, n. 333.

1157. The preceding three traditions appear in *Tafsīr*, XXIII, 43 (*ad* Qur. 37:77). They are out of place here and probably were inserted by Ṭabarī as an afterthought when he remembered them from his commentary on the Qur'ānic passage.

1158. ʿAlī b. Mujāhid died in or about 182/798. See *TB*, XII, 106 f.; *Tahdhīb*, VII, 377 f.; Sezgin, *GAS*, I, 312.

1159. Muḥammad b. Ṣāliḥ b. Dīnār, an expert in the history of the Raids (*maghāzī*), died in 168/784–85. See *Tahdhīb*, IX, 225 f.

1160. The division of the earth in Jubilees is understandably different.

1161. In Muslim times, the names of Sayḥān and Jayḥān were given to two rivers in Cilicia. See *EI*[2] , II, 502 f., s. v. Djayḥān. Sayḥān has no known Biblical or other literary antecedent. The reference here no doubt originated in the by then familiar pairing of Jayḥān with Sayḥān. A connection with Sihon, the king of the Amorites, is unlikely but not entirely impossible in the context.

and regions beyond to the region from where the eastwind blows.

The eras (thereafter) were: from the Flood to the fire of Abraham;[1162] (from the fire of Abraham) to the mission of Joseph; from the mission of Joseph to the mission of Moses; from the mission of Moses to the reign of Solomon; from the reign of Solomon to the mission of Jesus, the son of Mary; and from the mission of Jesus, the son of Mary, to when the Messenger of God was sent. [201]

These eras mentioned by al-Shaʿbī must be those used by the Jews, for the Muslims started the (use of an) era only with the hijrah. Before it, they had no era, except that the Quraysh reportedly used the Year the Elephant for dating, while all the other Arabs used their well-known (battle) days, such as the Day of Jabalah, the First Kulāb, and the Second Kulāb.[1163]

The Christians used the period of Alexander Dhū al-Qarnayn (as the beginning of their era. I think they still use that era today.[1164]

The Persians used (the reigns of) their rulers for dating. As far as I know, they now (use) the period of Yazdjard b. Shahriyār, because he was the last of their kings to rule Bābil and the East.

1162. Cf. Qur. 21:69. See Speyer, *Biblische Erzählungen*, 142–44; Schützinger, 106 ff.

1163. For the famous pre-Islamic battle days see, for instance, Egbert Meyer, *Der historische Gehalt der Aiyām al-'Arab* (Wiesbaden, 1970). See also *EI*², II, 895, s. v. al-fīl, for the Year of the Elephant, and II, 353 f., s. v. Djabala, for the Day of Jabalah.

1164. Note Ṭabarī's hesitancy with regard to the use of the Seleucid era and the era of Yazdjard in his time.

Bibliography of Cited Works

ʿAbbādī, *Ṭabaqāt: al-fuqahāʾ al-Shāfiʿiyyah*. Edited by G. Vitestam. Leiden, 1964. Veröffentlichungen der de Goeje–Stiftung 21.

ʿAbd al-Jabbār, *Sharḥ al-uṣūl al-khamsah*. Edited by ʿAbd al-Karīm ʿUthmān. Cairo, 1384/1965.

ʿAbd al-Qādir al-Baghdādī, *Khizānah: Khizānat al-adab*. Būlāq, 1299.

ʿAbd al-Qādir al-Qurashī: *al-Jawāhir al-muḍiyyah*. Hyderabad, 1332.

Abū Bakr al-Khuwārizmī, *Rasāʾil*: Constantinople, 1297.

Abū Dāwūd, *Sunan*. Cairo, 1369-70/1950-51.

Abū al-Faraj al-Iṣfahānī, *Adab al-ghurabāʾ*: Edited by Ṣalāḥ al-dīn al-Munajjid. Beirut, 1972.

Abū al-Faraj al-Iṣfahānī: See *Aghānī*.

Abū al-Faraj al-Iṣfahānī, *Maqātil al-Ṭālibiyyin*: Edited by al-Sayyid Aḥmad Ṣaqr. Cairo, 1368/1949.

Abū Isḥāq al-Shīrāzī, *Ṭabaqāt: al-fuqahāʾ*. Baghdad, 1356.

Abū Maʿshar, *Ulūf*: See Pingree, *Thousands*.

Abū Nuʿaym (al-Iṣfahānī), *Akhbār Iṣbahān*. Edited by S. Dedering. Leiden, 1931-34.

Abū Shāmah, *Rawḍatayn: al-Rawḍatayn fī akhbār al-dawlatayn*. Cairo, 1287-88. Edited by M. Ḥilmī M. Aḥmad. Cairo, 1956.

Aghā Buzurg al-Ṭihrānī, *Ṭabaqāt aʿlām al-Shīʿah*. Beirut, 1392/1972.

Aghānī: Abū al-Faraj al-Iṣfahānī. *Kitāb al-Aghānī*. Būlāq, 1285. *Aghānī*[3]. Cairo, 1345 ff.

Allard, *Attributs*: M. Allard. *Le problème des attributs divins*. Beirut, 1965.

Andrae, *Person*: Tor Andrae. *Die Person Muhammeds in Lehre und Glauben seiner Gemeinde*. Stockholm, 1918.

Anklesaria: See *Bundahishn*.

Arabian Nights: Edited by Muhsin Mahdi. Leiden, 1984.
Arberry, "A Baghdad cookery book": See *Ṭabīkh.*
Arberry (A. J.), *The Koran Interpreted.* London, 1965.
'Arīb: 'Arīb b. Sa'd al-Qurṭubī. *Ṭabarī Continuatus.* Edited by M. J. de Goeje. Leiden, 1897. (Reprinted in Vol XI of Ṭabarī, *History,* ed. Cairo.)
al-Aʿshā, *Dīwān.* Edited by R. Geyer. London, 1928. E. J. W. Gibb Memorial Series, N. S. 6.
Ashʿarī, *Maqālāt*: al-Ashʿarī. *Maqālāt al-Islāmiyyīn.* Edited by Hellmut Ritter. Wiesbaden, 1963. Bibliotheca Islamica 1.
Awn (P. J.), *Satan's Tragedy and Redemption.* Leiden, 1983.
Azharī, *Tahdhīb*: Al-Azharī. *Tahdhīb al-lughah.* Edited by ʿAbd al-Salām M. Hārūn, M. ʿAlī al-Najjār, and Ibrāhīm al-Ibyārī. Cairo, 1964-67.
Baḥshal, *History of Wāsiṭ: Ta'rīkh Wāsiṭ.* Edited by Gūrgīs ʿAwwād. Baghdad, 1387/1967.
Bakrī, *Muʿjam: mā istaʿjam.* Edited by Muṣṭafā al-Saqqā'. Cairo, 1364-71/1945-51.
Becker (C. H.), "Ṭabarī's sogenannte Catechesis Mahometana": *Zeitschrift der Deutschen Morgenländischen Gesellschaft* 55 [1901]: 96 f.
Bell (R.), *The Qur'ān.* Edinburgh, 1937-39.
Berēshīt Rabbā: Edited by J. Theodor and Ch. Albeck. Berlin, 1912-36.
Bergsträsser, "Quellen": G. Bergsträsser, "Die Quellen von Jāqūt's Iršād." *Zeitschrift für Semitistik* 2 [1924]: 184-218.
Bīrūnī, *Chronology: Al-Āthār al-bāqiyah ʿan al-qurūn al-khāliyah.* Edited and translated by C. Eduard (Edward) Sachau. Leipzig, 1878; London, 1879.
Bīrūnī, *Ṣaydanah.* Edited and translated by Hakim Muhammad Said. Karachi, 1973.
al-Birzālī. *History.* See General Introduction, n. 284.
Book of Adam and Eve: Translated by S. C. Mahan. London and Edinburgh, 1882.
Bowen: Harold Bowen. *The Life and Times of ʿAlí ibn ʿÍsà: the "Good Vizier".* Cambridge, 1928.
Brockelmann, *GAL* (*GAL*^{2}, *GAL*, Suppl.): C. Brockelmann, *Geschichte der arabischen Litteratur.* Weimar, 1898-1902 (Leiden, 1943-49; Leiden, 1937-42).
Brockelmann (C.), *Lex(icon) Syr(iacum)*^{2} . Halle, 1928.
Bukhārī, *Kunā.* Hyderabad, 1360.
Bukhārī, *Ṣaḥīḥ*: See Ibn Ḥajar, *Fatḥ.*
Bukhārī, *Ta'rīkh.* Hyderabad, 1360-78/1941-59.
Bulliet, *Patricians*: R. W. Bulliet. *The Patricians of Nishapur.* Cambridge, Mass., 1972.

Bundahishn: Das Bundehesh. Edited and translated by F. Justi. Leipzig, 1868; *Zand-Akāsīh. Iranian or Greater Bundahišn.* Edited and translated by B. T. Anklesaria. Bombay, 1956.
Cahen, "L'historiographie arabe": Cl. Cahen, "L'historiographie arabe des origines au VIIe s. H." *Arabica* 33 [1986]: 133-198.
Cambridge History of Iran: Vol. 4. Cambridge, 1975.
Cameron (A. J.), *Abū Dharr al-Ghifārī.* London, 1973.
Canard, *Ḥamdanides*: M. Canard. *Histoire de la dynastie des H'amdanides*, Vol. I. Algiers, 1951.
Canard: See Ṣūlī, *Akhbār.*
Charfi (Abdalmajid), "Christianisme": "Le christianisme dans le Tafsīr de Ṭabarī." *Mélanges de l'Institut Dominicain d'Études Orientales du Caire* 16 [1983]: 117-68. English translation in *Islamochristiana* 6 [1980]: 105-48.
Christensen (A.): *Les types du Premier Homme et du Premier Roi.* I^e^ *partie: Gajōmard, Masyaγet* Masyānaγ, Hōšang et Taχmōraw. Stockholm, 1917. IIe partie: Jim. Leiden, 1934. Archives d'Études Orientales, 14: 1–2.
Concordance: A. J. Wensinck and others. *Concordance et Indices de la Tradition Musulmane.* Leiden, 1936-69.
Crum: W. E. Crum. *A Coptic Dictionary.* Oxford, 1939.
Dhahabī, *ʿIbar: al-ʿIbar fī khabar man ghabar.* Edited by Ṣalaḥ al-dīn al-Munajjid and Fu'ād Sayyid. Kuwait, 1960-66.
Dhahabī, *Mīzān: al-iʿtidāl.* Edited by ʿAlī M. al-Bajāwī. Cairo, 1382/1963.
Dhahabī, *Nubalā': Siyar al-aʿlām al-nubalā'.* Cairo, 1956 ff.
Dhahabī, *Tadhkirat al-ḥuffāẓ.* Hyderabad, 1333-34.
Dhahabī, *ʿUluww: al-ʿUluww li-al-ʿAliyy al-Ghaffār fī ṣaḥīḥ al-akhbār wa-saqīmihā.* Edited by ʿAbd al-Raḥmān M. ʿUthmān. Cairo, 1388/1968.
Dhayl: Ṭabarī's *Dhayl al-mudhayyal*, ed. Leiden, III, 2295-2561, ed. Cairo, XI, 492-705.
Dīnawarī, *al-Akhbār al-ṭiwāl*: Abū Ḥanīfah al-Dīnawarī. *al-Akhbār al-ṭiwāl.* Cairo, n.d.
Dīnawarī, *Nabāt*: Abū Ḥanīfah al-Dīnawarī. *Kitāb al-Nabāt.* Edited by B. Lewin. Wiesbaden, 1974. Bibliotheca Islamica 26.
Dioscurides. Edited by M. Wellmann. Berlin, 1907-14.
Dozy: R. Dozy. *Supplément aux dictionnaires arabes.* Leiden, 1881.
Eche, *Les bibliothèques arabes*: Youssef Eche. *Les Bibliothēqes arabes.* Damascus, 1967.
Eclipse: See Miskawayh.
EI: Encyclopaedia of Islam. EI^2, *Encyclopaedia of Islam*, 2nd edition. Leiden, 1960 ff. *EI*^{2}, *Suppl(ement).* Leiden, 1980 ff. Also *Shorter En-*

cyclopaedia of Islam. Leiden, 1965.

Eilers, "Der Name Demawend": W. Eilers, "Der Name Demawend." *Archiv Orientální* 22 [1954]: 267-374, 24 [1956]: 183-224.

Encyclopaedia Iranica. Edited by Ehsan Yarshater. London, 1982 ff.

Ephraem Syri in Genesim: et in Exodum Commentarii. Edited and translated by R.-M. Tonneau. Louvain, 1955. Corpus Scriptorum Christianorum Orientalium, Scriptores Syri 152 and 153.

Ferré, "Vie de Jésus": A. Ferré, "La vie de Jésus d'après les Annales de Ṭabarī." *Islamochristiana* 5 [1979]: 7-29.

Firdawsī, *Shāhnāmah.* Edited and translated by J. Mohl. Paris, 1838-78. "Russian edition" refers to the edition by E. E. Bertels and others. Moscow, 1960-71.

Fitzmyer (J. A.), *The Genesis Apocryphon: of Qumran Cave I.* Rome, 1966.

Fraade, *Enosh*: S. D. Fraade. *Enosh and his generation.* Chico, California, 1984.

Fraenkel, *Fremdwörter*: S. Fraenkel, *Die aramäischen Fremdwörter im Arabischen.* Leiden 1886.

Fück, *Arabische Studien*: J. Fück. *Die arabischen Studien in Europa.* Leipzig, 1955.

Fück, "Neue Materialien": J. Fück, "Neue Materialien zum Fihrist." *Zeitschrift der Deutschen Morgenländischen Gesellschaft* 90 [1936]: 291-321.

GAL: See Brockelmann.

GAS: See Sezgin.

Genesis Apocryphon. Edited and translated by N. Avigad and Y. Yadin. Jerusalem, 1956.

Ghazi, "Raffinés": F. M. Ghazi, "Un groupe social: 'Les Raffinés' *(Ẓurafā').*" Studia Islamica 11 [1959]: 39-71.

Gilliot, "Les sept lectures." *Studia Islamica* 61 [1985]: 5-25, 63 [1986]: 49-62.

Ginzel: F. K. Ginzel, *Handbuch der mathematischen und technischen Chronologie.* Leipzig, 1906-14.

Gluck (T.), *The Arabic legend of Seth, the Father of Mankind.* New Haven, 1968 (unpublished Yale dissertation).

Götze (A.), "Die Nachwirkung der Schatzhöhle." *Zeitschrift für Semitistik* 2 [1923]: 51-94, 3 [1924]: 53-71, 153-77.

Goldziher, "Die literarische Thätigkeit": I. Goldziher, "Die literarische Thätigkeit des Ṭabarī nach Ibn ʿAsākir." *Wiener Zeitschrift für die Kunde des Morgenlandes* 9 [1895]: 359-71. Reprinted in Goldziher's *Gesammelte Schriften.* Edited by J. Desomogyi. Vol. III. Hildesheim, 1969. See General Introduction, n. 18.

Goldziher (I.), *Muslim Studies*. English translation by C. R. Barber and S. M. Stern. London, 1967-71.
Goldziher, *Richtungen*: I. Goldziher. *Die Richtungen der islamischen Koranauslegung*. Reprinted Leiden, 1952.
Goldziher (I.), *(Die) Ẓāhiriten*. Leipzig, 1884.
Ḥājjī Khalīfah, ed. Yaltkaya: *Kashf al-ẓunūn*. Edited by Sherefettin Yaltkaya. Istanbul, 1941-43.
Halperin (D.J.), "The Ibn Ṣayyād traditions": *Journal of the American Oriental Society* 96[1976]: 213-25.
Hamadhānī, *Takmilah*: Muḥammad b. ʿAbd al-Malik al-Hamadhānī. *Takmilat Ta'rīkh al-Ṭabarī*. Edited by A. Y. Kanʿān. 2nd printing. Beirut, 1961. (Reprinted in the Cairo edition of *History*, Vol. XI.)
Hamaker, *Specimen*: H. A. Hamaker. *Specimen catalogi codicum mss. orientalium Bibliothecae Academiae Lugduno-Batavae*. Leiden, 1820.
Ḥamzah al-Iṣfahānī, *Annales: Ta'rīkh sinī mulūk al-arḍ*. Edited by J. M. E. Gottschalk. Petersburg and Leipzig, 1844-48.
Hāshimī, *ʿIlal*: ʿAlī b. Sulaymān al-Hāshimī, *The Book of the Reasons behind Astronomical Tables. Kitāb fī ʿIlal al-zījāt*. Edited and translated by F. I. Haddad, E. S. Kennedy, and D. Pingree. Delmar, N. Y., 1981.
Heine (P.), *Weinstudien*. Wiesbaden, 1982.
Hemgesberg (H.), *Abu Huraira*. Frankfurt am Main, 1965.
D'Herbelot, *Bibliothèque: Orientale*. Paris, 1697.
History: refers to Ṭabarī's *Ta'rīkh*.
Horst: H. Horst, "Zur Überlieferung im Korankommentar aṭ-Ṭabarī's." *Zeitschrift der Deutschen Morgenländischen Gesellschaft* 103 [1953]: 290-307.
Ḥudūd al-ʿālam: Translated by V. Minorsky. London, 1937. E. J. W. Gibb Memorial Series, N. S. 11.
Ḥūfī: Aḥmad M. al-Ḥūfī. *Al-Ṭabarī*. Cairo, [1382/1963]. *Aʿlām al-ʿArab* 13.
Ibn ʿAbd al-Barr, *Istīʿāb: al-Istīʿāb fī maʿrifat al-aṣḥāb*. Edited by ʿAlī M. al-Bajāwī. Cairo [ca. 1380/1960],
Ibn ʿAbd al-Ḥakam, *Futūḥ Miṣr: The History of the Conquest of Egypt, North Africa and Spain*. Edited by C. C. Torrey. New Haven, 1922. Yale Oriental Series–Researches 3.
Ibn Abī ʿAwn, *al-Ajwibah al-muskitah*. Edited by M. ʿAbd al-Qādir Aḥmad. Cairo, 1985.
Ibn Abī al-Ḥadīd, *Sharḥ: Nahj al-balāghah*. Edited by Ḥasan Tamīm. Beirut, 1963-65. Ed. Cairo, 1379/1959.
Ibn Abī Ḥātim: ʿAbd al-Raḥmān b. Abī Ḥātim Muḥammad b. Idrīs al-Rāzī.

Kitāb al-Jarḥ wa-al-ta'dīl. Hyderabad, 1941-53.
Ibn Abī Ḥātim, *Taqdimah*: Hyderabad, 1371-1952.
Ibn Abī Ya'lā, *Ṭabaqāt: al-Ḥanābilah.* Edited by M. Ḥāmid al-Fiqī. Cairo, 1371/1952.
Ibn 'Asākir: refers to the Ṭabarī biography from Ibn 'Asākir, *Ta'rīkh Dimashq*, published in Ṭabarī, *Introductio etc.*, LXIX-XCVI.
Ibn 'Asākir, *Tahdhīb: Ta'rīkh Dimashq.* Edited by 'Abd al-Qādir b. Aḥmad b. Badrān and Aḥmad 'Ubayd. Damascus, 1329 ff. (Vol. 7: Damascus, 1351).
Ibn al-Athīr, *Kāmil.* Edited by J. C. Tornberg. Leiden, 1851-74.
Ibn al-Athīr, *Nihāyah*: Majd al-dīn b. al-Athīr. *al-Nihāyah fi gharīb al-ḥadīth.* Cairo, 1322.
Ibn Farḥūn, *Dībāj: al-Dībāj al-mudhahhab fī ma'rifat a'yān 'ulamā' al-madhhab.* Cairo, 1351/1932.
Ibn Ḥajar, *Durar: ad-Durar al-kāminah fī a'yān al-mi'ah ath-thāminah.* Hyderabad, 1348-50.
Ibn Ḥajar, *Fatḥ: al-Bārī bi-sharḥ al-Bukhārī.* Cairo, 1378-83/1959-63.
Ibn Ḥajar, *Lisān: al-Mīzān.* Hyderabad, 1329-31.
Ibn Ḥajar, *Tahdhīb: al-Tahdhīb.* Hyderabad, 1325-27. Cited as *Tahdhīb* in the notes to the translation.
Ibn Ḥanbal, *Musnad* (also cited as Ibn Ḥanbal): Aḥmad b. Muḥammad b. Ḥanbal. *al-Musnad.* Cairo, 1313.
Ibn Ḥazm, *Fiṣal: al-Fiṣal fī al-milal wa-al-ahwā' wa-al-niḥal.* Cairo, 1317-21.
Ibn Hishām, *Sīrah.* Edited by F. Wüstenfeld. Göttingen, 1858-60. Translated by A. Guillaume. Oxford University Press, 1955, reprinted Karachi, 1967.
Ibn Hishām, *Tījān.* Hyderabad, 1347.
Ibn al-'Imād, *Shadharāt: al-dhahab fī akhbār man dhahab.* Cairo, 1350-51.
Ibn al-Jawzī, *Da'f: shubah al-tashbīh.* Cairo, n. y.
Ibn al-Jawzī, *Manāqib: al-Imām Aḥmad b. Ḥanbal.* Edited by 'Alī M. 'Umar and 'Abdallāh b. 'Abd al-Muḥsin al-Turkī. Cairo, 1399/1979.
Ibn al-Jawzī, *Muntaẓam: al-Muntaẓam fī ta'rīkh al-mulūk wa-al-umam.* Hyderabad, 1357-59.
Ibn al-Jazarī, *Ghāyah*: Muḥammad b. Muḥammad b. al-Jazarī. *Ghāyat al-nihāyah fī ṭabaqāt al-qurrā'. Das biographische Lexikon der Koranlehrer.* Edited by G. Bergsträsser and O. Pretzl. Leipzig, 1933-35(37). Bibliotheca Islamica 8a-c. Reprinted Cairo, n. y.
Ibn al-Jazarī, *Nashr:* Muḥammad b. Muḥammad b. al-Jazarī. *al-Nashr fī al-qirā'āt al-'ashr.* Edited by M. A. Dahman. Damascus, 1345.
Ibn Kathīr, *Bidāyah.* Cairo, 1351-58.

Ibn Khaldūn, *Muqaddimah.* Translated by F. Rosenthal, 2nd printing. Princeton, 1967. Bollingen Series 43.
Ibn Khallikān, *Wafayāt: al-aʿyān.* Edited by Iḥsān ʿAbbās. Beirut, n. y. (last vol. dated 1972).
Ibn Khuzaymah: Muḥammad b. Isḥāq b. Khuzaymah. *Kitāb al-Tawḥīd wa-ithbāt ṣifāt al-Rabb.* Edited by Muḥammad Khalīl Harrās. Cairo, 1387/1968.
Ibn Mājah: *al-Sunan.* Edited by Muḥammad Fu'ād ʿAbd al-Bāqī. Cairo, 1381-82/1972.
Ibn Manẓūr, *Lisān: al-ʿArab.* Būlāq, 1300-8.
Ibn Mujāhid, *Sabʿah: al-Sabʿah fī al-qirā'āt.* Edited by Shawqī Ḍayf. Cairo, 1972.
Ibn al-Nadīm, *Fihrist*: Edited by G. Flügel. Leipzig, 1871-72. Translation by B. Dodge. New York and London, 1970.
Ibn Qayyim al-Jawziyyah, *Furūsiyyah.* Edited by ʿIzzat al-ʿAṭṭār al-Ḥusaynī. Beirut, n. y.
Ibn al-Rūmī, *Dīwān:* Edited by Ḥusayn Naṣṣār. Cairo, 1373-76.
Ibn Saʿd, *Ṭabaqāt.* Edited by E. Sachau and others. Leiden, 1904-40.
Ibn al-Shiḥnah: *Rawḍat al-manāẓir fī ʿilm al-awā'il wa-al-awākhir.* Printed in the margin of Ibn al-Athīr, *Kāmil* (Būlāq, 1290).
Ibn Taghrībirdī, *Nujūm*: Abū al-Maḥāsin b. Taghrībirdī. *al-Nujūm al-zāhirah fī mulūk Miṣr wa-al-Qāhirah.* Cairo, 1348 ff./1929 ff. Reprinted ca. 1967.
Ibn al-Ṭayyib, *Commentaire sur la Genèse:* Abū al-Faraj 'Abdallāh b. al-Ṭayyib. *Commentaire sur la Genèse.* Edited and translated by J. C. J. Sanders. Louvain, 1967. Corpus Scriptorum Christianorum Orientalium, Scriptores Arabici 24-25.
Ikhtilāf: refers to Ṭabarī's *Ikhtilāf* according to the editions of F. Kern (Cairo, 1320/1902) and J. Schacht (Leiden, 1933).
Irshād: See Yāqūt, *Irshād.*
Jāḥiẓ (al-), Ḥayawān: Edited by 'Abd al-Salām M. Hārūn. Cairo, 1356-66/1938-47.
Jeffery, *Materials:* A. Jeffery. *Materials for the History of the Text of the Qur'ān.* Leiden, 1937.
Jubilees: Edited by R. H. Charles, *The Ethiopic Version of the Hebrew Book of Jubilees.* Oxford, 1895. Translated by the same, *The Book of Jubilees or the Little Genesis.* London, 1902.
Justi: See *Bundahishn.*
Justi (F.), *Iranisches Namenbuch.* Marburg, 1895. Reprinted Hildesheim, 1963.
Juwaynī, *Shāmil:* Imām al-Ḥaramayn al-Juwaynī. *al-Shāmil fī uṣūl al-dīn.* Edited by ʿAlī Sāmī al-Nashshār, Fayṣal Budayr ʿAwn, and Suhayr M.

Mukhtār. Alexandria, 1969.
Juynboll (G. H. A.). *Muslim Tradition. Studies in Chronology, Provenance and Authorship of Early Ḥadīth.* Cambridge, 1983.
Karatay, *Catalogue:* F. E. Karatay. *Topkapı Sarayı Müzesi Kütüphanesi Arapça Yazmalar Kataloğu.* Istanbul, 1962-69.
Kern, "Ṭabarī's Ikhtilāf": F. Kern, "Ṭabarī's Ikhtilāf alfuqahā'." *Zeitschrift der Deutschen Morgenländischen Gesellschaft* 55 [1901]: 61-95.
Khalafallāh (Muḥammad A.). *Ṣāḥib al-Aghānī.* 3rd printing. Cairo, 1968.
Khalidi (Tarif). *Islamic Historiography.* Albany, N. Y., 1975.
Khalīfah, *History:* Khalīfah b. Khayyāṭ. *al-Ta'rīkh.* Edited by Akram Ḍiyā' al-'Umarī. Baghdad, 1386-87/1967.
Khalīfah, *Ṭabaqāt:* Khalīfah b. Khayyāṭ. *Kitāb al-Ṭabaqāt.* Edited by Akram Ḍiyā' al-'Umarī. Baghdad, 1387/1967.
Khallāl, *Musnad:* Abū Bakr Aḥmad b. Muḥammad b. Hārūn al-Khallāl. *al-Musnad min masā'il...Ibn Ḥanbal.* Dakka, 1975.
Khaṭīb, *Ta'rīkh Baghdād:* al-Khaṭīb al-Baghdādī. *Ta'rīkh Baghdād.* Cairo, 1349/1931. Cited here as *TB.*
al-Kindī, *Kīmiyā': al-'iṭr.* Edited by K. Garbers. Leipzig, 1944. Abhandlungen für die Kunde des Morgenlandes 29.
al-Kisā'ī, Muḥammad b. 'Abdallāh. *Qiṣaṣ al-anbiyā'.* Translated by W. M. Thackston. Boston, 1978.
Klijn (A. F. J.). *Seth in Jewish, Christian and Gnostic Literature.* Leiden, 1977.
Kosegarten (J. G. L.). *Taberistanensis...Annales Regum atque Legatorum Dei.* Greifswald, 1831-53.
Kraemer (Joel), *Humanism: in the Renaissance of Islam.* Leiden, 1986.
Kronholm (T.), *Motifs: from Genesis 1-11 in the genuine hymns of Ephrem the Syrian.* Lund, 1978.
Lane: *An Arabic-English Dictionary.* London and Edinburgh, 1863-93. Reprinted Beirut, 1968.
Laoust (H.): "Les premières professions de foi Ḥanbalites." *Mélanges Louis Massignon,* III, 7-35 (Damascus, 1957).
Laoust (H.), *(La) Profession de foi d'Ibn Batta.* Damascus, 1958.
Lassner, *Topography:* J. Lassner. *The Topography of Baghdad in the Early Middle Ages.* Detroit, 1970.
Laurens, *Barthélemi d'Herbelot:* H. Laurens. *La Bibliothèque Orientale de Barthélemi d'Herbelot.* Paris, 1978.
Le Strange, *Baghdad:* G. Le Strange. *Baghdad during the Abbasid Caliphate.* London, 1900.
Leemhuis, "Ms. 1075 Tafsīr": F. Leemhuis, "Ms. 1075 Tafsīr of the Cairine Dār al-kutub and Muǧāhid's Tafsīr." *Proceedings of the Ninth Congress of the Union Européenne des Arabisants et Is-*

lamisants. Leiden, 1981. Pp. 169-80. Publications of the Netherlands Institute of Archaeology and Arabic Studies in Cairo 4.

Lewis (J. P.), *A Study of the Interpretation of Noah: and the Flood in Jewish and Christian Literature*. Leiden, 1968.

Lidzbarski, *De propheticis...legendis:* M. Lidzbarski. *De propheticis, quae dicuntur, legendis arabicis*. Leipzig, 1893.

Lisān al-ʿArab: See Ibn Manẓūr.

Lommel (H.). *Die Yäšt's des Awesta*. Göttingen and Leipzig, 1927.

Loth, "Ṭabarī's Korancommentar": O. Loth, "Ṭabarī's Korancommentar." *Zeitschrift der Deutschen Morgenländischen Gesellschaft* 35 [1881]: 588-628.

Maqrīzī, *Khiṭaṭ: al-Mawāʿiẓ wa-al-iʿtibār bi-dhikr al-khiṭaṭ wa-al-āthār*. Būlāq, 1270. Reprinted Beirut, ca. 1970.

Maqrīzī, *Muqaffā:* See Ṭabarī, *Introductio etc.*, XCVI f.

Massignon, *Passion*²: L. Massignon. *La Passion de Husayn Ibn Mansūr Hallāj*. 2nd ed. Paris, 1975. English translation by H. Mason. Princeton, 1982. Bollingen Series XCVIII.

Massignon (L.), *Salmān Pāk: et les prémices spirituelles de l'Islam Iranien*. Tours, 1934.

Masʿūdī, *Murūj: al-dhahab wa-maʿādin al-jawhar*. Edited and translated by C. A. C. Barbier de Meynard and B. M. M. Pavet de Courteille. Paris, 1861-77. Edited by C. Pellat. Beirut, 1965-74.

Masʿūdī, *Tanbīh: Kitāb al-Tanbīh wa-al-ishrāf*. Edited by M. J. de Goeje. Leiden, 1894. Bibliotheca Geographorum Arabicorum 8. Reprinted Beirut, 1965.

Meyer (E.). *Der historische Gehalt der Aiyām al-ʿArab*. Wiesbaden,1970.

Mez, *Renaissance:* A. Mez. *Die Renaissance des Islāms*. Heidelberg, 1922.

Milik (J. T.). *The Books of Enoch*. Oxford, 1976.

Miskawayh, *Eclipse:* See the edition and translation of H. F. Amedroz and D. S. Margoliouth, *The Eclipse of the Abbasid Caliphate*. Oxford, 1920-21.

Mordtmann (A. D.). "Nachrichten über Taberistan aus dem Geschichtswerke Taberi's." *Zeitschrift der Deutschen Morgenländischen Gesellschaft* 2[1848]: 285-314.

Muʿāfā, *Jalīs:* al-Muʿāfā b. Zakariyyā' al-Nahrawānī. *al-Jalīs al-ṣāliḥ al-kāfī wa-al-anīs al-nāṣiḥ al-shāfī*. Edited by M. Mursī al-Khūlī. Vol. I. Beirut, 1981.

Mujāhid, *Tafsīr*. Edited by ʿAbd al-Raḥmān al-Ṭāhir b. Muḥammad al-Sūratī. [Qaṭar, 1976].

Muqātil b. Sulaymān, *Tafsīr*. Ms. Bursa (copy in G. Böwering's possession).

Muranyi, *"Kitāb al-Siyar":* M. Muranyi, "Das *Kitāb al-Siyar* von Abū

Isḥāq al-Fazārī." *Jerusalem Studies in Arabic and Islam* 6 [1985]: 63-97.

Muslim, *Ṣaḥīḥ:* Calcutta, 1265/1849.

Murtaḍā al-Zabīdī, *Itḥāf: al-sādah al-muttaqīn bi-sharḥ asrār Iḥyā' 'ulūm al-dīn.* Cairo, 1311. Reprint Beirut, ca. 1972.

Muth: F.-C. Muth. *Die Annalen von aṭ-Ṭabarī im Spiegel der europäischen Bearbeitungen.* Frankfurt am Main, 1983. Heidelberger Orientalistische Studien 5.

Najāshī, *Rijāl:* Abū al-'Abbās Aḥmad b. 'Alī al-Najāshī. *Kitāb al-Rijāl.* Bombay, 1317.

Nallino, "Le fonti arabe": C. A. Nallino, "Le fonti arabe manoscritte dell'opera di Lodovico Marracci sul Corano." *Raccolta dei Scritti,* Vol. II, 90-134 (Roma, 1940).

Naveh and Shaked, *Amulets:* J. Naveh and S. Shaked. *Amulets and Magic Bowls.* Jerusalem and Leiden, 1985.

Nawawī, *Tahdhīb: al-asmā'.* Cairo [1927?].

Cat. Nemoy: L. Nemoy. *Arabic Manuscripts in the Yale University Library.* New Haven, 1956. The Connecticut Academy of Arts and Sciences. *Transactions* 40.

Newby (G. D.), "The *Sīrah* as a source for Arabian Jewish history." *Jerusalem Studies in Arabic and Islam* 7 [1986]: 121-38.

Nöldeke (Th.) - Schwally (F.) - Bergsträsser (G.) - Pretzl (O.): *Geschichte des Qorāns.* Leipzig, 1909-38.

Noth, "Charakter": A. Noth, "Der Charakter der ersten grossen Sammlungen von Nachrichten zur frühen Kalifenzeit." *Der Islam* 47 [1971]: 168-99.

Oxford Latin Dictionary: Edited by P. G. W. Clare. Oxford, 1977.

Paret (R.), *Der Koran.* Stuttgart, etc., 1962. Also *Der Koran. Kommentar und Konkordanz.* Stuttgart, etc., 1971.

Pauly-Wissowa: *(Paulys) Realencyclopädie der classischen Altertumswissenschaft.*

Pedersen (J.), *(The) Arabic Book.* English translation by G. French. Princeton, 1984.

Pines, *Atomenlehre:* S. Pines. *Beiträge zur islamischen Atomenlehre.* Berlin, 1936.

Pingree, *Thousands:* D. Pingree. *The Thousands of Abū Ma'shar.* London, 1968.

Qifṭī, *Inbāh: al-ruwāh 'alā anbāh al-nuḥāh.* Edited by Muḥammad Abū al-Faḍl Ibrāhīm. Cairo, 1369-93/1950-73.

Qifṭī, *Muḥammadūn: al-Muḥammadūn min al-shu'arā' wa-ash'āruhum.* Edited by Riyāḍ 'Abd al-Ḥamīd Murād. Damascus, 1395/1975.

Qurṭubī, *Jāmi':* Muḥammad b. Aḥmad b. Abī Bakr al-Qurṭubī. *al-Jāmi'*

li-aḥkām al-Qur'ān. Cairo, 1387/1967.
Rāzī, *Tafsīr:* Fakhr al-dīn al-Rāzī. *al-Tafsīr al-kabīr (Mafātīḥ al-ghayb)*. Cairo, ca. 1353-1381/1934-62.
Rescher (O.), *Orientalische Miszellen*. Constantinople, 1925.
Ritter (H.). Review of E. Marin, *The reign of al-Muʿtaṣim*. *Oriens* 6 [1953]: 157 f.
Rodinson, "Recherches": M. Rodinson, "Recherches sur les documents arabes relatifs à la cuisine." *Revue des Études Islamiques* 1949(1950): 95-165.
Rosenthal (F.), *Gambling: in Islam*. Leiden, 1975
Rosenthal, "Hidden illness": F. Rosenthal, "ar-Rāzī on the hidden illness." *Bulletin of the History of Medicine* 52 [1978]: 45-60.
Rosenthal, "Hippocratic Oath": F. Rosenthal, "An ancient commentary on the Hippocratic Oath." *Bulletin of the History of Medicine* 30 [1956] 52-87.
Rosenthal, *Muslim Historiography*²: F. Rosenthal, *A History of Muslim Historiography*. 2nd edition. Leiden, 1968.
Rosenthal (F.), *"Sweeter than Hope": Complaint and Hope in Medieval Islam*. Leiden, 1983.
Rotter, "Überlieferung": G. Rotter, "Zur Überlieferung einiger historischer Werke Madā'inīs in Ṭabarīs Annalen." *Oriens* 23-24 [1974]: 103-33.
Ru'bah, *Dīwān:* Edited and translated by W. Ahlwardt. *Der Diwan des Reğezdichters Rūba ben El ʿAğğağ*. Berlin, 1903-4.
Sadan, *Mobilier:* J. Sadan. *Le mobilier au Proche Orient médiéval*. Leiden, 1976.
Ṣafadī, *Wāfī: al-Wāfī bi-al-wafayāt*. Edited by H. Ritter and others. Wiesbaden, 1931 ff. Bibliotheca Islamica 6.
Sakhāwī (al-), *Ḍaw': al-Ḍaw' al-lāmiʿ li-ahl al-qarn al-tāsiʿ*. Cairo, 1353-55.
Samʿānī, *Ansāb*. Hyderabad 1962-82.
Ṣarīḥ: refers to Ṭabarī's *Ṣarīḥ al-sunnah*. Edited and translated by D. Sourdel, "Une profession dc foi de l'historien al-Ṭabarī." *Revue des Études Islamiques* 36 [1968]: 177-99.
Schatzhöhle: Die Schatzhöhle (Meʿārath Gazzē). Edited and translated by C. Bezold. Leipzig, 1883-88. Reprinted Amsterdam, 1981. English translation by E. A. Wallis Budge. *The Book of the Cave of Treasures*. London, 1927.
Schoeler, "Überlieferung der Wissenschaften": G. Schoeler, "Die Frage der schriftlichen oder mündlichen Überlieferung der Wissenschaften im frühen Islam." *Der Islam* 62 [1985]: 201-30.
Schreiner, *Gesammelte Schriften:* M. Schreiner, "Beiträge zur Geschichte

der theologischen Bewegungen im Islam." *Zeitschrift der Deutschen Morgenländischen Gesellschaft* 52 [1898]: 463-563. *Gesammelte Schriften.* Edited by M. Perlmann, 366-464 (Hildesheim, 1983).

Schützinger (H.): *Ursprung und Entwicklung der arabischen Abraham-Nimrod-Legende.* Bonn, 1961. Bonner Orientalistische Studien, N. S. 11.

Sellheim (R.). *Materialien zur arabischen Literaturgeschichte I.* Wiesbaden, 1976. Verzeichnis der orientalischen Handschriften in Deutschland. Band XVII, Reihe A.

Sellheim (R.), "Neue Materialien: zur Biographie des Yāqūt." Forschungen und Fortschritte der Katalogisierung der orientalischen Handschriften in Deutschland. Marburger Kolloquium 1965, 87-118 (Wiesbaden, 1966).

Sezgin, *GAS:* F. Sezgin, *Geschichte des arabischen Schrifttums.* Leiden, 1967 ff.

Sezgin (U.), *Abū Mikhnaf.* Leiden, 1971.

al-Shīrāzī: See Abū Isḥāq al-Shīrāzī.

Shorter Encyclopaedia of Islam: See *EI.*

Simon (R.), Ignác Goldziher. Budapest and Leiden, 1986.

Soden (W. von), *Akkadisches Handwörterbuch.* Wiesbaden, 1965-72.

Speight: P. Marston Speight, "Attitudes toward Christians as revealed in the *Musnad* of al-Ṭayālisī." *The Muslim World* 63 [1973]: 249-68.

Speiser, *Genesis:* Translated by E. A. Speiser. New York, 1964. Anchor Bible.

Speyer, *Biblische Erzählungen:* H. Speyer. *Die biblischen Erzählungen im im Qoran.* Gräfenheinichen, 1939. Reprinted Hildesheim, 1961.

Stackelberg (R. von), "Bemerkungen zur persischen Sagengeschichte." *Wiener Zeitschrift für die Kunde des Morgenlandes* 12 [1898]: 230-48.

Steingass (F.). *Persian-English Dictionary.* London, 1892. 2nd printing, 1930.

Stern, "Abū Īsā": S. M. Stern, "Abū Īsā Ibn al-Munajjim's chronography." *Islamic Philosophy and the Classical Tradition. Essays presented... to Richard Walzer,* 437-66 (Oxford, 1972).

Subkī, *Ṭabaqāt:* Tāj al-dīn al-Subkī, *Ṭabaqāt al-Shāfiʿiyyah al-kubrā.* Edited by ʿAbd al-Fattāḥ M. al-Ḥilw (Helou) and Maḥmūd M. al-Ṭanāḥī (?). Cairo, 1383/1964.

Ṣūlī, *Akhbār al-Rāḍī wa-al-Muttaqī.* Edited by J. Heyworth Dunne. London, 1935. Translated by M. Canard. Algiers, 1946-50. Publications de l'Institut d'Études Orientales de la Faculté des Lettres d'Alger X and XII.

Suyūṭī, *Taḥdhīr: al-khawāṣṣ min akādhīb al-quṣṣāṣ.* Edited by Muḥammad al-Ṣabbāgh. Cairo, 1392/1972.

Ṭabarī, *Dhayl al-Mudhayyal:* See *Dhayl.*

Ṭabarī, *Firdaws*: ʿAlī b. Rabban al-Ṭabarī. *Firdaws al-ḥikmah.* Edited by M. Z. Siddiqi. Berlin, 1928.

Ṭabarī, *Introductio etc.*: refers to the volume of the Leiden edition containing *Introductio, Glossarium, Addenda et Emendanda.* Leiden, 1901.

Ṭabarī, *Tafsīr:* refers to *Jāmiʿ al-bayān ʿan taʾwīl āy al-Qurʾān,* cited here according to the edition Būlāq, 1323-29, with an indication of the sūrah and verse for facilitating the location of a given passage in other editions. See General Introduction, 105 ff.

Ṭabīkh: Muḥammad b. al-Ḥasan b. Muḥammad al-Kātib al-Baghdādī. *Kitāb al-Ṭabīkh.* Edited by Fakhrī al-Bārūdī. Beirut, 1964. Translated by A. J. Arberry, "A Baghdad cookery book." *Islamic Culture* 13 [1939]: 21-47, 189-214.

Tabṣīr: refers to Ṭabarī's *Ṭabṣīr ulī al-nuhā,* according to the Escorial manuscript 1514, fols. 81a-104b.

Tafsīr: refers to Ṭabarī, *Tafsīr.*

Tahdhīb: refers in the General Introduction to Ṭabarī's *Tahdhīb (Musnad ʿAlī* and *Musnad Ibn ʿAbbās).*

Tahdhīb: See Ibn Ḥajar, *Tahdhīb.*

Talmud (Babylonian): cited here in the traditional manner.

Tanūkhī, *Faraj:* Abū ʿAlī al-Muḥassin b. ʿAlī al-Tanūkhī. *Kitāb al-Faraj baʿd al-shiddah.* Cairo, 1357/1938.

Targum Neofiti. Edited by A. Diez Macho, *Neophyti l. Targum Palestinense Ms de la Biblioteca Vaticana.* Madrid and Barcelona, 1968-79.

Targum Pseudo-Jonathan: Edited by M. Ginsburger. Berlin, 1903. Also edited by D. Rieder. Jerusalem, 1974.

TB: See Khaṭīb, *Taʾrīkh Baghdād.*

Thaʿālibī, *Ghurar:* Abū Manṣūr al-Thaʿālibī. *al-Ghurar fī siyar al-mulūk.* Edited and translated by H. Zotenberg, *Histoire des rois des Perses.* Paris, 1900.

Thaʿlabī, *Qiṣaṣ: al-anbiyāʾ.* Cairo, n.y.

Ṭūsī, *Fihrist:* Abū Jaʿfar Muḥammad b. al-Ḥasan al-Ṭūsī. *al-Fihrist.* Edited by M. Ṣādiq Āl Baḥr al-ʿulūm. 2nd printing. al-Najaf, 1380/1961.

Ullmann, *Medizin:* M. Ullmann. *Die Medizin im Islam.* Leiden, 1970. Handbuch der Orientalistik, Erste Abteilung, Ergänzungsband VI, 1. Abschnitt.

Ullmann (M.): See *Wörterbuch.*

van Ess, *Erkenntnislehre*: J. van Ess. *Die Erkenntnislehre des ʿAduḍaddīn al-Īcī.* Wiesbaden, 1966.

van Ess, *Gedankenwelt:* J. van Ess. *Die Gedankenwelt des Ḥāriṯ al-*

Muḥāsibī. Bonn, 1961. Bonner Orientalistische Studien, N. S. 12.
von Grünebaum, "Bemerkung": "Eine Bemerkung zu den Anfängen der neupersischen Dichtung." *Wiener Zeitschrift für die Kunde des Morgenlandes* 44 [1937]: 224.
Wakin, *Documents*: J. A. Wakin. *The Function of Documents in Islamic Law*. Albany, N. Y., 1972.
Washshā', *Muwashshā:* Abū al-Ṭayyib Muḥammad b. Aḥmad (Isḥāq?) al-Washshā'. *Kitāb al-Muwashshā*. Edited by R. E. Brünnow. Leiden, 1886.
Wensinck, *Handbook:* A. J. Wensinck. *A Handbook of Early Muhammadan Tradition*. Leiden, 1927.
Wörterbuch: der klassischen arabischen Sprache. Edited by M. Ullmann. Wiesbaden, 1970 ff.
Ya'qūbī, *Ta'rīkh:* Edited by M. Th. Houtsma. *Ibn-Wāḍiḥ qui dicitur al-Ja'qūbī, Historiae*. Leiden, 1883. Reprinted Leiden, 1969.
Yāqūt, *Irshād: al-arīb ilā ma'rifat al-adīb (Mu'jam al-udabā')*. Edited by D. S. Margoliouth. Leiden and London, 1907-27. E. J. W. Gibb Memorial Series 6. Edited by Aḥmad Farīd al-Rifā'ī. Cairo, 1355-57.
Yāqūt, *Mu'jam: al-buldān*. Edited by F. Wüstenfeld. Göttingen, 1866-73.
Yasht: See Lommel.
Zarkashī, *Burhān:* Badr al-dīn Muḥammad b. Bahādur al-Zarkashī. *al-Burhān fī 'ulūm al-Qur'ān*. Edited by Muḥammad Abū al-Faḍl Ibrāhīm. Cairo, 1376-78/1957-58.
Zubaydī, *Ṭabaqāt:* Abū Bakr Muḥammad b. al-Ḥasan al-Zubaydī. *Ṭabaqāt al-naḥwiyyīn wa-al-lughawiyyīn*. Edited by Muḥammad Abū al-Faḍl Ibrāhīm. Cairo, 1373/1954.

Index

Occurrences in footnotes in the General Introduction are noted only by page reference. Occurrences in both text and footnotes on the same page of the Translation are indicated only by page reference. Routinely quoted large reference works are usually listed as passim *under the authors' entries.*

A

Abān b. Abī 'Ayyāsh Fīrūz 183 n. 145, 302 and n. 823
Abān b. Ṣāliḥ 183 n. 145, 302 and n. 823
'Abbād b. 'Abdallāh b. al-Jubayr 332
'Abbād b. al-'Awwām 199
'Abbād b. Ya'qūb al-Asadī 71, 367
al-'Abbādī (Abū 'Āṣim) 63 f., 101
al-'Abbās b. 'Abd al-'Aẓīm al-'Anbarī 151
al-'Abbās b. 'Abd al-Muṭṭalib 90–93
al-'Abbās b. al-Ḥasan (al-wazīr al-'Azīzī) 37, 112
al-'Abbās b. Muḥammad al-Dūrī 58
al-'Abbās b. Muḥammad (b. ?) al-Muḥassin, Abū al-Faḍl 122
al-'Abbās b. al-Walīd b. Mazyad al-Bayrūtī 23, 178
'Abbāsid(s), Hāshimite(s) 54, 62, 73, 80, 90, 92, 120, 131, 133, 169 n. 18
'Abdallāh b. (al-)'Abbās 109, 128, 130, 173, 183, 188, 190, 192, 199–203, 205–7, 212, 214–19, 221–23, 226–30, 232 n. 436, 233, 234 n. 442, 235, 243 f., 246, 250–55, 256 n. 555, 257–59, 261–64, 266 f., 269 f., 273–76, 281, 290–93, 295–97, 300, 302–7, 309, 313 f., 320, 324, 328 f., 331, 333 f., 336, 339 f., 344, 348, 353, 355, 357 f., 360, 364–66, 368, 370
'Abdallāh b. 'Abd al-Raḥmān, see Ibn Ḥujayrah
'Abdallāh b. Abī Awfā, see Ibn al-Kawwā'
'Abdallāh b. Abī Ja'far ('Īsā b. Māhān al-Rāzī) 253, 268, 272, 279, 288, 291, 296
'Abdallāh b. Abī Najīḥ 247, 267, 274, 281, 287
'Abdallāh b. Abī Ziyād (al-Ḥakam al-Qaṭawānī) 179
'Abdallāh b. Aḥmad b. Ja'far, Abū Muḥammad, see al-Farghānī
'Abdallāh b. Aḥmad b. Muḥammad, see Ibn al-Mughallis
'Abdallāh b. 'Amr b. al-'Āṣ 52, 245, 313

'Abdallāh b. Buraydah b. al-Ḥuṣayb al-Aslamī 180
'Abdallāh b. Dhakwān, Abū Zinād 284
'Abdallāh b. Dīnār 174
'Abdallāh b. Ḥamdān, see Abū al-Hayjā'
'Abdallāh b. Ḥanbal 17, 70
'Abdallāh b. al-Ḥasan, see Abū Shu'ayb
'Abdallāh b. Idrīs, see Ibn Idrīs
'Abdallāh b. 'Īsā b. Māhān, see 'Abdallāh b. Abī Ja'far
'Abdallāh b. Kathīr 246
'Abdallāh b. Lahī'ah, see Ibn Lahī'ah
'Abdallāh b. Mas'ūd 75, 109, 129, 206, 214, 219, 221 f., 230, 250, 254, 258, 262 f., 269, 273, 275, 281, 307 f., 315, 353
'Abdallāh b. al-Mubārak 199, 299
'Abdallāh b. Muḥammad b. 'Aqīl b. Abī Ṭālib 282 f.
'Abdallāh b. Murrah 315
'Abdallāh b. Rāfi', mawlā Umm Salamah 189, 212, 222, 224, 231
'Abdallāh b. Salām 151, 189 f., 210, 213, 221, 223, 286 f.
'Abdallāh b. Ṣāliḥ, Abū Ṣāliḥ 210, 213 f., 221, 223, 370
'Abdallāh b. Ṣayyād 185
'Abdallāh b. Sulaymān b. al-Ash'ath, see Abū Bakr b. Abī Dāwūd
'Abdallāh b. 'Umar 52 f., 75, 174 f., 202, 217, 245 n. 482, 295
'Abdallāh b. 'Uthmān b. Khuthaym 309
'Abdallāh b. Wahb 182, 198, 269, 280 f., 284, 287, 322, 325, 344
'Abdallāh b. Yazīd, see Abū 'Abd al-Raḥmān
'Abdallāh b. al-Zubayr 323 n. 934
'Abd al-'Azīz b. Abān 356, 365
'Abd al-'Azīz b. 'Abd al-Ghafūr 367
'Abd al-'Azīz b. Hārūn 104
'Abd al-'Azīz b. Muḥammad al-Ṭabarī, Abū Muḥammad 7, 107 f., 110, 125
'Abd al-'Azīz b. Mūsā, see Abū Rawḥ
'Abd al-'Azīz b. Rufay' 244
'Abd al-Ghafūr 367
'Abd al-Ghafūr b. 'Abd al-'Azīz al-Wāsiṭī 367 n. 1141
'Abd al-Ḥamīd b. 'Abd al-Raḥmān al-Ḥimmānī 364
'Abd al-Ḥamīd b. Bakkār al-Kalā'ī al-Bayrūtī 23
'Abd al-Ḥārith 320–22
'Abd al-Jabbār (al-Qāḍī al-Asadābādī) 68
'Abd al-Jabbār b. Yaḥyā al-Ramlī 25
'Abd al-Karīm b. Hawāzin al-Qushayrī 58
'Abd al-Laṭīf b. 'Abd al-Mun'im al-Ḥarrānī, Abū al-Faraj 100
'Abd al-Malik b. Abī Sulaymān 321
'Abd al-Malik b. 'Amr al-'Aqadī, see Abū 'Āmir
'Abd al-Malik b. Ḥumayd b. Abī Ghaniyyah 340, 365
'Abd al-Malik b. Marwān 198 n. 224
'Abd al-Mughīth 316
'Abd al-Mun'im b. 'Abd al-Karīm al-Qushayrī, Abū al-Muẓaffar 58
'Abd al-Mun'im b. Idrīs 286 n. 760
'Abd al-Qādir al-Baghdādī 171 n. 24
'Abd al-Qādir al-Qurashī 47
'Abd al-Raḥmān b. 'Abdallāh, see al-Mas'ūdī
'Abd al-Raḥmān b. 'Abdallāh b. 'Abd al-Ḥakam 28 f., 245 nn. 487, 490, 282 f.
'Abd al-Raḥmān b. Abzā 231
'Abd al-Raḥmān b. Aḥmad al-Ṭabarī 125
'Abd al-Raḥmān b. 'Awf 189 n. 177, 285 n. 748
'Abd al-Raḥmān b. Ḥujayrah, see Ibn Ḥujayrah
'Abd al-Raḥmān b. Hurmuz al-A'raj 283 f.
'Abd al-Raḥmān b. Jubayr b. Nufayr 182

'Abd al-Raḥmān b. Kaysān (= Abū Bakr al-Aṣamm ?) 102
'Abd al-Raḥmān b. Mahdī 201, 229, 244, 261, 281, 315
'Abd al-Raḥmān b. Muḥammad b. Ziyād, see al-Muḥāribī
'Abd al-Raḥmān b. Yaḥyā 256
'Abd al-Raḥmān b. Yazīd al-Anṣārī 283
'Abd al-Raḥmān b. Zayd b. Aslam 109, 269, 280, 287
'Abd al-Razzāq b. Hammām 229, 267, 277, 290, 292, 299, 301, 353
'Abd al-Ṣamad b. 'Abd al-Wārith 183, 202, 320
'Abd al-Ṣamad b. Ma'qil b. Munabbih 174, 206, 208, 210, 301, 351
'Abd al-Wahhāb b. 'Abd al-Majīd al-Thaqafī 260, 297
'Abd al-Wāḥid b. Sulaym 199
'Abd al-Wārith b. 'Abd al-Ṣamad b. 'Abd al-Wārith 183 n. 144
'Abd al-Wārith b. Sa'īd 304
'Abdah ('Abdān) al-Marwazī 227, 251, 268, 288
'Abdah b. Sulaymān 287
'Abdān b. Muḥammad al-Marwazī, see 'Abdah
Abel 307–17, 324, 331, 337
Abraham 293, 302, 344, 371
Abū al-'Abbās, see Ibn al-Thallāj
Abū 'Abdallāh, see al-Jaṣṣāṣ
Abū 'Abd al-Raḥmān 'Abdallāh b. Yazīd al-Ma'āfirī al-Ḥubulī 245
Abū 'Abd al-Salām al-Zubayr 230
Abū Aḥmad Muḥammad b. 'Abdallāh al-Zubayrī 259 f., 267, 303
Abū al-Aḥwaṣ 177, 285
Abū al-'Āliyah Rufay' b. Mihrān 279, 288, 291, 298
Abū 'Āmir 'Abd al-Malik b. 'Amr al-'Aqadī 282 f.
Abū 'Amr b. al-'Alā' 67
Abū 'Āṣim al-Nabīl, al-Ḍaḥḥāk b. Makhlad 247, 255, 267, 274, 281, 287
Abū 'Awānah al-Waḍḍāḥ 211, 227
Abū al-Azhar, see al-Mubārak b. Mujāhid
Abū Bakr (b. 'Abdallāh) 217, 268, 270
Abū Bakr b. 'Abdallāh, see Ibn Abī Maryam
Abū Bakr b. Abī Dāwūd (Sulaymān b. al-Ash'ath) al-Sijistānī 24, 29 f. 58, 59 f., 69, 110, 124
Abū Bakr b. Abī Ḥāmid 69, 123
Abū Bakr b. 'Ayyāsh 77, 176 f., 188, 212, 222 f., 230
Abū Bakr b. Dāwūd al-Ẓāhirī, see Muḥammad b. Dāwūd
Abū Bakr al-Dūrī 92
Abū Bakr b. al-Jawālīqī 43 f.
Abū Bakr al-Khuwārizmī (Muḥammad b. al-'Abbās al-Ṭabarkhazī) 13, 40
Abū Bakr al-Marrūdhī (Aḥmad b. Muḥammad b. al-Ḥajjāj) 72, 74
Abū Bakr b. Mujāhid, see Ibn Mujāhid
Abū Bakr al-Qaffāl, see al-Qaffāl
Abū Bakr b. Sahl al-Dīnawarī 79
Abū Bakr (al-Ṣiddīq) 63, 87, 90–92, 129
Abū Bishr, Ja'far b. Iyās 211, 237, 330
Abū Ḍamrah, Anas b. 'Iyāḍ 180
Abū Dāwūd (Sulaymān b. al-Ash'ath) al-Sijistānī 24, 59, 71, 197 n. 218
Abū Dāwūd, Sulaymān b. Dāwūd al-Ṭayālisī 259, 331, 353
Abū Dharr al-Ghifārī 231 f., 323, 344
Abū al-Ḍuḥā, Muslim b. Ṣubayḥ 201, 203, 219
Abū al-Faraj, see Ibn al-Thallāj
Abū al-Faraj b. Abī al-'Abbās al-Iṣfahānī 35. See also the following
Abū al-Faraj al-Iṣfahānī 24, 35, 48, 135
Abū al-Fatḥ, see Muḥammad b. Aḥmad al-Ḥāfiẓ
Abū al-Fidā' 70, 137
Abū Ghiyāth al-Ja'farī 98
Abū al-Ḥajjāj, see Mujāhid b. Jabr
Abū Hammām, al-Walīd b. Shujā' al-Sakūnī 291, 292 n. 790, 295 f., 303

Abū Ḥamzah, Muḥammad b. Maymūn al-Sukkarī 286
Abū Ḥanīfah 61, 66 f., 90, 102. Ḥanafite(s) 46, 173 n. 28
Abū al-Ḥasan b. al-Munajjim, see Aḥmad b. Yaḥyā b. 'Alī
Abū Hāshim, Ismā'īl b. Kathīr 201–3
Abū Ḥaṣīn, 'Uthmān b. 'Āṣim 176 f., 259 f.
Abū Ḥātim al-Rāzī 24, 26
Abū Ḥātim al-Sijistānī 42, 45, 58, 79
Abū al-Hayjā', 'Abdallāh b. Ḥamdān 38
Abū Ḥāzim, Salamah b. Dīnār 179 f.
Abū Hishām al-Rifā'ī, Muḥammad b. Yazīd 173, 176, 192
Abū Ḥudhayfah, Mūsā b. Mas'ūd 274
Abū Hurayrah 67, 176 f., 184, 189, 191, 197, 212, 222, 224, 230 f., 265 f., 283–87, 327, 331
Abū Idrīs al-Khawlānī 323, 325, 344
Abū Isḥāq ('Amr b. 'Abdallāh) al-Hamdānī 245, 316
Abū Isḥāq b. al-Faḍl b. Ḥayyān al-Ḥulwānī 122
Abū Isḥāq al-Shīrāzī 64
Abū Jabīrah 181
Abū Ja'far, see al-Ṭabarī
Abū al-Jamāhir, see Muḥammad b. 'Abd al-Raḥmān
Abū Kathīrah Rufay' 245
Abū Khālid, see Sulaymān b. Ḥayyān
Abū Khālid al-Wālibī 177, 260
Abū Kudaynah, Yaḥyā b. al-Muhallab 285
Abū Kurayb, Muḥammad b. al-'Alā' 18, 20 f., 30, 176 f., 180, 205, 227 n. 399, 244, 246, 252, 258, 261, 264, 266, 269, 285–87, 302, 305, 364
Abū Lubābah b. 'Abd al-Mundhir al-Anṣārī 283
Abū Mālik (Ghazwān al-Ghifārī) 206, 214, 219, 221 f., 250, 254, 258, 262 f., 269, 273, 275, 281, 307
Abū Ma'mar, see Ṣāliḥ b. Ḥarb
Abū Ma'shar, see Ziyād b. Kulayb
Abū Ma'shar, Najīḥ b. 'Abd al-Raḥmān 6, 210, 213, 221, 223, 278, 367
Abū Mikhnaf 53
Abū Mu'ādh, al-Faḍl b. Khālid 227, 251
Abū Mu'āwiyah, Muḥammad b. Khāzim al-Ḍarīr 177, 205, 315
Abū al-Mughīrah 313
Abū Muḥammad (authority of Hushaym) 363
Abū al-Muḥassin (Muḥsin) al-Muḥarrir 39
Abū Mujālid (Aḥmad b. al-Ḥusayn) al-Ḍarīr 68, 121
Abū Mūsā al-Ash'arī 260, 297
Abū al-Muthannā, see Aḥmad b. Ya'qūb
Abū Naḍrah, al-Mundhir b. Mālik al-'Abdī al-'Awqī 176
Abū Nahīk, 'Uthmān b. Nahīk 364
Abū Naṣr (Muḥammad b. Aḥmad al-Khallāl ?) 181, 256
Abū Nu'aym, see 'Umar b. Ṣubḥ
Abū Nu'aym, al-Faḍl b. Dukayn 175, 180
Abū Nu'aym al-Iṣfahānī 217 n. 344
Abū al-Qāsim al-Azharī 62
Abū Qilābah 53
Abū Qubays, see Mecca
Abū Rāfi' 355 n. 1074
Abū Rawḥ, 'Abd al-'Azīz b. Mūsā al-Ḥimṣī 24
Abū Rawq, 'Aṭiyyah b. al-Ḥārith 211, 227, 252, 258, 261, 264, 266, 269, 356
Abū Razīn al-'Aqīlī 204, 206 f.
Abū Sa'd (Sa'īd b. al-Marzubān) al-Baqqāl 188, 212, 222 f., 230
Abū Sa'īd 176
Abū Sa'īd (Aḥmad b. Muḥammad b. Ziyād) al-A'rābī 79
Abū Sa'īd 'Amr b. Muḥammad b. Yaḥyā al-Dīnawarī 52
Abū Sa'īd al-Baqqāl, see Abū Sa'd
Abū Sa'īd (Ismā'īl b. Ibrāhīm) al-Yaḥmadī 255

Abū Sa'īd 'Umar b. Aḥmad al-Dīnawarī 52, 83
Abū Sa'īd 'Uthmān b. Aḥmad al-Dīnawarī 52
Abū Sa'īd b. Yūnus, see Ibn Yūnus
Abū Salamah (= Mūsā b. Ismā'īl al-Tabūdhakī) 205, 328. See also Mūsā b. Ismā'īl
Abū Salamah b. 'Abd al-Raḥmān b. 'Awf 189, 265, 285–87, 327
Abū Ṣāliḥ, see 'Abdallāh b. Ṣāliḥ
Abū Ṣāliḥ in the chain al-Suddī—Abū Ṣāliḥ—Ibn 'Abbās: 206, 214, 219, 221 f., 250, 254, 258, 262 f., 269, 273, 275, 281, 307; in the chain al-Kalbī—Abū Ṣāliḥ—Ibn 'Abbās: 290 f., 293, 297, 303, 314, 324, 331, 333 f., 336, 340, 344, 348, 355, 358, 362, 365 f., 368; in the chain al-A'mash—Abū Ṣāliḥ—Ka'b 173, 211, 227; in the chains al-A'mash (also 'Āṣim or Abū Ḥaṣīn)—Abū Ṣāliḥ—Abū Hurayrah 265, 327 (also 184 or 176 f.). The separation of the Abū Ṣāliḥ of the first two chains as Bādhām from that of the last two chains as Dhakwān seems dubious at best. "Abū Ṣāliḥ" is no doubt a fictitious character.
Abū Sālim 180 n. 116
Abū Shāmah (Shihāb al-dīn Ismā'īl) 141
Abū Shu'ayb, 'Abdallāh b. al-Ḥasan 65
Abū Shuraḥbīl al-Ḥimṣī 24
Abū Sinān (Ḍirār b. Murrah) al-Shaybānī 217
Abū Sulaymān, 'Alī b. Sulaymān 322, 325, 344
Abū Taghlib b. Nāṣir al-dawlah 133
Abū al-Tayyāḥ, Yazīd b. Ḥumayd 179
Abū al-Ṭayyib al-Jurjānī 122
Abū Tha'labah al-Khushanī 182 f.
Abū Thawr, Ibrāhīm b. Khālid 71, 102
Abū al-Ṭufayl, 'Āmir b. Wāṣilah 244
Abū 'Ubayd al-Qāsim b. Sallām 95–97, 292 n. 791, 364
Abū Umāmah (= Ṣudayy b. 'Ajlān al-Bāhilī ?) 323
Abū 'Umar al-Zāhid, Ghulām Tha'lab 46, 108
Abū 'Uthmān al-Nahdī 262
Abū Yaḥyā Bā'i' al-Qatt (= al-Qattāt ?) 292, 295 f., 303
Abū Yaḥyā b. al-wazīr Ibn Khāqān 21 f., 36
Abū al-Yaqẓān, 'Ammār b. Muḥammad 175
Abū Yūsuf (Ya'qūb b. Muḥammad) 102, 173
Abū al-Zabīr, Muḥammad b. Muslim 295
Abū Ẓabyān, Ḥusayn b. Jundub 200, 203, 218 f.
Abū Zur'ah, Wahballāh b. Rāshid 29, 283
Abūshīl (= Methushael) 338, 346 n. 1035
'Ād 237
Adah 338
Adam 132, 184–86, 188–90, 213 f., 217, 223–25, 233, 241, 253, 255–311, 313–40, 342–44, 346 f., 351–54, 362, 364, 366–70
Ādam b. Abī Iyās 195, 265, 327
al-Adamī, see al-Ḥusayn b. Yazīd; Muḥammad b. Yazīd
'Adan, see Eden
'Adan ('Adab) bint Enoch 337 f.; See also Ednā, Ednī
Adānah, see Hadānah
'Adnā bint 'Azrā'īl 346. See also Ednā, Ednī
Afrawāk (Fravāk) b. Siyāmak 325 f.
Afrī bint Siyāmak 325
al-Afṭas, see Sālim
Aghānī, see Abū al-Faraj al-Iṣfahānī
Aḥmad b. 'Abdallāh b. 'Abd al-Raḥīm al-Barqī, see Ibn 'Abd al-Raḥīm
Aḥmad b. 'Abd al-Raḥmān b. Wahb 182, 322, 325, 344
Aḥmad b. 'Abdūn (Ibn Ḥāshir) 92
Aḥmad b. Abī Khaythamah 254, 339
Aḥmad b. 'Alī (b.) al-Bādā 100

Aḥmad b. ʿAlī b. Bayghjūr (Ibn al-Ikhshēd) 110
Aḥmad b. ʿAlī b. Nūḥ 119
Aḥmad b. Faraj, Abū ʿUtbah 25
Aḥmad b. Ḥammād al-Dawlābī 17 f.
Aḥmad b. Ḥanbal (Aḥmad b. Muḥammad), see Ibn Ḥanbal
Aḥmad b. Ibrāhīm b. Kathīr al-Dawraqī 260 n. 578
Aḥmad b. Ibrāhīm b. Shādhān al-Bazzār 100
Aḥmad b. ʿĪsā al-ʿAlawī 48
Aḥmad b. ʿĪsā al-Rāzī, Abū ʿAbdallāh 102
Aḥmad b. Isḥāq al-Ahwāzī 259 f., 267, 303
Aḥmad b. Isḥāq b. al-Buhlūl 46 f.
Aḥmad b. Kāmil, Abū Bakr, see Ibn Kāmil
Aḥmad b. Manīʿ 30
Aḥmad b. al-Miqdām, Abū al-Ashʿath 20, 333
Aḥmad b. Muḥammad b. Abī Bakr al-Wāsiṭī 100
Aḥmad b. Muḥammad b. Ḥabīb al-Ṭūsī 181, 198, 304
Aḥmad b. Muḥammad b. al-Ḥasan al-Iṣbahānī, Abū ʿAlī 23
Aḥmad b. Muḥammad b. ʿIsā 215 n. 334
Aḥmad b. Muḥammad b. Rustam, see al-Rustamī
Aḥmad b. Muḥammad b. Ziyād, see Abū Saʿīd b. al-Aʿrābī
Aḥmad b. Mūsā b. al-ʿAbbās, Abū Bakr, see Ibn Mujāhid
Aḥmad b. Thābit al-Rāzī 6
Aḥmad b. ʿUthmān, Abū al-Jawzāʾ 20
Aḥmad b. Yaḥyā b. ʿAlī b. Yaḥyā b. Abī Manṣūr, Abū al-Ḥasan Ibn al-Munajjim 65 f.
Aḥmad b. Yaʿqūb, Abū al-Muthannā (= al-Ḥasan b. al-Muthannā ?) 140
Aḥmad b. Yūsuf al-Thaʿlabī (al-Taghlibī) 96 f.
Aḥmad b. Zuhayr, see Aḥmad b. Abī Khaythamah
al-Ahwāzī, see Aḥmad b. Isḥāq
ʿĀʾishah 75, 140, 355
al-ʿAjjāj 12
Ajwab (Ajrab) b. Siyāmak 325
al-Akhfash, Abū al-Ḥasan 110
al-ʿAlāʾ b. al-Musayyab 209
al-Aʿlam, see Ibn Ṣāliḥ
Alexander Dhū al-Qarnayn 371
Alexandria 181, 283 n. 730
ʿAlī, see ʿAlī b. Sahl
ʿAlī b. Abī Ṭalḥah 215, 370
ʿAlī b. Abī Ṭālib 59–63, 87, 91–93, 119, 130, 173 n. 37, 235, 244 f., 260, 291, 316. ʿAlid(s), Shīʿah 11, 13, 26, 48, 56, 60–63, 90, 92 f., 99, 102, 123, 127
ʿAlī b. Aḥmad b. al-Ḥasan al-ʿIjlī 7
ʿAlī b. Dāwūd (al-Qanṭarī) 214, 370
ʿAlī b. Ḥamzah, see al-Kisāʾī
ʿAlī b. Ḥarb 332
ʿAlī b. al-Ḥasan (b. ʿAbdawayh al-Khazzāz ?) 256, 267
ʿAlī b. al-Ḥasan b. Shaqīq 198 f., 286
ʿAlī b. al-Haytham 211, 227, 356
ʿAlī b. ʿImrān 8
ʿAlī b. ʿĪsā (al-wazīr) 50, 73
ʿAlī b. Maʿbad 282
ʿAlī b. Mihrān 18
ʿAlī b. Muḥammad b. ʿAbd al-Malik, see Ibn Abī al-Shawārib
ʿAlī b. Muḥammad al-ʿAdawī, Abū al-Ḥasan, see al-Shimshāṭī
ʿAlī b. Muḥammad b. ʿAllān al-Ḥarrānī 37
ʿAlī b. Mujāhid 370
ʿAlī b. Rabban, see al-Ṭabarī
ʿAlī b. Rabīʿah 244
ʿAlī b. Sahl al-Ramlī 25, 174, 197, 230, 262 n. 601
ʿAlī b. Sirāj, Abū al-Ḥasan 27, 46
ʿAlī b. Sulaymān, see Abū Sulaymān
ʿAlī b. Thābit al-Jazarī 364
ʿAlī b. ʿUbaydallāh al-Simsimī 32
ʿAlī b. Zayd b. ʿAbdallāh b. Abī

Mulaykah b. Jud'ān 176, 291, 328, 357, 360
'Alid(s), see 'Alī b. Abī Ṭālib
'Alqamah b. Qays al-Nakha'ī 285
al-A'mash (Sulaymān b. Mihrān) 173, 177, 200 f., 205, 207, 211, 217–19, 227, 261, 265, 286, 305, 315, 327, 365
Amat al-Mughīth 316
'Āmir b. Wāṣilah, see Abū al-Ṭufayl
'Ammār b. al-Ḥasan 268, 272, 279, 288, 291, 296
'Ammār b. Muḥammad, see Abū al-Yaqẓān
Amorites 370 n. 1161
'Amr b. 'Abdallāh al-Hamdānī, see Abū Isḥāq
'Amr b. Abī Qays 306
'Amr b. Abī Salamah al-Tinnīsī 179
'Amr b. 'Alī b. Baḥr al-Fallās 290
'Amr b. al-'Āṣ 245 n. 490
'Amr b. Dīnār 285
'Amr b. Ḥammād 206, 214, 219, 221 f., 250, 254, 258, 262 f., 269, 273, 275, 281, 307, 322
'Amr b. Sharaḥīl, see al-Sha'bī
'Amr (b. Shu'ayb ?) 314
'Amr b. Shuraḥbīl b. Sa'īd b. Sa'd b. 'Ubādah 282 f.
'Amr b. Thābit b. Abī Khālid al-Wālibī 260
Āmul 10–13, 16, 127
'Amzūrah bint Barākīl b. Mehujael (= 'Emzārā bint Rākē'ēl) 346 n. 1035, 347
Anak, see Og
Anas b. 'Iyāḍ, see Abū Ḍamrah
Anas b. Mālik 175, 177–79, 288 n. 773
al-'Anbarī, see al-'Abbās b. 'Abd al-'Aẓīm; Yaḥyā b. Kathīr
'Anbasah b. Sa'īd b. al-Ḍurays 226, 260 (?)
Angel of Death 257, 328–30
al-Anṣār 181
Antioch(ian era) 184 n. 148
Anūshīl 338 n. 999
Aphrem (Ephraim Syrus) 312 n. 882, 315 n. 895
al-'Aqadī, see Abū 'Āmir; Bishr b. Mu'ādh
Arabian Nights 41
'Arafah, 'Arafāt, see Mecca
al-A'raj, see 'Abd al-Raḥmān b. Hurmuz
Aramaic, Mandaic, Nabataean, Syriac 45 f., 209 n. 300, 237, 274, 312 nn. 877, 878, 324, 335 n. 983, 366 n. 1137
Ararat, see al-Jūdī
'Arbā, see 'Adnā
'Arīb 38, 112
Aristotle, Aristotelian 121, 159
Arpakhshad 364 n. 1132
Arṭāh b. al-Mundhir 208
Asad b. 'Amr 287
al-Aṣamm, see 'Abd al-Raḥmān b. Kaysān
Asbāṭ b. Naṣr 206, 214, 219, 221 f., 250, 254, 258, 262 f., 269, 273, 275, 281, 307, 322
al-A'shā 172
al-'Asharah al-Mubashsharah 128, 130
al-Ash'arī, see Abū Mūsā
al-Ash'arī ('Alī b. Ismā'īl) 76, 102
Ashūt 317, 337 f.
'Āṣim b. Abī al-Najjūd Bahdalah 183, 184 n. 147, 244
'Āṣim b. Kulayb 267
'Asqalān 26
'Aṭā' b. Abī Rabāḥ 209 f., 214, 222 f., 293
'Aṭā' b. al-Sā'ib 190, 199, 201, 219, 290, 306
Athātī 317
'Athmah, see Ibn 'Athmah
'Aththām b. 'Alī 177
'Aṭiyyah b. al-Ḥārith, see Abū Rawq
'Aṭiyyah b. Sa'd b. Junādah 215, 246, 313, 329
'Awf (b. Abī Jamīlah) al-A'rābī 260, 297, 313

'Awn b. 'Abdallāh b. 'Utbah 210
'Awn b. Abī Shaddād 355, 368
Awrāsh b. Siyāmak 325
Awrāshī bint Siyāmak 325
al-Awzā'ī 23, 47, 66, 102 f., 178 f.
Ayād 317
Ayanhad 344 n. 1026
'Ayn Wardah 366 n. 1137, 367
Ayyūb b. 'Abdallāh al-Fihrī (al-'Āmirī ?) 230
Ayyūb b. 'Abdallāh b. Mu/ikraz 230 n. 421
Ayyūb b. Isḥāq b. Ibrāhīm 25
Ayyūb b. Khālid 189, 212, 222, 224, 231
Ayyūb al-Sakhtiyānī 53
Ayyūb b. Suwayd 178
Ayyūb b. Ziyād 198
'Azāzīl 254
Aždahāk, see al-Ḍaḥḥāk
al-Azharī, see Abū al-Qāsim
al-Azharī (Abū Manṣūr Muḥammad b. Aḥmad) 60
al-'Azīz (Fāṭimid) 141
al-'Azīzī, see al-'Abbās b. al-Ḥasan
'Azrā'īl b. Abūshīl b. Enoch 346
al-Azraq, see Isḥāq b. Yūsuf; Salamah b. al-Faḍl
'Azūrā, see Ḥazūrah

B

Bābil, Babylonia 292 n. 793, 318, 325, 341, 345, 350, 371
al-Bādā, see Aḥmad b. 'Alī
Bādhām/n, Abū Ṣāliḥ, mawlā Umm Hāni' 173 n. 37, and see Abū Ṣāliḥ
Badr 198 n. 224, 250 n. 511
Baghdad 11, 14, 16, 19, and General Introduction, *passim*. Bāb al-Ṭāq 66; Baradān Bridge 32 f.; Bridge of Ibn 'Afīf (?) 107 n. 369; al-Karkh 72; Khurāsān Gate 32; al-Khursī (al-Ḥarashī) Square 33; al-Mukharrim 33, 107; Round City 32; al-Ruṣāfah 80; al-Shammāsiyyah 32, 96; Shāri' 'Abd al-Ṣamad 7; Sūq al-'Aṭash 7, 33, 43, 77, 110; Sūq Yaḥyā 96; Suwayqat Abī 'Ubaydallāh 7; Tigris Bridge 96; Ya'qūb Square 32 f.
Baḥr b. Naṣr 284
Baḥshal (Aslam b. Sahl) 181 n. 133
Bā'i' al-Qatt, see Abū Yaḥyā
Bakjūr 110
al-Bakrī 367 n. 1142
al-Balad 49
Bālagh 317
al-Bal'amī 138
Banān 317
Bāqardā, see Qardā
al-Bāqarjī, see Ibrāhīm b. Makhlad; Makhlad b. Ja'far
al-Baqiyyah b. al-Walīd 24 f.
al-Baradānī 100 n. 344b
Barākīl b. Mehujael (Rākē'ēl) 326, 336 f., 342, 347
Baraknā bint Darmasīl b. Mehujael (= Bāraka bint Rāsūyāl) 343
Bāraq 317
Barāsb b. Siyāmak 325
al-Barbahārī (al-Ḥasan b. 'Alī b. Khalaf) 72
Barjīsīyā 237
al-Barqī, see Ibn 'Abd al-Raḥīm
Bashīr b. al-Muhājir 180
al-Baṣrah, Baṣran(s) 19 f., 25, 30, 45, 53, 76, 87, 95, 109, 179 n. 101, 204 n. 265, 245 n. 483
Batanūsh (Bath Anōsh, Bētēnōs, Bitenosh, Qīnūsh) 346 n. 1035, 347
al-Baṭīn, see Muslim
Bāwandids 11
Bawdh, see Nūdh
Bāwīl b. Mehujael 346
al-Bayāḍī (Abū 'Alī Muḥammad b. 'Īsā ?) 73
Bayrūt (Beirut) 23, 178 n. 98

Bēwarāsb 344 f., 348, 350, 354. See also al-Ḍaḥḥāk
al-Bīrūnī 184 n. 148, 185 n. 149, 298 nn. 808, 809, 350 nn. 1051, 1052
al-Birzālī 74, 92
Bishr b. Mu'ādh al-'Aqadī 20, 30, 193, 246, 251, 268, 270, 274, 302, 356, 365, 367, 369
Bishr b. 'Umārah 252, 258, 261, 264, 266, 269
Black Stone, see Mecca
Būdāsb (Bodhisattva) 345 n. 1030
Buddha 291 n. 788
Būdh, see Nūdh
Buhayl 292
Bukayr b. al-Akhnas 217
Bukhārā 238 n. 459
al-Bukhārī *passim*
Bukht Nāṣir (Naṣṣar) 352
al-Bunānī, see Thābit b. Aslam
Bundahishn 325 n. 941, 344 nn. 1024, 1026, 349 n. 1045, 351 n. 1056
Bundār, see Ibn Bashshār
Buraydah b. al-Ḥuṣayb 180

C

Cain 307–17, 331, 335, 337–41, 343, 346 f., 366
Canaan 368
Caspian Sea 11
Ceylon, see Sarandīb
Charakene, see Maysān
Chinese 238 n. 459
Christianity, Christian(s), people of the Gospel 45, 50, 77, 105, 159, 163, 184 f., 193, 208 n. 294, 292, 366 n. 1137, 371. Apostles 357 f.; *Book of Adam and Eve* 303 n. 833; Luke 358 n. 1090; Revelation 77. See also Greek(s); Jesus; *Schatzhöhle*
Cilicia 370 n. 1161
Coptic 45
Ctesiphon, see al-Madā'in

D

Dādhī bint Siyāmak 325
al-Ḍaḥḥāk (Aždahāk) 344 n. 1024, 350, 351 n. 1056, 352, 354 n. 1063
al-Ḍaḥḥāk b. Makhlad, see Abū 'Āṣim al-Nabīl
al-Ḍaḥḥāk b. Muzāḥim 109, 205, 209–11, 227, 251–53, 258, 261, 264, 266, 269, 356
Dahnā('), al-Dahnaj, Daḥnā 290–92, 306
Dallawayh, see Ziyād b. Ayyūb
Damascus 9, 26
Ḍamrah b. Ḥabīb al-Ḥimṣī 208
Ḍamrah b. Rabī'ah al-Ramlī 25 f.
Dānēl 346 n. 1031
al-Dānī 20, 94
Darābīs 317
David 328–31
al-Dawlābī, see Aḥmad b. Ḥammād
al-Dawraqī, see Aḥmad b. Ibrāhīm; Ya'qūb b. Ibrāhīm
al-Dawsī, see Ibn Abī Dhubāb
Dāwūd b. Abī al-Furāt 339
Dāwūd b. Abī Hind 265, 327
Dāwūd b. 'Alī al-Iṣfahānī (al-Ẓāhirī) 52, 68 f., 120–22
Dāwūd b. al-Ḥuṣayn al-Umawī 320
Dayr al-Jamājim 206 n. 279
al-Dhahabī *passim*
Dhakwān, See Abū Ṣāliḥ
Dhāt al-riqā' 86
Dhū al-Qarnayn, see Alexander
Dīnah bint Barākīl 326, 336, 337 n. 992
Dīnawar 73
al-Dīnawarī, see Abū Bakr b. Sahl; Abū Sa'īd 'Amr; Abū Sa'īd 'Umar; Abū Sa'īd 'Uthmān
al-Dīnawarī (Abū Ḥanīfah) 171 n. 24, 238 n. 459, 344 nn. 1024–26
Dioscurides 51
Ḍirār b. Murrah al-Shaybānī, see Abū Sinān

Dīs b. Siyāmak 325
Dunbāwand (Danbāwand, Damāwend) 318, 342, 350
al-Dūrī, see al-'Abbās b. Muḥammad; Abū Bakr al-Dūrī

E

Eber 368
Eden, 'Adan, Garden of Eden 291 n. 788, 312, 314
Ednā, Ednī 337 n. 998, 346 n. 1031. See also 'Adan, Adānah, 'Adnā, Hadānah
Egypt, Egyptian(s) 8, 14, 21, 23, 26–31, 34, 46, 64, 102, 124, 178 n. 93, 245 n. 485, 282 n. 712
'Emzārā, see 'Amzūrah
Enoch (= Idrīs) 336–38, 340, 343–46, 354, 358 n. 1088. Book of Enoch 337 n. 998
Enosh, Yānish 326, 335 f., 338 n. 999
Ephraim Syrus, see Aphrem
Ethiopic 45, 192 n. 194
Euphrates 43, 370
Eve 132, 273–81, 287 f., 290–92, 294, 296, 298 n. 811, 299 f., 302–4, 309 f., 314, 316–18, 320–22, 324, 327, 333 f., 363

F

al-Faḍl b. Dukayn, see Abū Nu'aym
al-Faḍl b. Ja'far b. al-Furāt 43, 52
al-Faḍl b. Khālid, see Abū Mu'ādh
Fā'id, mawlā Ibn Abī Rāfi' 355
al-Farghānī (Abū Muḥammad 'Abdallāh b. Aḥmad) 7 f., 22, 32, 36, 38, 64, 78 f., 89, 95 f., 101, 106 f., 112, 114, 126, 128 f., 131, 139
al-Farrā' (Yaḥyā b. Ziyād) 45, 110
Fārs 318, 326, 345
Fāṭimid(s) 141
Fayshān 370
Fērōz b. Yazdjard 369
Fēshdādh, see Ōshahanj
Firdawsī 163, 344 n. 1024, 345 n. 1028, 348 n. 1044, 349 n. 1045, 350 n. 1053
al-Firyābī, see 'Ubaydallāh b. Muḥammad
Fiṭr b. Khalīfah 177
Fravāk, see Afrawāk
al-Fuḍayl b. Sulaymān 179, 189
Fusṭāṭ, Mosque of 'Amr 28 f., 124

G

Gabriel 75, 232, 234, 237 f., 240 f., 258, 298, 322, 324, 333
Gayōmart, see Jayūmart
Ghadīr Khumm 91–93, 123 f.
Ghālib b. Ghallāb 209, 214, 222 f.
Ghazwān al-Ghifārī, see Abū Mālik
Ghiyāth b. Ibrāhīm 316
Ghulām Tha'lab, see Abū 'Umar al-Zāhid
Ghundar, see Muḥammad b. Ja'far
Gihon, see Jayḥān
Gog and Magog, see Yājūj
Gomer b. Japhet b. Noah 186, 318
Gordyaia, Gordyene 366 n. 1137
Greek(s), Rūm 46, 49, 133, 184, 366 n. 1137. Septuagint 346 n. 1034

H

Ḥabīb b. Abī Thābit 305
Hābīl, see Abel
Habtah 173 n. 28
Hadānah, Adānah 346. See also Ednā, Ednī
Hadaz 317
al-Ḥaḍramī 208 f. (=M. b. 'Al. b. Su., d. 297 ?)
Ḥafṣ b. Ghiyāth 209
Ḥafṣ b. 'Umar 29
al-Ḥajjāj b. (al-)Minhāl 190, 204, 211, 227, 291
Ḥajjāj b. Muḥammad 189, 192, 207, 212, 222, 224, 231, 246, 250 f.,

268, 270, 278, 287, 309, 357, 365, 367
al-Ḥajjāj b. Yūsuf 171, 326
Ḥājjī Khalīfah 10, 70, 82, 94, 115, 126, 134, 138
al-Ḥakam b. 'Utaybah 340, 365
Ḥakkām b. Salm al-Rāzī 226, 306
Ham 347, 357 f., 360, 365 f., 368–70
Hamadhān 73
al-Hamadhānī (Muḥammad b. 'Abd al-Malik) 38, 72, 139
Ḥamdānids 38
Ḥammād b. Abī Sulaymān Muslim 173, 190 (?)
Ḥammād b. Salamah b. Dīnār 190 (?), 204, 230, 262, 291, 328, 332
Hammām b. Munabbih 353 n. 1059
Hammām b. Yaḥyā 353
Ḥamzah (b. Ḥabīb) 96
Ḥamzah al-Iṣfahānī 184 n. 148, 349 n. 1045
Ḥanafite(s), see Abū Ḥanīfah
Ḥanbalite(s), see Ibn Ḥanbal
Hannād b. al-Sarī 18, 20, 176 f., 188, 212, 222 f., 230, 315
al-Ḥārith (= Iblīs) 252, 320 n. 916, 321 f.
al-Ḥārith b. 'Abd al-Raḥmān, see Ibn Abī Dhubāb
al-Ḥārith b. Muḥammad b. Abī Usāmah 247, 287, 290 f., 297, 303, 314, 324, 331, 333 f., 336, 340, 344, 348, 355 f., 358, 362, 364–66, 368
al-Ḥarīzī, see Ibrāhīm b. Ya'qūb al-Jūzajānī
Ḥarrān 363 n. 1119
al-Ḥarrānī, see 'Abd al-Laṭīf b. 'Abd al-Mun'im
Hārūn b. 'Abd al-'Azīz, Abū 'Alī 104, 106 f.
Hārūn al-Rashīd 211 n. 316
al-Ḥasan b. 'Abd al-'Azīz al-Hāshimī 80
al-Ḥasan (b. Abī al-Ḥasan) al-Baṣrī 90, 109, 176 n. 69, 268, 270, 271 n. 654, 302 (?), 314, 316, 320, 322, 332, 357, 363, 369
al-Ḥasan b. 'Alī al-Ahwāzī, Abū 'Alī 47, 97
al-Ḥasan b. 'Arafah 175, 364 f.
Ḥasan b. 'Aṭiyyah b. Najīḥ 286, 302
al-Ḥasan b. 'Aṭiyyah b. Sa'd b. Junādah 215, 246, 313, 329
al-Ḥasan b. Bilāl 25, 230, 262
al-Ḥasan b. Dhakwān 332
al-Ḥasan b. Dīnār 360
al-Ḥasan b. Ḥamzah al-Āmulī 119
al-Ḥasan b. al-Ḥusayn b. 'Alī, see al-Ṣawwāf
al-Ḥasan b. Mūsā al-Ashyab 247, 287
al-Ḥasan b. al-Muthannā (= Abū al-Muthannā Aḥmad b. Ya'qūb ?) 140
al-Ḥasan b. al-Ṣabbāḥ 52
al-Ḥasan b. Sa'd 267
al-Ḥasan b. 'Umārah 299
al-Ḥasan b. Yaḥyā al-Jurjānī 229, 267, 277, 290, 292 f., 301, 353
al-Hāshimī ('Alī b. Sulaymān) 184 n. 148
Hāshimites 295
Ḥawwā', see Eve
Ḥayān 317
Ḥayyān b. 'Ubaydallāh 205
Ḥazūrah, Ḥazūrā, 'Azūrā 317, 324, 335
Hebrew, see Jews
Herodotus 139
Hibat Allāh, see Seth
al-Ḥijāz 31
al-Ḥimmānī, see 'Abd al-Ḥamīd; Yaḥyā b. 'Abd al-Ḥamīd
Ḥimṣ 24 f., 215 n. 334
Ḥirā', see Mecca
Hishām b. 'Abd al-Malik 306 n. 855
Hishām b. al-Ḥakam 76
Hishām b. Hassān 292
Hishām b. Muḥammad b. al-Sā'ib al-Kalbī 110, 290 f., 293, 297, 303, 314, 324, 326, 331, 333 f., 336, 340 f., 344 f., 348, 352, 355, 358, 362, 363 n. 1120, 365 f., 368
Ḥismā 363
Hōshank Pēshdādh, see Ōshahanj
Hūd 237 n. 456

Ḥudhayfah b. al-Yamān 242
Ḥudūd al-'ālam 291 n. 788, 292 n. 792
al-Ḥulwānī, see Abū Isḥāq b. al-Faḍl
Ḥumayd b. Mas'adah 20
Ḥurqūṣ b. Zuhayr 123
al-Ḥurqūṣiyyah 123 f.
al-Ḥusayn b. 'Alī, see al-Ṣudā'ī
al-Ḥusayn b. Dāwūd Sunayd 192, 207 f., 246, 250 f., 256, 268, 270, 278, 287, 309, 357, 364 f., 367
al-Ḥusayn b. al-Faraj 227, 251
al-Ḥusayn b. al-Ḥasan b. Muḥammad b. al-Ḥasan b. 'Aṭiyyah 215, 246, 313, 329
al-Ḥusayn b. Ḥubaysh, Abū al-Qāsim 52, 120
Ḥusayn b. Jundub, see Abū Ẓabyān
al-Ḥusayn b. Muḥammad b. Bahrām 304
al-Ḥusayn b. Wāqid al-Khurāsānī al-Marwazī 300, 364
al-Ḥusayn b. Yazīd, see al-Qaṭṭān; al-Sabī'ī
al-Ḥusayn b. Yazīd al-Adamī 285
Hushaym b. Bashīr 256, 363
al-Ḥuṣrī 40
Ḥuyyay b. 'Abdallāh 245

I

Iblīs, Satan, Satans 84 f., 132, 188, 223 f., 249–59, 261–66, 272 f., 275–81, 292, 299 f., 303, 311, 316 n. 901, 320–22, 334 f., 337, 340, 342 f., 345 349–51, 360. See also al-Ḥārith
Ibn 'Abbās, see 'Abdallāh
Ibn 'Abd al-A'lā, see Yūnus
Ibn 'Abd al-Barr *passim*
Ibn 'Abd al-Ḥakam 28, 124. See also 'Abd al-Raḥmān b. 'Abdallāh; Muḥammad b. 'Abdallāh; Sa'd b. 'Abdallāh; Yūnus b. 'Abdallāh
Ibn 'Abd al-Raḥīm al-Barqī, Aḥmad and Muḥammad 179 f.
Ibn Abī 'Adī, Muḥammad b. Ibrāhīm al-Qasmalī 200, 218, 260, 297
Ibn Abī 'Arūbah, see Sa'īd
Ibn Abī 'Awn 40
Ibn Abī Bazzah, see al-Qāsim
Ibn Abī Dhubāb al-Dawsī, al-Ḥārith b. 'Abd al-Raḥmān 265, 327
Ibn Abī al-Furāt, see Dāwūd
Ibn Abī Ghaniyyah, Yaḥyā b. 'Abd al-Malik b. Ḥumayd 340, 365
Ibn Abī al-Ḥadīd 13, 74
Ibn Abī Ḥafṣah, see Sālim
Ibn Abī Ḥātim al-Rāzī 24 and *passim*
Ibn Abī Khaythamah, see Aḥmad
Ibn Abī Laylā, see Muḥammad b. 'Abd al-Raḥmān
Ibn Abī Manṣūr, see Muḥammad
Ibn Abī Maryam, Abū Bakr b. 'Abdallāh 217 n. 350
Ibn Abī Maryam, Sa'īd b. al-Ḥakam 180, 355
Ibn Abī Mulaykah, see 'Alī b. Zayd
Ibn Abī Najīḥ, see 'Abdallāh
Ibn Abī Rabī'ah, see Ibrāhīm b. 'Abd al-Raḥmān
Ibn Abī al-Shawārib, 'Alī b. Muḥammad 245 n. 483
Ibn Abī al-Shawārib, Muḥammad b. 'Abd al-Malik 245
Ibn Abī Ṭayyi' 141
Ibn Abī Unaysah, see Zayd
Ibn Abī Usāmah, see al-Ḥārith b. Muḥammad
Ibn Abī Ya'lā 21, 70, 72
Ibn Abī Zā'idah, Yaḥyā b. Zakariyyā' 246
Ibn Abī al-Zarqā', see Zayd
Ibn Abī Zinād, 'Abd al-Raḥmān b. 'Abdallāh b. Dhakwān 284
Ibn Abzā, see 'Abd al-Raḥmān
Ibn al-Akhḍar, see Muḥammad b. 'Umar al-Dāwūdī
Ibn 'Allān al-Ḥarrānī, see 'Alī b. Muḥammad
Ibn 'Āmir ('Abdallāh b. 'Āmir) 58
Ibn al-A'rābī, see Abū Sa'īd

Ibn ʿAsākir 9, 24, 83, and *passim*
Ibn ʿAskar, see Muḥammad b. Sahl
Ibn al-Athīr (ʿIzz al-dīn) 58, 70, 74, 77, 136 f., 158 f., 184 n. 148, 232 n. 436, 344 n. 1026, 345 n. 1029
Ibn al-Athīr (Majd al-dīn) 189 n. 174, 276 n. 677
Ibn ʿAthmah, Muḥammad b. Khālid 369
Ibn ʿAṭiyyah, see al-Ḥasan
Ibn ʿAyyāsh, see Abū Bakr
Ibn Ayyūb al-Qaṭṭān, Muḥammad b. ʿAbdallāh b. Muḥammad 62
Ibn al-Bādā, see Aḥmad b. ʿAlī
Ibn Bālawayh 30
Ibn al-Barqī, see Ibn ʿAbd al-Raḥīm
Ibn Bashshār, Abū Bakr Muḥammad b. Bashshār Bundār 16, 20 f., 30, 110, 174 f., 201, 219, 229, 244, 260 f., 282 f., 297, 313, 315, 320, 330, 353, 369
Ibn Baṭṭah 75
Ibn Bazīʿ, see Muḥammad b. ʿAbdallāh
Ibn al-Buhlūl, see Aḥmad b. Isḥāq; Muḥammad b. Aḥmad b. Isḥāq
Ibn Bukayr, see Yūnus
Ibn al-Dāʿī, see Murtaḍā
Ibn Durayd 79
Ibn Farḥūn 125 n. 428
Ibn Fuḍayl, see Muḥammad
Ibn al-Furāt family 43, 79. See also al-Faḍl b. Jaʿfar
Ibn Ḥajar 99, 161, 302 n. 823, and *passim*
Ibn Ḥammād, see Aḥmad
Ibn Ḥanbal (Aḥmad b. Muḥammad) 16 f., 19, 21, 28, 30 f., 34, 44, 48, 69–72, 74 f., 104, 123, 128, 189 n. 169, 197 n. 218, 199 n. 237, 283 n. 725, 304 n. 842, 306 n. 857, 323 n. 933. Ḥanbalite(s) 10, 13, 19, 30, 60, 62 f., 69–74, 76–78, 99–101, 104 f., 124
Ibn al-Ḥawārī 33
Ibn Hayyāj, see Muḥammad b. ʿUmar
Ibn Ḥazm 127 f.
Ibn Hishām 86, 317 n. 903, 331 n. 960, 356 n. 1077
Ibn Ḥujayrah (ʿAbd al-Raḥmān and ʿAbdallāh b. ʿAbd al-Raḥmān) 229
Ibn Ḥumayd, Abū ʿAbdallāh Muḥammad b. Ḥumayd b. Ḥayyān al-Rāzī 17–19, 172, 174, 177, 201 f., 211, 217, 219, 226 f., 244, 251, 254 f., 259, 263, 265, 273, 276, 279, 281, 284, 292, 296, 299 f., 306, 310, 315–17, 320, 323 f., 330, 332, 335–37, 343, 346, 358, 360, 366, 368
Ibn Ḥuṣayn, see ʿImrān
Ibn Idrīs, see ʿAbd-al-Munʿim
Ibn Idrīs (ʿAbdallāh b. Idrīs) 286
Ibn al-Ikhshēd, see Aḥmad b. ʿAlī b. Bayghjūr
Ibn al-ʿImād 27, 100
Ibn Isḥāq (Muḥammad b. Isḥāq b. Yasār) 17 f., 172 n. 26, 174, 201–3, 211 f., 254, 263, 265, 273, 276, 279, 281, 292, 296, 302 n. 823, 310, 317, 320, 323 f., 332 f., 335–38, 343, 346, 358, 360, 366, 368, 370
Ibn Jarīr, see al-Ṭabarī
Ibn al-Jawālīqī, see Abū Bakr
Ibn al-Jawzī 9 f., 31, 33 f., 40, 44, 60, 73, 75, 77, 100, 129, 138
Ibn al-Jazarī 20, 23, 27, 58, 67, 94, 97, 129, 173 n. 33, 175 n. 54, 176 n. 72, 177 n. 78, 183 n. 146, 227 n. 401, 242 n. 466, 246 n. 494
Ibn Jinnī 133
Ibn Judʿān, see ʿAlī b. Zayd
Ibn Jumhūr, see Muḥammad b. Jaʿfar
Ibn Jurayj (ʿAbd al-Malik b. ʿAbd al-ʿAzīz) 109, 189, 192, 207, 212, 222, 231, 246, 250 f., 287, 309, 365, 367
Ibn Kāmil (Abū Bakr Aḥmad b. Kāmil) 7, 15, 18, 27, 42–44, 50, 52, 58, 65–68, 70, 78 f., 91–96, 107, 115, 122, 124, 129, 131 f., 227 n. 399
Ibn Kathīr, see ʿAbdallāh

Ibn Kathīr ('Imād al-dīn Ismā'īl) 92 f., 129, 141
Ibn al-Kawwā', 'Abdallāh b. Abī Awfā 244 f.
Ibn Kaysān, see 'Abd al-Raḥmān
Ibn Kaysān, Abū al-Ḥasan Muḥammad b. Aḥmad 107
Ibn Khaldūn 137, 185 n. 150, 361 n. 1110
Ibn Khallikān 8, 10, 12 f.
Ibn Khāqān, 'Ubaydallāh b. Yaḥyā 21 f. See also al-Khāqānī
Ibn Khuzaymah, Muḥammad b. Isḥāq al-Nīsābūrī 28–30, 260 n. 588, 330 n. 957
Ibn Lahī'ah ('Abdallāh) 245
Ibn al-Maḥāmilī (Aḥmad b. Muḥammad b. Aḥmad) 98
Ibn Mahdī, see 'Abd al-Raḥmān
Ibn Mājah 283 n. 725
Ibn Manī', see Aḥmad
Ibn Manẓūr 60, 171 n. 24, 172 n. 26, 246 n. 495, 276 n. 677
Ibn Ma'rūf, see al-Qāsim b. Bishr
Ibn Mas'ūd, see 'Abdallāh
Ibn Miqdām, see Aḥmad
Ibn al-Mubārak, see 'Abdallāh
Ibn al-Mughallis (Abū al-Ḥasan 'Abdallāh b. Aḥmad b. Muḥammad) 52, 123, 132, 135
Ibn Muhrib, see 'Umar b. 'Abd al-Raḥmān
Ibn Mujāhid, see 'Alī
Ibn Mujāhid (Abū Bakr Aḥmad b. Mūsā b. al-'Abbās) 33, 67, 77, 95–97, 108 (Abū Bakr Muḥammad!)
Ibn Mukraz (Mikraz), see Ayyūb b. 'Abdallāh
Ibn al-Munajjim, see Aḥmad b. Yaḥyā
Ibn al-Musayyab, see Sa'īd
Ibn al-Mu'tazz 140
Ibn al-Muthannā (Abū Mūsā al-Zamin) 110, 175, 177, 179, 200, 218, 254, 259
Ibn al-Nadīm 8, 12, 33, 44, 52, 59, 65–67, 69, 94, 101, 106, 110 f., 113–15, 120, 129, 133
Ibn Qayyim al-Jawziyyah 125
Ibn Qusayṭ, see Yazīd b. 'Abdallāh
Ibn Rabban, see al-Ṭabarī ('Alī b. Rabban)
Ibn Rāmīk, Abū Bakr 115
Ibn al-Rūmī 40
Ibn Rustam (Abū Ja'far Aḥmad b. Muḥammad), see al-Rustamī
Ibn Rustam al-Ṭabarī, see Muḥammad b. Jarīr
Ibn Sa'd (Kātib al-Wāqidī) 77, 200 n. 245, 279 n. 694, 284 n. 739, 285 n. 752, 290 f., 297, 303, 314, 324, 333 f., 336, 340, 344, 348, 355, 358, 362, 365 f., 368
Ibn Salām, see 'Abdallāh
Ibn Ṣāliḥ al-A'lam 63
Ibn Ṣayyād, see 'Abdallāh
Ibn Shādhān, see Aḥmad b. Ibrāhīm
Ibn Shaqīq, see 'Alī b. al-Ḥasan; Muḥammad b. 'Alī
Ibn Shihāb al-Zuhrī (Muḥammad b. Muslim) 283, 370
Ibn al-Shiḥnah 70
Ibn Sinān, see Muḥammad
Ibn Sirāj, see 'Alī
Ibn Taghrībirdī 28, 129
Ibn Ṭarrār/Ṭarārah, see al-Mu'āfā
Ibn al-Ṭayyib 312 n. 882
Ibn al-Thallāj (Abū al-Faraj and Abū l-'Abbās) 43, 50
Ibn Thawr, see Muḥammad
Ibn 'Ufayr (Sa'īd b. Kathīr) 245
Ibn 'Ulayyah (Ismā'īl b. Ibrāhīm b. Miqsam) 260, 305
Ibn 'Umar, see 'Abdallāh
Ibn 'Uyaynah, see Sufyān
Ibn Wahb, see 'Abdallāh; Aḥmad b. 'Abd al-Raḥmān
Ibn Wakī', see Sufyān
Ibn Yamān 192
Ibn Yūnus, Abū Sa'īd 8, 27
Ibn Zayd, see 'Abd al-Raḥmān
Ibrāhīm b. 'Abd al-Raḥmān b. Abī Rabī'ah 355 f.
Ibrāhīm b. Aḥmad al-Mīmadhī 37
Ibrāhīm b. Ḥabīb al-Saqaṭī al-Ṭabarī, Abū Isḥāq 8

Ibrāhīm b. Khālid, see Abū Thawr
Ibrāhīm b. Makhlad, Abū Isḥāq al-Bāqarjī 66, 123
Ibrāhīm b. Muḥammad 8
Ibrāhīm b. Sa'd al-Jawharī 305
Ibrāhīm b. Ya'qūb al-Jūzajānī (al-Ḥarīzī) 26
Ibrāhīm b. Yazīd al-Nakha'ī 284–86
Idrīs, see Enoch
'Ikrimah 90, 109, 188, 190, 212, 217, 222 f., 226 f., 229 f., 233, 243 f., 255, 300, 320, 339, 353 364
'Ilbā' b. Aḥmad 300, 339
'Imrān b. Bakkār al-Kalā'ī al-Ḥimṣī 24
'Imrān b. Ḥudayr 245
'Imrān b. Ḥuṣayn 204 f.
'Imrān b. Mūsā al-Qazzāz 304
'Imrān b. 'Uyaynah 290
India 290–92, 295–97, 303, 342, 363 f.
Iqlīmā, see Qalīmā
Irad 338
Īrān 344 n. 1026
Iran(ian), see Persia
Iraq 19, 21, 23, 87, 159
'Īsā b. Ḥāmid b. Bishr 295 n. 78
'Īsā b. Māhān, Abū Ja'far al-Rāzī 253, 268, 272, 278, 288, 291, 296, 367
'Īsā b. Maymūn 247, 267, 274, 281, 287
'Īsā b. Mūsā, Abū 'Alī al-Ṭūmārī 33
'Īsā b. Rawwād b. al-Jarrāḥ 26
'Īsā b. 'Uthmān b. 'Īsā al-Ramlī 25
Iṣfahān/Iṣbahān 237 n. 457, 292
Isfitūr (Spityura) 351
Isḥāq b. al-Ḥajjāj al-Ṭāḥūnī 253, 299, 301
Isḥāq b. 'Īsā b. al-Ṭabbā' 200 n. 245
Isḥāq b. Manṣūr (b. Bahrām al-Kawsaj ?) 18
Isḥāq b. Manṣūr (al-Salūlī) 285
Isḥāq b. Shāhīn 210
Isḥāq b. Yūsuf al-Azraq 200, 209, 214, 218, 222 f.
Ismā'īl b. Abān 260
Ismā'īl b. 'Abd al-Karīm b. Ma'qil b. Munabbih 173 f., 206–8, 210, 301, 351
Ismā'īl b. 'Abd al-Raḥmān, see al-Suddī
Ismā'īl b. Abī Khālid 181
Ismā'īl b. Ibrāhīm, see Abū Sa'īd al-Yaḥmadī; Ibn 'Ulayyah
Ismā'īl b. Isrā'īl al-Sallāl 25
Ismā'īl b. Kathīr, see Abū Hāshim
Ismā'īl b. Mūsā al-Fazārī 20, 30
Ismā'īl b. 'Ubaydallāh 178 f.
Ismā'īl b. Umayyah 189, 212, 222, 224, 231
Israel (Children of), see Jews
Isrā'īl b. Yūnus 226, 245, 381

J

Jabal, see Tūlīn
Jabalah (Battle Day) 371
Jābalq 237
Jābars 237
Jābir b. Samurah 177
al-Ja'd, Muḥammad b. 'Uthmān 107
Ja'far b. Abī al-Mughīrah al-Qummī 217, 259, 299, 330 f.
Ja'far b. 'Arafah 73
Ja'far b. Burqān 197
Ja'far b. Iyās, see Abū Bishr
Ja'far b. Muḥammad al-Ṣādiq 98
Ja'far b. Rabī'ah 284
Ja'far b. al-Zubayr 323
al-Jahḍamī, see Naṣr b. 'Alī
al-Jāhiliyyah 303, 339 f.
al-Jāḥiẓ 40
Jahmī(s), Jahmiyyah 59, 72, 127, 197 n. 218. See also al-Mu'tazilah
Jam b. Wēwanjihān, see Jamshēd
Jam', see Mecca
Jāmi' b. Shaddād 204 f.
Jāmir, see Gomer
Jamshēd, Jam 348, 350–52
Japhet, Japhetite(s) 238 n. 459, 291 n. 788, 347, 360, 365 f., 368
Jared 336 f., 339, 342–44, 346
Jarīr (Banū) 13
Jarīr b. 'Abd al-Ḥamīd b. Qurṭ al-Rāzī

Jarīr (*continued*)
201, 211, 219, 227, 244, 284, 315, 321
Jarīr b. Ḥāzim 229, 268, 270, 304
Jarīrī(s) 64–67
al-Jarmī, see Muslim
al-Jaṣṣāṣ, Abū ʿAbdallāh 73
al-Jawharī, see Ibrāhīm b. Saʿd
Jayḥān 370
Jayūmart 185 f., 318 f., 325 f., 342, 369
al-Jazīrah 366
Jerusalem 26 f., 198 n. 224, 334, 370. Mount of Olives 294
Jesus, son of Mary 77, 185, 357 f., 371
Jews, Jewish, Judaism, Hebrew, People of the Torah, Torah 45, 50, 77, 159, 163, 184 f., 188, 190, 193, 208 n. 294, 211 f., 217, 233, 273, 276 n. 677, 277 n. 683, 292, 312, 315, 324, 331, 335–38, 343 f., 346, 359, 361, 366, 368, 371. Children of Israel 314, 316. Bible, Genesis 160, 163, 186 n. 153, 276 n. 677, 291 n. 788, 312 nn. 877 ff., 315 n. 895, 324 n. 937, 326 nn. 943 ff., 331 n. 959, 336 nn. 984 ff., 337 nn. 991, 993, 338 nn. 999 ff., 339 n. 1007, 343 n. 1019, 346 n. 1034, 347 n. 1038, 348 n. 1041, 356 n. 1080, 358 n. 1089, 360 n. 1103, 361 n. 1109, 366 n. 1137, 368 nn. 1144, 1147; Midrashic literature 163, Bereshit Rabba 276 n. 677; Talmud (Bab.) 259 n. 568, 365 n. 1135; Targum Neofiti 312 n. 879, 346 n. 1034, Targum Pseudo-Jonathan 259 n. 568, 276 n. 677, 312 n. 879, Septuagint 346 n. 1034
Jinn 166, 250–57, 272, 279, 300, 349 f.
Jonah 220 n. 361
Joseph 298, 371
Jubal, see Tūbāl; Tūbīsh
Jubayr b. Nufayr 182
Jubilees 317 nn. 903, 905, 326 n. 947, 335 n. 983, 337 nn. 992, 998, 338 n. 1000, 343 n. 1019, 346 nn. 1031, 1035, 347 nn. 1036, 1037, 370 n. 1160
Juddah (Jiddah) 291 f.
al-Jūdī, Ararat 294, 362, 366 f.
al-Jurayrī, Abū Masʿūd Saʿīd b. Iyās 151
Jurhum 364
al-Jurjānī, see Abū al-Ṭayyib
al-Juwaynī 76
al-Jūzajānī, see Ibrāhīm b. Yaʿqūb

K

Kaʿb (al-aḥbār) 173, 183, 211, 216, 227, 233, 241 n. 462, 243 f., 285
Kaʿbah, see Mecca
al-Kajjī, Abū Muslim Ibrāhīm b. ʿAbdallāh 64 f.
al-Kalbī, see Hishām b. Muḥammad
al-Kalbī, Muḥammad b. al-Sāʾib 110, 290 f., 293, 297, 303, 314, 324, 331, 333 f., 336, 340, 344, 348, 355, 362, 365 f., 368
Kamārā 238 n. 459
Kardouchoi 366 n. 1137
al-Karkh, see Baghdad
Kathīr b. Ghālib 12
Kenan 326, 336 f., 338 n. 1000
Khalaf b. Khalīfah 364
Khalaf b. Mūsā b. Khalaf al-ʿAmmī 175
Khalaf b. Wāṣil 231 f.
Khālid (ancestor of Ṭabarī) 12
Khālid b. ʿAbdallāh al-Ṭaḥḥān 210
Khālid b. ʿAbd al-Raḥmān 29
Khālid b. Makhlad 180
Khalīfah b. Khayyāṭ 159 and *passim*
al-Khalīl 47
Khallād b. Aslam 178, 204
Khallād b. ʿAṭāʾ 254
Khallād b. Khālid 23
al-Khallāl (Abū Bakr Aḥmad b. Muḥammad b. Hārūn) 58, 71 f., 75, 77, 151, 174 n. 45
al-Khāqānī, Muḥammad b. ʿUbaydallāh b. Yaḥyā b. Khāqān 14, 21, 36, 38 f., 122

Khārijite(s) 61, 123
Khaṣīf (Khuṣayf) b. 'Abd al-Raḥmān 267, 303
al-Khaṭīb al-Baghdādī 9, 32, 62, 98, 161, and *passim*
al-Khawlānī, see Abū Idrīs
Khazars 238 n. 459
al-Khazzāz, see al-Naḍr
Khumm, see Ghadīr
Khurāsān(ian) 15, 87, 98 f. Khurāsān Road 32, 73
Khusraw, see Kisrā
Khuwārizm 13
al-Khuwārizmī, see Abū Bakr
Kindah 209
al-Kindī 42
al-Kisā'ī 162
al-Kisā'ī ('Alī b. Ḥamzah) 67, 110
al-Kisā'ī (Muḥammad b. Yaḥyā) 67
Kisrā (Khusraw) 186
al-Kūfah, Kūfī, Kūfan(s) 18–21, 30, 57, 65, 87, 95, 102, 109, 183 n. 146, 244 n. 475, 286 n. 760, 341, 364
Kulāb (Battle Day) 371
Kulthūm b. Jabr 304 f.
Kurds 366 n. 1137

L

Labūdhā, Layūdhā, Lūbadhā 317
Lamech 315 n. 895, 336, 338, 346 n. 1034, 347 f., 368 n. 1145
Layth b. Abī Sulaym 71, 74, 175, 276, 364
al-Layth b. Sa'd 71 f., 198, 210 n. 310, 284
Lebanon 294
Lisān (al-'Arab), see Ibn Manẓūr
Lūbadhā, see Labūdhā
Luke, see Christianity
Luqmān 220

M

Ma'bad b. Hilāl 179
al-Madā'ın, Madā'in Kisrā 173 n. 33, 186
al-Madā'inī 53
al-Māḍī b. Muḥammad 322, 325, 344
Magian(s) 160, 185 f., 193, 369
Mahalalel 326, 336 f., 339, 341—43
al-Mahdī 316 n. 899
Mājūj, see Yājūj
Makhlad b. Ja'far al-Bāqarjī 66, 123
al-Makīn 137
Mālik b. Anas, Mālikites 27 f., 66 f., 102 f., 124, 306
Ma'mar b. Rāshid 201, 207, 252, 267, 290, 301, 302 n. 823, 353
Mandaic, see Aramaic
al-Mandal 292
Mansak 238
al-Manṣūr, Abū Ja'far 333 n. 970
Manṣūr b. Nūḥ 139
al-Maqburī, see Sa'īd b. Abī Sa'īd
al-Maqrīzī 9, 20, 23, 81, 87, 94, 141
Mārī, Māshī, Mīshī 319, 325 f.
Māriyānah, Māshyānah, Mīshānah 319
Marqīsīyā 237
al-Marrūdhī, see Abū Bakr
Marthad b. 'Abdallāh al-Yazanī 229
Marw 180 n. 119, 319
al-Marwazī, see 'Abdah
Mary, see Jesus
Māshī, Māshyānah, see Mārī; Māriyānah
Maslamah b. (al-)Qāsim al-Qurṭubī 16, 33 f.
Masrūq b. al-Ajda' 315
al-Masrūqī, see Mūsā b. 'Abd al-Raḥmān
al-Mas'ūdī ('Abd al-Raḥmān b. 'Abdallāh) 181, 204
al-Mas'ūdī ('Alī b. al-Ḥusayn) 7, 69, 135, 223 n. 375, 291 n. 788, 298 n. 810, 316 n. 901, 317 n. 903, 345 n. 1030, 366 n. 1138, 369 n. 1149
al-Mayānajī, see Yūsuf b. al-Qāsim
al-Maydūmī (Ṣadr al-dīn Muḥammad b. Muḥammad) 100
Maymūn b. Qays (Banū) 172
Maymūnah 197 n. 215
Maysān 292

Mayyās 47
Māziyār b. Qārin 11
Mecca 19, 28, 31, 77, 87, 95, 98 f., 175 n. 61, 292–95, 300, 308, 333, 335. Abū Qubays 333, 335, 362; 'Arafah, 'Arafāt 291, 294 f., 303 f.; Black Stone 297, 303, 362; Ḥirā' 294, 314; Jam' 291; Ka'bah, (Ancient) House 216 f., 293–95, 301–3, 308, 335, 362, 363 n. 1117, 367; Minā 304 n. 835; al-Muzdalifah 291, 303; Na'mān 304 f.; Qu'ayqi'ān 175; Sacred Territory 117, 362; Thabīr 309 n. 870, 310. See also Ṣūfah (Banū)
Medina, Medinese 31, 95, 102, 180 n. 115. Sacred Territory 117, 362
Mehujael 338
Meru (Mount) 291 n. 788
Mesene, see Maysān
Methuselah 336, 337 n. 998, 346–48
Methushael, see Abūshīl
Michael 259
Midrashic literature, see Jews
Mihrān b. Abī 'Umar al-Rāzī 217
al-Mīmadhī, see Ibrāhīm b. Aḥmad
al-Minhāl b. 'Amr 207, 209, 302
Mis'ar b. Kidām 260
Miskawayh 7, 38, 62, 77, 158
Moses 45, 344, 361 n. 1110, 371
Mosul(ites) 49, 133, 362
Mount of Olives, see Jerusalem
Mu'ādh b. Jabal 241
al-Mu'āfā b. Zakariyyā' al-Nahrawānī, Ibn Ṭarrār/Ṭarārah 9, 12, 47, 65 f., 79, 113, 119, 140
Mualeleth, see Mūlīth
al-Mu'allā b. Sa'īd, Abū Khāzim al-Bazzār 98–100
Mu'ammal b. Ismā'īl 174
Mu'āwiyah 198 n. 224
Mu'āwiyah b. Hishām 173
Mu'āwiyah b. Ṣāliḥ 182, 198, 215, 370
al-Mubārak b. Faḍālah 268, 270, 357
al-Mubārak b. Mujāhid, Abū al-Azhar 251
al-Mubarrad 107 f.
Mubashshir b. Ismā'īl al-Ḥalabī 208
al-Mufaḍḍal b. Faḍālah 357
al-Mufaḍḍal b. Salamah 107 f.
Mughīrah b. Ḥakīm al-Ṣan'ānī 175
Mughīrah b. Miqsam 284 f.
Muḥammad, the Prophet *passim*
Muhammad b. al-'Abbās, see Abū Bakr al-Khuwārizmī
Muḥammad b. 'Abdallāh b. 'Abd al-Ḥakam 28 f., 124 f., 178
Muḥammad b. 'Abdallāh b. 'Abd al-Raḥīm, see Ibn 'Abd al-Raḥīm
Muḥammad b. 'Abdallāh b. Bazī' 179, 189
Muḥammad b. 'Abdallāh b. Muḥammad, see Ibn Ayyūb al-Qaṭṭān
Muḥammad b. 'Abdallāh al-Ṭūsī 198 n. 226
Muḥammad b. 'Abdallāh b. al-Zubayr 323 n. 934
Muḥammad b. 'Abd al-A'lā al-Ṣan'ānī 20, 179, 201, 207, 252
Muḥammad b. 'Abd al-Malik, see Ibn Abī al-Shawārib
Muḥammad b. 'Abd al-Raḥmān, Abū al-Jamāhir 24
Muḥammad b. 'Abd al-Raḥmān b. Abī Laylā 302
Muḥammad b. Abī Manṣūr al-Āmulī 211, 231 f., 356
Muḥammad b. Abī Ma'shar Najīḥ 210 n. 311
Muḥammad b. Abī al-Qāsim b. Muḥammad b. 'Alī al-Āmulī 119
Muḥammad b. Aḥmad al-Ḥāfiẓ, Abū al-Fatḥ b. Abī al-Fawāris 63
Muḥammad b. Aḥmad b. Isḥāq b. al-Buhlūl, Abū Ṭālib 46
Muḥammad b. Aḥmad al-Khallāl, see Abū Naṣr
Muḥammad b. al-'Alā', see Abū Kurayb
Muḥammad b. 'Alī b. al-Ḥasan b. Shaqīq 199 n. 227, 286
Muḥammad b. 'Alī b. Muslim, Abū Ja'far al-Āmulī 119
Muḥammad b. 'Amr b. al-'Abbās al-

Bāhilī 247, 265, 267, 274, 281, 287, 327
Muḥammad b. 'Amr b. 'Alqamah 286 f.
Muḥammad b. 'Athmah, see Ibn 'Athmah
Muḥammad b. 'Awf al-Ṭā'ī al-Ḥimṣī 24, 175
Muḥammad b. Dāwūd b. 'Alī, Abū Bakr al-Ẓāhirī 58, 68 f., 71, 102 f., 122 f.
Muḥammad b. Fuḍayl 71, 200, 218, 321
Muḥammad b. Ḥafṣ al-Waṣṣābī 24
Muḥammad b. Hārūn, Abū Nashīṭ al-Bazzāz 203 n. 257
Muḥammad b. Hārūn al-Qaṭṭān (al-Rāziqī ?) 203
Muḥammad b. Hārūn al-Rūyānī 29
Muḥammad b. al-Ḥasan al-Kātib al-Baghdādī 41, 43, 50
Muḥammad b. Ḥumayd, see Ibn Ḥumayd
Muḥammad b. Ibrāhīm b. al-Mundhir al-Nīsābūrī 29
Muḥammad b. Ibrāhīm al-Qasmalī, see Ibn Abī 'Adī
Muḥammad b. Isḥāq, see Ibn Isḥāq
Muḥammad b. Isḥāq b. Khuzaymah, see Ibn Khuzaymah
Muḥammad b. Ismā'īl b. Isrā'īl al-Dallāl 25
Muḥammad b. Ja'far (Ghundar ?) 177, 260, 297, 313, 320
Muḥammad b. Ja'far b. Jumhūr 12
Muḥammad b. Jarīr, see al-Ṭabarī
Muḥammad b. Jarīr b. Rustam, Abū Ja'far al-Ṭabarī 13, 57, 92, 118 f.
Muḥammad b. Khalaf al-'Asqalānī 26, 53 f., 265, 327
Muḥammad b. Khāzim al-Ḍarīr, see Abū Mu'āwiyah
Muḥammad b. Ma'mar 282 f.
Muḥammad b. Maymūn al-Sukkarī, see Abū Ḥamzah
Muḥammad b. Mu'āwiyah al-Anmāṭī 199
Muḥammad b. Muḥammad b. Ibrāhīm, see al-Maydūmī
Muḥammad b. Mūsā al-Ḥar(r)ashī 20
Muḥammad b. Muṣ'ab al-Qirqisānī 267
Muḥammad b. Muslim, see Abū al-Zabīr; Ibn Shihāb al-Zuhrī
Muḥammad b. al-Muthannā, see Ibn al-Muthannā
Muḥammad b. Nāṣir, Abū al-Faḍl 100
Muḥammad b. Naṣr al-Marwazī 29 f.
Muḥammad b. Qays 278, 367
Muḥammad b. al-Rūmī 79
Muḥammad b. Sa'd, see Ibn Sa'd
Muḥammad b. Sa'd b. Muḥammad 6, 215, 246, 313, 329
Muḥammad b. Sahl b. 'Askar 173, 206 f., 210, 351
Muḥammad b. al-Sā'ib, see al-Kalbī
Muḥammad b. Ṣāliḥ 199 n. 234
Muḥammad b. Ṣāliḥ b. Dīnār 370
Muḥammad b. Sinān al-Qazzāz 183, 205, 255, 291, 328
Muḥammad b. Sulaymān al-Hāshimī 133
Muḥammad b. Thawr al-Ṣan'ānī 201, 207, 252
Muḥammad b. 'Ubaydallāh b. Yaḥyā b. Khāqān, see al-Khāqānī
Muḥammad b. 'Umar, see al-Wāqidī
Muḥammad b. 'Umar al-Dāwūdī, Abū Bakr b. al-Akhḍar 62
Muḥammad b. 'Umar b. Hayyāj 181
Muḥammad b. 'Umārah al-Asadī 260, 285
Muḥammad b. Yazīd al-Adamī 180
Muḥammad b. Yazīd al-Rifā'ī, see Abū Hishām
Muḥammad b. Zayd b. al-Muhājir b. Qunfudh 189
al-Muḥāribī, 'Abd al-Raḥmān b. Muḥammad 287, 367
al-Muḥāsibī 78
Mujāhid b. Jabr, Abū al-Ḥajjāj 52, 58, 71–77, 82, 109, 149, 151, 162, 174 n. 45, 175, 192, 200–3, 211,

Mujāhid (*continued*)
217 f., 227, 246 f., 254, 267, 274, 281, 287, 292, 295 f., 303, 364
Mujāhid b. Mūsā 178
Mujālid b. Sa'īd b. 'Umayr 181
al-Mukharrim, see Baghdad
al-Muktafī 37, 112
Mūlīth, Mualeleth 338
al-Mundhir b. Mālik see Abū Naḍrah
Muqātil b. Ḥayyān 109 f., 227 n. 339, 231, 233
Muqātil b. Sulaymān 162, 323 n. 933, 366 n. 1137, 367 n. 1142, 368 n. 1147
al-Muqtadir 59, 133
Murrah (b. Sharaḥīl) al-Hamdānī 206, 214, 219, 221 f., 250, 254, 258, 262 f., 269, 273, 275, 281, 307
Murtaḍā b. al-Dā'ī 123
Murtaḍā al-Zabīdī 82, 101, 105
Mūsā, see Moses
Mūsā b. 'Abd al-Raḥmān al-Masrūqī 364
Mūsā b. Abī 'Uthmān 284
Mūsā b. Hārūn al-Hamdānī 206, 214, 219, 221 f., 250, 254, 258, 262 f., 269, 273, 275, 281, 307, 322
Mūsā b. Ismā'īl, Abū Salamah al-Tabūdhakī 192 n. 185, 205 n. 270, 328, 339. See also Abū Salamah
Mūsā b. Khalaf 175
Mūsā b. Mas'ūd, see Abū Hudhayfah
Mūsā b. Numayr 256
Mūsā b. Sahl al-Ramlī 25, 199
Mūsā b. Ya'qūb al-Zam'ī 355
al-Musabbiḥī 141
Muṣarrif b. 'Amr 208 f.
al-Musayyab b. Sharīk 211, 227, 356
Muslim b. 'Abd al-Raḥmān al-Jarmī 256 n. 550, 267
Muslim b. (Abī) 'Imrān al-Baṭīn 261
Muslim b. al-Ḥajjāj 189 n. 169, 197 n. 216, 282 n. 718, 283 n. 731, 284 n. 735
Muslim b. Ṣubayḥ, see Abū al-Ḍuḥā
Muslim b. Yasār al-Juhanī 306
al-Mustawrid b. Shaddād al-Fihrī 181
Mutakallim, see Mu'tazilah
al-Mu'tamir b. Sulaymān b. Ṭarkhān 179, 333
al-Mu'taṣim 11, 66, 145, 163
al-Mutawakkil 50
Mu'tazilah, Mutakkalimūn 11, 49, 61, 65, 68, 72, 102, 110, 121, 127, 158 f. See also Jahmī(s)
al-Muthannā b. Ibrāhīm al-Āmulī 17, 190, 202, 204, 210 f., 213 f., 221, 223, 227, 253, 274, 299, 301, 355
al-Muwaffaq 68, 121
al-Muzanī 28, 67 f.
al-Muzdalifah, see Mecca

N

Nabataean, see Aramaic
al-Naḍr b. 'Abd al-Raḥmān, Abū 'Amr al-Khazzāz 364
al-Naḍr b. Shumayl 178, 204
Nāfi', mawlā Ibn 'Umar 75, 174, 295
Nāfi' (b. 'Abd al-Raḥmān) 96
al-Nahdī, see Abū 'Uthmān
Najabah b. Ṣabīgh 197
al-Najāshī 119, 123
Najīḥ b. 'Abd al-Raḥmān, see Abū Ma'shar
al-Nakha'ī, see 'Alqamah; Ibrāhīm b. Yazīd; Sharīk b. 'Abdallāh
Na'mah (Naamah), Noam 335 f.
Na'mān, see Mecca
Nasr 354
Naṣr b. 'Alī al-Jahḍamī 355, 368
Naṣr al-Qushūrī 59 f.
al-Nawawī 9 f., 63
al-Nawwāq, see al-Tawwāq
Nāzūk 73
Nile 370
Nīsābūr 30, 66
Noah 160, 294 n. 789, 297, 302, 326, 334, 340 f., 344, 347 f., 353–70
Noam, see Na'mah
Nod, see Nūdh
Nu'aym b. Ḥammād 199

Nūdh (Būdh, Bawdh, Nod) 291 f., 295, 303, 315, 334, 340
Nūḥ b. Abī Bilāl 67
Nūḥ b. Qays 355, 368

O

Og b. Anak 361
Ōshahanj 326 f., 341 f., 344 f.
Ottoman(s), see Turk(s)

P

Palestine 23, 25–27, 31
Persia, Persian(s), Iran(ian) 29, 45, 133, 137, 143 f., 159, 163, 184 n. 148, 318 f., 325 f., 341 f., 344 f., 348, 369, 371
Pishon, see Fayshān

Q

Qābīl, Qābīn, Qāyin, Qayn, etc., see Cain
al-Qadariyyah 127. See also Jahmī(s), Mu'tazilah
al-Qaffāl, Abū Bakr 30 f., 37
Qalīmā, Iqlīmā, Qlīmath 314, 316, 317 n. 903
Qardā, Qardū, Bāqardā 366
Qarmaṭians 73
al-Qartha' al-Ḍabbī 284–86
Qasāmah b. Zuhayr 260, 297
al-Qāsim b. 'Abd al-Raḥmān al-Sha'mī 323
al-Qāsim b. Abī Bazzah 199
al-Qāsim b. Aḥmad b. al-Shā'ir, Abū al-Ṭayyib 14
al-Qāsim b. Bishr b. Ma'rūf 189, 212, 222, 224, 230
al-Qāsim b. al-Ḥasan b. Yazīd al-Hamadhānī 192, 207 f., 246, 250 f., 268, 270, 278, 287, 309, 357, 364 f., 367
al-Qāsim b. Muḥammad 323, 325, 344
al-Qāsim b. Sallām, see Abū 'Ubayd
Qatādah b. Di'āmah 90, 109, 175, 177–79, 193, 235 n. 445, 246, 251 f., 255, 267 f., 270, 271 n. 654, 274, 290, 302, 320, 333, 353, 356, 365, 367, 369 f.
al-Qaṭawānī, see 'Abdallāh b. Abī Ziyād
al-Qaṭṭān, al-Ḥusayn b. Yazīd 285 n. 749
Qays b. Abī Ḥāzim, Abū 'Abdallāh 181
Qays b. al-Rabī' 267, 286, 302 f.
al-Qifṭī 8 f., 49, 111, 134, 136
Qīnūsh, see Batanūsh
Qu'ayqi'ān, see Mecca
Qur'ān (passages quoted) *1* 66 f., *1:1* 263–66, 327; *2:20* 194, *26* 96, *29* 214–16, 219, *30* 252, 254, 257 f., 266, 269–72, *31* 266–69, 271, *31 f.* 268, 270, *31–33* 272, *32* 273, *32 f.* 271, *33* 268, 272 f., *34* 255, 264, *35* 273–75, 279, *36* 279, 281, *37* 302 f., *117* 192, 225, 228, *125 ff.* 55, *156* 233, *189* 167, *210* 203, *213* 353, *282* 328; *3:36* 249, *40* 278, *189* 169; *4:1* 274, *12* 55, *43* 57; *5:6* 56, *18* 169, 27 311, 313 f., 320, 27–30 308, *31* 309, *31 f.* 311, *64* 59; *6:73* 237, *102* 198, *103* 165, *158* 242; *7:12*, *13* 264, *14–17* 84, *18* 278, *19* 275, *20* 279, *20 f.* 278, 280, *21* 276, 299, 22 276, 278, 296, 299, 304, *23* 302 f., *24* 279, 281, *26* 278, *54* 188, 225, *172*, 304–7, 329 f., *172 f.* 304, *189* 273, *189 f.* 320 f., *190* 322; *10:5* 232, *5 f.* 167; *11:7* 202, 207, 210 f., 223, 226 f., 37 355, 359, *38 f.* 359, *40* 297, 356, 359, 362–65, *42* 360 f., *42 f.* 361, *44* 363, *73* 237; *12:39* 195; *14:7* 167, *33* 233; *15:26* 258 f., 261 f., 27 252, *28* 258 f., *30 f.* 263, *33* 258 f., *34 f.* 273, *38* 334, *94* 165; *16:15* 214, 220; *17:1* 238, *11* 258 f., *12* 167,

Qur'ān (passages quoted) (*continued*) 231, 234, 244–47, *61* 259, *62* 84, *79* 58, 71–77, 149; *18:50* 251, 255 f., *60* 184, *86* 234; *19:62* 191, *98* 249; *20 : 6* 169, *117*, *117–19* 300, *120* 276, 280, 121 304; *21:22* 196, *29* 251 f., *30* 222 f., 229, *32* 116, 235, *33* 187, 235, *37* 214, 263, 287, *69* 371; *22:18* 278, *26* 293, *47* 192, *55* 191; *23:27* 297, 356, *91 f.* 196; *24:43* 223; *25:59* 225; *28:88* 193; *29:14* 348, *53* 243; *30:21* 273; *31:10* 214, *16* 220; *32:4* 212, *5* 192, 227 f.; *33:33* 339 f., 72 309; *36:37–40* 186, *38* 232, *40* 235; *37:6 f.* 223, *75–77* 369, *77* 368, 370; *38:71* 255, *71 f.* 262, *72* 263, *75–85* 265, *76* 264, *81* 334; *41:9 f.* 188, *9–11* 221, *9–12* 213, *11* 192, 214, 222, 270, *12* 193, 206, 214, 223; *50:15* 257, *38* 190, 218, *38 f.* 188; *51:56–58* 166; *52:4* 362, *9–11* 236; *54:9* 358, *11 f.* 360, 362, *13 f.* 361; *55* 33, *15* 252, *17* 234, *26 f.* 193, *33* 165, *50* 226; *56:27* 307, *28 f.* 277, *41* 307; *62:5* 120; *68:1* 218, 220; *70:40* 235; *71:5 f.* 358, *19 f.* 166, *21* 355, *21–24* 354, *26 f.* 359 *27* 358 f.; *78:10 f.* 167, *23* 184; *79:3* 52, *27–29* 230, *27–32* 216, *30* 206, 215, *30 f.* 215, *31 f.* 221; *81:1* 193, 232, *15* 235; *85:13* 243; *86:9* 168; *87:18 f.* 344; *88:17–20* 195; *91* and *92*; *94:4* 12; *95* 51; *96:5* 223; *100:1* 235; *112:2* 262, *4* 165
Quraysh, Qurashite(s) 98, 371
al-Qushayrī, see ʿÁbd al-Karīm b. Hawāzin; ʿAbd al-Munʿim b. ʿAbd al-Karīm
Quṭrub, Abū ʿAlī 110

R

Rabāḥ b. Zayd 199
al-Rabīʿ b. Anas 253, 268, 272, 279, 288, 291, 296
al-Rabīʿ b. Sulaymān 27, 102, 284
al-Rāfiʿī 63
Rākē'ēl, see Barākīl
al-Ramlah 25 f., 197 n. 213, 198 n. 224, 262 n. 601
al-Raqqah 282 n. 714
Rāsūyāl, see Baraknā
Rawḥ b. Aslam 332
Rawḥ b. ʿUbādah 285, 305
Rawwād b. al-Janāḥ 26
al-Rayy 16–18, 342
al-Rāzī, Abū Bakr 40, 51
al-Rāzī, Fakhr al-dīn 75
al-Rāziqī, see Muḥammad b. Ḥārūn al-Qaṭṭān
al-Rifāʿī, see Abū Hishām
al-Rīwandī, see Sahl b. Aḥmad
Rizqallāh b. ʿAbd al-Wahhāb al-Tamīmī 100
al-Ru'āsī 122
Ru'bah b. al-ʿAjjāj 12 f.
Rufayʿ, see Abū al-ʿĀliyah; Abū Kathīrah
al-Ruhūn 291 n. 788
Rūm, see Greek(s)
al-Ruṣāfah, see Baghdad
al-Rustamī, Abū Jaʿfar Aḥmad b. Muḥammad b. Rustam 107

S

Ṣābi', Sabian(s) 345, 347, 354
al-Sabīʿī, al-Ḥusayn b. Yazīd 285 n. 749
Sābūr 345
Sacred Territory, see Mecca; Medina
Saʿd b. ʿAbdallāh b. ʿAbd al-Ḥakam 28 f.
Saʿd b. ʿAbd al-Ḥamīd b. Jaʿfar 306
Saʿd b. Habtah 173 n. 28
Saʿd b. Muḥammad b. al-Ḥasan 215, 246, 313, 329
Saʿd b. ʿUbādah 282 f.
al-Sadūsī, see Sayf
al-Ṣafadī *passim*
al-Saffāḥ 215 n. 334
Ṣāfī al-Ḥuramī 38

Ṣafwān b. Muḥriz 204 f.
Sahl (Suhayl) b. Aḥmad b. Sahl al-Rīwandī 37
Sahl b. Sa'd al-Sā'idī 179 f.
Sahl b. Yūsuf (al-Sulamī ?, al-Anmāṭī ?) 314
Sa'īd b. Abī 'Arūbah 193, 246, 251, 268, 270, 274, 302, 356, 365, 367, 369 f.
Sa'īd b. Abī Sa'īd al-Maqburī 67, 210, 213, 221, 223, 266, 327
Sa'īd b. 'Amr al-Sakūnī 24 f.
Sa'īd b. Bashīr 369
Sa'īd b. al-Ḥakam, see Ibn Abī Maryam
Sa'īd b. Iyās, see al-Jurayrī
Sa'īd b. Jubayr 108 f., 173, 199, 207, 259–61, 267, 290, 299, 302, 304–6, 309, 321, 330 f.
Sa'īd b. Kathīr, see Ibn 'Ufayr
Sa'īd b. Ma'bad 267
Sa'īd b. Masrūq al-Thawrī 229
Sa'īd b. Mas'ūd 256
Sa'īd b. al-Musayyab 255, 281
Sa'īd b. Sa'd b. 'Ubādah 282 n. 716, 283
Sa'īd b. 'Uthmān al-Tanūkhī 24
al-Sakhāwī 100
Saladin 141
Salamah b. Dīnār, see Abū Ḥāzim
Salamah b. al-Faḍl 18, 174, 201 f., 211, 251, 254, 263, 265, 273, 276, 279, 281, 292, 296, 310, 316 f., 320, 323 f., 332, 335–37, 343, 358, 360, 366, 368
Salamah b. Kuhayl 175
Ṣāliḥ 237
Ṣāliḥ b. Ḥarb 295
Ṣāliḥ b. Mismār al-Marwazī 355
Ṣāliḥ (b. Nabhān), mawlā al-Taw'amah 250 f.
al-Salīl b. Aḥmad 133
Sālim b. Abī Ḥafṣah 321
Sālim b. 'Ajlān al-Afṭas 267
Sallām b. Miskīn 254 f.
Salmān al-Fārisī 262, 284–86, 356
al-Sam'ānī 29 and *passim*
Sāmānids 138
Samurah b. Jundub 320, 369
Samurah al-Ṣawwāf 309 f.
Sandal 317
Sarah 237
Sarandīb (Ceylon) 291 n. 788, 292
al-Sarī b. Ismā'īl 364
al-Sarī b. Yaḥyā 6
Sassanian 319 n. 912
Satan, see Iblīs
al-Ṣawwāf, see Samurah
al-Ṣawwāf, Abū 'Alī al-Ḥasan b. al-Ḥusayn 61, 70, 122
Sawwār b. Abī Ḥukaym 293
Sawwār b. al-Ja'd al-Yaḥmadī 255
Sayf al-Sadūsī 151
Sayf b. 'Umar 6, 53, 314 n. 890
Sayḥān 370
Schatzhöhle 163, 291 n. 788, 303 n. 833, 311 n. 874, 314 nn. 889, 893, 315 n. 895, 317 n. 903, 333 n. 972, 336 n. 990, 337 n. 995, 339 nn. 1006, 1007, 341 n. 1014, 362 n. 1113, 366 nn. 1137, 1138, 368 n. 1145
Seleucid era 371 n. 1164
Seth, Shīth, Shāth, Hibat Allāh 317, 324–26, 331, 333–36, 338–41, 343 f., 354, 365
al-Sha'bī, 'Amr b. Sharaḥīl 181, 265, 327, 364, 370 f.
Shabīb b. Bishr 255
Shabūbah 317
al-Shāfi'ī, Shāfi'ite(s) 27 f., 30, 49, 63 f., 66 f., 98, 102, 115 n. 396, 127 n. 432
Shahr b. Ḥawshab 217 n. 350
al-Shammāsiyyah, see Baghdad
Sharīk b. 'Abdallāh b. Abī Namir 250 f., 255 n. 542, 267
Sharīk b. 'Abdallāh al-Nakha'ī 175, 200, 209, 214, 218, 222 f.
Shaybān (Banū) 102
Shaybān b. 'Abd al-Raḥmān al-Naḥwī 285
Shaybān b. Farrūkh b. Abī Shaybah 254
al-Shaybānī, see Sulaymān b. Abī Sulaymān

al-Shaybānī (Muḥammad b. al-Ḥasan) 102, 114 n. 392
Shem 347, 360, 365 f., 368–70
Shī'ah, Shī'ite(s), see 'Alī b. Abī Ṭālib
Shibl b. 'Abbād ('Ubād) 274
al-Shimshāṭī, Abū al-Ḥusayn al-Mu'allim (= Abū al-Ḥasan 'Alī b. Muḥammad al-'Adawī ?) 133
Shu'ayb b. al-Layth 284
Shu'bah b. al-Ḥajjāj 177–79, 200, 202 f., 218, 259, 330
Shubayl b. 'Awf 181
Shujā' b. al-Walīd al-Sakūnī 291, 295 f., 303
Shuraḥbīl b. Sa'īd b. Sa'd b. 'Ubādah 282 n. 716, 283
Sihon 370 n. 1161
al-Sijistānī, see Abū Bakr b. Abī Dāwūd; Abū Dāwūd; Abū Ḥātim
Simāk b. Ḥarb 226
Sim'an bint Barākīl b. Mehujael 337, 342
al-Simsimī, see 'Alī b. 'Ubaydallāh
Sinai 294
Siyāmak b. Māshī b. Jayūmart 325 f.
Siyāmī 325
Slavs 238 n. 459
Solomon 371
South Arabia(n), see Yemen
Spityura, see Isfitūr
al-Subkī (Tāj al-dīn) 10, 138, and *passim*
al-Ṣudā'ī, al-Ḥusayn b. 'Alī 54, 189, 212, 222, 224, 231
Ṣudayy b. 'Ajlān al-Bāhilī, see Abū Umāmah
al-Suddī, Ismā'īl b. 'Abd al-Raḥmān 20, 206, 214, 219, 221 f., 250, 254, 258, 262 f., 269, 273, 275, 281, 307, 322
Ṣūfah (Banū) 309 n. 870
Ṣūfī(s), Ṣūfism 58, 79, 82–84
Sufyān (b. Sa'īd) al-Thawrī 53, 102, 162, 173–75, 192, 201–3, 207, 217, 229, 251 n. 517, 261, 303, 315, 365
Sufyān b. 'Uyaynah 17, 173 n. 35, 174 (?), 175, 219 (?), 290 n. 782, 299
Sufyān b. Wakī' b. al-Jarrāḥ 119, 176, 203, 207, 226, 267, 281, 305, 307, 314 f., 321, 331, 340, 365
al-Sufyānī 53 f.
al-Sulamī 58 n. 227
Sulaymān, see al-A'mash (200 n. 244, 218 f.)
Sulaymān b. 'Abd al-Raḥmān b. Ḥammād al-Ṭalḥī 20
Sulaymān b. Abī Sulaymān, Abū Isḥāq al-Shaybānī 210
Sulaymān b. 'Alī b. 'Abdallāh b. 'Abbās 295 n. 802
Sulaymān b. al-Ash'ath, see Abū Dāwūd al-Sijistānī
Sulaymān b. Bilāl 180
Sulaymān b. Dāwūd, see Abū Dāwūd
Sulaymān b. Ḥayyān, Abū Khālid 265, 327
Sulaymān al-Khāqānī 14
Sulaymān b. Mihrān, see al-A'mash
Sulaymān b. Muḥammad b. Ma'dīkarib al-Ru'aynī 24
Sulaymān b. Mūsā al-Umawī 192
Sulaymān b. Ṭarkhān, Abū al-Mu'tamir al-Taymī 179, 262, 333
al-Ṣūlī (Muḥammad b. Yaḥyā) 49
Sunayd, see al-Ḥusayn b. Dāwūd
Sūq Thamānīn 366
al-Sūs, Susa 341
Suwā' 354
al-Suyūṭī 73 n. 279
Syria, Syrian(s) 21, 23–27, 31, 53, 83, 87, 95, 102, 344. Syriac, see Aramaic

T

al-Ṭabarī, see Muḥammad b. Jarīr b. Rustam
al-Ṭabarī, Abū Ja'far Muḥammad b. Jarīr *passim*. See also Jarīrī(s)
al-Ṭabarī, 'Alī b. Rabban 40 f., 49 f.
Ṭabaristān 10–14, 29, 45, 62, 73, 127, 139, 305 n. 851, 318, 342
al-Ṭabarkhazī, see Abū Bakr al-Khuwārizmī

al-Tabūdhakī, see Mūsā b. Ismā'īl
Tāfīl 238
al-Ṭaḥāwī 115
Ṭāhirids 11
Ṭahmūrath 344 f., 348, 352
al-Ṭāḥūnī, see Isḥāq b. al-Ḥajjāj
al-Ṭā'if 306 n. 858
al-Ṭalḥī, see Sulaymān b. 'Abd al-Raḥmān
Talmud, see Jews
Ṭalq b. Ghannām 244
Tamīm b. al-Muntaṣir 181, 200, 209, 214, 218, 222 f.
al-Tanūkhī (al-Muḥassin b. 'Alī) 15, 51, 82, 84
Targum, see Jews and 366 n. 1137
Tārīs 238
Tarsus 267 n. 632
al-Taw'amah bint Umayyah b. Khalaf 250 f.
Tawbah 317
Ṭāwūs al-Yamānī 254, 276
al-Tawwāq (Nawwāq) 171
al-Ṭayālisī, see Abū Dāwūd
al-Taymī, see Sulaymān b. Ṭarkhān
Teheran, see al-Rayy
al-Tha'ālibī 349 n. 1048, 350 n. 1049
Thabīr, see Mecca
Thābit b. Abī Khālid al-Wālibī 260
Thābit b. Aslam al-Bunānī 332
Thābit b. Sinān 60, 134
Tha'lab 21, 46, 107
al-Tha'labī 162, 232 n. 436, 276 n. 677, 317 n. 903, 347 n. 1036
al-Tha'labī (Taghlibī ?), see Aḥmad b. Yūsuf
Thamānīn, see Sūq
Thamūd 237
Thumāmah b. 'Abīdah ('Ubaydah) al-Sulamī 295
Tigris 43, 370. See also Baghdad
al-Ṭirimmāḥ 46
Treasure Cave, see *Schatzhöhle* and 333
Tūbāl (Jubal) 339
Tubal-cain 335 n. 983, 338
Tūbīsh (Jubal) 338
Ṭulayq b. Muḥammad al-Wāsiṭī 30
Tūlīn (Jabal) 338
al-Ṭūmārī, see 'Īsā b. Mūsā
Tunis(ia) 245 n. 488
Turk(s), Turkish, Ottoman(s) 137, 139, 141, 143, 238 n. 459
al-Ṭūsī 92

U

'Ubādah b. al-Ṣāmit 198 f.
'Ubādah b. al-Walīd b. 'Ubādah b. al-Ṣāmit 198
'Ubayd b. Ādam b. Abī Iyās al-'Asqalānī 26, 198
'Ubayd b. Sulaymān al-Bāhilī 227, 251 (see n. 515)
'Ubayd b. 'Umayr al-Laythī 245, 285, 358
'Ubaydah b. al-Aswad 181
'Ubaydallāh b. 'Abdallāh b. 'Utbah 210
'Ubaydallāh b. 'Alī b. Abī Rāfi' 355
'Ubaydallāh b. 'Amr 282
'Ubaydallāh b. Muḥammad al-Firyābī 26
'Ubaydallāh b. Mūsā b. Bādhām/n 285
'Ubaydallāh (= 'Ubayd ?) b. Sulaymān 227 n. 402, 251
'Ubaydallāh b. Yaḥyā b. Khāqān, see Ibn Khāqān
Ubayy b. Ka'b 242, 332 f.
al-Ubullah 292
'Umān 45
'Umar b. 'Abd al-'Azīz 143, 201 n. 249, 245 n. 489, 266 n. 626, 315 n. 896
'Umar b. 'Abd al-Raḥmān b. Muhrib 277
'Umar b. Ḥabīb 199
'Umar b. Ibrāhīm al-Baṣrī 320
'Umar b. al-Khaṭṭāb 63, 87, 90–92, 130, 189 n. 177, 241, 242 n. 466, 306
'Umar b. Shabbah 53, 260
'Umar b. Ṣubḥ, Abū Nu'aym al-Balkhī 231 f.
Umayyad(s), Umayyad Shī'ah 24, 61, 120, 131, 133, 169, 171 n. 23, 326 n. 944

Umayyah b. Khalaf 250 n. 511
Umm Hāni' 173 n. 37, 206 n. 278
Umm Salamah 189, 212, 222, 224
'Uqbah b. 'Āmir 229
'Uthmān b. 'Affān 87, 90 f., 209 n. 302, 242 n. 466, 319
'Uthmān b. 'Āṣim, see Abū Ḥaṣīn
'Uthmān b. Maṭar 367
'Uthmān b. Nahīk, see Abū Nahīk
'Uthmān b. Sa'īd, see Warsh
'Uthmān b. Sa'īd b. Kāmil 256
'Uthmān b. Sa'īd (al-Zayyāt ?, al-Mursī ?) 252, 258, 261, 264, 266, 269, 285

W

Wadd 354
Wahb b. Jarīr 179, 229
Wahb b. Munabbih 174, 206, 208, 210, 277 f., 286 n. 760, 301, 331 n. 960, 351
Wahballāh b. Rāshid, see Abū Zur'ah
al-Wāḥidī (Abū al-Ḥasan 'Alī b. Aḥmad) 75
Wakī' b. Ḥudus ('Udus, 'Udas) 204
Wakī' b. al-Jarrāḥ 119, 200, 207, 218, 226, 267, 315
al-Wālibī, see Abū Khālid; 'Amr b. Thābit; Thābit
al-Walīd b. 'Abd al-Malik 178 f.
al-Walīd b. Mazyad 23, 178
al-Walīd b. Shujā' al-Sakūnī, see Abū Hammām
al-Walīd b. 'Ubādah b. al-Ṣāmit 198 f.
al-Walid b. Yazīd 278 n. 686
al-Wāqidī 110
Warqā' b. 'Umar b. Kulayb 247, 287
Warsh ('Uthmān b. Sa'īd) 96 f.
al-Washshā' 41
Wāṣil b. 'Abd al-A'lā al-Asadī 200, 218
Wāsim, Wāshim 292
Wāsiṭ 19, 121, 181 n. 133, 204 n. 258
Wēwanjihān, Vivangah, Ēwankihān 344 n. 1026, 345

Y

Yaghūth 354
al-Yaḥmadī, see Abū Sa'īd (Ismā'īl b. Ibrāhīm); Sawwār
Yaḥūd 317
Yaḥyā b. 'Abbād b. 'Abdallāh b. al-Zubayr 332
Yaḥyā b. 'Abd al-Ḥamīd al-Ḥimmānī 364 n. 1122
Yaḥyā b. 'Abd al-Malik b. Ḥumayd, see Ibn Abī Ghaniyyah
Yaḥyā b. 'Abd al-Raḥmān b. Mālik 181
Yaḥyā b. Abī Kathīr 285
Yaḥyā b. Ādam 176 f.
Yaḥyā b. 'Adī 105
Yaḥyā b. Ayyūb al-Ghāfiqī al-Miṣrī 229
Yaḥyā b. Ibrāhīm b. Muḥammad b. Abī 'Ubaydah b. Ma'n 181 n. 129
Yaḥyā b. 'Īsā al-Ramlī 25, 305
Yaḥyā b. Kathīr al-'Anbarī 151
Yaḥyā b. al-Muhallab, see Abū Kudaynah
Yaḥyā b. Sa'īd b. Farrūkh al-Qaṭṭān 219, 260 f.
Yaḥyā b. Wāḍiḥ 172, 177, 255, 300
Yaḥyā b. Yamān, see Ibn Yamān
Yaḥyā b. Ya'qūb b. Mudrik, Abū Ṭālib 172 f.
Yaḥyā b. Zakariyyā', see Ibn Abī Zā'idah
Yaḥyā b. Ziyād, see al-Farrā'
Yājūj and Mājūj 238
Ya'lā b. 'Aṭā' 204
Yām b. Noah 360 f., 368
Yānish, see Enosh
Ya'qūb b. 'Abdallāh al-Qummī 217, 259, 299, 330
Ya'qūb b. Ibrāhīm al-Jūzajānī (= Ibrāhīm b. Ya'qūb ?) 26
Ya'qūb b. Ibrāhīm b. Kathīr al-Dawraqī 260, 305, 363
al-Ya'qūbī 159, 163 n. 6, 317 n. 903, 333 n. 972, 341 n. 1014, 357 n. 1084, 362 n. 1113, 366 n. 1138

Yāqūt 9, 13, 18, 37, 66, 77, and *passim*
Yarid, Yārid, see Jared
Yasht 350 n. 1054, 351 n. 1056
Ya'ūq 354
Yazdjard b. Shahriyār 184 n. 148, 319, 369, 371
Yazīd (grandfather of al-Ṭabarī) 12
Yazīd b. 'Abdallāh b. Qusayṭ 281
Yazīd b. 'Abd al-Malik b. Marwān 143
Yazīd b. Abī Ḥabīb 229
Yazīd b. al-Aṣamm 197
Yazīd b. Hārūn b. Zādī b. Thābit 178, 181 f., 204
Yazīd b. Ḥumayd 179
Yazīd b. Hurmuz 266, 327
Yazīd b. Zuray', Abū Mu'āwiyah 193, 245 f., 251, 268, 270, 274, 302, 356, 365, 367, 369
Yemen, Yemenites, South Arabia(n) 45, 91, 205, 314, 337, 367
Yūnus b. 'Abdallāh b. 'Abd al-Ḥakam (?) 29
Yūnus b. 'Abd al-A'lā 27, 96 f., 127, 198, 269, 280 f., 287
Yūnus b. Bukayr 18
Yūnus b. Yazīd b. Abī al-Najjūd 283
Yūsuf b. Mihrān 291, 328, 357, 360
Yūsuf b. al-Qāsim b. Yūsuf al-Ma/iyānajī, Abū Bakr 37

Z

Zabbān (b. Fā'id ?) 183
Ẓāhirite(s) 52, 63, 68 f.
Zā'idah b. Qudāmah 244
al-Zajjāj, Abū Isḥāq 107
Zakariyyā' b. Isḥāq al-Makkī 285
Zakariyyā' b. Yaḥyā b. Abān al-Miṣrī 245
al-Zarkashī 105
Zayd b. Abī Unaysah 306
Zayd b. Abī al-Zarqā' 197
Zayd b. Arqam 209
Zayd b. al-Ḥubāb 364
Zaydites 11
Zillah 338
Ziyād b. Ayyūb (Dallawayh) 7, 53 f.
Ziyād b. Khaythamah 291 f., 295 f., 303
Ziyād b. Kulayb, Abū Ma'shar 284 f.
Zoroastrian(s), see Magian(s)
al-Zubaydī 42
al-Zubayr, see Abū 'Abd al-Salām
al-Zubayr b. Bakkār 98 f.
al-Zubayrī, see Abū Aḥmad
Zuhayr b. Ḥurqūṣ 123
Zuhayr b. Muḥammad al-Khiraqī 282 f.
al-Zuhrī, see Ibn Shihāb

www.ingramcontent.com/pod-product-compliance
Lightning Source LLC
Chambersburg PA
CBHW020118240426
43673CB00038B/526
* 9 7 8 0 8 8 7 0 6 5 6 3 7 *